Hospitality & Tourism

Twelfth Edition

An Introduction to the Industry

Robert A. Brymer
Florida State University

Kathryn Hashimoto
Sensei Associates

KENDALL/HUNT PUBLISHING COMPANY
4050 Westmark Drive Dubuque, Iowa 52002

Book Team
Chairman and Chief Executive Officer   Mark C. Falb
Director of National Book Program   Paul B. Carty
Editorial Development Manager   Georgia Botsford
Developmental Editor   Tina Bower
Vice President, Production and Manufacturing   Alfred C. Grisanti
Assistant Vice President, Production Services   Christine E. O'Brien
Prepress Editor   Angela Puls
Permissions Editor   Elizabeth Roberts
Designer   Jenifer Chapman
Senior Vice President, College Division   Thomas W. Gantz
Managing Editor, College Field   Greg DeRosa
Associate Editor, College Field   Cooper Gouge

Cover image © Jupiter Images.

ISBN 13: 978-0-7575-3105-7
ISBN 10: 0-7575-3105-9

Printed in the United States of America
10   9   8   7   6   5   4   3   2   1

Dedication

To my incredible wife Becky, the perfect partner in life God has given me.

—Robert Brymer

To my loving and supportive husband, George, and to Florida State University and the great Hospitality faculty who helped us through our evacuation from Katrina. Thank you.

—Kathryn Hashimoto

Brief Contents

Contents

Acknowledgments

The twelfth edition of this book is a collection of readings written by 45 authors representing 34 colleges and universities across the United States. These authors have written papers specifically for this book, and without their generous contributions the publication of this edition would not have been possible. They have truly created an outstanding edition, and we are very grateful for the special role each and every author played.

The following alphabetical list of authors includes their mailing and e-mail addresses at the time of publication.

Donna Albano
The Richard Stockton College of New Jersey
Professional Studies, Hospitality Management
P.O. Box 195 Jim Leeds Road
Pomona, NJ 08240-0195
Donna.Albano@stockton.edu

Susan W. Arendt
Iowa State University
Apparel, Educational Studies, & Hospitality
    Management
8A MacKay
Ames, IA 50011-1120
sarendt@mail.hs.iastate.edu

Bradley Beran
34 Slocum Hall
Syracuse University
Syracuse, NY 13244-1250
bcberan@syr.edu

Dr. Daniel Bernstein
Hospitality Management
Seton Hill University
Seton Hill Drive
Greensburg, PA 15601
Bernstein@setonhill.edu

Ernie Boger
Hotel & Restaurant Management Dept
University of Maryland Eastern Shore
Princess Anne, MD
epboger@mail.umes.edu

Sherie Brezina
Florida Gulf Coast University
Fort Myers, FL 33963
sbrezina@fgcu.edu

Ronald J. Cereola
College of Business
James Madison University
ZSH 612
MSC 0206
Harrisonburg, VA 22807
cereolrj @jmu.edu

Wanda M. Costen
University of Tennessee
Retail, Hospitality, and Tourism Management
1215 W. Cumberland Ave.
220D Jessie Han-is Bldg.
Knoxville, TN 37996-1911
wcosten@utk.edu

Dan Crafts
Missouri State University
901 5. National
PROF 440
Springfield, MO 65897
dancrafts@missouristate.edu

John C. Crotts
Department of Hospitality and Tourism
    Management
School of Business and Economics
66 George Street
College of Charleston
Charleston, SC 29424-00 1 USA
CrottsJ@cofc.edu

Chris DeSessa
Johnson & Wales University
89 Enfield Ave.
Providence, RI 02908
Chris.Desessa@jwu.edu

George G. Fenich
The Lester E. Kabacoff School of Hotel,
    Restaurant, and Tourism Administration
University of New Orleans
#462C Kirschman Hall, Lakefront
New Orleans, LA 70148
gfenich@uno.edu

Reg Foucar-Szocki
James Madison University
MSC 0202
Showker 224
Harrisonburg, VA 22807
foucarrf@jmu.edu

Heather Goldman
Department of Hospitality & Tourism
    Management
School of Business & Economics
College of Charleston
5 Liberty Street #332 (Beatty Center)
Charleston, SC 29401
goldmanh@cofc.edu

Susan Gregory
Hotel & Restaurant Management Program
    Coordinator
Eastern Michigan University
School of Technology Studies
202B Roosevelt Hall
Ypsilanti, MI 48197
sgregory@emich.edu

Christian Hardigree
University of Nevada, Las Vegas
William F. Harrah College of Hotel
    Administration
4505 Maryland Parkway
Box 456021
Las Vegas, NV 89154-6021
christian.hardigree@unlv.edu

Joe Hutchinson
University of Southern Mississippi Gulf Coast
Tourism Management
College of Business Administration
730 East Beach Blvd.
Long Beach, MS 39560
Jhutchlb@aol.com

Miyoung Jeong
5 MacKay Hall
Iowa State University
Ames, IA 50011
mjeong@iastate.edu

Doug Kennedy
University of Wisconsin-Stout
Hotel, Restaurant and Tourism Management
405 Home Economics Building
Menominee, WI 54751-0790
KennedyD@uwstout.edu

Keith Mandabach
University of New Mexico
Box 80003, 3hrtm
Las Cruces, NM 88003
kmandaba@nmsu.edu

Karl Mayer
William F. Harrah College of Hotel
    Administration
University of Nevada, Las Vegas
Las Vegas, NV 89154-0623
karl.mayer@unlv.edu

Cynthia R. Mayo
Delaware State University
1200 N. Dupont Highway
210 MBNA Building
Dover, DE 19901
cmavo@desu.edu

S. Denise McCurry, Esq.
MGM Mirage
3260 Industrial Road
Las Vegas, NV 89109
dmccurry/mgmmirage.com

Robert A. McMullin
Center of Hotel and Restaurant Management
200 Prospect Street
East Stroudsburg University
E. Stroudsburg, PA 18301
rmcmullin@po-box.esu.edu

Richard J. Mills, Jr.
Robert Morris College
1474 Coraopolis Heights Road
Coraopolis, PA 15108
mills@rmu.edu

Gail Myers
Suite Harmony Corporation
247 Houston Ave.
Crookston, MN 56716
GailJMyers@hotmail.com

Ken Myers
University of Minnesota, Crookston
Hotel, Restaurant, & Institutional Management
2900 University Ave.
Crookston, MN 56716
KMyers@mail.crk.unm.edu

Radesh Palakurthi
Oklahoma State University
210E - HESW
School of Hotel and Restaurant Administration
Stillwater, OK 74078
Palakur@okstate.edu

Charles G. Partlow
University of South Carolina
School of Hotel, Restaurant & Tourism
    Management
College of Hospitality, Retail & Sport
    Management
Columbia, SC 29208
cpartlow@sc.edu

Denis P. Rudd
Robert Morris University
Hospitality and Tourism
881 Narrows Run Road
Moon Township, PA 15108-1189
rudd@rmu.edu

Chay Runnels
Stephen F. Austin University
Department of Human Sciences
P.O. Box 13014
Nacogdoches, TX 75962
rnnnelsc@sfasu.edu

Yumi E. Satow
San Francisco State University
Department of Consumer & Family Studies and
    Dietetics
College of Health & Human Services
San Francisco, CA 94132
yes@sfsu.edu

Michael Scales
The Richard Stockton College of New Jersey
Professional Studies, Hospitality Management
P.O. Box 195 Jim Leeds Road
Pomona, NJ 08240-0195
scalesm@stockton.edu

Janet Sim
San Francisco State University
Hospitality Management Department
College of Business
1600 Holloway Avenue
San Francisco, CA 94010
jsim@sfsu.edu

John M. Stefanelli
University of Nevada, Las Vegas
William F. Harrah College of Hotel
    Administration
Department of Food and Beverage Management
4505 Maryland Parkway
Las Vegas, NV 89154-0623
john.stefanelli@unlv.edu

Nancy Swanger
Washington State University
Todd 475
Pullman, WA 99164
swanger@wsu.edu

Pat Tierney
San Francisco State University
Department of Recreation and Leisure Studies
600 Holloway Ave.
San Francisco, CA 94019
ptierney@sfsu.edu

Kirsten Tripodi
Fairleigh Dickinson University
45 Birch St.
Bloomfield, NJ 07003
kirsten@fdu.edu

Constantine Vlisides
University of New Haven
Tagliatela School of Hospitality and Tourism
West Haven, CT 06492
cvlisides@newhaven.edu

G. Burch Wilkes, IV
Pennsylvania State University
Professional Golf Management
Department of Recreation, Park and Tourism
    Management
College of Health and Human Development
201 Mateer Building
University Park, PA 16802
gbw104@psu.edu

John Wolper
University of Findlay
College of Business, Hospitality Management
Findlay, OH 45840
wolper@findlay. edu

Paula Wolper
University of Findlay
College of Business, Hospitality Management
Findlay, OH 45840
pwolper@findlay.edu

Alina M. Zapalska
Department of Management
U.S. Coast Guard Academy
27 Mohegan Avenue
New London, CT 06320-8101
Phone: 860-444-8334
Fax: 860-701-6179
Alina.M.Zapalska@uscg.mil

Hospitality and Tourism Industry

Part I

1
Welcome to Hospitality and Tourism

2
The Past, Present, and Future

3
Information Resources: Periodicals and the Web

4
Industry Associations and Rating Services

5
Career Realities and Opportunities

Kathryn Hashimoto
Robert Brymer

Welcome to Hospitality and Tourism

Learning Objectives

The purpose of this chapter is to give you an overview of the industry and of this book so that you will know what to expect

Chapter Outline

The Service-Tourism-Hospitality Connection
Hospitality and Tourism

*T*his book is about one of the fastest-growing industries in the world. It comes to you at a time when the wonderful world of hospitality and tourism has never been more exciting. Hospitality and tourism refers to those organizations that offer services like food, drink, lodging, and entertainment. However, many fields are incorporated in creating these service products. For example, people may not realize that sculptors are needed in food organizations to create ice and food sculptures for banquets and restaurants. Interior designers help create the fantasy of a casino's pirate fantasy or a Chinese restaurant's theme. Meeting planners can organize weddings at Disneyland or a meeting of the local bar association or a convention of ten thousand attendees. Hospitality enterprises need many different types of skills from artists to public relations to accountants.

On a broader scale, they are part of the service industry. There are four areas in which service is different from manufacturing. First, the service product is intangible. This means that unlike a table that you can take back and exchange, a service once offered cannot be taken back. Once a guest meets and interacts with the employee, "the moment of truth," the service experience is created for better or worse. Second and third, the service is inseparable from and variable by the provider. You, the provider, cannot totally separate yourself and your thoughts from how you behave with other people. In addition, as you change moods, the service that you deliver also changes from moment to moment because the service experience is created by each employee the guest encounters. Finally, service cannot carry inventory. The service experience is created at the moment of truth, and a good encounter cannot be carried until tomorrow. This means that we need special people who like people and truly want to help make the guests experience the best possible. The authors in this book will introduce you to an industry that is a "people" business. Chapter after chapter will reaffirm that, in the world of hospitality, taking good care of the guest is the single most critical element for success.

Hospitality and Tourism is systematically organized for the introductory student. The book begins with a broad overview exploring how and why the industry developed into the different components. Then it develops your knowledge for gathering information and some of the industry associations and rating services that will help you gather knowledge. You will also learn what associations you should be

aware of and join to learn the applications of the theory you learn in your classes. Chapter 5 alerts you to the realities and opportunities that you may not be aware of in hospitality. There are many fields that students have never thought of in terms of a career path. This first section gives you the overall knowledge you need to learn more about this exciting industry and understand the general scope. The second section, Hospitality & Tourism Businesses, gradually narrows the focus to include an introduction to companies and operations. The third section, Hospitality & Tourism Operations, explores six of the general areas of business; however, it explores the areas that are the same yet different in the service industry. The final section, Hospitality & Tourism Career Menu, reviews many specific career options available to prospective managers. (Please see Figure 1.1 for a graphic view of how the book is organized.) The goal is to provide a survey approach to hospitality and tourism, while offering the information needed to help students proceed into more advanced courses and readings.

The Service-Tourism-Hospitality Connection

For a better understanding of where the industry fits in the economy, please refer to Figure 1.2. Starting at the top of that chart—The Economy—you will see that the economy is made up of agriculture, manufacturing, and service. They are three separate parts of the economy, yet each plays a role in the service part of the economy. In the past, agriculture and manufacturing contributed the most to the economy. Agriculture focuses on growing the food that is necessary for survival. Once that production process is stable and people have enough to eat, the economy moves on to manufacturing. Manufacturing helps build products that make life easier. These are products that we can evaluate with our five senses like touch or smell. As other countries have developed cheaper labor, American manufacturing has changed. Now the service sector is the most dominant contributor.

This shift of dominance from agriculture and manufacturing to service has required people to acquire different skills. In an agricultural economy, people were engaged in growing crops and preparing them for consumer consumption. Service played a very small role because most of the focus was on climates and crops. In a manufacturing economy,

Figure 1.1 ┃┃┃ **Organization of the Book**

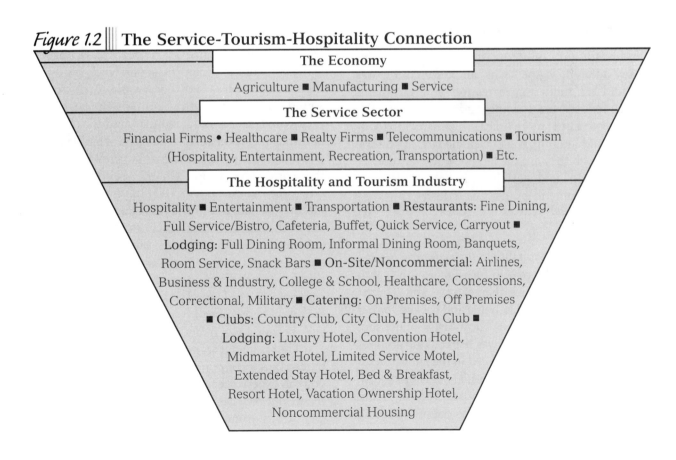

Hospitality and Tourism Industry

Welcome to Hospitality and Tourism ■ The History, the Present, and Future ■ Information Resources ■ Industry Associations ■ Career Realities

Hospitality and Tourism Companies

E-Hospitality ■ Independents ■ Chain Operation ■ Contract Management ■ Franchising and Referral Associations

Hospitality and Tourism Operations

Management ■ Marketing ■ Physical Facilities and Security ■ Human Resources ■ Law and Ethics ■ Revenue and Cost Management

The Hospitality and Tourism Career Menu

Attractions ■ Beverages ■ Casinos ■ Clubs ■ Cruise Ships ■ Culinary ■ Distribution ■ Education ■ Golf ■ Interior Design ■ International Hotel and Lodging ■ Consulting ■ Meeting and Events ■ Non-Commercial Food Service ■ Quick Service ■ Real Estate ■ Resorts ■ Restaurants ■ Senior Services ■ Travel and Tour

Figure 1.2 ┃┃┃ **The Service-Tourism-Hospitality Connection**

The Economy

Agriculture ■ Manufacturing ■ Service

The Service Sector

Financial Firms • Healthcare ■ Realty Firms ■ Telecommunications ■ Tourism (Hospitality, Entertainment, Recreation, Transportation) ■ Etc.

The Hospitality and Tourism Industry

Hospitality ■ Entertainment ■ Transportation ■ **Restaurants:** Fine Dining, Full Service/Bistro, Cafeteria, Buffet, Quick Service, Carryout ■ **Lodging:** Full Dining Room, Informal Dining Room, Banquets, Room Service, Snack Bars ■ **On-Site/Noncommercial:** Airlines, Business & Industry, College & School, Healthcare, Concessions, Correctional, Military ■ **Catering:** On Premises, Off Premises ■ **Clubs:** Country Club, City Club, Health Club ■ **Lodging:** Luxury Hotel, Convention Hotel, Midmarket Hotel, Limited Service Motel, Extended Stay Hotel, Bed & Breakfast, Resort Hotel, Vacation Ownership Hotel, Noncommercial Housing people were occupied with the process of creating a product, what machinery could be used to speed up the process. Service played a more important role because more people were involved in the process. In today's service economy, there is no tangible product—the product is mostly service, and the quality of that product rests in the mind of the guest. Therefore, people skills are critical to operations.

In a hotel, the room is the tangible product. However, in picking the hotel, the guest spends more money for the ambience and the service. By the same token, people go to a restaurant to eat, but just as important is the way they are treated. Think about your best experience in a restaurant. You enjoyed the food, of course. However, what if the server was rude? What would happen to your feeling about the restaurant experience? Herein lies the difficult and exciting part of this industry: forecasting the guests' service expectations. The skills necessary to survive in an agricultural economy and manufacturing economy are physical and mental. In the service economy, they are more interpersonal and intellectual. For many people, this is quite a change and a difficult transition. Figure 1.2 illustrates the relationship between the economy, service, and the hospitality and tourism industry.

Hospitality and Tourism

The hospitality and tourism industry includes many different segments, as can be seen in Figures 1.1 and 1.2, including recreation, entertainment, travel, foodservice, lodging, and many others. We will devote a little more time in this chapter to foodservice and lodging, the two single largest sectors. Even though they are the largest, however, they're closely related and work hand in hand with many other vital segments of this vast industry.

Foodservice

This part of the hospitality industry is growing at a dramatic rate. The reason for this growth is that consumers are changing their eating habits. In the 50s, the woman stayed at home and cooked for her husband and two children. The measure of her success as a wife and mother was her cooking abilities and how much time she labored in the kitchen. Going out to eat was only for special occasions. Now, there are a variety of households, ranging from singles to one-parent families to couples with no

kids to the two-parent family. To meet their economic needs, the adults in the family are working longer hours. Therefore, there is less time to spend buying groceries and preparing meals. As a result, more people are consuming meals away from their homes or are bringing prepared food home to eat. The increase in second-income families and the inadequate time to prepare meals is a significant factor in this trend.

However, this industry is far more than just food and service. For example, how many different reasons can you think of for going out to eat? Hunger, of course. What else? How about getting together with friends to socialize or impressing a special someone, or creating a romantic mood? Because there are so many different reasons for eating out, it makes sense that restaurants come in all types of price ranges and service qualities to meet the needs of their guests. For example, quick-service restaurants cater to our frantic on-the-go lifestyle. Family restaurants attempt to keep kids occupied with activities like placemats that they can draw on while they wait for their food. At the upper end of the spectrum are restaurants that serve great food and deliver exceptional service. In each of these different venues, understanding the guests' needs and providing the kind of food and good service they want is important.

However, there is another aspect of any service environment: ambiance or servicescape. Ambiance is made up of the décor, the sound level, the lighting, the furniture, and the symphony of dining sounds created by both the diners themselves—their conversation and laughter—and the clanking of dishes and silverware. What type of ambiance do you like when going out to eat? When Windows on the World reopened in 1996, the president of Windows, Joe Baum, announced at the employee orientation, "We are not in the restaurant business; we are in the entertainment business because we are creating a unique experience." He took the notion of a dining experience to the next level. Windows on the World went on to become the highest volume restaurant in the United States. Unfortunately, that ended on September 11, 2001, when the industry and the world lost many good people.

The restaurant segment of the foodservice industry can be a trip around the world. In any major city, you can experience food from almost any country in the world. New taste sensations are created as chefs blend different cuisines to produce what is called "fu-

When you go to a restaurant, the service is as important as the meal.

sion" cuisine. For example, the blending of the flavors from Chinese and French cuisine produces a new, unique taste. Creative themes and décor can enhance the eating experience by transporting the guest to any country in the world or make them feel like they are in the eighteenth or the twenty-third century. The diversity of the restaurant segment is immense. As a customer, you can spend five dollars for dinner or you can spend one hundred dollars for dinner. You can select from an assortment of five beverages or a selection of one thousand varieties of wine. You can also experience an operation that is owned by an individual who has one restaurant and works at it all the time or a restaurant that is one of a thousand restaurants owned by a corporation, where the owners are never around. For the employee, both entrepreneurial properties and franchises have advantages and disadvantages.

In addition, the foodservice industry is made up of more than just restaurants. The noncommercial foodservice industry feeds students—elementary, secondary, and college—as well as patients and corporate employees. The challenge is to offer food they will eat and that is nutritious. In some college dining programs, a cafeteria is set aside just for vegetarians. That goes a long way to meet and exceed the expectations of the customer. Many students will choose that university because they have a vegetarian cafeteria. Hospital foodservice is challenging

in that meals must be suitable for all kinds of diets that are required by patients. Many institutional dining facilities (hospitals, schools, companies) have gone to branding. Branding is taking a known brand like McDonald's and opening that facility in a hospital or a school. This trend brings to the operation the name recognition and appeal that goes with it, as well as the standards of operation for that brand.

An often overlooked segment of the foodservice industry is the private club segment. Private clubs are owned and run by its members. Therefore, the focus is on satisfying the needs of a small group of people. You know these people because they come in regularly and they expect that you will know their names and their preferences for drinks and food. These operations can provide an exciting, interesting place to work, especially if the club has a large foodservice facility that serves a la carte and has catering for special events. In addition to the foodservice operation, a manager could end up managing the challenges of other activities like a golf course or tennis courts.

Probably the largest segment of this industry is the quick-service or fast-food restaurants. As we mentioned earlier, quick service meets our needs for food when we are on the run. As you know, you can eat in or drive through, which affords a variety of eating options like eating at your desk or in the car on the way to classes. Quick-service restaurants are

One of the segments of the noncommercial food industry in schools.

continually trying to reinvent themselves, but the eating public continues to go for that hamburger, fried chicken, and pizza.

Another subdivision of the foodservice business is found in special events and catering. Special events include foodservice at outdoor concerts, golf tournaments, tennis tournaments, and huge events like the Olympics. These events are intense and many times more difficult to operate because the dining tents and kitchens are normally temporary. During the Winter 2002 Olympics, the foodservice people were providing one hundred thousand meals per day. The dining tent in the Olympic Village housed thirteen hundred seats, a huge kitchen, and a full-service McDonald's. Working in stadiums and arenas is a unique challenge because they contain almost every segment of the foodservice industry: concession stands, private clubs, luxury skyboxes, a la carte restaurants, and catering for special events. As a free bonus, you get the excitement of watching a major sporting event. As you can see, foodservice has a broad variety of venues that will be explored in this book. Knowing about all these different types will allow you to decide whether this is the career path for you.

Lodging

If you were to ask ten people to give you an example of the lodging industry, you might get answers like: a resort in the Bahamas or Hawaii; a small inn in Vermont; a bed and breakfast in Cape May, New Jersey; a small exclusive converted castle in France; a roadside motel in Akron, Ohio; a 1200-room luxury hotel in New York; a 100-room budget motel in Fresno, California; an all-suite hotel in Memphis; a mega hotel in Las Vegas; and an apartment hotel in London. All these answers, although different in some ways, represent examples of the lodging industry. The common bond is that they all have sleeping rooms.

However, the amenities and quality of service will vary from concept to concept. A Motel 6 will give you a clean room with bed and bath, whereas a Marriott might provide you with additional amenities like a fitness center and a swimming pool. A resort will allow you to walk around the grounds and play golf or go to the spa and have a clean room with bed and bath. Some will have extensive foodservice with two or three restaurants with different cuisines and twenty-four-hour room service. Some will have one restaurant that serves breakfast, lunch, and dinner. An apartment or residential hotel may provide the guests with a fully equipped kitchen. A bed and breakfast will serve only breakfast. Some will have no foodservice except for a vending machine with snacks and soft drinks. The profitability percentage of a sold guest room is usually higher than the profitability percentage of selling a meal. Therefore, many owners make the decision not to have foodservice in their properties because of the profitability picture and the difficulty of operating a foodservice facility. In some cases, lodging owners want to provide foodservice for their guests and will lease the foodservice facility.

Some lodging facilities will have five employees to service each room, whereas others will have two or more employees per room. The Peninsula Hotel in Hong Kong changes your linens and towels several times a day to provide the ultimate in service, whereas other hotels will ask you to throw the towels on the floor only when you want them changed to protect the environment. If you think about how much water and soap it takes to wash all those sheets and towels, you can see that even using towels one more day before washing them can make a big difference in water usage. In places that regularly have droughts like California, this is an important factor. It is amazing that there are over 50,000 lodging operations in the United States. What incredible opportunity.

The lodging industry is very broad and varied, with each segment requiring a different skill set. Can you imagine the amount of experience you would need to run one of those mega-properties in Las Vegas with four to five thousand rooms? You would actually be running a medium-sized corporation. You would need to have experience in all facets of hotel operations, excellent interpersonal and leadership skills, extensive food and beverage experience to run twelve to twenty-four different venues, plus excellent knowledge of the gaming industry. Obviously, to run a hundred-room or less property without food and beverage would require much less experience than the Vegas property. Some managers of these properties have less than five years experience in the lodging business.

The basic strategy in the lodging business is to sell rooms; that is pretty obvious. The challenge for marketing is to bring people in to buy rooms. Once the guest is at the property, a challenge might be to sell them the kind of room they desire at a price that represents value to the guest. Value, like quality, is determined by the guest, not the management of the property. A guest room is a perishable product. If it is not sold on any one night, that revenue is lost, so the challenge is to know how to sell that room based on the guests' expectation and their perception of value.

Summary

As you can see from our brief exploration of just food and lodging, there are many components of the hospitality industry that you may never have realized. In this book, you will find that there are even more opportunities for careers as we explore many segments. However, the bottom line in the hospitality business is managing the "moments of truth." A "moment of truth" is any time the guest comes in contact with anything that represents the operation. The perception of that contact could be positive or negative. Those contacts could be the condition of the parking lot, the friendliness of the voice on the phone when the reservation was made, the cleanliness of the entranceway, the greeting by the front desk person or a hostess, the speediness of the elevator, and so on. In a one-night stay or the time it takes to enjoy a meal, the guest could experience one hundred "moments of truth." The greatest challenge in the industry is to manage those "moments of truth" so that they are positive for the guest who then wants to return and tell their friends how wonderful their encounter was. These happy memories create the desire in our guests and everyone who hears their stories to come and experience the adventure. Hospitality, tourism, and service are interwoven in this exciting worldwide industry.

Enjoy your exploration into the industry, companies, operations, and careers. Welcome!

☛ Key Words and Concepts

Ambience or servicescape
Foodservice
Lodging
Moment of truth
Service
Service experience
Service product

1 ▊ Review Questions

1. Why is the hospitality industry referred to as a "people" business?

2. What are the three separate parts of the economy described by the author? Define each.

3. Describe the major shift in the economy concerning the manufacturing industries and the service industries.

4. What is the product in a service economy?

5. Who judges the quality level of service?

6. What are the skills necessary to survive in the service economy?

7. Describe the various segments of the hospitality industry.

8. Describe the current trends in the foodservice industry. How and why are they changing?

9. List three to five factors that influence decisions concerning a meal away from home.

10. What is fusion cuisine?

11. What is a challenge of the noncommercial food industry?

12. Describe the different attributes of the private club segment of the hospitality industry.

13. What are the common menu choices of fast-food restaurants?

14. What types of venues are likely to cater to or hold special events?

15. What makes working in stadiums and arenas a unique challenge?

16. Give six examples of different types of lodging.

17. What is the range of employees per guest room ratio? How does that vary within the lodging industry?

18. What are the different types of food services you will find in many hotels?

19. What type of lodging management skills would be needed to run a mega-property in Las Vegas?

20. What is meant by the concept that a guest room is perishable?

21. List five examples of "moments of truth" in a hospitality setting.

22. What is one of the greatest challenges related to managing moments of truth?

Dr. Reginald Foucar-Szocki
James Madison University

Dr. Ronald J. Cereola
James Madison University

The Past, Present, and Future

Learning Objectives

After studying this chapter you should be able to:
- ✓ Describe the role of Ellsworth Statler in the evolution of the lodging industry
- ✓ Explain the culture of Marriott, Inc.
- ✓ Detail Escoffier's impact on the role of the chef
- ✓ Point out qualities of Julia Child, Ray Kroc, Colonel Sanders, and Walt Disney that influence our industry today
- ✓ Understand the changing role of the U.S. economy and the scope of the hospitality and tourism industry
- ✓ Begin to think outside the box of what the industry might look like when you are ready to retire at age 70

Chapter Outline

The History of Lodging
Food: The Universal Language
A Man and His Mouse
Five Rings and So Much More
2050: A Hospitality Odyssey

*W*elcome to a great learning experience filled with new ideas, insights, and understandings about the wonderful world of hospitality. The focus of this chapter is to examine the past, present, and future of hospitality and tourism management. There are several ways we can explore the subject matter.

(1) Prepare you to be a contestant who knows bits and pieces on *Jeopardy*;
(2) Drown you in facts and figures; or
(3) Provide a balance of people, places, and things that make your professors love the multi-faceted business of hospitality and tourism management.

It should come as no surprise that Option 3 will be the direction of this chapter. We have selected a few of the colorful characters that shaped the business over the past century to present a snapshot of the present state of the industry and finish with what hospitality and tourism management might look like in 2050.

We will begin our tour of the lodging side of the industry with a gentleman named Ellsworth Statler, the most famous hotelier of the early twentieth century, and then learn about how a simple nine-seat A&W Root Beer stand turned into Marriott, Inc. On the food side, one of the great visionaries was Augustine Escoffier, who professionalized the role of chef/culinarian and created dishes that are still served a century later. Before Rachel Ray, Emeril, and Bobby Flay, there was Julia Child, who taught Americans how to cook. At the same time there was a milk shake mixer salesperson who founded McDonald's, a Colonel who had a recipe, and a man with a dream of a magical kingdom.

We'll continue our tour with the definitive hospitality and tourism event, the Olympic Games, and a passing of the torch from manufacturing to the service economy as the backbone of the U.S. economy. Lastly, we'll look at life after iPods, IMS, Facebook, the Travel Channel, and the Food Network to see what the field of hospitality and tourism management will look like in the future.

Again, there is no way to cover every person, place, and thing that makes our industry great. This is a simple snapshot; a single-dimensional model that we hope will be a springboard for future studies. We hope that after reading this book, you will turn our snapshot into a four-dimensional interactive Web-based model of hospitality and tourism.

The History of Lodging

Statler: The Lightbulb Goes On

In 1901, Buffalo, New York, was preparing to host the Pan American Exhibition. The Exhibition organizers expected about eight million people. An entrepreneur named Ellsworth Statler built temporary structures to house guests; this began his fascination with the hotel industry. He opened his first permanent hotel in Buffalo in 1907, offering "a room with a bath for a dollar and a half."[1] His target market was the ordinary traveler. Value, guest satisfaction, and cleanliness were his priorities. Statler was fascinated with ways to make hotel operations more efficient and is credited with the idea of building bathrooms back to back, minimizing the expenses and allowing a private bathroom for each guest, something that was new and in stark contrast to the water closets (WCs) of European hotels. He would spend hours with housekeepers and engineers, looking at ways to make the hotel more efficient and thus more profitable.

On December 11, 1916, Ellsworth acquired the operating lease of the Hotel Pennsylvania in New York City for an annual sum of $1 million.[2] It was the largest hotel in the United States at the time. More important than guest conveniences was his belief in his employees. Ellsworth Statler had a unique saying: "Life is service. The one who progresses is the one who gives his fellow human beings a little more, a little better service."[3] He was the first to give hotel staff a six-day week, paid vacations, and free health care. He devised a profit-sharing plan that matched a free stock share with each one purchased by employees. It is easy to see why Ellsworth Statler is called "the hotel man of the half century" and the father of innkeeping science. On October 27, 1954, Conrad Hilton purchased the Statler chain for $111,000,000 in what was then the largest real estate transaction in history.[4]

Marriott: Humble Beginnings

Meanwhile, another famous hotel line, Marriott, was in its infancy during the 1950s, building on 25 years of success in foodservice operations. Today, this dynamic organization has more than 2,700 lodging properties employing 133,000 associates in the United States and 65 other countries and territories.[5] This company began in 1927 as a nine-seat A&W Root Beer stand in Washington, DC.

J. W. Marriott, a devout member of the Church of Jesus Christ of Latter-Day Saints, did missionary work in New York City and Washington, DC. In the spring of 1927 he moved back to Washington, DC, and opened a nine-seat A&W Root Beer stand named the Hot Shoppe. His vision was simple: to treat all associates with respect and provide good customer value in a clean environment.

For 25 years Marriott scrupulously avoided putting his company in debt, even while opening 45 restaurants in nine states. Although the Hot Shoppes flourished, Marriott diversified his business interests by starting an airline catering business in 1937—"In-Flite Catering," serving Capital, Eastern, and American Airlines; and signing a contract with the U.S. government to provide foodservice to the U.S. Treasury; and with Miami International Airport. In the mid 1950s, Marriott landed its first institutional and school contracts, with Children's Hospital and American University, respectively.[6]

In 1956, the company moved into the hotel segment. The company's first hotel, the Twin Bridges Marriott, sat the foot of the 14th St. Bridge in Virginia and was managed by Bill Marriott, J. W.'s son. By the time the senior Marriott turned the company over to Bill in 1964, he had built 120 Hot Shoppe restaurants and a dozen hotels and had an $85 million-a-year business, all of which was virtually debt free. In ensuing years, J. W. Marriott would often tell the same joke, "When I came to Washington in 1927, I owed $2,000, now in 1964 I owe $20 million. Is that progress?"[7]

Bill Marriott still leads the company today and is credited with creating the "Marriott Way." His management style incorporates concern for all associates, hands-on management, and an unrelenting commitment to customer service. This explains Marriott International's dominance of the hospitality industry. Bill Marriott embodies the industry's professionalism, compassion, commitment to ethics, and social responsibility.[8]

So what is the current status of the lodging industry in the United States? The American Hotel & Lodging Association in their most recent projections suggests the following:[9]

- There are approximately 47,500 hotels in the United Sates with more than 4.1 million guest rooms.
- In 2005 revenue totaled $113 billion in sales and generated over $16.7 billion in pre-tax profits.
- The average room rate will be nearly $90. The most recent data show 2004 was $86.24—up from $82.52 in 2003.
- The industry pays $163.3 billion in travel-related wages and salaries and employs 1.8 million hotel property workers.
- One of every eight Americans is employed either directly or indirectly because of people traveling to and within the United States.

In 1937 J. W. Marriott began a foodservice contract with the U.S. Treasury.

The hotel industry is a rapidly expanding and highly competitive business with many opportunities for a variety of career opportunities.

Food: The Universal Language

The National Restaurant Association is based in Washington, DC, and its mission is to represent, educate and promote a rapidly growing industry that consists of 925,000 restaurant and foodservice outlets and employs 12.5 million people. Today, this organization is the voice of the foodservice industry.

Escoffier

However, before the industry had such a strong lobby, it was known for its cuisine. George Augustine Escoffier was the King of Chefs and the Chef of Kings. Born in 1846 near Nice, France, he revolutionized the culinary industry by simplifying cooking and kitchens and reinventing the culinary profession. The hotel kitchens of the late 1800s and early 1900s were terrible places to work—long and grueling hours in poorly designed space with little air flow. It was commonplace for the cooks to cool off by drinking beer. The limit was no more than three beers per hour. Alcoholism, swearing, and screaming were routine daily activities. Apprentices who wanted to learn the trade of cooking were particularly abused. The working conditions were not attractive, hazing was a rite of passage, and the industry was not attracting the best and the brightest.

Escoffier believed the best way to keep his palate as sensitive as possible was to avoid tobacco and alcohol. As a result, he created a nonalcoholic drink that contained barley, forbade cursing, and made all his employees take an abstinence oath. He encouraged his staff to learn as much about their profession as they could. Although this is the expectation today, it was a revolutionary concept in Escoffier's time.

Escoffier created the kitchen brigade to increase efficiency. Rather than separating the kitchen as had been the practice, in Escoffier's kitchen, elements were logically organized, and cleanliness became the cornerstone of kitchen practice. In the 1890s Escoffier partnered with Caesar Ritz and revolutionized European cuisine. At the turn of the century, Escoffier opened the Carlton Hotel in London, spending 20 years managing a team of 60 culinarians creating a la carte dining options. His first book, *Le Guide Culinaire* (1902), contained almost 5,000 recipes. To his credit, many of Escoffier's innovations are now standard in today's great foodservice operations.[10]

Just as Escoffier professionalized cooking, Julia Child personalized it. It is hard to imagine that people used to dine in restaurants only on special occasions. Today, half of all Americans purchase food to eat outside the home every day.

Julia Child

Julia Child, 1913–2004, was 6'2", enjoyed puffing on cigars, and worked for the federal government in the Office of Strategic Services (now the CIA). In 1948, Child enrolled in the Le Cordon Bleu Cooking School in Paris, where she met Simone Beck and Louisette Bertholle. The three of them opened a cooking school in Paris to bring classic French cuisine to American expatriates, which led to her popular cookbook, *Mastering the Art of French Cooking*. The theme of the book was that French cooking was not difficult if the cook had the correct skills and equipment.

In the early 1960s Child went to television station WGBH in Boston to promote her book. Instead of just talking about the book, she brought a hot plate, eggs, and a pan to show the audience how simple it was to prepare a French omelet. Shortly thereafter her show *The French Chef* became a staple of American television. Her message was simple: "above all have a good time."[11] In 1981, with vintner Robert Mondavi and others, she cofounded the American Institute of Wine and Food in California to "advance the understanding, appreciation and quality of wine and food."[12] Today, her kitchen is in the Smithsonian Institution; she was awarded the Presidential Medal of Freedom and recognized by the French Ordre de Mérite Agricole, Order de Mérite Nationale, and the Confrérie de Ceres. Most importantly she opened the doors for today's culinary stars such as Rachel Ray, Emeril, Bobby Flay, Martha Stewart, Mario Batali, and Jamie Oliver. All one has to do is to look at the Food Network to see the impact of Julia Child on the world of gourmet cooking

Ray Kroc Sold More Than Mixers

In 1954, Dick and Mac McDonald of San Bernardino, California, ordered eight multimixers from Ray Kroc. They told him how their restaurant sold the cheapest burgers, fries, sodas, and milkshakes in town and how people were standing in line to get their food. Kroc thought about how great it would be if there were these McDonald's restaurants all over the country with eight multimixers in each. Kroc strongly believed that people went to McDonald's to eat, not to dine. He formed a partnership with the McDonald brothers and slowly spread the Golden Arches across the country. In 1961 he purchased the exclusive rights to McDonald's for $2.7 million dollars.[13]

Kroc understood Fredrick Taylor's principles of scientific management. Fewer steps meant more customers could be served, and that meant more sales and more revenue. Every employee was told, "If you have time to lean, you have time to clean." His values were quality, service, cleanliness, and value. He demonstrated that detailed planning, standardized practices, and tight controls can introduce a complicated operation to more than 115 countries. Ray Kroc is the father of fast food, and his systems have been copied by restaurateurs around the world.

The Colonel Has a Recipe

In the 1930s, Harland Sanders made fried chicken dinners for people who passed by his service station in Corbin, Kentucky. Eventually, his popularity grew, and Sanders moved his enterprise to a motel and restaurant that seated 142 people. In the early 1950s, the Colonel perfected his method of pressure cooking chicken in eleven herbs and spices that enhanced the flavor and allowed the chicken to be cooked much faster than panfrying. The Colonel devoted himself to the chicken franchising business by driving across the country cooking batches of chicken for restaurant owners and their employees. If the people liked the food, he entered into a handshake agreement that stipulated that he would earn a nickel for each chicken the restaurant sold. By 1964, Colonel Sanders had more than 600 franchised outlets for his chicken in the United States and Canada. That year, he sold his interest in the U.S. company for $2 million.[14]

Both Kroc and the Colonel were passionate about an idea and believed in their ability to take that idea from concept to product. This is as relevant today as it was fifty years ago. So what is the current state of the foodservice industry? The National Restaurant Association has made the following predictions for 2006:[15]

- Sales: $511 billion.
- Locations: 925,000 — serving more than 70 billion meal and snack occasions.
- Employees: 12.5 million — the industry is the largest employer after the federal government.
- Restaurant-industry sales are forecast to equal 4 percent of the U.S. gross domestic product.
- Every dollar spent by consumers in restaurants generates an additional $2.34 for industries allied with the restaurant industry.
- The average household expenditure for food away from home in 2004 was $2,434, or $974 per person.
- The restaurant industry provides work for more than 9 percent of those employed in the United States and is expected to add 1.9 million jobs by 2016.
- Eating-and-drinking places employ more minority managers than any other industry.

Whether it is gourmet dining or fast food, the eating industry grows every year as people spend less time cooking and more time eating out.

A Man and His Mouse

During the fall of 1918, Walt Disney attempted to enlist for military service but was rejected because he was only sixteen years old. Instead, Walt joined the Red Cross and was sent overseas to France, where he spent a year driving an ambulance and chauffeuring Red Cross officials. His ambulance was covered from stem to stern, not with stock camouflage, but with Disney cartoons.[16] In 1932, the production entitled *Flowers and Trees* (the first color cartoon) won Walt the first of his studio's Academy Awards. In 1937, he released *The Old Mill*, the first short subject to utilize the multi-plane camera technique. On December 21, 1937, *Snow White and the Seven Dwarfs*, the first full-length animated musical feature, premiered at the Cathay Theater in Los Angeles. The film was produced at the unheard cost of $1,499,000 during the depths of the Depression, and is still considered one of the great feats and imperishable monuments of the motion picture industry.

Walt Disney's dream of a clean, organized amusement park came true when Disneyland Park opened in 1955. Walt also became a television pioneer beginning production in 1954 and presenting the first full-color programming with his *Wonderful World of Color* in 1961. Walt Disney is a legend; his worldwide popularity was based on the ideals of imagination, optimism, creation, and self-made success in the American tradition. He brought us closer to the future, while telling us of the past.

Before we look at the future, one event is synonymous with our industry and ties together the past, present, and future.

Five Rings and So Much More

A footrace was held at Olympia in Western Peloponnese for the first time in 776 BCE in honor of the Greek god Zeus. Coroebus, a cook from Elis, won the 210-yard race called the "stade." The victor was crowned with a wreath of wild olives and was granted special honors in his home city. This modest celebration, won by a hospitality employee, led to the modern Olympics.[17]

There is no better example of what our industry is all about than the Olympics. Every four years, the international summer or winter games are held. This grand event showcases a city and region. Preparing a city to welcome visitors and athletes from more than 100 countries can be an overwhelming task. The pageantry of the opening ceremonies, the parade of athletes, the lighting of the Olympic flame, and medal presentations are the easy part. We hospitality professionals know how to fit the pieces of the Olympic puzzle together. In short, the skills that are necessary to organize the Olympics are best learned in the hospitality and tourism area.

You've met some of the founders of the hospitality business, examined the current volume of

There is no better example of what the hospitality and tourism industry is all about than the Olympics.

business and its economic impact, and seen how the Olympics are the ultimate example of hospitality and tourism management. As we conclude the chapter, we share our thoughts about the future.

2050: A Hospitality Odyssey

If we could see the world of hospitality in 2050, we would immediately stop writing, access our brokerage accounts, and start buying shares in the Marriotts and McDonalds of the future, so that our posterity would be able to live like Bill Gates. Although we cannot actually see the future, we can make some educated guesses based on what we know about the past and present.

Mega-Resorts

It's 2007 and you're in Las Vegas after a 5½ hour flight on a cramped plane with way too little leg room. Here in one location, entire cities are recreated. You can dine on meals prepared by the world's greatest chefs and be entertained around the clock, with nonstop music, theater, dance, and other performing arts. Hotels are among the most modern, and the rooms are counted not in the hundreds, but in the thousands. You can shop in huge malls, ride roller coasters, experience cutting-edge IMAX and 4-D motion simulation rides, swim and surf in wave pools, enjoy exclusive spa treatments, attend conferences and meetings, walk through museums and view great works of art by Picasso and Monet, and even get married, without ever leaving your hotel. Amazingly, there is not just one of these mega-resorts, but dozens! This is the desert oasis called Las Vegas, today's mega-resort.

You wonder about the early Spanish traders en route to Los Angeles who passed through this then-unexplored Las Vegas Valley. They referred to the route through the valley as "jornada de muerte," the journey of death.[18] Could they have imagined that it would become the "City of Entertainment," the number one tourist destination in the world? Despite Wall Street pundits' periodic predictions of its demise due to overdevelopment, the city keeps prospering, building even bigger hotel resorts. Seventeen of the twenty largest hotels in the world are located in Las Vegas.[19] Each one of them is a destination in its own right. In recent years the Wynn Las Vegas opened, a $2.7 billion luxury hotel and destination resort. The Wynn Las Vegas features

2,716 luxurious guest rooms and suites, an 111,000-square-foot casino, an eighteen-hole golf course, 223,000 square feet of meeting space, a Ferrari and Maserati dealership; and 76,000 square feet of retail space. Among its twenty-two food and beverage outlets is the Alex Restaurant, internationally recognized by AAA as a Five Diamond restaurant offering fine French cuisine in a luxurious and opulent setting.[20]

It's 2010, and you have returned to the city to help plan the Hilton's newest property. It was a long flight, but the food was better, and your luggage arrived with you. The mega-resorts are even larger, more elaborate, and more activity inclusive. For some it's simply not enough to visit the city; they want to share in the unprecedented expansion of leisure and recreation that the future has presented. Partial, individual ownership in mega-resort complexes has burgeoned since the early 2000s. Many "visitors" now own one or more units in the many hotel condominium resort complexes that have been built over the last ten years around the Strip. Along with ownership comes access to the entertainment facilities, concierge services, and fine dining and beverage services, as well as other upscale amenities.

In recent years, innovative chefs have flocked to the city, drawn by the money as well as the promise of fame. These young, highly trained culinary artists, armed with solid business credentials, are well equipped to operate successful restaurants. They follow in the footsteps of Todd English (Olives at Bellagio); Emeril Lagasse (Emeril's New Orleans Fish House at MGM Grand), Michael Mina (Aqua at Bellagio); Wolfgang Puck (Spago's, Chinois at the Forum Shops at Caesars); Julian Serrano (Picasso at Bellagio), and Joachim Splichal (Pinot Brasserie at the Venetian).[21] Each of these newcomers is determined to make a mark on the culinary world in a city that contains the largest concentration of famed chefs.

Ride in My Beautiful Machine

It's 2015 and you have flown into the Mohave Air & Space Port, America's first Inland Spaceport.[22] You just deplaned from the world's largest aircraft, the Airbus A380. It was quite the experience flying on an aircraft the size of a football field along with 500 other passengers. You were lucky enough to go below and work out in one of the small onboard gyms, then catch a few winks in your private sleeper compartment. You should have bought your six-year-old son a souvenir from one of the onboard retail boutiques,[23] but maybe next time. Look, your luggage is actually at baggage claim before you are! You worried a bit about how they were going to serve all those passengers, as well as get them off the plane, but everything went very smoothly: "service with a smile." Wonder what they studied at college that enabled them to take care of all the details? Tomorrow, 20 civilians will take the first suborbital tour in space. Back in 2001, Dennis Tito went to the International Space Station, but he paid $25.8 million. This group paid $200,000 to see the cobalt blue sky turn to mauve and indigo and finally black. The civilian space tourism industry started with the X-Prize, a $10,000,000 reward offered to the first private company that succeeded in putting a person in space and then repeated the feat within two weeks.[24] On October 4, 2004, Spaceship One, designed by Burt Rutan, did just that. Almost immediately thereafter, Richard Branson announced the formation of Virgin Galactic Corporation, which would bring space tourism to the public.[25]

New Atlantis, 2025

The 2,000-mile trip went by rather quickly. Boeing's new 877 hypersonic aircraft travels at five times the speed of sound.[26] Hilton's Oceania I is part of New Atlantis, an artificial island floating in the Caribbean. The technology is based on the old oil rig platforms now made obsolete by the new fusion energy sources. As soon as scientists figured out how to redirect the ocean storms, these floating islands became great leisure opportunities. Just in time, too, as the global democratization of travel has started to stress traditional leisure travel destinations, especially the smaller islands. The concept of New Atlantis is the logical evolution of the cruise ship. The ships kept getting bigger, and by 2006 Royal Caribbean launched the world's largest cruise ship, Freedom of the Seas, a 3,600-guest ship with ice skating rinks, rock climbing walls, Broadway shows, surfing pools, and a host of other attractions.[27] However, Royal had already placed an order for a new mega class ship that was delivered in 2009. Dubbed Project Genesis, it cost over $1.24 billion and held up to 6,400 passengers.[28] From there it was just a short leap to the artificial leisure island. Among the first were the Palm Islands off the coast of Dubai, which were fully operational by 2010. Like New Atlantis, these islands sport luxury hotels, residential villas, unique water homes, shoreline apartments, marinas, theme parks and aquariums, casinos, restaurants, shopping malls, multiple golf courses and other sports facilities, health spas, cinemas, stadiums and theaters, and various diving sites on artificial reefs.[29] Also available on New Atlantis are fractional ownerships in residential vacation homes, modeled on the condo mega-resort hotel complexes that appeared in Las Vegas in the early 2000s. Many include planned communities with assisted living facilities for today's active retirees.

A Room with a View, 2035

It's only been 20 years since you witnessed the launch of the first commercial space tourist, and here you are in the new Hilton International Orbital Hotel. In 1964 Barron Hilton delivered a speech in which he envisioned hotels in space,[30] and in 1999 Hilton International endorsed the concept of using spent space shuttle launch vehicles as the building blocks for a space hotel,[31] but it was your Virgin Galactic report that convinced the company. Today you are meeting here with top executives from all over the hospitality industry, a fitting location for the unveiling of plans for the Lunar I resorts.

Foodservice hasn't changed much, and Escoffier would be pleased by the fact that every facility still needs an excellent chef. However, improved transportation technology, coupled with new techniques in food preservation and storage, has provided guests with a wider array of food choices, and "fresh" means fresh. Kitchens are truly "clean rooms," and both facilities and workers are automatically sanitized by new light wave technology. Cooking technology has made significant advances so that the food is prepared healthier and quicker; room service is no longer a 40-minute wait. Ordering room service is completely automated. Guests simply use a menu touch tablet to place their order, and because of the advances in kitchen technology, specialty "off-the-menu" orders are no problem. After dinner you can take advantage of the equipment in your mini-gym "closet."

Statler's bed and bath are still at the heart of the room, but they too have evolved. The beds are equipped with "space age" foam mattresses that contour to your body and with electronic sensors to monitor and induce deep restful REM sleep and noise canceling technology, so that you are sure to awake refreshed. Standard bathrooms include the same light wave sanitation devices used in the kitchen, voice-activated showers and wash basins to control flow and temperature, mini spas and of course a flat-panel multipurpose LCD monitor. Oh, and they also have variable environmental lighting make-up assistance (VELMA) that allows women to program the kind of light they want when applying their cosmetics. Yes, the rooms back on Earth are quite different. Up here the rooms are still very much like the 1990s, but looking out the porthole at the home planet, the view is unbelievable!

Welcome to Hilton Galactic Resort I, 2050

You just alighted from the lunar shuttle, and a sign in the space port says "Welcome to Galactic Resort I." The whole lunar leisure recreation complex would have been impossible without the strategic alliances with companies like Boeing Aerospace and Airbus, Virgin Galactic, Aramark, Disney, Universal, and MGM—Mirage. The high-tech giants like Intel and IBM are well represented, as are a host of other private companies from around the world. It had been a true international effort, the epitome of business going global.

You sure traveled a lot over the course of your career, that's one of the perks of the hospitality business. This trip, however, is strictly for pleasure, here with your entire family to enjoy the semi-weightless recreational environment. In fact, it has been six months since you retired from the Hilton organization, and this all-expense-paid trip is part of their recognition of your longtime service, loyalty, and contributions that ensured Hilton would remain a pioneer in the hospitality industry. Word is that a similar resort will be on Mars in 50 short years. You haven't walked too far when you spy the familiar Golden Arches and smile.

Endnotes

1. Dunn, Walter. (1972). *The History of Erie County*. Buffalo: Buffalo and Erie County Historic Society
2. Wikimeida Foundation, 2000. Retrieved February 1, 2006. http://commons.wikimedia.org/wiki/Category:New_York_City_from_1900_to_1939
3. Buffalo Historical Society Publications. (1930), 30(1), 2–4

4. http://www.hiltonworldwide.com/en/ww/company_info/corporate_history.jhtml. Retrieved February 1, 2006

5. http://marriott.com/corporateinfo/culture/heritageTimeline.mi (retrieved February 1, 2006)

6. http://marriott.com/corporateinfo/culture/heritageTimeline.mi

7. Cereola, Ronald J., Foucar-Szocki, Reginald, and Welpott, Stephen D. "J. W. Marriott, Jr.: The Spirit to Serve," *Journal of Hospitality and Tourism Education*, 6–11. 2004

8. Marriott, W. and Brown, K. (1989). *The Spirit to Serve*. Upper Saddle River, NJ: Prentice Hall

9. http://www.ahla.com/; retrieved February 10, 2006

10. http://en.wikipedia.org/wiki/Auguste_Escoffier; Wellman, Joseph Chef, http://escoffier.com/phpnuke/html/index.php; retrieved February 1, 2006

11. NPS Archives—Julia Child

12. www.aiwf.org/

13. Kroc, R. (1977). *Grinding It Out*. New York: Contemporary Books

14. Sanders, Harland. (1974). *Life as I Have Known It Has Been Finger Lickin' Good*. Carol Stream, IL: Creation House

15. www.restaurant.org; retrieved February 1, 2006

16. http://www.justdisney.com/walt_disney/; retrieved February 1

17. http://www.mapsofworld.com/olympic-trivia/ancient-olympics.html/

18. City of Las Vegas. (n.d.) February 17, 2006; Retrieved from http://www.lasvegasnevada.gov/FactsStatistics/history.htm

19. Chisholm, Charlyn. *Twenty Largest Hotels in the World*, (n.d.); Retrieved February 17, 2006 from http://hotels.about.com/cs/uniqueunusual/a/largesthotels_2.htm

20. Wynn Resorts. (n.d.). Retrieved February 17, 2006 from http://phx.corporate-ir.net/phoenix.zhtml?c=132059&p=irol-IRHome

21. Restaurant Report. (n.d.) Retrieved February 17, 2006 from http://www.restaurantreport.com/features/ft_lasvegas.html

22. Mohave Airport & Spaceport. (n.d.). Retrieved February 17, 2006 from http://www.mojaveairport.com/

23. PBS. *Chasing the Sun Airbus A380*. (n.d.). Retrieved February 17, 2006 from http://www.pbs.org/kcet/chasingthesun/planes/a380.html

24. X Prize. (n.d.). Retrieved February 17, 2006 from http://www.xprizefoundation.com/about_us/default.asp

25. CNN.com. (n.d.). Retrieved February 17, 2006 from http://www.cnn.com/2004/TECH/space/10/04/spaceshipone.attempt.cnn/a

26. Boeing.com. *Boeing Joins X-432 Hypersonic Research Vehicle Team*. (n.d.). Retrieved February 17, 2006 from http://www.boeing.com/news/releases/2003/q4/nr_031120a.html

27. Garrison, Linda. *Royal Caribbean International Names New Ultra-Voyager Cruise Ship*. (n.d.). Retrieved February 17, 2006 from http://cruises.about.com/od/cruisenews/a/041109rci.htm

28. MSNBC.com. *Royal Caribbean Orders Largest Ever Cruise Ship*. (n.d.). Retrieved February 17, 2006 from http://msnbc.msn.com/id/11199685/

29. The Emirates Network. *The Palm*. (n.d.). Retrieved February 17, 2006 from http://realestate.theemiratesnetwork.com/developments/dubai/palm_islands.php

30. Hilton, Barron. *Hotels in Space*. (1967). Retrieved February 17, 2006 from http://www.spacefuture.com/archive/hotels_in_space.shtml

31. Whitehouse, David. *Hilton Backs Space Hotel Built from Shuttle Tanks*. (3/15/99). Retrieved February 17, 2006 from http://www.gsreport.com/articles/art000116.html

☞ *Key Words and Concepts*

Condo-Hotel (condominium hotel)—A lodging property where all or part of the "rooms" or suites are owned by independent entities, either for the owners' personal use or for rental purposes. The day-to-day "hotel" operations are run by a management company for a fee on behalf of all the owners.

Democratization of travel—The concept that travel, in particular leisure travel, is no longer the sole province of the wealthy and that the practice of traveling for leisure has permeated through all levels or strata within society.

Environmental scanning—The acquisition and use of information about trend changes in technology, politics, culture, economics, competition, and social concerns, the knowledge of which would assist management in taking advantage of opportunities and minimizing risks when planning the organization's strategic plan for the future.

Franchise—A form of business organization in which a firm that has a successful product or service (the franchisor) enters into a contractual relationship with other businesses (franchisees) operating under the franchisor's trade name using the franchisor's methods and expertise, in exchange for a fee.

Mega-resort—A final or primary destination where one can find all aspects of the hospitality industry either in a highly compact region or within the confines of a specific hospitality property.

Profit-sharing plan—A benefit given employees, in addition to salary and wages, that permits them to share in a percentage of the profits of the company, distributed to them in either dollars or shares of ownership in the company. Profit sharing motivates employees to be more productive.

Scientific management—The movement started by Frederick Taylor (father of scientific management) in the early 1900s that involved creating efficiencies in the production process through time and motion studies. Taylor championed the idea that management not workers should control how "work" was done; therefore every step of the process needs to be broken down into the most efficient steps for them to follow.

Space tourism—The commercial development by private enterprise for the public at large of earth orbital and suborbital flights, beyond earth orbit experiences, and earth-based simulations of the foregoing for both training and entertainment purposes.

The Marriott Way—The management style that incorporates concern for all associates (employees), hands-on management, and an unrelenting commitment to customer service as articulated by Bill Marriott.

Contributor Information

Reginald Foucar-Szocki
James Madison University
foucarrf@jmu.edu
Dr. Reg Foucar-Szocki is the J. W. Marriott Professor in the Hospitality and Tourism Management program at James Madison University, Harrisonburg, Virginia, where he has taught since 1989. Reg believes the world is a special event, and hospitality management is the centerpiece for success.

Ronald J. Cereola, JD, MBA
James Madison University
cereolrj@jmu.edu
Dr. Ronald J. Cereola is an Assistant Professor in the Hospitality and Tourism Management program at James Madison University, Harrisonburg, Virginia. He teaches Tourism, Hospitality Services Marketing, Hospitality Law, and Entertainment Management.

2 ▌ Review Questions

1. Using the text chapter, identify the core value, belief, or priority of Statler, Marriott, Escoffier, and Kroc.

2. Examine the similarities that exist among your responses to question #1. Why are they important?

3. List the basic amenities in Statler's early hotel rooms and do the same for your most recent stay at a hotel. What has changed and what remains the same?

4. Both Escoffier and Kroc were in the foodservice niche of the hospitality industry. In what way were their contributions similar?

5. Why is "environmental scanning" important for the hospitality industry?

6. After reading the authors' vision of "artificial islands" and space tourism, how realistic are these opportunities for the hospitality industry? What will be the technical, political, economic, and cultural challenges that will have to be overcome to achieve that vision?

Miyoung Jeong
Iowa State University

Information Resources
PERIODICALS AND THE WEB

Learning Objectives

✓ To introduce students to different information
resources available in the field of the hospitality
and tourism industry for their efficient and
effective information search
✓ To familiarize students with key hospitality and
tourism publications
✓ To improve students' skills to search information through a variety of available resources

Chapter Outline

Comprehensive Information Resources
Periodicals
Industry e-Newsletters and Glossary
    Web Sites

They say that knowledge is power. The more information you know, the better the decisions you can make. How do you get knowledge? Well, of course, one way is to go to school . . . take classes . . . graduate . . . get a diploma. However, what if you want more information, what do you do? Where do you go? Learning is an on-going process. We are constantly acquiring new information through conversations with friends, colleagues, bosses, and family. Television, computers, newspapers, and other media are alternative ways to learn new things. Joining associations and being involved in the community and industry is another way. Networking is about meeting new people in the industry and maintaining contact so that you can talk to friends and discover new information. You never know when you might need some help or when they might come to you with a tempting idea. To compete with others, we need the best information available, and so this chapter is designed to help you know where to look.

The hospitality and tourism discipline is an applied science, with its various disciplinary concepts adapted mostly from general business, sociology, psychology, and food science. So, a broad knowledge base is important. Within all those different concepts, there is one that stands out, service. *Service* is the characteristic that makes it and its industry unique and differentiated from other disciplines and industries. As you will continually read throughout this book, service is the human interaction or that "moment of truth" when employee and guest come together. That is when we learn whether our employees have the right kind of information to do their job. As we strive to develop and improve our service quality, more information is needed.

The first step in understanding the true meaning of hospitality and tourism, one must have a direct working experience in related industries. Such direct industry experiences provide one with a rich source of real, subjective information about the discipline and industry as a whole. Thus, one's direct work experience becomes the *primary* source of information for understanding the discipline and industry.

We can also gain primary information from talking with our colleagues and managers. What clothes should I wear to work? What information do I need to finish the project? What career path can I have with your company? When we ask a question and gain answers, this is called primary data gathering. Some call this research, and it is. However, the word *research* tends to scare people with its reputation for difficult statistics. In fact, research is no more than trying to get information to solve a problem. You do "research" every day. You ask questions, gather information, and decide how to proceed—classic research process. Think about it. Should I get out of bed and go to class? After you

Networking is about meeting new people in the industry and maintaining contact so you can stay informed.

filter through the data in your head, you make a decision. A quest for knowledge about a career path is a research process. What field should I plan my career in? This book is designed to give you the information to start answering this question.

However, one may often look for more information from various perspectives about the industry to expand his or her understanding of current industry trends and industry-specific management/operational issues. When you want to look outside your personal contacts, you might want to explore what important industry people think about a topic or what objective research has been done in this area. Such published information can be obtained from industry newsletters, trade journals or magazines, and research journals, and these are generally called *secondary* information resources. Secondary data reflect the fact that you did not gather this information to answer your personal questions. Someone else had a similar question, and so they gathered the data. You came along and used this information to help answer your research question. Therefore, you were the second person to use the data, hence it is a secondary information resource. Keep in mind that depending on who gathered the data and how they gathered the information, the findings may be valid and reliable or they may not.

Example: The Center for Gambling Addiction finds that 80 percent of people who enter a casino will become addicted. Is this true? What questions should you ask about the Center before you accept their findings? Do they have a reason to want a certain outcome? If the researcher appears to be objective and unbiased, then the second question is, "Are they funded by another organization?" Does this organization have a reason to want the data to say certain things? If they are a center for gambling addiction, they want and need to show gambling addiction as a threat, that's why they are in business. However, the research findings may be objective and reliable. Unless you ask questions, you won't know whether the information you have acquired is good or bad. Just because something is in print, does not make it correct or objective. This is a hard lesson to learn because it is very easy to accept printed words at face value.

A good place to start is at the library. Know what is available in your area. Walk through the stacks and see what information can be found. You may be surprised at what you see. The offline resources offer traditional ways of obtaining necessary information, and they include printed materials such as newspapers, newsletters, magazines, and journals. Remember that not all journals, newspapers, magazines, and newsletters are online. There are many good resources that only come in paper. Especially, information on specialty topics may not be accessible to outsiders online, so you may have to rely on paperbound sources. For example, although there is a lot written on gambling, how casinos are actually run is not online. These specialty journals cater only to the casino employees and are only available by subscription. A library may have these periodicals and newsletters available for you to read. In addition, the library has special databases that contain academic literature that may be easier to find in the database for a preliminary search rather than on the Internet.

However, today more and more offline resources are being relocated to Internet sites by either totally eliminating their offline formats or offering both printed and online forms of information. Adoption of the Internet as a platform of information offering like this will accelerate exponentially by dint of its easy accessibility, convenience, ease of use, and currency. Even if many online information providers offer information to readers free of charge in return for the reader's registration for a free newsletter subscription (e.g., hotel-online.com, restaurant_hospitality.com, etc.), other providers set restrictions on information release by requiring membership (e.g., Hospitality Financial Technology Professionals).

With the advent of the Internet as a main hub for information searches, information resources have been divided into largely two categories based on where the target information is placed: online and offline resources. As a major information resource in the hospitality and tourism area today, the Internet makes our life much easier by offering ready access to countless information sources for one's education and career development. The online resources provide the information from various, specific Web sites accessible on the Internet. For example, to gather information about emerging trends or issues in the lodging industry for the upcoming year, hotel-online.com, a major hotel news Web site, is available for access on the Internet.

To make effective and efficient use of both online and offline information resources, the hospitality and tourism industry can be divided into four areas according to industrial characteristics.[1]

The hospitality industry can be divided into the four areas of travel, lodging, foodservice, and recreation.

1. **Travel.** The travel sector is defined based on how people travel from one place to another place, so-called different methods of transportation. This sector includes the airline, cruise, train, coach, and automobile industries. For instance, people tend to use a train, a coach, or an automobile when they travel domestically or for a short distance. For international or long-distance trips, the airplane is a typical transportation people use; so is the cruise ship. However, the cruise is used for more leisure and pleasure trips on water.

2. **Lodging.** The lodging industry, includes two major subindustries: (1) hotels and motels and (2) meetings, conventions, and expositions. The lodging sector is defined based on a place where people can stay while traveling, a hotel or a motel, and what business functions they participate in—meetings, conventions, or expositions. Meetings are typically held in a hotel or a motel in its conference rooms because a small number of people attend the meetings with a range of 50 to 300 people, whereas conventions or expositions are typically held in a destination's convention center due to their large scale of more than 500 participants.

3. **Foodservice.** Commercial restaurants and on-site foodservice operations are classified as the foodservice sector. The foodservice sector refers to places where people can eat out while they are away from home. Think about places you usually go for lunch or dinner, such as McDonald's, Chili's Grill & Bar, Panera Bread, a college dining center, or a residence hall. The first three places fall under the commercial restaurant and the last two under the on-site foodservice.

4. **Recreation.** This consists of attractions, parks, and recreation. The recreation sector focuses on places where people can enjoy themselves and activities that people can participate in. Such places as Niagara Falls, Grand Canyon, and Disney World are excellent examples for attractions. There are many national, state, and local parks in the United States in which people can participate in a wide variety of recreational activities and games including fishing, scenic drives, weekend getaways, camping, and excursions. Yosemite National Park is one of the well-known parks in the world.

In this chapter, we will review sources of information by three categories: (1) a comprehensive information resource, *Hospitality & Tourism Index*, (2) periodicals such as magazines and journals, and (3) industry newsletters and glossary.

Comprehensive Information Resources

Hospitality & Tourism Index

Many universities and colleges in the United States have already subscribed to the *Hospitality & Tourism Index (HTI)*, a comprehensive index for the hospitality and tourism industry. According to the EBSCO publishing Web site,[2] the HTI is

... a bibliographic database covering scholarly research and industry news relating to all areas of hospitality and tourism. This comprehensive index combines the records of three renowned collections: Cornell University's former *Hospitality* database, *Articles in Hospitality and Tourism* (AHT), formerly co-produced by the Universities of Surrey and Oxford Brookes, and the *Lodging, Restaurant & Tourism Index* (LRTI), formerly produced by Purdue University. Together, this collection contains more than 500,000 records from more than 500 titles, with coverage dating as far back as 1965. Sources are both domestic and international in range and scope, with material collected from countries and regions such as Canada, Australia, Europe and Asia. Subject areas covered include the culinary arts, demographics & statistics, development & investment, food & beverage management, hospitality law, hotel management & administrative practices, leisure & business travel, market trends, technology and more.

The EBSCO publishing company also provides users with a full-text HTI with additional costs. Key sources of this index include academic journals, market research/industry/country reports, magazines, trade publications, and more. A complete coverage list of the index is available on the EBSCO Web site.[3] Figure 3.1 is a front page of the HTI on the Internet that can be used to search potential pe-

Figure 3.1 ||| **Database of Hospitality and Tourism Index**

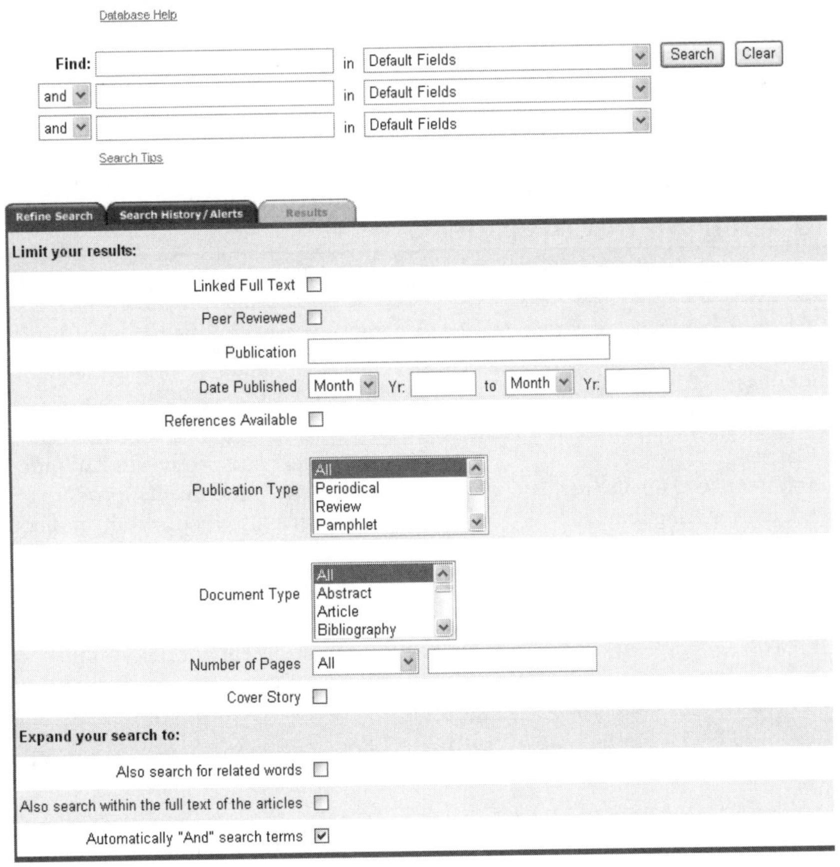

riodicals with key words and to refine the search process by setting limits of the search, such as date and type of publication and document. This index is believed to be the first place to start for searching information in the field of hospitality and tourism.

Periodicals

Periodicals refer to publications such as magazines, newspapers and journals that are published in regular intervals, usually daily, weekly, monthly, or quarterly.[4] Many periodicals in the hospitality and tourism industry are published either in magazines or in journals. All magazines are related to industry-specific publications written by experts in the field such as in *Lodging, Hospitality Technology,* and *Travel Weekly*. Articles in these magazines focus on industry trends both national and international, current operational and management issues, industry outlook, and/or consumers' buying patterns, based on the expert's experience and opinions, or brief interviews or surveys with target markets. Most journals are focused on reporting academic research done by educators and industry practitioners, such as articles published in *Cornell Hotel and Restaurant Administration Quarterly* and *Journal of Foodservice Management and Education*. The academic research, differs from expert opinions, requires more scientific evidence and process by identifying clear research problems or hypotheses, and provides valid results to the problems by analyzing collected data. Many of these publications have both online (their own Web sites) and offline (hard copy) platforms to disseminate information to potential readers. In this chapter, two types of periodicals (magazines and journals) are reviewed as classified by the industry sector and subject area.

Hospitality and Tourism Magazines

There are about sixty-three magazines in the hospitality and tourism area. Twenty-three of the magazines relate to the foodservice sector, twenty-three to lodging, ten to the hospitality sector in general (covering both lodging and foodservice), and eight to the travel/recreation sector. As shown in Tables 3.1 and 3.2, most magazines across the sectors generally cover current issues and trends, industry news, and industry events for the focal business sector. However, such publications as *Wine Spectator, Cruise Industry News Quarterly, Air Transport World,* and *Hospitality Technology* concentrate on a specific product, service, and/or subject area. Therefore, magazines are grouped by their focal subject for a better use of magazines in one's research.

Table 3.1 **List of Foodservice and Lodging Magazines and Their Main Coverage**

Industry	Title of Magazine by Subject	Coverage Area
Foodservice	Alcohol, beverage, & wine ▪ *Beverage World* ▪ *Cheers* ▪ *Wine Spectator*	A comprehensive online listing of beverage products and services; wine ratings; daily wine picks; dining & travel; vintage charts; wine shops
	Catering ▪ *Caterer & Hotelkeeper* ▪ *Catering Magazine* ▪ *Catering Update*	A fresh, expert perspective and an independent view on the news, issues, and events; product information; contract catering to food, drink, and equipment
	Equipment/supplies/recipes ▪ *Chef Magazine* ▪ *Cooking for Profit* ▪ *Food Arts* ▪ *Foodservice Equipment & Supplies*	New recipes; nutrition; up-to-date foodservice equipment; new energy-efficient technologies; foodservice facilities; equipment specifications

(continued)

Industry	Title of Magazine by Subject	Coverage Area
	Onsite foodservice • *Food Management* • *Foodservice Director*	Current issues and events on noncommercial foodservice industry; food safety and layout/design; issues, ideas, and events in institutional foodservice organizations
	Restaurants • *Efenbeonline* • *Foodservice & Hospitality* • *Nation's Restaurant News* • *Nightclub & Bar Magazine* • *Restaurant Business* • *Restaurant Hospitality* • *Restaurant Report* • *Restaurants & Institutions* • *Restaurants USA; Pizza Today*	Key issues and trends of the foodservice industry; new food and equipment products and trends; menu and recipe ideas; new technology; food safety; emerging new concepts; consumer attitudes and trends; labor and training; profiles of successful operations; buyer's guide to suppliers; franchise opportunities; community outreach
	Clubs • *Club Management*	Club leadership; marketing; food & beverage; golf course; sport/fitness; technology; facilities
Lodging	Hotels • *Crittenden Hotel/Lodging News* • *Hotel and Motel Management* • *Hotel Business; Hotel Resource* • *Hotelier; HotelOnline* • *Hotels; Lodging* • *Lodging Hospitality* • *Premier Hotels & Resorts*	Industry trends and issues on marketing, technology, operations, human resources, food & beverage, design & construction, legal, governmental affairs, finance; association news; suppliers; trade shows; hotel brands guide; employment opportunities; worldwide hotel project development; site selection; renovation
	Housekeeping • *Executive Housekeeping Today* • *Room Chronicle*	Housekeeping issues and trends; training; management; operational strategies; energy savings; engineering; front office; guest services; housekeeping; people skills; reservations; risk management; complaint handling
	Meetings/conventions • *Association Meetings* • *Convention Forum* • *Meeting and Conventions* • *Meetings Net; Meeting News* • *Meeting Professionals International* • *Successful Meetings*	Issues and trends on the meetings and events industry; industry news; industry jobs; venue and supplier search database; events in five focused areas, association, corporate, insurance/financial, religious, and medical; destination-specific information about facilities, resources, local attractions and events
	Special lodging segments • *Cruise Industry News Quarterly* • *Green Hotelier* • *Vacation Ownership*	Cruise industry news and trends; cruise operations; ports and destinations; social and environmental issues and trends; sustainable travel and tourism operation; issues and trends on the vacation ownership industry; showcase; guide to vacation ownership

Table 3.2 ‖ **List of Hospitality and Travel/Recreation Magazines and Their Main Coverage**

Industry	Title of Magazine by Subject	Coverage Area
Hospitality	Hospitality • *Hospitality Interactive* • *Hospitality Matters* • *Hospitality Net* • *Hospitality News Resources* • *Hotel & Restaurant*	Industry news; association update; job opportunities and demands; marketplace; hotel schools; industry links; profiles of top chefs, restaurateurs, and hoteliers
	Design • *Hospitality Design*	Hospitality design (hotels, resorts, restaurants, cruise ships, country clubs, nightclubs, conference centers, spas, senior living facilities); other hospitality-oriented projects
	Law • *Hospitality Law*	Hospitality legal cases; summaries of the latest court cases; employee policy development; practical ramifications of the latest cases; employment practices
	Marketing/consulting • *HSMAI Marketing Review* • *HVS International Journal*	Issues and trends of hospitality sales and marketing; industry events; insights from HSMAI leaders; member education. Global consulting and services on the hotel, restaurant, time-share, gaming, and leisure industries
	Technology • *Hospitality Technology* • *Hospitality Upgrade*	Technology news and trends; industry solutions; IT resources and research; software and hardware solutions; in-depth analyses by consultants; interviews with top industry executives; IT purchasing and maintenance
Travel/ Recreation	Airline/travel agent • *Air Transport World* • *Onboard Hospitality* • *Travel Agent*	Issues and trends on travel agents and airline operations, management, technology, safety & security, regulation, airport development, and air cargo; forum for news and views from the in-flight, cruise and rail hospitality industry
	Attractions • *Attractions Management*	Visitor attraction market; theme parks, museums; science centers; corporate brandlings
	Travel • *Business Travel News* • *Canadian Travel Press* • *Travel Weekly* • *Travel & Leisure*	Current issues and trends on business travel; industry meetings and events; international business travel; trade news; global perspective thorough in-depth coverage of airline, car rental, cruise, destination, hotel and tour operator, technology, economic, and governmental issues

Hospitality and Tourism Journals

As briefly mentioned earlier, journals are slightly different from magazines in that they have a relatively limited target audience, are more academic research oriented, and do not always carry up-to-date articles due to a long lead time for publication. However, articles in each journal tend to provide concrete conceptual frameworks for solving or analyzing real-world problems so that management can implement potential techniques or strategies borrowed from journal articles for its chronic operational issues. Journal articles often include sections for discussing how the study's procedures and re-sults can be applied to actual managerial situations. Table 3.3 shows a comprehensive list of journals and their main coverage.

Industry e-Newsletters and Glossary Web Sites

All industry magazines reviewed in this chapter have their own Web sites featuring additional information for readers. Approximately one-third of these magazines provide free daily or, at least weekly, electronic newsletters to those who have submitted their e-mail address to the publishing

Table 3.3 ||| List of Journals by Industry and Their Main Coverage

Industry/ Name of Journal	Coverage
Foodservice - *Journal of Child Nutrition & Management* - *Journal of Foodservice Management and Education* - *Journal of Nutrition Education & Behavior* - *Journal of Foodservice Business Research*	Child nutrition; school foodservice management; on-site foodservice industry; food behavior; sustainable dietary change; nutrition education; management and entrepreneurship; marketing, finance, and accounting; information systems and technology; legal matters; franchising; nutrition; food habits and food safety; global issues and cultural studies
Hospitality - *Cornell Hotel and Restaurant Administration Quarterly* - *FIU Hospitality Review* - *International Journal of Contemporary Hospitality Management* - *International Journal of Hospitality Management* - *Journal of Applied Hospitality Management* - *UNLV Gaming Research & Review Journal*	Marketing; finance; human resources; international development; travel and tourism; more general management; innovative international academic thinking; practical examples of industry best practice; consumer behavior; business forecasting and applied economics; operational management; technological developments; national and international legislation; gaming laws and regulations
Hospitality & Tourism - *Journal of Hospitality & Tourism Research* - *Journal of Hospitality and Leisure Marketing* - *Journal of Hospitality and Tourism Education* - *Scandinavian Journal of Hospitality & Tourism* - *Tourism & Hospitality Research* - *International Journal of Hospitality & Tourism Administration* - *International Journal of Tourism and Hospitality Research* - *Journal of Convention & Event Tourism* - *Journal of Human Resources in Hospitality and Tourism* - *Information Technology & Tourism* - *Journal of Teaching in Travel & Tourism* - *Journal of Vacation Marketing* - *Tourism Economics* - *Tourism Review International*	Strategic management; innovations in service strategies and customer satisfaction; lodging industry and human resources management; tourist decision making and behavior; marketing and administration; legal issues; finance; cross-cultural and multicultural management issues; property management and hotel/restaurant development; research methodology; pricing hospitality and leisure products; econometric analysis of the price/demand function; empirical and conceptual research of issues; recruitment and retention; workforce diversity; the latest teaching developments; international travel and tourism course curriculum; teaching for excellence; perspectives on the changing directions of travel education; capital provision; economic appraisal; mathematical modeling; regional economic effects of tourism developments; international tourism data analysis; tourism promotion; cultural awareness; destination selection processes; destination marketing; general contractors and subcontractors
Travel/Recreation - *Leisure Studies* - *Recreation* - *Tourism Culture & Communication* - *Tourism Recreation Research* - *Annals of Tourism Research* - *International Journal of Tourism Research* - *Journal of Sustainable Tourism* - *Journal of Tourism Studies* - *Tourism Geographies* - *Journal of Travel and Tourism Marketing* - *Journal of Travel Research*	Sociology; psychology; human geography; planning; economics; cultural attitudes toward the management of tourists with disabilities; gender aspects of tourism; sport tourism; age-specific tourism; recreational environments; ecology; economics; conservation development; regional planning and sociology; sustainable tourism; tourism product development; meeting services and conventions; tourist behavior and destination choice; marketing

company. Subscription of e-newsletters is one of the best ways to help oneself keep up-to-date with the progress of the hospitality and tourism industry including industry outlooks, news, trends, and challenges. It is recommended to subscribe to at least one e-newsletter in each industry sector to stay informed of this complex and ever-growing industry. Table 3.4 lists magazines by industry sector, along with their URL providing free daily or weekly newsletters.

Table 3.4 ||| **Free e-Newsletters by Industry Sector**

Industry Sector	e-Newsletter Providers
Foodservice	- *Beverage World:* http://www.beverageworld.com - *Food Arts:* http://www.winespectator.com/Wine/Free/FoodArts/FoodArts_Subscription/0,2613,,00.html - *Foodservice Equipment & Supplies:* http://www.foodservice411.com/fesmag/ - *Nation's Restaurant News:* http://www.nrn.com/ - *Nightclub & Bar Magazine:* http://www.nightclub.com/ - *Restaurant Business:* http://www.restaurantbiz.com/ - *Restaurant Hospitality:* http://www.restaurant-hospitality.com/ - *Restaurant Report:* http://www.restaurantreport.com/ - *Restaurants USA:* http://www.restaurant.org - *Wine Spectator:* http://www.winespectator.com/Wine/Home/
Lodging	- *Hotel Business:* http://www.hotelbusiness.com/main.asp - *Hotel Resource:* http://www.hotelresource.com/ - *HotelOnline:* http://www.hotel-online.com/index.html - *Hotels:* http://www.hotelsmag.com/ - *Lodging Hospitality:* http://www.lhonline.com/ - *Meeting and Conventions:* http://www.meetings-conventions.com/ - *Successful Meetings:* http://www.mimegasite.com/mimegasite/index.jsp
Hospitality	- *Hospitality Design:* http://www.hdmag.com/hospitalitydesign/index.jsp - *Hospitality Interactive:* http://www.hotelinteractive.com/ - *Hospitality News Resources:* http://www.hotelnewsresource.com/headlines.htm - *HVS International Journal:* http://www.hvsinternational.com/ - *Onboard Hospitality:* http://www.onboardhospitality.com/
Travel	- *Air Transport World:* http://www.atwonline.com/ - *Canadian Travel Press:* http://www.travelpress.com/ctp_kit/index.html - *Travel Agent:* http://www.travelagentcentral.com/travelagentcentral/

Like many other disciplines, hospitality and tourism has developed its industry-specific terminologies. One needs to know main concepts and terms pertaining to this industry to understand the industry's issues and/or develop careers in this industry. Eight glossary Web sites cover the industry in general and are specific to areas:

- General hospitality and tourism glossary
  - □ Libra Hospitality: http://www.librahospitality.com/club/dictionary/
- Travel industry glossary
  - □ California Arts Council: http://www.cac.ca.gov/?id=252

- Restaurant industry glossary
  - □ Wikipedia: http://en.wikipedia.org/wiki/Category:Restaurant_terminology
- Hospitality law glossary
  - □ Hospitalitylawyer.com: http://www.hospitalitylawyer.com/?PageID=21
- Hospitality information technology glossary
  - □ SearchCRM.com: http://searchcrm.techtarget.com/gDefinition/0,294236,sid11_gci537805,00.html
- Accounting glossary
  - □ NYSSCPA.org: http://www.nysscpa.org/prof_library/guide.htm
- Internet marketing glossary
  - □ Marketingterms.com: http://www.marketingterms.com/dictionary/

Summary

As a starting point to garner information about the hospitality and tourism industry, this chapter reviewed potential information resources available online as well as offline. Prior to visiting a specific journal or magazine Web site, one is recommended to browse the hospitality and tourism index first to identify recommended resources and read abstracts of articles to narrow down the information search. When using the HTI, students should have a clear idea of what field and what subject they are in to search information; otherwise, results of each search are uncontrollable and unmanaged due to an excessive number of search results. Additionally, most industry magazines and research journals can be valuable resources to support students' coursework and career development. Therefore, subscribing to industry e-newsletters is highly recommended to keep abreast with industry trends and build a strong connection to the industry early on. Knowledge is power, and knowing the sources of knowledge is a starting point.

Endnotes

1. Walker, J.R. (2004). Introduction. In J.R. Walker (Eds.), *Introduction to Hospitality Management*, (pp. 3–37). New Jersey, USA: Pearson Prentice Hall
2. EBSCO Publishing (2006). Hospitality & Index. Retrieved January 25, 2006, from http://www.epnet.com/thisTopic.php?marketID=1&topicID=85
3. *Hospitality & Tourism Index*. (n.d.). Retrieved January 25, 2006, from http://www.epnet.com/thisTopic.php?marketID=1&topicID=85
4. *Glossary*. (n.d.). Retrieved January 27, 2006, from novaonline.nvcc.edu/eli/lbr105/glossary.htm

Resources

Internet Sites

Magazines

Air Transport World: http://www.atwonline.com/
Association Meetings: http://meetingsnet.com/associationmeetings/
Attractions Management: http://www.attractions.co.uk/
Beverage World: http://www.beverageworld.com
Business Travel News: http://www.btnonline.com/businesstravelnews/index.jsp
Canadian Travel Press: http://www.travelpress.com/ctp_kit/index.html
Caterer & Hotelkeeper: http://www.qssa.co.uk/reed/subcentre/default.asp?title=cho&promcode=1452
Catering Magazine: http://www.cateringmagazine.com/home/
Catering Update: http://www.cateringupdate.com/
Cheers: http://www.beveragenet.net/cheers/2005/0512%5Fchrs/
Chef Magazine: http://www.chefmagazine.com/
Club Management: http://www.club-mgmt.com/
Convention Forum: http://www.conventionforum.com/
Cooking for Profit: http://www.cookingforprofit.com/magfeatures.html
Crittenden Hotel/Lodging News: http://www.crittendenonline.com/
Cruise Industry News Quarterly: http://www.cruiseindustrynews.com/index.php?option=com_content&task=blogsection&id=4&Itemid=43
Efenbeonline: http://www.efenbeonline.com/index.asp
Executive Housekeeping Today: http://www.ieha.org/publications/editors_corner.html
Food Arts: http://www.winespectator.com/Wine/Free/FoodArts/FoodArts_Subscription/0,2613,,00.html
Food Management: http://www.food-management.com/
Foodservice & Hospitality: http://www.foodserviceworld.com/fsh
Foodservice Director: http://www.fsdmag.com/
Foodservice Equipment & Supplies: http://www.foodservice411.com/fesmag/
Green Hotelier: http://www.greenhotelier.com/
Hospitality Design: http://www.hdmag.com/hospitalitydesign/index.jsp
Hospitality Interactive: http://www.hotelinteractive.com/

Hospitality Law: http://www.shoplrp.com/product/p-7800.HOSP.html
Hospitality Matters: http://www.hospitalitymatters.co.uk/
Hospitality Net: http://www.hospitalitynet.org/index.html
Hospitality News Resources: http://www.hotelnewsresource.com/headlines.htm
Hospitality Technology: http://www.htmagazine.com/HT/index.shtml
Hospitality Upgrade: http://www.hospitalityupgrade.com/
Hotel & Restaurant: http://www.hotelandrestaurant.co.uk/
Hotel and Motel Management: http://www.hotelmotel.com/hotelmotel/
Hotel Business: http://www.hotelbusiness.com/main.asp
Hotel Resource: http://www.hotelresource.com/
Hotelier: http://www.foodserviceworld.com/hotelier/archives/septFour/septFour.shtml
HotelOnline: http://www.hotel-online.com/index.html
Hotels: http://www.hotelsmag.com/
HVS International Journal: http://www.hvsinternational.com/
Lodging: http://www.lodgingmagazine.com/
Lodging Hospitality: http://www.lhonline.com/
Meeting and Conventions: http://www.meetings-conventions.com/
Meeting News: http://www.meetingsnet.com/
Meetings Net: http://www.meetpie.com/registration/persistent/mee05_mit_subscription_free.asp
Nation's Restaurant News: http://www.nrn.com/
Nightclub & Bar Magazine: http://www.nightclub.com/
Onboard Hospitality: http://www.onboardhospitality.com/
Pizza Today: http://www.pizzatoday.com/
Premier Hotels & Resorts: http://www.premierhotels.com/premier/
Restaurant Business: http://www.restaurantbiz.com/
Restaurant Hospitality: http://www.restaurant-hospitality.com/
Restaurant Report: http://www.restaurantreport.com/
Restaurants and Institutions: http://www.foodservice411.com/rimag/
Restaurants USA: http://www.restaurant.org
Room Chronicle: http://www.roomschronicle.com/
Successful Meetings: http://www.mimegasite.com/mimegasite/index.jsp
The Meeting Professionals International: http://www.mpiweb.org/cms/mpiweb/default.aspx
Travel & Leisure: http://www.travelandleisure.com/
Travel Agent: http://www.travelagentcentral.com/travelagentcentral/
Travel Weekly: http://www.travelweekly.com/
Vacation Ownership: http://www.vomagazine.com/
Wine Spectator: http://www.winespectator.com/Wine/Home/

Journals

Annals of Tourism Research: http://www.sciencedirect.com/science?_ob=JournalURL&_cdi=5855&_auth=y&_acct=
    C000050221&_version=1&_urlVersion=0&_userid=10&md5=e0c01093915f6542f4750140532315c7&chunk=xxx
Cornell Hotel and Restaurant Administration Quarterly: http://www.hotelschool.cornell.edu/publications/hraq/
FIU Hospitality Review: http://hospitality.fiu.edu/review/index.htm
Information Technology & Tourism: http://itt.ec3.at/
International Journal of Contemporary Hospitality Management: http://www.emeraldinsight.com/info/journals/ijchm/
    ijchm.jsp
International Journal of Hospitality & Tourism Administration: http://www.haworthpress.com/web/IJHTA/
International Journal of Hospitality Management: http://www.sciencedirect.com/science?_ob=JournalURL&_cdi=
    5927&_auth=y&_acct=C000050221&_version=1&_urlVersion=0&_userid=10&md5=39c3adc5ecc55a616cb22c83c4ce000b
International Journal of Tourism and Hospitality Research: http://www.anatoliajournal.com/index.htm
International Journal of Tourism Research: http://www.wiley.com/WileyCDA/WileyTitle/productCd-JTR.html
Journal of Applied Hospitality Management: http://www.robinson.gsu.edu/hospitality/jahm.html
Journal of Child Nutrition & Management: http://docs.schoolnutrition.org/newsroom/jcnm/
Journal of Convention & Event Tourism: http://www.haworthpress.com/store/TOC.asp?sid=
    76A1CPSPC0PG8JC19TH7QE3EQSBN8X0E&sku=J452
Journal of Foodservice Business Research: http://www.haworthpress.com/web/JFBR/
Journal of Foodservice Management and Education: http://www.fsmec.org/journal_current.html
Journal of Hospitality & Tourism Research: http://jht.sagepub.com/

Journal of Hospitality and Leisure Marketing: http://www.haworthpress.com/store/product.asp?sku=J150
Journal of Hospitality and Tourism Education: http://www.hlst.heacademy.ac.uk/Johlste/index.html
Journal of Human Resources in Hospitality and Tourism: http://www.haworthpress.com/web/JHRHT/
Journal of Nutrition Education & Behavior: http://www.jneb.org/
Journal of Sustainable Tourism: http://www.multilingual-matters.net/jost/
Journal of Teaching in Travel & Tourism: http://www.haworthpress.com/web/JTTT/
Journal of Tourism Studies: http://www.jcu.edu.au/fac1/public/business/jts/
Journal of Travel and Tourism Marketing: http://www.haworthpress.com/store/product.asp?sku=J073
Journal of Travel Research: http://jtr.sagepub.com/
Journal of Vacation Marketing: http://jvm.sagepub.com/
Leisure Studies: http://www.tandf.co.uk/journals/titles/02614367.asp
Scandinavian Journal of Hospitality & Tourism: http://www.tandf.co.uk/journals/titles/15022250.asp
Tourism & Hospitality Research: http://www.henrystewart.com/tourism_and_hospitality/
Tourism Culture & Communication: http://www.cognizantcommunication.com/filecabinet/Tourism_Culture/tcc.htm
Tourism Economics: http://www.ippublishing.com/general_tourism.htm
Tourism Geographies: http://www.tandf.co.uk/journals/routledge/14616688.html
Tourism Recreation Research: http://www.trrworld.org/
Tourism Review International: http://www.cognizantcommunication.com/filecabinet/Tri/tri.html
UNLV Gaming Research & Review Journal: http://hotel.unlv.edu/res_gamingJournal_main.html

Terminology

Glossary of Tourism Terms: http://app.stb.com.sg/asp/tou/tou08.asp
Hospitality Law Glossary: http://www.hospitalitylawyer.com/?PageID=21
Glossary of Hospitality Terms: http://www.librahospitality.com/club/dictionary/
Hospitality Information Technology Glossary: http://searchcrm.techtarget.com/gDefinition/0,294236,sid11_gci537805,00.html
Travel Industry Terminology: http://www.cac.ca.gov/?id=252
Restaurant Terminology: http://en.wikipedia.org/wiki/Category:Restaurant_terminology
Accounting Terminology: http://www.nysscpa.org/prof_library/guide.htm
Internet Marketing Terminology: http://www.marketingterms.com/dictionary/

⌐ Key Words and Concepts

Information resources—Places in which information can be placed. Here, information refers to any text, graphics, pictures, narratives, and opinions related to hospitality and tourism.

Journals—Academic research publications done by educators and industry practitioners.

Offline resources—Hard copy of periodicals (i.e., magazines, newspapers, journals, newsletters).

Online resources—Information can be retrieved from a Web site.

Periodicals—Publications such as magazines, newspapers, and journals that are published on a regular basis such as daily, weekly, monthly, or quarterly.

Contributor Information

Miyoung Jeong, PhD, is an assistant professor in the Hotel, Restaurant, and Institution Management (HRIM) program at Iowa State University. Corresponding e-mail: mjeong@iastate.edu

3▮ Review Questions

1. Why is it important to have both primary and secondary information resources?

2. What is the *Hospitality and Tourism Index*?

3. What are two different formats of information resources?

4. Describe similarities and differences between magazines and journals.

Chay Runnels
Stephen F. Austin University

Industry Associations and Rating Services

Learning Objectives

- ✓ To identify and recognize major industry associations
- ✓ To define the terms *industry association, bylaws, member benefits, rating services*
- ✓ To understand the importance of industry associations and recognize leading industry associations in the hospitality and tourism fields
- ✓ To understand the rating systems of lodging and restaurants in the United States

Chapter Outline

What Is an Industry Association?
Why Join an Industry Association?
Associations in the Food and Lodging Arena
Associations in the Travel and Tourism Arena
Hotel and Restaurant Rating Systems

What Is an Industry Association?

*I*ndustry associations are professional organizations that assist members by providing opportunities for networking, education and training, recognition, and support within a given industry. Some associations are formed for the purpose of promoting a particular industry to the public. For example, originally the Automobile Association of America (AAA) was primarily dedicated to assisting members with their driving plans for vacations. The automobile was the up-and-coming transportation mode during the 50s because it was economical to take the whole family for two weeks to see America and visit the family in other states. AAA provided people with rated places to sleep and eat along with attractions that would keep the children in the back entertained when they asked, "Are we there yet?" Other associations are formed to keep members informed about legislative issues that may affect their industry or business. The American Gaming Association filled a need to act as liaison between the federal government and the casino industry. With the bad reputation of the gaming industry in the early 1900s, the casinos needed to have a voice in Washington so they could help turn around their image and get information to the people who were voting on the issues. The hospitality industry has many associations that provide members with current information on industry trends while also keeping the general public aware of the industry through marketing and public relations efforts. The National Restaurant Association sends out periodicals each month to keep their members informed on what is happening in the industry. Then to aid their members on learning what is new in the supply side, they have an annual trade show convention in Chicago in May. This is the largest restaurant show in the country designed to allow suppliers to show off their newest product lines, to give workshops on different trends, and to allow industry people to network.

Associations in the hospitality field may be organized on several different levels. Associations may be created to meet the needs of individuals, businesses, and organizations in a certain geographic area. An example of this type of industry association would be an organization formed by bed-and-breakfast owners in a community or region. Many communities and cities have specific industry associations for lodging, foodservice, and tourism-related organizations. For example, there is the New Orleans Restaurant Association, which is a branch of the National Restaurant Association. This allows members to network and organize projects that are necessary for their city. After 9-11, the New Orleans Restaurant Association began a media campaign to set aside one night to take someone out to dinner to create awareness that restaurants were failing without customers and tourists. States also have hospitality and tourism associations that serve the needs of members on a statewide level.[1] (see Industry Association Profile). Large national associations may include not only individual and business members, but also colleges and universities, affiliated industry partners, vendors, institutional members, and student members. These large associations, like the *National Tour Association*, may have thousands of members. Finally, some industry associations are international. Membership in these global associations is often made up of smaller industry associations from around the world. Many international associations also have national, statewide, or local chapters. These chapters are smaller, affiliated groups that share the same or similar purpose as the "parent" association. The Council on Hotel, Restaurant and Institutional Education (CHRIE) is an association of educational hospitality programs around the world. There are states that are grouped together by region in the United States and the International Federations that are part of CHRIE but also operate independently in their own countries. These different regional groups offer special programs to help their students develop research studies as well as provide networking opportunities.

To find associations that are relevant to your interests, consult a set of books called the *Encyclopedia of Associations* in your library. Every association is listed by name, address, purpose, contact information, number of members, and areas of specialization. One of the volumes is searchable by topics. So, it is easy to find an association that suits your particular needs.

Determining Member Needs

No matter what the size or scope of membership, almost all industry associations will have governing documents that will include a mission and/or vision, bylaws, and a board of directors or advisors that oversees the organization.

Industry associations will have a mission—a statement of purpose—that should concisely describe why the association was formed and for what purpose. You should be able to look at an association's mission statement and immediately understand the purpose and scope of the organization. The **mission statement** is developed by the membership or governing board of an organization and often serves as the guide for the activities of the association. Industry associations will also have bylaws that govern the membership, board of directors or advisors, and any paid staff that the organization may employ. **Bylaws** are rules or laws that govern the association's actions and internal operations. Bylaws are typically developed internally by an association and adopted by the membership. With the membership's approval, bylaws may be amended or changed to meet the needs of an association. A **vision statement** is typically an umbrella statement about where the organization sees itself in the context of the industry as a whole. Vision statements tend to be broader in scope than mission statements and may include goals that the association hopes to achieve in the future.

Governing documents like bylaws and mission and vision statements help associations run smoothly. Many smaller industry associations have volunteer or part-time staffs. These associations rely on boards of directors or advisors to guide the organization's activities. Larger industry associations may employee both full- and part-time staff members to assist the association's board and membership in the day-to-day activities of the organization.

Why Join an Industry Association?

Everyone always says "networking is important." And it is. But, what does it mean? How do you "network"? Some students believe that if they become president of the student chapter of the restaurant association that they don't have to do any more than have the organization's name on their resume. However, networking is more than that. It is meeting someone for the first time, exchanging business cards, and getting to know them. Then it is time to follow up. E-mail them a week later to say what a pleasure it was to meet them and how you would like to learn more about what they do and their company. Call them and set up an appointment to talk. Afterward, send them another e-mail thanking

them for taking the time to talk to you. Make sure at the next meeting, you say "hello." This is the process for getting to know someone. In this way, people learn who you are, but it is a gradual process, not a one-shot deal. Then once you become friends, you can ask for help finding a job or learning about opportunities in their company, and they will spend the time to ask around. If you are a perfect stranger, why should anyone go out of their way to help? Networking is building relationships.

Why should you join an association? Let me give you a personal example. I used to teach in a large ski school for many years. I did my job and had a lot of fun. Then it came time for me to look for more responsibility. I didn't know anyone outside my ski school, so I bought a book of ski areas and sent out over 500 letters to people I didn't know. Well, I got back around 20 rejections and wasted a lot of time and effort, but finally managed to get a job. I thought to myself, "There must be a better way." So, I joined a number of associations, then volunteered for some committees, and talked to people. People began to know who I was. The next time I wanted a better position, I called five people and within two weeks, I had six interviews and one offer. What made the difference? Networking. My five friends were trusted by a lot of people, and when they vouched for me, people listened. Networking takes time and effort, but it makes life much easier when you need help. Associations provide the contacts, but you must provide the energy.

Most industry associations provide excellent networking opportunities for members through educational seminars, annual meetings, conventions, and conferences. Many industry associations maintain Web sites and are now providing e-mail updates in addition to printed newsletters. Becoming a member of an industry association may also give you a competitive edge in your chosen hospitality career path. Some associations extend **member benefits** to employees whose companies have institutional memberships or are affiliated with the association on some level. Member benefits may include newsletters, updates, and educational opportunities.

Although most industry associations charge annual dues, many are now offering reduced rates for student members. Student chapters are valuable experiences. First, you are meeting future colleagues who share your interests, and if they are working now, they are potential information sources about jobs and companies. Second, most student chapters

Business Profile
Texas Travel Industry Association[7]

Mission: To unify and develop industry leadership that will support and influence the growth of Texas travel and tourism.

Membership: 774 members including attractions, convention and visitor's bureaus, chambers of commerce, historical and cultural sites, educational institutions, ecotourism providers, hotels and guest ranchers, sports organizations, and transportation companies.

Structure: Governed by an Executive Committee, a Board of Directors and President and CEO Paul Serff. TTIA has three councils, eleven committees, and three task forces that allow members to focus various aspects of the travel and tourism industry in Texas.

Programs: TTIA works with lobbyists to address legislative issues facing the travel and tourism industry in Texas. The organization also develops marketing programs and projects to promote the travel industry in the state. Every year TTIA sponsors the Texas Travel Summit—a statewide conference that brings together tourism professionals and industry partners—and also hosts an annual Travel Fair for travel counselors and AAA representatives that allows attractions to share information about their destinations. With other state agency partners and ClearChannel radio, TTIA developed the "Rediscover Texas" campaign aimed at promoting Texas destinations during National Tourism Week each May. The organization also develops other marketing and promotional opportunities for members and industry leaders.

Publications: TTIA members receive a monthly newsletter, *TTIA Explorer,* as well as a membership directory that includes an annual listing of all association members. The organization also hosts a Web site with exclusive membership content and sends out regular e-mail updates and briefings to members, especially during the legislative session.

Education: TTIA partnered with Junior Achievement to create a tourism module for third- and fourth-grade students, awards scholarships to college students who are members of the organization, and also sponsors an internship program that allows members to post internship opportunities free of charge. In 2005, the organization launched the "Texas Education Vacation" program for educators that emphasizes place-based learning and casts a new light on Texas destinations.

Contact Information:
Paul Serff, President/CEO, 812 San Antonio, Austin, Texas 78701
Phone: 512-476-4472
Web site: www.ttia.org

invite guest speakers from industry so you have the opportunity to meet a professional who cares about helping students, otherwise they wouldn't be there. Third, become a leader. Leaders must interface with industry to obtain speakers and outside resources for the chapter. This is an excellent way to show your interest, demonstrate your leadership abilities, and network. Fourth, go to parent chapter meetings. Every student chapter has at least one industry liaison who is interested in helping you. Take advantage of that friendship. Have them introduce you around at the meetings. Talk to people about what they do and what kind of company they work for. This allows you the opportunity to learn the industry, meet new friends, and develop contacts. People begin to recog-

nize you as an interested, involved person, not just a student. When you become a member of an industry association, you are joining a network of professionals. There are many leadership opportunities in industry associations. You may be a chapter officer or hold a statewide position within a larger national association. Some associations have both state and regional annual meetings in addition to larger national meetings. These meetings are opportunities for professionals in the hospitality field to learn about industry trends and share ideas with colleagues. Also, many associations offer certifications in several areas. Although there are years of experience requirements, many associations will waive some years for someone obtaining a degree in the field. Working on a certification allows you to bond with others by studying together and to give you a competitive advantage by having a degree and a certificate from a reputable, national professional organization. The certificate gives you credibility from a practitioners' perspective and the degree provides you with the theoretical knowledge, internship experience, and many different perspectives on handling the same problem. It is the best of both worlds.

Associations in the Food and Lodging Arena

Because the hospitality industry is so diverse, many associations have been created to meet the needs of professionals in the different arenas. We will take a look at some of the major industry associations for professionals in food and lodging. Remember that many states have their own food and lodging industry associations.

Founded in 1919, the *National Restaurant Association* represents over 60,000 members and over 300,000 restaurant establishments. The organization offers memberships to restaurants, allied industries, educators and students, international companies, and not-for-profit organizations. The National Restaurant Association promotes the restaurant industry and related career paths, promotes dining out, and is committed to food safety in the industry.

With over 65,000 members the *American Dietetic Association (ADA)* promotes healthy lifestyles grounded in good nutrition and well-being. The *American Culinary Federation (ACF)* is the nation's largest organization for professionals working in the culinary arts, including chefs, bakers, and cooks. The ACF sponsors competitions, awards, and educational events for chefs, including a comprehensive certification program for chefs. Both the ADA and ACF have student membership categories. Other important food and nutrition–related industry associations include *American Association of Wine and Food, International Food Service Executives Association,* and *Catering and Institutional Management Association.*

Professional organizations are also an important part of the lodging industry. The *American Hotel & Lodging Association (AHLA)* promotes the interests of hoteliers throughout the United States and internationally. The AHLA offers student memberships and extensive educational opportunities for members. Other lodging-related organizations include *International Hotel Association, International Executive Housekeeper's Association,* and *Hospitality Sales and Marketing Association International.* Each of these organizations sponsors conferences, conventions, and educational opportunities for those interested in the lodging industry.

The American Hotel & Lodging Association promotes the interests of hoteliers throughout the U.S. and internationally.

Associations in the Travel and Tourism Arena

A number of associations in the travel and tourism arena have been organized to serve the needs of tourism professionals. Many of these associations also promote the industry externally—by encouraging people to travel and visit destinations. The *Tourism Industry Association of America (TIA)* works with partnering organizations to promote travel within and to the United States. Through press releases, advertisements, and other marketing efforts, TIA encourages travel throughout the country with its "See America" campaign.

The World Tourism Organization (UNWTO/OMT), is a specialized agency of the United Nations. The organization is a leading international organization in the field of tourism. According to the mission of the UNWTO, the organization "serves as a global forum for tourism policy issues and practical source of tourism know-how."[2] The organization also encourages sustainable and regional tourism worldwide and sponsors tourism related research internationally. Other tourism industry associations like the *International Association of Convention and Visitor's Bureaus (IACVB)* and the *National Tour Association (NTA)* provide services to members in a very specific segment of the industry. These organizations promote travel and tourism awareness and also encourage travel to the United States. *Club Managers Association of America, Meeting Professionals International,* and *American Association of Travel Agents* also are leading tourism-related industry associations that offer networking and educational opportunities to their members. *Travel and Tourism Research Association* works with educators, tourism marketing professionals, and other industry associations to promote research in the field, and provide networking opportunities and career information.

Finding a Place to Belong

As you can see, many hospitality industry associations have been organized to assist professionals in their chosen fields. Joining an industry association could

- Help you develop your professional skills
- Foster a sense of belongingness in a large and diverse industry
- Provide important networking opportunities
- Communicate information about issues, trends, and legislation affecting the industry

In addition to personal and professional development, many associations also recognize industry leaders and innovators and set standards within the hospitality profession. Some industry associations provide mentoring programs and scholarship opportunities for early and midcareer professionals. No matter what part of the industry you are interested in, there is an association for you.

Hotel and Restaurant Ratings Systems

Just as industry associations set standards for professionals in the hospitality field, **hotel and restaurant ratings systems** also set standards with definite criteria. Although there are no government rating systems of the hotel or restaurant industry in the United States, the American Automobile Association (AAA) and *Mobil Travel Guide* both provide independent rating services for hotels and restaurants.[3] AAA and *Mobil Travel Guide* use professionally trained inspectors to evaluate and rate hotel and restaurant properties based on a system of standards and guidelines. The goal of the ratings system is to provide an indicator for excellence in hospitality. According to Shane O'Flaherty, Vice-President of Quality Assurance, *Mobil Travel Guide*, "the Mobil Five-Star Award indicates that a dining or lodging experience is one of the best in the country. These properties consistently provide an unparalleled level of service and quality that distinguishes them from their peers."[4]

Whereas *Mobil Travel Guide* assigns stars to properties that meet certain criteria, the AAA uses a classification system that awards diamonds to qualifying properties. The Five-Diamond award is the highest award bestowed on a restaurant or hotel by AAA. The AAA inspects over 57,000 properties in the United States, Canada, Mexico, and the Caribbean, and less than one-half of one percent of the evaluated properties receive the coveted five-diamond award each year. In 2006, more restaurants were added to the list than hotels, bringing the number of five-diamond ranked properties to 150. According to Michael Petrone, director, AAA Tourism Information Development and head of the

AAA Diamond Ratings®, this reflects trends seen in the hospitality and tourism industry. It's not surprising to Petrone that "the greatest numbers of Five Diamond restaurants are in areas of high tourism. As a nation, we are becoming more enlightened diners. Consumer demand is resulting in an emerging trend for more high quality dining experiences in our travel and vacations."[5]

Do Ratings Matter?

As the use of the Internet for trip and travel planning increases, more and more Web sites use rating systems to help consumers make decisions on where to stay and where to dine. As previously mentioned, the AAA and *Mobil Travel Guide* are among the oldest and most respected evaluators of hotels and restaurants. Some travel agents continue to rely heavily on ratings, whereas others trust their own experience with properties—rated or unrated. When a hotel or restaurant loses a star or diamond or is downgraded from a higher category, industry experts take note. "When a hotel's been downgraded, we pay attention," says Walter Littlejohn, president of Teaneck, N.J.—based Great Vacations. "Then we start to look for properties in the same area that are newer or have higher ratings."[6]

How the Ratings System Works

Hotel and restaurant inspectors evaluate properties based on a set of guidelines. The AAA Diamond Ratings System uses the following criteria for restaurants:

- One-diamond restaurants must meet basic standards for management, quality, and cleanliness. These restaurants tend to have limited service menus and offer food at an economical price.
- Two-diamond restaurants have expanded menus and feature upgraded service and atmosphere. These restaurants are family friendly and may have enhanced or themed décor.
- Three-diamond restaurants employ professional chefs and offer entry-level fine dining. They exhibit a degree of refinement, and there is an emphasis on quality and service.

- Four-diamond restaurants are distinctive and are focused on fine dining. Often expensive, these restaurants are for those seeking a high-quality experience.
- Five-diamond properties are "world class" and leaders in innovative menu selection and fine service. These properties are distinctive and feature "haute cuisine" and impeccable service.

Summary

Industry associations are professional organizations that assist members by providing opportunities for networking, education and training, and support within a given industry. Associations in the hospitality field may be organized on several different levels: community, statewide, regional, national, or international. They may include only one segment of the industry or encompass the hospitality and tourism industry as a whole. Industry associations will have governing documents that will include a mission and/or vision, bylaws, and a board of directors or advisors that oversees the organization. Hospitality and tourism industry associations are important because they provide a voice for the industry and also provide many benefits to members. Industry associations may also set standards and guidelines for the hospitality industry.

Just as industry associations set standards for professionals in the hospitality field, hotel and restaurant ratings systems also set standards with definite criteria. Although there are no government rating systems of the hotel or restaurant industry in the United States, the American Automobile Association (AAA) and *Mobil Travel Guide* both provide independent rating services for hotels and restaurants. *Mobil Travel Guide* assigns stars to properties that meet certain criteria, and the AAA uses a classification system that awards diamonds to qualifying properties. Both the AAA and *Mobil Travel Guide* use professional inspectors to determine what properties will receive star or diamond ratings. The highest awards given by both organizations are highly sought by world-class hotels and restaurants.

Endnotes

1. 2006 Hospitality Associations. (2005, December). *Lodging Hospitality*, 16–18
2. Retrieved January 15, 2006 from http://world-tourism.org/aboutwto/eng/menu.html
3. Rowe, M. (December, 2003). *Lost in Translation*. Meetingsnet.com, 34

4. Mobil Travel Guide Announces the 2006 Mobil Five-Star and Four-Star Winners. Retrieved February 21, 2006 from http://rez.mobiltravelguide.com/mtg/template.jsp?id=20413; http://rez/mobiltravelguide.com/mtg/template.jsp?id=2041

5. Graziani, J. (2006, November) *AAA Names 13 New Five Diamond Lodgings, Restaurants for 2006*. Retrieved January 15, 2006 from http://www.aaanewsroom.net/Main/Default.asp?CategoryID=8&ArticleID=407

6. Webber, S. P. (2000, February). Stargazing. *Travel Agent*. 298. Retrieved February 1, 2006 from the Business Source Premier Database

7. Personal conversations with Scott Owings, director of Membership, Texas Travel Industry Association, February 21, 2006

Resources

Internet Sites

The National Restaurant Association: http://www.restaurant.org
The American Hotel & Lodging Association: http://www.ahma.org
International Executive Housekeeper's Association: http://www.ieha.org
Hospitality Sales and Marketing Association International: http://www.hsmai.org
Meeting Professionals International: http://www.mpiweb.org
American Society of Travel Agents: http://www.astanet.com
International Association of Convention and Visitor's Bureaus: http://www.iacvb.org
Tourism Industry Association of America: http://www.tia.org
Travel and Tourism Research Association: http://www.ttra.org
American Automobile Association: http://www.aaa.com
Mobil Travel Guide: http://www.mobiltravelguide.com

☞ *Key Words and Concepts*

Bylaws
Hotel ratings system
Industry association
Member benefits
Mission statement
Networking
Restaurant ratings system

🔖 *Contributor Information*

Chay Runnels
Department of Human Sciences
Stephen F. Austin State University
P. O. Box 13014, Nacogdoches, Texas 75962
E-mail: runnelsc@sfasu.edu
Chay Rees Runnels is a lecturer in the Hospitality Administration program at Stephen F. Austin State University in Nacogdoches, Texas. Prior to teaching at SFA, she worked with the Texas Heritage Trails Program as regional coordinator, Texas Forest Trail Region. The Texas Heritage Trails Program is a grassroots, heritage tourism organization that received the 2005 Preserve America Presidential Award. Her experience includes working with numerous nonprofit tourism industry associations, museums, and heritage tourism organizations.

4 ▋ Review Questions

1. What are some of the benefits to joining an industry association in the hospitality or tourism field?

2. How can you determine for what purpose an industry association is formed? What are some of the basic governing documents of an industry association?

3. Explain the process of rating a hotel or restaurant property. What are the oldest, most-respected rating organizations in the United States?

4. If a hotel or restaurant is downgraded in a rating system, travel agents may take notice. Do you think industry ratings matter? Why or why not?

Doug Kennedy
University of Wisconsin-Stout

Career Realities and Opportunities

Learning Objectives

✓ To develop an understanding of the factors that contribute to the success and growth of the hospitality industry

✓ To learn what type of personal skills and traits are essential for having a career in the field of hospitality

✓ To become familiar with the positive and negative aspects of a career in hospitality

✓ To understand the role various strategies and activities play in preparing oneself for a career in the field

✓ To develop criteria for evaluating prospective employment opportunities with hospitality organizations

Chapter Outline

What Are the Needs of the Hospitality Industry?

Preparation for a Career in Hospitality

Pursuing a Career

Job Offers

New Job Expectations

*D*o I want a career in the hospitality industry? This is a big question for you. You wouldn't be reading this unless you have already given it some thought. You wouldn't be in school taking this course unless you were serious about this for your future. So, let's explore this idea. What does this industry need? And do I have the "tickets" to be a contributor? Beyond that beginning, you need to understand the pros and cons of working in this type of business. Like any business or industry, there is good news and bad news. We want to focus on how you need to prepare yourself in the coming years to have a career in hospitality, while you are still in school. We also need to spend some time reflecting on how this investment in time and money is going to pay off for you. How can you size up what are the best opportunities for you? It is critical to have an understanding of the process for obtaining that first career position after school, career fairs, resumes, interviews, and job offers. We will even explore starting out on the job: what you can expect and how you should handle yourself in those first weeks and months in your new organization.

What Are the Needs of the Hospitality Industry?

The hospitality industry is a very unique industry. That is good to know and that says something about you. Not just anyone can work and be successful in this business. Many try their hand in it on a part-time basis while going to school, but only as a means to a source of income. What are the drivers of the growth and success of this expanding industry? The hospitality industry is a service-driven business that meets many of the basic needs of people in our society. We provide enjoyment for many, and therefore there is great demand for hospitality services as our society becomes more affluent and can afford to eat out more, travel more, and recreate more. This demand continues to grow and can only be satisfied if there are enough skilled and talented individuals willing to take on leadership positions in this unique service business.

Without the existence of our industry, people would lead pretty boring lives. With the stress and hectic pace people face today in their jobs and personal lives, we provide the "soothing ointment" for their wounds. We give them the opportunity to recharge their batteries. It may be for a short lunch, a weekend getaway or a 21-day cruise. So, there are a number of factors creating this demand. How can you cash in on it?

Certain commonalities have emerged in the numerous industry segments.

1. This is a service-driven business! With all the time deprivation that is out there today, people want to be taken care of. Many hospitality businesses have found success simply because they have learned how to serve the guest. Others have met failure for the inability to do this well.

2. It is a competitive environment. Many restaurants, hotels, cruise lines, casinos, and other hospitality venues are available for the consumer to select from. The drive to excel and distance oneself from the competition is very evident in an industry that is dominated by many entrepreneurs.

3. When the majority of the customer transactions take place is unique, it is hard to make sweeping generalizations, but it is a fact of the hospitality lifestyle that many of these needs are met when most of society is not working. That means as a rule, the hospitality workforce has a different work schedule from the rest of the world. We work when everyone else plays—weekends and holidays. This means the general manager of the property should be front and center when the property is experiencing the greatest customer transaction counts. Those hospitality organizations that operate from this mind-set will be the most successful.

Traits/Skills Needed to Succeed in Hospitality

A desire to serve others is a strong characteristic of successful people. Wanting to give our guests a quality experience is an important trait. It comes down to something as simple as wanting to help. Whether it is giving them directions to an area attraction or clearing and cleaning a table so they can be seated in a restaurant, this type of activity must be a source of satisfaction for you. Liking to be with others and a desire to interact with them is something that is intrinsic to most positions in this business. Being friendly, sincere, patient, and a good listener are critical skill sets for anyone contemplating success in this field. Now, these skills take time and practice to develop, and there will be days when they will be tested to the limit. But these are essential elements of the skills portfolio you will need.

Other required traits relate more to the management side of things. As a manager of a hospitality business, you will have to be able to pay attention to the fine points. A missing detail, no matter how small, can derail the whole "hospitality" experience for the guest. Another critical criterion is to develop a problem-solving mentality. Solving problems is why managers' positions exist. The hospitality industry will provide continuous problems yearning for solutions. If you enjoy solving problems, this is one aspect of the industry that will be enticing for you. This is an inexact business. Many times managers are dealing with perishable products, demanding customers, and challenging employees. This combustible combination will present many problem-solving opportunities for the hospitality manager.

Pros and Cons of Working in This Field

The rewards of working in this field are many. To start off, there is the satisfaction of providing people with a service that they may not be able to get anywhere else. But if you are looking for something more tangible, you have come to the right place.

This is one of the best industries to be able to experience the "American Dream." This is a profession where one can start at the bottom and literally work their way up the ladder of additional responsibility and rewards. This can happen in a variety of settings, large, medium, or small. It can happen in a large corporate setting, if that is your desire, or maybe working for a franchisee in a medium-sized company. There are many small operators who can provide great starting careers. You may even decide at some point to hang your own hospitality "shingle" as an entrepreneur. But you may want to do that only after you have learned the ropes from an established hospitality business. This is an industry where the rewards are commensurate with the responsibility. There is an opportunity to come into a tremendous amount of responsibility early in your career. You just have to be careful it is not too much, because the demand for talent in this industry is always increasing. People who are willing to work hard and learn from their experiences have been known to rise to great heights.

Like all work environments, there is a downside that has to be put into perspective. So just how bad is it? There are three areas to be aware of in hospitality.

1. The work can be very hands-on, and at times involve physical labor. This isn't all bad because

The desire to give guests a quality experience is an important trait.

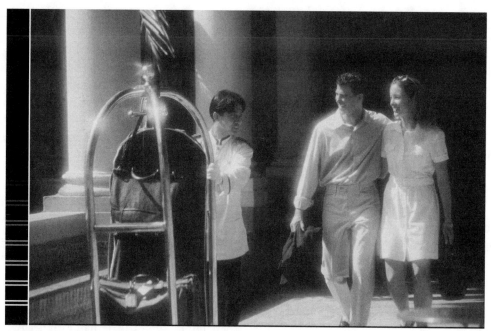

Practical experience in the hospitality industry can start as early as high school.

as a manager it gives you better empathy and appreciation for the hard work of your employees. It is a way to keep you close to the customer, which is critical to understanding your business. If, however, there is never any quiet time to plan and manage, this can be a major issue. In a labor-intensive business, you can plan on being a "working" manager in this field if not always, at least in your formative years.

2. Another area to contend with is the long hours. They are certainly different, and they can be long. In the words of an industry leader when addressing future managers in his organization, he said something to the effect that you work "long and hard." Many companies in the hospitality arena are looking to recruit qualified management. Those organizations that offer a better "quality of life" are going to find that they will be able to attract a better breed of managers. This is certainly a factor to be aware of as you research companies you may desire to work for after graduation. Be sure to ask current management employees the hours they work; don't just rely on what the recruiter says.

3. One of the biggest challenges facing managers in hospitality is the nature of the workforce. As we discussed earlier, many people get their first work experience and training in our industry.

They are passing through on their way to a different career path. Yet while they are here, we need to motivate them to serve our customers courteously and efficiently. There is also a group of workers who are less qualified and end up in this industry by default. Then, there are the hospitality professionals, those people who want a career in this industry. The challenge for the hospitality manager is to understand the differences in motivation and nurture and develop these workers into a quality, service-oriented workforce.

Preparation for a Career in Hospitality

One of the distinct advantages that hospitality graduates have over graduates in other fields is that the hospitality grad has the best of both worlds when they finish their schooling. Most graduates have no or very little practical work experience in their chosen field. A hospitality grad can have as much as four to six years of practical experience in the industry. This means working in the industry while in school or at least during the summers. It also means being able to get good grades at the same time. This is good multitask training. The prospective hospitality employer can have confidence that their new hire won't back away from the industry. With practical work experience and their degree, the hospitality graduate understands the pros and cons of the industry.

For now your job is to be a student. It is your number one priority! There will be time for work and play, but being a student is a vocation with which you have had a lot of experience. Use this time to further build lifetime learning behaviors. Planning, organization, and time management are crucial to your success in school and in life. So really focus on those skills now. Plan out your semester for each class. Don't let assignments go till the last minute. Plan in your study time, your work time, your recreation time, and your class time. Ask questions in class. This is your education and you are paying for it, now or in the future, so get the most out of it. You will be surprised later in your career that the skills and habits you develop during this time can be extremely advantageous in helping you advance your career. It is your investment in your future career.

Work Experience to Get While in School

This is the time to build your resume. If you don't have one, start one. If you have one, update it every year when you return to school. This is your time to explore the various segments in the industry. There are a number of approaches, all of which can lead to success for you. Some students have an opportunity to work for an organization that can give them a variety of job experiences and even some exposure to management. This can be a reason to stick with one employer while in school. Just be sure you are challenged and learning new things, not just staying "comfortable." Others will want to use these years to try different aspects of hospitality—moving from lodging to a restaurant or different positions within a hotel or restaurant.

For some, summers can be a very good chance to try new positions because the school year may be too hectic. Summer allows a student to try different businesses or even work in a different part of the country or world. There is a lot less at risk moving for a summer job versus a career. By working toward a hospitality degree and having a growing resume, you will be surprised how many doors open to you. You can find a job on your own or do an internship. Take the opportunity to learn what it is

like to work and live in a different area if you are so inclined. Hospitality students are in high demand, especially during this peak season.

Probably the biggest challenge to working and going to school at the same time is that it forces you to manage your time better. It is not for everyone, but it can provide variety and a change of pace for you to help you be more effective in both your studies and your work. Just remember that your first priority is to finish your degree and get good grades. The biggest win/win of the arrangement can be that you are able to apply and observe what you are learning in the classroom to what is taking place in the hospitality field. This is indeed the best of both worlds!

Resume Building Experiences While in School

Being involved in student organizations is a plus for building your resume. It shows you are a joiner and can work with others. It is especially helpful to be active in hospitality-related student groups. This way you can get to know other students in your major who have common interests with you. They can help you with information about various classes and teachers and share job information about various segments of the industry and particular employers. Later, on graduation, your peers can open doors to exciting possibilities. Even better is to seek out leadership positions. Finding industry speakers and food donations creates an environment to network with practitioners. Employers are looking for leaders, and a leadership position in a group of your peers shows your abilities to prospective employers. It is also valuable to get involved in some organization that does volunteer work in the community. It is a character-building experience and allows you to develop team-building skills.

Pursuing a Career

There are several key questions that you will need to address for yourself. First, what segment of the industry is right for you and secondly, who are the better employers in each sector? You may not be able to find answers to these questions until you have experienced a variety of employment settings. Start becoming a student of the industry now. Read various trade publications. Track different company performances and history during your time in school. Attend open houses and talks given by hospitality em-

Figure 5.1 || A student organization usually has a Web site to attract members, a constitution,
and a schedule of meetings.

What Is RTMA?

RTMA is the UW-Stout Restaurant and Tavern Management Association. As a group, we visit local food and beverage establishments, and get an opportunity to speak with the restauranteur, take a tour, and often sample the menu. Joining RTMA looks great on a resumé and is also an excellent way to network and make contacts in the industry.

Feel free to e-mail us for more information!

Constitution of the Restaurant & Tavern Management Association

Article I: *Name*
The name of this organization shall be the Restaurant & Tavern Management Association.

Article II: *Purpose*
The purpose of this Association shall be:

1. To assist in the development of educational resources in the hospitality industry through workshops and off campus industry tours.

2. To strengthen members leadership abilities through members acceptance of responsibility for organizing the Restaurant & Tavern Management Association activities.

Fall 2005 Schedule

Meetings this semester will be held Sunday evenings at 6 p.m. in the Northwoods Room.

DATE	TYPE/DESCRIPTION	LOCATION
September		
25	General Meeting . . . First meeting of the semester	Northwoods Room (lower level of MSC)
October		
16	Movie Night	
23	No Meeting . . .	
30	General Meeting/Zanza Bar Tour . . .	Northwoods Room (lower level of MSC)
November		
13	General Meeting/Progressive Dinner . . .	Northwoods Room (lower level of MSC)

20	Leinenkugel's Tour . . .
	   We will meet at 2 p.m. in the Northwoods Room;
	   be sure to bring your ID—you must be 21 to sample
	   but you need not be 21 to come with us.
		Northwoods Room
		(lower level of MSC)

December		

4	General Meeting/Bowl-a-Thon
	   General meeting followed by our annual
	   Bowl-a-Thon fundraiser . . . more details to come
		Northwoods Room
		(lower level of MSC)

11	General Meeting/End-of-the-Semester Social	Northwoods Room (lower level of MSC)

Figure 5.2 Your school's career service office will have a suggested career preparation to-do list year by year for you to follow.

Freshman Year

Develop your resume—Learn what an effective resume looks like. Learn what experiences you should have between now and graduation that will stand out on your resume. You will need a resume when applying for summer jobs, Co-op/Internship, and full time positions upon graduation.

- Attend resume workshop posted on our Web site
- Read resume writing materials found in our office or Web site
- Learn what a Co-op/Internship is by visiting our Web site or office
- Learn why you should attend our annual Career Conference in October

> **DID YOU KNOW?**
>
> Approximately 50% of students that do a Co-op receive a job offer from that employer. Plan to do a Co-op during your Junior year.

Sophomore Year

Register with our office at Stout CareerLink found on our Web site and begin the process of preparing for your Co-op/Internship.

- Update your resume
- Make appointment with a counselor to review your resume
- Attend workshop on "How to find a Co-op/Internship" posted on our Web site
- Attend annual Career Conference in October and network with potential employers
- Attend company Open Houses listed on Stout CareerLink to find out about Co-op/Internship opportunities
- Get involved with a student organization related to your major

> **DID YOU KNOW?**
>
> Approximately 200 employer representatives visit campus at the Career Conference in October.

On-Campus Interviewing Timeline

Visit our Web site for interviewing schedules. www.uwstout.edu/careers

Prime time for interviews on campus are October, November, February, and March.

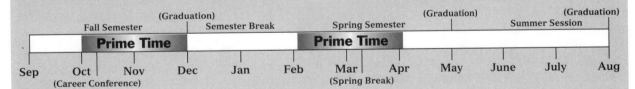

Junior Year

Sign up early for on-campus interviews on Stout CareerLink and approach organizations for Co-op/Internship. The most important part of Co-op/Internship job hunting is the interview. Remember that the best candidate is not always the one who gets the position. Often it is the person who interviews the best.

(continued)

Figure 5.2
(continued) | Your school's career service office will have a suggested career preparation to-do list year by year for you to follow.

- Attend an interview workshop to learn about:
  - □ Researching employers for successful interviews
  - □ Dressing professionally
  - □ Questions that will be asked and how to answer them
  - □ Questions you might ask
  - □ How to write a good thank you letter

DID YOU KNOW?

Co-ops receive, on average, $11.87 per hour. Students have done Co-ops in 26 states and in 4 countries.

- Read interviewing materials found at our office or Web site
- Update resume and make appointment with a counselor to learn how to conduct an effective job search
- Attend annual Career Conference in October and network with potential Co-op/Internship employers
- Stay involved with a student organization related to your major
- Attend "Professionalism: Social and Work Environment" class (HT-427/627)

Senior Year

Sign up early for on-campus interviews on Stout CareerLink and approach organizations for full-time employment upon graduation. Make an appointment with a counselor to become aware of the many ways to find employment either in the Midwest or around the nation.

- Update your resume
- Attend an interview workshop if you have not already done so
- Attend "Professionalism: Social and Work Environment" class (HT-427/627) if you have not already done so
- Contact your references and let them know you are looking for full time employment
- Read Alumni and "Life After College" information on our Web site
- If you find employment, let us know by filling out our employment survey on our Web site or in our office

DID YOU KNOW?

Over 400 employers recuit Co-ops and Seniors each year.

ployers. Attend annual career conferences. Be sure to talk to employer representatives, even if you are not looking for work at that time. It is a good skill to practice so you are comfortable with that format when it really counts. Definitely take advantage of the resources your school offers, whether they are your advisor or the career services office.

Can an Internship Work for Me?

The first rule of thumb in this area is that some internships are good and some are bad, but you will always learn something from them. They can be obtained through your career services office, your department, or on your own. Remember, attending a school with a hospitality program gives you kind of a built-in employment brand for this industry. With the Internet your potential is limitless when it comes to obtaining an internship.

I have heard some very insightful comments from students who have done internships. Some of the critical ones are "don't wait till the end of your time in school to do an internship" and "consider doing more than one internship while in school." The former comment implies that what you learn during the internship can make your classroom learning more meaningful. The latter comment was made after a poor internship experience or one where the student learned that they did not like that segment of the industry.

Students need to avoid the trap of thinking their internship will be ideal and answer all their questions. It won't be perfect; after all it does take place in the real world. It may also create more questions for you than answers. But you will learn from it, and it will go on your resume. It can be a base on which you can develop future job opportunities. You will observe various management styles in action, some of which you will want to adopt and many you will want to avoid. It may even bring a job offer after graduation. This way you and the employer will be in a better position to make an informed decision about your suitability for the job and your fit within their organization's culture.

Securing an Interview

The goal of your resume is to get you an interview with an employer of your choosing. To make this happen, your resume must be eye-catching and appealing. For a student a one-page resume will suffice. The employment objective at the top of the resume is your message to the employer telling them what type of position you want. This is the first test of compatibility between you and the employer. Are they going to be able to meet your needs in a career, and are you what they want? Your objective can be narrow or specific, depending on where you are careerwise. For most students, an objective that states "an entry-level management position in a hospitality organization" will keep a lot of doors open.

There are many schools of thought on resume development and delivery in our ever-changing techno world. Your school's placement office can be a strong resource in putting together a resume that will get you interviews. The fact remains we are in a time-starved era, so your resume needs to speak loud and clear, and fast! Human resource professionals do not have a lot of time to pore over resumes, so clear formatting will help yours stand out. However, style alone will not carry the day; there has to be substance. You can only use so many action words on a resume, and then it will take actual experience to back them up. Let the area detailing your work experience stand out. Details about dates, positions, duties, and scope of responsibility are critical. This is your track record and the best predictor of your future success in a work environment.

During an Interview

There is an old saying that you only get one chance to make a first impression. Recruiters will develop a first impression about you and will use the rest of the interview to confirm or reject that initial feeling they had about you. How is this first impression developed? There are a number of initial indicators for the

Figure 5.3 A resume worksheet can help you list all the vital information you will need to have as part of your resume.

Basic Resume Format and Information

Name

Address (Permanent and Temporary)

Telephone

E-mail

Career Objective

Education

Work Experience

Special Skills

Honors/Accomplishments

Experiment with different font and print types to make the resume extremely attractive to the eye and easy to read and follow.

Dress and appearance are critical in an interview.

interviewer. Dress and appearance are critical, especially in the hospitality industry. The recruiter will be asking themselves, how will this applicant come off to our guests? Just as important is the initial greeting you have with the interviewer. Do you look them in the eye and offer a sincere cordial greeting and firm handshake? This will not happen overnight, but it is a skill you should work on throughout school whenever you meet people in a professional setting.

Today in many interviews the employer wants to understand how you will perform on the job under certain circumstances. To get at this, they will present you with a series of lifelike events that happen daily on the job and ask how you would respond to them. In some cases you may have had actual experience in dealing with similar situations earlier in your work life and will be comfortable answering such inquiries. Other questions may represent your first exposure to a certain situation. The key is to remain calm and think through how you would answer the question.

An interview is a two-way street. The goal of both participants is to get enough information about each other to make an informed decision. Making a quality decision about going to work or not for a particular employer is just as important for you as it is for the employer as to whether they are going to hire you. You should develop a list of questions that you want answered prior to the interview. At some point toward the end of the interview, you may be asked if you have any questions for the employer. There is nothing wrong with pulling your list out at this point and reviewing it to see if there are any unanswered questions. There are different schools of thought about asking about salary in the initial interview. This shows the employer you are prepared and an active participant. Ideally, you should have some idea of the salary range for the position after the first interview. Remember to send a thank-you note to the interviewer. This is not done often and can leave a lasting impression.

Job Offers

Before you start the interviewing process, write down your criteria for accepting an offer. This will put you in a better position to evaluate potential offers. Having clearly defined expectations ahead of time will help you make a better decision when the time comes.

If you get more than one offer, you may be faced with decision deadlines in having to respond to an offer before you have finished other interviewing processes. Your best line of defense is to be honest with the recruiter. If you cannot accept the offer within their time frame, tell them you are still in the process of evaluating other opportunities. Tell them this in no way means their offer isn't a good one, but that you can only make this critical decision when you have all the facts in front of you. You can ask for a reasonable extension, but you may be faced with losing this opportunity. Don't be rushed into a decision. Do what is in your best interests. This is the time when you will have the maximum leverage with an employer, and if they really want you, they should be able to wait a reasonable time. Again, rely on the expectations you set at the beginning of the process and let them guide you during this stressful time.

Before embarking on your job search, find out what the market is offering someone with your background for that position. Your school's career services office or your department can provide you with data and research sources to help you come up with a reasonable range. Although you need to be realistic, you do not want to accept an offer that is below what you think you are worth because in the long run it will affect your performance on the job.

Is This Employer Right for Me?

Many employers will offer prospective candidates the opportunity to come onto their properties for a "preview day" to observe the working conditions and talk to existing employees about the company and the position. One of the best ways to research a company is by doing an internship with them. But if you are not able to experience either of these situations, there is another way to judge a prospective employer. Assess how they managed the employment process. Were they timely? Did they keep their word? What was your impression of the people in the company you interacted with? The answers to these questions are some strong clues in helping you to evaluate a prospective employer.

New Job Expectations

Starting a new job can be a stressful time in one's life. Therefore it is very important to try to get some rest and relaxation before beginning this new venture. You will want to be at peak performance levels, as you will have much to absorb in the coming days and weeks ahead. This isn't the only time rest will be useful. You will always need to understand the importance of being able to strike a balance between your work life and other aspects of your life. It is important to make time for the other areas too, so you can be at your best when at work.

The first few days on the job, you will meet many new people and be exposed to many new things. Some organizations will have very detailed and structured training programs with each day and each hour of the day set aside for specific activities. Other organizations will "wing it," as they may not have a program or the resources to develop one. In the end you are responsible for your training, so don't hesitate to ask questions and take the initiative. This will make people in your organization see that you are committed to doing a good job. However, much of the training in the hospitality business takes place on the job versus in a classroom. At times the rush of the business will take precedence, and your training will be put on hold. Find a mentor to help you through the hurdles.

Finally, there will be good days and bad days on the job. Do your best to maintain a positive attitude. Remember that some of the best learning can only happen over time through our experience. Things may seem overwhelming at first, but eventually you will look back and marvel about all you have learned in such a short period of time.

Summary

You are about to embark on a journey that can lead to a long-term successful career in a dynamic and thriving industry. The hospitality industry is a very unique industry, and it demands certain skill sets like strong interpersonal skills, attention to details, and the desire to be a problem solver. Although the industry has different hours than most, it has many rewards to offer someone who is willing to work hard and "earn their stripes."

Your number one priority over the coming years is to be a student—a good student. This is both from an academic skills standpoint and from the standpoint of understanding this industry. Build your resume now while in school. Develop a variety of experiences that will help you land a great starting position when you finish your schooling. Definitely pursue one or two internship experiences to add to your portfolio. Utilize all the services of your school's career office and your department to assist you in the interviewing and the job acceptance process as you finish your studies. Be prepared to take the good work and study habits you developed during school with you into the hospitality industry so that you are ready to advance your career.

Resources

Internet Sites

Adventures in Hospitality Careers: http://www.hospitalityadventures.com
Career Management International: www.cmi-lmi.com
Entertainment, Hospitality, Travel, and Resort Jobs: http://www.nationjob.com/hotel
GotAJob: Part-Time Jobs: http://www.gotajob.com
Hcareers.com: http://www.hcareers.com

Hospitality Career Net: http://www.hospitalitycareernet.com
Hospitality Jobs Online: http://www.hospitalityonline.com
Hospitality Jobs Worldwide: http://www.hjww.net
Hospitality Net: http://www.hospitalitynet.org
Hotel Career Solutions: http://www.hotelcs.com/
Hotel Jobs: http://www.hoteljobs.com
Hotel Restaurant Jobs: http://www.hotel-restaurantjobs.com
Lodging Careers: www.lodgingcareers.com
SOS Hotels Job Board: http://www.soshotels.com

⌐ *Key Words and Concepts*

Balance—A delicate mixture of your time spent at work and off; one needs to spend enough time at work to succeed and achieve personal goals, but time off work is important to maintain good health and get sufficient exercise and rest.

Career fair—An event where many recruiters come together on a college or university campus to meet and interview students for employment opportunities—often internships and entry-level management.

Employment brand—This refers to the image a particular company has as an employer in the eyes of prospective employees. It can also refer to the image an applicant has in the employer's mind based on their prior education and work experience.

Feedback—The exchange of words, used often to provide praise or constructive remarks.

"Fit"—What you and potential employers want to know—do your values line up with their organization, and how successful will you be in their work environment.

Internship—Paid or unpaid temporary employment experiences designed to expose the student worker to the employer's business operations by providing them the opportunity to work in a variety of functions with a number of the organization's managers.

Labor-intensive business—This describes a key element of the hospitality industry. Many of the services provided by the industry require high levels of personal service and attention to the guest. This is a major cost factor for the industry that must be managed and controlled.

Mentor—Someone who is experienced in the business that one can talk to for advice and counsel; usually not one's immediate supervisor.

Multitasking—The ability to handle a variety of tasks at one time.

Open houses—Receptions sponsored by employers to offer students the opportunity to learn about their companies in an informal setting with the company's recruiters.

Placement office—An office on most college and university campuses that helps students develop resumes, practice interviewing skills, and can assist with job searches.

Quality of life—This refers to a benefit an employer can offer to their employees by providing them adequate time off from work each week to attend to matters in their personal lives.

Service-driven business—This describes the fact that the hospitality industry relies on guest service as a key reason for people to patronize it.

Skill sets—These are attributes or traits a person possesses or develops that lead to successful performance on the job.

Student of the industry—This term describes someone who takes an active interest in a segment or segments of the hospitality industry by reading trade publications, talking to professionals in the industry, and tracking industry trends and events.

Student organizations—These are groups of students that come together in their free time to organize activities to support their common vocational interests.

Time management—This is a practice of making the best use of one's time by treating it as a precious commodity and planning and organizing one's life to ensure all essential tasks are able to be accomplished in an efficient manner.

Contributor Information

Doug Kennedy
KennedyD@uwstout.edu
Assistant Professor
Undergraduate Program Director
Hotel, Restaurant and Tourism Management
University of Wisconsin-Stout
405 Home Economics Building
Menominee, WI 54751-0790

Doug worked in the restaurant industry for over 30 years in operations, training, human resources, real estate, and the law. He is currently an assistant professor and program director for the hotel, restaurant, and tourism management program at the University of Wisconsin-Stout, where he has worked as an adjunct and full-time instructor for 9 years. With over 500 students in the major, this program has been in existence for over 35 years and has produced thousands of hospitality professionals.

5 | Review Questions

1. What are some of the services provided by hospitality organizations that are driving the industry's growth?

2. List several advantages and disadvantages of working for both a small and a large employer in the hospitality industry.

3. List various skills and traits necessary for successful job performance in the hospitality industry.

4. List some of the rewards and downsides of working for a hospitality company.

5. What advantage does a hospitality graduate have compared to most college graduates when it comes to the job market?

6. Write out a schedule of the times of the activities you do in a typical week (including sleep). Analyze how many hours you spend each week in the various activities (work, class, study, relax, exercise, sleep, etc.). Do you need to make any changes?

7. What are the pros and cons of staying with the same hospitality employer while you are in school?

8. List at least four hospitality trade publications you could use to keep up on industry trends.

9. How would you go about finding an internship in hospitality?

10. Go to your school's placement office Web site. List what services they offer to you as a student.

11. How would you answer the following question in a job interview? "What would you do if a guest in our dining room informs you she cannot find her purse?"

12. How can you find what salary ranges various entry-level management positions in the hospitality industry have?

13. Make a list of the key factors you will weigh in deciding whether or not to accept a job offer.

14. Do an Internet search of various hospitality companies. What are the features of the various training programs they offer?

15. What is the role of a resume?

16. What are some of the activities you can partake in to broaden your hospitality career knowledge base?

17. What are three questions you could ask a potential employer to determine if you would "fit in" well with their organization?

Hospitality and Tourism Businesses

Part 2

6

Independent and Entrepreneurial Operations

7

Chain Operations

8

Franchising, Referral Organizations, and Third-Party Distribution

9

E-Hospitality: Technology in the Hospitality Industry

10

Contract Management

Dan Crafts
Missouri State University

Independent and Entrepreneurial Operations

Learning Objectives

✓ To explain entrepreneurship and its roles and contributions to the economic life of the hospitality and tourism industry

✓ To describe entrepreneurial skills that will contribute to the hospitality entrepreneur's success

✓ To describe the techniques for assessing and developing opportunities in the hospitality and tourism industry

✓ To discuss how entrepreneurs generate and assess ideas for entrepreneurship in the hospitality industry

✓ To investigate the required resources and sources that may be used to evaluate and plan an entrepreneurial venture in the hospitality and tourism industry

✓ To review the development process for a venture plan for a hospitality and tourism business

✓ To explore career choices for entrepreneurship in the hospitality and tourism industry

Chapter Outline

Characteristics of an Entrepreneur
The Entrepreneurial Process
Company Evolution

Introduction

*O*ver the past two decades the United States has seen an increase in entrepreneurial ventures that has set the standard for how business will be conducted for the new century and beyond. This new generation is often called the **e-Generation**, not because they were raised on electronics, but because they are the equity generation. They are building their wealth through the development of their own businesses. If the sales of the top 16 entrepreneurial companies over the last ten years were combined, they would be as large as the tenth largest country in the world.[1]

In 1970 the **U.S. Small Business Administration** reported that only 200,000 new companies had been created compared to today's 3.5 million new start-ups of all kinds of businesses. In 1970 women were limited to small home-operated businesses and typically employed less than one million people nationwide—representing less than 5 percent of all businesses. Today women represent almost 50 percent of all business owners and employ well over 20 million people.[2] You can read in newspapers and magazines about how women and minorities are starting and/or reinventing businesses into very large multimillion dollar ventures.

Characteristics of an Entrepreneur

Entrepreneurs are willing to take action and pursue opportunities that others typically view as too risky, nothing but problems and threats. These individuals exhibit behavior that is dynamic, risk-taking, creative, and definitely growth oriented. The entrepreneur is willing to put part of their compensation at risk in return for the right to pursue entrepreneurial ideas and see their equity grow. The sky is the limit in terms of what the entrepreneur expects to achieve with the growth of their company and their return on investment. This requires that the entrepreneur expand their business on an ongoing basis. Expansion could include statewide, regional, national, or international expansion. An example of successful hospitality entrepreneurial company would be Starbucks. The coffee company started small but grew to be quite a large operation with premium coffees, pastries, and so on.

Smaller entrepreneurial operations are sometimes referred to as **independent owners**. A primary distinction of independent company owners, such as the local coffee shop is that they prefer to operate with a more limited scope than Starbucks. They have purposefully decided on a smaller scale

An independent coffee shop operates with a more limited scope than an entrepreneurial company such as Starbucks.

of operation. The local coffee shop owners will stay with the approach that has made them successful as an independent. Surely the independent wants to see their business grow. However, same-store sales growth might be more to their liking rather than seeing their company grow into a giant franchise machine with hundreds of outlets. It should be noted that even though a business owner has purposefully opted for a smaller-scale operation, many of the independent operators have a favorable outlook on larger companies. Lee Cohen, co-owner of the independent coffee house *The Daily Grind*, stated, "I don't resent Starbucks, I learn from them." John Moorby, owner of the independent coffee house *Uncommon Grounds*, stated, "I have a positive outlook on Starbucks. They are educating the public on what good coffee can be."[3]

Whether a businessperson is an entrepreneur whose company has experienced significant growth or an independent business owner working to manage a narrowly defined scope of business, they actually have more things in common than features that separate them.

First, a lot of people who are working 40 hours a week already feel like they are maxed out. This is especially true for the almost 70 percent of U.S. workers who do not like their work. On the other hand, if a person is self-employed, they put in very long days, which usually do not end until late into the night. Their weekends are spent planning and preparing for the next week. The 40-hour week becomes a distant memory. This is a fact of life that many aspiring entrepreneurs do not grasp until the reality sets in that their life is no longer their own.[4] They are beginning to understand that business ownership is not a job, it is a lifestyle. Walt Disney summed up the entrepreneurial spirit best when he said, "I don't make movies to make money. I make money to make movies."[5] Entrepreneurs simply like the chase and the challenge.

Gary Blankenship, owner of the Walnut Street Inn, sums up his thoughts of the work lifestyle at his inn:

> To me being an innkeeper is an incredible way to immerse yourself in life. While opening your home to strangers you will be shocked and pleased, disappointed and thrilled, embarrassed and proud, defeated and motivated, but you will never be bored, lonely or feel totally out of control. Why do I do it? Because serving the public has rewards greater than anything I have ever done. We soothe the soul of the tired business traveler. We allow romance to rekindle and burn bright again. We become close friends with perfect strangers, and then send them on their way, a little more content with their lives than when they checked in. Then we do it again.[6]

Entrepreneurs share common traits. They have an intense commitment and level of perseverance; they always see the cup as full—that's right, full (half full of air and half full of water). When you research all highly successful business owners, they all share one thing in common above all else. They have unquestioned integrity. They are also totally dissatisfied with the status quo and are trying to improve almost any business deal they encounter. Wally Amos of Famous Amos Chocolate Chip Cookies said, "You can do anything you want to do. The beginning is the most important part of the work."[7] Ray Kroc, founder of McDonald's, stated that the principle reasons for his success were

(1) the ability to react positively to challenges and learn from his mistakes,
(2) taking personal initiative, and
(3) perseverance and determination.[8]

J. W. Marriott did not start with a great idea or a brilliant strategy but with a simple desire to build something from the ground up—most important—build it to last. From a very small single A&W Root Beer stand—hardly the invention of electricity or the personal computer—he developed a multibillion dollar hotel empire. The basic belief he built his company on was there can be no distinction between a company's core values and the core values of its leadership. J. W. Marriott's core values are a commitment to continuous improvement and overcoming adversity, a good old-fashioned dedication to hard work and having fun while doing it.[9]

The Entrepreneurial Process

Simply put, the entrepreneurial process is a way of thinking, reasoning, and acting that is focused on opportunity. For an entrepreneur to succeed they must first go beyond an idea and determine if a good **business opportunity** exists. The opportunity must have a market with a customer base that can be defined and is going to provide lasting growth. The entrepreneur must be able to determine the size of the market (current and potential). Evaluating the potential profit margins is another effective way to separate an opportunity from an idea. The entrepreneur must know the profit margins the market will yield along with calculating a realistic break-even point before entering the market.

Resources such as finances, assets, and personnel must be available in addition to a well-conceived business plan. Doing a lot with very little in the beginning of the entrepreneurial process is a way of life for an entrepreneur. Determining what the capital requirement will be for the venture is a key activity for any venture. This is not only essential for the entrepreneur to determine whether an adequate return on investment can be made but also for the potential investor to determine how much of their capital they are willing to risk in the project—or none at all. Will the amount of money that has been asked for solve the identified problem for an existing venture or achieve the goals associated with a new opportunity?

What has been proposed in the venture's business plan must be a good fit. The business plan is the document that will take a potential investor to a departure point where they will conduct their own investigation and determine the risk/return balance of the proposed project. Beyond the investigation of the opportunity, the potential investor will also scrutinize the abilities of the founder of the venture and the management team.

There is very little dispute among the experts that the **entrepreneurial team** is a key element when the scope of the opportunity is larger. It must be anchored by a leader who teaches faster and better than the competition, deals with adversity, is dependable, honest, and builds an entrepreneurial culture. One of the most successful venture capitalists in the United States, John Doerr, holds to a rule—he would prefer a Grade A entrepreneur and team with a Grade B idea, over a Grade B team and a Grade A idea.[10] The leader must be able to time all three of these critical entrepreneurial dimensions—opportunity, resources, and team. Opportunity is a moving target, resources are limited, and the team must be carefully orchestrated to survive the venture's infancy and prosper.

The Business Plan

After the opportunity and resources for the venture have been identified, along with assembling a team with diverse skills and backgrounds, it will be time to put together the **business plan**.

Investors will be looking closely at the characteristics of the team to assess whether they are a group with integrity, if they are capable of developing and applying creative solutions to unforeseen challenges, the team's ability to respond positively to problems, and whether the team will be a cohesive unit as well as work cooperatively with the investor(s) during troubled times. As the business grows and develops, will this team be able to add value? The investor will be asking whether they should place their capital in the venture and go into business with this team. And, as J. W. Marriott would ask, "Will we have fun?"[11]

Certainly there will not only be varying views of the actual market, but also the way in which the market should be approached. The reconciliation of these matters and the answers to the previous questions will determine whether the venture will be great, average, poor, or no venture at all. Without a well-defined opportunity, adequate resources, and a cohesive team to run the right plays at the right time, the business plan is not going to be successful.

The key to developing a successful business plan is to make sure it is a fit for the service industry in which we operate. A service business such as those found in the hospitality industry typically has simple financial projections Usually, **fixed expenses** are equal to the total costs, and the owner's objective is to make sure **sales revenue** exceeds **fixed expenses** while holding key **variable expense** ratios in line. Investors and lenders will look for proof that the plan's **revenue forecasts** can be met, because the business succeeds or fails based on that forecast.

The individual parts of a typical business plan are

I. Executive Summary/Introduction

In many cases this is the only section that will be read by a potential investor. In this section you will explain the concept and the business approach that will be applied. Discuss the opportunity and the strategies that will be used to capture the opportunity. The target market will be described and show its forecasted levels of business over time. Tell the readers what makes the proposed business unique and what advantages it will have over the competition. Report to the prospective investor what is the projected value of the business if it were harvested in 5, 10 or 15

A successful business plan needs to have a well-defined opportunity, adequate resources, and a cohesive team.

years. Outline the organization's team members and the strengths they bring to the venture.

II. The Industry, Company, and the Services/Products

Explain the details of the hospitality industry segment in which the company will operate, review the services and products the company will provide. Describe how the team expects to enter marketplace and illustrate projections for the company's growth.

III. Market Research and Plan

Identify the customers and guests the business will serve. Detail the size of the **target market** and its **trends**. Review what the competition is doing to maintain their share of the market. Explain what **share of the market** the planned venture will garner. The investor should have a clear picture of the **strategies** that will be implemented to market the business. The prices for product and service will be listed in this section.

IV. The Economics of the Business

Show the venture's projected levels of **gross profit**, **adjusted gross income**, and so forth based on a forecast of expenses, sales, and **return on investment**. Show the investor the projections of fixed and variable expenses as well as demonstrate how

long it will take the venture to **break-even** and generate a positive **cash flow**.

V. Operating and Development Plans

Describe the business cycle in which the venture will operate, its geographic location, planned facilities (or planned renovations and improvements), special zoning (required for bed-and-breakfast operations), and regulatory or legal issues (liquor license).

VI. The Team

Provide an **organizational chart** that illustrates the position of each team member within the organization along with an up-to-date resume of the key team members. Review the proposed compensation of each of the team members and the level of ownership each member has in the venture. Reveal other investors, officers of the corporation, and any supporting or professional advisors or services retained.

VII. Critical Risks, Problems, and Assumptions

The team will need to describe any risk and consequences (**third-party liquor liability**). Explain all assumptions about venture forecasts. If there is something typically considered as too risky (high rate of restaurant failures), then explain how the team will overcome this hurdle.

Although this is going to expose the venture's weaknesses, it is important not to leave this section out of the plan. If the team is aware of inherent weaknesses of a venture, then the potential investor is more than likely going to know it as well. There are only four perceptions that will result from leaving this section out and they are all bad: (1) the investor will think the team is naïve or stupid—or both, (2) the team is trying to hide something, (3) the team does not have enough expertise to recognize the weakness or the skill level to deal with it, or (4) the team presents to a potential investor that falls into category three. Even though in the short term this individual may invest in the project, they will not be an effective business partner for the long term who can give effective advise or share expertise in problem solving.

VIII. Financing the Venture

The entrepreneur will need to consider finances from the simple approach of getting as much financing as possible, as early in the project as possible, and doing so without taking on a lot of unnecessary risk. The financing strategies executed for the venture should meet the entrepreneur's business and personal goals. Each of the financing options should be evaluated to determine if they meet the entrepreneur's particular needs. The team should avoid the temptation to take the money from a financing source simply because they are making the financing so easy to obtain (refer to VII, option 4). To accomplish this, the entrepreneur will need to develop a financing plan that answers several key questions. How much capital does the venture need? When is it needed? How long will the funding last? How is this process managed and by whom? Where and from who can this money be raised?

Considering the last question raises three additional questions. When thinking about raising money for the business, the team must ask: (1) Do we need outside capital? (2) Do we want outside investors? and (3) Who would invest? Regardless of the source from which the venture receives funding, one of the primary considerations is to determine how the investor will add value to the venture beyond the influx of money they have provided (refer to VII, option 4).

Investors can be **angel investors**, **venture capitalists**, **Small Business Administration Loans (SBA)**, **Small Business Investments Companies (SBIC)**, **Initial Public Stock Offerings (IPO)**, and **Employee Stock Options (ESOP)**.

Regardless of your approach to raising capital, there are a few tips you should know. First, there are a lot of sources for capital, and they should be qualified to ensure they are a fit for your company. Not all who are willing to invest will be good partners, and the entrepreneur should be prepared to say no and stay focused on their best-suited sources. The aspiring entrepreneur would also be wise not to divulge what other sources of venture capital they have access to. You should never meet with an associate or junior representative from a source of capital twice unless they bring a partner with them. In this case, the entrepreneur will likely be wasting their time, and in the worst-case scenario, they would be giving away key pieces of information about their opportunity one meeting at a time. Stress your business concept in the executive summary. Stay away from a lot of number crunching and table/graph presentations—they don't matter. What matters to the investor are the long-term

value proposition and your business model that will support it. You should present as much information as you can that illustrates the demand for your business in the target market and specifically the market segment you have identified. Prepare very detailed resumes and current references for all the key team members in your company.

As you move forward with qualified investors, you should align yourself with those who are as hungry as you are. Never say no to an offer price. You should make that decision together with your CPA and attorney. Do not stop promoting your idea until you actually see the money. Again, some unethical investors may actually be baiting the entrepreneur in an effort to gain more information about the business they have planned.

Make the process of obtaining capital a top priority. Throughout the process be concise and straightforward in the answers you give about your proposed business—never lie. Don't even stretch tiny details that seemingly have no significance. They matter, and when an investor catches wind of any sort of inconsistency in your presentation, they will terminate the negotiations immediately. In that regard you should also know it is a small world, and word travels fast.

This is going to be much more difficult than you originally imagined. Just remember you can do more and last much longer than you originally thought you could. Develop your plan and execute it.

IX. Proposed Company Offering

The proposal finally spells out how much financing is desired and a description of how the team will spend the money to move the venture forward and bring in a return on investment that meets with the requirements of those who are providing the financing. The entrepreneur will indicate in this section what percent of the business the investor will hold after making their investment.

To orchestrate this process efficiently, the entrepreneur will need to count on a financial advisor, typically a banker, to provide timely information. Making this decision is going to be one of the most important decisions that the entrepreneur will make. The banker should be evaluated based on their banking knowledge, a shared sense of urgency for the venture, knowledge of the business, willingness to share what they know, the financial stability of the bank, and a willingness to take a chance or work around a policy when the situation deems it necessary.

Company Evolution

After the business is funded and has been operational for a period of time, it will become necessary for the company to create new products and services and evolve to meet the changing demands of the target market. As the company evolves through these changes, the team will need to anticipate new rounds of financing as well as control the distribution of company ownership. For this to happen, the leadership of the business will need to be represented with a good balance between finance, marketing, and operations. If the team identifies opportunities that will allow the company to grow at a fast pace and beyond the capabilities of the current leadership team, then it may become necessary to bring in external expertise to facilitate the new opportunity.

Harvesting the Business

If on the other hand the entrepreneur decides that a newly identified opportunity to accelerate the growth of the company is not within a framework that is suitable, then it may be time to **harvest the business**. The accumulation of wealth for an entrepreneur will become reality only if a great company is developed. For all the pieces of the puzzle to be in place to bring a great company to a point at which it can be harvested requires that the entrepreneur start a business venture with the end in mind. Starting with the end in mind serves several purposes. It establishes the goals that must be achieved over the course of many years and creates a motivating force that keeps the entrepreneur going. The harvest may be what is necessary for the business to keep going. Socially and economically important when doing so will allow employees of the business to keep their jobs. And with the harvest, a new venture is typically launched by the entrepreneur. It is more than just signing the bottom line and walking away. When planning the harvest the entrepreneur must be patient, have a vision of what is next, be realistic in terms of valuation of the business, and seek outside advice from financial experts such as the banker who is already familiar with the business.

It is common to see entrepreneurs who have harvested their business focus on assisting the next generation of entrepreneurs. The entrepreneurial system is too fragile to entrust it to just anyone. Therefore the entrepreneur who has harvested their business must now turn their attention to the proposal of the new entrepreneur and make it better.

Endnotes

1. Research Institute of Small and Emerging Businesses, *Human Capital Study.* Washington, D.C., 2004, p.19
2. U.S. Small Business Administration, Office of Women's Business Ownership. Report: *Defining "Women-owned" Small Business*, Federal Acquisition Regulation (FAR) 19.001. Washington, D.C., www.smallbusiness.gov
3. Degroot, J., *Independent Coffee Shops Hold Their Own vs. Chains*, Retrieved January 31, 2006 from www.bizjournals.com/albany/stories/2000/07/24/focus1.html
4. Bibby, N., Independent vs. Franchise Business Opportunity. *The Bibby Group Excellence in Franchising and Entrepreneurship News Letter*, Shreveport, LA, 2006, pp. 1–2
5. Lammers, T. & Longsworth, A., Guess Who? Ten Big Timers Launched From Scratch, *INC.*, September 1991, Boston: Goldhirsch Group, Inc., p. 69
6. Blankenship, G., *What It Takes to Be an Innkeeper*, Missouri State University and Bed and Breakfast Inns of Missouri Aspiring Innkeeper's Workshop, Springfield, MO, Workshop Manual, 2006, p. 8
7. Amos, W., Founder of Famous Amos Chocolate Chip Cookies Web site, *Wally's Wit and Wisdom Quote of the Week*, www.wallyamos.com, Kailua, HI, 2006
8. Kroc, R., Ray Kroc—Big Wheels Turning: The Future of Business, *Time*, Time 100 Builders and Titans, www.time.com/time/time100/builder/profile/kroc.html, 1998
9. Marriott, J. W. & Brown, K. *The Spirit to Serve: Marriott's Way* (New York: HarperCollins Publishers, 1997). Also see www.yeartosuccess.com/google.cgi, www.hrm.uh.edu/?PageID=204 and www.wikipedia.org/wiki/J._Willard_Marriott
10. Doerr, J., John Doerr's Start Up Manual, *Fast Company*, (February–March 1997), p. 84. www.fastcompany.com
11. Ibid

Resources

Internet Sites

www.NOLO.com
www.womenbiz.org

Suggested Readings

Cohen, William *Model Business Plan for Product Businesses*
McGarthy, Terrance *Business Plans That Win Venture Capital*
Pinson, Linda, and Jinnett, Jerry *Steps to Small Business Start-up*
Small Business Administration (SBA) *The Business Plan Road Map to Success Workbook, Small Business Administration*

⚷ *Key Words and Concepts*

Adjusted gross income—Gross income adjusted by business and other specified expenses.

Angel investor—An investor who provides lower levels of capital to entrepreneurial projects in the early stages. Many times a former entrepreneur who has harvested their business.

Breakeven—The level of sales at which the business will make neither an income nor a loss.

Business plan—A detailed plan that identifies the opportunity, the resources needed, the team make-up, the market, the operating plan, the risks, required finances, and an exit plan for a specific proposed business venture.

Cash flow—Cash receipts minus cash payments over a period of time.

e-Generation—Refers to the generation of new entrepreneurs who are accumulating their future wealth through the development of equity in a business venture.

Entrepreneur—A term often used to define risk-taking behavior that results in the creation of new opportunities for individuals and organizations.

Entrepreneurial team—A mix of individuals with relevant experience and expertise necessary to pursue a defined business opportunity.

ESOP—Employee stock option plan administered through a trust established by the company to distribute stock to its employees.

Fixed expenses—Expenses that over the short run (a year or less) do not vary with revenue.

Gross profit—Sales revenue minus sales cost.

Harvest the business—The entrepreneur makes the determination to sell their business.

Independent business owner—Similar to the entrepreneur with the distinction that they prefer operating a single business operation on a smaller scale than a entrepreneur.

IPO—Initial public stock offering. Stock sales registered through the Securities and Exchange Commission for typically younger companies.

Market share—The portion of the overall market that a company can quantify as recurring sales on a consistent basis. Divide actual product sales by total available product in a particular product market.

Opportunity—The premise of a business proposition that has gone beyond a good idea and shows a viable market with income potential.

Organization chart—A diagram that describes the basic arrangement of work in a business.

Resources—People, financial, assets such as physical plant and equipment used by the entrepreneur to pursue opportunities and convert them into wealth.

Return on investment—Measure of profits achieved calculating the ratio of net income to total assets (simplest version).

Revenue forecast—An estimate of money earned from sales or in exchange for goods or services over a period of time (typically on a monthly or annual basis).

SBA—Small Business Administration. Often underwrite loans through commercial lending institutions for small business financing.

SBIC—Small Business Investment Companies. Federally funded private venture capital firms funding primarily expansions of new or risky ventures.

Strategies—Long-term operational goals and direction of a business.

Third-party liquor liability—An expense incurred as the result of a lawsuit by an injured party to bring suit for loss or injury as a result of being served alcoholic beverages to level of intoxication.

Trend—A general course of action, direction, or behavior pattern that can be identified as a focus of marketing efforts.

U.S. Small Business Administration—Provides counseling, business plan assistance, and available financing for small business concerns in the United States.

Variable Expense—An expense that varies on a linear basis with sales or revenue.

Venture Capitalist—An investor who provides capital for medium- to high-risk entrepreneurial venture for a higher than normal rate of return.

Contributor Information

Dan Crafts
Missouri State University
901 S. National
PROF 440
Springfield, MO 65897

Dr. Dan Crafts is an Associate Professor of Hospitality and Restaurant Administration at Missouri State University. He has held multiunit management positions in the restaurant industry and the general manager position in the lodging business as well as owning and operating a full-service catering company. Recent entrepreneurial activities include hosting entrepreneurial workshops for aspiring hospitality business owners from across the United States. Dr. Crafts is former recipient of a Moot Corp. Entrepreneurial Fellowship at the University of Texas at Austin. His contact information is dancrafts@missouristate.edu.

6 ▐ Review Questions

1. How has the economy changed in the United States and around the world over the last 10 to 20 years? Why do you believe this to be so and where do you think we will go from here?

2. What can the entrepreneur do to get the odds of success on his/her side?

3. How would you describe the attributes of the most effective managers you have worked for? The worst? Explain why you believe there are differences in the two styles.

4. Over time we have seen entrepreneurs come up with some very innovative ways of managing their resources. Why must the entrepreneur be so effective in this regard?

5. Why do you suppose Walt Disney said "I don't make movies to make money. I make money to make movies"?

Radesh Palakurthi
Oklahoma State University

Chain Operations

Learning Objectives

- ✓ To learn the definition of a hospitality chain operation
- ✓ To understand the difference between a hospitality chain and a brand
- ✓ To know the different business models of hospitality chain operations
- ✓ To know the advantages and disadvantages of hospitality chain operations
- ✓ To know the big hospitality chains in the lodging and foodservice industries

Chapter Outline

Structure and Business Models of Chain Operations

Advantages of Chain Operations

Disadvantages of Chain Operations

The Big Chains in Hospitality

Joan Tortza is a bright, young, enterprising undergraduate student in Hospitality Administration at a reputed national university. Ever since Joan started the program, she had harbored a passionate desire to start her own restaurant. With her excellent culinary abilities, people skills, and superior knowledge of management techniques (gained through hard work at school and internships), she was confident that she would be successful. During the end of her senior year, Joan put together a business plan for her proposed restaurant concept for the capstone class in strategic management. Joan's professor for the course was very impressed and offered an opportunity to present her plan to potential investors in the hospitality industry. Soon after graduating from school, Joan was making presentations to groups of investors that asked her pointed questions about the feasibility of her business plan.

Joan was eventually able to convince one local group of investors about the soundness of her proposed restaurant concept, and they agreed to convert one of their existing restaurant that was not performing up to standards into the concept proposed by Joan. After months of planning and renovation, the new restaurant opened with much fanfare. It was instantly a huge success, confirming that Joan's assessment for the need for such a restaurant concept was on the mark. In fact, the restaurant concept was so successful that the investors decided, with Joan's approval, to open a chain of additional restaurants using the same name and restaurant concept theme. Within a couple of years after graduation, Joan was overseeing four of her restaurants in the region. Needless to say, Joan was very happy with her success.

One fine day, a customer at one of her restaurants approached Joan to ask if she was interested in expanding her operations nationwide. Joan could not believe what she was hearing because the thought had crossed her mind. However, she was restrained by her original agreement with the investment group and also their relatively limited resources to expand rapidly nationwide. Additionally, the cash flow from her four restaurants was not high enough to expand rapidly in many markets simultaneously. If she decided to use only the profits from her restaurants to expand, the expansion would be very slow and other people with more money to invest could beat her to the market. The customer suggested that Joan consider the franchising route. In such a business model, many individuals or investors from across the country would make the capital investment to buy the land, build the restaurant, license Joan's restaurant name and logo, and agree to operate the new restaurants according to Joan's standards. In return, Joan would receive part of the new restaurants' sales as franchise fees and royalties, even though she had not made any additional investments. She could also charge them a management fee if they decided to allow Joan's employees to operate the restaurants. Although Joan was thrilled with the prospect of turning her four-restaurant concept into a national chain, she was immediately concerned with all the management issues that might crop up in the process. After all, the devil is in the details, isn't it? For example, Joan wondered if such rapid expansion would enable her to maintain control over the quality of the restaurant products that she now has. How about the fact that she now will have to deal with hundreds of investors (franchisees) from across the country, all with different personalities and financial goals? Will she be able to find an adequate number of employees with the required skills to run her restaurant concept nationwide? What about legal responsibilities of her company and the franchisees? Reflecting on such issues, Joan sat down to do some careful planning to set the course for the future of her company.

*T*he preceding vignette offers a scenario in developing chain operations. It describes one of the ways by which a hospitality chain operation can be created and the underpinning issues involved in growing it. The vignette also describes a chain operation without unfolding the specifics. The purpose of this chapter is to throw light on hotel and restaurant chain operations and discuss the nuances of structuring such chains.

A chain operation can simply be defined as a business under one management or ownership. More specifically, chain-operated hotels, restaurants, and other similar businesses are owned by the same company and offer similar goods and services, but are found in different geographic locations. Although there is no magic number in commerce that converts similar operations into a chain, generally, six similar type operations could be considered to be a chain. The scope of a chain operation could be regional, national, or international. A few examples of international hospitality chain operations include McDonald's Restaurants, Burger King Restaurants, Holiday Inn Hotels, and Marriott Hotels.

Structure and Business Models of Chain Operations

Although the concept of a chain operation is easy to understand, structurally it may become more complex with increasing size. The complexity comes from the ownership and management contracts that form the basis of the relationships between the unit operators and the corporate office. Additionally, the distinction between a chain and a brand confounds the issue. A brief description of each of the business models is described here.

Simple Form

In its simplest form, a chain can consist of a single owner/investor that has full equity stake in all the units owned by a company. In such a chain, the parent company fully owns and operates all the units in its chain. All the profits obtained by running the chain belongs to the parent company. All the employees of the unit operations are the employees of the parent company. For accounting purposes, the parent company may consolidate the sales and costs of all the unit operations to determine the total profit or loss for the parent company. Any market-

ing campaigns conducted would be at the expense of the parent company and would be performed for the benefit of all the unit operations. Usually, this type of structure is found in local or regional chain operations, and they constitute a large percentage of the smaller chains in hospitality. Figure 7.1 illustrates the simple form of structure of chain operations in hospitality.

Mixed Franchise Form

In this type of a chain, there is a mix of ownership with some units being owned and operated by the parent company (known as the franchisor) and the rest owned and operated by many other owners/investors (known as franchisees). Depending on the size of the chain, the number of franchisees can be large. The percentage of the total units owned that are franchised also determines the number of franchisees. Many of the franchisees may own multiple units through business partnership entities of their own. It is not uncommon for some of the franchisee partnerships to own more units than the parent company. The franchisor derives their revenues through multiple revenue streams:

- Franchising Fees (Franchise application fees and a flat fee as a percentage of gross sales)
- Incentive Fees (An additional fee based on the level of profitability of the unit operation)
- Royalty Fees (A fee for using the name, logo, and standard operating systems of the parent company)

Figure 7.1 ||| **Simple Form of Chain Operations in Hospitality**

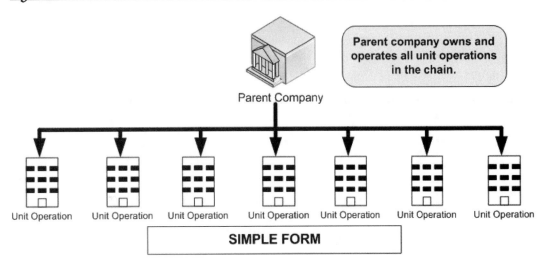

- Marketing Fees (An additional fee to pay for marketing the entire chain through different campaigns)
- Other Fees (For project consulting, employee training, and inventory/supplies management)

It should be noted that although all such fees are reported as revenue for the franchisor, the gross sales of the non-company-owned (franchisors) units is not reported as revenue of the parent company. Although the fees charged by the parent company can be a major part of the costs of a franchisor, the benefits derived can also be substantial. For example, the franchisor will not have to worry about the soundness or feasibility of the business concept because it is already a proven business model. Additionally, the operating systems are already laid out with clear plans for design, operations, and personnel management. Even though the marketing for the units is undertaken by the parent company (franchisor), the entire chain's brand name is emphasized rather than any individual unit. Figure 7.2 illustrates the structure of a mixed franchise form in hospitality.

Management/Franchise Form

When the parent-company (franchisor) also engages in offering professional management services for its non-company-owned (franchised) units, the company can be said to be using the management/franchise form of chain operations. The difference is that in this form, the parent company has an additional

stream of revenue called "management fees" (i.e., fees that it charges the non-company-owned units for managing their operations). The parent company also charges the costs involved in running the units directly to the units. The employees of the unit operations that are managed but not owned by the parent company are the employees of the parent company (franchisor). Some management/franchise parent companies also help fund the investment projects of the franchisees such as opening a new unit or renovating an existing unit. All such functions may be conducted through a separate financial subsidiary of the parent company. Any profits obtained from such funding are retained by the parent company. Many such financing operations of the franchisors are currently more profitable than the franchise operations because of the low interest rates on loans. Many regional and national chain operations use this business model. A point to note in this model is that the franchisees may be free to hire any other professional operations management company rather than the parent company. In such a case, the unit will be owned by an investor and managed by an outside company that will operate the business strictly by the standards established by the parent company. The fee structure of the outside management company may be similar to that of the parent company. However, the outside management company may be operating many other operations that belong to other chains. In fact, the outside management company may also be either a partial or full business partner in

Figure 7.2 ‖‖ **Mixes Franchise Form of Hospitality Chain Operations**

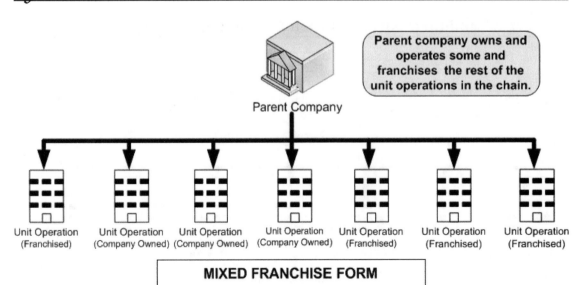

Parent company owns and operates some and franchises the rest of the unit operations in the chain.

Parent Company

| Unit Operation (Franchised) | Unit Operation (Company Owned) | Unit Operation (Company Owned) | Unit Operation (Company Owned) | Unit Operation (Franchised) | Unit Operation (Franchised) | Unit Operation (Franchised) |

MIXED FRANCHISE FORM

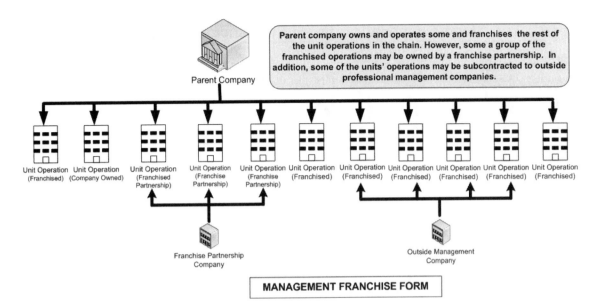

Figure 7.3 | A Management/Franchise Form of Hospitality Chain Operations

some unit operations it manages. Figure 7.3 illustrates the management/franchise form of structure in hospitality.

Brand Management Form

When a mega-corporation owns multiple chain operations under the same parent umbrella structure, it prefers to refer to each of such chain operations as a brand rather than a chain to emphasize the importance of the distinctive brand image of each of the brands in its portfolio (see Figure 7.4). For example, Marriott International owns nine hotel chains (along with other related brands such as vacation clubs and time-share properties): Marriott Hotels & Resorts, JW Marriott Hotels & Resorts, Renaissance Hotels & Resorts, Courtyard by Marriott, Residence Inn by Marriott, Fairfield Inn by Marriott, Marriott Conference Centers, TownePlace Suites by Marriott, SpringHill Suites by Marriott, and The Ritz-Carlton Hotels. Each of the brands has a distinctive position and covers specific market segments of the lodging industry. For example, the JW Marriott Hotels & Resorts is an elegant and luxurious brand for business and leisure, whereas the Residence Inn by Marriott is designed to be a "home away from home" and caters to travelers who stay for an extended stay of five or more nights.[1] Each chain within the brand management form operates similarly to the management/fran-

chise form in terms of the franchisor–franchisee relationships. The chain's units may be operated by the parent company directly, sole-owners as franchisees, partnership-owners as franchisees, or a management company as a third-party operator for a franchisee. The large size of the mega-corporation may also allow it to raise funds through the financial markets to make direct investments in real estate across the globe. In such a case, the parent corporation may buy land, build new establishments, or buy existing establishments and convert them into one of their brands. Such investments also allow the mega-corporation to offer the invested properties on a lease to third parties that may choose to operate the establishment or hire a professional management company to run it for them. The complexity of such relationships may be compounded when the mega-corporation chooses to enter into a joint venture or other similar partnership with a foreign entity to enter and expand in foreign countries. Figure 7.5 shows the partial portfolio of Marriott International.[2] It can be seen that the company owns, manages, leases, and franchises its properties, although at a different level for each brand. The company uses different brand strategies for each chain within its portfolio. For example, although almost all units in the Fairfield Inn chain are franchised, none of the units are franchised in the Ritz-Carlton chain. Instead, all the Ritz-Carlton hotels are managed through full ownership or direct management con-

Figure 7.4 ‖ **The Mega-Corporation Form Structure of Hospitality Operations**

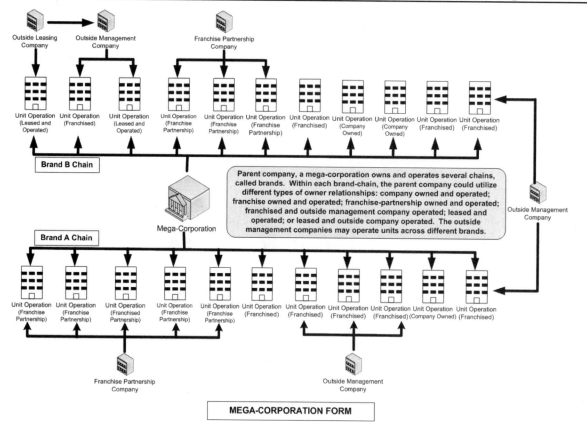

Figure 7.5 ‖ **Partial Portfolio of Lodging Chain Operations of Marriott International**

Partial Portfolio of Marriott International (At the End of 3rd Quarter, 2005)

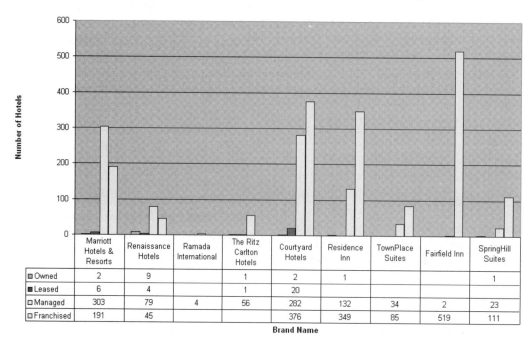

	Marriott Hotels & Resorts	Renaissance Hotels	Ramada International	The Ritz Carlton Hotels	Courtyard Hotels	Residence Inn	TownPlace Suites	Fairfield Inn	SpringHill Suites
▣ Owned	2	9		1	2	1			1
▪ Leased	6	4		1	20				
▢ Managed	303	79	4	56	282	132	34	2	23
▢ Franchised	191	45			376	349	85	519	111

Brand Name

Source: http://www.Marriott.com; Company Reports

Table 7.1 ||| **Top Ten Franchisees and Managers of Hotel Chains**

Companies That Franchise the Most Hotels		
Company	**Total Franchised**	**Total Hotels**
Cendant Corp.	6,396	6,396
Choice Hotels International	4,977	4,977
InterContinental Hotels Group	2,971	3,540
Hilton Hotels Corp.	1,900	2,259
Marriott International	1,658	2,632
Accor	949	3,973
Carlson Hospitality Worldwide	864	890
Global Hyatt Corp.	505	818
Starwood Hotels & Resorts	310	733
Worldwide Louvre Hotels (Societe du Louvre)	307	887
Companies That Manage the Most Hotels		
Company	**Hotels Managed**	**Total Hotels**
Marriott International	889	2,632
Extended Stay Hotels	654	654
Accor	535	3,973
InterContinental Hotels Group	403	3,540
Tharaldson Enterprises	360	360
Global Hyatt Corp.	316	818
Interstate Hotels & Resorts	306	306
Starwood Hotels & Resorts	283	733
Hilton Hotels Corp.	206	2,259
Worldwide Louvre Hotels (Societe du Louvre)	227	887

Source: HOTELS' Giants Survey, 2005.

tracts. This ensures full control of the quality of this upscale brand.

Similar to Marriott Corporation, other mega hotel chains also follow a strategy of their own in terms of managing and franchising their properties. Table 7.1 shows the top ten hotel franchisees and managers of hotel properties in the world. In the table it can be seen that all the major chains prefer to extensively franchise their hotels and manage them to a lesser extent. Some of the chains such as Cendant and Choice Hotels franchise all the hotels in their chain. On the other hand, the Tharandson Enterprise prefers to manage all the hotels in the company.

Advantages of Chain Operations

Hospitality chains operations have many advantages that can broadly be classified into the following categories.

Market Reach

How many times have we wished that one of our local favorite restaurants also traveled with us so we never have to miss the food we love? That is precisely the need that chain operations aim to fulfill by replicating a successful product in as many geographic regions as they can. In this way, chain operations have an advantage over single independent restaurants because they "reach" out to many markets with the same concept. Reaching new markets means increased sales and thereby increased profits (hopefully!).

Economies of Scale

Economies of scale refers to the cost advantages that a company can derive because of its large size. Because chain operations have multiple units, all products and supplies they buy are also multiples of the requirements of a single independent unit. Therefore, a chain operation will be able to negotiate better rates for its products and supplies from vendors compared to a single-owner unit. In addition, chain operations will also be able to derive cost savings through synergy. For example, a single-unit operation may have to have a different functional department (marketing & sales, finance, human resources, etc.) for running the operation, whereas in a chain, the same single functional department may manage many units in the chain. In other words, the chain operation could have the same departments (and staff) help run many units in the chain (say regionally). Therefore, the chain operation is able to spread the costs of such functional departments across many units compared to a single-unit operation and thereby reduce the overall unit cost of such functions for all units in its chain. Such synergies can only be derived in a chain operation.

Streamlined Operations

Chain operations often standardize the products and services offered to streamline their operations. The standardization also extends to operating procedures resulting in commonly understood requirements for managing all resources (people, finances, and equipment). Such standardization makes it easy for consolidation and reporting of performance across the chain. It also makes it easy to compare unit performance across the chain and assign accountability to individuals.

Marketing Power

The marketing power of chain operations comes from increased visibility gained through greater market reach. The greater visibility allows the chain to use mass media such as TV, radio, and newspapers for marketing purposes. It also allows the chain to embark on multiple marketing campaigns at the same time in different geographic regions. An added benefit of such campaigns is that successful campaigns in one geographic region can be repeated in other regions ensuring a more effective use of marketing dollars.

Service Options

Chain operations are often able to provide additional services both to the customers and the unit chain operations. Such services range from providing a reservations service to full-fledged consulting for running the operations. For the customers, the chain may provide a loyalty program to make sure they spend most of their product-related expenses with the chain. They may also have a full-fledged customer relationship management (CRM) program that keeps track of the customers' expenses and their likes and dislikes. For the unit chain operations, the parent company may offer preopening services, architectural and construction consulting services, employee training and certification services, operations and revenue management services, information technology consulting services, owners and franchisee services, and guest satisfaction survey services.

Access to Finances

The larger size of the chain operations may mean the company may have multiple options for raising money for growth. The cheapest way to fund growth may be through operational cash flows, which will be higher in chain operations compared to a single and independent operation. However, the chain may be able to borrow money from banks, savings and loans, and other financial institutions such as insurance companies. The chain may also be able to borrow money by issuing bonds on the stock market. All such funds raised can be used to fund operations, make capital investments for growth, or in turn be lent to the unit operations for a fee and a reasonable interest rate. Such increased assess to finances means that a chain may be able to grow more rapidly than a non-chain operation.

Professional Management

Because of the enhanced legal requirements and the complexity of operations in a chain, many such companies are realizing that it is prudent to hire professionals such as students graduating from hospitality management programs. With professionalism and specialization comes a better understanding of company's operating needs. In that regard, chain operations are becoming incubators of good management practices in hospitality.

Disadvantages of Chain Operations

Depending on the perspective of the owner (or the parent company/franchisor) and the operator (or the franchises/management company), some of the advantages listed earlier can also be seen as drawbacks for managing hospitality chain operations. The disadvantages can broadly be listed under three categories as discussed in the following.

Operational Constraints

Although the parent company may want standardized operations throughout the chain to control costs and efficiency, it may put a lot of restrictions on the franchisees or owners that may want to vary in some small ways. For example, the ownership contracts may disallow independent marketing in the local areas by any unit operations without prior approval by the parent company. The type of marketing and the collateral used may also be restricted by the parent company. Such restrictions are only enforced to ensure a consistent image of the brand in the minds of the consumers in all geographic areas where the chain operates. In final analysis the power of the brand comes from maintaining the image of the brand, and hence, the parent company is often very stringent with their requirements. In fact, all chain operations have some form of quality-assurance program where they perform surprise inspections of their unit operations to ensure compliance with all company rules and regulations. Units that repeatedly violate the company requirements are dropped from the chain after proper notice.

Financial Strain

Another disadvantage of belonging to a chain operation may be the strain put on the financial resources of the company. Not only do unit operations have to contribute to the parent company through royalties, incentive, franchise, marketing, and other such fees, but they may also incur additional expenses if the parent company requires additional capital investments to comply with a new requirement they initiated across the chain. For example, if the parent company of a 300-hotel chain decides that the lighting in the guest bathrooms must be increased from 400 lumens to 500 lumens for better visibility and safety, each hotel may have to incur thousands of dollars in expenses to refit each guest bathroom in the hotel they operate. If one such hotel in the chain has 250 rooms, and it costs about $300 to make the lighting change in each bathroom including equipment, labor, and downtime costs, this particular hotel will have to spend $75,000 to meet the parent company's requirements. Extending the calculation, across the chain, it may cost up to $22.5 million to meet this new parent company requirement.

Legal Forces

The complex structure of most chain operations along with many types of owner–operator contracts and partnerships often plagues it with legal woes. Invariably a difference of opinion or perspective on the same issues may have no other recourse than the local courthouse. Consider again the example of the guest bathroom lighting enhancement requirement described earlier. This cost of improving the bathroom lighting at the unit level will have to come at the expense of the profit of the unit operations, and that is always a contentious issue between the parent company and the unit managers. The parent company may have a more holistic view of the costs associated because they believe that such an investment may pay off through lower guest accidents in the bathroom that may in turn reduce insurance costs and legal expenses. If the unit managers can be convinced of the justification of the costs, then the cost of making the lighting changes in the bathroom will be seen as an investment rather than an unjustified cost rained on them by the parent company. However, if the costs are seen as unjustified, the unit operations may first try to wield control by collective representation through unions or partnerships. If that fails, the parent company may have to deal with the issue in a court of law.

The Big Chains in Hospitality

Lodging

The increasing globalization of the hospitality industry is rapidly being reflected in the geographic profiles of large hospitality corporations, especially in the hotel industry. It is now commonplace for major hospitality corporations to consider the entire global market as their potential domain. Table 7.2 lists the number of countries each of the major hotel corporations operated in 2005. The top five companies operated in more than half the nations in the world.

In addition to the countries in which the hotel companies operate, the country in which the companies are based is also truly global in scope. Table 7.3 lists the top 15 hotel chains in the world in terms of number of rooms.[3] In the table, for example, the world's largest hotel company, InterContinental Hotels Group, is based in the United Kingdom, and Accor, the fourth largest, is based in France. Al-

Table 7.2 ‖ Top 15 Hotel Corporations Operating in Most Countries

Company Name	Number of Countries
InterContinental Hotels Group	100
Accor	90
Starwood Hotels & Resorts	82
Best Western International	80
Hilton Group plc	78
Carlson Hospitality Worldwide	70
Marriott International	66
Le Meridien Hotels & Resorts	56
Golden Tulip Hospitality/THL	47
Cendant Corp.	44
Global Hyatt Corp.	43
Choice Hotels International	42
Rezidor SAS Hospitality	41
Club Mediterranee	40
TUI AG/TUI Hotels & Resorts	28

Source: HOTELS' Giants Survey, 2005

though many of the other larger chains are based in the United States, the ownership profile is changing rapidly with cross-national mergers and acquisitions such as the Hilton brand, which is now partly based in Herts, England, and in Beverly Hills, California, under two different ownership companies.

Foodservice

Unlike the hotel industry, the foodservice chains are currently dominated by American quick-service restaurants. Table 7.4 lists the top 12 foodservice chains in the world.[4] The top eight chains have substantial international operations with most of their growth actually coming from the overseas markets. It is interesting to note that although McDonald's Restaurants is still ranked first in terms of sales, the Subway Restaurants chain is the largest in terms of the number of units. It can also be seen that the more traditional quick-service concepts, such as Burger King and Wendy's, are either in mature or decline stage. Newer restaurant concepts such as

Table 7.3 ‖ Top 15 Hotel Chains in Terms of Number of Rooms (2005)

Rank 2004	Rank 2003	Company Headquarters	Rooms 2004	Rooms 2003	Hotels 2004	Hotels 2003
1	1	**InterContinental Hotels Group** Windsor, Berkshire, England	534,202	536,318	3,540	3,520
2	2	**Cendant Corp.** Parsippany, N.J., USA	520,860	518,747	6,396	6,402
3	3	**Marriott International** Washington, D.C., USA	482,186	490,564	2,632	2,718
4	4	**Accor** Paris, France	463,427	453,403	3,973	3,894
5	5	**Choice Hotels International** Silver Spring, Md., USA	403,806	388,618	4,977	4,810
6	6	**Hilton Hotels Corp.** Beverly Hills, Calif., USA	358,408	348,483	2,259	2,173
7	7	**Best Western International** Phoenix, Ariz., USA	309,236	310,245	4,114	4,110
8	8	**Starwood Hotels & Resorts Worldwide** White Plains, N.Y., USA	230,667	229,247	733	738
9	11	**Global Hyatt Corp.** Chicago, Ill., USA	147,157	89,602	818	208
10	9	**Carlson Hospitality Worldwide** Minneapolis, Minn., USA	147,093	147,624	890	881
11	10	**Hilton Group plc** Watford, Herts, England	102,636	98,689	403	392

Source: HOTELS' Giants Survey, 2005

Table 7.4 ||| **Top 12 Foodservice Chains in the World in 2005**

2005 Rank	2004 Rank	Chain	Segment	2004 Systemwide Sales ($Mil)	2004 Change in System Sales	Number of Franchised Units	Number of Company Units	Total Units
1	1	McDonald's	Burger	$24,391.00	10.30%	10,989	2,684	13,673
2	3	Wendy's	Burger	$7,712.00	3.10%	4,605	1,328	5,933
3	2	Burger King	Burger	$7,700.00	−10.50%	6,982	642	7,624
4	5	Subway	Sandwich	$6,270.00	10.00%	17,909	1	17,910
5	4	Taco Bell	Mexican	$5,700.00	5.60%	4,590	1,281	5,871
6	6	Pizza Hut	Pizza/Pasta	$5,200.00	2.00%	5,790	1,729	7,519
7	7	KFC	Chicken	$5,000.00	2.00%	4,275	1,240	5,515
8	9	Starbucks	Snack	$4,804.10	38.30%	1,982	4,394	6,376
9	10	Dunkin' Donuts	Snack	$3,380.00	15.00%	4,418	0	4,418
10	8	Domino's Pizza	Pizza/Pasta	$3,173.20	5.70%	4,428	580	5,008
11	11	Arby's	Sandwich	$2,836.00	4.70%	3,100	235	3,335
12	12	Sonic Drive-In	Burger	$2,770.00	13.90%	2,374	542	2,916

Source: *QSR Magazine*: QSR 50 Survey, 2005

Starbucks and Sonic Drive-In are rapidly growing. Not unlike the hotel industry, the foodservice industry also has a penchant for franchising, with some of the chains such as Subway and Dunkin' Donuts franchising almost all their restaurant.

Summary

In an increasingly competitive world, chain development strategy offers an opportunity for hospitality companies to take control of costs and harness their strengths. With the short time it now takes for the diffusion of innovation and migration of ideas across the world because of rapidly evolving telecommunication facilities, the world is swiftly shrinking and creating immense business opportunities for growth globally. As people around the world share the same information and ideas, they may also develop the same preferences for hospitality products and services. In such an environment, growing through the application of chain development strategy is prudent for business. Needless to say, the concept of hospitality chain operations will only get stronger in the future.

Endnotes

1. *Marriott Hotel and Resorts Brand Factsheets*, 2005 at http://www.marriott.com
2. *Marriott International Annual Report*, 2005
3. *HOTELS' Corporate 300 Report*, Giants Survey, July 2005
4. *QSR 50 Survey*, 2005 at http://www.qsrmagazine.com/qsr50/charts/systemwide_sales.html

Resources

Internet Sites

Hotel Chain

Marriott Corporation: http://www.marriott.com
Intercontinental Group: http://www.ichotelsgroup.com/
Accor: http://accor.com/gb/index.asp
Starwood Hotel & Resorts: http://www.starwoodhotels.com/
Best Western International: http://www.bestwestern.com/
Hilton Groups plc: http://hiltonworldwide.hilton.com/
Le Meridien Hotels & Resorts: http://www.lemeridien.com/

Carlson Hospitality Worldwide: http://www.carlson.com/
Golden Tulip Hospitality/THL: http://www.goldentulip.com/site/?ShowLanguage=EN
Cendant Corp.: http://cendant.com/
Global Hyatt Corp.: http://www.hyatt.com/hyatt/index.jsp
Choice Hotels International: http://www.choicehotels.com/
Rezidor SAS Hospitality: http://www.rezidorsas.com/
Club Mediterranee: http://www.clubmed.com/cgi-bin/clubmed55/clubmed/welcome.jsp
TUI AG/TUI Hotels & Resorts: http://www.tui-group.com/en/ir/group/

Foodservice Chain

McDonald's: http://www.mcdonalds.com/
Wendy's: http://www.wendys.com
Burger King: http://www.bk.com/
Subway: http://www.subway.com/subwayroot/index.aspx
Taco Bell: http://www.tacobell.com/
Pizza Hut: http://www.pizzahut.com/
KFC: http://www.kfc.com/
Starbucks: http://www.starbucks.com/
Dunkin' Donuts: http://dunkindonuts.com/
Domino's Pizza: http://www.dominos.com/Public-EN/
Arby's: http://www.arbys.com/
Sonic Drive-In: http://www.sonicdrivein.com/index.jsp

☞ Key Words

Franchise
Business structure
Business organization

☞ Key Concepts

Chain operations: Chain-operated hotels, restaurants, and other similar businesses are owned by the same company and offer similar goods and services, but are found in different geographic locations.

Business model: Hospitality chain business models can be of four types—simple form, mixed franchise form, management/franchise form, and brand management form. In a simple form, a chain can consist of a single owner/investor that has full equity stake in all the units owned by company. In a mixed franchise form chain, there is a mix of owner-ship with some units being owned and oper-ated by the parent company (known as the franchisor) and the rest owned and operated by many other owners/investors (known as franchisees). If a management/franchise form the parent company (franchisor) also engages in offering professional management services for its non-company-owned (franchised units), the company can be said to be using the management/franchise form of chain operations.

Brand: In a brand management form a mega-corporation owns multiple chain operations under the same parent umbrella structure. A mega-corporation that owns multiple chains under the same umbrella would prefer to refer to treat each of the chains as a separate brand to emphasize the different images projected by the chains.

Chain advantages: The advantages of a chain operation include market reach, economies of scale, more streamlined operations, greater marketing power, more service options, greater access to financing, and more profes-sional management.

Chain disadvantages: The disadvantages of chain operations include greater operational constraints, higher financial strain, and more legal woes.

🖾 *Contributor Information*

Radesh.Palakurthi@okstate.edu

Dr. Palakurthi is a professor and the coordinator of the master's program at the School of Hotel and Restaurant Administration at Oklahoma State University in Stillwater, OK. Dr. Palakurthi has a doctorate from Penn State University, MBA from San Jose State University, MS from Purdue University, and a BS from Florida International University. Dr. Palakurthi has previously taught at University of North Texas, San Jose State University, and The Wellington Institute of Technology in Petone, New Zealand.

7 Review Questions

1. What is the definition of hospitality chain operations?

2. What is the difference between a hospitality chain and a hospitality brand?

3. What are the different business models used in hospitality chain operations?

4. Describe the differences between the different business models used in hospitality chain operations.

5. Describe the relationship between a franchisor and a franchisee in hospitality chain operations. When can the franchisors be more powerful than the franchisees?

6. What are the additional sources of revenue available to an owner in a mixed franchise form compared to a simple form?

7. How would you describe a megacorporation in hospitality? Explain how its operations are more complex than other forms of business models.

8. What are some of the advantages of hospitality chain operations?

9. What are some of the disadvantages of hospitality chain operations?

10. List the top ten hospitality chain operations in the lodging and foodservice industries.

Susan Gregory
Eastern Michigan University

Franchising, Referral Organizations, and Third-Party Distribution

Learning Objectives

✓ To describe the role of franchising in the hospitality industry

✓ To identify the benefits and constraints of franchising from the franchisor's and franchisee's perspective

✓ To explain the role of referral organizations and third-party distribution systems in the hospitality industry

✓ To identify the common elements found in franchising, referral organizations and third-party distribution systems

✓ To discuss the trends affecting franchising, referral organizations, and third-party distribution systems in the hospitality industry

Chapter Outline

Franchising in the Hospitality Organization
Referral Organizations
Role of Franchising or Referral
    Organization Advisory Committee
Third-Party Distribution Systems

*I*n previous chapters you learned about independent, entrepreneurial, and chain operations. This chapter will add more options to the types of business structures that are available: franchises, referral organizations, and third-party distributions. These three structures are similar in that each business model offers a system or method of marketing a product or service under a trademark or brand name. Marketing can increase the amount of exposure a business would receive in the marketplace over what they would receive if they were on their own competing for guests. Marketing activities are direct in the case of franchisees and referral organizations and indirect through a middleman as in the system called third-party distribution.

Franchising in the Hospitality Organization

Franchise is a network of business relationships. It is a method of distributing goods and services that allows a franchisee the right to establish and operate a unit or units and to use the franchisor's name and/or business system. These contractual rights require the franchisee to abide by all the standards and operational rules that are established by the franchisor. It's a proven way of doing business and quickly creates a strategic marketing identity and image in the minds of customers for a new business. For the franchisee, being part of the network can also mean a shorter learning curve in a new business. An independent businessperson is not solely dependent on their own ideas and creativity. They don't have to "reinvent the wheel" because the marketing and operations expertise are already in place. If there are problems, the franchisor and other franchisees bring a wealth of knowledge and experience to the system.

In 2004 the U.S. Census Bureau estimated that 3.9 billion dollars in sales were generated by the top 200 franchise companies by their company-owned units and franchisees. The largest franchise organization is McDonald's. The IFA Web site has a list of industries that offer franchises.[1] In a time when America has lost its competitive edge in manufacturing, franchising has become a major export for the United States. In developing regions of the world, it has become a stabilizing force creating business ownership and personal wealth among the citizens. There has been over a 50 percent growth in the rapidly expanding economies in Asia and East-

ern Europe since 1999.[2] Since 2004, they have seen a 14 percent growth in the number of franchise units built. As a result, franchising is helping America balance its trade deficit.

Franchising is a method of growing a business that sells goods and services at multiple locations under a common name. Some hospitality businesses have used franchising as a means of expanding their brand name, creating broader name recognition, without operating the business themselves. A **franchisor** licenses its brand name, operating system, or even its marketing expertise to another business entity (individual or group). This allows people who are novices in the field to start a business without the expertise in the field they should have to run a successful enterprise. They agree to follow the policies and rules set out in a franchise agreement. In some cases, the franchisor provides everything for the business, even management training. This allows someone to become a manager and be an owner quickly. The **franchisee** pays the franchisor an initial fee and then continuing fees (sometimes called royalties or maintenance fees) over the course of the contract.

According to a survey conducted by the Gallup Organization for the International Franchise Association (IFA),[3] 90 percent of franchise owners consider their franchise business to be successful or very successful. Franchise owners also indicated that they work hard for their money and made on average over $91,000 per year. These owners felt that owning the franchise was the key to their success.

Types of Franchises

There are two types of franchises—**product distribution** franchises and **business format**. A **product distribution franchisee** sells products or services that the franchisor manufactured. The most common product or services are cars, soft drinks, gasoline, and insurance. These items usually require some preparation by the franchisee before they are sold. Travel agencies operate in this fashion, especially for cruises. A product distribution franchisee may represent several different franchisors and sell their products or services on an exclusive or semi-exclusive basis. The product distribution franchisor provides its trademark and logo to the franchisee but usually not a business operating system.

Business format franchising provides the trademark, the logo, and the complete system for delivering the product and/or service and operating

Industry Spotlight—Rio Wraps Southwestern Grill

Tom Stegeman, a graduate of Central Michigan University Hospitality Service Program, was the V.P. of Development for the Asia Pacific Region of A&W Restaurants with responsibility for over 220 international locations ranging from Bangladesh to Australia. In 1999 Tom decided it was time to start his own franchise and partnered with brothers Mark and Joe Sheena to start Rio Wraps Southwestern Grill.

Rio Wraps Southwestern Grill opened their first quick-service restaurant in the Detroit area of Michigan. Today there are 26 restaurants, of which 20 are franchised, with plans for five more restaurant openings this year in Michigan and Florida. Their philosophy is to deliver fresh flavorful food at a fair price in a clean and entertaining environment. The core menu is made of tacos, nachos, quesa Rio's, salads, and classic and deli wraps. Rio Wraps likes to say that they offer a unique alternative to the standard deli fare, and a quality value-oriented twist over other Tex-Mex, south-of-the-border concepts. They focus on quality, variety, value, uniqueness, and atmosphere offering "not fast food . . . it's fresh food fast."

Tex-Mex, a small segment of the quick-service industry, has experienced rapid growth in recent years. This has provided an opportunity for Rio Wraps Southwestern Grill take the concept and add their own flavor while maintaining a southwest theme. They offer entrepreneurial minded people an opportunity to build a business with multiple units and costs comparable to other quick-service franchise concepts. Their restaurants average 1,400 to 1,800 square feet and gross sales of $350,000 to $450,000 a year. The advantage a small franchisor like Rio Wraps Southwestern Grill has is the ability to customize their relationship with their franchisees. In addition to purchasing the use of the brand name and operating systems, they offer services ranging from site selection and design to management and employee training and consulting services. Their franchisees bring a variety of skills and experiences, and by customizing services they can better support their needs and ultimate success. For more information about the Rio Wraps Southwestern Grill concept go to www.riowraps.com

the business. Operations that use business format franchising range from restaurants (most common) and hotels to real estate services and tax preparation services. The franchisor provides a detailed system from physical appearance of the business, product and service standards, to policies and procedures that ensure consistency from one location and franchisee to another. The confidential operating and procedures manuals guide franchisees in how to market their franchise; employee staffing from recruiting, hiring, and training, to employee dress code; and product ordering, preparing, and delivering the product and/or service. For instance, McDonald's provides all the manuals and has created Hamburger University to train their managers. In addition, to maintain consistency, there may be a list of vendors that provide the approved food. No others are allowed. When the largest McDonald's was opened in Moscow, Russia, it took years of preparation for the opening. They had to provide seeds for the lettuce, tomatoes, and potatoes and then teach the Russian farmers how to grow them. Then, they did the same with the beef cattle and the bakers for the rolls. All this was to maintain the same product consistency. Brand consistency in product and service provides the greatest business advantage for franchisor and franchisee.

Table 8.1 ||| Franchising Fast Facts[4]

- Over 1,500 franchise companies operating in the United States with more than 320,000 retail units
- 75 industries use franchising to distribute goods and services to consumers
- Average investment is less than $250,000
- Royalty or maintenance fees range from 3 percent to 6 percent of gross sales
- Franchisors average slightly less than 100 units
- Average length of contract is 10 years
- When a property changes franchise affiliation, it is referred to as reflagging

Table 8.2 ||| **Top 10 Types of Franchises**

Top 10 Franchise Companies (by # of units)
1. McDonald's Corporation
2. 7-Eleven Inc.
3. Subway Sandwiches & Salads
4. H&R Block, Inc.
5. Burger King Corp.
6. Jani-King International Inc.
7. Taco Bell Corp.
8. RadioShack
9. Pizza Hut Inc.
10. Domino's Pizza LLC

Franchise agreements can be for a **single-unit** (sometimes called direct unit) or for multi-units. **Multi-unit** agreements allow a franchisee to purchase additional units, growing their business with a brand that they are familiar with, lowering the financial risk for both the franchisee and franchisor. Multi-unit franchisees may have more leverage with the franchisor as they negotiate additional agreements and contract for services. **Area development** agreements grant the franchisee exclusive rights to a geographic area for opening up new locations within a specified time period. A **master franchisee** agreement is similar to an area development agreement with the addition of the ability to sell locations within a specified geographic area to persons or groups to open single-unit franchises. A master franchisee becomes a franchisor to these single-unit franchise owners.

Franchisor's Role

A franchisor can be a large public (McDonald's) or private company (Carlson Companies) located anywhere in the world (Accor—Paris, France or Wendy's International—Dublin, Ohio) and be a small start-up company (Rio Wraps—Detroit, Michigan) or a large conglomerate (Cendant Corporation—Parsippany, New Jersey). The franchisor licenses the right to conduct business under their brand name. Brand recognition is one of the biggest advantages that franchisors have to sell to franchisees. A brand name communicates expectations to consumers and is closely controlled by the franchisor. Franchisors provide the franchisee with support while exercising control over the way they operate under the brand. A consistent brand image is developed through franchisors' marketing activities that are paid for by franchisees in the form of a marketing fee. Marketing fees are pooled together to provide advertising, public relations, and other activities that promote the brand name.

Franchisors also provide operating methods and procedures to franchisees in the form of technical and management training to maintain consistent quality of products and services. The franchisor owns the concept name and how the franchisee's business deals with consumers. Product and service development is controlled by the franchisor to ensure that every franchise offers the same type and quality of products and services. The types of support provided by the franchisor vary from one organization to another and are outlined in the Uniform Franchise Offering Circular (UFOC). Franchisors like to say that you are in business for yourself, but not by yourself.

There are several **advantages** and **disadvantages** to developing a franchise.

Advantages

- Ability to grow business with minimum capital
- Do not have to manage each location, becomes responsibility of franchisee
- Franchisees are motivated to be profitable and in turn a portion is paid to franchisor

Disadvantages

- Royalty or maintenance fees are less than what the franchisor could make if they operated the business
- Franchisees are independent operators and may have a different perspective on how the business should be operated or compliance with contract
- Franchisee may not have the skills to profitably operate the business

Franchisee's Role

The franchisee agrees to operate under the franchisor's trademark or brand name providing only approved products or services using the franchisor's operating methods. The franchisee normally owns the land and building. The franchisee is responsible for securing capital for acquiring the physical assets and franchising fees and operating the business, though a franchisor may provide access to capital for expansion or updating of existing franchise units over time. In addition, they are responsible for human resource activities like hiring, training, and compensating their employees.

There are several **advantages** and **disadvantages** to owning a franchise:

Advantages

- Brand name recognition makes it easier to compete with established independent operators
- Access to training and operations manuals, site selection tools, and store design
- Purchasing power when negotiating for equipment and supplies
- Research and development of new product and service offerings

Disadvantages

- Loss of independence—must follow franchisor's policies and procedures
- Judged by management of other franchisees in system (reputation)
- Income expectations balanced with cost of franchising

Referral Organizations

Referral organizations are similar to franchise organizations in that they have the same name and provide similar core services. The typical referral organization is a nonprofit affiliation owned by members of independently owned and managed lodging operations. Typically, administrative expenses are covered by fees paid by its members. Rules, regulations, policies, and governance are determined by the voting members. Another difference is that **referral organizations** are comprised of member properties that are linked together for marketing purposes and therefore have fewer rules and regulations than franchise properties. The physical appearance of each member will be different, but they all provide similar products and have the same service standards.

Combining their marketing resources allows them to have a wider reach for advertising while creating a brand image. For example, The Luxury Romantic Collection by Great Hotels of The World is a small group of hotels that have joined together because they have a common image. So, guests select the image first and then decide which of the members has the best location for their romantic fantasy. Not only can they go to one Web site for information about each hotel, but people can make reservations at the site as well. Everybody wins. Referrals allow independently owned businesses to compete more efficiently with franchise brands and still maintain their uniqueness.

The largest referral organization is Best Western International, which is the world's largest hotel chain. They operate under a single brand name with 4,200 properties around the globe. Through **referral organizations**, members band together to market their business under a common trademark or brand. Their size allows them to leverage their combined purchasing power when buying products for quantity pricing and to share ideas for improved operating methods.

Referral organizations, such as Best Western International and Kampgrounds of America (KOA) maintain their individual property uniqueness found in their charm and local appeal while meeting global quality standards. Best Western International and KOA offer members the unique advantage of retaining their independence while providing the benefits of a full-service affiliation that includes marketing programs, training support, and purchasing power. A downside of this operating method is that travelers may be confused about different types of properties, differing quality and service levels, and a wide range of rates. These are some of the challenges of all referral organizations.

Role of Franchising or Referral Organization Advisory Committee

All major franchise and referral organizations have some structured way of gathering information from members through a **franchisee advisory board**. Franchise advisory boards address issues of both the franchisor and franchisees or referral organization and its members. Franchisee advisory groups can be a valuable source of marketing, operations, and product/service development ideas. Changes in products and services, such as new menu rollout are discussed along with policies and procedures for their implementation. Often the best ideas come from operators. One of McDonald's earlier franchisors, Jim Delligatti of Pittsburgh, Pennsylvania, invented the Big Mac in 1968, and another franchisor, Herb Peterson, developed the Egg McMuffin in 1973. Today, both of these sandwiches continue to be popular, profitable staples in the McDonald's product offerings.

Third-Party Distribution Systems

Third-party distribution systems act as middlemen between the buyer and supplier. In the hospitality industry this most often refers to Internet-based companies that provide travel reservations, such as "Travelocity.com," "Expedia.com," "Priceline. com," or "Hotwire.com." The third-party distribution company becomes a representative to the hospitality service provider. They do not own the products or services that they are selling; their role is to connect buyers with sellers. Some buy the product like blocks of rooms from the hotel for wholesale prices and then turn around and sell those rooms to the end user at discounted prices. Sometimes this results in a price war, with hotels competing for their own rooms. In New Orleans, hotels want to create a referral organization for New Orleans to compete with these third-party distribution companies.

Third-party distribution systems can also operate reservation services on behalf of corporate, franchise, and independent lodging properties. For a fee or commission, these organizations provide reservations to the public. Examples of hospitality third-party distributors are "Expedia.com," "Orbitz. com," and "Travelocity.com." These Internet sites sell a variety of travel products and services: lodging, transportation (car rental, airline, train and bus tickets), and entertainment (theater, amusement parks). Think of these companies like a grocery store in that they advertise their Internet site to the general public. Once a customer visits the Internet site, each individual brand or property competes for the customer's business based on location, price, and amenities. Third-party distribution systems provide a means for independent or non-affiliated business to create brand awareness and compete with affiliated (corporate or franchise) properties. Affiliated properties have one more marketing tool for promoting their specific property in addition to brand systemwide promotional activities.

Hotwire.com

Hotwire.com is one of many third-party distribution companies that become a representative to the hospitality service provider.

Participating hospitality businesses provide a set number of rooms/tickets in a price range or established price. The third-party operator acts as a representative of the hotel and sells the room/ticket to the general public. The customer pays the third-party distributor, and they in turn pay the lodging, transportation, or entertainment operator minus the commission.

Summary

Franchises, referral organization, and third-party distribution systems are other ways to manage your business. Each system operates differently giving the owners unique opportunities. Six of the top 10 largest franchisors are hospitality organizations. Chances are that you have visited one of these businesses and/or worked for a hospitality franchised operation. Franchising offers many advantages to the owner/manager, employee, and customer: consistency in brand offerings, standardization of policies and procedures and service standards. As a future hospitality professional, you have many career options and employment choices. Owning a franchise is one way that you can go into business for yourself without doing everything yourself. On the other hand, if you operate a small going concern, perhaps referral organizations will give you marketing power without the necessity of merging with a large corporation. Finally, third-party distribution systems may give you a central reservation system and additional visibility to aid in obtaining more guests. Depending on what you need, each of these methods is a possibility when exploring your options.

Endnotes

1. www.franchise.org
2. International Franchise Association. (2005). *Industry facts.* Downloaded, January 15, 2006
3. International Franchise Association. (2005). *Franchise Development Super Session Series.* Atlanta, GA April 21–22
4. Olson, Paul. (2005). The Franchise Times: Top 200. *Franchise Times*, Oct 2005 p. 49
5. Thomas, Dave, Seid, Michael. (2000). *Franchising for Dummies.* New York: Hungry Minds

Resources

Internet Sites

Accor: www.accorhotels.com
Best Western: www.bestwestern.org
Cendant Corporation: www.cendant.com
International Franchise Association: www.franchise.org
KOA: www.koa.com
Rio Wraps Southwestern Grill: www.riowraps.com

☞ *Key Words and Concepts*

Franchise advisory board
Franchisee
Franchisor
Referral organization
Third-party distribution system

 *Contributor Information*

www.emich.edu/sts/hrm
Susan Gregory is a professor and coordinator for the Hotel and Restaurant Management Program at Eastern Michigan University.

8 Review Questions

1. What are some of the names of local hospitality franchise operations in your city?

2. Are there any local franchisors in your community or state?

3. What are the advantages for an independent business owner to join a franchise or referral organization?

4. As an employee, what are the advantages of working for a franchise operation (affiliated) over working for a nonaffiliated business and vice versa?

5. As a consumer, describe how you have used a third-party distribution company.

6. What is the difference between a franchise and a referral system?

7. How can you find out what services a franchisor offers to its franchisees?

8. Why are franchise restaurants popular with consumers?

Wanda M. Costen
University of Tennessee

E-Hospitality: Technology in the Hospitality Industry

Learning Objectives

✓ To describe the different types of technology used in the hospitality industry
✓ To identify which technological applications are used in which segments of the industry
✓ To explain how technology usage affects a hospitality organization

Chapter Outline

What Is E-Hospitality?
Technology and Consumer Behavior
Technology in Lodging
Technology in Foodservices
Technology in Conventions and Meeting Planning
Other Uses of Technology

*E*ver since the advent of computers, the world of technology has been rapidly changing. Microchips keep getting smaller and smaller, and all the products that use them are shrinking as well. Luckily, along with the shrinking size comes the reduction in pricing making everything better and more affordable. This means that the average person can afford voice mail, e-mail, security systems, and computers. Not only can they buy these products and many more, but because of the size, they have become portable as well. People can get their voice and e-mail messages anywhere in the world. You can check the security of your house by accessing your house Web site. And, computers come in all sizes. Because people are using more technology, they expect high tech when they travel as well. Therefore, hotels and even restaurants offer wireless availability.

The dropping prices also allow businesses to use high-tech equipment to speed up operations, coordinate activities, and secure their properties. Hotels have programmed key cards and property management systems that allow a guest to turn the lights, TV, and heating/cooling systems off and on. Restaurants have systems to speed up ordering and check and credit card operations. Of course, the Internet has totally changed the way people shop, explore their options, and make reservations. This means that hospitality businesses need Web sites, online reservations, and property tours to accommodate this new way of attracting customers. As you can see, e-hospitality is growing faster than any other business.

What Is E-Hospitality?

Technology seems to be one of the most important components affecting business today. E-hospitality is the term used to reflect all aspects of technology in the hospitality industry. Technology encompasses everything from voice mail systems and electronic door locks to property management and menu engineering systems. Technology affects each segment and department of the hospitality industry. The purpose of this chapter is to expose you to the various types of technology used in different segments of the industry. It is important to understand the role of technology in the hospitality industry because research shows that technology positively influences organizational performance, employee productivity, and customer satisfaction.[1]

Unfortunately, the hospitality industry typically lags behind other industries in terms of adopting technology. This is usually because of the hospitality industry's slow response to information technology growth. Other industries have leveraged technology and increased efficiency and productivity. Leveraging technology is the process of using technology in ways that maximize its benefits. For example, most business managers have e-mail capability. Leveraging the use of this technology would include not only communicating using e-mail, but also attaching memos, policy changes, and new procedures. This process would reduce the amount of paper used in the organization, as well as the time it takes to implement changes to policies and procedures. Reducing implementation time increases the efficiency of the organization. Because many hospitality managers have little technological training, they are less comfortable adopting new technology.[2] Consequently, decision makers in the hospitality industry are only typically willing to invest in technology that is visible or has a direct impact on the bottom line. Visible technology falls into the "low end" of the technological spectrum. These applications are primarily clerical/administrative or operational and include computers, e-mail, fax machines, printers, and Internet access. Unfortunately, however, computer usage primarily duplicated the paper system that it replaced. For example, technology is not primarily used to allow the front office system to "talk to" the foodservice cost management system or the reservations system.

Technology and Consumer Behavior

According to the U.S. Department of Commerce, since the year 2000, more people are using the Internet to make purchases. See Table 9.1 for information on travel consumer behavior.

Consumers primarily use the Internet to find out information. Therefore, access to the company's Web site, quality of the content, and structure are the most important attributes that consumers use to evaluate a company's Web site. Access measures how easy it is for consumers to find a company's Web site. The quality of the content measures how current the information is and whether that information is readily understandable and useful to the consumer. The structure of the site is a measure of

Table 9.1 ‖ **Travel Planning on the Internet** (in millions)[21]

	2000	2001	2002	2003	2004	2005
Online travelers	59.4	64.5	63.9	64.1	63.8	79.0
Online frequent travelers[a]	30.8	32.0	33.8	32.6	31.7	47.2

[a]The Travel Industry Association of America defines frequent travelers as those who make 5+ trips/year.

how the site is organized, including the usefulness of links and placement of important information. Additionally, information completeness and ease of use are the two characteristics that most influence consumer behavior intentions. Information completion is whether consumers find the information they are seeking, and ease of use is how user-friendly the Web site is and whether consumers are able to conduct their desired transactions. When consumers are satisfied with the information they obtain from an organization's Web site, they are more likely to purchase that product.[3]

E-Commerce

E-commerce is the process of using the Internet to establish a distribution channel that allows companies to work with customers, suppliers, and partners.[4] A distribution channel is a way of getting a company's products or services to the consumer. E-commerce changes these relationships, as well as the flow of information. One way that e-commerce changes relationships is that the Internet allows people to retrieve the information they need when they need it.[5] Thus, consumers no longer have to contact a supplier to purchase an item. In the hospitality industry, this means that consumers can log onto the Internet and purchase a hotel room whenever they want, without the hassle of trying to find the telephone contact information for a reservation center. E-commerce influences the flow of information in that a consumer no longer has to interact directly with a company representative to get the information they need. Although the company does control the information that is posted on its Web site, how and when that information gets to the consumer is now at the consumer's fingertips.

Hospitality companies, and lodging properties in particular use multiple distribution channels, each with different rates, to sell their rooms. Hospitality companies sell their services through their own company Web sites, third-party Web sites, and company telephone reservations systems. The different rates are due to the costs associated with each channel. A third party often charges a fee for distribution, and there are obvious labor costs associated with a company's telephone reservations system. No one distribution channel consistently has the lowest price, so consumers are likely to use the Internet to seek out the rates available from various providers that best suit their needs.[6] In 2005, many benchmark lodging properties noticed that 50 percent of their business was generated from the Internet.[7] A study of Internet use in the lodging industry indicated that hotel company Web sites received 75 percent of the market, while third parties (Travelocity, Orbitz, Expedia, etc.) received the other 25 percent. However, economic issues are forcing lodging companies to provide more inventory to third-party distributors. The Internet has given the consumer access to a wide assortment of lodging options, and therefore the hotel room is now a commodity. Each room that is priced similarly is seen as equivalent, regardless of the quality of the property. To distinguish its product, lodging companies now have to invest in customer-oriented amenities and offers of free services. These investments ultimately affect the bottom-line profit of the company and are quickly becoming the cost of doing business. As a result, hotel companies will most likely begin to rely more on third-party Web sites to sell their room inventory in the near future. Relying on third parties could potentially reduce the bottom-line profit of hotel companies because the company will no longer have exclusive control over room rates.

Technology in Lodging

Some of the greatest strides in technology in the hospitality industry have occurred in the lodging segment of the industry. In general, there are four types of information technology (IT) applications in the lodging industry:

50 percent of the business of benchmark lodging properties came from the Internet in 2005.

1. Front office information technology applications include reservation management, room management, and guest accounting systems.
2. Back office technology includes human resources systems, financial reports, and inventory systems.
3. Restaurant and banquet management systems include cost control, menu and recipe management, beverage control, sales forecasting, and menu pricing.
4. Guest-related systems are those related to the call accounting system, energy management systems, guest-operated devices, and automated guest services like an automated wake-up call system.[8]

Technology can be used to increase employee productivity, reduce administrative and communication costs, enhance revenue, and increase guest services. The property management system is an example of how technology can increase guest services. Today's property management systems provide the front desk, room service, and other guest agents with a guest's name. This information gives the employee the opportunity to call the guest by name, thereby establishing a rapport with the guest. Technology geared toward employee productivity includes voice mail, interactive TV guides, and management e-mail. Interactive TV guides provide the customer the opportunity to check out of the hotel, which reduces the number of people with whom the front desk needs to interact. Ultimately this technology increases employee productivity. Internet bookings, teleconferencing, cell phone rentals, and ATMs are technology applications that generate additional revenue. Guest services technology includes in-room modems, in-room Internet access, and in-room fax machines.

Generally, the more upscale the lodging property, the greater the number of technological applications the property has adopted. Casino and convention hotels implement the most technology designed to enhance guest services (in-room Internet access and in-room modems and fax machines). Not surprisingly, convention hotels also implement significantly more technology that increases employee efficiency and enhances revenue. The most frequently adopted technological application in lodging companies is Internet bookings, followed by management e-mail systems and Internet access in hotel rooms.[9]

Technology has reached almost unbelievable heights in international hotels. In Dubai's Burj Al Arab, curtains, lighting, and heating in a guest room are voice controlled. The room even can sense when it is occupied! The latest lodging technology systems monitor and control smoke detectors, room entry, alarm systems, heating, air conditioning, television, and lighting all from a central location. Hallway sensors allow lights to be turned off unless someone enters the hallway. Motion sensors signal the system and turn on the lights as needed. This technology significantly reduces energy costs while maintaining safety. Today, some five-star lodging properties have interactive plasma TVs that not only allow the guest to check out without going to the front desk, but also order room service, schedule a spa treatment, or get a tee time.[10]

Technology in Foodservice

Technology in foodservice has typically been restricted to the back-of-the-house, but that is rapidly changing. The back-of-the-house is the term used to classify positions that have little or no guest contact. In foodservice these positions are located in the kitchen, such as chef/cook or dishwasher. Therefore, back-of-the-house foodservice technology refers to the technology that assists kitchen operations. Food and beverage cost control, recipe management, menu pricing, and sales forecasting are some of the types of technological systems currently in use in foodservice establishments. There is a new trend, however, in that cutting-edge foodservice operators are using their Web sites to facilitate online reservations and better serve their customers.

Pizza delivery restaurants seem to be taking the lead in on-site technology. When a customer calls into almost any national pizza delivery restaurant, the store is able to pull up pertinent information about the customer quickly. The data management system contains not only the name and address of the caller (retrieved by phone number), but also information about previous orders and delivery instructions. This same system is integrated with sales and marketing and allows the restaurant to send out direct mailers and promotional coupons to specific customers. For example, a store owner can run a query, download all the customers who have not ordered a pizza in the past 90 days, and send those customers a promotional advertisement.

Full-service, upscale restaurants are also using technology to enhance their customer service and guest experience. The Charlie Palmer Group uses an electronic wine list at its restaurants in Las Vegas, New York City, and Washington, D.C. The list, which contains 4,000 bottles, is presented on a personal data assistant (PDA) and given to the customer at the table. Each wine listing contains information on food and wine pairings, as well as background information about some of the wineries. This system has increased wine sales by 36 percent.[11]

In Atlanta, Nava uses wireless handheld terminals that allow cocktail servers to send drink orders immediately to the bar. By the time the cocktail servers get to the bar, the drink is ready! Additionally, this particular system sends each food order to the particular area in the kitchen. For example, each component of the order is sent to the grill, hot appetizers, or garde manger. These wireless handhelds can also be used to print out the guest check and scan credit cards at the table. According to the General Manager, John McDaniels, these wireless handheld terminals make the restaurant more efficient and more profitable.[12]

Smart phone technology is on the cutting edge of restaurant technology internationally. Smart phones are cell phones with PDA capabilities. In Asia and Europe, customers can use their smart phones to order and pay at some restaurants. This smart phone technology has huge implications for the restaurant industry, especially quick-service restaurants. Imagine going into a quick-service restaurant and beaming in your order while paying for it at the same time! This technology could help reduce labor and training costs, while simultaneously increasing customer satisfaction.[13]

Technology in Conventions and Meeting Planning

With the advent of teleconferencing, conventional wisdom suggested that technology would reduce the number of meetings held each year. To the contrary, technology has actually stimulated the need for technology shows and enhanced the demands of other shows. As a result, convention centers have needed to broaden their technological capabilities.

Fifty percent of the convention centers and convention and visitor bureaus (CVBs) that participated in a study in 1998 posted information for event planners and attendees online via their Web site. Approximately 60 percent provided Internet access to meeting planners and attendees in exhibit halls or meeting rooms and offered network setup. In terms of security, 45 percent of the participants used smart cards to limit access to secure areas of the convention center. Furthermore, 70 percent had teleconferencing capabilities, and 65 percent had videoconferencing capability.[14] This information means that convention center and CVB clients expect to have access to a variety of technological applications. In order to remain competitive, these organizations need to ensure that they can meet the needs of these technologically savvy clients.

In 2000, 70 percent of the major convention centers in the United States had T1 Internet connections capable of transferring 1.54 megabits of data per second. A large number of these centers also have T3 connections, which are **30** times *faster* than T1s! These connections allow exhibitors to use the Internet as part of their display in an exhibition hall. The Dallas Convention Center implemented the first wireless networking system in a convention center in 1997. Wireless systems provide Internet access without connecting a cable to a computer. According to the Technical Director, Cindy Coyle, this wireless system is actually cheaper than the wired communication systems offered by the local telecommunications provider.[15]

Other Uses of Technology

It seems clear that technology aids in sales and marketing, given the increased numbers of consumers booking travel online. Technology also influences other areas in hospitality companies. Many companies today use intranet systems to train employees and disseminate company information. An intranet system is similar to the Internet, only it is only accessible within the company by people granted access. Human resource departments have set up computers in the back-of-the-house to allow employees to access and update their benefits information.

With the success of Monster.com, e-recruiting is now revolutionizing the way companies find new employees. In 2000, 45 percent of the *Fortune* 500 companies used the Internet to actively recruit.[16] Using the Internet reduces the costs of advertising for open positions. Two of the most sophisticated Web sites for seeking a position in the hospitality industry in North America are Hcareers[17] and Hospitality Career Net.[18–19] See Figure 9.1 for a more thorough listing of online hospitality employment sites.

How Technology Adds Value to an Organization

In many manufacturing companies, technology is often adopted to reduce labor costs. By contrast, technology in the service industry is used to support, not replace, the employee. One of the challenges facing hospitality companies is how to train employees on the technology being implemented in the organization. Because a lot of the training in this industry occurs on the job, technological skills often are not shared in a systematic way.

One of the key reasons to adopt new technology is to increase bottom-line profit. Research shows that there is a positive relationship between IT and company performance and profit. Implementing IT systems cannot only reduce costs, but also increase productivity, revenues, and ultimately customer service. The effective use of technology can also create a sustainable competitive advantage and become a way for hospitality companies to differentiate themselves.

Summary

Although there is much discussion about the potential impact of technology on the hospitality industry, few companies are actually investing in technology designed to assist the organization in accomplishing its strategic goals and creating a sustainable competitive advantage. The most technologically developed segment of the hospitality industry is the lodging segment. However, a 1998 study revealed that almost 70 percent of the 4,520 lodging properties studied had adopted few or none of the existing technology available in the marketplace.[20] With a significant amount of the lodging customers coming from the business segment, lodging companies will have to adopt some of the customer-oriented technology available to meet or exceed their customers' expectations.

In the foodservice segment, technology designed to improve the efficiency of employees, who have face-to-face contact with guests, is still cost prohibitive. However, many restaurants interface with their food suppliers and order products online. Additionally, forecasting and cost control modules assist foodservice managers in obtaining more profit.

Many of the convention centers in the U.S.' largest cities are increasing their technological capa-

Figure 9.1 ||| **Hospitality Employment Web Sites**[22]

www.hotelresource.com—This site lists job openings in front office, food and beverage, maintenance, and hotel management.

www.hospitalityonline.com/jobs—This site lists lodging management and front line positions by location, company, and position.

www.hospitalityadventures.com—Contains U.S. and international positions listed by location, company type, or company name.

www.casinocareers.com—Information about career opportunities in the casino segment of the hospitality industry.

www.foodservice.com/jobs.htm—This site is the largest and most active Web site for foodservice professionals.

www.e-hospitality.com—This site provides important information about the hospitality industry, as well as job listings, recruitment information, and salary information.

bilities. Not only are technology shows on the rise, but many clients are now requesting advanced technological support. To drive business, convention centers will need to begin to invest in cutting-edge technology.

Overall, the hospitality industry is poised to take advantage of the benefits offered by technology. In the coming years, more hotel rooms will have wireless technology, and restaurant servers will be taking your order with a handheld!

Endnotes

1. Siguaw, J., Enz, C., and Namasivayam, K. (2000). Adoption of information technology in U.S. hotels: Strategically driven objectives. *Journal of Travel Research, 39*, 192–201
2. Law, R. and Jogaratnam, G. (2005). A study of hotel information technology applications. *International Journal of Contemporary Hospitality Management, 17* (2), 170–180
3. Jeong, M., Haemoon, O., and Gregoire, M. (2003). Conceptualizing web site quality and its consequences in the lodging industry. *International Journal of Hospitality Management, 22*, 161–175
4. Garces, S., Gorgemans, S., Sanchez, A. M., and Perez, M. (2004). Implications of the Internet—an analysis of the Aragonese hospitality industry. *Tourism Management, 25*, 603–613
5. Lee, S., Barker, S., and Kandampully, J. (2003). Technology, service quality, and customer loyalty in hotels: Australian managerial perspectives. *Managing Service Quality, 13* (5), 423–432
6. O'Connor, P. and Murphy, J. (2004). Research on information technology in the hospitality industry. *International Journal of Hospitality Management, 23*, 473–484
7. Rama, M. (2005, May 16). Third party web sites threaten brand loyalty, bottom lines. *Hotel and Motel Management*, 23
8. Ham, S., Kim, W. G., and Jeong, S. (2005). Effect of information technology on performance in upscale hotels. *International Journal of Hospitality Management, 24*, 2005
9. Siguaw, et. al., 2000
10. Room for technology. (2002, May). *Hospitality Focus*, 15–16
11. Gerst, V. (2004, May 1). Dining in the digital age. *Restaurants and Institutions, 114*, 56–58
12. Gerst, 2004
13. Allen, R. (2005, November 28). Call it a hunch, but industry should invest in smart-phone technology for ordering. *Nation Restaurant News, 39*, 21
14. Kamp, A., and Petersen, D. (1998, October 19). Technology offerings play a major role in success. *Amusement Business, 110*, 26–28
15. Chapman, B. (2000, September 1). Really wired. *Successful Meetings, 49*, 105–110
16. Rushmore, S. (2000, June 1). 'E-' is for employment. *Hotels, 34*, 40
17. www.hcareers.com
18. www.hospitalitycareernet.com
19. Rushmore, S., 2000
20. Namasivayam, K., Enz, C., and Siguaw, J. (2000). How wired are we? The selection and use of new technology in U.S. hotels. *Cornell Hotel and Restaurant Quarterly, 41* (6), 40–48
21. Adapted from Travel Industry of America. (2005). *Travelers' use of the Internet for travel planning*
22. Adapted from Nagubandi, A. (2003, March 10). It's hospitality here. *The Hindu*. Retrieved on 20 January 2006 from http://global.factiva.com.proxy.lib.utk.edu:90/ha/default.aspx

Resources

Internet Sites

www.hospitalitynet.org—Contains current industry news and information, as well as job opportunities and hotel schools.

www.ahla.com—This is the American Hotel and Lodging Association Web site. It is the premier Web site for the lodging industry. This site contains information on professional certifications, career opportunities, conferences, and more.

www.restaurant.org—This is the National Restaurant Association Web site. It is the premier Web site for the foodservice industry. This site contains information about professional certifications, career opportunities, current news, and more.

www.cmaa.org—This is the Club Managers Association of America Web site. Here you will find important information about a career in club management.

www.mpiweb.org—This is the Meeting Professionals International Web site. It contains information about careers, educational programs, and the meeting planners' profession.

🔑 Key Words and Concepts

Back-office technology
Data management systems
Distribution channel
E-commerce
Front-office technology
Guest-related systems
Restaurant and banquet management systems
Smart phones
Third parties

📇 Contributor Information

wcosten@utk.edu

WANDA M. COSTEN earned her PhD in sociology from Washington State University. She also has an Executive MBA from Pepperdine University and her undergraduate degree is from the United States Military Academy at West Point. She is currently an assistant professor in the Retail, Hospitality, and Tourism Management Department at the University of Tennessee. Dr. Costen's research interests include racial and gender inequality in organizations, women and leadership, and strategic human resources. Her work has been published in *Journal of Management Inquiry, Journal of Human Resources in Hospitality and Tourism,* and *Gaming Research and Review Journal.* Dr. Costen has partnered with business organizations to help them develop diversity initiatives and training programs. She also has ten years of business management experience in sales, operations, and human resources.

9 Review Questions

1. How does the hospitality industry compare to other industries in terms of adopting new technology?

2. What Web site characteristics influence a customer's decision to purchase something on the Internet?

3. How is e-commerce affecting the profitability of hotels?

4. What are the four types of technology used in the lodging industry?

5. What are some of the benefits of using a data management system in a restaurant?

6. How does technology impact the human resources function?

7. How does technology add value to a hospitality organization?

Janet Sim
Yumi Satow
San Francisco State University

Rob Heiman
Kent State University

Contract Management

Learning Objectives

Students will be able to:

- ✓ Understand contract management and components of a basic contract concept
- ✓ Explain types of management companies in the lodging industry: management franchise management vs. independent management companies
- ✓ Understand contract terms, types of management fees, and their implications
- ✓ Explain recent trends of hotel management companies and owner participation in operational decisions
- ✓ Define terms in contract foodservice management
- ✓ List the largest contract management companies
- ✓ Understand the diversity of work environment in the contract foodservice industry
- ✓ Know job challenges and career opportunities in the noncommercial foodservice segments

Chapter Outline

Hotel Contract Management
Foodservice Management Contracts

*I*n this section on "Hospitality and Tourism Businesses," many different forms of businesses were discussed. Independent and entrepreneurial operations were multiplied into chains. To become even larger, franchises were developed and small businesses were combined into referral associations. Using current technology, e-hospitality has been advanced to improve marketing and operations. In this last chapter of the section, the possibility of contracting other companies to manage businesses and services is explored.

Contract management encompasses the management of services in a very broad range of settings by agreeing to a contract that is a mutually binding legal relationship. In the hospitality industry, it means that a contract has been negotiated between the operator who furnishes management services to operate the foodservice and/or lodging operation and the owner who pays for these services. The owner usually either does not have the expertise or the desire to manage the hospitality operation and must therefore buy the service from a management company. This allows an owner to receive benefits from the business without having to personally manage the operation. However, this also means relinquishing the day-to-day control over the business.

The basic contract concept consists of three components:

1. the operator has sole and exclusive right to manage the property without ownership interference;
2. the owner pays all operating and financing expenses and assumes ownership risks; and
3. the operator is indemnified from his or her actions except for gross negligence or fraud.

Thus, the concept assigns all operating responsibilities to the operating company and all financial responsibilities to the owner.[1] Therefore, the owner needs to be very careful in selecting a management company that is responsible for all aspects of the operation.

Hotel Contract Management

The hotel industry has undergone a constantly changing situation in the last two decades. In the 1970s and 1980s, the hotel industry prospered, and the number of hotels expanded rapidly. Much of this development was undertaken by people who were not experienced in hotel operations, but understood the importance of providing shelter to weary travelers. As a result, the hotel owners invited management companies to furnish management services to operate the foodservice and/or lodging operations for a given monetary consideration.

With the increasing demand for hotel rooms, the number of hotel management companies also multiplied rapidly. Then came the recession and the Persian Gulf War. The cost of travel increased with the rising gas shortages, and people no longer had as much discretionary income to spend, so travel slowed down. This left many hotels in the middle of construction with the reduced demand. Other hotels struggled to compete in the over-saturated market. The hotel industry was faced with financial difficulties and distressed properties. Although the 1980s were characterized by contracts weighted toward operators, the 1990s revealed a resurgence of owner rights. When the properties were losing money, the owners wanted to take back control in hopes that they had enough business expertise to turn the tide. As the economic turbulence subsided, the trend in the latter part of the 1990s was to either expand internationally or consolidate at home.[2] As prosperity returned, owners once again relinquished control. However with a broader range of management companies competing for business, owners have the advantage of getting management contracts with greater flexibility on terms, such as the right price for the right length of time.[3]

Types of Management Companies

There are two types of hotel management companies. First, most chain organizations such as Marriott International or Sheraton Corporation serve as management companies for hotels under their franchises. Others are independent management companies that operate properties under several franchises.

In the August 2003 issue of *Lodging Hospitality*, the top hotel management contract companies were ranked, based on the total rooms managed. Starwood Hotels and Resorts was ranked at the top, managing 137,281 rooms, International Hotels and Resorts was ranked second managing 73,447 rooms, and Wyndham International was ranked third managing 43,387 rooms. However, all management companies are not the same.

To be competitive, successful companies have taken on new roles, such as forming financial programs with brokerage houses and offering loans to owners who wish to seek financial support. These giants also make equity investments in participating properties. Some of these companies offer special services to handle a wide range of management services.

Length of Contract Terms

Management companies used to operate hotels under long-term management contracts because they were perceived as the experts. Some of them have kept their contracts for as long as three decades. In the 1990s, when the trend was for owners to take back operations, lengths of initial contract terms and number of renewals decreased for both chain and independent operators. These shorter terms and fewer renewal periods have created flexibility for owners but increased the operator's sense of urgency to perform well.

Length of term correlates with whether the operator represents a brand name. A survey conducted by the Hotel Asset Managers Association (HAMA) in 1999 showed a bimodal distribution in that two distinct groups have emerged. One set of contracts for independent operators favors an initial term of less than six years. The other set of operators representing brand operators provides for an initial term of 20 or more years.[4]

Management Fees

Management companies typically receive a base fee and often an incentive fee. *Base fee* is a percentage of total revenue, averaging between 2 to 3 percent of gross revenue. Management contracts, which provide automatic base fees, are a thing of the past, as it did not motivate the management companies to perform their best. Therefore, there is a continuing downward trend in base fees.

Unlike base fees, which are based on generated income, incentive fees are motivational tools. *Incentive Fees*, which began in the late 1980s, are generally based on performance improvement after at least a year. Incentive fees are typically calculated as a percentage of the amount over a specific goal, a percentage improvement in gross operating profit, or a percentage of net operating income.[5] The most common method of structuring incentive fees is to set those fees as a percentage of a given net-income line after expenses. There is an inverse correlation between the level of the base fee and the levels of incentive fees. Thus, the lower the base-fee percentage, the higher the incentive-fee levels.[6] This means that management companies can make more profit, but they must work hard to improve operations.

Although contracts continue to have low base fees, incentive fees continue to be more important, particularly for full-service hotels. With the management fee weighted toward net income rather than total revenue, it is in the management company's best interest to operate as profitably as possible. Competition among operators for more contracts has also intensified, setting off a fee war among operators who find themselves having to bid lower and lower on fees to obtain additional contracts.

Loan and Equity Contributors

Another aspect of changing hotel management is that management companies have become owners by purchasing shares or equity in the company. Loan and equity contributions from the management companies have been a source of negotiation for a long time. With increased competition in the industry, management companies may have to invest more equity or loans in the hotels before they get major contracts with longer terms and higher incentive fees. This is appealing to the owners, because the management company now has a vested interest in making sure the company succeeds. Of course, many management companies would rather not make any equity contributions to the properties because they are at a high risk level with their money. On the other hand, equity participation inspires them to perform better, because their own money is at stake. Therefore, they become owners and risk-takers, not just fee-takers. Johnson[7] reported an inverse correlation between contract length and operator contributed equity. Independent operators who generally sign short-term contracts have a greater propensity to contribute equity.

Owner Input in Operational Decisions

Hotel owners are now taking a much more active role in overseeing functions of their management companies. To protect against poor management, the owner may require the management company to agree on a performance clause. Such a clause may specify that if management does not achieve a pre-agreed level of financial results for a specified number of consecutive years, the owner then has the right to terminate the contract.[8] The owners' rights to approve budgets is nearly universal. Perhaps the

Hotel owners are taking a more active role in overseeing functions of their management companies.

greatest change in the 1990s' hotel management contracts involves owners' increased ability to review and approve key management positions, budgets, and marketing plans.[9] Because owners are more involved in operations, it is important that both the owner and the operator meet regularly, monthly, or quarterly to discuss the strengths and weaknesses of operating plans and results for the upcoming period as well as any other issues that either side deems important.

In summary, management companies have been pressured to achieve higher and more structured performance standards, shorter contracts, and lower base fees. With increasing competition among a wide range of management companies, owners are mandating greater flexibility on terms and are shifting to below-the-line incentives rather than negotiating management fees from the revenues.[10] This forces the management companies to be joint risk takers in operating the venture.

Foodservice Management Contracts

Contract foodservice management is one of the least known career opportunities to students who are studying hospitality management. Managed services consist of foodservice operations in the noncommer-cial or the institutional segment of the foodservice industry, such as hospitals, schools, colleges/universities, business and industry, vending, leisure/recreation, and correctional facilities. These parts of the hospitality industry have staggering numbers of units to prove their importance. Total sales for these segments are in excess of $75 billion, generated from more than 200,000 locations.

Historical Background

Providing food for workers and employees can be traced back to very early times when the Pharaohs fed the people building the pyramids. This would be a very early example of today's business and industry foodservice where the employer provides food on premise for the employees. Foodservices have been documented in facilities as early as 1834, when the Bowery Savings Bank in New York offered food to its employees. Foodservice today is a very integral part of many organizations. It has grown to offering food in very appealing and upscale environments in most of the noncommercial segments of foodservice industry. Foodservice in many of these dining areas has grown beyond the employee cafeteria to include catering, retail operations, executive or private dining, take-home meals, convenience stores, and more. Contract foodservice management has grown from a nondescript, boring career option into one of the most exciting, challenging segments of the hospitality industry.

Contract Foodservice Companies

The contract foodservice management firm that arranges with the host firm to provide management for their foodservice operations is often referred to as a *contractor*. These *host* facilities that receive services are usually located in the noncommercial or the institutional segment of the foodservice industry. The host firm is usually referred to as the *client* of the contractor. As the word *"contract"* implies, there is a legal document between a host company (often known as the client company) and a contract company to provide services. The services involve operating the foodservice department and managing the foodservice employees. In the same contract, the management fees and terms are also negotiated between the contract company and host firm. Host firms employ contractors to manage their foodservices for a variety of reasons, such as financial considerations that the contractor may guarantee the budget or human resource benefits that the contractor is able to offer competent or well-trained foodservice managers.

Not all foodservice organizations hire contractors. When host firms choose to operate their own foodservices, they are known as *self-ops*. Therefore, the manager of a self-operating foodservice is an employee of the host firm. Depending on the segment of foodservice, contracted service versus self-op service will vary proportionally. For example, in business and industry, there is an 80/20 ratio (80 percent contracted and 20 percent self-op). It is just the opposite in the hospital segment, with 30 percent contracted and 70 percent self-op.

Food Management has been compiling and publishing a listing for the noncommercial foodservice industry's 50 largest contract management companies annually since 1998. In the September 2005 issue of *Food Management*, the following were the top five contract management companies in total sales volume (in millions) in 2004:

1. Aramark Corp., Philadelphia, PA, $6,882
2. Compass Group Americas Division, Charlotte, NC, $6,400
3. Sodexho, Inc., Gaithersburg, MD, $6,000
4. Delaware North Companies, Buffalo, NY, $1,700
5. Centerplate, Spartanburg, SC, $607

Diversity

The contract management companies, whether they are very large or small, offer a great diversity in work environments from hospitals or schools to sports stadiums. Diversity comes in several forms. Unlike some other parts of the foodservice industry, the contract services do not have two facilities that are exactly alike, whether they are two schools, two business and industry locations, or two colleges. Therefore, each location offers a unique challenge. In addition, contract services offer a wide variety of job options as well as choice of work hours: daytime (business and industry), nighttime (stadium or arena), or something in between. Most restaurants do not offer this type of variety under one roof. As contract services increase and expand into other areas, such as housekeeping, laundry, and building maintenance, one needs to increase the knowledge and skill base to keep abreast of this change.

Career Advantages

There are many advantages in choosing a career with a noncommercial contract firm that operates in the foodservice industry. One advantage is that the career offers excellent opportunities for upward mobility. One can develop a whole career potential, from entry-level assistant manager to corporate executive. By working with only one firm, one is able to learn the organization well, build seniority, and capitalize on long-term benefit plans such as company stock option opportunities or retirement programs. Another advantage of a career with a contract firm is the availability of corporate support services, such as standardized training programs and support from specialists in marketing, accounting, financial analysis, or human resources.

Perhaps the greatest advantages of a career in the noncommercial sector are the number of work days, frequent weekends off, and the number of hours worked in most segments. Most noncommercial managers work fairly regular work schedules, and most of the work hours are in the daytime.

Job Challenges

There are also some challenges. Relocation is a big consideration, because many people do not want to relocate. The contract management companies move their managers often. It may only be across town, but one may expect to be at another location about every 12 months or every few years when contracts get terminated. In the beginning of one's career, this can be very positive because it provides a broad base of experiences, and it may help prevent managers from becoming "stale."

Another unique challenge of contract management services is the client liaison, or the "other boss" at the client or host organization. Yet, every foodservice director still has his/her traditional boss, the district manager with the contract company. This results in two bosses. Most of the time, the "bosses" do agree, and the foodservice director knows where they stand. However, there are occasions when the foodservice manager receives different messages from the two bosses and gets caught in the middle. These situations are definitely a challenge to the manager. One must remember that the client liaison is one very unique part of contract services. Restaurants in the commercial sector generally do not have liaisons.

Another possible perceived disadvantage is providing foodservice to the same people every day. This is different from most of the other areas of hospitality, where the guests are more transient. It certainly is a challenge to get the same customers to come back to the same foodservice facility every day. Meeting these challenges promotes creativity, which makes these jobs so unique in the foodservice industry.

Career Paths and Opportunities

The growth rates in many noncommercial foodservice segments offer many entry-level opportunities for college graduates. The typical path starts with entry-level management, usually assigned to a "training" account. Most companies have a training period, which lasts two to three months. The next level is typically assistant manager, possibly referred to as production manager, assistant catering manager, or service manager. These titles may vary with the size and complexity of the client account.

An assistant manager should expect to be considered for promotion to foodservice director in approximately four to five years, after the beginning of his/her career. In approximately five to six more years, a foodservice director could expect to be selected for the next position, which is district manager. If one does not choose day-to-day operations as the district manager, there are other positions in marketing/sales, human resources, and accounting/finance, which may also be appealing or challenging. One's experience with the company thus far is often at that important juncture when some harder decisions must be made to determine which direction one's career should take.

Contract foodservice management companies have been referred to as the "best kept secret" in the hospitality industry. Contractors are active in all segments of the noncommercial and institutional foodservice industry. If you have read the preceding pages, it is no longer a secret. There is a vast array of career options within contract management. College graduates can pursue a successful career in this challenging industry.

Summary

Contract management between the operator and the owner is a mutually binding legal relationship. The owner usually does not have the desire to manage the hospitality operation and must therefore buy the service from a management company. With increasing competition among a wide range of management companies, management companies have been pressured to achieve higher performance standards, shorter contracts, and lower base fees. Contract foodservice management companies are active in all segments of the noncommercial and institutional foodservice industry. There is a vast array of career options within contract management.

Endnotes

1. Eyster, J. (1988). *The negotiation and administration of hotel and restaurant management contracts*. School of Hotel Administration, Cornell University, Ithaca, NY
2. *Hotels*. (2000, July). *34*(7), 4
3. Ibid
4. Johnson, K. (1999, April). Hotel management contract terms: Still in flux. *The Cornell Hotel and Restaurant Administration Quarterly, 40*(2), 34–39
5. Sangree, D. J., & Hathaway, P. P. (1996, October). Trends in hotel management contracts. *Cornell Hotel and Restaurant Administration Quarterly, 37*(5), 29

6. Johnson, K. (1999, April). Hotel management contract terms: Still in flux. *The Cornell Hotel and Restaurant Administration Quarterly, 40*(2), 34–39

7. Ibid

8. *Hotels.* (1995, September). *Tips on selecting a management company. 29*(9), 40

9. Johnson, K. (1999, April). Hotel management contract terms: Still in flux. *The Cornell Hotel and Restaurant Administration Quarterly, 40*(2), 34–39

10. *Hotels.* (2005, October). *Management renaissance: Expansion of big-name brands and a new crop of contenders is heating up the management contract race world wide. 39*(10A), 36–42

Resources

Lodging Hospitality. (2003, August). *Lodging's 400 Top Performers—TOP MANAGEMENT COMPANIES. 59*(11): 44

Food Management. (2005, September). *FM's Top 50 Management Companies,* p. 42

McCool, A. C., Smith, F. A., and Tucker, D. L. (1994). *Dimensions of Noncommercial Foodservice Management.* New York: Van Nostrand Reinhold

Warner, M. (1994). *Noncommercial Institutional and Contract Foodservice Management.* New York: John Wiley & Sons

☞ *Key Words and Concepts*

Base fee

Client of the contractor

Contract management

Contractor

Diversity in work environments

Host facilities

Incentive fee

Loan and equity contributors

Noncommercial foodservices

Performance clause

Relocation

Self-ops

📖 *Contributor Information*

Dr. Janet Sim, Professor and Chair

Department of Hospitality Management

College of Business, San Francisco State University

1600 Holloway Avenue

San Francisco, CA 94132

Tel. (415)338-2673; Fax (415)338-0997

jsim@sfsu.edu

Ed.D. University of San Francisco

M.S. Iowa State University

B.S. University of Colorado

Dr. Yumi Satow, Assistant Professor

Department of Consumer & Family Studies and Dietetics

College of Health & Human Services

San Francisco State University

San Francisco, CA 94132

yes@sfsu.edu

Rob Heiman

Hospitality Foodservice Management

100 Nixson Hall

Kent State University

Kent, OH 44242

330-672-2075

FAX: 330-672-2194

rheiman@kent.edu

10 ▋ Review Questions

1. How do you define contract management?

2. What are the three components of a basic contract management concept?

3. What are the recent trends of hotel management companies?

4. What are the two types of hotel management companies?

5. What have been the common lengths and trends of contract terms?

6. Define "base fee" and "incentive fee." What are the current trends of fee structures?

7. Explain the meaning and significance of management companies as loan and equity contributors.

8. Explain why it is important for owners to have input in operational decisions.

9. How do you define "contractor," "host," "client," "self-op," and "noncommercial sector"?

10. How do foodservice contract management companies offer diversity in work environments?

11. What are the career advantages to choosing a career in the noncommercial segments of the foodservice industry? What are the career paths and opportunities?

12. What are the job challenges to choose a career with contract management company?

Hospitality and Tourism Operations

Part 3

11

Operations Management

12

Applied Marketing and Sales of Hospitality and Tourism Services

13

Law and Ethics

14

Revenue and Cost Control

15

Human Resource Management

16

Physical Plant Management

Operations Management

Richard J. Mills, Jr.
Robert Morris University

Learning Objectives

✓ To identify the importance of operations management
✓ To define the role of the manager in the hospitality and tourism industry
✓ To discuss the consequence of the recent materialization of management as a field of work and study
✓ To show how management is a set of balanced, problem-solving techniques rather than a group of inborn abilities and traits
✓ To view planning as an organizational process that goes on at all levels
✓ To define and use key planning concepts used in this chapter
✓ To outline the general procedure of staff planning and identify and describe the major tools that are used in that process

Chapter Outline

What Is Operations Management?
The Hospitality Manager's Role
Basic Qualifications for a Successful Operations Manager
Levels of Management
Management Functions
Leadership and Directing in Hospitality and Tourism Management
Future Concerns for Hospitality and Tourism Management

*B*ecause you are in a school of higher learning and pursuing a degree, we assume that you want to be a manager. When asked why he wanted to be a manager, a student replied, "Because you can shut the door, put your feet up on the desk, go to sleep, and get paid lots of money. You have to work if you're not a manager because everyone is always watching you." Is this your definition? How would you define a manager?

What Is Operations Management?

Students considering a career in hospitality and tourism management must, first and foremost, identify the meaning of management and, second, identify the meaning of operations. It is equally important for them to understand that there are different levels and areas of responsibility in the work of operations managers and supervisors. To begin, the word *management* has two meanings. First, management is used as a collective noun to identify those in charge of directing business affairs. Management is a group of persons or individuals who receive their authority and responsibility from ownership or a directive from organizations to oversee the entire operation. Therefore, one definition of manager is a position within the company. Managers use this authority, along with the resources that are supplied from the business, to produce a product or service that creates an operation. Or in other words, an operation is the process of creating the service and products. Second, management is a service. From the sale of products and services, the operation itself becomes an additional product that engages management compensations, employee wages, and dividends paid to owners. Management in this context is the behaviors and interactions with other members of the business that productively unites everyone together for a common purpose. Operations management then becomes an appointed position within the company who oversees the process to create the best product/service.

One distinguishes management operations into categories of managing itself, consulting, or just doing routine operative tasks. Managing the operations requires diplomacy and knowledge about human motivations to maximize an individual's potential contribution. One of the hardest tasks of managers is to create an environment where people can get on doing their jobs with the resources they need. This requires a consulting task where you arbitrate or offer alternatives to problems. It also means that you need to understand each aspect of the operations so that you can ask relevant questions and offer pertinent suggestions. Finally there are the everyday tasks like meetings, communications, and analyzing accounting information. Therefore, as a student, the first task at hand is to define what management *does*, and second, how these managerial tasks are learned, applied, and implemented. This defines the different operations that encompass the hospitality and tourism industry today. To be successful in the hospitality and tourism industry, it is imperative that students have a basic understanding of what management actually *performs* and why particular managerial styles, leadership skills, and personal qualities enhance the direction and overall outcome of any operation.

The Hospitality Manager's Role

There have been many definitions applied to the term *management*, but the one that seems to get directly to the point is: *Management is the process of getting tasks accomplished through people.* A manager is a person who is responsible for the work of others, deciding the tasks people should perform, and ultimately how they can accomplish these goals to the best of their abilities. It is strongly suggested that managers accomplish their goals by acquiring skills and knowledge and passing these qualities on to employees by acting as a coach or facilitator.

Identifying *whom management is* may be easier than defining *what management does*. The products of management are not easily recognizable. The products are not readily visible, such as a hamburger or an ironed tablecloth, but management is responsible for both. The average employee may not see what management *does*, but management does produce. It is the corporate culture of the business, that is, the way people feel when they work there. Do employees enjoy going to work? Do they feel that management respects them? Do they get praise for their accomplishments as well as coaching for improvement? Do they trust their managers? Studies have shown that satisfied employees have a direct impact on the bottom line. The production success of management is evident in a successful business and, often, in the failure of another, even though both have equal resources. It is well recognized that the value of a business is based on its management talent as well as its physical assets.

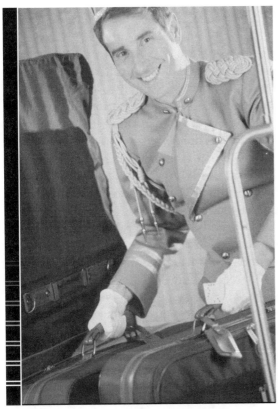

Studies have shown that satisfied employees have a direct effect on the bottom line.

Supervision, in a service business, is more complex than that in a factory, and for this reason, hospitality supervisors face a unique challenge. Manufactured products and labor drive the hospitality manager. Often, the workers are fatigued, tired of doing the same thing every day, and dull working under constant conditions. Service employees work under different conditions. The "product" of their work is a satisfied guest. Although many circumstances are controlled through careful planning and training, there are always unforeseen situations. As a result a good employee is not one who reacts to problems, but one who seeks out potential issues and solves them before they become problems. The work situation changes from guest to guest and changes with each individual guest. This keeps the supervisor constantly alert and under pressure. However, with empowerment and teamwork, a good supervisor allows the employees to do their jobs and assists where necessary.

Managing Change

Management is a very modern institution, and ultimately, it must view the problems of work in an ex-

panding and increasingly wealthy society. This new way of viewing problems has become one of the strongest forces in the last 100 years of the development of civilization. Because of rapid development in this period, our view of management problems has changed dramatically. Management continues to change or adapt itself to the dynamic society in which it operates, and those who aspire to a career in management must be prepared to adjust to these changes.

Management styles change with the fluctuations in society. It used to be a case where management told people what to do and how to do it. If they did not do the job, there were always plenty of people who could step in on a moment's notice. A person went to "work" and had a "job." There is a different set of rules for managing today's workers. Today's managers do not have the same set of goals that were evident in colonial America or the sweatshops in the Industrial Revolution. These rules would be intolerable for today's managers housed in computer-age, air-conditioned, sanitary workplaces. Today, the goal is for a person to have a "career"—a place to earn money doing something they like to do.

Basic Qualifications for a Successful Operations Manager

Technical Skills

Technical skills involve having the knowledge of, and the ability to, perform a particular job or task. One requirement of a competent operations manager is that he/she thoroughly understands the specific, technical aspects of the operation of his/her unit or department. Operations managers, and often middle managers, are directly involved with the operation of a department and must possess the technical skills and specific know-how of the particular systems they supervise. Operations managers train and direct employees on a daily basis and require a high level of technical skill and knowledge. These skills include:

- Developing standard operating procedures
- Using participative management principles
- Effective training
- Safety assurance
- Stimulating personnel to use efficient methods

- Motivating men and women to do a better job and be proud of their products and services.

For example, it would be difficult for an executive chef to supervise workers in a kitchen without knowledge of culinary arts and kitchen procedures. Similarly, a front office manager in a hotel needs to know the operation of the computer system at the front desk and the procedures for registering a guest.

Judgment

Judgment can be described as having "good sense." Individuals who hope to be qualified leaders must possess the ability to make sound and wise decisions. Sound thinking accompanies creative thinking, innovative brilliance, and invention. Change for the sake of change can be detrimental unless change is balanced with common sense.

Being negative is never a substitute for judgment. If an individual approaches an idea with a negative history, the idea, no matter how creative, may be perceived as one that *will not work*. Enthusiasm and a positive attitude are important talents required of a leader whose judgment and decision-making activities will be tested daily.

Conceptual Skills

The organizational manager must have the ability to conceptualize the company or department as a whole and understand how the different parts work together. This involves technical skills utilized for problem solving, decision-making, planning, and organizing. Managers with conceptual skills are able to look at problems from a broad perspective and see them from different points of view. Conceptual skills are important at all levels of management, but they are essential for top managers who make decisions that can dramatically affect the future of the hotel or restaurant company.

We can talk about the difference between "worker" bees and managers. You are probably very familiar with a "worker" bee. This is a person who goes to the cafeteria every day and complains about how *they* didn't do or *they* had so many problems that they should just blow up the company and start over again. This person comes to management constantly complaining and talking about all the problems. A potential manager identifies the problems like the worker bee does, but then they look for solutions.

Interpersonal Skills

Interpersonal or human skills involve the ability to understand people and work well with them on an individual basis and also in groups. Interpersonal skills include a manager's ability to lead by example, motivate employees to want to perform to the best of their abilities, and communicate with those around them. Examples of good managers show that these people know their employees' names and use them and help when the shift is shorthanded like bussing tables or picking up debris off the floor, rather than telling someone else to do it. Professionals who understand the skills that underlie successful interpersonal behavior must recognize body language skills. For example, making eye contact with another individual or recognizing facial expressions or hand movements are all useful when interacting with others. In these times, it is important to know other cultures because most hospitality operations have at least two or more ethnicities as employees. So, understand that direct eye contact is important for Americans, but many Asian and Spanish cultures feel this is a sign of disrespect. Observing people's nonverbal reactions can avert potential miscommunication issues. Because all managers must deal directly with people, and in particular guests, interpersonal skills are essential at all levels of management.

Integrity and a Sense of Ethics

An organizational manager must have a set of principles or ethics to enhance interaction with others. Ethics should govern the general behavior of managers and guide them in making business decisions. The quality of one's integrity manifests itself in many ways, but the honesty and sincerity of an effective organizational manager must be unquestionable. This quality applies to *true leaders* and must not be compromised. Operational managers are responsible for the ethical treatment of five different groups of people: customers, employees, suppliers, owners, and the community at large. Basically, ethical behavior means fair and consistent treatment toward members of each of these groups. A personal code of ethics is imperative for a qualified organizational manager to ensure truth, a lack of bias, consistency, and respect when interacting with others.

Levels of Management

It is agreed that all managers carry out the same functions; these functions become less important, relative to the others, as the manager moves up or down the organizational ladder. This shifting emphasis distinguishes the different levels of management. Although the line between the levels is often blurred, management is separated into three levels: *top management, middle management, or supervisory management.*

Top Management

Top management includes only a limited number of senior executives within the organization. In small properties, like an individually owned and operated enterprise, the owner–manager is the sole member of top management. But in large corporations or organizations, members of top management usually have titles such as Chairman of the Board, Chief Executive Officer, Chief Operating Officer, President, or Executive Vice-President. Top managers determine the direction of the company by recognizing and identifying the basic mission and objectives of the company. They develop goals and established plans for the purpose of reaching the company's overall objectives or operational outcomes.

Middle Management

In middle management, the department heads, perhaps 2 to 20, are next highest in responsibility. Several titles frequently used for middle managers are Regional Director, General Manager, Rooms Division Manager, and Food and Beverage Director in the hotel or hospitality industry. Although this group is larger in number than top management, there are still fewer middle managers than supervisory managers.

Supervisory Management

The line supervisor, who is the first manager up the managerial ladder and the last one down, is the most difficult to identify as management. Typical titles of supervisory managers are Front Office Manager, Executive Housekeeper, or Restaurant Manager. Supervisory managers implement the goals and plans of the organization by directing work of the line-level employees, who provide guests with products and services. They are closer to the operative employees than they are to other managers. In many instances, they have earned their promotions because of excellent operative skills. The ambiguity of who they are is reinforced by the lack of management title.

Different managers rely on different skills: the sales manager is expected to be more outgoing; a good server may become a host; a skillful bartender may be promoted to chief or head bartender; and a room attendant may become the floor inspector. Different managerial positions call on different elements of the personal and professional package that each individual brings to the position or job.

Management Functions

Planning

Planning is based on the establishment of goals and objectives. Thus, management must decide how to accomplish these goals. Planning is often referred to as the primary management function, and the result of inadequate planning is chaos. Successful companies train at all management levels to ensure successful goals.

Organizing

Managers must determine what activities are to be done and how employees are grouped to accomplish specific tasks. Reservations, housekeeping, or maintenance are examples of how groups of individuals are organized to perform a specific task. Additionally, at a higher level, many large hotel companies are divided into several divisions, according to the geographic location of their property or the product or service they provide.

Staffing

Staffing is the process used to service guests at a lodging, food, beverage, or tourism establishment. Managers involved with staffing have several responsibilities:

- They determine the number and type of employees needed.
- They recruit and select employees.
- They develop and implement training programs.
- They determine compensation and benefits received by employees.

Controlling

Controlling is the process of comparing the performance of employees in a workforce to the objectives and goals that have been set by the company. The purpose of any control system is to ensure that the company is headed in the right direction and capable of making corrections when necessary. There are three distinct types of control:

1. *Preliminary controls* take place before an event occurs, such as the planning of a major banquet.
2. *Concurrent controls* take place during an actual event, such as a server's responsibility.
3. *Postactional controls* take place after an event has taken place, as when a general manager reviews a monthly "profit and loss" statement for a hotel.

Leadership and Directing in Hospitality and Tourism Management

Leadership Qualities

An organizational manager must instill and influence others for the purpose of channeling their activities toward assisting the hotel or restaurant's goals. Leadership can be viewed as having two separate components or elements: success and effectiveness. A successful leader demonstrates a quality that followers want to emulate; an effective leader instills a desire to follow in the right direction. Leadership may be defined in several ways. Often these qualities consist of the leader, the group, and the situation. Leadership is a *personal* and a *human* experience, as animals and computers cannot lead. Leadership is both an *art* and a *science* and is subjective in nature. There are fundamentals of leadership that can be learned and are based on research and observation. Leadership is *active,* as leaders must do something; leadership is one element of a three-part dynamic; the leader, the group, and the situation are always in *interaction* and tension with one another.

Why People Follow a Leader

People enter an organization and perform their work for various reasons. They follow the leader of the organization for the purpose of being financially and socially successful. The most basic reason that people work is to provide themselves and their dependents with food, shelter, and clothing. This is often identified as a *selfish* reason for working. In contrast, there is a more positive motive for *following the leader.* This is most evident when people seek work for societal goals. Making enough money to achieve both needs and wants supports the aspirations of the worker. Personal satisfaction is therefore necessary for individuals to pursue work.

Through hard work and diligence, one is rewarded with independence, encouragement, praise, and recognition.

Followers must freely accept the efforts of the leader for leadership to occur. Followers must voluntarily align their will with that of the leader. A leader must manifest good qualities without threats of discipline or punishment for followers to function within their own free will. It is only when followers make a true choice to follow the leader that true leadership occurs.

Future Concerns for Hospitality and Tourism Management

Enthusiasm for the Industry

An enthusiasm for the industry is often identified as having the business "in their blood." For the purpose of developing a desire to work in this industry, it may be necessary to have a passion for the business. Leaders are the best "cheerleaders" for their organization and their people. They display enthusiasm or passion and instill it in others. They possess poise, stability, clear vision, and articulate speech. Their enthusiasm is often described as *infectious* and motivates workers that are in their presence.

Successful managers are confident that their abilities are up to the task of their actions and are able to gain the trust and support of workers. A manager must first be enthusiastic, with a passion for the position, and second, the manager should be confident. It is obvious when these qualities are displayed; self-confidence helps the manager adjust to the ever-changing direction of the industry.

Developing Your Own Style

We are impressed and often amazed with the ability of certain people and their leadership style. All are unique, and top managers are uncommonly different; they are extraordinary people who can adjust from one role to another without losing momentum or hesitation in thought or action. The roles of managers may also reflect the styles of the managers. A leader possesses standards and values within the organizational culture. The manager is responsible for what happens in the organization in such areas as personnel choices, marketing, financial, and public affairs decisions. The manager is the chief tactician, strategist, spokesperson, negotiator, observer, and the one who ultimately represents the organization beyond whom decisions do not pass without a final determination.

Summary

There is an interrelated set of functions carried out by managers at all levels of the organization and also with the workers. Management is relatively new and has emerged as a field of study only in the last 100 years. As a separate practice, management grew up to meet the changing needs of society and eventually affect several areas, including the hospitality industry.

Future events will transform the nature and structure of hotel operations, but one fact remains even in an environment of constant and rapid change. The future is in the hands of management; through a collective experience and wisdom, management must find solutions to meet the needs of an ever-changing society and industry. The managers will plan and implement strategies to deal with them successfully and introduce the new, while holding onto the best of the old.

Management is a profession with a body of knowledge gained through practical application of management principles. Excellent management means better individual operations and, therefore, a better and more efficient industry. The destiny of the industry is in the hands of competent, passionate managers with exemplary leadership skills and professionalism. Management must keep pace with the dynamics of the society.

Resources

Internet Sites

Baldridge National Quality Program: http://www.quality.nist.gov/
Center for the Study of Work Teams: http://www.workteams.unt.edu/
Creative Learning: http://www.creativelearningcentre.com/default.asp

Suggested Readings

Brymer, Robert A. *Hospitality and Tourism.* 11th ed. Dubuque, Iowa: Kendall/Hunt Publishing, 1977

Fisher, William P. & Muller, Christopher C. *Four-Dimensional Leadership.* Upper Saddle River, NJ: Pearson Prentice Hall, 2005

Nykiel, Ronald A. *Hospitality Management Strategies.* Upper Saddle River, NJ: Pearson Prentice Hall, 2005

Powers, Thomas F. *Introduction to Management in the Hospitality Industry,* 2nd ed. New York/Chichester/Brisbane/Toronto/Singapore: John Wiley & Sons, 1979

Powers, Tom and Barrows, Clayton W. *Management in the Hospitality Industry,* 8th ed. Hoboken, NJ: John Wiley & Sons, 2006

Vallen, Jerome J., & Abbey, James R. *The Art and Science of Hospitality Management.* East Lansing, MI: The Educational Institute of the American Hotel & Motel Association, 1987

⊶ Key Words and Concepts

Conceptual skills—The ability to see the company or department as a whole and understand how the different parts work together

Control—Comparing the performance of employees in a workforce against the objectives and goals that have been set by the company

Empowering—Where a contemporary leader has created the organizational work environment in which staff members are trained in necessary skills, enabling them to handle most customer service encounters; management must support the decisions made by the staff members

Ethics—A set of principles that managers apply when interacting with people and their organizations; fair and equal treatment, truth, lack of bias, consistency, and respect of others

Interpersonal skills—The ability to understand people and work well with them on an individual basis and in groups

Labor intensive—The business or industry that employs a large number of employees to provide customers with a product or service

Leadership—The influencing of others to channel their activities toward reaching the goals of the business

Management—The process of getting tasks accomplished through people

Organizing—The efforts involved with determining what activities are to be done and how employees are grouped together to accomplish specific tasks

Planning—The establishment of goals and objectives and deciding how to accomplish these goals

Staffing—Supplying the human requirements necessary to service guests

Technical skills—The skills involving knowledge of and the ability to perform a particular job or task

🖳 *Contributor Information*

mills@rmu.edu

Richard J. Mills, Jr., has many years of both professional and academic experience. He is currently a certified sous Chef through the American Culinary Federation and has worked in the industry as a professional cook and chef for twelve years. He is presently teaching in the Hospitality and Tourism department at Robert Morris University, Moon Township, PA. Richard Mills holds two master's degrees, an MLS and an MA, and has taught, researched, and published several journal articles in the field of hospitality and tourism. In addition to journal publications Mr. Mills also coauthored a catering text entitled "Introduction to Catering: Ingredients for Success" published in 2000 by Delmar Publishing. Mr. Mills has also designed and implemented various courses at the undergraduate level, including food production management and quantity food production at several colleges and universities. He is currently pursuing his doctorate degree in the Communications and Rhetorical Studies at Duquesne University in Pittsburgh, PA.

11 Review Questions

1. What is the author's definition of management?

2. What do managers do within operations?

3. What is the difference between management and operations?

4. How has management changed historically?

5. List the basic qualifications for a successful operations manager.

6. Define technical skills as a management function.

7. Define judgment as a management function.

8. Define conceptual skills as a management function.

9. Define interpersonal skills as a management function.

10. What five groups should managers be concerned with when ethics are applied?

11. What are the three traditional levels of management?

12. What are the primary duties of top management?

13. What are the primary duties of middle management?

14. What are the primary duties of supervisory management?

15. What are the four functions of operations management?

16. Define planning as a management function.

17. Define organizing as a management function.

18. Define staffing as a management function.

19. Define controlling as a management function.

20. List some basic leadership qualities that operations managers should be concerned with.

21. List some basic reasons why people follow. What role does leadership play?

22. From the author's perspective why is enthusiasm for the industry important?

23. What does developing your own style mean?

24. What are some future concerns for operations managers?

Heather Goldman
John C. Crotts
College of Charleston,
South Carolina

Applied Marketing and Sales of Hospitality and Tourism Services

Learning Objectives

✓ To develop a marketing framework
✓ To present marketing as an active relationship development process
✓ To link hospitality supply and demand to repeat patronage, account penetration and long-term buyer–supplier relationships
✓ To provide students a realistic view of the knowledge and skills they will need

Chapter Outline

The Marketing Mix
Target Markets
The Sales and Marketing Process
Distribution Channels
Future Trends

*C*onsider for a moment: The association meeting planner who has just finished a successful convention, the restaurant patron who has dined again at his/her favorite bistro, the outbound tour operator who has just put together a line of tour products for a destination. At some point, all three of these customers were no more than a lead or prospect. In each case, the marketing and/or sales department of the convention hotel, restaurant, and the convention and visitors bureau did something right in gaining these persons' attention and winning their business.

In today's competitive environment, it takes more to be successful than to simply advertise that you are open for business. It takes sales to convert product attributes into benefits in the mind of the client. Make no mistake, the hospitality and tourism industry is competitive, and clients have tremendous freedom of choice. To create a level of awareness, interest, desire, and ultimately action (AIDA) in the consumer, it takes marketing professionals to probe and understand the client's needs and provide solutions that are better than the competition. The goal of all organizations is to supply a product that the customer demands. For example, hotels (who have supply) want to sell rooms and other services to guests (who provide demand) at rates that produce a profit. Doing it in such a way that creates satisfied loyal customers is the key to long-term profitability.

This chapter follows a framework that presents marketing as an active relationship development process that links hospitality supply and demand to create repeat patronage, account penetration, and ultimately long-term buyer–supplier relationships. This framework is designed to provide students a realistic view of the knowledge and skills they will need to master to be successful as hospitality marketing professionals. Your first job in hospitality sales will likely have little resemblance to your last, and the framework provides a road map for your future. In today's harried business environment, the marketers should never overlook the important skills and knowledge areas that must be learned to grow and evolve.

To create a successful strategy or plan for the future, we need to be aware of activities in the local market and the industry as a whole that affects a firm's abilities to successfully compete in the marketplace. With this awareness comes knowledge, which begets opportunity. We will address factors one might consider when establishing their strategies for a profitable return, based on a concept known as "environmental scanning."

To attract consumers, a hotel must understand the many different reasons why people come to the property.

The Marketing Mix

Owner/operators of hospitality and tourism enterprises must develop a marketing strategy to influence customers to buy their products and services. Only when customers begin to recognize the value of the product or service and begin buying it does the business hold opportunity for success. Therefore, without information, the consumer cannot act; without a promotional strategy, the marketer cannot sell. However, even a combined product and promotional approach is considered insufficient to succeed in today's competitive environment. Place and price of the offering must also be considered. One must recognize that a successful marketing mix, like a recipe, is a blending of several ingredients to reach and satisfy customers at a profit.

The key to understanding the concept of the marketing mix is that it is a carefully developed reasoning process that is built solely around the customer. By understanding the customers' perspective, a manager can prepare a recipe for success (a mix of inducements to buy) that fits the needs and preferences of the target markets more than the competition. Elements the manager has to work with are commonly referred to as the 4 Ps: product, place, price, and promotion.

1. Design or offer a **product** (good or service) that customers need and want.
2. Offer the product in a **place** (location, channel of distribution) that is both convenient and available to consumers.
3. **Price** the product in terms of its value to the customer and the price of competitors' goods and services.
4. Communicate the offering to potential customers through appropriate and cost-effective **promotion** activities (advertising, direct sales, and other forms of communication channels).

Target Markets

Individual versus Group

Would you prefer individual guests coming to your hotel, those who pay full price but who leave possibly never to return? Or would you be willing to offer a reduced price to a group of individuals? To attract individual consumers, the hotel or restaurant must understand many different reasons for people to come to the property. Some consumers are seeking value only; others convenience; others still seek amenities and an unforgettable experience. Therefore, it is more difficult to ensure guest satisfaction. On the other hand, organizational buyers make larger purchases in advance. For example, corporate travel agents (e.g., Carlson Wagonlit, American Express, among others) may prearrange all travel for a select company (e.g., IBM, Blackbaud, Hershey's, etc.). In doing so, the agents are able to negotiate discounted prices, specific room types, and packaged activities because they have a large volume of business they are bringing to the hospitality establishment. Organizational buying is usually done by several people in the decision-making process.

Among all hotel firms, a ratio exists of how much individual (transient) business the company receives as compared to group business. The elasticity of demand (whether an increase in price results in a decrease in demand) is significant to monitor. Traditionally, individual business travelers are an inelastic clientele—meaning that they will travel regardless of price—as compared to a vacationing family, who may cancel its annual trip due to increased costs (e.g.,

higher gas prices) or a weakening economy. Regardless, hotels wisely opt to diversify their client base to react to curves in demand in the market.

Transient Business

Because potential guests are scattered within many different geographic areas, advertising and public relations are important. Advertising creates and controls one message and simultaneously conveys it to a large group of people. This may include print media like magazines or newspapers, television, radio, or billboards. Public relations is similar except that the advertiser does not have control over the message. To remind potential guests about the property, sales promotions create items like T-shirts or key chains with the logo and name engraved on them to keep the name visible in the short term. Quite often all these are created together for a broader reach.

In recent years, online marketing has begun to emerge as a key component in the total communications package. However, although technology continues to infiltrate and indeed augment within our industry, certain segments still vastly benefit from tangible, traditional marketing pieces. Transient guests may appreciate the opportunity to pick up a brochure or CD about the venue at their local visitors' center when they enter a new city. These guests may also wish to receive information in the mail prior to their visit. CDs are easy to update after completing renovations, changing menu options, adding recent photography and are relatively cost effective.

Where we are perhaps witnessing the swiftest change is the realm of e-marketing (electronic marketing). Currently, we are living in the "opt-in" world, whereby for a marketer to contact you, you must check the box on the screen, answering that you would indeed like to take part. One of the challenges with e-marketing is that many individuals opt in initially, but their spam filters are set too high, and the marketing e-mail does not come through. The other common challenge is that with the overabundance of e-mail marketing in today's world, it is paramount for an organization to distinguish itself among the masses. However, e-mail remains expedient, relatively inexpensive, and measurably effective as a marketing tool.

A hospitality organization, for example a cruise line, must first choose where it wants to market electronically: their corporate Web site (i.e., Norwegian, Royal Caribbean, Crystal), travel agencies (i.e.,

American Express, Carlson Wagonlit), and/or third-party online booking agents (i.e., Expedia, Orbitz, Priceline). Additionally, the cruise line may choose to insert their advertisements in online newspapers and magazines (e.g., *NY Times, Travel and Leisure*) for maximum exposure. Certain ratios can be very effective tools in monitoring the success of online distribution channels as well as the competitive set. The look-to-book ratio (or the number of requests to a booking engine per reservation made) becomes essential when monitoring the effectiveness of online contributions.

Another tool for marketing to individual travelers (and groups as well) is that of public relations. In addition to positive features about the property appearing in newspapers, magazines, Web sites, TV, and radio, public relations also includes industry outreach. Sponsorships, promotions, community involvement, and special events all help increase a property's visibility. In 2003, Holiday Inn ingeniously launched a major campaign allowing guests to bring in their previously stolen towels from HI hotels around the world, with a tale of what they were used for. The tales were included in a coffee table book, with profits going to the nonprofit "Give Kids the World." A positive, philanthropic spin on petty theft! Whether a grand opening, a special holiday promotional package, completion of renovations, or a special acclaim for the property, it is imperative to share the news with your feeder markets.

Targeting key groups of industry journalists is also a worthwhile venture. A new General Manager or Executive Chef for the hotel? A ghost story about one of the rooms around Halloween? Are you the only hotel with a kosher kitchen in your area? Ideally, a master list of noted publication editors should be created. To gain further media exposure, hospitality organizations may opt to allow employees one day off to donate their time to a local charity, involve youth in a concert or choir on property, provide room night packages or meals for silent community auctions, or invite hospitality students from local schools to take a "behind-the-scenes" tour of your hotel. Finally, during low season, why not invite media to stay as guests at cost? You may earn a complimentary article about your property and at the very least, you put a few more "heads in beds."

Group Sales

Fundamental to many hospitality organizations are Group Sales Departments. This department's sole responsibility is to solicit and book business from groups of (typically) 10 or more people. For example, some groups are very price sensitive. The SMERF market (social, military, educational, religious, fraternal) may be a major feeder, depending on the location and type of the hospitality organization. Modifications in recent years have substituted *medical* for *military* and added an *E* on the end (SMERFE) for Environmental. Traditionally, SMERFE clients may be

Group sales are fundamental to many hospitality organizations.

unwilling to pay higher room rates, but they can be good for business because they meet frequently, book both smaller and larger functions, and boast a vast network of referrals within the SMERFE market itself. SMERFE and association attendees may also bring their families with them for planned destination meetings, thereby spending more money in ancillary outlets (gift shops, restaurants, game rooms, etc.). The government segment works within established per diems. Government travelers have little rate flexibility, but may visit during low season and often utilize a large number of rooms. The tour and travel segment is also generally considered price-sensitive but yields a large volume and steady business throughout the year.

Capturing profitable group business and cultivating an ongoing relationship is no small undertaking. One of the challenges of booking business is to maintain a sense of rate integrity. Rate integrity refers to the knowledge that your price is competitive with similar hotels and that guests perceive value. Remember, once rates are randomly lowered, it is next to impossible to raise them again and retain integrity in the market. Some clients will be purely rate focused However, if rate integrity is maintained, the salesperson can have the negotiating edge. If the client persists in being offered a rate reduction, there are several alternatives:

1) Shift the group's dates to a slower month.
2) Move to slower nights of the week.
3) Package more amenities, activities, food, and beverage so that the ancillary revenues will offset the discounted room rate.
4) Offer a multiple booking package. The ultimate goal is to increase sustainable market share in low demand periods and increase revenues (rooms and ancillary) and loyalty in high demand periods.

The Sales and Marketing Process

Two distinct types of marketing exist—direct and indirect. Direct sales implies that the sales force will have direct contact through personal interactions with prospective clients. This would also include direct marketing initiatives through various types of technology, including the Internet. Often a S.W.O.T. analysis (Strengths, Weaknesses—based on their internal organizational and Opportunities, Threats—based on their external environment) is a useful tool when conducting research.

On the other hand, an indirect marketing team focuses their efforts on third-party intermediaries who will be the contact for the end users. Examples of these wholesalers may include tour operators, independent meeting planners, or destination management companies (DMCs). The benefit to having strong relationships with DMCs, from a meeting planner's perspective, is that the DMC will have lists of local reputable suppliers. Therefore, marketing hotel sales teams often have strategic relationships with their local DMCs.

Requests for Proposals (RFPs)

Another facet to the sales process is the Request for Proposals, or RFP for short. For example, imagine a planner has all the specifics about a meeting—name, date, alternate date, number of rooms, meals required, meeting space required, special events, budget, etc.—and she is considering three locations and only high-end resorts. So she writes an RFP and sends it via e-mail (or possibly fax) to all the four-star hotels in St. John, Virgin Islands; Key Largo, FL; and Honolulu, HI. Those hotels in turn check the availability for sleeping rooms, meeting space, and so on and compile a package rate (encompassing all the requested experiences for the stay) and send it back. The sales contact should always follow up to ensure the client received the information and to see if there are questions. Additionally, the manager should request a history of the group pickup from previous meetings elsewhere. The group's history is a valuable tool to measure that the number of blocked rooms on the contract was nearly accurate to the number of rooms actually picked up by the client. Typically a 5 to 10 percent attrition rate is acceptable, depending on the property, but more will significantly and adversely affect the hotel's forecasted budget. At this time, the marketing representative may also offer to host the meeting planner for a site visit to the property, where he/she can experience firsthand the facilities, services, and ambiance.

Organizing a Marketing Team

Promotions need to be measurable. For every new print ad distributed, the marketing team should be able to track the resulting revenue derived. Reservationists ask each guest on call-in what prompted them to think of that hotel. Alternately, if booked online, the advertisement may have a tracking number, which individuals input before making a reservation. The direct sales force is responsible for making their weekly, monthly, quarterly, and annual quotas. Traditionally, these are determined by the budget, forecast, historical reports, sales manager, director of sales, and general manager's inputs. Together, they determine what defines a SMART goal (Specific, Measurable, Attainable, Realistic, and Timely). Sales teams can be divided by market segment, geographic regions, industries (i.e., pharmaceuticals, insurance, automotive, incentive houses, consulting firms) or size of group.

Maximizing Technology

Technology has driven many positive changes in both direct and indirect marketing initiatives. One tool readily available to sales managers is a sales management software system, such as Breeze, Delphi, or OPERA. These are tremendous tools that contain all the meeting space parameters, availability for conference rooms as well as sleeping rooms, clients' contact information, and even personal information (spouse's birthday, last visit to the hotel, etc.), trace dates for recommended next date of contact, and what should be discussed (i.e., "Contact David about coming out to the hotel for lunch so you can show him the renovated meeting space and talk about booking next year's meeting with us"). Smaller, independent properties may still function with paper function books and notecards to trace individuals for future contacts, as well as paper files, but even the few of these who remain tend to be moving toward paperless systems.

Distribution Channels

Distribution channels consist of manners through which travel providers advertise, sell, or confirm purchase of their products to clientele. For example, it would be logistically challenging and not cost effective for a car rental agency to have physical sales offices in every city in the United States. Instead, they have central reservation systems (CRSs) whereby clients can call a toll-free number to request more information. The local agency will then pay a commission to the national office and will provide transportation for the paying guest.

The hotel industry has followed the lead of the airlines on many fronts. The airlines began to eliminate the use of travel agents directly to cut distribu-

tion costs and began offering online direct marketing and booking capacities to purchasers. Today, many airlines and hotels offer the "lowest price guaranteed" so that individuals will be sure to visit the host Web site vs. booking through an intermediary (examples are Expedia, Orbitz, Priceline). So, marketers know that reservations are booked through call centers, Web sites, online travel agencies, and traditional travel agents, with direct Web sites being the largest provider since 2004. E-commerce (the selling of goods and services via the Internet) is thriving, though security is still a concern for many when required to release their confidential credit card information. Paperless ticketing is still being perfected, and online travel searchers must continually wade through amateurish, uninformative, or outdated information as well as a maze of hyperlinks and constant pop-up ads. Ultimately, the number of travel distribution channels is vast, and there are many opportunities for marketers.

Future Trends

With the continued globalization of our customers, we as marketers must continually adapt our targeting approaches to the current trends. As such, we must take into consideration gender, race, age, educational background and economic status of our clients. Now, additionally, we must consider their sexual orientation, physical abilities, social status, and perhaps even religious or spiritual positioning. For example, we may not wish to target college fraternity groups to host their holiday formal parties on the same dates we are expecting to have groups of religious conservatives in house practicing prayer for many hours of the day. Pharmaceutical companies even often specify in their contract requests that they are unable to be "in house" at the same time as a competitor. A wise policy for all hoteliers to follow—consulting with prospective clients—prior to booking them simultaneously may avoid conflicts of interest. With DINKs (Double Income No Kids), OPALs (Older People with Active Lifestyles), and SITCOMs (Single Income Two Children One Mortgage), we must grow more savvy and sensitive as to who is our target market and who we wish it to be. The steadily growing number of Hispanics in management positions in the workforce will mean new adaptations and customizations to their specific needs (i.e., travel ads for vacation destinations in Spanish is one example). After all, "We are all equal does not mean we are all the same" (Carmen Baker, VP Diversity, Carlson Hotels Worldwide).

As we have witnessed in the last decade, it will become even more imperative for companies to create strategic alliances with one another. High-end (luxury) properties partner with Baccarat for their crystal in their restaurants, Rolls-Royce for their transportation, Tiffany for their VIP gifts, and Armani for their toiletries in the bathrooms. We will continue to see such liaising but soon with larger parties. Airlines and hospitality, car rental agencies, travel distributors, real estate developers (such as Cendant, who has now broken into these four divisions) will become industry behemoths, bundling packages for travelers at every turn. For independent operators, they will continue to align themselves with umbrella companies (e.g., Preferred Hotels and Resorts, Leading Hotels of the World, Small Luxury Hotels of the World, Relais & Chateaux, among others). Although they may not all share a central reservation or even a referral system, they do subscribe to established standards for membership and court clientele with similar interests and lifestyles. Though outward alliances will be numerous in the years to come, diversification within individual companies and their product offerings will morph as well. Hotel companies will continue to launch new brands within their portfolios in attempts to offer something for everyone. Starwood Hotels and Resorts is an example of this (Figure 12.1).

By first accurately identifying a client base, they have then successfully launched and adapted new products (first W Hotels and now Aloft) customized to their target market, meeting with resounding success.

Summary

Both challenging and rewarding, a career in hospitality sales and marketing continues to evolve. As with all successful managers, fulfillment and success are often derived through lifelong learning and exposures to new ideas. Ultimately, the goal is to produce the highest yield on investment for owners, and simultaneously, exceed customers' expectations. Research supports that buyers prefer to work with those sales and marketing individuals who are creative, genuine, knowledgeable, and perceptive in their professional liaising.

Figure 12.1 ||| **Starwood Hotels and Resorts Brand Tiering**

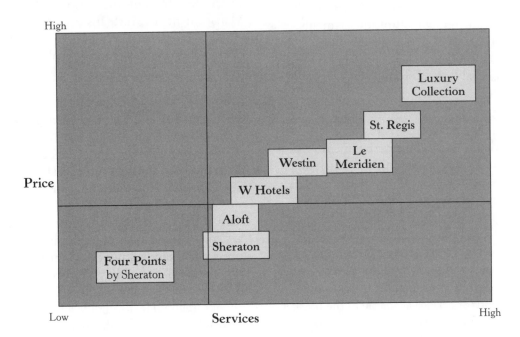

⚙ Key Words and Concepts

AIDA—Awareness, Interest, Desire, Action—the catalysts on behalf of customers to pay and experience once (or the motivation to repeat visit) a hospitality product or service.

CRM—Customer Relationship Management—the process by which companies track detailed requests and personal information about their clientele to customize the sales process and enhance the guest's experience.

Distribution channels—Manners through which travel providers advertise, sell, or confirm purchase of their products to clientele.

DMC—Destination management company—An organization that collectively assists with all travel planning, including accommodations, transportation, events and excursions, for groups of visitors arriving from outside the local market.

Elasticity of demand—A measurement of whether an increase in price results in a decrease in demand.

Look-to-book ratio—Number of requests to a booking engine per reservation made.

Macro environment—The external, global factors exerting pressure on the hospitality organization, typically categorized by identifying the STEEP criteria.

Micro environment—The immediate, internal surroundings within a hotel (or other hospitality entity), including multiple departments and their standard operating procedures.

Rate integrity—Maintaining confidence in rate tiers, financial strategies, and value of product to price.

RFP—Request For Proposal—distributed by planners, this tool solicits availability of specific dates, rates, and entertainment options at various hotels within a specified geographic market.

SMERFE market segmentation—Social, Military (or Medical), Educational, Religious, Fraternal and Environmental—standardized industry categories of group clients targeted through sales and marketing initiatives.

Supply and demand—Supply is the amount of product and/or service available in the market (e.g., hotel rooms, restaurant seats, cruise berths), whereas demand is the amount of desire from consumers to partake of that product and/or service.

S.W.O.T. analysis—Strengths, Weaknesses, Opportunities, Threats—a traditional company's assessment of the status of their product and services, both internally (via strengths and weaknesses) and externally (via opportunities and threats) as they relate to the competition.

The 4 Ps of the marketing mix—Product, Price, Place, Promotion—identifying the good/service, sales amount, location for distribution and manner of marketing within the outreach process.

⚙ Contributor Information

Heather Goldman is an instructor in the Department of Hospitality and Tourism Management at the College of Charleston specializing in hotel and resort management. Prior to this position, she was in sales and marketing with the Biltmore Estate in Asheville, NC, representing the Biltmore House, Gardens, Winery, and Historic Farm Village as well as the renowned Inn on Biltmore. Prior to joining Biltmore, she was on the opening team as a Director of Sales and Marketing with a new Hilton brand hotel in the greater Chicago area. In the years preceding this, Heather nationally represented Starwood Hotels and Resorts, based out of Miami. Heather earned an MBA specialized in International Hospitality Management at IMHI (Insititut de Management Hotelier International), a joint program through Cornell University's Hotel School and Essec Business School in France.

John C. Crotts, PhD, is a professor and chair of the Hospitality and Tourism Management Program at the College of Charleston. Prior to this position, he lectured in the Advanced Business Programme on tourism subjects at Otago University, Dunedin, New Zealand, and was Director of the Center for Tourism Research and Development at the University of Florida. His research encompasses the areas of economic psychology, tourism marketing strategy, and management of cooperative alliances. Dr. Crotts received his PhD in Leisure Studies and Services from the University of Oregon. He also holds a bachelor's degree in Sociology from Appalachian State University, an MS in Education from Mankato State University, and an EdS in Adult Education from the Appalachian State University.

12 Review Questions

1. What are the 4 Ps in the marketing mix? Explain how each contributes to a successful business model.

2. Who provides supply and who demand in the hospitality industry?

3. What are the five criteria (known as STEEP) in the environmental scanning process? Why is it important to build awareness to these macro factors affecting tourism?

4. How does marketing to the individual transient guest differ from marketing to the group traveler?

5. Name the various market segments affiliated with group sales clients. Do all hotels target the same segments? Elaborate on your response.

6. Give an example of one common complaint a meeting or event planner might have concerning the sales-service delivery process. How might this be overcome?

7. With the growing presence of direct online booking of travel and reservations, how has the role of a DMC changed, and why/why not is it beneficial to maintain strong professional connections with these individuals?

8. Imagine you are the proprietor of a highway economy hotel. Would you allocate a majority of your marketing funds for online distribution? If not, how would you promote your hotel? Explain your answer.

9. What is your understanding of "diversity," and how can it be interwoven into hospitality and tourism?

10. Describe the personal profile and skills necessary for a successful sales and marketing individual.

Christian E. Hardigree
University of Nevada, Las Vegas

S. Denise McCurry
MGM Mirage

Law and Ethics

Learning Objectives

✓ To have a working knowledge of the impact of the legal system on the hospitality industry
✓ To be able to recognize what area of the law would apply to a specific fact scenario

Chapter Outline

Litigation in General
Areas of Law
Employment Law
Business Formats
Ethical Considerations

The legal implications of the hospitality industry are virtually limitless. The law permeates every aspect of a hospitality organization, ranging from the formation of the organization, to the daily operations of food and beverage, to personal injuries on property, to the contracts formed with guests and others. It would be futile to attempt to cover in one chapter every aspect of how the law applies to our industry. As you proceed through your educational experience, you will likely have an opportunity to take a course or two dedicated to hospitality law, which will likely go into much greater depth of the legal and ethical implications of our industry. This chapter serves as a mere introduction to the legal terms and concepts that you will encounter during your academic and work experience. We also pose ethical considerations that accompany many of the legal quandaries that you may face.

Litigation in General

Litigation is a scary process largely because most people do not understand it. Typically we think of "law shows" on television, where the police investigate a crime, catch a suspect, and have a trial all within a 60-minute program. Such shows have taken artistic license to have an interesting and entertaining television program. Unfortunately, those shows only offer a miniscule glimpse into the litigation process, focusing primarily on the criminal realm. These shows are also "fast forwarded" to keep the audience entertained.

In reality, a case can take four to seven years from the date of the injury until the date of trial and even longer if the matter is appealed. Because full-blown litigation can take so long, many cases are resolved by an agreed-upon settlement, the outcomes of which are generally kept confidential. Cases that are settled are virtually impossible to track due to the confidentiality of the terms of settlement, so we are typically limited to jury verdicts to predict future case outcomes.

A large portion of the public perceives hospitality businesses as "cash cows." There is also an ever-growing sentiment that when someone is injured, it must be the landowners' "fault." When these two perceptions are combined, the hospitality industry becomes a target for people to make claims against and/or sue our businesses. Some people have legitimate claims for which they should be remunerated. However, an increasing number of incidents are either exaggerated and/or completely staged in an effort to extort money from the business. For example, in March of 2005, a 39-year-old woman named Anna Ayala planted a human finger into a bowl of Wendy's chili, claiming that she bit into it while consuming her food.[1] She was ultimately sentenced to nine years in prison for her part in the scam, and her husband, Jaime Plascencia, was sentenced to 12 years for obtaining the finger from a coworker following a workplace accident.[2] Despite being cleared of any wrongdoing on its part, Wendy's estimated that it lost approximately $2.5 million in revenue due to the bad publicity that followed the incident.

The Wendy's incident serves as a reminder to the hospitality industry that we are a target of unscrupulous people. As such, issues relating to retention of evidence become paramount. A scam similar to the Wendy's scam was attempted in 2004, when a woman and her son planted a dead mouse in the woman's vegetable soup. In that case, a forensic examination of the mouse revealed that it had died of a skull fracture, did not have any soup in its lungs, and had not been cooked.[3] Had the waitstaff simply thrown the mouse away, the restaurant would not have been able to defend itself and prove the scam. This case illustrates how necessary it is for hospitality businesses to anticipate issues and to retain evidence to determine potential liability.

When a Claim Arises

Once someone incurs an injury, whether in the form of personal injury, breach of contract, or stolen property that person may have a "cause of action" that arises. A "cause of action" is the term used to identify the legal theory under which the injured party believes that someone else should be held responsible for their injuries. Many times an injured person will contact the business to fill out an incident report or claim. Some hospitality facilities will have risk management departments to handle these types of claims, whereas other facilities may simply have a manager who handles such claims. In some instances, the person claiming injury will simply go to a lawyer and then proceed with formal litigation, never contacting your business regarding their claims.

Each cause of action has a minimum time frame during which it must be formally brought as litigation or the cause of action is lost. This is known as a "statute of limitations." The statute of limitations varies for each legal theory, state by state. For example, if someone fell in your coffee shop because an employee spilled oil on the floor and did not clean it up, the cause of action would be negligence. In most states, the statute of limitations for negligence is two years. So the customer would have two years to file their litigation, otherwise they lose the right to proceed. If children are involved, the statute of limitations for the injured child may not begin to accrue until the child reaches the age of majority.

The statute of limitations is important because it tells the property owner or manager that they need to retain documents (i.e., incident reports, security reports), as well as other evidence (i.e., the dead mouse, videotapes of the incident) for at least the statute of limitations for use in the event that litigation is filed. The fact that an incident occurs on the property owner's property is sufficient to give the owner notice of a potential claim. There is no obligation that injured parties attempt to resolve the matter with the facility prior to proceeding to litigation. In some instances, the first time a company knows they are a party to litigation is after they have been served with the formal lawsuit.

Risk Management

Rather than incurring the expense of hiring an on-staff attorney or in-house counsel, many facilities simply create a claims department to handle claims made against the property. Sometimes the people in charge of the claims department have a legal background, perhaps even a law degree, but more frequently, they are individuals who have simply worked in the business for many years in different departments. Many such claims departments, or risk management departments, are simply responsive to situations, as opposed to being proactive. Rather than conducting internal audits to identify problems and resolve them prior to injuries, these types of departments frequently just respond to claims and litigation. Even those companies that do conduct internal audits prior to an incident will undertake a cost/benefit analysis when assessing potential liability of a property. They assess whether the costs associated with fixing a hazard are too costly in comparison to the likelihood or risk of injury and/or lawsuit.

Those facilities that do engage in proactive risk assessment find that they can better quantify, assess, and manage risk, as well as improve the performance of their personnel. Certainly it makes sense to avoid situations that may create liability rather than simply reacting to suits after they have been filed. However, because it is difficult to quantify the savings to a facility, and risk management/claims departments are non-revenue-generating areas of an organization, they tend to be under-funded, under-staffed and sometimes under-appreciated.

Civil versus Criminal Law

Civil litigation is usually initiated when the aggrieved party is seeking monetary damages for some wrongdoing; whereas the outcome of a criminal matter would be an individual charged with a crime and potentially incarcerated and/or placed on probation. The main difference between the two areas of law relates to the definition of the "plaintiff." In civil hospitality cases, the plaintiff is generally an individual who seeks damages as a result of a claim that they have suffered a physical, mental, or monetary injury. In criminal cases, the plaintiff is that state, and they are seeking to limit the freedom of the defendant. Most hospitality cases that a manager will have to deal with relate to civil litigation, largely stemming from the areas of contracts, torts, intellectual property, and employment law.

Let us look at some of the issues that are most commonly litigated in hospitality.

Areas of Law

You will come in contact with various areas of law in the hospitality industry. In fact at times you may feel that the law, both statutory and case law, has invaded every aspect of the hospitality industry. Keep in mind that different states and jurisdictions may have variations on some of these concepts that differ from each other. This serves as a general introduction to the most common concepts you will encounter.

Respondeat Superior

An employer can be held responsible or liable for the acts of its employees as long as those employees are acting within the scope of their employment. Liability attaches when the employee is under the control of the employer, and the act causing the injury is within the scope of employment (i.e., in furtherance of the employer's business or interests). In order to determine whether to hold an employer liable for the acts of its employee, the question that needs to be answered is: Was the employee at the time of the incident, *acting within the scope of their employment*? Another way to look at this is whether the actions that caused the injury arose out of or in the course of employment. Generally an employer will not be held liable for the acts of an employee while traveling to and from work; this is known as the "going and coming rule." An exception exists, however, when an employer sends an employee on a special errand that is undertaken outside the usual working hours. For example, if a bartender is asked to run to the grocery store for bar supplies and has a car accident on the way to the store. In that instance, the employer may be held liable to the injured person because the bartender was acting in furtherance of the employer's business interest.

Traditionally, an employer will not be held liable for the actions of an employee that is in furtherance of that employee's private or individual interest. These independent acts of the employee fall into the legal categories of frolic (major deviations) and detour (minor deviations). Generally the law holds an employer responsible for employees on a detour and only responsible for those employees on a frolic if the employer has reason to know of the frolic. In either instance, the employer may be held liable for the individual actions of their employees.

Additionally, employers are not responsible for the acts of a competent, valid independent contractor. The primary difference between an independent contractor and an employee is the amount of control that the employer has over the daily job duties that each is required to perform. An employer may control the general type of work that an independent contractor undertakes, but does not control the manner and method by which the independent contractor's work is accomplished.

Torts

Torts are a large classification of different types of civil wrongs that result in injury or damages to either people or property. Hotels and restaurants have a responsibility or duty to people on their property to keep the premises in a reasonably safe condition and to protect against physical dangers such as wet floors, construction, or spills. Hotels and restaurants also have a duty to protect their guest from harm or danger caused by other people such as employees, other guests, and even criminals. One of the most common torts is negligence.

Negligence occurs when a duty owed to someone on the property is not upheld, resulting in a breach of the duty that causes injury or damages to an individual. Hotels and restaurants owe a duty of reasonable care to their guests. A hotel or restaurant that has been sued for negligence can raise the defense that the injured party was to some extent responsible for their injury. This is called contributory negligence or comparative negligence. Individuals have a duty to take reasonable precautions to protect

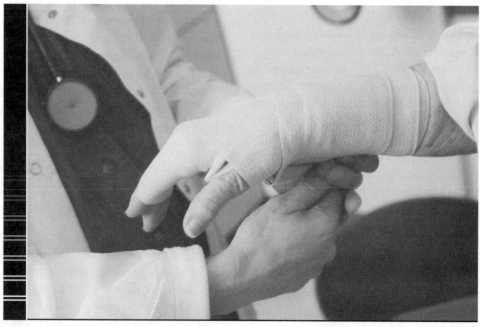

A person may sue a hotel for negligence if they believe they suffered an injury because the hotel did not uphold their duty.

themselves from harm or danger. An individual must act in a manner to protect himself in a similar fashion as someone of like age, intelligence, and experience would do under similar circumstances. For example, assume there is a wet substance that was spilled on the floor of a hotel lobby, and a guest of the hotel, seeing the spill, chooses to walk through it, slips and falls and is injured. The hotel may have breached its duty of reasonable care by not cleaning up the spill quickly enough. However, the hotel guest contributed to his injury by failing to avoid the spill, which he saw and attempted to traverse. In such cases, the guest has also failed to protect himself by taking reasonable precautions, and thus his recovery may be limited.

Privacy Torts

Some of the other torts that may affect you in the hospitality industry are a group of torts called the privacy torts. The privacy torts are **intrusion, appropriation, right of publicity, the unreasonable publication of private facts,** and **false light.** The unreasonable intrusion on the seclusion of another requires the intentional intrusion, physical or otherwise, on the solitude or the seclusion of another. The individual who alleges that their right to privacy had been invaded must establish that they had a reasonable expectation of seclusion or solitude. For example, a dance revue show that is the feature attraction for Hotel A is being filmed for an upcoming television special. The performers in the show do not have a reasonable expectation of privacy on stage. But if one of the cameramen filmed the female dancers changing costumes in the changing room, that would be intrusion.

The use of the name or likeness of an ordinary, uncelebrated person without their permission for advertising or other commercial purpose is appropriation. For example, Todd takes a picture of Betsy and gives the photograph to his friend Bill, who is the owner of Bill's Brew Pub. Bill uses Betsy's picture without her permission or knowledge to advertise for an upcoming ladies' night.

The right of publicity is essentially the same concept as appropriation, except that it protects the use of the name or likeness of a celebrity for commercial purposes.

Defamation

A hotel or restaurant can be held liable not only for causing a physical harm or injury such as broken bones, but can also be held liable for the harm caused by the language of its employees. An individual may be able to sue for defamation when a false statement is made about an individual and that statement is overheard or made to a third person, resulting in damage to the reputation or business interest of the individual. For example, employee A says to guest B, "You're a thief!" If this statement was overheard by the business partner of guest B, and the business partner dissolves their partnership, then guest B can sue employee A (and maybe the employer).

Intellectual Property

There are different types of intellectual property rights that can be obtained by businesses and individuals. These would include patents, copyrights, trademarks, and trade secrets. Intellectual property refers to creations of the mind: inventions, literary and artistic works, and symbols, names, images, and designs used in commerce.

Patent is the grant of a property right to an inventor issued by the U.S. Patent and Trademark Office. A patent enables its holder to exclude others from making, using, or offering for sale the invention.

A trademark is a word, name, symbol, or device that is used in trade with goods to indicate the source of the goods and to distinguish them from the goods of others. Trademark rights may be used to prevent others from using a confusingly similar mark, but it cannot be used to prevent others from making the same goods or from selling the same goods or services under a clearly different mark.

A copyright is a form of protection provided to the authors of "original works of authorship," including literary, dramatic, musical, and artistic works both published and unpublished. A copyright gives the owner the exclusive right to reproduce the work, to prepare derivative works, to distribute copies of the work, to perform the copyrighted work publicly, or to display the work publicly. Keep in mind the copyright protects the form of expression rather than the subject matter of the writing. For example, the description of a hotel in a coffee table book could be copyrighted, but the copyright would only prevent others from copying the description not from writing a description of their own.

An example of a trade secret may be the identity of a customer of a hotel, casino, or restaurant. For example, casino host Joan leaves Casino A and takes employment at Casino B, taking the customer list with her. Casino A can then sue both Joan and Casino B for a violation of their trade secret.

Employment Law

Employment law is a vast area law that can be complex and tedious. This is an area of law that came about primarily to establish and protect the rights of employees. Some of the pivotal laws that have been enacted in this area are the Civil Rights Act, Fair Labor Standards Act, Family Medical Leave Act, Equal Pay Act, The Americans with Disabilities Act, and the National Labor Relations Act.

The 14th Amendment to the U.S. Constitution forms the basis for the Civil Rights Act and Title VII, laying the groundwork for basic equal rights in employment today. The Equal Protection Clause states that all people are entitled to equal protection under the law. Under Title VII it is illegal to discriminate against an individual in reference to any term, condition, or privilege of employment based on their religion, race, color, sex, or national origin. Title VII prohibits both intentional discrimination and neutral job policies that disproportionably exclude minorities.

Fair Labor Standards Act (FLSA)

The FLSA was first enacted by Congress in 1938. FLSA regulates the minimum compensation that an employee should be paid on an hourly basis, the maximum number of hours an employee should be required to work weekly, overtime pay, child labor, and record keeping. FLSA covers both full-time and part-time employees.

Individual states can create laws that are more favorable to the employee than that under federal law. For example, in 2006 the minimum wage under FLSA was $5.15 an hour. However, in California, the state's minimum wage was $6.75. Thus a business in California would have to comply with the state's minimum wage rather than the federal government's prevailing wage.

Family Medical Leave Act (FMLA)

The FMLA was passed by Congress in 1991. The purpose behind FMLA was to balance work and family by allowing employees to take leave. As well, FMLA minimizes the potential for employers to discriminate against employees based on gender. FMLA involves the entitlement to leave, the maintenance of health during leave, job restoration after leave, and it sets requirements for notice and/or certification to get FMLA leave. For an employee to be eligible under FMLA, he or she must have worked for the employer for 12 months, have worked 1,250 hours during the 12 months prior to the start of the FMLA leave, and work for an employer with 50 or more employees.

An employer covered under FMLA must grant an eligible employee up to a total of 12 work weeks of unpaid leave within a 12-month period. An eligible employee may only request leave under FMLA for the birth or adoption of a child, a serious medical condition for themselves or an immediate family member. Leave requested to care for an in-law is *not* covered under FMLA.

Equal Pay Act (EPA)

The EPA requires that men and women be given equal pay for equal work in the same establishment. The EPA does not require that the jobs be identical, but they must be substantially equal. It is the job content, not job titles, that determines whether jobs are substantially equal.

An eligible employee may request up to 12 weeks unpaid leave after the birth of a child, under FMLA.

Employers may not pay unequal wages to men and women who perform jobs that require substantially equal skill, effort, and responsibility and that are performed under similar working conditions within the same establishment. Pay differentials are permitted when they are based on seniority, merit, quantity or quality of production, or a factor other than sex.

Keep in mind that on June 10, 1963, President John F. Kennedy signed the Equal Pay Act (EPA) into law. At the time, full-time working women were paid on average 59 cents to the dollar earned by their male counterparts, according to government data. Since 1963, when the Equal Pay Act was signed, the closing of the wage gap between men and women has been at a rate of less than a half penny a year.

Americans with Disabilities Act

Title I of the Americans with Disabilities Act prohibits private employers, state and local governments, employment agencies, and labor unions from discriminating against qualified individuals with disabilities in job application procedures, hiring, firing, advancement, compensation, job training, and other terms, conditions, and privileges of employment.

The ADA covers employers with 15 or more employees, including state and local governments. Under the ADA an individual with a disability is a person who

1. Has a physical or mental impairment that substantially limits one or more major life activities
2. Has a record of such impairment
3. Is regarded as having such impairment

An individual with a disability must be qualified to perform the essential functions of the job, with or without reasonable accommodation, to be protected by the ADA. The ADA makes it illegal for an employer to discriminate against a qualified applicant or employee because of her disability.

An employer is required to make a reasonable accommodation to qualified applicants or employees with a known disability so long as it would not impose an "undue hardship" on the operation of the employer's business. Reasonable accommodations may include

- Acquiring or modifying equipment or devices
- Job restructuring

- Part-time or modified work schedules
- Reassignment to a vacant position
- Adjusting or modifying examinations, training materials, or policies
- Providing readers and interpreters
- Making the workplace readily accessible to and usable by people with disabilities

Business Formats

There are various types of business formats such as sole proprietorships, partnerships, and the various types of corporations. Each of these business formats has advantages and disadvantages. Prior to creating a business format, you should consult an attorney. However, this will provide you with a brief look at the benefits of each format.

Both sole proprietorships and partnerships have no separate existence from the owner of the business. A sole proprietorship essentially means that a person does business in their own name and there is only one owner, whereas a partnership is two or more people doing business together, sharing in profits and losses. Neither sole proprietorships nor a partnerships limits the liability of the business owner(s) because neither is a separate entity apart from the owner(s). Thus, if a sole proprietorship or a partnership were to be sued, then the owner(s) of the business would be personally liable for any judgment or debt that is incurred by the business.

The lack of protection for the business owner(s) in a sole proprietorship and a partnership is one of the reasons why business owners prefer to form corporations. A corporation is a separate legal entity that has the same rights as an individual person. The primary advantage to forming a corporation is that the officers and stockholders of the corporation can avoid being held individually/personally liable for the action of their business.

Ethical Considerations

In addition to the legal implications of the various issues discussed earlier, a good manager must also balance these considerations with what is ethical. In 2005, the business world was rocked by corporate scandals such as Enron and Tyco. So what importance does a good hospitality executive place on the ethical considerations of their day-to-day tasks? Again, an entire book could be devoted to this arena, and you may have the opportunity to take an ethics course during your academic pursuits. Let us consider a few scenarios:

If you know your floor is uneven and sloping, only 1 of every 100,000 people will misstep or fall, and it will cost 15 percent of the annual profits to fix the floor, should you fix it? A risk management analysis may indicate that the risk is not great in comparison with the cost of fixing it. But what about the ethical considerations involved?

As a purchasing agent, you receive a case of high-end champagne delivered to your home at the holidays from one of the purveyors from whom you regularly submit orders. Because you use their company anyway, the champagne really isn't a "bribe," but could it be considered a "kickback"? Is it ethical to keep it? It may be not illegal, but what perception is created if the purchasing agent keeps it?

Your state law only requires you to pay employees $5.15 an hour for their work. Fifty percent of your employees work in non-tipped positions and thus cannot easily supplement their income with tips. You know that it is difficult for a family to survive on such low hourly pay. You have an obligation to the company to keep your labor costs low. But should you consider paying the non-tipped employees a higher wage? How do you balance your obligations to the stockholders and your obligations to the employees?

Summary

As we have seen, the law permeates every aspect of a hospitality organization. It is difficult in today's world to discern what is "legal" without having an attorney on hand to continuously ask questions, a luxury that most businesses do not have available. Rather than fear the unknown arena of litigation, good managers must arm themselves with some basic knowledge of the law and the legal process. That same manager must also consider the ethical implications of their day-to-day decisions. Through trial and error (sometimes many errors), eventually a good manager will be able to manage in a pro-active and ethical manner to create a safe and supportive hospitality environment.

Endnotes

1. Retrieved from http://www.msnbc.msn.com/id/7594873 on December 22, 2005
2. Retrieved from http://www.cbsnews.com/stories/2006/01/18/national/main1218315.shtml?CMP=OTC-RSSFeed&source=RSS&attr=HOME_1218315 on January 20, 2006
3. Retrieved from http://home.hamptonroads.com/stories/story.cfm?story=71183&ran=107750 on December 22, 2005

Resources

Internet Sites

The U.S. Equal Employment Opportunity Commission: www.eeoc.gov
The U.S. Department of Labor: www.dol.gov

⌐ Key Words and Concepts

Americans with Disabilities Act (ADA)
Appropriation
Cause of action
Copyright
Corporation
Defamation
Defendant
Detour

Equal Pay Act (EPA)
Ethics
Fair Labor Standards Act (FLSA)
False light
Family Medical Leave Act (FMLA)
Frolic
Intrusion
Negligence

Partnership
Patent
Plaintiff
Right of publicity
Risk management
Respondeat superior
Sole proprietorship
Statute of limitations
Torts
Trademark
Trade secret
Unreasonable publication of private facts

▦ Contributor Information

Christian E. Hardigree is an associate professor in the William F. Harrah College of Hotel Administration at the University of Nevada, Las Vegas. She is also an attorney licensed to practice law in both Georgia and Nevada. In addition to her academic career, she maintains a practice as a litigator mainly in cases defending hotels, restaurants, and nightclubs. She can be reached at UNLV, William F. Harrah College of Hotel Administration, 4505 Maryland Parkway, Box 456021, Las Vegas, Nevada 89154. Her e-mail address is christian.hardigree@unlv.edu

S. Denise McCurry is the Vice President of Litigation Risk Management for MGM Mirage. Denise McCurry has also served as an Alternate Judge for the City of Las Vegas Municipal Court. She is licensed to practice law in Nevada. Her e-mail address is denise_mccurry@yahoo.com

13 Review Questions

General Questions

1. Define the following terms based on your reading:

   Plaintiff

   Defendant

   Cause of action

   Statute of limitations

   Respondeat superior

2. What are the benefits of having a formal risk management department? Why do most properties not have a risk management department?

Situational Questions

1. Your hotel puts up a sign outside the ladies bathroom that states "Wet Floor." The hotel does not barricade access to the bathroom. A hotel guest sees the sign, enters the bathroom, and slips and falls. Do you think your hotel should be responsible? Why or why not? What cause of action would the guest claim? What defense would you use?

2. You own a restaurant. One of your bartenders likes to flip the alcohol bottles while he is making drinks. On one occasion, the bottle slips and strikes a patron in the face, cutting her face. Do you think your restaurant should be liable? Why or why not?

3. A card dealer is dealing cards to gamblers at a blackjack table. One of the gamblers becomes irritated and calls the dealer a bad name. The dealer punches the gambler in the face, knocking him unconscious. Should the casino be liable for the dealer's actions? Why or why not? What if the dealer waited until after shift and attacked the gambler in the parking lot? Would that affect your analysis? How?

4. Both a male and a female have applied to work in the laundry area of your hotel. This job entails some heavy lifting, and you are concerned that the female will not be able to lift the same amount as her coworkers. Could you decide not to offer her the job? Why or why not? Could you pay her less than her male coworkers based on the lifting requirements? Why or why not?

5. Your mother has been diagnosed with cancer, and you have requested to take FMLA leave to care for her. Should your employer grant your request to take FMLA leave?

Daniel Bernstein
Seton Hill University

Revenue and Cost Control

Learning Objectives

✓ To learn how revenue is evaluated in a hotel and restaurant
✓ To be able to calculate and use the ratios that are used for success
✓ To learn how to maximize revenue through selling
✓ To learn how to control costs in the hotel and restaurant industry

Chapter Outline

Revenue in the Hotel Industry
Revenue in the Restaurant Industry
Maximizing Revenue through Selling
Cost Control in the Hotel Industry
Cost Control in the Restaurant Industry
Careers in Revenue and Cost Control

*T*he two main ingredients in making a profit are increasing revenue and lowering cost. A company may often appear to be profitable because they have high revenues. However, failure to control costs may actually cause the company to lose money and eventually go out of business. This chapter will introduce different types of revenue in the hotel and restaurant industry and introduce means of utilizing cost control. Because of the unique nature of this industry, different formulas for measuring hotel and restaurant revenue are used.

Revenue in the Hotel Industry

It is important for students to understand that in reality, most of the everyday tasks completed by managers are done for the financial well-being of the firm. Specifically, most hospitality managers increase shareholder value by decreasing expenses and increasing revenues. If the manager is not concerned with the success of the company, he or she will not likely be employed for long.

There are various means of measuring revenue in the hotel industry so people can assess how suc-

Certain seasons present more favorable weather conditions, and will affect occupancy.

cessful they are as managers. Before one measures their success, they must have a working knowledge of expectations. Of course, hotel managers would like to sell out every room, every night, but this is not always possible. Many factors can affect hotel occupancy over which the hotel manager may have very little or no control. These factors are often external (outside) forces such as seasonality and competition. Certain seasons present more favorable weather conditions, which may increase occupancy. For example, Arizona, California, and Florida have high occupancy during the winter and lower occupancy in the summer when weather conditions are less favorable. Another factor that may affect occupancy is competition. New hotels in your market niche may compete for the same customers. These external factors may adversely affect hotel occupancy, and therefore, a manager must carefully plan to overcome these problems.

Tools for Measuring Revenue

To aid in the strategic plan, three tools for measuring revenue are

1. Occupancy percentage
2. Average daily rate
3. Yield management

Occupancy Percentage is a ratio relating the number of rooms sold to the number of rooms available (Figure 14.1). How does a hotel manager know if their hotel is running at an acceptable occupancy percentage? Numerous factors may assist them in determining an acceptable occupancy percentage. First a hotel manager should be aware of national averages of occupancy percentages. There are various resources for obtaining this data, such as the A.H. & L.A. (American Hotel & Lodging Association). Secondly, hotel companies average occupancy percentages that they expect you to meet.

What if you work for an independent hotel, without any specific guidelines about expected occupancy percentages of your hotel? Find out percentages of comparable hotels in your area. Another way of estimating what your occupancy percentage would be is by looking at a daily audit report. When comparing occupancy percentages from past records, it is important to know what to compare. If you want to know how well your hotel will do for December 15th this year, you may assume that you should look at December 15th of last year. But that would not be

Figure 14.1 ||| Occupancy Percentage

Room (Units) for Sale
900 (Rooms available for sale) $\times$ 365 (days per year) = (328,500 Rooms)

Occupancy Percentage
Number of rooms sold / Number of rooms available for sale
674 (number of rooms sold) / 900 (rooms available for sale) = 74.88% (occupancy %)

accurate. December 15th of this year and December 15th of last year were on different days of the week. Hotel occupancy percentage often fluctuates by days of the week. Often business hotels have lower occupancy percentages on weekends. Resort hotels tend to be the opposite, with high occupancy percentage on the weekends and lower occupancy percentage on weekdays. So, if you want to estimate how well your hotel will do for December 15th this year you should compare by the days of the week. If December 15th was on a Thursday this year you would compare it to the third Thursday in December last year. The only time you would compare the same date from year to year would be holidays such as Christmas, which is always on December 25th. In this case, the day of the week is of little significance compared to the actual date.

Another calculation that the hotel manager should look at in reference to occupancy is people in a room (Figure 14.2). Most hotels charge more for double occupancy than for single. The reason is that hotels incur additional costs like the use of another bed, length of time for a housekeeper to clean a room, free continental breakfasts, and happy hours.

However, some hotels charge per room instead, though most hotels price by the number of guests in a hotel room.

The second measurement of hotel revenue we will discuss is **average daily rate**, also known as ADR. The average daily rate is computed by dividing room revenue by the number of rooms occupied (Figure 14.3). This formula is necessary when you sell rooms for more than one rate, which is often the case with most hotels. This is how we measure how well we are maximizing revenue through double occupancy and through the selling of more expensive rooms. If your most expensive rooms are $250 per night and the lowest priced rooms are $100 per night and if average daily rate is barely above $100 per night, you are not maximizing your room revenue. You may be selling mostly your least expensive rooms or not charging for double occupancy. This is lost revenue for the hotel, which will affect your hotel bottom line. A hotel can have high occupancy but a low average daily rate. Both are important in calculating how well your hotel is at selling rooms.

The $110 rate is simply the average price of rooms sold that night. It may very well mean that

Figure 14.2 ||| Double Occupancy Ratio

Number of Guests – Number of Rooms Occupied / Number of rooms occupied
1011 (number of guests) – 674 (number of rooms occupied) / 674 (number of rooms occupied)
337 (number of guests – number of rooms occupied) / 674 = .50

What this means is that 50 percent or half of the rooms occupied, 337 rooms had double occupancy, and 50 percent of the rooms or half of the rooms single occupancy, 337 rooms.

337 rooms $\times$ single occupancy (1) = 337
337 rooms $\times$ double occupancy (2) = 674
674 rooms   1011 guests

Figure 14.3 ||| Calculating Average Daily Rate

$74,140 (room revenue) / 674 (rooms occupied) = $110 (ADR)

Over half of independent restaurants go out of business within the first three years of operation.

not a single room sold for $110 that night. In an extreme circumstance, a 900-room hotel may have their one most expensive room selling for $1,000 that night. If that was the only room they sold that night, the average daily rate would be $1,000. That would be impressive, except that your occupancy percentage would be less than 1%, which would certainly not be impressive. They want to maximize revenue by selling as many rooms as possible at as high a room rate as the market will allow.

The third and final measurement of hotel revenue we will discuss is **yield management**. Occupancy percentage and average daily rate combined are a utilization of yield management attempts to restrict occupancy. You might question why would we want to restrict occupancy. The answer is that we can restrict occupancy by holding out for a higher room rate. For example, due to seasonality, a hotel might change their rates January 1, April 1, July 1, and September 1. Any potential guest who makes a reservation from April 1 through June 30, will be restricted from making a reservation after June 30, unless they are willing to pay the higher rate. Hotels that fail to adjust rates according to changing conditions will likely lose out in maximizing revenue. It is often easy for anyone to estimate that hotel occupancy may seem high, but only the hotel manager will know if yield management principles were realized in attaining optimum revenue.

Revenue in the Restaurant Industry

Revenue concerns may be even more crucial in the restaurant industry than in the hotel industry because the restaurant business failure rate is very high. Over half of independent restaurants go out of business within the first three years of operation. Why do independent restaurants fail at a greater rate than chain restaurants? Independent restaurants cannot purchase in mass volume or afford to spend money on advertising. However, the entry level costs are lower for independent restaurants, which is why more may try to enter the restaurant business by this method.

There are various means of measuring revenue. **Prime cost** is a term restaurants use for food and beverages expenses and payroll. They are referred to as prime costs because these are your two largest expenses in the restaurant industry. If you cannot control your two largest expenses, smaller expenses that you controlled efficiently will not likely matter. Most restaurants fail financially because they could not control their prime costs.

Labor costs, also referred to as payroll cost, consist of salaries and wages and employee benefits. Low labor costs may not be an indicator of efficient management. If by controlling labor costs you are understaffed, customers will complain about poor

Figure 14.4 ‖ Food Cost Percentage

Cost of food sold / Food Sales = Food Cost %
$30,000.00 (cost of food sold) / $100,000.00 (Food Sales) = 30% (Food Cost)

This formula determined that food cost was 30% of food sales. That means that $70,000.00 or 70% was profit out of this $70,000.00.

service and not return. On the other hand, being overstaffed will likely result in having employees standing around doing very little. A good manager should be upset at seeing employees being paid to do nothing.

The best means for evaluating labor needs is to have a formula to determine how much labor you need based on the number of customers. Peak hours for breakfast may be 6:00 am to 9:00 am, for lunch 11:00 am to 2:00 pm and for dinner 5:00 pm to 9:00 pm. A restaurant manager would increase staff service during those hours and reduce employees in between meals. Restaurants often have to simply estimate customer levels during different meals. When estimations are incorrect, a restaurant manager can control labor costs by sending some servers and bus persons home. Most bus persons and servers do not like coming to work just to be sent home. But this is a necessary tool in controlling labor costs in the restaurant industry.

Employee benefits are another concern in controlling labor costs. In the 1970s and 1980s it was unheard of for hourly restaurant workers in the restaurant industry to receive health benefits. In the 1980s, I was a restaurant and hotel manager and did not receive health benefits from either position. Today, most full-time hourly workers receive some type of health benefits. If your restaurant offers health benefits and another doesn't, your restaurant may be able to attract better quality workers. To control costs and avoid paying health benefits, a manager may choose to hire less full-time workers and more part-time workers.

Food cost includes the cost of food sold, given away, stolen, or wasted. Restaurant managers determine what food they need to purchase by buying food based on their recipes, menu, and customer demand. Recipes also ensure that menu items are consistent in taste. Restaurant managers can adjust food costs by being creative about menu items. A leftover broiled chicken can become a chicken salad special tomorrow. Also restaurant managers can determine the popularity of menu items from POS (point of

sale) equipment, which determines the percentage of sales of each particular menu item. However, food can also be wasted by a failure to follow recipes or improper cooking of food. Another concern is employees who remove food from the restaurant. Restaurants that secure food well and have enough managers can lessen food theft. Another factor is employees who serve food to customers and purposely do not charge for the food. Food giveaways may be accidental from servers who undercharge or forget to collect payment from customers.

Restaurant managers can measure how effective they are by measuring their food cost percentage (Figure 14.4). Most franchise restaurants will have established desired food cost percentages from the corporate office. Previously discussed concerns, such as food given away, stolen, or wasted food, will make it more difficult to attain desired food cost percentage.

Without the necessary labor, it will be difficult to produce revenue for the restaurant. If you do not manage food purchasing, food waste, food giveaways, and food theft, this will adversely affect the amount of revenue you will bring into your restaurant. Controlling food cost will increase your revenue, which will increase your level of success as a restaurant manager.

Maximizing Revenue through Selling

Most hotels and restaurants in this competitive environment must determine methods for maximizing revenue and gaining a competitive edge. Among the methods utilized by hotel and restaurant managers are discounting, up-selling, and the top-down approach.

Discounting

Discounting is a method of reducing an item from the regular price. A student might question, how does one charge less and make more? Hotel managers must concern themselves with the perishability factor. A hotel room that has a rack rate of $100 nets zero dollars in revenue if it doesn't sell that night. That is a loss of $100 in revenue potential for that room. If that hotel room with a rack rate of $100 is discounted to $80, and it sells at $80, that is $80 in additional revenue for the hotel. It is better to get $80 for a hotel room than zero dollars. Each hotel room has a perishability factor of 24 hours or one day. If you do not sell room 100 on December 30, you can never sell that same product again. Yes you can sell the same room the next day, but you can never sell room 100 on December 30, after that date. It should be noted that hotel managers must set a specific amount to which they may discount no further. If a hotel room regularly sells for $100, there is a price that would be so low that they would actually lose money from renting that room. Also, if a hotel attracts a certain clientele, severe discounting may attract a different type of clientele. Regular hotel guests may decide to stay elsewhere in the future.

A restaurant manager must concern themselves with discounting when considering the perishability factor of food. Food has a limited shelf life and must be used when it is fresh or must be discarded. Restaurants must develop methods of discounting menu items to encourage customers to purchase these items. Often customers walk into a restaurant not knowing what to order. Customers like to order a menu item that is deemed special and think they are getting a bargain. Instead of reducing the price of a menu item, they may charge the regular price but give a free dessert with the meal. Therefore the discount is not with the meal, but with a free dessert. Discounting is used more often at lower-priced restaurants and less fine dining restaurants.

Up-Selling

Up-selling is a technique that is used to get the consumer to purchase more expensive items. Quite often, it is simply a reminder question. "Would you like a large order of fries with that hamburger?" or "For only $20 more, you can be upgraded to a pool-side room." Up-selling is not selling more items, it is selling the same amount of items at a higher price per item. More profitable hotel rooms up-sell their most expensive rooms. Restaurants' most profitable menu items are often the most expensive items with largest profit margin. So up-selling is in the best interest of the hotel or the restaurant.

In selling a hotel room, prospective customers come to a hotel or make a reservation by Internet or phone. Your first objective is to sell rooms. Your next objective should be to maximize revenue by selling the features of the more expensive rooms.

Up-selling to a pool-side room will increase ADR and maximize revenue.

More expensive hotel rooms may be a more deluxe room or have a desirable location. This up-selling technique, if used effectively, should help to increase your average daily rate (ADR), which in turn maximizes revenue.

Up-selling can be used for customers who are unsure of what they wish to order. An effective means of up-selling is to recommend one of the more expensive items or purchasing in larger quantities to the customer. Fast-food restaurants have done this in the past by asking customers if they wish to "Super Size" their order.

Top-Down Approach

The **top-down approach** is a method of attempting to sell the most expensive item first and then offering a less expensive item next, and so on. In the restaurant industry, the top-down approach is similar to up-selling and would consist of the restaurant server recommending more expensive items. They can further reinforce these recommendations by informing the customer, "This is my personal favorite" or "This is the chef's specialty." This increased check average and greater tips will likely lead to more satisfied servers. This will likely benefit the restaurant by reducing employee turnover. This in turn will maximize revenue by reducing employee recruitment costs. Discounting, up-selling and the top-down approach can all be effective tools in maximizing revenue in the hospitality industry.

Cost Control in the Hotel Industry

Cost control in the hotel industry is an important component in maximizing profits. Without proper cost control procedures, a hotel may appear to be successful financially in terms of room sales, but miss out on controlling expenses. Two means of controlling expenses are in the area of energy management and labor costs.

Energy Management

Energy management, in a hotel, deals with heat, air-conditioning, water usage, electric usage, and gas usage. Hotels can control heat and air-conditioning by regulating minimum and maximum temperatures in individual guest rooms. Water usage can be regulated by use of low-flow toilets and showerheads, which dispense less water. Also sprinkler systems can be shut off outside when it is raining. Using lower wattage bulbs in guest rooms can control electric usage. Regulating temperatures based on changing weather conditions can control gas usage. If it is 60 degrees on a winter day in a cold climate, the heat can be lowered. Being aware of changing conditions can help to regulate energy costs.

Labor Costs

Labor costs in the hotel industry are different than controlling labor costs in the restaurant industry. Hotels have less peak specific periods during a day, unlike restaurants, which have meal periods. Labor costs are more likely to be controlled by seasonality over long periods of time. If a hotel is operating at 90 percent occupancy during the summer and 50 percent occupancy during the winter, staffing should be adjusted accordingly. In a hotel that has low occupancy during a particular period, they can reduce the number of guest service agents at the front desk. Guest service agents can also handle reservations, reducing reservations staff. Housekeeping can be reduced by fewer full-time housekeepers and more part-time staff.

Cost Control in the Restaurant Industry

Volume Purchasing

Controlling food costs, as discussed earlier, is essential in the success of your restaurant. One means of controlling food costs is through **volume purchasing**. Restaurants can save money per pound or unit by purchasing in bulk. The supplier is willing to reduce the price so that they can keep repeat business. An astute steward should know based on sales projections how much food needs to be purchased. For example, a restaurant sells an average of 380 hamburgers a week, and each hamburger is four ounces (380 hamburgers times 4 ounces equals 1,520 ounces) (1,520 ounces divided by 16 ounces in a pound equal 95 pounds of hamburger meat). So the restaurant steward purchasing 100 pounds of hamburger meat would be a good amount to buy. You should always purchase slightly more than you need. As we talked about before, food is sometimes wasted, given away, or stolen. You do not want to cut it so close for the restaurant that you run out of supplies. Few things look as unprofessional as a restaurant that runs out of food.

Two additional concerns about volume purchasing are the perishability factor and the storage factor. Although a restaurant may save money from volume purchasing, it must concern itself with the perishability factor. Saving money on purchasing volume will be offset if the food spoils and has to be discarded. A volume purchase for dry goods, canned goods, and frozen foods makes more sense because there is little or no concern about perishability of those food items. The second concern is storage because your volume purchasing will be limited by the size of your storage area. Larger restaurants with larger storage areas can be more profitable than smaller restaurants with smaller storage areas. Larger restaurants may sell the same exact item for the same price as a smaller restaurant, but the profit will be greater for the large restaurant due to volume purchasing.

Portion Control

Portion control is a very necessary component of cost control in the restaurant industry. If a restaurant does not use portion control, they will never know exactly how much profit margin they are making on each item. Portion control is not just about profit margins, it is also about uniformity. If you don't use portion controls, individual menu items may taste different each time.

Two means of measuring portion control are As Purchased (AP) and Edible Portion (EP). In the case of meat, such as a sirloin steak, AP would mean what the steaks weighed when purchased. This is before waste of fat and bones are removed. The more the meat is cooked, the more it shrinks. The weight of the meat after waste is removed and it is cooked is known as EP, edible portion. If a recipe calls for 50 pounds of sirloin EP, you would need to know the yield factor before you decide how much to buy (Figure 14.5).

Figure 14.5 ||| Yield Factor

50 lbs / .72 yield percentage = 69.44 (quantity)
Quantity = 69.44 lbs rounded up to 70 lbs.

If we know the sirloin has a yield percentage of 72% or 28% waste, we would know based on this formula to purchase 70 pounds of sirloin steak AP to yield 50 pounds of sirloin steak EP.

These methods of cost control in the restaurant industry—volume purchasing, portion control, (AP) as purchased, (EP) edible portion and yield percentage costing—are essential tools of a restaurant manager concerned with cost control.

Careers in Revenue and Cost Control

A majority of management and supervisory positions in the hotel and restaurant management industry involve revenue and cost control. We will explore the hotel positions first (Table 14.1), then the restaurant industry (Table 14.2).

Table 14.1 ||| Key Hotel Management Positions in Revenue and Cost Control

Title	Department	Revenue and Cost Control Description	Advancement Opportunities
Executive Housekeeper	Housekeeping	In charge of all renovation and purchasing housekeeping supplies	Supervisor of more than one operation or corporate position
Catering Manager	Food & Beverage	Purchases and supervises the receipt and storage of food and beverage for the hotel	Director of Food and Beverage
Director of Food and Beverage	Food & Beverage	Oversees entire food and beverage operation	General Manager
Director of Sales	Sales	Sells convention facilities for meetings, banquets, and receptions; sells rooms to volume purchasers such as corporate travel directors of large companies	Resident Manager

(continued)

Table 14.1 (continued)

Title	Department	Revenue and Cost Control Description	Advancement Opportunities
Resident Manager	Administration	Takes over for manager in his or her absence. Usually handles duties assigned by the manager	General Manager
General Manager	Administration	Supervises all activities with the hotel. Responsible for the coordination of all departments	Managing Director
Food and Beverage Controller	Accounting	Controls food and costs through menu planning and pricing, purchasing decisions, storage issues	Assistant Controller
Credit Manager	Accounting	Oversees accounts receivables from time of extension of credit until cash is collected	Assistant controller
Assistant Controller	Accounting	Functions as office manager with responsibility for preparation of financial statements	Controller
Controller	Accounting	Acts as financial advisor to management in achieving profit objectives through detailed planning controlling costs and effectively managing hotel assets and liabilities	Area or Regional Controller

Table 14.2 | Key Restaurant Management Positions in Revenue and Cost Control

Title	Department	Description	Advancement Opportunity
Beverage Manager	Beverages	Orders for and stocks bar; maintains inventories of liquor and glassware	Food Production Manager
Cook or Sous Chef	Kitchen	Prepares and portions out all food served	Executive Chef
Executive Chef	Kitchen	Responsible for all quantity and quality food preparation; supervision of sous chefs and cooks and menu recipe development	Assistant Manager
Purchasing Agent	Management	Orders, receives, inspects, and stores all goods shipped by suppliers	Assistant Manager
Assistant Manager	Management	Performs specified supervisory duties under the manager's direction	Foodservice Manager
Foodservice Manager	Management	Responsible for profitability, efficiency, and quality of the entire foodservice operation	Multiunit Regional Manager
Personnel Director	Management	Responsible for hiring and training of foodservice personnel and benefits	Regional Personnel Manager

Summary

In this chapter, we learned about revenue and cost control in the hospitality industry. Hotel and restaurant managers must utilize revenue and cost control to survive. In discussing revenue in the hotel we learned about occupancy percentages, ADR (average daily rate), and yield management. In the restaurant industry, we learned about the prime costs of labor and food costs. In order to maximize revenue, we discussed selling through methods like discounting, up-selling, and top-down. In our discussion on cost control we learned about energy management and labor cost. For the restaurant industry, we also learned about controlling food costs through volume purchasing and portion control. Finally we discussed the many rewarding and challenging opportunities in hospitality and tourism revenue and cost control.

Resources

Internet Sites

A Directory of Knowledge Management Web Sites: www.knowledge-manager.com

American Hotel & Lodging Association (AH&LA): www.ahla.com; click information center

A–Z topics/Business and Financial Management/Running your own business: www.restaurant.org/business/topics_financial.cfm

Council of Hotel, Restaurant & Institutional Educators (CHRIE) (Affiliation of hotel and restaurant educators): www.chrie.org

Financial Information Advertising: www.restaurant&results.org

Financial Management HQ-Financial Management: www.financialmanagementhq.com

Gecko Hospitality (Hospitality Financial): www.geckohospitality.web.aplus.net

Hospitality Careers: www.hcarres.net

Hospitality and Food Service Management: www.cccd.edu/hospitality/resources.htm

Hospitality Financial and Technology Professionals (HFTP): www.hftp.org

Hospitality net-in depth-decision support-Revenue Management: www.hospitalitynet.org

Hotel Resource: Hotel and Hospitality Industry Resource: www.hotelresource.com

Hotel Real Estate: www.lodgingeconometrics.com

Microsystem Inc. —Fidelio—Property Management Point of Sale: www.micros.com

Profitable Hospitality Resources and Solutions for Restaurants and Hotels: www.profitablehospitality.com/links/index.htm

Restaurant Report—top 50 Food and Hospitality Industry Web Sites: www.restaurantreport.com/top100/index.htm

Suggested Readings

A Guide to College Programs in Hospitality and Tourism, 3rd ed. New York: John Wiley & Sons, 1993, p. 13–14

Chatfield, R. and Dalbor, M. *Hospitality Financial Management*, Upper Saddle River, NJ: Prentice Hall, 2005, p. 10

Dittmer, Paul R. *Principles of Food, Beverage, and Labor Cost Controls*, 7th ed. New York: John Wiley & Sons, 2003, p. 9, 12, 549

Vallen, G. K. and Vallen, J. J. *Check-In Check-Out, Managing Hotel Operations*, 7th ed. Upper Saddle River, NJ: Prentice Hall, 2005, p. 609

☛ *Key Words and Concepts*

AP (as purchased)	**Occupancy percentage**
ADR (average daily rate)	**Perishability**
Cost control	**POS (point of sale)**
Discounting	**Portion control**
EP (edible portion)	**Revenue**
Energy management	**Top-down approach**
Food cost	**Units**
Intangibility	**Up-selling**
Labor cost	**Volume purchasing**
Mom & pop	**Yield management**

Contributor Information

Bernstein@setonhill.edu

Daniel Bernstein is currently in his second year as program director and associate professor of Hospitality Management at Seton Hill University in Greensburg, Pennsylvania. Daniel Bernstein has over 15 years of teaching experience in higher education at different universities throughout the United States. Daniel Bernstein holds the following degrees: doctorate (EdD) in Educational Administration from the University of South Dakota, master's (MBA) in Hospitality Industry from the University of New Haven, and a bachelor's (BA) in English from Adelphi University. Daniel Bernstein has previous hospitality management experience as a restaurant owner, restaurant manager, hotel manager, hotel marketing director, and hotel front desk manager. Daniel Bernstein has previous publishing experience in hospitality management journals, magazines, and newspapers. Daniel Bernstein has done previous consultant work in the hotel and restaurant industry.

14 ▊ Review Questions

1. An occupancy percentage measures the ratio of what two factors in determining the answer?

2. Why do hotels want to determine the difference between rooms occupied and double occupancy?

3. What is another term used in the industry for rooms?

4. How can a hotel have a high occupancy percentage and a low ADR (average daily rate)?

5. What is the "rule of thumb" in determining if your ADR calculation is accurate?

6. How can controlling room rates and restricting occupancy be effective tools in yield management?

7. Why do you think the failure rate is higher for independent restaurants than franchise restaurants?

8. Why do more restaurants fail than hotels?

9. What are the two factors that make up prime cost in the restaurant industry?

10. How has labor cost changed over the last 20 years in relation to health benefits?

11. Why should restaurant managers not staff at the same levels throughout the day?

12. Name three methods of food cost incurred in which potential revenue is lost?

13. Hotels that are considered business hotels, would likely discount their rates during what part of the week?

14. In up-selling a particular item in the hospitality industry, the seller must emphasize this characteristic of what they are selling.

15. The top-down approach attempts to sell in the hotel what priced rooms first?

16. Name three areas within the hotel where effective energy management principles could be utilized to reduce energy costs.

17. Name the statistics in the hotel industry that may cause labor costs to vary.

18. Why would it not be cost effective to purchase food for a restaurant from a supermarket?

19. What are the incentives for restaurants to purchase larger quantities of various food items?

20. Why is the perishability factor important in the hotel industry?

21. Why should restaurants use portion control as a means of controlling costs?

22. What are three factors that reduces meat from AP (as purchased) form to EP (edible portion)?

23. Why is service an intangible?

24. Why is it important for hospitality managers to be able to visualize intangibles?

25. What are the job description responsibilities of a cook or sous chef?

John Wolper
Paula Wolper
University of Findlay

Human Resource Management

Learning Objectives

✓ To describe the functions of the human resource department
✓ To recognize the role any manager plays within human resource functions
✓ To describe the role legislation plays in human resource management
✓ To discuss the role human resources plays in guest satisfaction in the hospitality industry
✓ To develop a vocabulary of human resource terminology

Chapter Outline

How Human Resources Is Involved in Every Supervisory/Management Position
Human Resource Department Functions
Career Path
Human Resource Management Strategies

*W*hat is human resource management? It is the department within the organization that handles the paperwork regarding selection, termination, legal mandates, benefits, training, and compensation. In the past this department handled these responsibilities following policies formulated by top management. Today, human resource (HR) managers no longer just follow policy. They are also responsible for formulating policy and assisting with strategic planning related to department functions. Although the HR department performs these functions, there is more to human resource management than paperwork. These departmental functions will be discussed; however, the reader must understand that HR goes beyond the functions of any department and is the responsibility of all supervisors/managers and every worker within the organization. Human resource management is concerned with the management and caring of the hospitality businesses' most important asset—the people who work for the organization.

J. W. Marriott, founder of the Marriott Corporation, is noted for saying that if a company takes care of the people who work for it, then the people will take care of the company. This translates into a well-balanced 360-degree company/employee/customer relationship that can be evaluated at any of the three levels. To play a productive role in the organization HR must be involved in activities to enhance the ability of the company to meet the needs of the guest while satisfying the needs of the worker. As in every department, customer satisfaction is the bottom line. Simply stated, *human resource management is the process of how organizations treat their people to accomplish the goals and objectives of the firm.*

How Human Resources Is Involved in Every Supervisory/Management Position

The HR department works in concert with all management at every level. HR plays a critical role in keeping all managers and supervisors appraised of changing legislative and court judgments that affect management functions. Even in traditional areas that are considered the purview of the HR department, management from other departments plays a role in accomplishing a key task. For example, the HR department may be responsible for recruiting prospective employees, performing initial interviews, completing reference checks, and completing the appropriate paperwork. However, the manager or supervisor of the department where this employee will work makes the outright decision regarding the hiring of an individual. This is not the only area that must employ a combined effort, and from this you can see that the HR department and all managers must work closely together to achieve the employment goals of the organization, which should be to hire the very best you can and keep them for as long as possible. Economies of scale are critical to the cost effectiveness of the HR tasks, no matter who is responsible, yielding appropriate cost control management. Retention is vital to reducing hiring costs.

In a small organization there is no formal HR department. Those responsibilities are relegated to the operational management or ownership. Here the organization's management staff is responsible for all of the HR functions along with all the other management functions relegated to their duties. Managers in a unit of a multi-unit chain find themselves responsible for the day-to-day functions; however an HR department at corporate headquarters backs them up. In the latter instance, the management staff must play a more active role in HR activities due to the distance from the corporate HR staff. Looking at this example more closely, we observe that the selection procedure, in this multi-unit situation, finds the management responsible for all selection functions, such as recruiting, interviewing, completing reference checks, making the final decision and completing the paperwork. The HR department at corporate office plays more of an advisory role and is responsible for the upkeep of the appropriate files and keeping unit managers aware of current accepted hiring practices as well as legal issues. As you can see from this example, it is critical that all management personnel have a thorough understanding of the functions involved in the management of human resources.

This is a shift from what we were accustomed to in years past. Corporate offices were attempting to control too many of these critical functions, and they often failed. Today, the cost of making mistakes does not afford organizations the luxury of simply hiring someone else to do the job. Although attitudes still exist in the hospitality industry that it is easy to replace an employee, especially a good one, they are seriously rethinking these passé thoughts, as they are very outdated and costly to the company.

Human Resource Department Functions

Planning

As a management function, planning is one of the most important activities. This certainly is the case in the HR area. The HR department must not only attempt to predict future employment needs, but they must also look at future trends to prepare the staff and assist the company in growth. It can be seen that this is a dimension where the HR department cannot work in a vacuum. They must work with all departments to assess employment needs. Additionally, they must be kept updated regarding industry shifts to enable them to assist the workforce in handling the ongoing changes. Moreover, they must remain competitive with wages to attract the best and the brightest to our industry.

Before an organization can determine how many people are needed to meet the demands of the business, planning functions are necessary to determine what work must be accomplished, how the work should be completed, and the skills necessary to complete the job. There are tools available to the HR professional to fulfill these tasks. The first is *job analysis*. This is the information that focuses on what work needs to be accomplished. It is a process of determining the tasks and skills necessary to complete a job. This analysis allows us to write job descriptions and job specifications. *Job descriptions* identify the purpose, duties, and conditions under which jobs are performed. *Job specifications* are the qualifications, knowledge, and skills necessary to perform the position. Job descriptions and specifications are the basis for advertising positions, selection, training, and evaluating.

The task of determining how the job should be performed is the function of *job design*. This looks at how the job is organized and how it can be planned to provide both productivity to the organization and the most job satisfaction to the employee. Once essential qualifications needed for the job are identified, you can then determine the type of position in the organization and how many people are necessary to fill the vacancy. Additionally, these tools assist us in determining where and how to recruit, the criteria to select employees, and the training methods necessary.

Staffing

Once the organization determines the number and type of employment positions available, the task of staffing for these positions begins. This includes recruiting candidates for the positions and selecting the best person for the position. This must all be achieved within the guidelines set forth in both fed-

The main concern while interviewing is to ensure fairness and achieve the best match for the job.

eral and state laws. A thorough job of recruiting must be performed to afford the organization the best choice of available candidates. Selection is not as easy as putting an ad in the paper and choosing a new employee from the stack of applications. The key element is finding the right employee for the job. The labor market demonstrates fluctuations dependent on the economy at any given time. When the economy is tight, there are more applications; however, when the economy is booming, it is often difficult to find qualified personnel to fill the vacancies. Not only does the economy affect the number and quality of the potential applicants, the sometimes negative perception concerning employment in the hospitality industry can also affect the pool of qualified applicants. We employ many entry-level employees in minimum wage jobs; this makes the challenge significantly greater for finding the right employee for every position. Given these variables, the current labor market conditions and shifting dynamics inherent in the labor force, a company today must go well beyond the traditional want ad and look for innovative ways to attract good employees. The scope of this introductory article prohibits the vast pool of creative methods in finding and keeping good employees; however, it is safe to say that several hospitality firms have had much success with a variety of programs designed to attract and retain competent workers and managers.

One increasingly popular tool is the Internet, with many Web sites available for the job seeker to research companies and pursue lists of jobs available. There are also services available to showcase the talents of the job seeker to any interested employer. Other nontraditional methods are also utilized and continue to grow in popularity as the employment markets tighten. Many companies today will have prospective applicants apply online for a candidate to be considered for employment. In this way, companies can better manage their applicant pool in accordance with their ongoing needs.

Once the company receives the individual's application, the task of interviewing begins. Many interviewing styles may be used; however, the overriding concern is to ensure fairness to the applicants and achieve the best match for the job. The interviewers must be sure they do not ask any questions that could be considered illegal or discriminatory in nature. Courses in human resource management will reveal key areas for design of the interview in depth. Often one of the functions of the HR department is training the managers interviewing applicants in the proper methodology to conduct the interviews. One must also try to structure the interview in such a way that you can compare the candidates' qualifications without bias. Increasingly, behavioral or situational interviewing methods are used. These methods show greater validity (via statistical accumulation) in choosing the right person for the job. Other tools being used to help in the decision-making process are checking references and administering a number of pre-employment tests. Many organizations today are employing outside firms to administer appropriate personality and honesty tests to obtain unbiased information suitable to a particular job and or company. The goal of this process is to find employees that will enjoy their work and fit well into the organizational structure.

Turnover and Employee Loyalty

Failure to adequately perform the recruiting and selection processes will often lead to unnecessary turnover. Turnover is the term used to describe the situation when an employee leaves and must be replaced. Turnover is an expensive occurrence, as the company must not only go through the entire recruitment and selection process once again, but it must also retrain a person for the position. Frequently, this ongoing training may produce negative effects of inefficiency until the new employee can achieve the expected level of productivity that the departed employee demonstrated.

Another expense to the organization is the time a manager needs to oversee this process. The replacement also takes a manager away from other responsibilities in situations where a manager performs all the recruiting and selection duties. Previously, turnover was an accepted occurrence in the hospitality industry because there were always new bodies to fill the shoes of the departing employee. However, this is not always the case. Therefore, more companies are emphasizing the need to select new hires wisely and to put programs in place to retain the existing employees.

Retention programs can focus around activities such as softball leagues and opportunities for socialization. Still, it is widely believed that the best methods to enhance employee retention is an atmosphere of fair treatment, one where employees enjoy working, one where they feel they make a difference and are rewarded based on their own individual needs. Because employee satisfaction is an ongoing process, managers will need to continually monitor the climate as new generations come into the labor market. The tangible and intangible assets of the job are becoming increasingly important to successful retention programs coupled with creative packaging that either entices and/or satisfies the employee. A *value-added relationship* is the term of the day, not only from a consumer perspective but an employee perspective as well.

Legislation

Organizations, in managing their employees must comply with many laws, regulations, court decisions, and mandates arising from the social legislation, most notably after 1960. Personnel departments had to become much more professional and more concerned about the legal ramifications of policies and practices enacted by their organizations. All management and supervisory personnel must continuously be updated and coached with regard to the legalities of the ever-changing fabric of our work environment.

Sweeping federal legislation that forever changed the standards for employment in the United States was passed under the Johnson administration. The act that provided the impetus for this change was the Civil Rights Act of 1964. This act prohibits discrimination on the basis of race, color, religion, sex, or national origin and has become the cornerstone piece of legislation protecting workers and their rights.

Key governmental agencies generally affect many HR activities. The HR professional must be familiar with many of these agencies and their functions. Among the more important ones to be familiar with are the actions of the Equal Employment Opportunity Commission, Occupational Safety and Health Administration, the Immigration and Naturalization Services, the Department of Labor, and the various state and city equal employment commissions and human or civil rights commissions. If the individual entrusted with the legalities of employment fails to maintain an awareness of current laws and regulations either through an HR department or individual actions, organizations may find themselves faced with costly lawsuits and significant fines. Much of this can be avoided by constantly monitoring the legal environment, by complying with changes, and by careful management of employees.

Evaluation

Employee evaluations take place after an employee has been selected, trained, and on the job for a period of time. Today, most jobs have a 30- to 90-day evaluation period. It is during this period that certain benefits may be withheld and the promise of offering continued employment non-binding. This means that termination may occur for stipulated reasons anytime during that evaluatory period. Evaluations have many organizational purposes. They can be used to determine if the employee may require more training, is in the best job for them, or is ready for a promotion, incentive pay, or any situation based on job performance. The best reason to evaluate an employee's performance is for official feedback; however, this should be the official documentation. The employee should be receiving feedback concerning their performance on a regular basis. A significant reason for discontent on the job, results from an employee not being aware of how they are doing on the job, and this feedback must be completed in a timely fashion. This is just like a student's desire to know where they stand regarding a grade in any given class. Evaluations play a significant motivational effect on employees by encouraging the employee to improve on their performance based on the outcomes of the evaluation. The HR department's role in this process is one of providing the form and filing the evaluations for future reference as well as training managers how best to complete the process. Evaluations are usually completed and administered by the employees' supervisor.

Employee evaluations also are used as backup documentation necessary if an employee is terminated based on performance. Although there are provisions for "employment at will" that allow an employer to terminate employment at the employer's discretion, most employers prefer to have a policy in place where an employee's performance is scrutinized, warnings are given, and an opportunity for retraining is provided before that termination takes place. This is also known as a progressive discipline policy. In this scenario the evaluations serve as documentation if the former employee brings discrimination charges forward.

In many organizations employee evaluations are the link between performance and pay raises. This makes it critical that the evaluations are performed in an impartial manner to ensure consistency regarding compensation across all areas of the organization. This approach of identifying employees who are performing at or above expected levels and providing them with increased wages is referred to as merit pay. You must make every effort to evaluate the employee on the promised anniversary date, as it is one of the most contentious complaints employees levy against their supervisors. Failing to evaluate and process the appropriate paperwork is essential to maintaining a professional posture and image.

Compensation and Benefits

Employees receive compensation for the work that they do in three ways—direct compensation (often referred to as base pay), merit pay, and benefits. The motivational effect of wages is often debated, but within the scope of this discussion employers continually look for better methods of materially rewarding people for the work they do. This results as a catalyst for improved productivity and a better motivational tool. Each form of compensation was introduced as a motivational tool. Benefits are introduced in this fashion and used to motivate or entice persons to work for their company; however, today benefits are often taken for granted and act more as a dissatisfier, if they are absent, than as a motivational tool. The predominant focus on wages today is that of merit pay, where only expected and above expected performance is rewarded above a base level.

One of the greatest challenges for the HR department today is finding and devising benefit packages that employees find attractive and that are affordable to the company. One of the most expensive components of any benefits package is the health insurance. As the cost of health care continues to rise rapidly, it becomes increasingly more difficult for companies to find insurance carriers with reasonable premiums. Companies are looking for innovative methods to solve this dilemma and must be sensitive to both the needs of the employees and the profitability of the company. As in other HR areas, some companies have found the way to balance both needs by outsourcing some portion of the HR functions as added dimensions. Each company must weigh the advantages and disadvantages of this move and proceed with the path that is best for that organization. HR professionals also look for a range of benefits that help employees meet personal goals and concerns. It should be duly noted, as in other HR areas, that the overriding principle in compensation is one of fairness and equity and is the law!

Health and Safety

Organizations are obligated to provide employees with a safe and healthy work environment. Requiring them to work with unsafe equipment or in areas where hazards are not controlled is a highly questionable and often costly practice. It is also the responsibility of managers to ensure that employees are safety conscious and maintain good health. Preventative safety is one of the best ways to avert an unsafe environment for the employee and often the customer. Both manager and the HR specialist are involved in health and safety practices in an organization. HR specialists coordinate programs, develop safety-reporting systems, and provide expertise on investigation, technical, research, and prevention methods. Managers coach, monitor, investigate, and observe employees practicing safety in the functional areas of the operation. Communication and good record keeping is vital in this area as it is with any area of the business. A newer piece of legislation is the **Americans with Disabilities Act**, or **ADA**, put into law by the Clinton administration. It calls for "reasonable" accommodations for both employees and customers who are functionally challenged. The term *functionally challenged* covers a wide array of physical and spatial challenges.

Career Path

There are many routes to take to achieve a career in HR in the hospitality industry. As mentioned previously, in a multi-unit chain the HR functions are handled by the management team at the store level. However, at the corporate level there would be persons in those positions that specialize in a particular HR area, such as benefits or compensation. Today as changing laws affect our industry as well as the need for specialization, an education in HR is becoming increasingly important. Many people still find themselves in HR by starting in operations; however, increasingly a background in HR is helpful to find a position in this department at the corporate level. If you are interested in HR, taking some specific classes or double majoring (HR and Hospitality Management) in college will help you to evaluate your interest and will help you secure a position in the field. You will need experience and more specialized training to become a department head.

Human Resource Management Strategies

To place into perspective the importance of human resource management strategies, it is critical to remember that the hospitality industry is a very labor intensive one. This changing environment is a result of the industry's cyclical growth, downturns, automation and technology, available labor supply, new concepts within the organization, mergers, acquisitions, and new approaches to conducting business. Any management strategies in the human resource area must be flexible to accommodate the strategic changes that are often faced by hospitality businesses. Some of the human resource management strategies focus on personnel management, organizational behavior, labor relations, and community relations. Each strategy is designed to focus on the specific aspects of an organization's needs. Further study on these specific topics will reveal the need to build in flexibility when employing strategies. The primary goal of any human resource strategy is the acquisition and retention of employees. Without the appropriate strategies, many hospitality organizations may find it difficult to maintain their labor supply and thus keep their competitive and strategic edge. You will learn more about this topic later and about the importance of succession planning in any organization.

Summary

Much of what has been discussed in this brief overview of HR essentials is procedural in nature. Nonetheless, truly taking care of employees involves much more than a daily routine can provide.

Hospitality organizations are dynamic entities. So are the individuals we seek to hire and to effectively represent our organizations. Companies must be positioned to meet the needs of their employees every day. There can be no exception to this imperative. If your company does not provide and care for the employee, and consequently the customer, in meeting their expectations, then failure is imminent. Longitudinal studies indicate a direct relationship with a hospitality business's failure with that of poor management. The numbers of annual failures are staggering with a clear majority of these failures pointing to poor management practices. There is always someone else out there who is able, willing, and ready to meet the challenges presented through the human resource functions.

The source of strength for successful companies is their ability to assess their surroundings and to adapt and change. In fact, a proactive posture generally accompanies these successful organizations. They are the industry leaders who remain in the forefront representing the most successful hospitality businesses in the world today. The future is very dynamic, and you have a wonderful opportunity to be a part of all the excitement and promise that is yet to come. Don't forget we are a people business, and we must take care of all the people that both work for and utilize our places of business.

In conclusion, we should never forget that people have to eat and sleep, and that is our business. We will always have work, but choose wisely and act professionally. Remember, we are lifelong learners and this process never stops. Keep yourself current and involved with your most important asset—your employees! It has been said many times before, "Take care of your employees and they will take care of your customers!"

Resources

Internet Sites

The Society for Human Resource Management: www.shrm.org
The International Association for Human Resource Information: www.ihrim.org
Workforce Management: www.workforce.com

☛ *Key Words and Concepts*

Americans with Disabilities Act	Interviewing
Civil Rights Act of 1964	Job analysis
Evaluation	Job descriptions
Human resource management	Job design

Job specifications
Merit pay
Progressive discipline policy
Recruiting
Selection
Strategic planning
Turnover
Value-added relationship

Contributor Information

wolper@findlay.edu
Dr. John M. Wolper is an associate professor of business and Director of the Hospitality Management Program housed in the College of Business at The University of Findlay in Findlay, Ohio.

pwolper@findlay.edu
Paula Wolper is an assistant professor in the Hospitality Management Program housed in the College of Business at The University of Findlay in Findlay, Ohio.

15 ▍ Review Questions

1. What is human resource management?

2. Who typically does the actual hiring of employees?

3. Why should all managers have a fundamental knowledge of human resource management?

4. Define the following:

    a. Job analysis

    b. Job description

    c. Job specifications

    d. Job design

5. What is the difference between job descriptions and job specifications?

6. What is the goal of the selection process?

7. Why do a growing number of companies today have you apply online?

8. Describe an effective recruiting tool that you have seen used in the hospitality industry.

9. What are the challenges of staffing?

10. Please identify two negative effects of turnover.

11. Please discuss a retention technique that a hospitality company could use to help prevent turnover. Why do you think it would work?

12. Discuss the importance of the Civil Rights Act of 1964.

13. Please give five reasons for management to complete employee evaluations.

14. Why is it important for an employee to be evaluated on a timely basis?

15. What is a progressive discipline policy?

16. What are three different forms of compensation?

17. Describe a challenge that a company may face when designing benefits packages.

18. What is the Americans with Disabilities Act?

19. What role does a manager play with regard to health and safety?

20. Please list two ways a company can take care of their employees.

21. What methods can be used to help ensure that management is selecting the right person for the position?

Robert A. McMullin
East Stroudsburg University

Physical Plant Management

Learning Objectives

✓ To be introduced to the importance of the physical plant
✓ To understand the value of curb appeal
✓ To understand the importance of communication between hospitality managers and independent contractors and corporate and property facility personnel with regards to property repairs will be covered
✓ To be exposed to human resources issues of the facilities department
✓ To understand the financial relationship between repairs and cost will be explored
✓ To be introduced to engineering systems, types of maintenance repairs, security, and the Americans with Disabilities Act
✓ To be able to develop the need and importance of facilities management and the relationship to guest satisfaction

Chapter Outline

Manager Roles and Responsibilities
Engineering Systems
Maintenance
Security
Americans with Disabilities Act

*T*he hospitality industry and education places great emphasis on service, marketing, and profitability to be competitive. However, one salient facet of the industry that is often overlooked is the "curb appeal" or attractiveness of the physical operations. Potential guests like to see a picture of the facility before they make a decision and the traveling public can be fickle in choosing to patronize a hospitality entity. Quite often, they judge the quality of the potential experience based on what they think of the visual appeal. Along with the physical attractiveness of the facilities, physical operations can enhance guest satisfaction. How clean and well kept the property is also reflects on the perception of the guest. Therefore, learning and understanding the physical plant operations are imperative for hospitality management. The maintenance and design of a good working property can affect the service you deliver, or how your facility is marketed, ultimately having a great impact on profitability.

Primarily, the physical plant is comprised of landscaping, grounds, exterior and interior building structure, building systems, furnishings, fixtures, and equipment (FF&E). Landscaping and exterior appeal sets the tone of attractiveness of a hospitality facility. Many hospitality organizations spend great sums in marketing guests, but the greatest hook is visual appearance. Hospitality properties should have clean, bright, and well-lit signage to allure travelers along with attractive landscaping.

However, other elements of the physical plant that are experienced by guests include plumbing, electricity, heating, ventilation, and air conditioning (HVAC). Managers of hospitality properties need knowledge and experience in understanding the effects of the physical plant and the actual outcomes to guests if equipment fails. In addition, management needs to be able to communicate with contractors, maintenance, and/or engineering staff to effect proper repairs without jeopardizing the guests' stay.

Manager Roles and Responsibilities

The scope and depth of the knowledge a facility manager must have depends on the type of property and size. Budget and economy lodging operations have relatively small and simple physical plants, whereas convention, resort, and luxury properties may resemble small cities. Other hospitality enterprises like restaurants and country clubs may rely on the property's general manager's communications with independent contractors or corporate personnel to repair their facility. Therefore, depending on the facility, there are many different backgrounds a physical plant manager must have.

The role and responsibilities of the hospitality facility manager or maintenance engineer typically includes detailed knowledge about the following areas:

1. Systems and building design
2. Building and system operations
3. Guestroom furnishings and fixtures maintenance
4. Equipment maintenance and repair
5. Equipment selection and installation
6. Contract management
7. Utilities management
8. Waste management
9. Budget and cost control
10. Security and safety
11. Contractual and regulatory compliance
12. Parts inventory and control
13. Renovations, additions and restorations
14. Staff training
15. Emergency planning and response

The aforementioned responsibilities present challenges for many hospitality facilities managers or maintenance engineers. Each skill level varies depending on work experience and background. For example the facilities manager may have to work with various contractors when the property decides to renovate or restore its facility.

In many hospitality situations, the facilities manager will have some detailed technical background from contracting firms, trade or technical schools, or other similar related employment. Although a technical background in plumbing, electrical, or HVAC equipment is good, they may have little conceptual knowledge of the hospitality industry. This can create problems with communication as the different hospitality departments attempt to communicate their problems and facilities managers try to understand so that they can fix the problems. In some cases, it feels like each department is speaking a different language, and in some ways they are. This can place an additional burden on the management staff and lodging property because the facility management needs to work closely with the executive housekeeper, front office manager, and food and beverage manager.

Bridging the communication gap is an important task for the general manager of a property because the property can lose its attractiveness.

In addition to working closely with other departments, the facilities manager must understand the financial relationship between maintenance, repair, and cost. For example, the facility manager needs to track energy costs while trying to find ways to decrease this expenditure. This position requires the need to analyze records, such as work orders, equipment data cards, equipment history records, architectural plans, and instruction and/or repair records. The facility manager needs to evaluate the cost of a repair while remaining committed to bring costs within a budget. In accounting terms, the actions of the facility manager is reported on the line item of the income statement called property operations and maintenance (POM). The challenge for the facility manager is to improve the quality of the physical plant while using minimal financial resources. Meanwhile the facility manager has to study the relationship of how equipment is used and consumption of energy usage from utility bills like electric, gas, and water. Therefore, the facility manager must work closely with the property controller, too. If the facility manager can maintain the same level of property efficiency while finding ways to reduce costs, this would have a positive effect on the hospitality property's financial statements. In addition, a clean, well-kept property is more attractive to potential guests, and there will be fewer problems. As a result, it will improve guest satisfaction.

Another significant financial responsibility of the facility manager is the evaluation of capital projects. These projects require a major cash outlay when either replacing or acquiring new equipment. The facilities manager along with other key hospitality management must judge the initial cost, durability, safety, and energy consumption of capital equipment. There are other accounting concerns like depreciation and tax implications. The process of judging the selecting and analysis of capital projects are called life cycle costing, which considers the following:

- Initial costs—for example, cost of the item itself including costs of installation, interconnection, and modification of supporting systems or equipment.
- Operating costs—for example, costs of energy or water to operate the equipment and supporting systems or those systems affected by the equipment; maintenance labor and supplies or contract maintenance services.
- Fixed costs—for example, insurance, depreciation, and/or property tax changes resulting from the equipment or system.
- Tax implication—for example, income taxes and tax credits such as investment, tax credits, and depreciation deductions.[1]

Engineering Systems

Management in the hospitality industry needs to understand the basic design and operations of the various engineering systems. This improves the communication between the facility manager and the rest of management. Having direct daily communication is imperative to relay any information on malfunctioning equipment so it can be repaired, while not disturbing the patrons or interrupting other management in completing their own tasks. The basic elements of the engineering systems include several areas.

Management should know the basic operations of water and wastewater systems, refrigeration systems, heating, ventilation and air-conditioning systems, or site power production, and safety and security systems, so he/she can intelligently explain what needs to be accomplished by the facilities management team.

Water and Wastewater Systems

Water supply is necessary for food and beverage and lodging establishments. Management should be familiar with the operation of backflow devices, which prevent water from re-entering a building. Other relevant systems include a storm sewer system for the disposal of rainwater and a sanitary sewer system for the removal of waste products. Another key system for restaurants is a grease separation or grease trap. Grease needs to be separated from wastewater to prevent water backup.

Refrigeration Systems

Hospitality managers should be knowledgeable about refrigeration systems. In the compressive refrigeration system, undesired heat is picked up in one place and carried to another place, where it is dumped or disposed. In many lodging establishments individual heating and air conditioning units are in each room. These are self-contained units that need to be maintained on a regular basis for guest comfort. Heat pumps work on a similar process except the unit is outside the room. This is a favorable way of heating and cooling for residential properties. The major components of the refrigeration cycle are:

1. Refrigerant, which is a fluid with a low boiling point that starts as a liquid, absorbs heat, and becomes a gas, and then is placed under pressure to become a liquid again.
2. The evaporation is the section of the circuit in which the refrigerant evaporates or boils to soak up heat.
3. An expansion value allows the refrigerant to soak up heat, allowing pressure to be lowered aiding the refrigeration cycle.
4. A compressor is a pump supplying the power to move the refrigerant through the system.[2]

Heating, Venting, and Air Conditioning Systems

Heating, ventilation, and air-conditioning (HVAC) systems provide levels of comfort based on heating, cooling, and humidity for guests, staff, and management. The key components of an HVAC system is pipes (hollow cylinder or tubular conveyance for a fluid or gas), ducts (any tubular passage through which a substance especially a fluid is conveyed), pumps (a machine or device for transferring a liquid or gas from a source or container through tubes or pipes to another container or receiver), thermostats (converts the temperature into a signal that is sent to the HVAC unit conditioning the space), and valves (devices that regulate the flow of gases, liquids, or loose materials through structures, such as piping or through apertures by opening, closing, or obstructing parts of passageways). Systems can be decentralized and operate as individual units or be centralized as one system working collectively.

Electrical Systems

Some hospitality properties operate an on-site power production, but most operations have electricity delivered by local utilities. In either case you should have a familiarity of electrical systems because you may experience brownouts (partial loss of electricity) or blackouts (total loss of electricity) that could disrupt your electrical service. Furthermore, management needs to understand electrical utility rates for cost control. Why should I be familiar with this? The utility is responsible for providing power at a correct voltage and frequency. The utility provides power through an electric meter that measures the rate and amount of power consumed, which generates the electric bill. The measure of the use of electrical energy is the watt. Amperes measure the rate of electrical flow through a device or appliance. The volt is the unit of electrical potential. Heating, ventilation and air conditioning (HVAC) systems should provide suitable temperature and humidity levels for guests, staff, and management. The HVAC system is an infrastructure of pipes, ducts, pumps, thermostats, valves, and pressure sensors. These systems can be decentralized and operated as individual units, or centralized as one system working collectively. Hospitality industry properties are supplied with alternating current (AC) from the local electric utility. If you do not have sufficient current your property may experience lights flickering or reduced illumination. Why do I need to know this? The goal of the facilities manager is to provide a suitable level of guest comfort but reduce electrical use.

Safety and Security Systems

Safety and security systems are another key responsibility of management. The entire management staff should be committed to a safe and secure environment in protecting guests, staff, and management. This can be accomplished by communicating safety and security needs at management staff meetings. There are far-reaching issues in the time, training, and financial investment of safety and security systems. One of the major concerns in this area is protecting people and assets. Guests should be made aware of their surroundings and encouraged to use all protective devices a room has installed. Most hospitality lodging establishments have two or three locks in each door. Guests should be informed that all should be used along with a door port viewer to prevent room invasions by potential criminals. Guests should be informed never to open doors to strangers and always contact the front office with any concerns.

Negligence in this area could result in legal situations. Hospitality management should know the operations of fire protection equipment, including detection, notification, suppression, and smoke control systems. In knowing these procedures, hospitality employees can aid in the deterrence of fire emergencies. Another key is security systems such as electronic lock systems, closed-circuit television, elevator controls, and exit alarms. These procedures aid in protecting the guests from unwanted intruders and safely evacuating the guests if an emergency arises. Procedures should be developed in case of emergencies. Each hospitality property should have plans for terrorists' acts, bomb scares, robberies, and extreme weather situations such as blizzards, hurricanes, tornadoes, and floods.

Maintenance

Regular Maintenance

Hospitality buildings are heavily used 24 hours of every day, seven days a week by guests, staff, and management. Each facility should have budgeted funds to reinvest in their property. Equipment will wear down, break down, and become obsolete. Management should have a tier plan to keep the property running efficiently.

- Routine maintenance is the general everyday duties of the facility staff, which requires relatively minimal skills or training. Examples of these duties include picking up litter, emptying trash cans, raking leaves, and shoveling snow.
- Preventive maintenance, sometimes referred to as PM, requires more advanced skills of the facility personnel. Examples of PM include inspections, lubrication, minor repairs or adjustments, and work order investigation.
- Guestroom maintenance is an activity applied to guestrooms of a lodging establishment. This is a form of prevention in ensuring guest comfort. Usually trained facilities personnel will remove several rooms a day from the rooms inventory and inspect them for the following:
  1. changing of filters in HVAC systems
  2. Test operation of TVs, electronic equipment, plumbing, and electrical equipment
  3. Ensure the guestroom is free of any maintenance issues.[3]

When a facilities manager plans, he/she must take into consideration scheduling regular maintenance, which requires advanced planning, significant amount of time to perform, specialized tools and equipment, and coordination of the departments affected. Each task should be assigned as part of each employee's schedule every day so that it does not get lost or forgotten when problems occur.

A plan for a disaster such as a hurricane should be in place in every hospitality facility.

Emergency Maintenance

Emergency and breakdown maintenance occurs when equipment fails based an unforeseen occurrence like flooding or thunderstorms. Hospitality properties cannot prevent equipment breakdown, but they can use preventative maintenance procedures to possibly keep breakdowns from occurring. Having contingency plans can aid when breakdown occurs. For example, when there is a power failure, backup electrical generators can keep the guests calm so that they can get to safety. Especially the day of a big banquet, the kitchen staff does not want to find out the refrigeration unit died, and everything is slowly defrosting without a backup refrigeration unit available. Or during a heat wave, guests and staff will not appreciate the facilities staff if there are no additional air-conditioning units when one fails. Therefore planning for common emergencies is necessary. With natural disasters like hurricanes, flooding, and snow, one cannot plan every detail. However, a disaster plan should be developed to prepare as carefully as possible. Many hotels and convention centers have been rethinking their disaster plans as the year of 2005 brought problems to all parts of the country. It is now becoming a major part of planning for all hospitality organizations.

Contract maintenance is necessary for certain equipment needs when repair and the skill level is beyond your facility staff. Some can be on retainer where they promise to handle emergencies as they happen for an annual fee, such as repair of refrigeration units where a repairman must come out. Cases for this type of contract might be washers and dryers for housekeeping or computer systems. Others contract for specific visits on a routine basis such as pest control. Some contractual arrangements can be available to assist in emergency or breakdown situations.

Security

Generally in the lodging industry we welcome guests to our properties and have them lower their guard, relax, and feel at home. However, it is not always possible to know when a person is a welcome guest or a pretender. Without security measures, strangers could go up the elevators and break into rooms or worse. Yet lodging facilities are a public building, and so guests need to be aware of safety measures as well. Many establishments provide "Traveler Safety Tips" on check-in or in the room.

However, in addition to the customer's awareness, equipment can be in place to increase security. For example, guestrooms should be equipped with phones to enable guests to place emergency phone calls. Many hotels put phones by the elevators or in hallways to make sure a guest can have access. The facilities staff should install guestroom doors that self-close and lock automatically. Doors should be equipped with deadbolts, view ports, security chains, or bars. Guestroom windows and sliding glass doors should be able to lock. Windows and sliding doors should only be able to open, but not wide enough for an intruder to enter. In many cases, a simple bar that fits into the floor track of the sliding glass doors ensures safety.

Guests should be encouraged to use in-room safes or safety boxes available at the front desk. This provides an extra level of security for guest valuables.

All lodging facilities should have a key control system for both manual and electronic keys. When keys are lost, stolen, or not returned the lock system should be evaluated. One approach to key control is referred to as the "five Rs."[4]

- Rationale—Criteria used to develop the keying schedule and to identify who will have various levels of access.
- Records—Involves guest information with regard to occupancy, status, and access.

- Retrieval—Actions by staff to recover keys from employees and guests.
- Rotation—Involves moving locks from room to room as a preventative security plan.
- Replacement—As keys are lost or locks compromised, replacement is necessary.

Historically older lodging properties with manual locks need to follow the aforementioned program. Even electronic locks have been comprised, which means the system should be evaluated from time to time.

Hospitality management and facility staff should work together to provide the highest means of safety and security to the guest and their own staff. This provides a safe environment for all.

Americans with Disabilities Act

An important consideration in the hospitality industry is the Americans with Disabilities Act (ADA) of 1990. This act spells out reasonable accommoda-

The Americans with Disabilities Act requires that reasonable accommodations are made for people with physical disabilities or sensory impairments.

tions to make for people with disabilities. Most people think that the ADA is only for people with physical handicaps or sensory impairments. However, think about which other people could use some help. How about, your grandmother who is fine, but a ramp instead of steps would make it easier for her to gain entry into a building or a railing by the bathtub would make it easier to get out. Or, you break your leg and have a cast, wouldn't it be easier to use some of the wheelchair equipment? So this act requires a percentage of rooms to have special equipment, but many people have special circumstances when an ADA room would be appropriate. With vans that are equipped to allow wheelchair entry, wider parking spaces are needed to accommodate someone exiting from the side of the van. For people with hearing and visual impairment, this act covers emergency situations like visual and audible alarms like strobe lights. Additionally, many believe that complying with ADA standards is very expensive. However, many accommodations have simple inexpensive alternatives. Do you have two or three stairs but no ramp? Use a temporary metal ramp that can be folded and stored nearby and then put in place for the occasion. Some hospitality facilities will hire consultants to evaluate their facility to ensure their compliance with ADA laws.

Summary

The facilities staff is a critical department of a hospitality enterprise. The way the property looks, how it works, and the comfort of the guest is critical. Many of these factors will ensure repeat business and guest satisfaction. If measures are not taken to ensure guest comfort and safety, you may find yourself in financial and legal problems.

Endnotes

1. Usiewicz, Ronald A., "Physical Plant Management and Security." (2004). In *Hospitality Tourism*, edited by Robert A. Brymer, 148–149. Dubuque, IA: Kendall/Hunt Publishing
2. Stipanuk, David D., *Hospitality Facilities Management and Design*, 2nd ed. (2002). East Lansing, MI: Educational Institute of the American Hotel, Lodging Association, p. 231
3. Ibid., p. 32
4. Ibid., pp. 152–156

Resources

Internet Sites

PM Engineer: www.pmengineer.com
International Facilities Management Assoc.: www.Ifma.com
FM Data: www.fmdata.com
Buildings Magazine: www.buildings.com
Burnham Boilers: www.burnham.com
American Solar Energy Society: www.ases.org
Green Globe 21: www.greenglobe21.com
National Fire Protection Association: www.nfpa.org
Water Web: www.waterweb.org
Water Online: www.wateronline.com
Electric Power Research Institute: www.epri.com
Air Conditioning and Refrigeration Institute: www.ari.org
Laundry Today: www.laundrytoday.com
Associated Landscape Contractors of America: www.alca.org
National Gardening Association: www.garden.org
American Institute of Architects: www.aia.org

Suggested Readings

American Hotel & Lodging Association (Producer). (1995). *Curb Appeal: Creating Great First Impressions* (Videotape). Available from the American Hotel & Lodging Association, P.O. Box 1240, 1407 S. Harrison Road, East Lansing, MI 48826-1240

Borsenik, F. D., & Stutts, A. D. (1991). *The Management of Maintenance and Engineering Systems in the Hospitality Industry* (3rd ed.). New York: John Wiley & Sons

Palmer, J. D. (1990). *Principles of Hospitality Engineering.* New York: Van Nostrand Reinhold

Stipanuk, D. M. (2002). *Hospitality Facilities Management and Design* (2nd ed.). East Lansing, MI: Education Institute of the American Hotel and Lodging Association

Usiewicz, R. A. (2004). Physical Plant Management and Security. In R. A. Brymer (ed.), *Hospitality & Tourism, An Introduction to the Industry* (11th ed., pp. 147–156). Dubuque, IA: Kendall/Hunt Publishing Company

☛ Key Words and Concepts

Alternating current (AC)

American with Disabilities Act (ADA)

Amperes

Capital projects

Contract maintenance

Curb appeal

Engineering systems

Furnishings, fixtures and equipment (FF&E)

Guestroom maintenance

Heating, ventilation and air conditioning (HVAC)

Life cycle costing

Property operation and maintenance (POM)

Refrigerant

Routine maintenance

Preventive maintenance (PM)

🖅 Contributor Information

rmcmullin@po-box.esu.edu

Dr. Robert A. McMullin, CHE, teaches hotel operations classes at East Stroudsburg University of Pennsylvania. Professor of Hotel, Restaurant & Tourism Management, East Stroudsburg University of Pennsylvania.

16 ▊ Review Questions

1. Why is maintaining your hospitality facility so important?

2. What comprises the physical plant?

3. What is curb appeal? Discuss why this affects your properties image.

4. What are the responsibilities of the physical plant manager or maintenance engineer?

5. What is the relationship between the general manager and maintenance engineer with regard to the physical property?

6. What is the financial relationship between repair, guest satisfaction, and cost?

7. Name and discuss the engineering systems.

8. Name and define the three types of maintenance.

9. What is life cycle costing? Why is it important?

10. Why is security so important to a hospitality facility?

11. What is the importance of the Americans with Disabilities Act?

Hospitality and Tourism Career Menu

Part 4

17

Ronald J. Cereola
Reginald Foucar-Szocki
James Madison University

Attractions

Learning Objectives

After studying this chapter you should be able to:

- ✓ Define an attraction
- ✓ Explain how attractions benefit local economies
- ✓ List the ways attractions are classified
- ✓ Describe the characteristics for each classification of attractions
- ✓ Classify examples of attractions according to their product offering or benefits they provide
- ✓ Apply your knowledge of why people travel and attractions to match and select appropriate attraction products

Chapter Outline

What Are Attractions?
Attraction Classification
Product Attributes of Attractions

What Are Attractions?

Attractions promote travel to destinations.

*G*o to *Google.com*, type *"attractions"* in the search box, select the *image* function, and click *search*. Look over the various pictures presented to you in the next few pages, and you are likely to see pictures of Disney World and other theme parks such as Six Flags, natural environments such as Bryce Canyon and San Diego ocean beaches, cultural landmarks in the form of Scottish castles, and adventure experiences on the Jurassic Coast Railway and Southern California hot-air balloon excursions. Venturing further into the Web pages you will see pictures of assorted museums, mountains and lakes, themed mega-resorts and hotels such as NYNY in Las Vegas, and even a few proverbial "biggest ball of twine" roadside stops. Consider for a moment, the diversity of the items that appeared on your computer screen. What do they all have in common? They are places, activities, and experiences sought out by leisure travelers. Some are wildly popular, whereas others may be just interesting stops along their way to the final destination. They are in the vernacular of the hospitality industry "attractions." *Attractions are the places we visit and the things we do while we are traveling for leisure.*

Attractions help satisfy needs.

Attractions are the lifeblood of tourism. Families take vacations to theme parks, or the shores of Southern California to enjoy the ocean, the mountains of Vermont and New Hampshire for recreational skiing, and to Washington, D.C. to visit the capital monuments and museums. Attractions are an integral part of the need satisfaction that fuels the desire to travel. Whether the need is belongingness (family vacation in Disney), physiological (rest and recuperating at the shore) or self-actualizing (visiting cultural and historical sites of Washington, D.C.), it is an attraction that the traveler will seek out to help fulfill that need. In short, attractions assist in satisfying the needs that motivate travel.

Attractions are economic engines.

They provide economic benefit to the region in which they are located. The money spent for the theme park admission may only be a small percentage of the leisure traveler's expenditure but then consider all the other amounts the traveler will spend on lodging, food and beverage, purchasing souvenirs, rental cars and other forms of transportation, guided tours, ancillary activities as well as shopping in local stores and malls. These expenditures provide economic benefits such as employment for the local residents who in turn use their wages to generate additional economic activity. Without the attraction these jobs might not exist. In addition to providing employment, attractions also support local governments when they generate income, sales, and excise taxes.

Attraction Classification

The most common methods of classification are *Status (importance or interest to the traveler), Origin, Lifespan, Ownership, Profit Orientation, and Product Attributes.*[1]

Status

Attractions are often broadly characterized as either *primary* or *secondary* attractions. A primary attraction is essentially the main reason a visitor travels to the destination and spends several days. As a result, pri-

Attractions such as the Washington Monument satisfies the self-actualizing need of the tourist.

mary attractions are usually supported by extensive ancillary facilities: lodging, food and beverage, transportation, extensive retail, and other hospitality services. An excellent example of a primary attraction is Disney World in Orlando, Florida. Visitors, especially families, make the trip and stay for several days. They purchase multi-day passes to the Disney theme parks and may stay in one of the many Disney owned properties, eat at Disney food outlets, use the Disney transportation system, and shop for their needs at Disney retail outlets. Because Disney World has tremendous drawing power, significant non-Disney owned hospitality facilities have developed around the theme park and have contributed to the growth of the Orlando area in Florida.

In contrast, a secondary attraction is of lesser importance to the traveler and might be considered simply something nice to do while on the way to or in the area of the primary attraction. Again, using the Orlando area as an example, there are many secondary attractions like Gatorland, which even advertises itself as the "best half-day attraction minutes away from Sea World, Walt Disney World and Universal Studios."[2]

Origin

Attractions may be classified according to whether they are *natural* or *man-made*. Natural attractions are those that occur in nature without human intervention. They include mountains, coastlines, lakes, islands, forests, deserts, rain forests, and other landforms and seascapes. Man-made attractions owe their very existence to the intervention of humans. Examples of pure man-made attractions are theme parks, shopping centers, sports and entertainment facilities, festivals, casinos, and museums. Often, human intervention combines with nature to create a mixed origin attraction such as the Hoover Dam constructed on the Colorado River, which created Lake Mead. The surrounding area, referred to as the Lake Mead National Recreation Area, is a premier inland water recreation area managed by National Park Service and encompasses over 1.5 million acres of land with 700 miles of shoreline. The area generates over 500 million dollars directly for the local economy and is within a day's drive of more than 23 million people from Los Angeles, California, to Phoenix, Arizona, making it one of the fastest-growing tourism destinations in the country.[3] Some natural attractions are made more accessible by man-made attractions that are constructed on or about the natural formation, such as the rain forest cable tours available in Costa Rica and other parts of the world. In these locations various forms of cable transportation and other viewing facilities have been constructed to permit visitors access to the natural attraction that would otherwise be relatively inaccessible to the visitor. The excitement of traveling along the cable itself has become one of the "things to do" for visitors to the area.[4]

Lifespan or Time Oriented

Attractions can be classified according to their lifespan or whether they are *relatively* permanent or temporary. Natural attractions such as lakes, mountains, and other landforms and seascapes are permanent attractions. However, permanent attractions can also be man-made, such as an amusement park, a zoo, or a historical monument. Although these attractions can be demolished and moved, they are relatively permanent in comparison to temporary attractions, which are short lived or can be easily relocated. Examples of temporary attractions are concerts, conferences, trade shows, parades, award shows, certain sporting events like the Super Bowl, and festivals. Permanent attractions are sometimes referred to as *site* attractions, whereas temporary attractions are referred to as *event* attractions.

Ownership and Purpose

Approximately 85 percent of all recreational land in the United States is under *public ownership* managed by the federal and state governments for the benefit of the public at large. The National Park Service, part of the Department of the Interior, manages the majority of federal lands under the auspices of the National Park System, which includes parks, monuments, and preserves. The world's first national park—Yellowstone—was created in 1872, at which time Congress set aside more than one million acres as "a public park or pleasuring ground for the benefit and enjoyment of the people."[5] This American invention marked the beginning of a worldwide movement that has subsequently spread to more than 100 countries and 1,200 national parks and conservation preserves. Today there are more than 388 units in the National Park System encompassing more than 83 million acres.[6] All represent some nationally significant aspect of the American natural or cultural heritage.

Closely aligned with ownership is the purpose for which attractions are operated, either as *nonprofit*

The Hoover Dam is a popular mixed-origin attraction.

or *profit-seeking* entities. Generally, nonprofit entities that own man-made attractions, such as museums, or natural attractions, such as nature preserves, do not have tourism as their primary goal. Rather, their interest is that of preservation of the natural environment or a historical, cultural, or religious consequence. Profit-seeking entities, on the other hand, are seeking to provide a return on investment to the private owners. There is a delicate balance for both types of owners. Profit-seeking entities cannot engage in unrestrained use and development without fear of the public backlash resulting from despoiling the environment or encouraging unrestrained commercial development of the surrounding area. In addition, it would not be in the long-term interest of the private owners to exhaust or physically depreciate the attraction through overuse, thereby shortening its useful life. For nonprofits the balance is between their preservation goals and generating sufficient revenues to maintain the attraction, while at the same time permitting public access at an acceptable level. The National Park Service faces this very same dilemma. How do they provide the widest array of access to the public while at the same time avoiding the overcrowding that would destroy the natural beauty of the environment, which is the very reason visitors come to the parks.

Product Attributes of Attractions

We can also categorize attractions based on what the attraction has to offer to the tourist as leisure activity. Common classifications include topography, culture and heritage, planned play environments, and events and entertainment.

Topography

The topography of an area is significant as an attraction and has an added benefit to the tourist in that scenery is free. Topography attractions consist of three areas of interest: *landforms*, *wildlife*, and *ecology*.[7]

Landforms, such as beaches, mountain vistas, and deserts can all be visually appreciated free and in many instances be utilized for little or no dollar costs to the traveler. Often because climate is closely aligned with topography, these attractions experience heavy seasonal demand. The beaches of Florida are in "high season" when the northern states are in their winter season, whereas despite their ability to make snow, the ski slopes of the West and New England are largely dependent on a snowy winter for a successful ski season. The challenge for these seasonal attractions is to manage the heavy demand during peak season and to create additional off-season activities to create demand during slow times.[8]

In addition to scenic beauty, topography is closely tied to recreational activities as well as wildlife viewing and ecological activities. In recent years concern for the environment has created a heightened awareness of the effects of tourism on the natural environment.[9] Efforts to control access and the types of tourism activities centered on natural attractions have been implemented by federal and state governments in the United States as well as by their counterparts around the world.[10] At the same time this heightened awareness has created environmentally friendly or ecotourism opportunities centered on natural attractions. A prime example of this is the whale-watching excursions that permit visitors to Maui, Hawaii, to see and hear the humpback whales during their annual migrations in December and January.

Culture and Heritage Attractions

Since the early days of mankind, travel has been closely linked to culture and heritage. The preservation for future generations, of artifacts and sites, in particular those associated with a people's origins, religion, war, art, as well as science and myth, are commonplace among the world's cultures. Cultural attractions are very popular among travelers. In fact, most U.S. adult travelers attend a cultural activity or event while on a trip. Most often attended are performing arts events, and/or museums.[11]

Museums

Visitors are attracted to museums both out of curiosity and for education. The Grand Tour, a root of modern tourism, was a long, arduous, albeit cultural journey through Paris, Venice, Florence, and Rome and a capstone educational experience for the elite of the sixteenth century. Today a visitor can approximate the experience by visiting the plethora of museums around the world, such as The Metropolitan Museum of Art[12] or The Museum of Natural History,[13] both in New York, wherein many great art works reside. In addition to exhibits, awaiting the visitor of museum attractions are programs and events, which include lectures, performances, workshops, and films. Many have been designed for children, the tourist of tomorrow.[14]

Religious Attractions

Rivaling museums in their numbers and diversity are religious attractions primarily consisting of ca-

thedrals and churches, temples, and mosques. There are also geographic areas that consist of entire cities and the surrounding locales of religious significance, such as the Holy Land in Jerusalem, where many of the principle religious sites for Christianity, Judaism, and Islam converge, or the city of Mecca in Saudi Arabia, where millions of Muslims from around the world make an annual pilgrimage. Modern tourism has its roots in religion. During the Middle Ages, individuals made pilgrimages to visit religious sites, and many of the same are still visited by tourists today. Much like travelers today, these pilgrims came from every strata of society.

Historical Attractions

The phrase often quoted by George Santayana, "Those who cannot learn from history are doomed to repeat it," is at the heart of historical attractions. They are the efforts to preserve the events of the past that demand remembrance. Primarily consisting of monuments and structures such as the Pyramids of Egypt, the Statue of Liberty, Tiananmen Square, or the Great Wall of China, they also encompass area attractions of historical significance such as battlefields. A recent survey reveals that 41 percent of travelers say they visited a designated historic site such as a building, landmark, home, or monument during their trip. Three in ten visited a designated historic community or town.[15] All too often, war provides tourism opportunities. American Civil War sites such as Gettysburg, Pennsylvania, are extremely popular, and many Civil War attractions involve battlefield reenactments (events), which heighten the visitor's understanding and appreciation of the historical significance as well as increasing visitor involvement.[16]

In addition to battlefield attractions there are numerous memorials in Washington, D.C. such as the Vietnam Veterans Memorial,[17] whose principal exhibit is The Wall containing the names of those who gave their lives, visited by over 3 million people in 2004, as well as the Korean War Veterans Memorial.[18] Lest you start to believe that historical attractions are just about war, there are numerous attractions celebrating historic ideas that changed the world and in particular America, many of which are found at the National Mall in Washington, D.C. There a tourist can visit the Thomas Jefferson Memorial, the Lincoln Memorial, the Washington Monument, and the Franklin Delano Roosevelt

Memorial.[19] In December 2005 the National Capital Planning Commission (NCPC) unanimously approved a preliminary design for the Martin Luther King, Jr. National Memorial to commemorate the life and work of Dr. Martin Luther King, Jr. and to honor his national and international contributions to world peace through non-violent social change.

Planned Play Environments

Planned play environments provide recreation and entertainment and are a significant sector of the tourism market. The ancient Greeks and Romans traveled for both theater and sport.

Sporting Facilities

Sports, recreation, and travel go together. The array of sporting and recreational attractions available to the traveler is almost endless. Fishing, hunting, cycling, mountain climbing, hang gliding, horseback riding, boating, surfing, snorkeling, and scuba diving are but a few, and for each there is a sporting attraction where one can engage in their desired rec-

reational activity to their heart's content. Among the most popular sporting and recreational activities are skiing and golf. In 2003, approximately 10 million Americans spent 58 million days on the slopes of more than 500 ski resorts across the United States. About 10 percent of the U.S. population are snow sport enthusiasts, making the ski industry a multibillion dollar business. Twenty-five percent of all ski excursions are multi-day visits more than 500 miles from home. In the United States, the ski resorts of the Rocky Mountain West are the prime ski attractions, accounting for approximately 30 percent of all lift tickets sold in the United States.[20]

If ski and snow sports are a bit too adventuresome, consider golf. There are over 25 million golfers in the United States. Reportedly, a golf facility is the only significant sports activity that will influence a meeting planner's choice of destination.[21] In a recent year, one in eight U.S. travelers played golf while on a trip of 100 miles or more away from home. Sixteen percent of travelers who played golf said that golf was the most important reason for taking the trip. Golf is a time to be among friends and a time to compete, to relax, and to do business, as well as to just enjoy the beauty of the natural surroundings.[22]

The ski resorts of the Rocky Mountain West account for approximately 30 percent of all lift tickets sold in the U.S.

Golf's Home

Scotland is known worldwide as "the home of golf." Dutch sailors are thought to have introduced "kolf" to Scotland, a game originally played by them with a stick and ball on the frozen canals in winter. It was transformed on the public links land becoming the game we know today.[23] Visitors have been coming to Scotland for golf holidays for over 100 years to play world-famous championship golf courses such as The Old Course St. Andrews, Royal Troon, Carnoustie, Muirfield, Turnberry, and Gleneagles.[24]

Theme and Amusement Parks

Theme and amusement parks are likely the most often recognizable attractions to the general public. Theme parks offer escape and replicate both real as well as "unreal" places that may or may not exist beyond the gates. Amusement parks, on the other hand, have rides, games, and exhibitions. Today the

The Tallest Fastest Roller Coaster on Earth

The 456-foot Kingda Ka ride at Six Flags Great Adventure park, a one-hour drive from Philadelphia, will reach 128 mph on its 50.6-second journey. The 18 riders on Kingda Ka's four cars will feel weightless at some points as they are propelled to 128 mph in just 3.5 seconds before being shot vertically to 456 feet. After reaching the top, they will plunge straight back down while turning in a 270-degree spiral before climbing a 129-foot-high hill and returning to the start point. A chest harness with two locking devices will be used to secure passengers.[26]

distinction has been blurred as both tend to contain elements of each in their offering.

According to the Travel Industry Association of America approximately one in ten (9 percent) trips includes a visit to a theme or amusement park, equating to over 92 million person-trips taken in the United States in 2002. Households visiting a "theme park" spend an average of $845 per trip, excluding transportation to their destination. On average, overnight theme park trips last 5.3 nights. A large share

(55 percent) of household trips involving a visit to a theme park includes children under age 18.[25]

Of course not every visitor to a theme park is looking for the intense experience of a thrill ride. Theme parks must continue to be family friendly by offering a wide spectrum of attractions suitable for all ages and taste. Universal's Seuss Landing[27] is a whimsical attraction that appeals to young and old alike and is suitable for the less adventurous. In addition to diverse product offerings, modern theme and amusement parks need to be clean, visually appealing, and family friendly.

Gaming

The modern Las Vegas-style casino resort has created a hybrid between gaming and entertainment. Moving along the Las Vegas Strip, one is presented with an Egyptian Pyramid, a Medieval Castle, New York City and the Statue of Liberty, the Eiffel Tower, ancient Rome, and Venice, as well as an Arabian Oasis. All of these might be classified as an adult theme park given the numerous adult-oriented attractions contained therein, of which gaming only happens to be one activity.

Shopping

Shopping is one of the most popular trip activities for U.S. adult travelers.[29] This should be no surprise for

Figure 17.1 ||| **Top 20 Casino Markets by Annual Gross Revenue 2004**

1	Las Vegas Strip	$5.333 billion
2	Atlantic City, N.J.	$4.806 billion
3	Chicagoland, Ind./Ill.	$2.346 billion
4	Connecticut (Indian)	$1.646 billion
5	Tunica/Lula, Miss.	$1.199 billion
6	Detroit	$1.189 billion
7	Biloxi/Gulfport, Miss.	$911.45 million
8	Reno/Sparks, Nev.	$903.54 million
9	Lawrenceburg/Rising Sun/Elizabeth/Vevay, Ind.	$885.90 million
10	St. Louis, Mo./Ill.	$848.41 million
11	Shreveport, La.	$835.51 million
12	Boulder Strip, Nev.	$791.69 million
13	Kansas City, Mo.	$701.39 million
14	Downtown Las Vegas	$663.28 million
15	New Orleans	$608.80 million
16	Laughlin, Nev.	$595.32 million
17	Black Hawk, Colo.	$524.04 million
18	Lake Charles, La.	$462.07 million
19	Council Bluffs, Iowa	$481.18 million
20	Charlestown, W. Va.	$360.24 million

Source: The Innovation Group 5/05.[28]

anyone who has visited Disney World in Orlando, Florida. As you stroll along Main Street in the Magic Kingdom and the other streets of the park, you are flanked on both sides by retail opportunities. It may be that part of the genius of Walt Disney was his disguising a retail mall within a theme park. Approximately 91 million people, or 63 percent of adult travelers in 2000, included shopping as an activity on a trip.[30] In a reverse of the Disney strategy, the West Edmonton Mall in Alberta, Canada, contains the Galaxyland Amusement park (the world's largest indoor theme park), the World Waterpark (the world's largest indoor water park), the Ice Palace (a national Hockey League-size ice arena), an exact Replica of the Santa Maria (which is available for weddings and special functions), an 18-hole, par 46 miniature golf course, and the 354-room Fantasyland Hotel.[31] The West Edmonton Shopping Mall is listed in the Guinness Book of World Records as the "largest shopping center in the world." The mall's Web page refers to the center as an "entertainment and shopping center, Alberta's *number one* tourist *attraction.*"[32]

Lest you think that the West Edmonton Mall is an anomaly consider the Mall of America located in Minnesota, which in addition to 520 stores contains The Park at MOA™, which has 30 rides including the Timberlane Roller Coaster, the Underwater Adventures® Aquarium, LEGO® Imagination

Center, Dinosaur Walk Museum, A.C.E.S. Flight Simulation, and the NASCAR Silicon Motor Speedway. On the MOA Web site you can plan your entire visit including air, hotel and auto packages. The MOA even hosts meeting facilities at its Executive Meeting and Events Center.[33]

Events

Events are temporary attractions. Relative to permanent site attractions, they are generally easier and less expensive to develop, although that may not always be the case in every instance, such as with the Olympics and other large-scale events, including the Super Bowl. Events include such activities as fairs and festivals, live entertainment offerings as in the performing arts, sports exhibitions, parades, pageants, and other celebratory gatherings such as New Year's Eve "First Night" celebrations. In many instances events give birth to site attractions. The sporting facilities specially constructed for the Olympics live on as site attractions for future sport exhibitions.

Sporting events, both professional and intercollegiate, are significant attractions for travelers. Over 75 million U.S. adults attended an organized sports event as either a spectator or as a participant while on a trip of 50 miles or more, one-way, in the past

Events like festivals are temporary attractions.

five years.[34] One of the fastest growing sporting events is NASCAR stock car racing.[35] NASCAR races are broadcast in over 150 countries. With 75 million fans it holds 17 of the top 20 attended sporting events in the United States.[36]

The performing arts have always been events that attract travelers. They include theater, dance, and music of all forms. Some destinations such as Branson, Missouri, and Monterey, California, are well associated with music festivals that serve as primary tourist attractions for the area. New York City's Broadway theater district is just one of the performing arts attractions the city offers to visitors. A legendary musical performance event was the 1969 Woodstock Festival and Concert. Though planned for 50,000 people, it is believed to have been attended by over 500,000 individuals.[37]

The modern-day epitome of an "event" is the Super Bowl, which occurs annually at the end of January each year. The first Super Bowl was between the Green Bay Packers and the Kansas City Chiefs. Tickets cost only $12, and the game had less then 50 percent attendance. Today, ticket costs are measured in the thousands of dollars and are difficult to come by, as the game is sold out. On average, 80 to 90 million Americans are tuned into the Super Bowl at any given moment. Cities compete to host the game in a selection bidding process similar to ones used by the Olympics and soccer's World Cup. Entertainment has become a major component of the event. A number of popular singers and musicians have performed during the pre-game ceremonies, the halftime show, or even just singing the national anthem of the United States. Among the notables have been Stevie Wonder, Paul McCartney, Aretha Franklin, The Rolling Stones (Super Bowl XL 2006), and of course the infamous "wardrobe malfunction" by Janet Jackson and Justin Timberlake in 2005.[38]

Industrial Attractions

Industrial attractions consist of operating concerns, manufacturing and agricultural, whose processes and products are of interest to visitors. For example, many manufacturing concerns provide tours of their facilities. Ethel M in Las Vegas conducts free interactive tours where the visitor can watch them make chocolate confections. You can tour the kitchen, walk through the enrobing and molding rooms, then finally try a free sample. Of course, your tour ends in their retail outlet.[39] The Boeing

Everett factory tours are conducted to showcase the Boeing Company and the Everett product line, the 747, 767, and 777 aircraft. Visitors can see airplanes in various stages of flight test and manufacture. The facility also contains conference space for 250 people, special event space for groups of up to 700 people, as well as a 240-seat theater and a 125-seat restaurant and retail space. There is also an aviation education program for children K–12th grade.[40] Virtually every state has one or more factory tours that would qualify as industrial attractions. Some charge a fee but most are free. You can get a comprehensive listing, by state, of available factory tours on the Web at Factory Tours USA.[41]

Wine tourism is defined as visitation to vineyards, wineries, wine festivals, and wine shows for which grape wine tasting and/or experiencing the attributes of a grape region are the prime motivating factors for visitors.[42] Wine tourism is experiencing steady growth edged along by the growing public interest in wines. The 2004 movie *Sideways* spurred the creation of wine tours mirroring the journey of the film's two main characters through Santa Barbara, California, wine country[43] (note how the movie is a convergence between culture and tourism). Napa and Sonoma in California, both major wine-producing areas in the United States, have flourishing wine tourism industries centering around vineyards and wine-tasting attractions. The Beringer vineyard is just one of many vineyards that provide tours and tasting to visitors.[44]

Summary

Attractions are the places we visit and the things we do while we are traveling for leisure. Attractions promote travel to destinations and are an integral part of the traveler's need satisfaction process. Attractions are economic engines that provide empsloyment and support to local governments through income, sales, and excise taxes.

For attractions to be viable tourism components, they must be supported by the areas *infrastructure*: roads, airports, and other transportation facilities; municipal services such as water, police, and fire protection; medical, power, and communication resources as well as *hospitality* services; lodging, food, and beverage facilities. In addition, the people of the area must have hospitality service skills and be open and amenable to the tourism industry and genuinely friendly to the visitor.

Endnotes

1. Mill, Robert C. & Morrison, Alastair M. (2002). *The Tourism System*. Dubuque, IA: Kendall/Hunt

2. Gatorland.com. Retrieved February 11, 2006 from *Welcome to Gatorland*. (n.d.). http://www.gatorland.com/

3. National Park Service. (n.d.). *Lake Mead National Recreation Area Strategic Plan 2001–2005*. Retrieved February 11, 2006 from http://www.nps.gov/applications/parks/lame/ppdocuments/ACFB12.doc You can discover more about the recreational tourism opportunities in the Lake Mead National Recreation Area by visiting the National Park Service Web site http://www.nps.gov/lame/index.htm

4. *Hacienda Baru National Wildlife Refuge*. (n.d.). Retrieved February 11, 2006 from http://www.haciendabaru.com/tours.htm

5. National Park Service. (n.d.) *NPS Management Policies*. Retrieved February 11, 2006 from http://parkplanning.nps.gov/document.cfm?projectId=13746&documentID=12825

6. National Park Service. (n.d.). *The National Park System Acreage*. Retrieved February 11, 2006 from http://www.nps.gov/legacy/acreage.html

7. Goeldner, Charles R., Ricthie, J. R. Brent, McIntosh, R.W. (2000). *Tourism: Principles, Practices, Philosophies*, 8th ed. New York: John Wiley & Sons

8. Middleton, Victor T. C., & Clarke, J. (2001). *Marketing in Travel and Tourism*. Oxford: Butterworth Heinemann

9. Weaver, David. (2001). Criteria and Context. *Ecotourism*. Milton, Australia: John Wiley & Sons

10. Weaver, David & Lawton, Laura. (2002). *Tourism Management*. Milton, Australia: John Wiley & Sons

11. Travel Industry Association of America. (n.d.). *Cultural Events/Festivals*. Retrieved February 11, 2006 from http://www.tia.org/pressmedia/domestic_a_to_z.html#c

12. The Metropolitan Museum of Art. (n.d.). Retrieved February 11, 2006 from http://www.metmuseum.org/home.asp

13. The American Museum of Natural History. (n.d.). Retrieved February 11, 2006 from http://www.amnh.org/

14. The Metropolitan Museum of Art. (n.d.). Retrieved February 11, 2006 from http://www.metmuseum.org/home.asp for more on The Grand Tour visit http://www.metmuseum.org/toah/hd/grtr/hd_grtr.htm

15. Travel Industry Association of America. (n.d.). *Shopping*. Retrieved February 11, 2006 from http://www.tia.org/pressmedia/domestic_a_to_z.html#s

16. Civil War Traveler.com. (n.d.). Retrieved February 11, 2006 from http://www.civilwar-va.com/ You can explore the Civil War historic monuments and battlefield attractions of Virginia, North Carolina, South Carolina, Pennsylvania, West Virginia, and Washington D.C. at *Civil War Traveler.com*. This site contains one of the most comprehensive virtual experiences of Civil War attractions

17. National Park Service. (n.d.). *Vietnam Veterans Memorial*. Retrieved February 11, 2006 from http://www.nps.gov/vive/

18. National Park Service. (n.d.). *Korean War Veterans Memorial*. Retrieved February 11, 2006 from http://www.nps.gov/kwvm/

19. National Park Service. (n.d.). *National Mall*. Retrieved February 11, 2006 from http://www.nps.gov/mall/monuments/monument.htm

20. Aron, Adam A., (2004). Marketing the Thrill of Skiing, the Serenity of the Mountains, the Luxury of Travel. In Bob Dickinson & Andy Vladimir. (Eds.), *The Complete 21st Century Travel & Hospitality Marketing Handbook* (pp.191–201) Upper Saddle River, NJ: Pearson Prentice Hall

21. Cook, Roy A., Yale, Laura J., & Marqua, Joseph J. (2002). *Tourism: The Business of Travel*. Upper Saddle River, NJ: Prentice Hall

22. Travel Industry Association of America. (n.d.). *Golf and Tennis*. Retrieved February 11, 2006 from http://www.tia.org/pressmedia/domestic_a_to_z.html#g

23. United States Golf Association. (n.d.). *What Is the Origin of the Word Golf*. Retrieved February 11, 2006 from http://www.usga.org/questions/faqs/usga_history.html

24. Scotland the Home of Golf. (n.d.). Retrieved February 11, 2006 from http://golf.visitscotland.com/

25. Travel Industry Association of America. (n.d.). *Theme/Amusement Park Travel*. Retrieved February 11, 2006 from http://www.tia.org/pressmedia/domestic_a_to_z.html#t

26. Six Flags Theme Parks, Inc. (n.d.). *Tallest Fastest Roller Coaster on Earth*. Retrieved February 11, 2006 from http://www.sixflags.com/parks/greatadventure/Rides/KingdaKa.html

27. Universal Studios. (n.d.). *Suess Landing*. Retrieved February 11, 2006 from http://www.univacations.com//themeparks/IOAsuesslanding.asp

28. American Gaming Association. (n.d.). *Industry Information Fact Sheets: Statistics Top 20 Casino Markets by Annual Revenue 2004*. Retrieved February 11, 2006 from http://www.americangaming.org/Industry/factsheets/statistics_detail.cfv?id=4

29. Cook, Roy A., Yale, Laura J., & Marqua, Joseph J. (2002). *Tourism: The Business of Travel*. Upper Saddle River, NJ: Prentice Hall

30. Travel Industry Association of America. (n.d.). *Shopping.* Retrieved February 11, 2006 from http://www.tia.org/pressmedia/domestic_a_to_z.html#s

31. West Edmonton Mall. (n.d.). *WEM Trivia.* Retrieved February 11, 2006 from http://www.westedmall.com/about/wemtrivia.asp

32. West Edmonton Mall. (n.d.). *Welcome to West Edmonton Mall's Website.* Retrieved February 11, 2006 from http://www.westedmall.com/about/default.asp

33. Mall of America. (n.d.). Retrieved February 11, 2006 from http://www.mallofamerica.com/home.aspx

34. Travel Industry Association of America. (n.d.). *Profile of Travelers Who Attended Sports Events.* Retrieved February 11, 2006 from http://www.tia.org/Pubs/pubs.asp?PublicationID=80

35. NASCAR. (n.d.). Retrieved February 11, 2006 from http://www.nascar.com/

36. Wikipedia. (n.d.). *NASCAR.* Retrieved February 11, 2006 from http://en.wikipedia.org/wiki/NASCAR#fn_1#fn_1

37. Wikipedia. (n.d.). *Woodstock Festival.* Retrieved February 11, 2006 from http://en.wikipedia.org/wiki/Woodstock_festival

38. Wikipedia. (n.d.). *Super Bowl.* Retrieved February 11, 2006 from http://en.wikipedia.org/wiki/Super_Bowl

39. Ethel M Chocolates, Factory Tour. (n.d.). Retrieved February 11, 2006 from http://www.ethelm.com/jump.jsp?itemID=117&itemType=CATEGORY

40. Boeing. (n.d.). *About Us.* Retrieved February 11, 2006 from http://www.boeing.com/companyoffices/aboutus/tours/index.html You can find more on Boeing's factory Tours at http://gonw.about.com/od/attractionsWA/a/futureofflight.htm

41. Factory tours USA. (n.d.). Retrieved February 11, 2006 from http://factorytoursusa.com/Index.asp

42. Hall, C. Michael, Johnson, Gary, Cambourne, Brock, Macionis, Niki, Mitchell, Richard & Sharples, Liz, (2002). Wine Tourism: An Introduction in C. Michael Hall, L. Sharples, B. Cambourne, & N. Macionis, (Eds.), *Wine Tourism Around the World* (pp. 1–22) Oxford: Butterworth Heinemann

43. Chiff.com. (n.d.). *Sideways, The Virtual Wine Tour.* Retrieved February 11, 2006 from http://www.chiff.com/a/sideways-wine-tour.htm

44. Beringer. (n.d.). *Winery Tours.* Retrieved February 11, 2006 from http://www.beringer.com/beringer/winery/index.jsp

Resources

Internet Sites

American Gaming Association: http://www.americangaming.org

American Museum of Natural History: http://www.amnh.org

Beringer: http://www.beringer.com

Civil War Traveler: http://www.civilwar-va.com/

Disney Theme Parks: http://disney.go.com/home/today/index.html

Google: http://www.google.com

Factory Tours USA: http://factorytoursusa.com

Gatorland: http://www.gatorland.com

Mall of America: http://www.mallofamerica.com

Martin Luther King National Memorial: http://www.mlkmemorial.org/

National Park Service: http://www.nps.gov

Maui Mountain Cruisers: http://www.mauimountaincruisers.com/

NASCAR: http://www.nascar.com

National Football League: http://nfl.com/

Olympic Movement: http://www.olympic.org/

Pacific Whale Foundation: http://www.pacificwhale.org

Travel Industry Association of America: http://www.tia.org

The Holy See: http://www.vatican.va/

Universal Theme Parks: http://www.universalorlando.com/

☞ Key Words and Concepts

Amusement park—Commercially operated enterprise that offers rides, games, and other forms of entertainment.

Attractions—The places we visit and the things we do while we are traveling or visiting.

Cultural tourism—Travel directed toward experiencing the arts, the heritage, and the special character of people and place.

Economic growth—An increase over time in the capacity of an economy to produce goods and services and (ideally) to improve the well-being of its citizens.

Events—Temporary attractions.

Gaming/Gambling—Casino-style activities offered on a cruise ship or at a resort.

Grand tour—A kind of education for wealthy noblemen. It was a period of European travel that could last from a few months to 8 years.

Heritage tourism—The practice of people traveling outside their home community to visit historic sites, to participate in local festivals, to enjoy local arts and crafts, sightseeing, and recreation.

Industrial attractions—Consist of operating concerns, manufacturing and agricultural, whose processes and products are of interest to visitors.

Life span—An attraction classification according to their life span or time-related criteria based on their duration.

Man-made attractions—Owe their very existence to the intervention of humans.

Museum—Typically a nonprofit, permanent institution in the service of society and of its development, open to the public, which acquires, conserves, researches, communicates, and exhibits, for purposes of study, education enjoyment, the tangible, and intangible evidence of people and their environment.

Natural attractions—Those that occur in nature without human intervention.

Nonprofit organization—Economic institution that operates like a business but does not seek financial gain.

Origin—Classifies if the attraction is natural or man-made.

Planned play environments—Provide recreation and entertainment sporting facilities, such as ski and golf resorts; commercial attractions that include theme and amusement.

Secondary attraction—Of lesser importance to the traveler, and might be considered simply a stop along the way to get to the primary attraction.

Shopping—Searching for or buying goods or services.

Status—Level of the importance or interest the attraction holds for the traveler.

Theme parks—Offer escape, as a result of modern technology they replicate both real as well as "unreal" places that may or may not exist beyond the gates.

Topography—Can be broadly subdivided into three areas of interest: *landforms*, *wildlife*, and *ecology*.

World's first national park—Yellowstone—was created in 1872.

🔖 Contributor Information

Ronald J. Cereola, JD, MBA
James Madison University
cereolrj@jmu.edu
Dr. Ronald J. Cereola is an assistant professor in the Hospitality & Tourism Management program at James Madison University, Harrisonburg, Virginia. He teaches Tourism, Hospitality Services Marketing, Hospitality Law, and Entertainment Management.

Reginald Foucar-Szocki
James Madison University
foucarrf@jmu.edu
Dr. Reg Foucar-Szocki is the JW Marriott Professor in the Hospitality & Tourism Management program at James Madison University, Harrisonburg, Virginia, where he has taught since 1989. Reg believes the world is a special event, and hospitality management is the centerpiece for success.

17 Review Questions

1. Define an attraction.

2. Explain how attractions benefit the community in which they are located. Provide an example.

3. For each of the following methods of classifying attractions, indicate the characteristics of each classification and provide an example for each type.

   a. Status

   b. Origin

   c. Life span

   d. Ownership

4. What are the methods for classifying attractions by product attributes? Provide an example for each.

5. What is the relationship between an attraction, infrastructure, and hospitality services in the surrounding area?

6. Revisit questions #3 and #4 and provide examples not found in the chapter for each.

7. Using *Google.com,* search the Internet for an attraction (as per the chapter introduction) and select one of the search results. Classify your choice using as many of the classification techniques described in the chapter as possible. Support your answer with a brief explanation for each.

Kirsten Tripodi
Fairleigh Dickinson University

Bar and Beverage Operations

Learning Objectives

To enable first-year hospitality students to:

✓ Become familiar with bar and beverage terminology
✓ Become familiar with career opportunities in bar and beverage management
✓ Understand the importance of responsibility regarding the sale of alcoholic beverages
✓ Appreciate the profitability and cost factors involved in beverage sales
✓ Gain an understanding of trends in beverage management

Chapter Outline

Glamour
Reality
Products
Profitability
Career Opportunities
The Future

The Merriam Webster On-Line Dictionary defines a bar as "a counter at which food or especially alcoholic beverages are served."[1] Bar and beverage management is considered by many to be one of the most interesting, challenging, and profitable areas of hospitality management. Many types of hospitality operations have a bar or beverage operation as part of their offerings to their guests or members. For the introductory hospitality student, the career possibilities are both varied and full of opportunity. Often relying on a substantial profit margin for the sale of alcoholic beverages, beverage operations are often very lucrative.

Glamour

Bar and beverage operations are connected to entertainment in many ways. Indeed, the act of going to a bar is a form of social entertainment. Many bars offer entertainment, which may be as simple as darts or as complicated as full-blown live entertainment productions of world-famous artists. The bar business has a glamorous side, which can be enticing. Working at night in a fast-paced part of the industry that caters to (and often hires) beautiful people who have disposable income can be like living in another world for many. Often, a lot of cash is changing hands, and for tipped employees, there is certainly a great deal of money to be made. Contact with entertainers and interesting promotional possibilities are perks. Due to the unique nature of alcoholic beverages, the legal implications and the control issues involved in its sale make this area of hospitality challenging. Success given these challenges is a sign to future employers that you have exhibited all the skills of a great hospitality manager in a fast-paced and competitive environment, that is to say, it is a great proving ground.

Like other segments of the hospitality industry, many students and the public are familiar with bar and beverage operations as guests. We see the entertainment and fun that guests are exposed to. Bar and beverage managers, like most other hospitality managers, are often too busy to enjoy the environment at work that they once enjoyed as a guest.

Reality

Alcohol Is a Drug

Many bar and beverage operations depend on the sale of alcoholic beverages. Alcohol is a legalized drug that can very much alter a person's perception of reality. Alcohol is addictive, and certain ingredients in some alcoholic beverages have hallucinogenic properties (absinthe, gin, and tequila). As a host in your home, you would never put a guest into

The act of going to a bar is a form of social entertainment.

a situation in which they might hurt themselves or someone else. This responsibility is the same for the guest/host relationship in a hospitality business situation. Serving alcohol changes that relationship to enhance the level of responsibility. As business owners and managers, we have a social responsibility not only to our guests, but also to society at large regarding the serving of alcohol.

Legal Responsibilities

In addition to the social responsibility and the guest/host relationship, there are legal requirements regarding the service of alcohol. Hospitality businesses in the United States are subject to a duty of care for guests and the public that has evolved under the common law from the inns of England in the Middle Ages.[2] Dram shop legislation refers to the legal onus on the provider of the alcoholic beverage. In the case of an injury that was caused by an intoxicated person, alcohol is considered to be so reality altering that the person is not held responsible for their own actions. The results of the actions of an intoxicated person are rather the legal responsibility of the provider of those beverages.

Many companies take this responsibility very seriously. In addition to in-house training, many have opted for additional training by experts in Responsible Alcohol Service. Generally, these programs include certification for employees who have passed an exam of some sort. Using a recognized program of this sort can mean substantial savings in terms of liability insurance, as the insurer recognizes that the business has taken steps to train employees to be aware of the consequences and legal ramifications of irresponsible alcohol service.

Managing a Cash Business

A business that involves cash is full of opportunities for employees to make costly mistakes or to be less than honest. Checks and balances must always be in place, and managers must be aware and proactive whenever possible. There are techniques for controlling costs, which range from computer regulated shots, which cannot be activated unless a sale is rung into an interfaced POS terminal, to enforcing the proper use of measured portions (shot glasses or measured pourers) to management vigilance. From a marketing standpoint, guests in certain types of establishments may be adverse to some of the more mechanized controls.

Theft

Regular inventory reconciliation is a commonly used technique for controlling costs. The drawback of using this method is that it is reactive rather than proactive, which is to say that it can only detect a problem after it has occurred. Security systems and surveillance equipment can also be used to reduce theft via pilferage or overpouring. It is important that these systems work together and work well in combination with the management teams' vigilance. There can be no substitute for awareness and constant training for all members of the staff. The nature of the inventory makes it inviting. Who wouldn't want a nice bottle of champagne in their refrigerator for a special occasion, especially one that did not cost anything? The unauthorized taking of inventory constitutes theft. This is referred to as pilferage if the item is stolen for consumption by an employee. Managers must also be aware that there are more ways for employees to steal. Overpouring (using more than the recipe amount of the alcohol for a beverage) constitutes a loss for the business and is theft. Tipped employees can be encouraged to add more to a beverage in return for a bigger gratuity. Left unchecked, tipped employees can even give drinks away.

A competent manager will also be aware that employees who are completely honest can cost a business profit through sloppiness (waste) and poor training (poor knowledge of recipes and standards).

Licensing

In the United States alcohol sales are regulated by individual states, which often allow municipalities to issue licenses and determine laws so long as those laws exist within the confines of any existing state regulations. In most states, background checks are completed regarding those applying for such a license to determine that those persons are of acceptable character.[3] The number and locations of licenses are often stipulated per municipality. There is a certain distance that any establishment must be from churches and schools. Quite often, liquor licenses are very expensive and can be revoked for a number of violations. Once revoked, it sometimes cannot be replaced, and the business will suffer. Serving minors or the already intoxicated can cause a licensing problem, but so can paying your bills late or failing to keep adequate records regarding sales and purchases of alcoholic beverages. The rights to a license must be protected at all times by the owners, managers, and staff of an establishment serving alcoholic beverages.

Opportunities to BYO (Bring your own) beverages do exist in many venues. Corkage fees can also be charged by an operation that holds a license to sell alcoholic beverages, should a guest prefer to bring their own selection of beverage into the establishment. Of course in a BYO situation, the legal responsibilities vary from municipality to municipality.

Licensing regulations and requirements may vary from state to state in the United States, therefore the prudent beverage manager will always have a copy of those regulations on premises for reference and will be familiar with them.

Products

Many different products are sold in beverage operations. As with sales positions in any other industry, the most knowledgeable salespersons can offer the best information and service to their guests.

Wine

Wine is an alcoholic beverage made from fermented grapes. It is sold around the world and has gained in popularity in the past two decades. Wines vary from "dry" to "sweet." Dry refers to the absence of sweetness. Wines can also be distinguished by the grape from which they are made or the year the grapes were grown and harvested (vintage). A varietal is a wine that is made primarily from one grape. In general, white wines are made from white (green) grapes and are usually served cold. Red wines are made from red grapes and are served at room temperature. Particular years in certain geographic locations are either ideal or less than ideal for the harvesting of these grapes. An ideal year will create a better wine, which can demand a higher price. Truly ideal vintages (years) age well, which means that the wines can get better with age, if stored properly. Depending on the quality of the vintage and the wine, at a certain point the wine will deteriorate, so it is important for collectors and beverage managers who are responsible for aging (cellaring) to be very knowledgeable about the products they are responsible for.

As you might expect, sparkling wines have gas (bubbles) and a different cork to manage that carbonation. Sparkling wines made in certain regions around the world may carry the name of that region, as does champagne and Asti, or they may be referred to as sparkling wines. They are served chilled and often offered for celebratory occasions.

Blush wines are a light pink color and are served chilled.

Fortified Wine

Sherries, ports, marsalas, and madieras are wines that have brandy added to them. They are usually offered alone in a glass after dinner. These alcoholic beverages are also popular as commonly used ingredients in cooking.

Beer

"Beer is a generic term for all alcoholic beverages that are fermented and brewed from malted barley, hops, water and yeast."[4] Beer is the largest-selling alcoholic beverage in the world. Beer is served ice cold in the United States, but many draught beers from the United Kingdom are meant to be served at room temperature. Beer is served in bottles or on draught. The bottles take up a great deal of space and can add significant cost or recycling issues to the beverage manager's day. Draught beer is more profitable, but the systems and storage required can be costly to add if not planned for when the establishment is being built or renovated.

Coffee

Coffee is a brewed beverage that has gained in popularity in the past 10 years. An entire industry has developed around this beverage. Cafes, storefronts, and retail operations feature some derivation of this non-alcoholic beverage served at a substantial profit.

Spirits

There is usually a selection of each category of spirits available at different price points. House brands, sometimes referred to as well brands as they are positioned in the well or speed rail for maximum efficiency (close reach for the bartenders), are the least expensive and are sold when no brand name is specified. Call brands, premium brands, and super premiums represent the alternatives to the house brands in increasing order.[5] Mixed drinks or cocktails often include a spirit. When the drink is simply a spirit and a mixer (soda or juice most often), the drink can be referred to as a highball.

White spirits are defined by the fact that they are colorless. This group of spirits includes vodka, gin, rum, and tequila. Brown spirits include whiskies of differing types. American, Canadian, Irish,

Scotch, and Bourbon are all examples of these whiskies or brown spirits. "After the process of distillation was discovered, it was inevitable that man should use the product closest at hand, easiest to obtain, and least expensive for distillation."[6]

Brandy and Cognac

Brandy is the general term for the distilled spirit of grapes. Often served after dinner, these beverages are made around the world. Cognac and Armagnac are brandies that are made in a particular geographic region of France.

Aperitifs

Aperitifs are served to stimulate the appetite. They are either spirit based or wine based and can be served chilled or at room temperature.[7]

Cordials and Liqueurs

These sweet alcoholic beverages are served after dinner, often at room temperature, but sometimes over ice (on the rocks).

Bottled Water

Health trends have had a huge impact on the bottled water market. A non-alcoholic, healthy alternative beverage, waters (both sparkling and still) have led the trend in non-alcoholic beverages. Less than 30 years ago, it was virtually unheard of for water to be paid for in a hospitality establishment. Today, bottled water has reached a point in popularity where it has become a multi-billion dollar industry.

Profitability

Cost Control

"A beverage list (covering beer, wine, and distilled spirits) must be given the same careful thought and attention to detail and market trends that is involved in the planning of a food menu."[8] Balancing the size of the inventory with the needs of the guests can be a difficult task. Increasing inventory (either levels or variety) means that more of the operation's funds are tied up in the storeroom and not immediately earning money. Preventing loss and theft require constant vigilance, control systems, and proper pricing techniques.

Katsigris and Porter, in their book, *Pouring for Profit*, identified several necessary steps to control-

ling costs and profit in beverage management. Budgeting for profit, pricing for profit, establishing product controls, and establishing cash controls are all vital parts of the control process, which requires an in-depth understanding of the operation at hand, the market, the product, and security.[9]

Pricing Trends

"The well-known fact that the price of two martinis in the average bar will buy a whole bottle of gin or vodka at the liquor store, if you wish to drink at home, is indicative of what the bar business is all about."[10] The price of a drink is determined by the cost of the drink. This means that the recipe for the drink and the cost of each individual ingredient must be considered. Mixers, such as juices and sodas, cost significantly less than does alcohol, so the cost of the bottle divided by the portion of the bottle used will determine the bulk of the cost for most drinks. The price is then based on the profit margin that a facility requires to cover its overhead costs and the profit that the owners desire. This must also be balanced with the demands of the market.

Beer, particularly draught (on tap) beer, can cost less than $.25 for a 16 oz. portion (pint), and sell for $1.50 to $5.00 depending on the establishment. Wine is often marked up two and one-half times at the low end (house brands) to one-half times for a high-end wine. Recently there has been a trend toward limiting the markup for wines to a more acceptable level given that the public is more aware of the pricing of wines at retail than ever before.

Career Opportunities

From attractions management to travel and tour operations, every chapter in this book is connected to bar and beverage operations in some way. Attractions such as Disney World and beach destination resorts quite often offer alcoholic or some type of non-alcoholic beverage service for their guests. Beverage service is usually available in private clubs for their members. Full-service hotels have lounges, restaurants, banquet and meeting facilities, room service, and minibar operations. Restaurants and private clubs also have available alcoholic beverages for their guests, as do some noncommercial food-service operations. Corporate dining rooms and catering operations usually include beverage service as do the vendors in airports and stadiums. It is hard to imagine a successful casino or cruise line that is not

Working as a bartender is a great way to earn money while in school, and add experience to your resume.

able to provide alcoholic beverages. Various methods of transportation from airlines to trains and even charter buses often proffer alcoholic beverages.

During School

For many students and indeed for hospitality students, bar and beverage operations are a great way to earn money while you're still in school. Work schedules can often be made flexible to accommodate class schedules, and gratuities can help to defray the cost of tuition or add to spending money. Bar backs, bartenders, minibar attendants, and cocktail servers as well as baristas are the entry-level line positions usually available. These positions require some knowledge about serving differing types of beverages. Bartenders and bar backs are usually found behind a "front bar" that is in view of guests and often has seating for guests. There are also service bars, where only employees of the establishment can order drinks for the guests in the restaurant, lounge, or room service. Bartenders mix the

drinks and are sometimes referred to as mixologists. Bar backs support the bartenders by leaving the bar to restock supplies; this way the bartenders can always be available to guests. Cocktail servers are out "on the floor" in a lounge environment; they order drinks from the bartender for their guests at the table. Minibar attendants restock the in-room refrigerators that have beverages and snacks in higher end hotels. These attendants are responsible to report the guest usage so that the guest can be properly charged. Baristas are found in a coffee bar or juice bar. Both types of non-alcoholic beverages have grown in popularity and availability in the past ten years. Companies such as Starbucks and Jamba Juice lead this part of the industry.

Customer service skills honed in this type of establishment in conjunction with the knowledge of the beverages served are useful skills to fall back on for the rest of your life. Particularly for hospitality students, this is a challenging beginning to a rewarding career.

After Graduation

Entry-level supervisory positions in the area of beverage management can be found in virtually all the types of operations in hospitality. In a large hotel or casino, there might be several layers of management after that initial position. In smaller operations a beverage career can successfully morph into a food and beverage career for a more mature, full-service manager, who will have more comprehensive management responsibilities. High-end wines are usually sold in full-service restaurants that employ wine consultants (sommeliers) who are experts. These sommeliers work for the establishment ordering the wine and managing the wine list and are tipped for their advice to the guests as well as salaried employees. Sommeliers are highly specialized employees who usually hold a credential that identifies them as experts.

Beverage management is a long-term career for a select few. The demands of the late night hours are more conducive to a younger, single management team.

Several core competencies are critical for success in beverage management. Cleanliness, friendliness, awareness of potential problems, and knowledge of products and services are all important. Having a great eye for detail and great interpersonal communication skills are a must in this part of the industry as they are in all other segments of hospitality.

The Future

In his book, *How to Manage a Successful Bar*, Christopher Egerton-Thomas asserts, "[T]he future trend is fairly easy to guess. The health industry will not go away. Countries that are not traditionally wine suppliers are getting into bold, massive, well-organized stride in their search for world markets."[11] It certainly seems as though the trend toward health has changed the beverage industry forever. After the controversial *60 Minutes* segment on the relative health of the French people and their diet, many medical journals have reported on the health benefits of wine in moderation. Water and non-alcoholic beverages, particularly those made with fresh fruits and vegetables, have gained in popularity and are not likely to decline in a health-aware market. As the population ages, these trends are likely to expand rather than contract.

For the beverage professional it is critical to remain on the cutting edge at all times. This is perhaps best achieved by reading trade journals and keeping up with technological breakthroughs by attending trade shows and speaking with vendors on a regular basis.

Summary

This chapter is just a brief overview of bar and beverage management. Many hospitality programs offer one or more courses in this exciting area of the hospitality industry. Hopefully, this introduction will inspire you to learn more, both while you are a student and afterward.

Bar and beverage management is an exciting and sometimes glamorous area to specialize in the hospitality industry. Due to the nature of the products (often alcohol), managing this type of hospitality operation can be more challenging than others in many ways. Management positions are available opportunities in virtually every type of hospitality operation.

Endnotes

1. *Merriam-Webster's on-line dictionary*. (n.d.). Retrieved January 22, 2006 from http://www.m-w.com/dictionary/BAR
2. Jeffries, J., and Brown, B. *Understanding Hospitality Law, (4th ed.)* East Lansing, MI: Educational Institute of the American Hotel & Lodging Association, 2001
3. Egerton-Thomas, C. *How to Manage a Successful Bar*. New York: John Wiley and Sons, 1994
4. Lipinski, B., & Lipinski, K. *Professional Beverage Management*. New York: John Wiley and Sons, Inc., 1996, p. 191
5. Egerton-Thomas, C. *How to Manage a Successful Bar*
6. Grossman, H., Revised by Harriet Lembeck. *Grossman's Guide to Wines, Beers, and Spirits*, 1983, John Wiley & Sons, Inc.
7. Lipinski and Lipinski, *Professional Beverage Management*
8. Lipinski and Lipinski, *Professional Beverage Management*, p. 288
9. Katsigris, C. and Porter, M. *Pouring for Profit: A Guide to Bar and Beverage Management*. New York: John Wiley & Sons, 1983
10. Egerton-Thomas, C. *How to Manage a Successful Bar*, John Wiley and Sons, 1994, p. 7
11. Ibid., p. 135
12. Jeffries and Brown, *Understanding Hospitality Law*, p. 3
13. Ibid
14. Barth, S., Hayes, D., and Ninemeier, J. *Restaurant Law Basics*. New York: John Wiley & Sons, 2001, p. 224

Resources
Responsible Alcohol Training Sites

The Bar Code Program by the Educational Foundation of the National Restaurant Foundation: http://foodserviceworkforce solutions.com/content.asp?topicID=75&contentID=616

ServSafe Alcohol offered by the Educational Foundation of the National Restaurant Foundation: http://www.nraef.org/servsafe/alcohol/book/

TIPS (*Training for Intervention ProcedureS*): http://www.gettips.com/index.shtml

Non-Alcoholic Beverages

Jamba Juice: http://jambajuice.com/

Starbucks: http://www.starbucks.com/default.asp?cookie%5Ftest=1

Credentials

Master Sommelier Program: https://www.mastersommeliers.org/apply;jsessionid=EC30F11F427EE2ACC42AAB6A79
FFABB1

☞ Key Words and Concepts

BYO—Bring your own beverage to a public establishment that is not licensed to sell it.

Cellaring—The process of storing a wine that will age to a better, more drinkable, and mellow wine.

Core competencies—Those skills that are necessary for success.

Corkage—A fee charged to bring your own beverage selection if it is not available at the establishment. This is ostensibly used to cover the cost of the beverage service (glasses, ice…) or the profit that would be gained from a sale and/or the ownership of the license.

Cost control—The ability to maintain a profit based on proper ordering and securing inventories before, during, and after their sale.

Common law—A system where the courts can apply the "generally accepted rules and principles enunciated by courts in earlier similar cases."[12]

Dram shop legislation—Statutory (as opposed to common law) cause of action against the provider of alcoholic beverages for those who are injured as a direct result of the intoxication.[13]

Duty of care— "A legal obligation requiring a particular standard of conduct."[14]

In-house training—That training provided by the company, usually by the management team as a normal part of the training process of a new employee.

Inventory reconciliation—A physical count of inventory that is matched to the sales figures to determine discrepancies that can point to problems with the control systems.

Liability insurance—Most businesses carry liability insurance in case of accident. If you have auto insurance, this is a type of liability insurance coverage. Some businesses are self-insured, which means that they have to absorb the costs of legal judgments or settlements.

Minibar—In-room units (usually refrigerators) that contain snacks and beverages for the guest's convenience at a charge. These are found in full-service hotels.

"On the floor"—An expression to indicate the sales floor or where food and beverages are sold. Usually refers to the area where guests can sit at the tables.

POS terminal—Often referred to as a cash register, this type is connected to a computer system that manages the revenue. POS stands for point of sale, and there may be many terminals in one operation.

Price points—The set pricing for categories of beverages that, when compared to the costs to the establishment, determine the cost percentages, hence the profit margins for those categories.

Profitability—What is left over from a sales transaction after all the costs are deducted is the profit. Profitability is the measure of how a business performs financially.

Shot—A measure of alcohol to be used in a recipe. Standards of measure may differ from establishment to establishment, but 1 oz., $1\frac{1}{4}$ oz., or 2 oz. are often used. To control costs and ensure consistency, a shot glass or jigger can be used or a measured pourer.

Social responsibility—Alcohol so alters one's perception of reality that it is not responsible to allow an intoxicated person to be put into a position where they could harm themselves or someone else. The sale or service of alcohol creates a social responsibility to both the guest and society at large to act in a manner to protect everyone from harm.

Sommelier—A wine expert employed by a beverage serving establishment to help the guests select the best wine for their meal.

Spirits—Alcoholic beverages also known as hard liquor. This category includes gins, vodkas, tequilas, rums, and whiskies (all types).

🎨 *Contributor Information*

Kirsten Tripodi is the Director of Professional Development Metropolitan Campus/ Professor—International School of Hospitality and Tourism Management, Fairleigh Dickinson University. She can be reached at kirsten@fdu.edu

Kirsten Tripodi has more that 25 years of hospitality operations experience.

Professor Tripodi has worked in various capacities including Restaurant Associates (Rockefeller Center); The Ritz-Carlton (Central Park South and Buckhead); and The Mayfair Regent (Park Ave.). Professor Tripodi specialized in food and beverage operations and training for most of her career.

Professor Tripodi earned her master's degree from Cornell University's School of Hotel Administration. She is currently pursuing her PhD in Higher Education at Seton Hall University.

18 Review Questions

1. Why is it important that alcohol is considered to be a drug?

2. What are some steps that a responsible company can take to ensure that alcohol is being served responsibly?

3. What are the benefits to being socially responsible regarding the service and sale of alcoholic beverages?

4. What is the most effective sales tool for beverages?

5. Given so many "harsh realities" to balance the glamour of the beverage business, why do you suppose that it remains a popular career path for hospitality graduates?

6. Why do you suppose non-alcoholic beverage establishments were included in this chapter?

7. What are some current trends that may give us a clue as to the future of this segment of the industry?

8. How can a beverage manager stay abreast of changes in the industry that can affect their business?

19

Kathryn Hashimoto
Sensei Associates

Casinos

Learning Objectives

✓ To develop some objective facts about the casino industry
✓ To understand the differences between casinos and other organizations
✓ To comprehend the layers of a casino organizational structure
✓ To understand that especially casinos have different levels of service for different customers

Chapter Outline

Differences between Casino Operations and Traditional Hospitality Enterprises
Organizational Structure
Power Structures
Levels of Service

*W*hy learn about casinos? Don't all hospitality operations run pretty much the same way? Well, not exactly. Certainly, a good manager can function in many environments. However, this industry has some differences that are important to understand. We'll begin externally by examining the impact of casinos on the surrounding communities and then examine the internal organizational and power structures. Have you heard the one about all guests are created equal? Not in a casino. Think you might want to work in one? Let's talk about the possibilities at the end of the chapter.

Casinos are a unique industry because their reputation has been less than socially acceptable. However, despite this perception, the American casino business has grown by leaps and bounds. The casino industry came of age in 2005 by following the trends of manufacturing corporations, and several companies merged creating three of the largest gaming companies in the country: Harrah's Entertainment and Caesars, MGM Mirage and Mandalay Resort, and Penn National Gaming and Argosy. When politicians see the amount of money generated by the gaming industry, everyone wants a piece of the action. As a result, legislators push to have gambling legalized. In the year 2005, more than 445 commercial casinos were operating in 11 states generating nearly 29 billion dollars in gross gaming revenue. This was up 7 percent from the previous year. In addition, some form of casino gaming was approved in 30 states across the country. These casinos hired over 350,000 direct employees who earned more than $12 billion in wages.[1]

Gaming can be an economic gold mine in other ways, as well. Typically, gambling establishments begin by developing an infrastructure to bring in outsiders to the area. In fact, the trend in casino development moves toward increasing amenities with more restaurants, shopping complexes, spas, and world entertainment venues. In fact, over twice as many casino visitors say they come for the food, shows, and entertainment than for the gaming.[2] This creates jobs for the locals and generates many different tax bases for the government. Then, to meet the needs of the visitors, the new tax revenues are used to improve the infrastructures that support the traffic. As the commercial base expands, new businesses open to support the growing number of tourists and locals. As a result, gaming is a very strong economic development tool. Casino development creates an upward spiral that increases jobs,

adds more taxes from businesses and tourists, and decreases taxes for the townspeople. When residents see the projected economic impact, the positive aspects of gaming are impressive.

However, as with any growth in tourism, this expansion comes with costs. The main problem is rooted in the business itself. Casinos generate millions of dollars a day in hard currency. For example, to convert the customers' paper money to chips and back again, the casinos have many areas called "cages." They act as mini-banks. However, on average, one cage may have five million dollars in cash. That does not even include all the money that is on the tables, in the slot machines, or on the patrons!

Think about being around that kind of money! Does it make you contemplate some different ideas? Everyone does. This brings about the negative aspects of the industry. It is perfectly normal to watch millions of dollars changing hands and think what it would be like to have some of it for your very own. Politicians, employees, customers, or local people are not exempt from this fantasy. Because of the enormous amount of money all in one place, organized crime has always been reputed to be a part of

Casinos generate millions of dollars every day in hard currency.

gambling. This resulted in bribery and graft in politicians and criminal activity like money laundering and illegal criminal operations, creating a negative image for gambling. However, as more respectable business people like Howard Hughes and Baron Hilton invested their money in these properties, casinos gained respectability. Although the criminal background will always be part of the excitement of a casino, strict regulations on employees and owners, as well as the large business conglomerates, have helped to alter the reality.

There are two main problems for employees and players: wanting the casino's money and spending too much of your own. Some people want the cash they see in the casinos. If they cannot win it, stealing is another option. This is one of the perceived problems that many anti-gaming advocates use to deter people from voting for gaming. They assume that crime increases in the areas where casinos operate. This is simple logic. With any increase in population density, problems are going to arise. On the other hand, with some more thought, this becomes counterintuitive. Casino owners understand that this open display of cash is a temptation. Therefore, security and surveillance are a major part of any casino operation to deter people from thinking along these lines for too long. The casinos do not want big winners to get robbed because it is bad for business. People who do not feel secure are not going to come back. Reinforcing this premise are newer longitudinal studies that show crime increases during the introductory phases of casino development, but then the rates actually decrease over the long term.

The second aspect of the money problem revolves around the fact that some people get caught up in trying to win the jackpot and stay too long. A select few will become pathological gamblers. Problem gamblers tend to follow similar patterns. Usually, they win big early in their careers, and then they chase their losses. This means that if you lose, you double the bet to get the money back. This is a bad strategy and rapidly increases gambling debts. However, less than 2 percent of the population is at risk of becoming addicted. Some researchers have stretched this percentage to 40 percent to 50 percent of the population. However, the key point to remember is that it all depends on how you define problem. Is it when you spend $10 more than you budgeted or is it when you steal to get money to gamble? Keep in mind that this is a very small percent of the population. On the whole, over 98 per-

cent of the people who come to a casino will not suffer any ill effects from the experience. Because of the large amounts of money generated, gaming has inherent bonuses and risks. Understanding both sides of the issues is important for each person so that they can decide how they stand.

Differences between Casino Operations and Traditional Hospitality Enterprises

Controlling the Money

With all these people spending their cash, the primary focus of casino management is to track the money. With $100 bills and $10,000 chips floating around the floor, controlling and securing the flow of cash is the name of the game. Computers, accounting departments, security, and surveillance are very important in this process. With all this money, there is a serious temptation to walk away with cash that is not yours. Therefore, the organizational structure is set up to accommodate the primary directive: track the money.

Accountants use computers to access credit information and verify customer accounts. Casino floor people can quickly determine credit lines for vouchers by searching the computer online or calling the credit department. Because money watching is the most important activity in the casino, accounting terminology is important. When casinos talk about profits, they describe them in terms of the process. For example, the "drop" is the total amount of cash plus the value of the markers (credit slips) the casino takes in. This is similar to gross revenues. However, the "handle" is the total amount of money that has continuously changed hands before it is actually won or lost. For example, a person can start with $5, then win $45, and lose $50. The casino counts it as a "handle" of $100. However, the casino "win" for this person would be "0." "Win" is comparable to net revenues.

Why is this important? This is part of tracking the money. The money has to be accounted for each time it changes hands. If a casino cannot follow the money trail, they may be losing cash without knowing it. To begin the process, patrons can play with dollars or they can exchange the dollars for chips. Chips are easier to use. For example, $10,000 converts instantly into a single chip. It's definitely less bulky to carry around the casino. Also, the casinos would like you to carry around the chips. It makes it easier for them to keep track of their money. Psychologically, the chips make sense for the casinos. When a person throws a chip onto the table, the gambler does not perceive it as "money." Spending chips operates on the same psychological principles as credit cards. Signing a piece of paper does not "feel" like spending money. On the other hand, handing over $100 bills to a clerk empties your wallet, and you know you have spent your paycheck. The last step in tracking the money is when the customer leaves the casino. Gamblers must cash in their remaining chips because you cannot play in one casino with chips from another "house" (casino). This allows the casino to track the cash flow from the time it enters the casino to the final moment when the gambler leaves.

Following the money trail also means a big job for security and surveillance. The temptation to cheat the casino is particularly strong, and stealing is not just limited to the clients. Think of it. You are a dealer. In front of you could be stacks of chips worth $250,000 in different denominations. One chip, the size of a half dollar, is worth $5,000. Okay. You are an honest person, and you have a code of ethics that says you do not steal from other people. Then you get in a car accident and need a car, but you haven't saved enough money to buy one. If you took just one chip . . . a small one . . . $5,000 . . . that's small money for a casino, and it would help you get back on your feet again. Would you be tempted? The assumption is that anyone would.

Therefore, the casino has two departments to watch everyone. These are the security and surveillance, or "eye in the sky," departments. The security people walk the casino floor and make sure everything is aboveboard. Their surveillance counterparts are in an office above the gaming floor. They watch hundreds of cameras embedded in the ceiling of the casino. Every square inch of the casino can be watched, photographed, and recorded on videotape. Surveillance can zoom into a table and read the face of a coin at that table. A call to security can have cheaters picked up on the floor. Anytime there is trouble, surveillance can rewind and view what happened on the casino floor. Also, there are customer safety people who help protect the customers. As we said before, it is very tempting to palm a $50,000 chip, so security and surveillance people design procedures to minimize the risk.

Organizational Structure

In addition, because everyone is watching everyone else, the hierarchy of power in the casino comprises several layers to act as additional security. All levels of management are responsible for making sure no one under him is taking money that does not belong to him. Typically, there are two main divisions with many layers of management: table games and slots.

Table Games

We define table games as any game played on a table. This encompasses the most prevalent games like blackjack, baccarat (*bah-ka-ra*), roulette, and craps that are played against the house (casino). The front-line personnel for the table games are the dealers, who are responsible for keeping the games moving and for making sure the games are played according to the rules. They also watch the games for players who cheat. For each two to four tables, there is a floor person, who looks for irregularities and handles most customer conflicts. Several floor people and their respective dealers work in an area called the "pit." The pit boss is the most senior gaming supervisor in the pit. This person is responsible for maintaining the record of customer activity and handling the financial accounting like fills, credits, and closing inventory. A fill is when a table needs more chips. Overlooking all the different pits is the shift manager. He/she does the scheduling, oversees the operations for a specific time, and supervises the floor and dealers. Finally, there is the casino manager. Status reports, radical changes in operations, suspicions of misconduct, personnel, and long-term planning are the domains of the casino manager. Because of these layers, the games are well protected.

Slots

Traditionally, the table games were where the "real" gamblers played, usually men. However, casino operators realized that wives and girlfriends needed something to do while the men gambled. Otherwise, the women would get bored and insist that the men leave the games before they were ready to go. Slot machines were the perfect decoys. The women could sit, chat, and "pretend" to gamble in a ladylike fashion. These are games that include slots, video poker, and other computerized games. Because computers have revolutionized the industry, all the table games in the casino usually have a video

Slot machines were initially designed to keep women occupied, but have become a huge profit center for casinos.

equivalent. Instead of playing around a table with a dealer, the computer chip is the competition. This is less threatening for novices, and it gives them a chance to practice the games. Some machines allow a person to play any table game at a single machine. The screens are user friendly and touch sensitized for game selection. The quarter slots are the most popular denomination. If you think that's not much, imagine four spins per minute . . . 240/hour . . . more than 1,000 in less than five hours . . . with three coins in a 25-cent machine, that's 75 cents per spin . . . in less than five hours, a person could wager $750 on a quarter slot machine. In the high stakes groupings, there are slots for $5, $25, $100, or $500. As it turns out, slots have become a bigger profit center than anyone could have imagined. In many casinos, slot machines account for 60 percent to 70 percent of the win. (Remember win? It does NOT refer to how much the gambler wins.) As casino managers realize this is a gold mine, more slots are added to the casino floor.

Slot departments have several layers of managers. On the floor, the slot attendants supervise an assigned area to cater to customer needs like change, payouts, and problems with the machines. Slot shift managers are in charge for a specific period and oversee slot personnel, verify major slot payoffs, and sign major jackpot slips. Finally, the slot manager handles slot operations, verifies authenticity of major payouts, looks for unusual variations in op-

erations, and works on promotional programs. Each manager has the responsibility of making sure the patrons have gambling change and ensuring the safety and honesty of each machine.

The primary goal of casino management is to follow the money. With cash being the primary product of a casino, it is imperative that many layers of management be used to ensure the honesty of everyone involved. More management positions are available as a result.

Power Structures

In any organization, the department that directly brings in revenues is considered a profit center. This means that they have more control in the everyday operations than other departments. In the hotel, the rooms division directly generates the money, and therefore, they are the most influential. What happens when a rooms division manager moves to a casino/hotel? Many casino operations use rooms and F&B as marketing tools or "comps." "Comps" are free items that players can receive as bonuses for playing at the casino. Therefore, in casino/hotels, the rooms division manager does not always have control over how many rooms are in inventory or what price the clients will pay. There must always be a block of rooms for "comping"; therefore, 100 percent occupancy is *not* optimal planning. The casinos like to have a certain percentage, say 10 percent of the room inventory, available at all times. As a result, the power positions, types of responsibilities, and goals will change when a person moves from a traditional hotel to a casino/hotel.

Levels of Service

Comps

Depending on how much money you wager, the casino has different levels of service and rewards. Like other hospitality operations, casinos treat each patron according to their level of involvement. However, casinos offer a much wider variety of services for free ("comps"), and the level of service can be radically different. "Comps" are based on a special formula that each casino generates. To create the information, they have to track a player's "action" or amount of play. When a casino "tracks" a player, they watch and record information like length of time at the casino, amount of money wagered, how often they come, and credit line. Because this is a time-consuming, labor-intensive process, historically high rollers (people who bet large sums of money) were the only ones who received ratings and, therefore, "comps." However, with the age of computers, the casino generates player information quickly and easily. Therefore, they can track any individual for "comps." Although they rate each person individually, casinos can categorize levels of "comps" to three major groups of people.

Low Rollers

"Low rollers" are people who play the nickel, dime, and quarter slots. They only gamble small amounts of money. For example, bus programs were created to accommodate low rollers and can include round-trip bus fare, $20 in tokens for the slot machines, and a complimentary lunch at the buffet. Although this might seem like an extravagance for the casinos, it pays off. On average, each person on the bus will leave approximately $40 to $50 of their own money at the casino. This is the McDonald's principle. Price low, but sell volumes.

Middle Rollers

This relatively new category of player was added with the arrival of computers. Previously, casinos ignored these players because there were too many of them, and it was hard to find a way for the casino people to keep track of them all. Now players can request that they be "tracked" at the casino's Players' Club. The casino immediately puts personal information into the computer and hands back a Player's Club Card. All a gambler has to do is insert the card into each slot machine he/she plays. Once inserted, the gambler's personal information file keeps track of play. It also keeps track of playing time, machines used, and amount bet. So no matter where the customer goes in the casino, management can follow their "action."

High Rollers

"High rollers" are people who gamble large amounts of money at the tables. At one casino in Las Vegas, there is a penthouse suite with 10,000 square feet of floor space, a butler, a swimming pool, Jacuzzi, and an optional chef. To expedite the "high roller's" request, there is a special casino person called a "host." The sole purpose of the host is to be available for a particular high roller while he/she is in town and make sure that everything is in order. "Instant gratification" is the name of the game. They will obtain anything for this guest on demand, no questions asked. Everything is "comped." In addition to free room and board, casinos invite "high rollers" on "junkets." These are special event parties where the casinos obtain top seats to heavyweight title fights, Super Bowl games, or professional golf tournaments. The casino will invite these "high rollers" to join them, free, provided that they spend a certain number of hours playing at the casino. So as you can see, they treat "high rollers" with a great deal of respect and lots of service. The levels of service can be met because they carefully track the money. Each patron is followed around the casino, and the casino notes and documents each monetary action with employees and computers. The number of different managers and marketing people guarantee that each person will be treated to the level of their spending habits.

Summary

To evaluate this business effectively, one must understand two relationships: (1) the pros and cons of gaming as an industry and (2) the differences between the traditional hospitality operations and a casino-driven one. Of course, this chapter has only dealt with the casino positions that are different from the traditional hospitality operations. There are still all the regular positions in marketing, accounting, and human resources, etc. Because of the multiple layers of managers, there are many opportunities for people who want to be a part of this industry. The main thing to keep in mind when evaluating a career in gaming: money is the product. As a result, this makes it different from other hospitality operations. Knowledge about the industry is the first step to making good career choices.

Endnotes

1. Chalmers, W. (2005). *2005 State of the Industry Report.* The Governor's Conference on Tourism, Las Vegas, NV, December 18, 2005
2. Ibid

Resources

Internet Sites

www.foxwoods.com
www.mohegansun.com
www.casinocareers.com
www.harrahs.com
www.bellagio.com
www.theborgata.com
www.state.nj.us/casinos
www.wynnlasvegas.com
www.americangaming.org
www.indiangaming.org
www.gamingfloor.com/Associations.html

☞ Key Words and Concepts

Casino manager

Chips

Comps

Dealers

Drop

"Eye in the sky"

Fill

Floor person

Handle

High rollers

Low rollers

Middle rollers

Pit

Pit Boss

Security department

Shift manager

Slot attendants

Slot manager

Slot shift managers

Slots

Surveillance department

Table games

Win

📇 Contributor Information

khashimo@uno.edu.
Before teaching in marketing and hospitality departments for 20 years, Kathryn Hashimoto managed training and marketing for resort operations for 10 years. She has edited/written three books with another three textbooks to be published in 2006 and has published/presented numerous articles on gaming. She is a full-time faculty member at the University of New Orleans.

19 Review Questions

1. Describe your opinion of casinos and their impact on society.

2. Why are legislators interested in gaming?

3. List at least five ways gaming can bring revenue to an area/state.

4. What is the history associated with crime and casinos? How is it different today?

5. What does the research show about crime in casino areas? How does this differ from perception?

6. What is the main problem for both employees and players in a casino?

7. What is meant by "chase your losses"? Is it an effective strategy?

8. What tools are used in casinos to control the money?

9. Define the following casino terms:

    a. Action

    b. Pit

    c. Fill

    d. House

    e. Handle

    f. Cage

    g. Drop

10. How do chips compare to credit cards?

11. How does a surveillance system work in the casino?

12. Who does the surveillance team watch?

13. Sketch the hierarchy of positions in the table games segment of a casino.

14. Compare and contrast the rooms division in a hotel with the rooms division in a casino.

15. What are the differences in people who are classified as:

   a. "Low rollers"

   b. "Middle rollers"

   c. "High rollers"

16. When, why, and to whom is a casino manager likely to comp room nights?

17. What is the role of the "host" assigned to a high roller?

18. What is a "junket"?

19. How has the casino industry perfected the relationship between level of service given and the level of money spent by the consumer?

20. Could other hospitality segments benefit from this service to money-spent ratio? If so, which segment(s)? Give an example.

Susan W. Arendt
Iowa State University

Catering Industry

Learning Objectives

After reading this chapter, the student will be able to:
- ✓ Define catering
- ✓ Identify skills and traits needed to be a successful caterer
- ✓ Compare and contrast on-site and off-site catering
- ✓ Describe different catering locations
- ✓ Identify potential areas of concern for a caterer
- ✓ Recognize trends in catering
- ✓ Identify professional organizations related to the catering industry

Chapter Outline

Characteristics of a Successful Caterer
Types of Catering Operations
Catered Venues
Purposes for Catering
Concerns in Catering
Benefits and Challenges in Being a Caterer
Emerging Trends
Career Path: Getting Started

Probably all of you have been introduced to the catering industry in some aspect of your life. Whether you attended a wedding where the food was catered, enjoyed a party with a catered menu, or ate a meal on an airplane, you have already experienced the catering industry. Catering is a growing segment of the hospitality industry with over 80,000 caterers in North America alone.[1]

In this chapter, you will be introduced to the catering industry, the different types of catering operations, and what it takes to be a caterer. Real-life catering examples are given, and a mini case study will engage your critical thinking skills to solve a catering dilemma.

What is a caterer? What is catering? What is the catering industry? A definition of each term is provided.

Caterer: The person or people who provide food and services.

Catering: The act of supplying and serving catered food. There are different degrees of catering from limited-service catering, where food for an occasion is provided, to full-service catering, where food and all food-related equipment, service, and even decorations and music are provided. Catering may be done on-site or off-site.

Catering Industry: An area within the foodservice industry that cuts across many segments of the industry including independent caterers, restaurants, hotels, and clubs.

Characteristics of a Successful Caterer

A caterer needs to possess many characteristics to be successful. Although food preparation is important, managing business aspects and fostering client relationships are just as important. Table 20.1 identifies several skills, knowledge, traits, and behaviors needed for successful caterers.

Planning

Planning is a major essential skill for any caterer. All aspects of the catering event must be meticulously planned according to the nature and degree of the event. This may include menu planning and preparation only or may also include setup and service of the meal. Organization skills assist with efficient and effective use of time and other resources—from an organized kitchen to an organized billing method. Both

Table 20.1 ‖ Successful Caterer Characteristics

Skills and Knowledge	Traits and Behaviors
• Planning • Organizing • Communicating • Marketing • Business skills • Cooking skills • Time management skills	• Confident • Flexible • Efficient • Dependable • Detail-oriented • Creative • Entrepreneurial • People-oriented • Handle stress • Leadership

written and oral communication skills are needed to obtain business and keep business. Catering contracts are one form of written communication, whereas face-to-face interactions with clients are an oral form of communication. Marketing food and services to attract the desired client base also is required. Business skills and knowledge, such as accounting, are needed to run a profitable catering business. Time management skills relate to timing of food preparation, transportation, and delivery.

Confidence and Flexibility

Confidence will assist a caterer in both the marketing and sales aspects of the business. A caterer must have confidence in his/her abilities and convey this to the client when selling catering services and when things do not go as the client had expected. A caterer who is flexible will have a much easier time meeting the needs of clients and running a successful catering business. Flexibility is needed because clients change their minds, because employees get ill, and because accidents do happen.

Efficiency and Attention to Detail

Efficiency is described as getting the most out of the resources utilized. Efficient caterers use their resources with care and concern. Human resources (employees) also are considered. Dependability is essential. A caterer often helps create an experience for their clients. The last thing a caterer wants the client or guests to remember is how long they had to wait to be served a meal because the caterer was late. The success of one event will sell future events for the caterer.

Great attention to detail is required. A missed serving utensil on a buffet line, a missed detail in the catering contract, or a missed turn on the drive to the service location can be costly to a caterer. Creativity in menu development, room design and layout, and food display compliment a caterer's repertoire.

Leadership

Leadership, along with an entrepreneurial sense, is needed to start, grow, and sustain a catering business. A caterer must enjoy working with and for a diverse group of people. Interacting with clients and exceeding client expectations are paramount to a successful catering business. Additionally, good working relationships with employees will help maintain an efficient and effective catering staff.

A good rule of thumb in the catering business is to expect the unexpected. Incidents such as limited water supply for handwashing at the site, not being able to locate an off-site event, or running short on food at an event can be extremely stressful. Therefore, in the catering business, the ability to handle and manage stress is essential.

Types of Catering Operations

The two primary types of catering are on-site and off-site. (These are sometimes referred to as on-premise and off-premise.) An additional type, mobile, also is addressed. The major differences between each type are where the food is prepared and where it is served.

On-Site Catering

On-site catering means the food is prepared at the same location it is served. Examples of on-site catering include hospitals, schools and universities, hotels, clubs, and attractions foodservice. Hospital foodservice departments have expanded services over the years to include catering for various meetings and events held at the hospital. These may include hospital board meetings, auxiliary functions, or fund-raising events. Schools and universities may cater small items such as a platter of cookies for a teacher's meeting to larger functions such as athletic banquets. Larger hotels generally will have conference rooms utilized for wedding parties and meetings. Generally the mandate in these operations is for meals and foods to be purchased and catered through the hotel dining department. Attraction foodservices, including zoo restaurants and cafes or museum foodservice operations, often will cater on-site for special events. Other caterers own or lease a building and will do some catered events there.

Larger hotels generally have on-site catering that is required with the use of one of their rooms.

Off-Site Catering

Off-site catering is exciting as often locations are chosen because of their beauty or the fact that they can accommodate a large number of guests. Parks, open fields, private homes, or even parking lots may be utilized. However, these sites can provide challenges for a caterer due to limited electrical service, water sources, trash facilities, working spaces, and questionable security. If an event is held outside, pest control and weather conditions also may be of concern.

Restaurants may provide off-site catering as another source of revenue. Corporate meetings and social events provide the largest opportunities for off-site catering done by restaurants. Larger grocery stores and supermarkets offer limited catering services, often providing food, beverages, and paper goods. Clients also can utilize supermarket floral departments for decorating purposes.

Off-site catering businesses can be home-based whereby the caterer produces all food and conducts business from their home. In contrast, an off-site catering business could be located in a leased or purchased space.

With off-site catering, caters may choose to use their own equipment or the client's equipment. Some caterers transport steam tables for hot holding of buffet items, utensils, guest tables, skirting, china, glassware, and flatware, all items needed for the event. Still others will provide only the food and utilize the equipment at the remote site. Of course, there are caterers that may be somewhere along this continuum and those that provide several options to clients. Still other caterers will transport food items in a variety of forms, raw and cooked. For example, a caterer doing an outside spring brunch buffet may bring most items prepared but set up an omelet or pancake station to prepare the menu item in front of the customer. This enhances the overall customer experience but can certainly pose unique challenges for the caterer.

Labor utilized at off-site catering events also varies from caterer to caterer. Some will bring their own staff to set-up, serve, and clean up. Others will provide food and minimal services while the client provides additional help needed for the event to run smoothly.

Mobile Units

Mobile catering utilizes a variety of movable units. Trucks custom built for some production and all service often are used. These trucks contain heating and holding equipment. A large window will open on the side of the truck for customer access, and some will have a picnic table attached on the back. Smaller mobile carts are used seasonally and may be manually pushed or motor operated. Street vendors often sell hot dogs, gyros, and other sandwiches from these units. The benefit of a mobile unit is the ability to sell from multiple locations so if sales are not stellar at one site, the caterer can move to a different spot. Many mobile caterers will target customers at construction sites or open-air markets due to limited competition and high customer traffic flow.

These three catering options are not distinct. A restaurant operation or other foodservice establishment may employ a dual catering strategy. They may offer both on-site and off-site catering to clients. Some caterers will have a small mobile unit that they use only seasonally but continue catering throughout the year either on- or off-premise.

Catered Venues

Generally when we think about catered events, special event celebrations and ceremonies come to mind (weddings, birthday parties, and corporate functions). Fund-raising events may be extremely elaborate (see Box 20.1) and may rely on caterers. Private parties, whether in a client's home or at a different location, are other venues for catering. Catered meals may be contracted for meetings to allow meeting participants to eat at the meeting site, which generally takes less time and is more controlled than allowing participants to leave. Airlines also utilize catering to provide meals to passengers, referred to as in-flight catering. Food preparation for in-flight catering is said to resemble a food manufacturing plant as compared to a catering kitchen.[2]

LSG SkyChefs and Gate Gourmet are two big name providers of in-flight catering. In 2005, Gate Gourmet produced an average of 534,000 meals per day.[3]

Purposes of Catering

There are several reasons a pre-existing foodservice establishment might decide to add catering to their service mix. Catering can help an establishment generate additional revenue and increase their client base. For a restaurant doing $1,000,000 in sales, the

Box 20.1
Classic Cars for Classic Kids Fund-Raiser

With the theme "You Rock, They Roll," the Classic Cars for Classic Kids Fund-Raiser was held in San Diego in November 2004 and proved a huge success.[8] The event was held at Evans' Garage of classic cars. Poodle skirts and lettermen sweaters were abundant at the event. The 50s party netted $378,000 to be used for bus service at the Preuss School, a charter school for low-income sixth through twelfth graders. Tracey Amernick, Director of Catering of Bahia Resort Hotel in San Diego, submitted this winning entry for the NACE Best Off-Premise Event (budget under $35,000).

first year of catering can add an additional $200,000 in net profits.[4]

Zoos and museums are good examples of businesses that have started catering to fund other activities. A zoo restaurant may produce food for a wedding to be held at the zoo (likewise a museum might produce food for an event on-site). Monies generated through catering can be used to cover other expenses at the zoo or museum.

Outsourcing of foodservice can provide opportunities for caterers (see Box 20.2). Outsourcing occurs when an organization does not manage their own foodservice operations but rather "contracts it out." A factory or business may not have a foodservice operation on-site or may not view providing foodservice as a primary mission to their organization. To feed hungry employees at lunchtime, a local restaurant or hotel may cater in food for the business. This is a mutually beneficial relationship and allows the corporation to concentrate on their business priorities.

Concerns in Catering

The catering industry is susceptible to various threats, which can cause concern for the caterer. A discussion of three concerns follows: financial, food safety, and governmental regulations.

Financial

A caterer or catering business has financial concerns related to expenses and revenues. A caterer must be able to forecast expenses accurately to ensure coverage of costs and still earn a profit. Expenses incurred by a caterer include insurance, rent, employee compensation, and food costs, to name a few. Appropriate pricing strategies are needed to guarantee a profit.

Collecting on client accounts to ensure revenues are realized is essential. A catering contract is the legal document between the caterer and client. The contract will specify when payment is due. Often the client will pay a deposit at the time they sign the contract. The deposit is generally a percentage of the total charges ranging from 10 percent to 50 percent.

Food Safety

Food safety is defined, as "a suitable product which when consumed orally either by human or animal does not cause health risk to consumer."[5] Like all foodservice operators, caterers must be responsible for ensuring food safety. Although catering may pose some unique challenges such as maintaining temperatures while transporting of food or holding temperatures on a buffet, these can be addressed. Good employee hygiene along with time and temperature monitoring are essential to prevent contamination of foods. For this reason, caterers will want to make certain that good hand-washing facilities are available for employees. Equipment for holding and maintaining adequate temperatures is a must. Additionally, time and temperature monitoring procedures need to be in place and enforced.

Alcohol Service

If alcohol is being provided and served by a caterer, additional concerns arise. Liquor license requirements, alcohol service legislation, and server age restrictions must be considered. Liquor license requirements vary by state; therefore a caterer should seek out information specific to their state liquor license requirements. Legislation prohibits service of alcohol to underage persons and those that are intoxicated. Servers of legal age must be properly trained and understand alcohol regulations.

Additionally, a caterer needs adequate storage facilities and equipment for alcoholic beverage service. Items including glassware, portable bars, and cooling units are needed. A reliable inventory monitoring method should also be in place to record usage and detect any suspicious inventory activity (including theft).

Governmental Regulations

A caterer must learn and understand local and state requirements regarding zoning permits, occupational license, license to sell food, health permits, and taxation to name a few. Realizing that these vary from location to location and state to state, a caterer must take initiative to find out information specific to his/her city. Federal requirements including equal opportunity employment, unemployment, immigration requirement, and taxes related to employment must be considered dependent on the size of the operation.

Benefits and Challenges in Being a Caterer

As with any profession, there are benefits and challenges to being a caterer and working in the catering industry. Being a caterer allows involvement in multiple aspects of the hospitality industry. Working in a catering department of a large hotel will likely provide opportunities in foodservice, culinary arts, lodging, decoration, design, marketing, and sales. This said, other advantages are the variety of work, variety of potential settings in which work is done, and the variety of people (both employees and clients). Benefits also are noted for the caterer who starts his/her own business and possibly works from home. Being your own boss and freedom to set your own hours make this an appealing option for some. Catering is exciting and fun work as clients are often celebrating a joyous occasion. The caterer is provided the opportunity to "take part" in this excitement by providing memorable experiences for clients and their guests.

Fluctuations in the catering business may be considered one challenge. Holidays and wedding seasons are busiest for caterers whereas business generally slows down after the first part of the year. The financial risk involved in starting and maintaining a self-owned catering business is another challenge. As with many foodservice positions, catering can require long hours and great physical demands. Some find dealing with client complaints to be a challenge, whereas others thrive on handling the day-to-day stress of catering.

Professional Organizations

The National Association of Catering Executives (NACE) promotes the catering profession while providing education and networking opportunities for its members. It is the oldest and largest catering professional organization with almost 3,000 members from the United States and Canada. Membership is available to students of junior and senior classification who are majoring in food and beverage. The NACE Web site can be accessed at www.nace.net.

Another organization, the International Caterers Association (ICA), started in 1981 and is dedicated to providing education, mentoring, and service to professional caterers. Membership is available to students as well as caterers, chefs, event planners, and

Working in the catering department of a large hotel may provide opportunities in foodservice, culinary arts, lodging, decoration, design, marketing and sales.

bridal consultants. The ICA Web site can be accessed at www.icacater.org.

Emerging Trends

The catering industry is affected by food trends and event planning trends. Food trends include ethnic cuisines and Asian Fusion. Dessert buffets with a seated and served meal, individual tableside ordering, and "Retro Desserts" are current trends.[6] Dessert buffets with seated, served meals allow guests to experience being served while given some freedom in dessert selection and reprieve from sitting. Individual tableside ordering is illustrated in Box 20.2: Pretty in Pink. Guests are given multiple menu options, which proves labor intensive for the caterer and staff. "Retro Desserts" include cherries jubilee and bananas foster that can be easily flamed, thus providing an exciting experience for guests. "Retro Desserts" are served from a station or from a rolled cart to allow guests to get an "up-close" look. Themed parties like Casino Night, Murder Mystery, and 70s Party lend themselves to themed food items also.

Career Path: Getting Started

Although there are no educational requirements to become a caterer, there are academic courses and programs that can help a caterer succeed. Some as- piring caterers choose a culinary school or program to hone their cooking skills, whereas others choose to study restaurant management, hospitality management, or business. Still others choose to go into catering after having extensive experience in the foodservice industry.

Recognize that starting a catering business will take money. Bode (2003)[9] gives these estimates for expenses and related costs:

- $1000 can get you started if you plan to utilize your home kitchen. However, it may cost $100,000 or more to equip a professional kitchen.
- Revenues between $200,000 and $2,000,000 can yield $50,000 to $1,000,000 pretax profit.

Still others note additional expenses related to transportation, noting that new refrigerated trucks cost $25,000 or more.[10]

If you choose to work for a hotel, restaurant, or other operation in catering, positions may include catering manager, catering coordinator, or conference and banquet manager. This allows you to work in the industry without assuming as much financial risk as you would if you were in business for yourself.

A student interested in catering should seek foodservice and catering work experiences or internships. Both NACE and ICA have student memberships offering valuable networking, mentoring, and educational opportunities.

Box 20.2
Nordstrom's Miami Store Grand Opening: Pretty in Pink

To celebrate their new store opening in Miami, Nordstrom's hired Joy Wallace and her team (Joy Wallace Catering Production and Design) to cater the event, Pretty in Pink.[7] There were 1,500 guests in attendance. Menu options were elaborate, including choices like petite tenderloin medallions crusted with fresh herbs and cracked pink peppercorns presented on a bed of caramelized onions; yellowtail snapper fillets rubbed with cumin, black peppercorns, sugar, and kosher salt; and saffron breast of chicken sliced and presented on a bed of candied kumquats, lemon rinds, cinnamon, cilantro, caramelized shallots, and black olives. One station included an avocado bar where guests were served a pitted avocado and given choices of toppings like sour cream, capers, and crispy red tortilla strips. Guests enjoyed special treats including Jelly Bellies, red Gummy Bears, and Red Hots. To make certain guests had a memento of the occasion; the take-home treat was a carmeled apple, nutted, sprinkled, chocolate-chipped, and wrapped in a special cellophane bag with a Nordstrom's sticker. Because the buffet tables were wrapped in hot pick vinyl, no sterno was used for fear of fire.

Summary

The catering industry is dynamic and entails more than just providing food to clients. Caterers have many options available including whether to work independently or link with a larger organization.

Caterers can be involved in providing limited services or providing a wide range of services including customizing menus, decorations, and entertainment. The opportunities are endless, and the future for catering is bright.

Case Study: Off-Site Catering

Dawn is the manager of a foodservice unit within a large midwest university dining services department. She and her staff are responsible for feeding 600 university students three meals a day while bringing in extra revenues through catering. There are other dining units within the university dining services department located across campus. The entire university dining system prepares over 15,000 meals a day for students and staff. Recently Dawn received a catering request for an upcoming football game day—a picnic for 1,000 people at the football stadium located 1 mile from her unit. Hamburgers, hot dogs, potato salad, baked beans, and condiments are on the menu. Game day arrives, and the picnic menu items are loaded on the truck for transportation to the football stadium. The aroma of hot dogs, hamburgers, and baked beans wafts through the truck. Upon arrival, Dawn and two other dining service employees begin to unload the truck slightly ahead of schedule. However, a slight mishap occurs as the beans are being rolled down the truck ramp on a cart. The employee accidentally catches the cart's wheel on the edge of the ramp and spills all the beans. Picnic service is to begin in 40 minutes.

Questions:

- What are some factors Dawn should consider before deciding what to do?
- What are Dawn's options?
- What are the advantages and disadvantages of each option?

Endnotes

1. www.icacater.org
2. Jones, P. (2004). *Flight catering* (2nd ed.). New York: Elsevier Ltd.
3. www.Gategourmet.com
4. Bode, S. (2003). *Successful catering*. Ocala, FL: Atlantic Publishing Group
5. www.fsis.usda.gov
6. Hansen, B., & Thomas, C. (2005). *Off-premise catering management* (2nd ed.). Hoboken, NJ: John Wiley & Sons
7. *ICA communicater cover story*. (2005). Retrieved November 6, 2005, from http://www.icacater.org
8. *Catered event of the year* (n.d.). Retrieved November 6, 2005, from http://www.nace.net
9. Bode, S. (2003). *Successful catering*. Ocala, FL: Atlantic Publishing Group
10. Hansen, B., & Thomas, C. (2005). *Off-premise catering management* (2nd ed.). Hoboken, NJ: John Wiley & Sons

Resources

Internet Sites

www.nace.net
www.icacater.org

⚶ Key Words and Concepts

Caterer
Catering
Catering contract
Catering industry
Client
In-flight catering
Mobile catering
Off-site catering
On-site catering
Outsourcing

🖾 Contributor Information

Susan W. Arendt
sarendt@iastate.edu
Susan W. Arendt is an assistant professor at Iowa State University, where she teaches Quantity Food Production Laboratory and Human Resource Management. Her research interests include leadership and student learning.

20 ▌ Review Questions

1. What characteristics are needed to be a successful caterer? Why?

2. List three ways off-site catering and on-site catering are similar.

3. List three ways off-site catering and on-site catering are different.

4. List at least three catering locations and describe special considerations for those sites.

5. What are the benefits to a restaurant that adds catering services?

6. Identify four major concerns for caterers and why these are of concern to a caterer.

7. Identify three challenges for caterers and how a caterer might address these challenges.

8. Identify current catering trends and what impact they have on caterers and clients.

9. Identify two professional catering organizations.

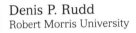

21

Denis P. Rudd
Robert Morris University

Alina M. Zapalska
U.S. Coast Guard Academy

Private Clubs

Learning Objectives

✓ To understand the sectors of the club management industry
✓ To identify the role that private clubs play in the hospitality industry
✓ To explain the importance and economic contribution made by clubs
✓ To identify future employment opportunities in the club industry

Chapter Outline

Historical Perspective
Economic Impact
Current Environment
Types of Clubs
Employment
Ownership
Management

Clubs are the windows into the boardroom of America.

John H. Rudd, Sr.
Senior Vice President of the Statler Hotel Corp.

Historical Perspective

*T*he ancient Egyptians had clubs that fulfilled the religious, business, and social needs of the Pharaoh and religious leaders and their people; the Greeks had their Hetairai, a loose association of like-minded individuals who gathered together for religious, political, commercial, and athletic reasons and developed clubs specifically for dining; the Romans developed a more formal club and were the first to integrate social gatherings into the Roman baths.

Although the roots of the ancient club can be traced back thousands of years, the beginning of the modern club surfaced in London during the 1700s with the introduction, growth, and development of the London coffeehouses. These clubs were actually special rooms in taverns that operated on an invitation-only basis for their members. One of the most famous clubs of the time was the Bread Street Club. Members met at a tavern, and individuals such as William Shakespeare and other literary notables of the Elizabethan time frequented these establishments. The Royal and Ancient Golf Club of St Andrews, Scotland, founded in 1758 and said to be the birthplace of golf, is the forerunner of the modern country club. During Queen Victoria's reign, clubs were only for members of the upper class, but that changed. The notion of clubbing, mentioned as early as the 1600s in the Diary of Samuel Pepys, developed in England when groups who regularly met in taverns began to assume a more permanent character. By the middle of the nineteenth century, the middle class was able to join clubs. Clubs were developed for the working man, allowing them to escape from their tiring days, their wives, children, and from the gin palaces and public houses. The working men's club movement was a way to keep the middle-class man sober. Many of these clubs provided amusement and refreshments as well as newspapers and books and were aimed to morally and socially improve the working men and to educate them.

In America the earliest known social club was the Fish House in Philadelphia. This club emphasized drinking and socializing, but by the mid 1700s, clubs had been established in Annapolis, Boston, Charleston, New Orleans, Philadelphia, and New York. Many of these American clubs were based on British antecedents. During the 1800s one of the most famous clubs formed was the first women's club called Sorosis. This club was for ac-tresses, artisans, supporters of the union's causes, and those interested in the arts. In most cases these women's clubs focused on social services and promoted women that were in the business and professional fields.

Within the heady industrial development that so profoundly transformed the American economy and American society in the decades following the Civil War, the proliferation of the new American clubs revealed the strength and social stature of their founders, most of whom were newly wealthy entrepreneurs. The new clubs provided a place where peers could meet and discuss mutual problems and solutions. As American urban centers expanded and became more industrial, the desirable residential districts were located further and further from the business and industrial centers. Busy businessmen could no longer go home for lunch. A downtown club could provide the pleasant environment and excellent noontime meal that later became an important part of the American club. Once considered the playground of the rich and famous, the club became a center for the American family and its recreational activities.

A **club** is defined as a group of persons organized or united for social, literary, athletic, political, or other purposes. People join clubs to engage in social discourses and to surround themselves with others who have similar interests. Growing steadily each year are the ever-increasing markets for private clubs. Catering to a multitude of clientele, clubs have existed for many millennia and include various interest groups, recreational activities, and organizations. With over 14,000 private clubs in the United States alone, clubs have created an atmosphere conducive to friendliness and comfort.

Economic Impact

The Club Managers Association of America (CMAA), the premier industry professional association for 6,500 managers of approximately 3,000 membership clubs, compiled the 2003 *Economic Impact Survey*.[1] The survey reported CMAA member-managed clubs generating annual gross revenues of over $10.16 billion per year with food and beverage revenue contributing $3.26 billion. Average CMAA-managed club income is approximately $3.98 million dollars, of which $1.28 million is attributable to the food and beverage department. Also, these clubs contributed $304 million in property taxes while also producing $312 million in sales tax revenue. CMAA-managed clubs employ over 263,000 people, boasting payroll of approximately $4.0 billion; provide over $300 million for charities, with approximately 83 percent of this money moved into local community charities; and report an excess of $10.4 million in student scholarships.

Current Environment

The competitive landscape has increased significantly over the past several years placing never before experienced pressure on membership at private clubs. Specifically, industry experts have drawn a general consensus identifying the changing golf course marketplace and population demographics as key culprits.

Frank Vain, president of The McMahon Group, a consulting firm to the private club industry, says the biggest challenge is the evolving golf marketplace that "has experienced a total reversal in market composition. Going back to the 1920s, about 80 percent of the golf courses were private. Public golf was almost unheard of, and up until the 1990s, most of the existing public courses were not comparable to private courses."[2] Vain's group now estimates that currently about 75 percent of U.S. golf courses are public and is projected to plateau at 80 percent around 2010.

Furthermore, these public facilities have grown in quality commensurate with their numeric growth. Steve Graves, president of Creative Golf Marketing, a membership-marketing firm, comments that private clubs today are in direct competition with up-scale daily fee courses. "These clubs are not your typical municipal courses that we all grew up around," suggested Graves, "these courses are being built and designed by the best in the industry and offer equal and many times better golf courses than a typical private club. [Therefore] the upscale daily fee courses present an adequate golf experience without the high monthly cost associated with being a member of a private club."[3] Vain further accentuates the point, "Most of the new course construction has been in the high-end arena with the conditions, accessibility and slope rating that can rival the private club experience, except there are no initiation fees, dues or assessments. There is a whole generation of people growing up not having or needing a private club still able to call themselves golfers. This was simply not possible 20 years ago."[4]

Additionally, the influence of technology, ease of travel, and the transient lifestyle produced by the

Golf courses have gone from 80 percent private in the 1920s to about 75 percent public today.

corporate career ladder has created a different societal need and, hence, a change in the population demographics. Leesa Mitchell, CMP, operator of Members Solutions, a consulting firm that has been involved in marketing high-end daily fee operative clubs, states,

> Many clubs have failed to change in correlation to the changing needs of our society. Many clubs are looking for the "tried and true" program to recruit and retain members. In my opinion, the fact of the matter is those programs do not exist. Every club has a different situation, different demographic and different trend line. In recruiting and retaining members, those are the areas that many clubs have been failing to recognize and utilize in their planning. Turning a deaf ear to demographics and related trending is not the route to go and creates a challenge in recruitment and retention, as well as maintaining a positive satisfaction level of existing members.[5]

In crisis situations, shortcuts often abound and glow with appeal. The private club industry is not immune. Graves articulates that one of the most disturbing national trends within the industry are clubs resorting to the "path of least resistance" by drastically reducing initiation fees or completely waiving initiation fees to compete. The harder path, and ultimately more fruitful, is to set member retention, recruitment, and satisfaction as the club's highest priorities. Gregg Patterson, general manager of The Beach Club of Santa Monica, California, states that because members have options with their leisure time and money, then a key realization for the club manager becomes that this is a "consumer oriented world." Patterson states, "All clubs need to find out what their members want and go after it aggressively. Every member has similar wants—goods, services, programs, facility and a sense of community but the expression of those wants changes with time."[6]

Therefore, it is of critical import for the club manager to stay abreast of the consumers' need and want continuum. Case in point is the busier American lifestyle with children's athletic events, community functions, and alternative entertainment activities that serve to place more scrutiny on a family's discretionary dollars. Thus, a main reason for problematic retention and recruitment is lack of use of the facilities. Vain concluded that in light of this scenario too many clubs "have failed to update their product to appeal with the growing age brackets of baby boomers."[7]

Given the preceding discussion, a consensus is again drawn as to the options available to success. A club manager may take a more formal route such as hiring a membership director focused specifically on retention and recruitment. Utilizing third-party firms in the consultation arena, drawing on survey information cultivated in-house or from broader industry outlets. Use this information to tweak or remodel the product to fit the niche that is unique to each club situation.

Types of Clubs

Although all clubs share a common bond being the fee/due-paying member, the private club industry has evolved into a vast landscape of variety. Listed and described are some of the most common clubs in existence today.

Country Clubs

Around 50 percent of all private clubs are country clubs and often provide elaborate social amenities along with their outdoor recreational facilities. Activities in a typical country club usually center on the golf course, yet many clubs also provide members with outdoor facilities for swimming, tennis, horseback riding, and other interests. Members might hold weddings, reunions, or other social events there. Recently many upscale housing projects have encouraged the building and growth of country clubs to

Profile

A Club Manager's Perspective: *Dan Brennan, Edgeworth Club*

The Edgeworth Club[8] was formed in 1893. Under the bylaws its purpose was to promote interaction and friendship among its members and their social enjoyment, and for the purpose of furnishing facilities for athletics and other innocent sports, and the erection and maintenance of a building or buildings thereafter. Sports that were emphasized at the club were tennis, bowling, and golf. The architectural style of the Edgeworth Club is decidedly Elizabethan, which lends itself particularly to the ground on which it was built and the uses for which it was designed. The Edgeworth Club hosted the Wightman Tennis Cup matches, a prestigious international tennis event. Since then its emphasis has been on tennis and paddle tennis. The club is the principal location for charity events in the raising of funds for health associations and other organizations, as this is an important part of the club personality. Similarly, the century-long tradition of the ventricle presentations involves club members in all phases of the writing, directing, and acting in these entertainments.

attract neighboring communities and new residents. There are two types of memberships at country clubs: full memberships, which entitle the club member to the full use of the facilities the club offers, and social membership, which permits the member to use specific facilities, such as the restaurant, lounge, bar, tennis courts, and so on. Social membership sometimes requires that club members use the club's facilities at certain times or days. Equinox Country Club in Manchester, Vermont, and the California Country Club in Whittier, California, are two examples of country clubs. In the past country clubs were seen as the last bastions of the upper-class elite. In some cases this is still true; however, in most instances the stuffy cigar smoke and the Mayflower context are no longer used to determine whether an individual should be qualified for membership.

Entering into the year 2006 and beyond has been quite difficult for many of the private clubs nationwide. Member expectations have changed dramatically. The private club members of today have the same high expectations for service and food as they had 30 years ago, but they want it faster and more casual. Private club members of today are searching for the value in their investment and have put aside family tradition and legacy as reasons for joining a given club. The age of technology has played a large part in that. Club members are constantly on the go. They want to eat fast and be able to use their laptop or cell phone while they dine. The older established clubs across the country have been fighting that change. Many have figured out how to permit it without giving up their status.

Members want to make reservations online; they want to use e-mail for committee reports and meetings. The Edgeworth Club has been able to make the progression into the "high-tech" society. Managing a club that encourages their senior staff to be progressive with technology is quite challenging. In the computer age, members want their schedules and statements online. They want to have the club at their fingertips 24 hours a day. There is the challenge to purchase the right hardware and software that best fits your club. We must keep in line with the updates. What we purchase today is obsolete in three to five years. How do we ask long-term employees of 20 years to change their habits and become "high-tech"? Putting the emphasis on education has never been more important in the club industry. The Club Managers Association of America has done a wonderful job in preparing managers for the present as well as the future.

As clubs move along trying to figure out what is right for them, we also must maintain our private club status. Sometimes going to "high-tech" can open up a whole new set of problems. Does the club membership understand the privacy laws? Do they want to put the club in jeopardy of losing their private club status? What are the tax implications? It is so important to keep up with education and to hire the right person to lead your club. Hiring intelligent, well-educated, and well-rounded individuals to manage the various departments in and around the club is of the utmost importance. They are the leaders who make the club successful. No one person has ever successfully run a private club, been successful financially, and kept their job longer than three years doing it all by themselves.

Yacht Clubs

These clubs are designated for establishments near or on the water and generally promote and regulate boating and yachting. The Montauk and Rochester yacht clubs are examples of this type of organization. Most yacht clubs own and operate a marina for their members, which may include the operation of a clubhouse with dining and recreation facilities.

Military Clubs

Military clubs cater to the enlisted man, the non-commissioned officer, and the officer. Military bases in the United States and overseas provide these clubs for the welfare and the benefit of the soldiers. They provide extended amenities for their club members, such as guest quarters, recreational activities, food and beverage operations, and entertainment. In the past the clubs have been run by military personnel, but recent changes in resource allocation have required the military to contract civilian firms to provide services. These facilities are located around the world and include the Bamberg Officers' Club in Bamberg, Germany, and the Fort Benning Officers' Club in Fort Benning, Georgia. An example is the 911th Airlift Wing of the U.S. Air Force. Before 1974 they had two military clubs on base. The NCO Club was for the enlisted members of the base, and the Officers' Club was designated for the officers of the base. Due to the downsizing in the military and the costs of running two clubs, the 911th NCO and Officers' Club became a Consolidated Open Mess (Club) in February 1974. Today's club is open to officers and enlisted members of all branches of the armed forces—Air Force,

Army, Navy, Marines, and Coast Guard—and is currently 1,133 members strong. Being a member of the club is a tradition at the 911th Airlift Wing. Members join the club for several reasons, but the biggest include camaraderie and a place to share military experiences with other armed services members. It is also a gathering place for the numerous retirees in the area. The 911th Club hosts several events each month for its members ranging from official functions to holiday celebrations, as well as membership nights, sports parties, meet-and-greets, birthday parties, wedding receptions, and other functions. The club offers excellent dining opportunities and does promotions with giveaways.

Professional Clubs

Professional clubs are for people in the same profession for social and business interaction. The Engineer's Club of St. Louis is a professional club that appeals to engineers from the St. Louis area.

Social Clubs

Similar to the Everglades Club in Palm Beach, Florida, social clubs concentrate on serving the social needs of members who are normally from similar socioeconomic backgrounds.

City Clubs

As the name implies, city clubs are usually located in urban communities and range from luncheon-only clubs that serve segments of the business population to fully integrated dining and athletic clubs. Unlike most private clubs, city clubs may rent out guest rooms, organize themselves around a specialized profession, or associate with a particular college or university. City clubs fall into the following categories: professional, social, athletic, dining, fraternal, and university. The Duquesne Club has achieved the number one ranking among America's ten thousand private clubs according to a national survey conducted by the Club Managers Association of America.

Athletic Clubs

Athletic clubs, such as the Palm Beach Bath and Tennis Club and the Toronto Cricket and Skating Club, provide an outlet for working out, athletic activities, dining, and meeting.

Dining Clubs

Usually located in large office buildings, dining clubs offer their members top-quality foodservice in urban surroundings. Examples include the Toronto Hunt Club and the Union Club of British Columbia.

Profile

The Duquesne Club[9] was founded as a "voluntary association" in 1873 and incorporated as "a club for social enjoyment" in 1881. Membership was limited to 300, and annual dues were $50. Only two years later, many of Pittsburgh's most illustrious citizens had been admitted, including Andrew Carnegie, Henry Clay Frick, B. B. Jones, Frank B. Laughlin, Andrew W. Mellon, Henry Oliver, Jr., and George Westinghouse. Many of their portraits can be seen hanging in the Founders Room. By 1902, membership limits had been raised to 1,100, and in 1980 members voted to elect women to membership. Today, the club has 1,457 active resident members, 465 senior resident members, and 448 non-resident members.

First situated on Penn Avenue between 8th and 9th Streets, in 1879 the Club leased a brick house on its present site. Membership flourished, and shortly thereafter the club commissioned architects Longefellow, Alden, and Harlow (who later designed the Carnegie Institute) to plan the new club-house. The firm submitted an elegant plan in the Richardson Romanesque style reflecting the success of H. H. Richardson's Allegheny County Courthouse and Jail.

The club occupied its new quarters in 1889. In 1902, LA&H designed a matching addition, which broadened the facade and expanded the club's space. Upon completion, it was reported that the Duquesne Club was the best-appointed club in America. In 1994, the club opened a 22,000-square foot state-of-the-art health and fitness center located in the adjacent Gimbels building. This facility has been an outstanding success and offers members one of the most extensive fitness facilities in the area. With 325 employees, excellent facilities, central location, and a perennial membership waiting list, the Duquesne Club remains one of America's preeminent and most respected private clubs and is considered a Pittsburgh treasure by its members.

Melvin Rex, general manager, explains, "Obtaining good managers can be difficult, but at the same time it can be threatening to some upper level managers. I think the best way to run an establishment is to surround yourself with the finest people that you can possibly attain. Some managers are intimidated by hiring someone that might be more educated than them. You have to be confident in yourself."[10]

Melvin Rex witnesses the turnover rate in general managers on a daily basis and commented by saying, "General managers have an employment expectancy rate in private clubs of about two and a half to three and a half years. Half of these managers leave for various reasons such as money or better positions at more accredited establishments and the other half of the managers are terminated. Being a club manager is highly stressful. These members, in a way, own the club. In life, it is difficult to satisfy another person like your husband or wife. If you have 2,600 members, then you have 2,600 opinions to satisfy."[11]

The Duquesne Club just received the honor of being the number one city club in the United States. Melvin Rex says he keeps his managers well informed by "... using a program that I call accountability management. I use this plan to set annual goals for my executive staff. For instance, the goal for the executive chef is to reduce turnover." I asked if it was for financial reasons, because I know that training employees is highly expensive. Mr. Rex acknowledged, "It's not just from an economical standpoint. You will have a more consistent product when you obtain an experienced staff."[12]

Figure 21.1 | The Duquesne Club: Facility Description

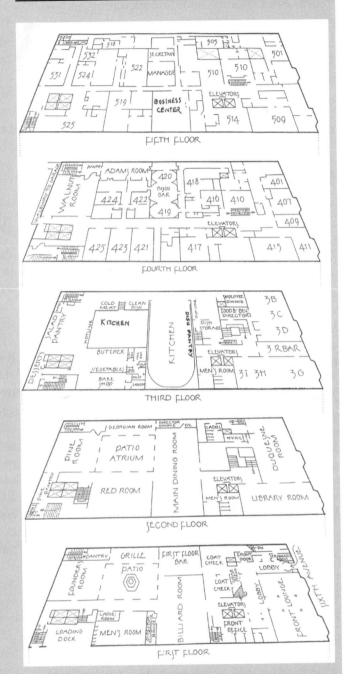

Basement: Laundry, Print Shop, Carpenter Shop, Paint Shop, Engineering Department, and Locker Rooms

Fraternal Clubs

Fraternal clubs, like the Elks Club and the Veterans of Foreign Wars, provide fraternal organizations with a central location for meetings, dining, and social activities.

University Clubs

These clubs are reserved for the activities of faculty, alumni, and guests. The Harvard, Yale, Princeton Club of Pittsburgh, and the University of Toronto Faculty Club are perfect examples.

Employment

As club types, country clubs are the largest employers, followed by golf clubs and city clubs. Taken together, the total employment in country clubs is four times the number employed in golf clubs and almost 10 times the number of those employed by city clubs. The ratio of full-time and part-time non-seasonal employees is almost exactly the same for both golf clubs and country clubs. Approximately 43 percent of all employees in these clubs are full-time and non-seasonal. This contrasts sharply with city clubs, where 74 percent of the employees are full-time non-seasonal employees. Similar ratios were found among full-time and part-time seasonal employees in both golf and country clubs. However, among city clubs, only one-third of the seasonal employees are part time.

Ownership

Club ownership includes two categories: equity clubs and proprietary clubs.

Equity Clubs

Equity clubs are nonprofit clubs and are the oldest form of club management, yet they are still the most common form of ownership today. These clubs are owned and organized by the members for their own enjoyment. The board of directors then establishes the policies and budget and does the hiring and firing of executives, such as the club manager. Any profits that are generated from the dues or club operations must be reinvested in the club's services and facilities and cannot be returned to the members.

Proprietary Clubs

Proprietary clubs are operated for profit and are owned by a corporation, company, business, or individual. These clubs became popular in the 1970s and 1980s and provided an expansion of club membership and stringent admission requirements. Club members purchase a membership from the club's owner(s) and have limited input and control over the activities or management of the daily operations of the club. In some cases contract organizations run the facility for the owner. The club manager reports to this organization or the owner of the facility. Depending on the type, interest, and development of all clubs, the category of ownership may vary.

Management

As a student one of the most challenging experiences in life will be to choose a career. If you're looking for a career that is creative and combines business skills, human resource management, marketing, and public relations, welcome to the world of club management. It is one of the fastest-growing industries and hospitality fields and will provide you with outstanding career opportunities in the future. Club management is similar to that of hospitality management because it offers similar facilities. The largest difference is that the club, unlike a hotel or restaurant, is actually looked at as being owned by the members. The member pays a fee each year, which can vary drastically depending on the nature of the club. In turn, the members feel that they are the owners of the facility. Having one boss may be difficult, but imagine having thousands! This sometimes can put the manager in a difficult situation.

The manager of a club is actually governed by a constitution and the bylaws of the club. The board of directors and club president are elected by their peers to ensure the goals and mission of the club are carried out effectively, and they create the constitution and bylaws that govern members' policies and standards. Club management structure is similar to that of company structure. There is a president, vice president, treasurer, secretary, and different committees. The manager of a club, usually referred to as the chief operating officer or the general manager, has to answer to and abide by the rules set forth by the governing body and is responsible for all areas of club operation. Although the board of directors and president may be responsible for the policy setting and implementation, it is the club manager's job to hire personnel to run the day-to-day operations of the club.

Continuing Education

The sprawl of the club industry, in all its variety, onto the cultural and business landscapes has served, as Perdue, Ninemeier, and Woods[13] astutely observed, to increase the industry's sophistication, thereby prompting managers to utilize new technologies and products to offer improved services all the while operating in an extremely competitive environment and labor market. As a result of these changing dynamics, the need for lifelong learning has emerged as a key element for individuals, organizations, and societies in maintaining their competitive position.[14]

It is to this end that the CMAA and its Canadian counterpart, the Canadian Society of Club Managers, have been instrumental in keeping its members, and thus the industry as a whole, in a learning mode. These organizations have served as a bridge to bring academia and club management together producing collaborative efforts in the valuable forms of management development/professional credentialing programs, teaching, conference participation, and applied research.

Club Managers Association of America (CMAA)

Many club managers belong to the Club Managers Association of America (CMAA). This organization is the oldest and most widely respected association representing the club management professional and is comprised of more than 6,500 professional managers from the most prestigious private country, city, yacht, and military clubs in the United States and around the world. In the early 1920s professional club managers recognized the impact clubs had on the American way of life and the need for a professional association of these clubs. In February of 1927 the first annual meeting of the CMAA took place.

CMAA actively promotes and advances cooperation among individuals directly engaged in the club management profession, as well as other associations in the hospitality industry. In addition CMAA encourages the education and professional advancement of its members and assists club officers and managers through their management to secure the utmost in efficient and successful operations. The organization recognizes its responsibility to assist students in gaining a better understanding of the private club management profession and in selecting a career in this sector of the hospitality industry.

Member Club Facts and Figures

Club Type and Location:
- 80 percent of CMAA members' clubs are golf and country clubs.
- 13 percent of CMAA members' clubs are city clubs.
- 68 percent are IRS classified tax-exempt-501(c)(7) organizations.

Club Income:
- Gross revenues equaled $10.16 billion for all clubs in 2003.
- Food and beverage revenues equal $3.26 billion.
- The average club income is $3.98 million.

Club Employees:
- Clubs employ more than 263,188 employees.
- Club payrolls equal $4 billion.

Club Outreach Programs:
- Clubs raised $300 million for charities in 2003.
- In 2003, clubs gave a total of $10.4 million in student scholarships.
- Most of CMAA's 50 chapters sponsor scholarship funds.

Economic Impact of Clubs:
- The average club spends $1.4 million in the local community.
- The average club spends $2.11 million within the state as a whole.
- Overall, club operations generate $4.38 billion for state economies around the country.
- A typical club pays $131,848 in property taxes.[15]

A student chapter of CMAA can be offered at any school that offers an undergraduate or graduate program in hospitality. As chapter members students participate in professional development programs, site visitation at local clubs, hands-on club operations and demonstrations, and leadership development programs. The CMAA provides its student chapters with an internship directory, which provides more than two hundred internships at private clubs around the world.

National Club Association (NCA)

The mission of the **National Club Association** is to serve the club community by protecting, preserving, and enhancing the interests and well-being of private social and recreational clubs.

Specifically NCA strives to

- Provide support and information to assist club leaders in addressing legal, governance, and business concerns.
- Help clubs strengthen their financial health and protect their assets.
- Ensure recognition and advancement of club interests through lobbying and other government relations activities, seeking to preserve the independence of clubs to operate.
- Assist clubs in complying with laws and regulations.

Summary

Clubs provide a unique managing experience that combines many elements of the hospitality and tourism industries. Club managers must be versatile and open to the changing needs of the club members and the world around them. The most important job of a club manager is to provide club members with a positive experience every time they attend a function at the club. If managers fail to do this, attendance and membership will drop off, and the club will cease to exist. Service is the key to a club manager's success, and service is the core of the business. Club managers must remember that they "serve the world."

Endnotes

1. *Economic Impact Survey 2003.* Club Managers Association of America. http://www.cmaa.org/EconImpactSurvey/2003EconImpactSurvey.doc. Retrieved June 29, 2005
2. *Club Management Forum.* Virginia: Club Managers Association of America, 2000. http://www.cmaa.org/conf/conf2000/time.htm (January 2, 2001)
3. Ibid
4. Ibid
5. Ibid
6. Ibid
7. Ibid
8. Edgeworth Club
9. Brown, Mark M., Lu Donnelly, and David G. Wilkins. *The History of the Duquesne Club.* Pittsburgh: Art and Library Committee, 1989
10. Ibid
11. Ibid
12. Ibid
13. Perdue, J., Ninemeier, J. D., & Woods, R. H. Comparison of present and future competencies required for club managers. *International Journal of Contemporary Hospitality Management.* 14, no. 3 (2002): 142–146
14. Barrows, C. W. & Walsh, J. Bridging the gap between hospitality management programmes and the private club industry. *International Journal of Contemporary Hospitality Management* 14, no. 3 (2002): 120–127
15. WWW.CMAA.org

Resources

Internet Sites

Algonquin Club of Boston: http://algonquinclub.memfirst.net/Club/Scripts/Home/home.asp
American Club in Singapore: http://www.amclub.org.sg/
American Society of Golf Course Architects: http://www.golfdesign.org/
Ariel Sands Beach Club: http://www.arielsands.com/
Army Navy Country Club: http://ancc.org/
Association of College and University Clubs: http://www.collegeanduniversityclubs.org/
Atlanta Athletic Club: http://www.atlantaathleticclub.org/
Ballantyne Country Club: http://www.crescent-resources.com/communit/charlott/ballanty/default.asp
Bear Creek Golf Club: http://www.bearcreekgc.com/Club/Scripts/Home/home.asp
Belmont Country Club: http://www.belmontcc.org/Club/Scripts/Splash/splash.asp
Boca Raton Resort & Club: http://www.bocaresort.com/
California Yacht Club: http://calyachtclub.com/cms/index2.htm
Capitol Hill Club: http://www.capitolhillclub.com/

Cedar Rapids Country Club: http://www.thecrcc.com/
Club Managers Association of America: www.cmaa.org
Club Services: http://www.clubservices.com
ClubCorp: http://www.clubcorp.com
Country Club of Lansing: http://www.cclansing.org/
Country Club of St. Albans: http://www.stalbans.com/
Golf Course Builders Association of America: http://www.gcbaa.org/
Golf Course Superintendents Association of America: http://www.gcsaa.org/
International Association of Golf Administrators: http://www.iaga.org/
International Club Network: http://www.privaccess.com/
International Health, Racquet, & Sportsclub Association: http://csdemo12.citysoft.com/IHRSA/viewPage.cfm?pageId=2
International Military Community Executives Association: http://www.imcea.com/
Ladies Professional Golf Association: http://www.lpga.com/
Lighthouse Point Yacht and Racquet Club: http://www.lpyrc.com/
National Association of Club Athletic Directors: http://www.nacad.org/
National Club Association: http://www.natlclub.org/
Professional Golfers Association of America: http://www.pga.com/
Sanctuary Golf Club: http://www.sanctuary-sanibel.com/
The ACE Club: http://www.theaceclubonline.com/
The Virtual Clubhouse/Club Management Magazine: www.club-mgmt.com

Supplemental Reading

Barnhart, C. L., ed. *The American College Dictionary*. New York: Random House, 1990

Crossley, John C. and Lynn M. Jamieson. *Introduction to Commercial and Entrepreneurial Recreation*. Champaign, IL: Sagamore Publishing, 1997

Membership issues: Opinions on What Works in Today's Private Club Industry. http://www.boardroommagazine.com/fa59.cfm. Retrieved July 1, 2005

Perdue, Joe., ed. *Contemporary Club Management*. Alexandria, VA: Club Managers Association of America, 1997

Perfect Storm: What Does It Mean for Private Clubs. http://www.boardroommagazine.com/fa58.cfm. Retrieved July 1, 2005

Singerling, James, Robert Wood, Jack Nimemeier, and Joe Purdue. "Success Factors in Private Clubs." *Cornell Hotel and Restaurant Administration Quarterly* 38.5 (Oct. 1997)

"The CMAA Student Advantage: A Commitment To Your Future." Alexandria, VA: Club Managers Association of America, 1999. http://www.cmaa.org/student/adv_bro/index.htm (Jan. 4, 2001)

Walker, John R. *Introduction to Hospitality*, 3rd ed. Upper Saddle River, NJ: Prentice Hall, 2001

☞ *Key Words and Concepts*

City clubs—Establishments that are in urban areas and cater to businessmen or women, provides dining services and occasionally athletics.

Club—A group of persons organized for social, literary, athletic, political, recreational, or other purposes.

CMAA—Club Managers Association of America formed in 1920.

Country clubs—Hospitality establishments that provide elaborate social events, offer dining, pool, tennis, and golf.

Equity clubs—Those facilities, owned by their membership, are nonprofit; oldest form of clubs.

Full membership—Entitles a member to full use of the club, all amenities, during any hour of operation.

Member—Regardless of type of club, each is made up of members, who have applied for and been accepted into membership.

Military clubs—Cater to enlisted men and women and the noncommissioned officers; provides a social outlet; often has golf.

NCA—National Club Association.

Proprietary clubs—Those owned by a corporation, company, business, or individual; they are for-profit businesses.

Service—The reason why private clubs exist; members receive high-end, personalized service at their club.

Social membership—Entitles a member to limited use of a country club, typically dining, pool, and tennis, but not golf; reduced initiation fee and dues structure.

Yacht club—Establishments near or on the water; activities center around sailing and boating; dining also available.

Contributor Information

Denis P. Rudd, Ed.D., CHA, FMP, is university professor and Director of Hospitality and Tourism Management at Robert Morris University Pennsylvania at both the Coraopolis and Pittsburgh campuses. Dr. Rudd received his Bachelor's Degree in Finance and Commerce from Rider College, Lawrenceville, New Jersey, a Master's in Business Administration, a Master's in Education Counseling, Specialist in Higher Education Administration, and a Doctorate in Educational Counseling from the University of Nevada, Las Vegas.

Dr. Rudd is a fifth-generation hotelier who began his career at his family's hotel in Windham, New York, at the Osborn House, a 150-room resort. In 1995 he accepted the position as professor and Director of Hospitality and Tourism Management for Robert Morris College Coraopolis and Pittsburgh, Pennsylvania. Dr. Rudd has recently published three texts entitled *Introduction to Casino and Gaming Operation*, the first introduction text on casino and gaming operations, published by Prentice Hall, and *Club Operations*, and *Convention Technology*. In addition Dr. Rudd has received certification as a CHA and FMP from the National Restaurant Association and the Educational Institute of the American Hotel Motel Association and PTC, from the International Meeting Planners Association. In 2005 Dr. Rudd was honored by being appointed the first university professor of Robert Morris University.

21 ▮ Review Questions

1. What types of facilities are likely to be found at a country club?

2. What types of services are likely to be offered at a city club?

3. Describe the types of military clubs and the purposes they serve.

4. What is the mix of full-time to part-time staff at country clubs?

5. What is the mix of full-time to part-time staff at city clubs?

6. What is the mix of year-round to seasonal staff in country clubs?

7. What is the mix of year-round to seasonal staff in city clubs?

8. Define an equity club.

9. Define a proprietary club.

10. Sketch an organization chart that shows which positions report to whom.

11. What is CMAA? Visit their Web site at www.cmaa.org.

12. What is NCA?

13. What are the goals of NCA?

Assignment 1

Visit Club Managers Association of America's Web site, ClubNet (www.cmaa.org). This Web site offers links to home pages for numerous private clubs throughout the United States. Visit as many of these home pages as possible to gain an understanding of the variety of private clubs available as well as the quality facilities that are provided for members and their guests.

ClubNet also describes the numerous professional development opportunities available for club managers through CMAA. Peruse this section of ClubNet to better understand how professional development and learning is a lifelong pursuit.

As you look ahead and plan your career, how will you pursue professional development and continuous educational opportunities?

Assignment 2

According to an article in *Club Management* by Chris White (December 2000), the growth of the spa industry can provide opportunities for the private club sector. The spa industry has grown across the United States due to a number of reasons delineated by White (p. 94):

- Baby boomers' desire to slow the effects of aging
- The high costs of conventional, remedial health care as compared to preventive health care
- The increasing concern for the quality of the lengthening average life span
- Increasing amounts of personal disposable income

The variety of types of spas is also expanding. Spas no longer have to be the destination, resort, or cruise line spas also known as vacation spas. Day spas, who tend to cater to local clientele and offer hair salons, skin care, body treatments, and massage, are a growing segment. White emphasized in this article that the day spa market may provide enormous opportunities for private clubs, particularly involving massage, body treatments, and possibly skin care.

What is your opinion of these expanded services for private clubs? What other types of amenities might be added that would be popular with private club members? How could these services be effectively marketed to the membership? What are potential disadvantages of offering "day spa" types of services?

Assignment 3

Many clubs are increasingly experiencing quite varied demographics among their membership resulting in contrasting membership expectations and demands. For example, although clubs may still have a population of older members who have perhaps been with the club for many decades, younger members, often with children, are also a growing segment. The older members may still enjoy dressing up for an evening of fine dining, but this may not be realistic or pleasurable for a family with three young children. How does a club cater to differing member preferences? The solution of operating different facilities to cater to the preferences of all members may work for some clubs but would be too costly and unrealistic for many operations.

If you were the new general manager of a club with these dilemmas (varied member preferences/limited budget and the membership resistant to increases in dues), what would you suggest? Think of going before the club's board with at least three options to possibly increase member usage of the food and beverage facilities. What will you propose?

Chris DeSessa
Johnson & Wales University

Cruise Line Industry

Learning Objectives

✓ To discuss the benefits of cruising
✓ To explain what is included in the price of a cruise
✓ To name two possible disadvantages of cruising
✓ To describe factors that determine the price of a cruise
✓ To name the possible positions that one can aspire to in the cruise industry
✓ To list some of the current and future trends in cruising

Chapter Outline

History
The Ship
Types of Cruise Lines
The Big Seven Cruise Lines
Activities
Cruising Areas
Career Opportunities
Trends

*W*elcome aboard to the wonderful world of cruising. The cruise industry is the fastest growing segment of the travel industry. Over 10 million people throughout the world took a cruise last year. For many, a cruise represents a vacation that allows one to do as little or as much as he or she wants. The amount of Americans taking cruises continues to grow every year. Since 1980, there has been an 8.1 percent increase per year in people taking cruises. More huge ships are being built so the competition between cruise lines is very competitive. The top states producing the most cruise passengers are Florida, California, Texas, Massachusetts, New York, Pennsylvania, New Jersey, Illinois, Ohio, and Georgia. There are many reasons for the popularity of cruises.

Historically, cruise ships were for people to sit in a deck chair and eat 24 hours a day. Now, you can book a fitness cruise with spa treatments, healthy dietary cuisine, and exercise programs for everyone. Cruise lines continue to build more new ships with more shopping, health clubs, casinos, and restaurants. There are also more destinations to travel to and more ports to depart from. Cruises to nowhere are designed to allow people to gamble, learn to cook or lose weight, or visit new sites without packing or unpacking. In addition, cruise companies have expanded their choice of itineraries to include more exotic ports of call and have introduced more innovative onboard facilities such as cyber-cafes, multiple themed restaurants, and state-of-the-art meeting facilities to attract a more diverse clientele.

And, not all boats are the large Carnival cruises that carry 1,000 people. Some are small boats that sleep four or six people, which can go up rivers to see places one cannot get to by any other means of transportation. There is a cruise for every budget, age group, eating habit, and activity level. It is easy to see why a cruise is the choice for many vacationers.

Americans love to cruise. They represent about 70 percent of the people who take cruise vacations. For many, a cruise represents both value and peace of mind. Unlike a land-based vacation, the hassles of paying for meals and entertainment and deciding where to eat are eliminated. There is security in knowing that everything is taken care of and no money for necessities is needed once you are on the boat. On board the problem of carrying money is eliminated because on board one is part of the "cashless society" that allows the passenger to sign for extra expenses. You can relax and enjoy yourself. In addition, because there are a lot of people on the boat, you can meet new friends, have drinks, party, and know that you are steps away from your bed when it is over.

The price of the cruise includes one's accommodations, all meals and in-between snacks, entertainment, lectures, social functions, movies, and the use

Americans represent 70 percent of the people who take cruise vacations.

of a ship's facilities, including entry into the casino and fitness centers. Sometimes the price also includes the price of flights to the ship and transfers (transportation between airport or hotel and the cruise port). Because 84 percent of U.S. adults have never cruised, there remains an enormous untapped market for cruises and great potential for the cruise industry in the years ahead.

Some people have the misconception that everything is included in the price. Therefore, it is important to clarify in advance what is not included. With a little common sense, most of these are obvious. Drinks and gambling debts are not included along with shopping. In addition, the following are not included in the price of a cruise: photos, health spas, Internet cafes, tipping (on some ships), phone calls, seasickness inoculations, and shore excursions.

History

The concept of cruising has changed dramatically over the years. Not so long ago cruising was for the very rich or very poor. Cruise ships were divided into classes. Many of our ancestors came to America via cruise ship. Their experiences were less than joyful because they were in the part of the ship known as "steerage," which was little better than barebones accommodations. They were housed at the bottom of the boat with no windows or air. Their recreation deck was the only place they could get sun. The movie *Titanic* with Leonardo DiCaprio portrayed what it was like in steerage. It also portrayed the problem if something happened to the ship but it did allow poor people to be able to cross the ocean. Of course the very rich could cross the oceans in elegance cruising in first-class accommodations on such famous ships as: The S.S. *France*, *Queen Mary*, and the ships of the White Star Line.

Many of the early cruises were for transportation. Before airplanes cruise ships were the main method of crossing from one continent to another. Although the cruise could be luxurious, it was still basically walking around the deck, sitting in lounge chairs, and eating. Up until the 1960s recreational cruising was considered a vacation option for senior citizens. That all changed with the creation of the hit television series, *The Love Boat*. TV viewers then saw cruising as a getaway to exotic ports such as Acapulco, where romance filled the air and passengers were pampered with dinners with the captain and adventures with fellow passengers. The series portrayed passengers as young or young at heart,

adventuresome, and available. Certainly, a more exciting image was created.

Another important event that changed the image of cruising was when Carnival Cruise Lines introduced the idea of a cruise ship as a destination in itself with its introduction of "The Fun Ships." The cruise ship itself was the focal point of activities with myriad scheduled fun activities from morning until night. Passengers still were concerned with visiting ports but many especially veteran cruisers were more concerned with the ships more than the ports visited. The ships contained everything that a small city would have minus the crime. People could go rock climbing or skeet shooting. They could get a massage or facial at the spa or work out at a state-of-the-art health club. Modern-day cruise ships have mini golf courses, basketball courts, rock climbing walls, nightclubs, merry-go-rounds, skating rinks, and surfing. Clients can take a tour of the galley (kitchen) or the bridge (area where the captain and crew navigate the ship). Or, as before, they could sit in a lounge chair and soak up the sun with occasional dips in the pool.

The Ship

Ships come in various sizes. The modern cruise ship can be the height of a 10-story building and cover the space of three football fields. Some clients prefer large ships because of the many amenities. Some ships can hold as many as 3,000 people. Others prefer the intimacy of a smaller ship. The size of a cruise ship is registered in gross tonnage (GRT). Some large ships cannot pull into ports, so passengers must be ferried to shore. A tender is a smaller boat that will ferry passengers from the larger ship to shore. Some of the tenders can hold more than 400 passengers.

Cruise passengers do not want to wait in long lines for service, so clients enjoy ships with plenty of room. The spaciousness of a cruise ship is measured by dividing the tonnage by the number of passengers. This is referred to as space ratio and represents a rough approximation of how much space there is on a ship. The front of the ship is referred to as the bow, and the rear is called the stern. The left side of the ship facing forward is the port, while the right side is the starboard.

Cabins

Throughout your trip you will rest and relax in your cabin, sometimes called a stateroom. The cost of a cruise also depends on the location, size, and special amenities of your cabin. A deck plan is a chart that displays the location of cabins and public rooms. (Figure 22.1) With larger ships, you have a choice of levels of floors, depending on how close to the activities one wants to be. On modern ships all passenger cabins are above the water line. Only the crew's quarters are below the water line.

Figure 22.1

CARNIVAL TRIUMPH. & CARNIVAL VICTORY.
Deck Plan and Staterooms

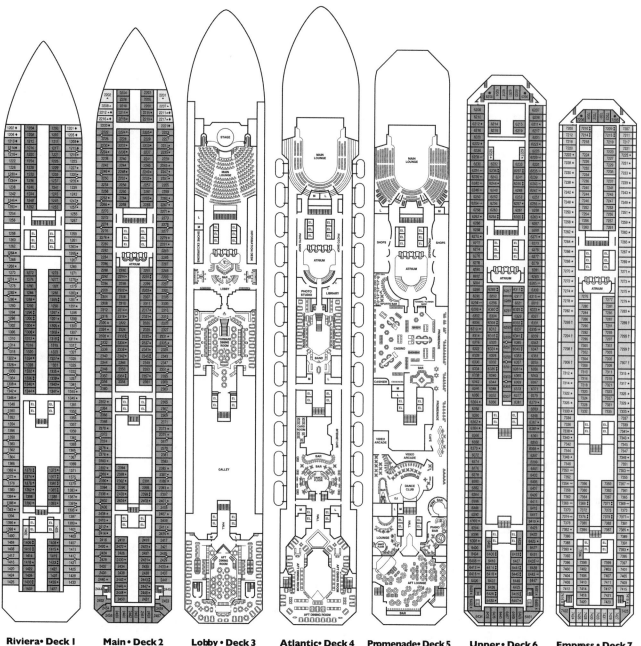

Riviera• Deck 1   **Main • Deck 2**   **Lobby • Deck 3**   **Atlantic• Deck 4**   **Promenade• Deck 5**   **Upper • Deck 6**   **Empress • Deck 7**

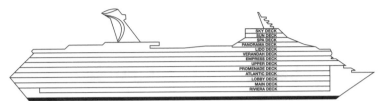

Gross Tonnage: 101,509 Length: 893 Feet Beam: 116 Feet Cruising Speed: 21 Knots
Guest Capacity: 2,758 (Double Occupancy) Total Staff: 1,100 Registry: The Bahamas and Panama

Stateroom Symbol Legend

- ⦂ 2 Uppers   • 1 Upper
- ▲ Twin Bed and Single Convertible Sofa
- ★ Twin Bed/King and Single Convertible Sofa
- ■ Twin Bed/King, Single Convertible Sofa and Upper
- † Twin Bed/King and Double Convertible Sofa
- × Queen-Size Bed   ∞ Queen-Size Bed, Single Convertible Sofa and Upper
- ♦ Stateroom with 2 Porthole Windows
- ◁ Connecting Staterooms *(Ideal for families and groups of friends)*
- ✳ Twin beds do not convert to a king-size bed

Catagory 6B staterooms with partially obstructed views:
UPPER DECK: 6201, 6202, 6203, 6204, 6205, 6206
EMPRESS DECK: 7201, 7202, 7203, 7204, 7205, 7206
LIDO DECK: 9201, 9202, 9203
PANORAMA DECK: 1001, 1002, 1003, 1004

Suites with standard-size balconies:
LIDO DECK: 9205, 9206

Staterooms are available that are modified for wheelchair users. Please contact Carnival Reservations department, Guest Access Services, at 1-800-438-6744, ext. 70025, for details.

Important Note: Please visit carnival.com for exact deck plan of each ship.

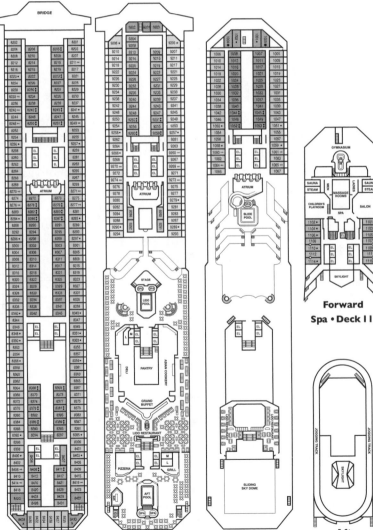

Verandah• Deck 8   **Lido • Deck 9**   **Panorama• Deck 10**

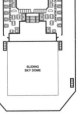

Spa • Deck 11

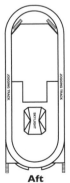
Aft

Sun • Deck 12

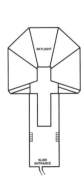
Sky • Deck 14

Cabins that have a porthole or window are referred to as outside or exterior cabins. These are more expensive. Some cabins have a porch or veranda to enjoy the scenery. Inside or interior cabins do not have a porthole or window. Inside cabins do have access to natural light.

Other considerations that may affect the choice of a cabin may be proximity to elevators, stairs, and public areas and the propensity for seasickness. Like any hotel, when an elevator or stairs is next door, it is very noisy all day and all night as people constantly are on the move.

Each deck on a ship is identified by a name or letter. Normally the higher the deck, the more expensive the cabin. Also cabins in the middle of the ship (amidship) are more expensive. These are more preferable to passengers who are prone to seasickness because there is less ship movement in the middle of a ship. Modern day cruise ships have wing-like projections called stabilizers that are used in rough seas.

Beds on a cruise ship are referred to as berths. One can decide between king, queen, and twin. Many cabins have bunk bed type accommodations, which are referred to as upper/ lower berths and are perfect for accommodating children on a cruise.

Types of Cruise Lines

The Cruise Lines International Association (CLIA) is the world's premier cruise marketing and training association comprising 19 major cruise lines and 16,500 travel agencies. Its goal is promoting the desirability, diversity, and high value of the cruise vacation experience. CLIA divides the cruise lines into three types: contemporary, luxury, and premium depending on quality, service, amenities, and itineraries.

Contemporary brands are geared to a mass market. Many of the contemporary brand cruise lines visit the same ports. Some distinctions between luxury and premium brands may have to do with the quality of food, level of service, and number of passengers on a ship. Another important factor for comparison would be the cruise itinerary. Premium cruise brands may visit more exotic ports. In comparing the passenger-to-crew ratio between two ships, one may get a rough estimate of the level of service.

The Big Seven Cruise Lines

All seven of the larger cruise lines offer a well-packaged cruise that includes a variety of itineraries, plenty of food, a variety of activities, and large-scale Broadway production shows. The lines differ in the facilities, space, food, and service. Each cruise line has its own niche. The Big Seven cruise lines are listed in Table 22.1.

Activities

A passenger can do as little or as much as he/she wants on a cruise. Most ships have gyms, theatres, movie theatres, libraries, pools, basketball and volleyball courts, jogging tracks, and art and photo galleries. These are all included in the price of a cruise. The role of a cruise director is to ensure that clients have the opportunity to have a good time. Many activities are geared toward clients meeting each other: a typical cruise may have a singles party, grandmothers bragging party, dance lessons, trivia contests, passenger talent shows, scavenger hunts, and poolside

Table 22.1 ‖ **Big Seven Cruise Lines**

Line	No. of ships (may change by publication date)	Brief profile
Carnival Cruises	20	Largest, most popular cruise line
Celebrity Cruises	10	Top rated; youngest, most innovative fleet
Costa Cruises	11	Europe's no. 1 cruise line
Holland America	13	Five-star premium ships
Norwegian Cruise Line	13	Free-style cruising; Hawaii cruising
Princess Cruises	14	Best-known name; the "Love Boats"
Royal Caribbean International	20	Leader in shipboard activities

Most cruise ships have gyms with classes that are included in the price of the cruise.

games. Other activities are geared towards teens or younger children. Typically a passenger will have an opportunity to attend a Broadway-type production before or after dinner. Another option could be to attend a first-run movie in the ship's movie theatre. Oftentimes a cruise line will deliver an activity sheet to a passenger's cabin at night so that the client is aware of activities for the next day (see Figure 22.2).

When a cruise ship is planning to enter a port, the cruise director may give a port talk on sights to see or places to shop. Cruise lines also offer shore excursions, which are half day or full day trips that can be bought on the cruise ship and are recommended by the cruise line. Sometimes these excursions can be previewed and bought ahead of time.

Cruising Areas

Cruises can range from a three-day getaway cruise from Miami to the Bahamas or an Around the World 180-day cruise. The Caribbean (and Bahamas) continues to be the number one destination for cruises, with 46.4 percent of the cruises traveling to those islands. Other leading cruising areas are Eu-

rope with 19.7 percent, Alaska with 8.3 percent, and Mexico and the West Coast with 7.1 percent of the market share.

Most Caribbean seven-day cruises depart from Miami and usually visit three ports, a private island (where clients can enjoy water sports and beachside activities), and two to three days at sea. One has the option of visiting the Eastern Caribbean, Western Caribbean (which is geared toward beach lovers), or Southern Caribbean. A good choice for a first-time Caribbean cruiser who is more concerned with the itinerary than the ship could be a port-intensive cruise departing from San Juan, Puerto Rico, and visiting six islands. The ship is already in the Caribbean, so it is easy to visit so many islands.

Cruises to Europe have become popular because a client only has to unpack once. Clients also like the fact that they go back each night to the familiar surroundings of their cabin and cruise ship. Alaska cruises became very popular following 9/11 because passengers felt safer cruising in U.S. waters.

Clients also have the option of taking "theme cruises." Some popular themes for cruises might be sports, music, food, wine tasting, and murder mystery. Other options include adventure cruises or expeditions to such places as the Galapagos Island, around-the-world cruises, and river cruises on such rivers as the Mississippi and the Rhine.

Career Opportunities

When one thinks of working for a cruise line, there are two options: working on the ship or on land. The cruise industry generated almost 295,077 American jobs in 2003. This is expected to grow due to the increased popularity of cruising and the number of newer and larger ships that are being built. When one thinks about positions on a ship, one must realize that a modern cruise ship is a restaurant, hotel, resort, and activities center. Many of the positions offered at those land-based establishments are also offered on a cruise ship.

Most cruise ships are registered in other countries such as Panama and Liberia, referred to as a "flag of convenience." When flying a "flag of convenience" of another country, the cruise line does not have to follow United States' standards in regard to taxes and minimum wage requirements. Traditionally cruise lines tend to hire residents from less-developed countries for positions such as waiters, cabin stewards, and bartenders because resi-

Figure 22.2 ‖ **Activities Sheet**

)Ⅽ CarnivalCapers

Your daily guide to FUN.

Food & Drink Showcase

Breakfast
Continental Breakfast
6:00am .... Emile's Lido Deck 9
Breakfast Buffet
6:00am - 10:30am
Open Sitting Breakfast
6:30am - 8:30am ..... Silver Olympian Dining Room

Lunch
Noon - 3:30pm .... Lido Deck 9
Choose from the *Grand Buffet*, Chinese food from the *Oriental*, hot fresh pizza from the *Pizzeria*, seafood delights from *Fish and Chips*, burgers and more from *The Grille* which will remain open until 6:00pm& 11:30pm - 1:00am speciality sandwiches available from *The Deli* which will remain open until 11:00pm
Taste of the Nations today serving "Caribbean"

Dinner - Dress code tonight is casual
Early Sitting Dinners
5:45pm .... Silver Olympian Dining Room
6:15pm .... Golden Olympian Dining Room
Late Sitting Dinners
8:00pm .... Silver Olympian Dining Room
8:30pm .... Golden Olympian Dining Room
The Silver Olympian Dining Room is located on Decks 3 and 4 aft.
The Golden Olympian Dining Room is located on Decks 3 and 4 forward.

The Origami Sushi Bar
5:30pm - 8:30pm .... Promenade Deck 5

Alternative Dining
We are pleased to offer an alternative dining venue with varied selections from the grill and salad bar.
6:00pm - 9:30pm .... Emile's, Lido Deck 9
Open 24 Hours
Pizzeria.
Room Service. .... Dial 8000

Today's Drink Special
Try our exotic special of the day
" *Island Delight* " *for only $6.75 in a colorful souvenir glass*
Margherita Party $3.50 Cabinet Bar
5-6PM & 7:15-8:15pm
Flavored Margarita not included in special price.
BEVERAGE SERVICE
You must be 21 to drink alcohol.

Harry's Supper Club
A cruise on the Carnival Liberty is not complete without a visit to Harry's, the best restaurant at sea. For a nominal fee of $30, we assure you of the finest steaks, sea food and luxury desserts. All of this, is complemented by six star service, a world class selection of wine and live music all of which will make **your visit to Harry's a night to remember.**
For a reservation, please call 1078 between 10am & 10pm. Dress code: Smart Elegant
Located on Panorama Deck 10

Presidential Wine Club
Join Today! For information about this new and exciting club collect a brochure from any of the following bars: Paparazzi Wine Bar, Deck 5 Aft Formalities, Deck 5 Fwd,Promenade Casino Bar.
Deck 5 Mid Ship

Wake Up Calls
You can program a wake up call by pressing the pre program wake up call button on your phone. Please enter the required time followed by the star (*) sign for AM or the pound (#) sign for PM. For example: if you want to wake up at 7:30 in the morning, please enter 730 (*) or 7:30 in the evening, please enter 730 (#). Please do not pick up your handset while you are programming a wake up call. If you have trouble programming your phone, please call room service at 8000.

Infirmary
Over the counter items such as Tylenol, motion sickness pills and Band-Aids available at the Information Desk, Gift Shop or Room Service.
The Infirmary is Open: 8am - 8pm. (Dial 4444)
Doctor's Hours: 8am - 11am & 3pm - 6pm.
In case of **EMERGENCY - Please Dial 911**
After Hours: Call Information Desk (Dial 7777)
A Nurse is always on Call for Emergencies.
Location: Deck 0, Forward, near the gangways

Going Ashore
Today in St Thomas we will be docking at a Navel base, the cost of a Taxi downtown is $4 per person one way, to Paradise Point is $5 per person from where we will be docked.

Phoning Home
We're now featuring even lower satellite calling rates. Calls to the U.S.,Canada and the Caribbean are only $6.99 per minute! International calls are only $9.99 per minute. Consult your stateroom directory for dialing instructions.

Beach Towels
Fresh beach towels will be placed in your stateroom the night before each port of call. Please use these towels while ashore and on the ship's open decks. Please return the towels to your stateroom steward when you are finished with them. A charge of $22 will be billed to your Sail & Sign account for each towel not returned. Basketballs & Volleyballs are available from the Lido Deck towel hut from 8:00am - 6:00pm. Your S&S Card will need to be left as a deposit.

Swimming Pools *Swim at your own risk*
8:00am - 8:00pm .... Fwd Pool, Lido Deck 9
8:00am - 10:00pm .... Aft Pool, Lido Deck 9
Whirlpools
8:00am - 10:00pm .... Lido Deck 9 Fwd
8:00am - 8:00pm .... Spa Carnival, Deck 11 Fwd
8:00am - 12:00am .... Lido Deck 9 Aft
Please note the aft whirlpools
are for ADULTS ONLY.

Smoking Areas
Guests are welcome to smoke in the following areas: Czar's Palace Casino, The Stage, The Piano Man Bar, The Hot and Cool Dance Club and the Starboard (right) Side of the Open Decks. Cigar smoking is only allowed in the Cabinet Cigar Bar located on Deck 4 aft.

Tonight we start with an open mic Karaoke
7:00pm - 8:30pm...........Victoria Lounge
Then at 11:30pm we move to Lido Deck
where will start the auditions for:
ARETHA FRANKLIN
ELTON JOHN
BRITNEY SPEARS
ELVIS PRESLEY
You will judge who will appear in
our Carnival Legends Show!
LEGENDS..........LIDO DECK 9 11:30PM

Tuesday, December 13th, 2005
Captain: Agostino Fazio / **Hotel Director:** Dany Petranko / **Cruise Director:** Brent Mitchell
Sunrise 6:44am / Sunset 7:44pm

WELCOME TO ST THOMAS U.S.V.I

Arrival In St thomas 7:00am. All Guests Must Be Back On Board 5:30pm
Carnival Liberty Sets Sail At 6:00pm
Make sure you have your Sail & Sign Card & Photo ID with you at all times &
always stay on ships time.
The gangway to disembark is located on DECK 0 FORWARD.
In Case Of Emergency, Please Call Our Agent ⚓ ᴇᴀsᴛᴇɴᴅ1.ᴄ☼ᴍᴘᴀɴʏPhone: 340 774 1780Fax: 340 775 4008Email
Address:shipagent@islands.vi. prophetwico@islands.vi

)ⅭCarnival.

Today-At-A-Glance

December 13th, 2005

6:00am	The Gymnasium Opens	Deck 11 Forward
7:00am	**Approx Arrival In St Thomas**	
	Shore Excursion Desk open til 9am	Deck 3
7:30am	The Jardin Cafe Opens	Promenade Deck 5 Aft
8:00am	Shopping Desk Open till 9:30am	Deck 5 Mid Ship
	Spa Carnival Opens	Deck 11 Forward
4:00pm	The Jardin Cafe Opens	Promenade Deck 5 Aft
	Formalities Opens	Lido Deck 9
4:30pm	TV Trivia	The Cabinet Deck 4 Aft
5:00pm	The Photo Gallery Opens	Atlantic Deck 4 Fwd
	The Library Opens till 6pm	Atlantic Deck 4 Fwd
5:15pm	Piano Music & Cocktails	Lobby Deck 3
5:30pm	**All Guest must be back Onboard**	
6:00pm	Slots Opens	Promenade Deck 5
	Golf Information	Excursion Desk Deck 3
6:30pm	Full Casino Opens	Promenade Deck 5
	The Gift Shops Open	Promenade Deck 5
7:00pm	Shore Excursion Desk open til 9pm	Deck 3
	Karaoke Fun	Victoria lounge
	Jazz Music	The Cabinet Deck 4 Aft
	Art Gallery Open	Satin Room, Dk 3 Fwd
	Music During Dinner	Harry's Supper Club
	Friends Of Bill W Meet	The Library Deck 4
7:30pm	Butch's Liberty Slide Class	Venetian Palace
	Shopping Desk Open	Deck 5 Mid Ship
	Piano Music & Cocktails	Lobby Deck 3
8:00pm	**Cheap as Chips Bingo**	**Venetian Palace**
8:30pm	**ShowTime**	**Venetian Palace**
9:30pm	Country Western & Rock & Roll	The Stage Deck 4 Aft
	Jazz Music	The Cabinet Deck 4 Aft
	Piano Music & Cocktails	Lobby Deck 3
10:00pm	**Cheap as Chips Bingo**	**Venetian Palace**
	Piano Party	Piano Man Bar Deck 5
	Calypso Sounds	**Venetian Palace**
10:30pm	**ShowTime**	**Venetian Palace**
11:30pm	Legends Show Auditions	The Cabinet, Deck 4 Aft
24 Hours	internet cafe	The Cabinet, Deck 4 Aft

CARNIVAL LEGENDS

Tonight we start with an open mic Karaoke
7:00pm - 8:30pm.......................Victoria Lounge
Then at 11:30pm we move to Lido Deck
where will start the auditions for:

ARETHA FRANKLIN
ELTON JOHN
BRITNEY SPEARS
ELVIS PRESLEY

You will judge who will appear in
our Carnival Legends Show!
LEGENDS........LIDO DECK 9 11:30PM

Main Show

From The Heart
Of **Motown** , We
Present Top
Entertainer

Marcus Anthony

8:30pm & 10:30pm

Venetian Palace

Do Not Miss This!

The Venetian Palace is a non smoking lounge

Music and Dancing

Calypso Sounds with Tropical Fire
4:00pm - 5:00pm.........................Lido Deck 9
10:00pm - 11:15pm......................Lido Deck 9

Beautiful Piano Music with Luigi
5:15pm - 6:15pm....................Flowers Lobby Deck 3
7:30pm - 8:30pm....................Flowers Lobby Deck 3
9:30pm - 10:30pm..................Flowers Lobby Deck 3

Jazz & Cigars with the Christian Forrest Trio
7:00pm - 8:00pm......................The Cabinet, Dk 4
9:30pm - 12:30am.....................The Cabinet, Dk 4

Music During Dinner with Play That
7:00pm - 11:00pm............Supper Club Deck 10

Country Western & Classic Rock & Roll Music
9:30pm - 12:30pm................The Stage, Deck 5 Aft

The Latest Dance Sounds with DJ Mikey
10:30pm - Late...Hot & Cool Dance Club Deck 5 Aft

Fun Around the Piano with Duane
10:00pm - Late................The Piano Man Deck 5 Aft

Karaoke Party
Join your host Ross and be a singing star.
7pm - 8:30pm..................Victoria Lounge Deck 5 Aft

TV Trivia Quiz
A chance to win a gold trophy.
4:30pm....................................Cabinet Deck 4 Aft

Butch's Liberty Slide Dance Class
Come for a Yee Ha good time!
7:30pm..Venetian Palace

Cheap as Chips BINGO
Triple Cards for only $10
JACKPOT PRIZE OF
$850

8:00pm & 10:00pm - Venetian Palace

Seaside Theatre

Big Screen
Concert Video: Tom Jones
5pm & 6:30pm
Family Movie Harry Potter
7:30pm

Karaoke Party
11:30pm
Seaside Theatre, Lido Deck 9

SPA carnival

Spa open
from 8am-10pm, gym open
from 6am-10pm
Port Day Special: Massage, Facial and
Foot Massage only $99
Body Blitz Only $89
2 for 1 BCA's

Fitness Classes:
7:30am Boot Camp Meet @ spaReception
8am...................................Pathway to Yoga (fee)
9am..Cardio Circuit
6pm.....................................Pathway to Pilates (fee)
7pm...Stretch & Relax
Call #1199
Specials valid in port.

Photo Gallery
5:00pm - 11:00pm .... Atlantic Deck 4 Forward
Pictures are the best way to preserve memories from
your cruise. Today, don't forget to give us a Smile on
the way out: we'll be at the pier with our cameras
ready to capture one of the best memories of the
cruise! So, enjoy, St.Thomas and later in the evening
come to see us at the photo gallery.
Tonight look for the **OLD FASHION STYLE** portrait
set up on promenade deck 5 You don't want to miss
it! ... Come and have some fun dressing up in old
west style clothes for one of the best memories of
the cruise you ever had.
Tonight Casual portraits:
7:15pm to 8:30pm and 9:30pm to 10:30pm - Lobby
deck 3 and Promenade deck 5

Jardin Cafe
Try the best specialty coffees at sea. Enjoy a freshly
made ice cream shake, tasty pastry or chocolate
covered strawberries. Nominal charges apply.
7:30am - 10:00am & 4:00pm - 1:00am..Deck 5 Aft

Formalities
Order fresh flowers for the one you love, have your
cabin decorated for a special occasion and rent a
tuxedo for formal night.
4:00pm - 10:00pm ...... Promenade Deck 5 Forward

Important Notice - Please Read
It is forbidden for any knives, replica weapons or replica
swords (which can be purchased ashore)
to be brought on board the vessel.

Shore Excursions
Last Chance to book your Shore Excursion for
beautiful St Thomas plus limit ed space available for
our remaining ports of call.
7:00am - 9:00am, 7:00pm - 9:00pm
The shore Excursion Desk is located on Lobby Dk3

CZAR'S PALACE CA$INO

Slots Open at 6pm
Full Casino Opens at 6:30pm
Caribbean Stud Poker /Diamond Edition
Progressive Jackpot Linked to other Carnival
Vessels Come check it out

Join the Ocean Players Club today. It's your
passport to discounts and special deals. See
your Casino Host for Details

Use your Sail & Sign Card to put credits onto
your slot machine. It's your own Casino Bank
account. **Coinless Gaming** is here. See
your Casino Host for details.

Sign up for tomorrow's
Blackjack Tournament!

Art Gallery Open
Stop by and see a few of the great artworks
available for auction later this cruise. Visit with
your art staff and collect your FREE raffle tickets
for upcoming drawings for fine art prizes!
7:00pm-10:00pm - Satin Room, Deck 3 forward

Carnival Golf.com
Don't miss the last chance to sign up for Jolly
Harbour golf course in Antigua. This course is set
in a tropical parkland, that has easterly breezes
cools you on the lush green fairways as you
challenge any of the seven lakes around the
course.
6:00pm - 8:00pm.............Tour Desk Lobby Deck 3

"The Web" Internet Cafe
INTERNET HAPPY HOUR 50% off!
50% off Time Charges!!! just login today between
6pm - 8pm to take advantage of this special offer.
*Please see the Internet café Manager for details
and restrictions.* Your Laptop or ours!! Wireless
access available everywhere!!!. The Web, Deck 4
Aft. Inside The Cabinet Lounge

CLUB O² (15 - 17 YRS)
Teens ages 15 – 17 come and join Abra your
CLUB O2 Director for activities exclusively for you.
Pick up a CLUB O2 schedule in WITHOUT
BATTERIES or at the Pursers desk.

PORT SHOPPING INFO DESK
Visit Michael at his desk for VIP Shopping
Stickers, Free Raffle Tickets, Coupons & Port
Shopping Info. Remember to take your St.Thomas
Port & Shopping Map, listing all the Carnival
approved stores today, 8:00am-9:30am & 7:30pm-
9:00pm - Deck 5 midship

NuEmage Air Brush Tattoos
Its Fun & Best of all it only temporary
8am-11am, 4pm-7pm & 8:30pm-11pm..Lido Deck

On Board Gift Shops
Open from 6:30pm - 10:30pm
Located on Promenade Deck 5

Beverly Hills Gold 14kt 70%
off the US retail.

St. Thomas Rum ball Tasting

dents from those countries are willing to work for less pay. Many Americans are not willing to work for low pay. That all changed in 2005 when Norwegian Caribbean Line's ship *The Pride of America* was the first ocean-going passenger vessel in nearly 50 years to sail under the American flag. As such, NCL was required to hire an all-American crew. NCL fully touts its NCL American brand.

Hospitality students with a degree can aspire to some of the better positions on a cruise ship. The top position in the rooms department is the hotel manager. The chief purser is responsible for personnel services and accounting. The cruise director is responsible for ensuring that guests are enjoying themselves. He is in charge of arranging activities and procuring entertainment for the ship. The chief steward is in charge of guest accommodations. These positions are similar to those in land-based operations. The top position in the restaurant side of the cruise ship is the executive chef. The food and beverage director and the maitre d' report to him. Many cruise lines promote from within, so an em-

Traditionally cruise lines hire residents from less-developed countries for positions such as waitress, because they are willing to work for less pay.

ployee may start as a child's activities director and work his way up to cruise director. Many workers sign up for six months at a time.

Each cruise line has policies concerning crew members fraternizing with guests. Some lines will allow its officers to mingle with the guests in selected areas. The crew does have its own deck, which consists of cabins and shared space for activities. Oftentimes the crew shares living accommodations. Working on a ship might seem glamorous, but it does involve many hours of work per day. Members of the crew may get some time off when the ship is in port. At that time they may attend to their personal needs or take some time off at the beach. There are advantages to working on a ship. First of all, one gets to meet people from all parts of the world. Because the crew's accommodations and meals are taken care of, one does not have to spend a great deal of money while on the ship, so one has the opportunity to save money. The downside is that the crew is away from their family and friends for long periods of time.

Because life aboard a cruise ship may not be for everyone, it may be a good idea for a college-age student to seek summer employment on a cruise ship. Some larger cruise lines may hire youth activity directors for the summer. Other smaller cruise lines may hire one to act as both a steward and a waiter. Some cruise lines may have opportunities for internships during college.

On shore one can work at the company's headquarters in the areas of marketing and sales, reservations, and finance and accounting. There are also a limited amount of positions working as a sales representative in major cities across the country. This position would entail visiting travel agents and groups highlighting the features and benefits of your product.

Trends

As seagoing vacations continue to grow in popularity, cruise lines have introduced new ports of call around the world. In 2006, travelers will find a portfolio of new cruises to the far reaches of the globe. The 19 cruise line members of the Cruise Lines International Association (CLIA) take travelers to 1,800 ports of call on more than 150 ships of varying styles, from yachtlike luxury ships carrying 150 passengers to mega vessels carrying more than 3,000 guests.

Other trends in cruising include

- A new generation of ships—68 debuted between 2000 and the end of 2005.
- Voyages to Antarctica.
- "Freestyle cruising" is designed to make cruising less regimented. Freestyle cruising offers clients the flexibility in choosing dining options, attire, activities, and times of disembarkation.
- Growth of drive market cruising. In the past most cruise ships departed from Miami and Los Angeles. Now clients have the option of departing from ports that are within driving distance of their home. Now it is possible for passengers to start their cruise from such cities as Galveston, Boston, Mobile, and Philadelphia on designated sailings.
- New types of pool decks. Royal Caribbean is changing the concept of the pool deck when it introduces a pool deck that will emulate many of the features of a water park. On its ship, *The Freedom of the Seas*, the coolest spot aboard the ship will be the H_2O zone, which will be a fabulous interactive water park that will offer surfing at sea. Other water-spouting attractions will be a waterfall, umbrella jets, and spray cannons.

So if you like value, fun, pampering, variety of activities, and interesting itineraries, come join "the wonderful world of cruising."

Resources

Internet Sites

Carnival Cruises: www.carnivalcruiselines.com
C.L.I.A.: www.cruisingorg/
Royal Caribbean International: www.royalcaribbean.com

☞ *Key Words and Concepts*

Berth
Bow
Bridge
Cabin
CLIA
Deck plan
Flag of convenience
Galley
Gross registered tonnage
Purser
Space ratio
Stabilizer
Stern
Tender

🖼 *Contributor Information*

Christopher DeSessa is an associate professor at Johnson & Wales' Hospitality College. In 1999 he won the National Tourism Foundation's Teacher of the Year Award. He has worked as a reservations agent for an airline, tour escort, and training director for a travel agency. For 23 years he also worked for one of the nation's oldest travel agencies.

22 Review Questions

1. What are the major departments of a ship?

2. What are the different career opportunities in the cruise industry?

3. What are the major trends in the cruise industry?

4. Please list the names of at least five cruise lines.

5. Where are the major cruise areas of the world?

6. What is the name of the organization that promotes the cruise industry?

7. What is included in the price of a cruise?

8. Please list reasons why people like cruises.

9. Please list five activities on a cruise ship.

Keith Mandabach
New Mexico State University

The Culinary World

Learning Objectives

✓ To describe a basic history of the culinary profession
✓ To define a wide array of culinary career options
✓ To identify strategies/recommendations for training and career paths
✓ To offer suggestions and stories from successful chefs
✓ To provide a list of resources for the novice culinarians

Chapter Outline

The Growing Culinary World
History of the Culinary World
Career Opportunities
Strategies to Build a Successful Culinary Career

What does it take to be a success in the culinary world and what do you do when you work as a chef?

Ratings for television food networks and cooking shows featuring glamorous chefs appear to have increased interest in cooking or culinary careers. The programs certainly piqued viewers' curiosity about what it is like to work in the culinary field. Others might be seriously considering becoming a chef and dedicating their life to the culinary world or as the industry describes them "wannabe chefs." Many have never worked in foodservice (some may never even have cooked an egg), but made an emotional decision that it might be fun to run a restaurant, write cookbooks, or have a cooking show on television. Readers are cautioned that as glamorous as the shows make the chef appear, the individuals that star on television did not instantly become the famous "chef." They worked long hours, studied, and trained to reach the positions they are in today.

Successful chefs formally apprenticed, attended a culinary school or college, trained under qualified chefs, and/or any combination of the three. They all certainly spent a great deal of time and effort mastering the basic culinary skills such as mastering knife skills and the correct methods to operate kitchen equipment. Each chef learned the correct methods of kitchen preparation including sautéing, frying, roasting, poaching, and broiling. In addition, these individuals understood and applied the principles of menu planning, recipe modification, food sanitation/safety, culinary human nutrition, and the science of cookery. Before one becomes a chef, one must be a cook, preferably a great one, and that is not always an easy task.

A great professional cook who aspires to become a chef must develop skills beyond simply following the steps outlined in a recipe. Cooking involves unique organic material (food products) that change over time. Complex factors also affect the process. These might include altitude, humidity, temperature, acidity, water chemistry, gauge or thickness of cooking pot or pan, regulation of cooking temperature, cooking techniques, and storage methods for the food. As one masters the art of preparation, one must utilize effective critical thinking skills to produce a tasty, attractive end product (something that people will enjoy eating). Being a chef is also being a business manager, and thus one must develop leadership skills and master the use of the computerized point-of-sale (POS) system in restaurants or computerized property management system (PMS) in hotels.

Computer systems assist today's chef in business operating essentials. Chefs utilize the systems in menu planning, recipe development, marketing, purchasing, inventory control, cost control, scheduling management, accounting, and human relations. In our computer-savvy world, the computer system is utilized in every facet of the operation. Knowledge of business skills is often as important as the technical skills a chef possesses. No matter how well one cooks, if the restaurant is not profitable, it will not stay in business. The chef must also anticipate food trends and the public's changing tastes. But most importantly in the end, a chef must enjoy the work. Most chefs work long hours, holidays, and weekends and this requires a unique dedication to the profession and a passion for making people happy. To those whose hearts are in the profession, the rewards can be fantastic. Chefs feed the world, and it is an honored profession.

The Growing Culinary World

The culinary world will continue to grow and is a solid career choice. Within the United States, the industry employs 12.2 million people and is expected to add 1.8 million new jobs between 2005 and 2015. "American consumers will spend around 47 percent of their food dollar in the restaurant industry in 2005."[1] There are over 900,000 restaurants in the nation and more are needed to keep pace with increasing demand. In 2005, predicted sales are expected to reach $476 billion. On a typical day in 2005, the restaurant industry will post average sales of nearly $1.3 billion. On an inflation-adjusted base, restaurant industry sales are expected to increase 4.9 percent in 2005, which equal 4 percent of the U.S. gross domestic product.[2]

History of the Culinary World

There is a long history of chefs and cooks whose lives were dedicated to improving the state of the culinary arts. Most traditional histories of cuisine have focused on the Western world's contribution to the field and rightfully emphasize the influence of

French cuisine on professional cookery. The French contribution is important not just because of the chefs who codified Western cuisine but also because of their leadership styles, cultivation, and insistence on the finest-quality ingredients, including French wine. There have been many French chefs, including Pierre François de La Varenne (1st French Cookbook), Jean-Anthelme Brillant-Savarin (book about the physiology of taste), Marie-Antoine Carême (the "Chef of Kings" was the father of Grande Cuisine), George Auguste Escoffier (wrote a cookbook that established standards of preparation for the world's chefs and developed the brigade system of kitchen management), Fernando Pont (clarified changes in cooking styles and taught his principles of cookery to the French from his classic restaurant the Pyramid), and Jacques Pépin (the ambassador of nouvelle cuisine, who stressed method and technique in his writings). Each became legends in their own time because of their professional attitude and their contributions to their communities and nation. They were respected for leading upstanding lives in addition to their awesome culinary skills.[3]

The European renaissance brought new interest in spices and foods from Asia. The West quickly adapted the advanced culinary habits of the East. In the 1400s the culinary and trade center of the world was Italy. A prominent chef of the Medici family published the first printed cookbook in 1475. When Caterina de Medici married the soon-to-be Henri II of France, she brought the entire kitchen staff to France. The French soon adapted the subtleties of spices and the new ingredients to create the classic French cuisine. Spain succeeded Italy as the great world power and also contributed to French cuisine by sending another French queen, Anna of Austria, to France with her Spanish chefs when she married Louis XIII. They introduced the classic brown sauces and roux (flour and butter) thickening agent to French cuisine. They also brought the foods of America, including the confusing tomato, to France.[4]

French Contributions

By 1651, the "French Grand Cuisine" would be codified by Pierre François Varenne in *Le Cuisinier Francais*. At the same time that France was codifying its cuisine, the products of America, among them the tomato, the potato, the pepper, chocolate, and coffee, were being assimilated into the European diet. The French also developed a training system for the chef and the steward (procurer of the food for the chef). Apprentices were indentured to learn the trade in kitchens that were smoky, dirty, and ill lit. Food was not simply something to eat but a spectacle to be produced. Ornate serving pieces complemented long complex dinners featuring at least one boiled salted meat, two soups, ten entrees, four roasts, four little hot entremets, and two pastries. Menus were presented in placard form and paraded before the dishes.[5]

The next century would see greater excesses. Chef Marie-Antoine Carême served massive royal dinners to members of the royal court. A big change occurred when the first French restaurant opened Les Rendezvous in 1765. Prior to this time, the catering industry was regulated by the caterer's guild. Over the guild's objections, a bouillon maker from Paris named Boulanger opened a shop selling a dish made with sheep's feet in wine sauce. It was designed to restore one's health and thus eventually became a restaurant. By the time of the French Revolution, hundreds of restaurants were open.[6]

American Contributions

American culinary traditions up until the American Revolution were tied to England, except for areas where Dutch (New York) or Germans (Pennsylvania) had settled. Americans ate quite well compared to the rest of the world. At times the early American diet may have been a bit bland and dominated by meat, but it was a definite improvement over what the majority of Europeans were eating. The most dedicated early American gourmet was Thomas Jefferson. He integrated the inside cookhouse into the design of Monticello. This integration produced warmer food because the food did not have to travel as far from the kitchen to the table. He also purchased one of the first cast iron ovens in America. He was one of the first Americans to make ice cream and hired the first French chef for the White House. Along with all the culinary innovations, Jefferson also cultivated grapes and made wine.[7]

America was an emerging nation as was its culinary style. Although European cuisine at this time was incorporating many of the new American foods into its meals, Americans learned fresh ways to merge Old World and New World foods. The Americas' greatest contribution to fine cuisine was cocoa, and one cannot imagine life without chocolate. America's tomato, corn, potato, and chili pepper are also now part of the basics of the world's cuisine.

Advice from Successful Chefs

Chef Gary Needham has worked in every segment of the industry except on-site dining. He has been a pastry chef, bakery operator, line cook, sous chef, and chef for restaurants, hotels, and resorts. He also worked in research and is now the chef owner of the award-winning Silver Oak Bistro in Washington, New Jersey. Chef Gary likes to simplify his advice to aspiring culinarians:

- Find out if you love the business before you spend the money on school.
- Listen to your clientele, they will tell you where you are as a chef.
- Be true to who you are as a chef.
- Don't try to please everybody's palate—just your own.
- Create a daily mantra for yourself. Mine is "Keep it fresh, keep it good."
- Enjoy cooking and talking to customers and staff; they are all your extended family.
- This business is hard work but very rewarding when you bring happiness into people's lives through a good meal.

Meats such as turkey and buffalo and a variety of fruits were also gifts from the new continents.[8]

In addition, technological revolutions taking place throughout the world were having a major effect on the culinary world. The innovation of the stove in 1807, by an American in England, allowed for major improvements in the cooking process and for kitchens to be located within a hotel or restaurant. Improvements were made in food preservation by canning and vacuuming seasonal items making them available year-round. Improvements in the transportation industry improved the portability of ice and made crude refrigeration possible. It became possible not only to transport food products quickly, but also to offer the products in a relatively healthy state at market.[9]

Although these inventions would affect the processes of cooking and serving food, the transportation industry would have a greater influence by increasing demand for good food. Restaurants opened to serve the needs of the residents and travelers. New York's Delmonico's was the first "in" American restaurant, and it offered cuisine beyond the nineteenth-century imagination. Ices and ice creams utilizing American fresh fruit were offered for the first time. They served foods in the French style with American adaptations. This was just one of many American restaurants whose food and service rivaled Parisian cuisine.[10]

Career Opportunities

There are a wide variety of career opportunities and places to work where a culinary professional will find satisfying work These include many multiple opportunities in four related industry career areas: commercial foodservice operations, culinology®, culinary education, and on-site dining. Each area has its own rewards, and all are connected and require the acquisition of technical (cooking) and managerial skills. In this book, we have covered catering, quick-service operations, restaurant operations, and bar/beverage operations.

Commercial Foodservice

Commercial foodservice is the part of the culinary area most of us are most familiar with and includes all forms of restaurants, hotels, clubs, bars, catering, sports venues, food markets, and ships. Most culinary careers begin in this discipline. Entry-level positions are usually cooks, pantry people, or kitchen helpers (many chefs started in the industry washing dishes). Although the size and type of establishment may differ by preparation style and method, those working in this area are producing purposeful food for profit.

Restaurants

This is the golden area of opportunity for aspiring culinarians. Many of our premier chefs and restaurant owners work in premier cutting-edge independent establishments. The work is very intense because the public is demanding. Usually the owner and/or chef will be very involved in everything from purchasing the freshest ingredients to production and service on the line. It is hard work, and to be successful in this world, one must have the stamina and vision to satisfy the public with every plate that is served.

Some dining companies also operate in these markets, and although it is a huge business, it is a small world. To get a job in this area, one must have a contact or friend or find a way to get "in" because everyone wants to get a job in the "best" place. Networking and reputation are important in all areas of the culinary world.

Premier dining spots are not the only area of opportunity. Large national chains (Chili's, Red Lobster, Olive Garden, Bennigan's, etc.) provide career paths for aspiring culinary managers in casual dining that eventually will reach general manager levels. Instead of chefs, most companies have culinary or kitchen managers. Clear-cut formulas are provided for management and for food service. Research teams in the head office develop proven recipes, and the computer systems are usually state of the art. Quick-service restaurants also offer financial rewards that many upscale facilities do not.

Hotels/Clubs/Resorts

Culinary careers in hotels, clubs, and resorts are often very similar in the way they operate, and it is not unusual for a chef to move from one area to the other. In this segment, the chef manages multiple-leveled restaurants, catering, and room service. Because of the multiple venues a chef must manage, communication and the ability to see the entire operation are two keys to success. In addition, chefs are often required to play public relations roles with guests, members, and the corporate officers. It is also important to understand the practicalities of budgeting, and computer skills are a must. Careers are often grown in this segment either through a corporation or mentor, and if one makes solid contributions on the way up the ladder, career success is possible.

On-Site or Non-Commercial Foodservice

Often as culinary careers develop, individuals find opportunities in other related areas of the industry. Commercial properties by their very nature require 24-7 attention, and for this reason a popular career path is to move into the on-site dining segment. Once labeled non-commercial or institutional, those working in this area might provide food to employees at an office building or manufacturing plant, manage the dining services of an educational facility, carefully supervise the food of health-care operation, or integrate high-quality foodservice in the life of a retirement community. In addition opportunities in on-site dining also include producing healthy food for those incarcerated in detention facilities, managing foodservice operations for the military, or coordinating events and food for a religious facility. This area also includes planning and delivery of food for sporting events including the Olympics, sports stadiums, recreational facilities, and camps.

Culinology®

For many who find their love of food and innovation challenged by the repetitive nature of commercial foodservice, on-site dining, or those who begin their culinary careers as food scientists, an alternative might be Culinology®. This term describes those involved in a variety of capacities in food product development, production, manufacturing, marketing, and distribution. The term was coined in 1996 by the Research Chefs Association to describe research chefs and food scientists (technologists). However all those involved in the development and distribution of food products now fall under this umbrella of Culinology®. The field embraces those involved in product, recipe, and menu development and innovation, food manufacturing, technology system (computer) development and application, purchasing, procurement, and media (television, newspapers, magazines, Internet).

Chef Educator

All chefs must teach and train their staffs and thus many at some time consider careers in education. For whatever reason, the number of culinary schools has more than doubled in the last ten years. In addition to traditional private and community college culinary schools, a variety of opportunities exist for chef educators. High school culinary arts programs hire experienced culinarians. Four-year universities are also expanding foodservice offerings, and public and private training programs addressing special needs are also growing.

Strategies to Build a Successful Culinary Career

Getting started in a culinary career is a daunting prospect, and aspiring culinarians might research the topic by reading stories and strategies in three great books: *Becoming a Chef, If You Can Stand The Heat* and *So You Want to Be a Chef: Your Guide to Culinary Careers.* These books provide a wealth of information and ideas about the culinary world and stress the challenges of the career. After your reading, the first step is to land an entry-level position and find out if the career is right for you. Almost all entry positions require a variety of hours, and one must accept the fact that weekends and holidays are normal workdays in the industry. Kitchens are also hot places to work, and entry-level positions will often have little of the glamour of higher level positions. Expect to wash dishes, do cleaning tasks, and have uncertain schedules. But no matter how menial, the right entry-level job is one that you are proud of.

Successful entry-level workers must be ready to learn, be a self-starter, and most importantly work

Culinary World Career Options

Commercial

- Restaurants: Fine dining/upscale, casual dining/multi/unit, value-driven restaurants/chain restaurants/limited service or quick service
- Hotels/resorts
- Clubs including country clubs/city clubs/social clubs/ethnic/religious/military
- Catering: Social/business/wedding/social/personal chef services
- Bars/taverns/sports/nightclubs/gentleman's/dance
- Sports arenas/sports clubs/racetracks
- Food markets: Supermarkets/gourmet markets/bakeries/pastry shops
- Ships: Cruise/excursion

On-Site Dining *(sometimes called noncommercial or institutional)*

- Industrial: Commercial/office/manufacturing/mining/special projects
- Education: Schools/universities/colleges
- Health care: Hospitals/nursing homes/retirement centers
- Detention: Federal/state/county/municipal
- Military: Base dining/social dining/deployed dining/recreation/sports
- Religious institutions: Churches/synagogues/mosques/retreats/camps

- Recreation: Sports arenas/Olympics/major events/residential camps/day camps/parks
- Vending: Machines/off-premise catering support

Culinology®

- Food Manufacturing: Research chef/chef nutritionist/food scientist/food service production specialist/food technologist/food stylist/procurement/marketing
- Distribution: Sales/chef demonstrator/purchasing specialist
- Corporate: Research chef/consultant/opening team specialist/menu developer/test kitchen/equipment evaluator or tester/ingredient evaluator/trade show specialist/marketing
- Technology specialist/food service point-of-sale system developer/system evaluator/installation specialist/support specialist/marketer
- Media: Television/magazines/newspapers

Education

- Chef educator: High school/culinary school/technical college/university/trade school/apprenticeship
- Trainer: Corporate/private/government-sponsored training programs

clean and neat. Sanitation is one of the most essential skills in any kitchen. Follow the adage "clean as you go" not just in your work space but also in your personal appearance. Kitchens are energized workplaces, and one must take care to respect co-workers and bosses. Come to work on time, ready to work and learn and master whatever tasks are assigned to you.

After sanitation, safety is most important. The three most common injuries are falls, cuts, and burns. Falls are usually caused by wet floors; clean up spills as they occur. Learn to use a knife properly and proper sharpening skills. A sharp knife is harder to cut yourself with. Burns are most often caused by carelessness or using wet towels to hold hot pans. Treat every piece of kitchen equipment— pots, pans, utensils—as if they were all hot all the time, and most burns can be avoided.

Education

Many individuals find their entry-level positions very satisfying and begin to advance their career, mastering skills and stepping up the ladder to more responsibility and higher pay. Many might seek to improve themselves beyond the training they are getting on the job and seek a formal training structure to improve their culinary and business skills. Some of these might have stepped into the culinary world to earn money for school or to support their families and have discovered they like and want to advance their careers, but are unsure of the best path. The immediate choices are culinary schools, colleges, and formal apprenticeships. The American Culinary Federation has a list of accredited programs and has detailed standards that list skills that must be mastered for the program to grant a certificate or degree. Almost all the programs require work experience that range from 400 to 1600 hours.

Public: Two-Year/Certificate Community College/Technical Schools

Although a detailed list of schools is beyond the scope of this chapter, the resource section lists information on a large number of schools. Students have many choices to acquire a quality culinary education at a variety of prices and venues. Students should always consider their local community college program in addition to the high profile culinary programs.

Private Schools: Two-Year Associate Degree and Certificate

The highest profile private culinary schools are the Culinary Institute of America (CIA), Johnson and Wales University, The Schools of Culinary Arts at the Art Institute, and Le Cordon Bleu Schools, and all have more than one campus. Other smaller quality private programs are the New England Culinary Institute and Kendall College. These are not all the private programs, and a more comprehensive list is available at *Peterson's Guide to Culinary Programs* listed in the resource section of this chapter. Whether large or small, the objectives of these programs are to provide high profile quality culinary education, and all require internships. Some require work experience prior to enrolling. Costs at these schools are significantly higher than public programs and thus it is wise to have had experience in the industry prior to enrolling.

Certification and Accreditation

Some culinary schools are accredited by the college accrediting agencies, and some are accredited by trade school agencies. Coursework from schools with trade school accreditation usually will not transfer to accredited academic degree programs so it is wise to find out what kind of accrediting agency granted the diploma before enrolling. The American Culinary Federation inspects and certifies culinary programs in the United States, and a list is included on their Web site. This is a voluntary program, and schools that are trade school accredited can be certified as accredited by the ACF if they complete the standards required.

College Two- and Four-Year Management Programs

These are usually part of hotel and restaurant management two-year or four-year degree programs at community colleges or universities. Most emphasize foodservice or restaurant management and are both public and private. Almost all have a variety of cooking classes in the curriculum. Many students who advanced to college directly from high school complete a four-year management degree, intern in culinary positions, and then go directly into culinary positions, culinary school, or apprenticeship programs after graduation. For those who have completed a four-year degree and have experience in the industry, CIA Greystone has a specific program designed for four-year graduates.

Advice from Successful Chefs

Chef Ronald Kuralt is Executive Chef and Dining Services Manager of Corporate Services in Columbus, Georgia, an on-site dining operation. Kuralt feels his work in on-site dining is a good fit for his talents. He utilizes his culinary leadership skills managing within the system provided by Sodexho. The position also offers many opportunities to showcase his culinary expertise and shine in special events and parties. Chef Kuralt chose this business because he enjoyed the hard work and the team effort it takes to serve great food.

- There is always going to be a need for trained culinary professionals.
- Work in the business, determine if you really love it, then go to a good culinary school.
- Remember school does not teach you everything you need to know about cooking, and it certainly does not make one a chef.
- Develop a career plan focused on continuous learning.
- Job changes contribute to learning but do not change jobs too often.
- Working for a quality hotel company or chain allows one to move and learn and not have to quit a job.
- Build a network of contacts to promote your career.
- Learn how computerized systems can be used to complete your daily purchasing, scheduling, sanitation and food production duties.
- The support of wives, significant others as well as family support can be a major positive force in many chefs' careers.

Bachelor Four-Year Culinary Arts Degrees

Currently there are over 20 accredited bachelor degree programs. Nicholls State, University of Nevada-Las Vegas, Walnut Hill College, the Art Institutes, CIA, Johnson and Wales, St. Louis University, Kendall College, and SUNY Cobleskill are a few of the best-known programs. All offer intensive culinary degrees with the general education components that allow them to grant a bachelor's degree. These programs were designed in response to industry demand. These programs are designed to provide graduates the quality of an intensive culinary degree with a stronger business and general education component. All these programs have classes that focus on computers/point-of-sale systems and require extensive verbal, written, and mathematic communication skills as well as expanded business accounting and management requirements.

Apprenticeship Programs

This method of training has historically been the world's standard culinary training method. The apprentice program in the United States is modeled after the European system and was approved formally in 1971. The U.S. program is managed by the American Culinary Federation and administered by the U.S. Dept. of Labor Bureau of Apprenticeship and Standards. Individuals work in establishments under approved chefs, attend educational sessions, and rotate through the varied work experiences for a two- or three-year period.

The key to finding the right apprenticeship is finding the right chef and property to work with. Many seek these training programs to replace going to college or culinary school because they get paid as they learn. Others actively search for apprenticeships after they complete school. The first step is to attend a meeting of your local chapter of the ACF or go to the ACF Web site, find your local chapter, and contact the president or apprenticeship chair. Not all chapters have apprentices. The ACF Web site also lists which programs are involved in apprenticeships. Sometimes the apprenticeships utilize the local community college to provide the educational component, and the chef at your school might also have information.

This is a systematic method of training, and traditionally includes working all the classical kitchen positions, and is a brilliant method to polish one's skills. Sometimes an apprentice will rotate between different properties to complete the skills. Whatever the setting, the novice chef should expect to experience a step-by-step approach based on moving from general to specific skills and follow a structured curriculum. Apprentices are provided an overview of the industry and first trained in sanitation and safety. In the kitchen, apprentices imitate chef demonstrations of basic knife cuts or cooking tasks. Eventually the imitation becomes experience, apprentices match level of skill required, and a student is said to have mastered a competency.

Apprentices might start in stewarding (dishes, pots, porter), move to the pantry, grill cook, butcher shop, bakery, line cook, vegetable cook, fish cook, broiler cook, roast cook, sauce cook, and rounds cook. Toward the end of the apprenticeship, many assume positions of garde-manger (cold kitchen chef), sous chef, or steward. Eventually, the student or apprentice will complete the competencies required and complete the program. To graduate apprentices must successfully complete both written and hands-on tests and acquire the Certified Culinarian or CC after their name from the ACF.

Certification

After mastering or completing the programs and continuing their careers, many individuals seek certification from the American Culinary Federation (ACF). Non-traditional students returning to school might be pleasantly surprised that the organization accepts on-the-job experience in its certification process. An excellent strategy for building a culinary career would be to investigate skill requirements and strive to master skills and requirements for certification. The first step to achieving certification is becoming a member of the ACF and contacting the local certification chair. In addition to educational requirements and knowledge tests, applicants must also pass a hands-on test for some of the levels of certification.

The ACF Web site identifies the skills necessary to attain certification at a variety of levels of the culinary profession with written and practical certification testing requirements including Certified Master Chef (CMC), Certified Master Pastry Chef (CMPC), Certified Executive Chef (CEC), Certified Executive Pastry Chef (CEPC), Certified Culinary Administrator (CCA), Certified Culinary Educator (CCE), Certified Chef de Cuisine (CCC), Personal

Certified Executive Chef (PCEC), Certified Secondary Culinary Educator (CSCE), Certified Working Pastry Chef (CWPC), Certified Sous Chef (CSC), Personal Certified Chef (PCC), Certified Culinarian (CC), or Certified Pastry Culinarian (CPC). The ACF is the premier national organization for chefs and cooks, and its Web address is listed in the resource section. *The Soul of a Chef: The Journey Toward Perfection* by Michael Ruhlman provides a fascinating description of the master chef certification exam and details the challenges chefs face when they attempt to reach the highest level.

Other Options

The ACF certifies for a wide range of positions, but other organizations also provide opportunities to enhance your career. The National Restaurant Association (NRA) also has a certification program as does the International Food Service Executives Association (IFSEA). NRA holds the premier restaurant show in the world (currently in May in Chicago) and is the organization to join for restaurant chefs. IFSEA is primarily an on-site and military organization that provides outstanding support within their organizations. The Club Managers Association also provides excellent networking opportunities for its chefs. There are two personal chef organizations, and the International Association of Culinary Professionals offers support for personal chefs and for those in Culinology®.

Within the Culinology® field, the Research Chefs Association provides certification opportunities and networking. For educators, Foodservice Educators Network International (FENI), Center for Advancement of Foodservice Education (CAFÉ), the ACF, and International Council of Hotel, Restaurant and Institutional Educators all provide support and certifications for culinary educators.

Summary

The culinary arts field is an exciting and growing career path. The history of the profession is tied to national and economic growth and has been heavily influenced by French and European chefs. Immigrant chefs trained in Europe were the dominant force in American cuisine. These professionals adapted American ingredients and began the process of blending the ethnic variety that was America into the food they served. They formed professional associations that promoted training in the culinary

Advice from Successful Chefs

Chef E. J. Harvey, the chef/owner of the Seagrille, part owner of The Band of Thieves Restaurant and the Nantucket Chowder Company on Nantucket Island, Massachusetts, says his favorite parts of his day are the beginning and the end. His day usually starts with organizing and planning the food production for the day. He starts the bread dough, and mixing and baking the bread provides him with a real sense of love. Creating the stocks, then the finished soups and sauces for the operation, and getting the staff set up for the busy day's business is also a tranquil time. The end of the day provides time for reflection and satisfaction. Every day his team successfully serves a large number of customers a wide array of food. After it is over the spirit of camaraderie that is evident in his team makes the hard work worthwhile, and he kicks back and reflects in the shadows of the day.

- The culinary profession is constantly changing.
- All students should work in the industry before attending culinary school.
- Develop a palate by tasting a wide variety of foods and do not prejudge a dish before you taste it.
- It is important to travel and experience different countries, cultures, and their cuisines because the word *fusion cuisine* is more than a word.
- Finally don't expect to graduate from school and be handed a top job.
- You must work hard and earn the respect of the people around you as well as keep your sense of humor.
- Be a professional and remember that manners are important.

Chef Harvey says that "my goal was always to become a chef, and I never lost sight of it no matter how many gatherings, holidays, or family events I missed. But I never put my family off. We might have Thanksgiving dinner on Friday, but we always celebrated. I set out to be a successful chef, and I carried that vision to my family and to the community. It would mean nothing to me to be successful if I did not have the respect of my community and the people around me, most importantly my family. I have been blessed with a very supportive wife and children. Without them it might have been very easy to lose my focus and thus my success."

arts and a professional approach to a culinary career that eventually became the American Culinary Federation. The ACF codified professional culinary training in schools and apprenticeships and implemented clear-cut professional standards that eventually lead to national standards for schools.

Aspiring culinarians have a variety of career choices and educational paths. Before going to culinary school it is a good idea to work in the industry and learn through on-the-job training. There are several options for culinary schools, and it is important to investigate the schools before making a final decision on where to spend one's tuition dollars. Another choice is apprenticeship, and students should contact the American Culinary Federation for information on where the nearest program is. The ACF also has a professional certification program that allows a culinarian to document career achievements.

Endnotes

1. Kim, K. (2004, December 14). National Restaurant Association announces record sales projected in year ahead for nation's largest private sector employer. *National Restaurant Association.* Retrieved August 9, 2005 from http://www.restaurant.org/pressroom/pressrelease.cfm?ID=979
2. National Restaurant Association. (2005c). *The cornerstone initiative.* Retrieved October 13, 2005 from http://www.restaurant.org/cornerstone/index.html
3. Gislen, W. (2006). *Advanced professional cooking.* New York: Wiley
4. Ibid

5. Dornenburg, A. & Page, K. (2002). *Becoming a chef.* Hoboken, NJ: Wiley
6. Ibid
7. Root, W., & Rochemont, R. (1976). *Eating in America.* New York: Morrow
8. Ibid
9. Ibid
10. Ibid

Resources

Books

Davis, Dawn. *If You Can Stand the Heat: Tales from Chefs and Restaurateurs.* New York: Penguin Putnam, 1999

Dornenburg, Andrew, Page, Karen, and Bergin, James. *Becoming a Chef Journal.* New York: Van Nostrand Reinhold, 1996

Brefere, Lisa M., Drummond, Karen Eich, and Barnes, Brad. *So You Want to Be a Chef: Your Guide to Culinary Careers.* Hoboken, NJ: Wiley, 2006

Ruhlman, Michael. *The Soul of a Chef: The Journey Toward Perfection.* New York: Penguin Putnam, 2001

Schools

The Art Institutes Schools of Culinary Arts All Campuses: http://www.artinstitutes.edu/culinary/

Culinary Institute of America: www.ciachef.edu

Culinary Institute of America at Greystone: http://www.ciachef.edu/california/

John Folse Culinary Institute: http://www.nicholls.edu/jfolse/

Johnson and Wales (all campuses): http://www.jwu.edu/

Kendall College Culinary: http://www.kendall.edu/Academics/CulinaryArts/tabid/70/Default.aspx

Le Cordon Bleu International (all campuses): http://www.cordonbleu.net/International/English/dp_main.cfm

Le Cordon Bleu USA: http://www.lecordonbleuschoolsusa.com/

New England Culinary Institute: http://www.neci.edu/home.html

Peterson's Guide to Culinary Schools: http://www.petersons.com/culinary/

Networking and Support Organizations

American Culinary Federation (ACF)
800-624-9458
www.acfchefs.org

American Dietitic Association (ADA)
800-877-1600
www.eatright.org

Educational Institute of the American Hotel and Lodging Association
517-372-4567
www.ei-ahla.org

American Institute of Wine and Food (AIWF)
800-274-2493
www.aiwf.org

American Personal Chef Association (APCA)
800-644-8389
www.personalchef.com

American Society for Healthcare Food Service Administrators (ASHFSA)

Association for Career and Technical Education (ACTE)
800-826-9972
www.acteonline.org

Black Culinarian Alliance (BCA)
800-308-8188
www.blackculinaries.com

Club Managers Association of America (CMAA)
703-739-9500
www.cmaa.org

Confrerie de la Chaine des Rotisseurs
973-360-9200
www.chaineus.org

Dietary Managers Association (DMA)
800-233-1908
www.dmaoline.org

Foodservice Educators Network International (FENI)
312-849-2220
www.feni.org

International Association of Culinary Professionals (IACP)
502-581-9786
www.iacp.com

International Caterers Association (ICA)
888-604-5844
www.icacater.org

International Food Service Executives Association (IFSEA)
702-838-8821
www.ifsea.com

National Association of College and University Food
    Services (NACUFS)
517-332-2494
www.nacufs.org

National Restaurant Association (NRA)
The National Restaurant Association Educational
    Foundation (NRAEF)
202-331-5900
www.restaurant.org

Research Chefs Association (RCA)
404-252-3663
www.culinology.com

School Nutrition Association (formerly the American
    School Food Service Association)
703-739-3900
www.schoolnutrition.org

Society for Foodservice Management (SFM)
502-583-3783
sww.sfm-online.org

United States Persona Chef Association (USPCA)
800-995-2138
www.uspca.com

Women Chefs and Restaurateurs (WCR)
877-927-7787
www.womenchefs.org

Women's Foodservice Forum (WFF)
855-368-8008
www.womensfoodserviceforum.com

☞ Key Words and Concepts

American Culinary Federation
Apprenticeship
Commercial food service
Culinary arts
Culinary school
Culinology®
Grande cuisine
On-site or non-commercial foodservice
Point of sale (POS)
Property management system (PMS)

▣ *Contributor Information*

Dr. Keith Mandabach, CEC AAC is an associate
professor at the School of Hotel Restaurant and
Tourism Management of New Mexico State
University. He has extensive industry experience
as a resort and convention hotel executive chef,
culinary educator, and consultant. He holds a
doctorate in educational leadership and cultural
studies from the University of Houston, has a
master's in hospitality management from the
Conrad Hilton College, and is a Certified Executive Chef and member of the American Academy
of Chefs. Dr. Mandabach has received numerous
professional awards and is a regular speaker,
consultant, reviewer, and researcher for academic
and industry journals and symposiums. He can be
reached at kmandaba@nmsu.edu.

23 Review Questions

1. What are three of the skills necessary to master to become a successful chef?

2. Why is a culinary career a solid career choice?

3. Describe "Grande Cuisine."

4. What are the three areas that present career opportunities in the culinary world?

5. Why is the commercial food service segment the area most culinarians start their career?

6. Why do many chefs move from the commercial food service segment to the on-site segment?

7. Describe at least two opportunities in the Culinology® field?

8. What do all the chefs and the author of the chapter advise one to do before applying to culinary school?

Donna Albano
Michael Scales
The Richard Stockton College
of New Jersey

Distribution Services

Learning Objectives

✓ To describe career possibilities in the hospitality distribution services industry

✓ To identify and explain trends affecting the hospitality distribution services industry

✓ To describe elements unique to each segment of the hospitality distribution services industry

✓ To describe the role of a distributor sales representative in the hospitality distribution services industry

✓ To explain the purpose of hospitality industry trade shows and expositions

✓ To identify the size and the scope of hospitality industry's linens needs

Chapter Outline

Career Opportunities
Food and Beverage
Foodservice Equipment and Supplies
Linens
Furniture, Fixtures and Equipment
 (FF&E)
Technology
Trends in Distribution Services

There are many career possibilities in distribution services. The hospitality industry utilizes thousands of goods and services in daily operations. Distribution services are the backbone of the hospitality industry. Career choices and opportunities in the hospitality industry expand beyond the popular segments of lodging and food and beverage. The peripheral career opportunities in the hospitality industry are many. This chapter can help you answer some important career questions like

- What segment(s) is/are of most interest?
- How do I discover career opportunities?
- How do I plan a longer-term career?
- Do I want to work for myself or for someone else?
- Do I want to work domestically or in a position elsewhere in the global hospitality industry (or both)?

Career Opportunities

Some of the careers in distribution services include purchasing agents, information technology, accountants, human resources, warehouse managers, delivery drivers, food inspectors, and street sales. Many of these positions require salespeople to meet face-to-face with hospitality operators weekly or more often. The sales representatives also provide information on cost-cutting ideas, introduce new or improved products, and assist in menu development. It is typically the personal interaction that creates a working relationship between the hospitality industry and its vendors.

Food and Beverage

Food Distribution

Food items are delivered daily to operations throughout the world. Price, quality, and quantity of food products are determined by chefs and kitchen managers each day. From the hot dog vendor at the ball game to the fine dining restaurant to hospitals and schools, all these operations must purchase food products for mass production. There are many career opportunities in the food and beverage distribution industry. Many food vendors seek out former restaurant managers and employees with knowledge of food products and operations to fill positions in this industry. Food distributors (also

known as vendors or purveyors) supply fruits and vegetables, meats and poultry, seafood, dairy products, coffee and beverages, bread and baked goods, dry, canned, and frozen products, and everything else needed for the food service operator.

Food product suppliers work directly with farmers, meat and poultry packaging plants, fish and seafood houses, dairies, and food processing plants. Many are small businesses that may carry a certain type of food. Dairy products and fresh baked goods and breads are normally delivered to restaurants and foodservice operations every day. These are sometimes considered standing orders in which the operators receive the same quantity of food products each day. Fresh produce (fruits and vegetables) distributors typically purchase products daily from a central distributor and act as an intermediary delivery directly to the food service operators for a profit. Some seafood distributors operate the same way, whereas many purchase large amounts of fish and butcher or fillet the fish on premises to be delivered daily. Meats and poultry are also often butchered on premise according to the foodservice operators' specifications. Meats and poultry products are generally delivered three to four days a week. Dry, canned, and frozen food products as well as coffee and beverages can be delivered once or twice a week.

Some food distributors carry a full line of food products, including produce, meats and poultry, seafood, dairy products, coffee and beverages, bread and baked goods, dry, canned, and frozen products. SYSCO, one the largest foodservice distributors in the United States, provides a full line of food products, along with foodservice equipment, paper products, and cleaning supplies. SYSCO also provides services to foodservice operators in kitchen design and cost-cutting consultation.

U.S. Foodservice™ and SYSCO are two companies that employ sales representatives and are considered "total suppliers."[1] These companies supply everything from brand-name products to equipment and supplies.

Many chain foodservice operations and multi-unit operations purchase products exclusively from system distributors. System distributors are commonly owned by the same corporations that own the chain foodservice operations. This allows the chain operation to control the quality and consistency of products and also enables the organization to purchase in large volume at reduced prices.

Corporate Profile: U.S. Foodservice™

U.S. Foodservice™ is one of the leading broad-line foodservice distributors in the United States, with yearly revenues exceeding $17 billion. U.S. Foodservice™ is one of the largest broad-line foodservice distributors in the United States. The company distributes food and related products to over 250,000 customers, including restaurants, health-care facilities, lodging establishments, cafeterias, schools, and colleges. U.S. Foodservice™ markets and distributes more than 43,000 national, private label, and signature brand items and employs more than 28,000 foodservice professionals.

Today, as the twenty-first century unfolds, U.S. Foodservice™

- Markets and distributes more than 43,000 national, private label, and signature brand items across America

- Supports over 250,000 food service customers, including restaurants, hotels, health-care facilities, cafeterias, and schools

- Employs more than 29,500 foodservice professionals

- Embraces a customer base of independent and chain businesses[2]

Liquor Distribution

Many restaurants sell alcoholic beverages in addition to food. Wine, beer, and spirits are typically purchased on a weekly basis. From fine wines to kegs of beer, the distribution of alcoholic beverages starts with the producers and ends on the guests' palates. The liquor distribution industry supplies these products to the hospitality industry. Although state, county, and local laws dictate sales of alcoholic beverages, most liquor distributors operate the same way.

Liquor distribution sales representatives work closely with wine producers and distributors. A liquor sales representative typically attends wine tasting and training seminars to properly represent the products they sell. These sales representatives often pass along this knowledge to restaurant, club, bar, and catering operators with the hopes of getting the wines they represent included on the operation's wine list. It can be a very competitive industry.

Wine pairing is another very important way liquor distributors provide a service to the hospitality industry. Many sales representatives work with restaurateurs to pair wines with food menu items. For this position a sales representative must be familiar with not only domestic and international wines, but also liqueurs, beers, and spirits. This segment of the industry offers other positions in purchasing, accounting and finance, warehouse management, and marketing.

Promotions are also a big part of liquor distribution. A huge part of selling these products is getting guests to try them. Many bars and restaurants will work with sales representatives and the marketing department to promote certain alcoholic beverages on specific nights, giving away free or reduced-price samples just as the food industry does in grocery stores. These promotions may also include entertainment, product logo giveaways (such as T-shirts, caps, and key chains), and interactive games.

Foodservice Equipment and Supplies

There are many career opportunities in the foodservice equipment and supply industry. All foodservice operations purchase non-food products from vendors. Everything from a broiler oven to a mop handle to paper towel rolls must be purchased for the efficient operation of a foodservice operation. This industry offers thousands of products that help operators maintain their workplaces. The equipment and supply industry works directly with foodservice operations in many ways, from supplying kitchen equipment to new businesses to providing paper and cleaning products to existing hospitality enterprises. Many suppliers also offer consulting advice in areas such as kitchen design and layout, equipment, menu design, and sanitation needs. How many juice glasses will a new restaurant with 300 seats need? How can I budget for dishwashing detergent next year? Should I purchase a conventional or convection oven? This industry provides expertise in answering these questions.

One company that specializes in providing equipment and supplies is Edward Don & Company. Edward Don & Company is a leader in foodservice equipment distribution and provides foodservice equipment and supplies to restaurants, government institutions, hospitals, hotels, and schools. Edward Don & Company also offers bar and fountain supplies, catering and cooking equipment, tableware, tables and chairs, paper goods, cleaning products, sanitation supplies, and 12,000 other products. The company distributes its products nationwide. Edward Don also designs and builds full-service kitchens for the foodservice industry. The company, owned by the Don family, was founded in Chicago in 1921.[3]

Another organization in the foodservice equipment industry is Restaurant Equipment World, Inc. Restaurant Equipment World, Inc. is a world leader of online restaurant equipment sales, installation, design, and export. The company owns and operates a network of 175+ product specific Web sites with a database of more than 20,000 catalog items with photos. Restaurant Equipment World, Inc. has been in business for over 28 years, and their site features REX—the restaurant equipment search engine.

Foodservice equipment distributors also provide products for daily use, particularly paper goods such as take-out cups and containers, toothpicks, lobster bibs, aluminum foil, cocktail napkins, and toilet tissue, to name a few. These sales representatives also sell cleaning products including dishwashing detergent, bleach, hand soap, and de-greasing products.

Career opportunities in this industry include accounting/finance, administration, customer service, human resources, marketing, operations, information technology, and sales. Sales positions include management and non-management positions in street sales, national accounts, and project managers for foodservice equipment division.[4] The vast majority of distributor sales representatives earn income based on some combination of total sales collected and percent of gross margin on products sold. Like other sales positions in and outside the hospitality industry, the more they sell, the more they earn. Many distributor sales representatives receive additional financial incentives if they achieve certain company goals: increasing average order sizes or sales of a particular product, maybe upping sales of private-label items. To create ongoing relationships with distributors, sales representatives are expected to provide useful information and present products to hospitality managers while letting the managers make decisions. It is the steady long-term customers that will make distributor sales representatives successful.[5] Distributor sales representatives are generally provided a geographical area in which to sell their wares. These areas are typically referred to as territories. The sales representatives provide service to existing customers while constantly trying to acquire new customers in their territories. This is an extremely competitive industry that requires skilled professionals with impeccable personal and organizational skills. These individuals must also be self-motivated and driven. Much of their time is spent alone traveling the territory and working with technology, specifically e-mail and cell phones, taking and placing orders to meet daily deadlines.

Linens

With the demand for upscale services growing at a rapid pace, the purchasing, receiving, issuing, storing, and cleaning of linens, towels, tablecloths, and uniforms has become an intricate component of cre-

Company Profile: AC Linen

Located in the heart of "Always Turned On" Atlantic City, AC Linen is the current name of a laundry operation that has been around since the late 1890s. This facility now does some work for each of the city's 13 gaming halls and handles the laundry for eight of the Atlantic City casino properties.

This operation is housed in a 14 million, 63,000-square-foot complex that is energy efficient, computerized, and fully automated.

AC Linen washes and dries about 100,000 pounds of laundry each day, and its daily load includes about 25,000 sheets and 30,000 bath towels. Laundry is processed around the clock guaranteeing a one-day turnaround for the casino hotels. The facility is open 24 hours a day, seven days a week.

The current facility operates at about 40 percent to 50 percent of its capacity, and the company has the ability to add more washers and dryers as its customer base grows. The company employs more than 200 workers and boasts annual revenues of $12 million.

Restaurants and banquets are only a small portion the soiled linens created every day in a hospitality operation.

ating a favorable guest experience. Linen ranging from very luxurious to normal types is used by various hospitality operations depending on their requirements.

In addition to purchasing laundry, hospitality operations have several choices when it comes to how they handle the laundry as well. Many peripheral industries are related to the rental and cleaning of hospitality laundry. Guestrooms, restaurants, banquets, fitness centers, and employees all create soiled linens, towels, tablecloths, and uniforms. Although many lodging properties in the United States operate an on-premises laundry, many others have their laundry cleaned and processed by outside contractors. Linen is a very important part of our hotel's image. Lodging customers measure quality as the sum of many little things, all of which are important.

Career opportunities in this peripheral hospitality segment of the industry could include working for a company that sells apparel and uniforms, bedding, linens, or an off-premise laundry company.

Furniture, Fixtures, and Equipment (FF&E)

Purchasing furnishings, supplies, and equipment is a function that can be performed by a corporate-level purchasing department, a purchasing manager

or agent at a hotel, or performed by a third-party purchasing agent. The Internet has made the job of purchasing easier and faster, but someone or some team must still ensure that the materials purchased are the right quality and quantity.

In hospitality, there are three distinct types of purchasing. Two areas—operating supplies and disposables and food-and-beverage items—are purchases that can be performed through computerized programs. Purchasing these standardized products is migrating toward business-to-business Internet purchasing.

Purchasing furniture, fixtures, and equipment requires a different process. Because almost every item is non-standard or custom-made, cost-effective FF&E purchasing demands professionals who fully comprehend the variables and use expertise to create the best value.

There are other intangibles that a purchasing professional addresses. Verifying that the manufacturer has liability insurance can save the hotel owner millions of dollars in potential liability claims. Coordinating time and routing of freight by balancing cost, construction and installation schedules, and packaging can save money.

Purchasing is an administrative function requiring technical knowledge about the products being purchased and the market dynamics that affect prices and supply.[6] A career in purchasing food and beverage for a hotel or restaurant would require some experience in food production and management as well as knowledge of how a kitchen operates. Keeping aware of market trends and new products is also important. Knowledge of grading criteria, labeling, and standards of quality is also important. A purchasing agent is required to judge if a fair price is being quoted by a distributor and match orders to purchase specifications.

Learning how to deal effectively with suppliers and master the managerial aspects of purchasing is necessary if you are interested in a career in the purchasing department of a hospitality company. A skilled purchasing agent knows how innovative purchasing techniques can contribute to profits, efficient operations, and guest satisfaction.

Technology

The hospitality industry utilizes many systems and technologies to serve guests more efficiently and effectively. Information technology helps hospitality businesses reach their goals of delivering exceptional guest satisfaction. Hospitality information technology can range from computers and hardware to telephone systems and software. Hospitality industry technology systems range from electronic mail to global or international information systems, hotel information technology systems, energy management systems, call accounting systems, guest reservation systems, security systems, sales and marketing systems, and restaurant and foodservice information technology systems. This automation help make hospitality operations as efficient as possible while enhancing the guest's experience when used correctly.

The links between point-of-sale (POS), property management (PMS), inventory and purchasing, sales and catering (S&C) and business intelligence (BI) systems are both tighter and more flexible. As technology becomes less of a limiting factor, the challenge is relying on hospitality managers to make the best use of these tools for a more effective operation.

The Property Management System (PMS) is the center of information processing in a hotel. It is a computer based lodging information system that connects both the front of the house and back of the house activities. Computerized property management systems can simplify check-in, track the status of rooms, and manage guest accounts. The PMS can also interface with electronic locking systems, energy management systems, and call accounting systems.

The point-of-sale systems (POS) are computerized systems used to track food and beverage charges and other retail charges that may occur in a hospitality facility. The POS can provide software for food/beverage management, inventory control, labor tasks, POS, and time and attendance. The POS equipment can include time clocks, handheld terminals, and credit card authorization/settlement readers.

If you have an interest in a career in technology in the hospitality industry a number of jobs are available in implementation of systems, product development, and Web design. Companies that specialize in hospitality technology are generally looking for those candidates that have hospitality industry experience and a background or training in technology. Some companies specializing in sales and service of property management systems look for a hospitality and/or computer support background, knowledge of computers by training clients, troubleshooting/resolving problems, and teamwork skills.

Jobs that are available in companies that specialize in sales and service of point-of-sales systems are administration, customer service, database administration, implementation specialist, product specialist, service technicians, research and development, sales and marketing, and software development. Many of the qualifications include prior experience with installation or support of POS/PMS or computer software and hardware and customer service. Additional skills include excellent verbal and written communication skills and excellent customer service skills.

Another category of peripheral hospitality careers are professionals that do nothing but design, promote, and manage exhibits and trade shows. Trade shows and expositions can be held in hotels, convention centers, or larger public venues. They are usually sponsored by companies or associations and can be public, professional, or retail oriented.

The hospitality industry holds many trade shows and expositions. Two of the most popular in the United States are The International Hotel/Motel & Restaurant Show and The National Restaurant Association Hotel-Motel Show. The International Hotel/Motel & Restaurant Show, the world's largest showcase and exchange of industry products, trends, and developments, attracts every segment and facet of the industry. This show unveils more than 1,400 products and services and draws more than 35,000 attendees each year.[7] The annual

Job Description:
Project Manager

Summary: Overall responsibility for providing from start to finish installation services on contracts for company products of four or less POS terminals; responsibility, except scheduling, for installation services on contracts for company products of five or more POS terminals, including the following essential duties and responsibilities:

Essential Duties and Responsibilities: Include the following. Other duties may be assigned.

- Review with the Software Services Manager system installation contracts and review the plan to complete the project.

- Review with the Account Manager what was sold and key features or issues that must be addressed in the installation.

- Survey and collect necessary information from a customer necessary to configure and install the purchased system.

- Coordinate with respective managers, departments, and customer all steps necessary to install a POS system.

- Keep Software Services Manager apprised of any changes to task dates as the project progresses.

- Write the database for the customer's systems, load, and test it.

- Diagrams the customer's system configuration.

- Trains and test customer skills in using their system.

- Documents time used, activity with the customer and collects all necessary paperwork and data files per company policy.

- Provides on-site assistance/guidance when the customer begins using the product.

- Assists in qualifying/quantifying software "bugs" in the products the company sells. Forward information and data to the Software Services Manager for follow-up.

- In rotation, provides after-hours Help Desk assistance to customers outside business hours.

National Restaurant Association's Hotel-Motel Show is the largest single gathering of restaurant, foodservice, and lodging professionals in North and South America. As the industry's premier business venue, it offers attendees the best opportunities of the year for networking and exploring new trends, as well as insight on myriad industry issues via seminars and special events.[8] Professional exhibitors and designers belong to an organization called the Trade Show Exhibitors Association (TSEA). This association acts as the industry voice for exhibit and event marketing professionals. For over 30 years, TSEA has provided knowledge to marketing and management professionals who use exhibits to promote and sell their products, as well as to those who supply them with products and service.[9] Additional careers in this field include trade show marketing, tradeshow sales and meetings, and exhibits coordinator.

Trends in Distribution Services

Working as part of the distribution systems industry, it is important that professionals stay abreast of the many trends that affect the hospitality industry. The following trends will no doubt impact hospitality operations in the near future.

In 2005 the New York City health department began a campaign against trans fats. Restaurant inspectors determined that 30 percent of the city's 30,000 eateries used oils that contained trans fats, which has been linked to cholesterol problems and increased risk of heart disease. This campaign could develop in foodservice industry changes across the United States, much in the same way no-smoking bans are changing the industry through legislation.[10]

Menu trends will include an increase in ethnic cuisines such as Thai, Mexican, and Caribbean.

Professional Profile: David Kasinetz

"I would not have the success I have today if it were not for my restaurant management background."

David Kasinetz is a Sales Manager for Advanced Hospitality Systems. He first worked for Darden Restaurants as a manager for Red Lobster on completing his Bachelor of Science degree in Hotel and Restaurant Management from Widener University. David also studied Business Administration at The Pennsylvania State University. After several years he went to work for Pepperidge Tree Restaurants in Philadelphia. As technological changes began to occur in the restaurant industry, David followed his longtime interest in computers and made a career change to Comtrex Systems Corporation as a sales consultant. David excelled in selling point-of-sales (POS) systems to food and beverage establishments. He left Comtrex for Advanced Hospitality Systems in 1997, where he has continued to be on the forefront of food and beverage technology. David admits, "I would not have the success I have today if it were not for my restaurant management background." His experience gives him the unique ability to work with clients on issues and concerns adapting and customizing POS systems for food and beverage operations. Mr. Kasinetz says his daily activities involve traveling; attending trade shows; conducting software demonstrations; preparing return on investments analyses; hiring, training, and managing a sales and administrative staff; and creating innovative marketing materials. David has also been a guest lecturer in hospitality management at both the University of Delaware and The Richard Stockton College of New Jersey.

Required Skills—Excellent communication skills, enjoy public speaking, computer skills, MS office applications, must be a great listener, salesmanship.

Required Knowledge—Understanding of hotel and restaurant operations, basic computer networking concepts.

Highlights of Job—I enjoy travel and attending trade shows and every day meeting new and interesting people and helping them increase their profits.

Recommendations—Most high paying sales jobs are commission based. Do not expect to have great success immediately. It takes a few years to build a pipeline of prospects, but eventually you will reap the rewards. Learn as much as you can while working in operations. Pay attention to food and beverage cost/labor cost, be detail oriented, and enjoy the hard work. Restaurant management will prepare you for different opportunities down the road. It's invaluable experience.

There will also be an emphasis in displaying ingredients such as whole grains, antioxidants, and other healthful aspects of food. Antioxidant-rich white tea will become an ingredient in many desserts, whereas other desserts will be based on single-origin chocolates from Ecuador, Venezuela, and Madagascar. Exotic tropical fruits will also be prominently featured on many menus.

Restaurant patrons wish to become more educated while dining out. This will require menus to include more information about nutritional content, origins of food products, and unique and innovative ingredients.[11]

The beer industry has changed in the past few years; new products and market placement have become extremely competitive within the industry. The beer industry markets their products directly against their competitors. Many producers have also expanded their product lines by creating products to increase the market of beer drinkers such as low carbohydrate beer, low-alcohol and no-alcohol beers, flavored beers, and alcoholic ciders, lemonade, and iced teas known as "hard" beverages. Imported beers have always been popular in the United States; today many of the most popular imported beers have increased their television marketing. Microbreweries have also become more prominent appealing to the market as an upscale beverage as compared to the mass production breweries taking market shares away from the large breweries. One mass producer of beer is attempting to emphasize beer's social value by marketing the art of the brewing process and the selection and use of natural ingredients, much as winemakers do.[12]

The National Restaurant Association announced award-winning kitchen innovations in 2006 including the MooBella Ice Cream System, a new creation that utilizes the space of a typical vending machine and produces real ice cream in 96 varieties, made to order in 45 seconds, as well as a refrigerator that improves food safety management by combining a thermometer and a programmable timer that emits a 70-decibel alarm when the current temperature of the food drops below 41°F or time expires. The timer retains data for proof of HACCP compliance.[13]

Keeping abreast of trends in hospitality information technology is important for managers and business to stay competitive and to deliver the best service product possible. For example, signature capture is more common, but mostly in cashier-desk operations (where the guest can sign on a small countertop unit) and in handheld terminal environments. It's becoming more common to have food and beverage (F&B) and retail operations on the same POS software, especially for casinos and sports stadiums. This more accurately reflects the wide-ranging nature of guests' transactions at these locations, requires fewer different systems to buy and manage, and makes it easier to transfer staff and stock between outlets.[14]

iConnect employs thin technology, desktop applications, a 15-inch flat-screen monitor, multi-media sound, and a full-size mouse and keyboard making it familiar and easy to use. Guests can surf the Internet and access e-mail accounts, but there are plenty of mind-blowing benefits as well. Installed in all 1,406 guestrooms, Gaylord Palms Resort & Convention Center, located near Walt Disney World theme parks in Kissimmee, Florida, is the first to offer this complimentary technology. With a click of a mouse, guests can send requests for fluffy pillows, arrange for valet services, peruse restaurant menus or send an intra-hotel message 24/7. Technologically delivered services are not a value-added amenity but a necessary attribute of today's core hotel product.[15]

Summary

In conclusion, the possibilities in distribution services are many. The hospitality industry purchases thousands of goods and services every day. It is the distribution services professionals that are responsible for supplying the hospitality industry of all its purchasing needs. It is the backbone of the hospitality industry. There are many career choices and opportunities in the hospitality industry within the distribution services segment including food distribution, liquor distribution, equipment and supplies, and technology, to name a few. The peripheral career opportunities in the hospitality industry are many.

Endnotes

1. Pavesic, David, & Magnant, Paul. (2005). *Fundamental Principles of Restaurant Cost Control.* Upper Saddle River, NJ: Pearson Prentice Hall

2. U. S. Foodservice. (2006). http://www.usfoodservice.com/html/index.html

3. Edward Don. (2006a.) Retrieved January 12, 2006 from http://hoovers.com/edward-don/—ID__44487—/free-co-factsheet.xhtml

4. Edward Don. (2006b). Retrieved January 12, 2006 from http://www.don.com/AboutDon/joblistings.aspx

5. Restaurant Biz. (2006). Retrieved January 23, 2006 from http://restaurantbiz.com/index.php?option=com_content&task=view&id=13282&Itemid=93

6. Pavesic, David, & Magnant, Paul. (2005). *Fundamental Principles of Restaurant Cost Control.* Upper Saddle River, NJ: Pearson Prentice Hall

7. International Hotel and Motel Show. (2006). Retrieved January 26, 2006 from http://www.ihmrs.com/content/home.htm

8. National Restaurant Association. (2006). Retrieved January 12, 2006 from http://www.restaurant.org/show/

9. Trade Show Exhibitors Association. (2006). Retrieved January 28, 2006 from http://www.tsea.org/page_1.php

10. USA Today. (2006). Retrieved January 12, 2006 from http://www.usatoday.com/news/health/2006-01-12-nyc-health_x.htm

11. Sun Times. (2006). Retrieved January 23, 2006 from http://www.suntimes.com/output/news/cst-nws-eattrends16.html
12. Wharton School of Business. (2006). Retrieved January 25, 2006 from http://knowledge.wharton.upenn.edu/article/1363.cfm
13. National Restaurant Association. (2006). Retrieved January 12, 2006 from http://www.restaurant.org/show/
14. Inge, Jon. (2005) Technology Trends in F&B Refining the Recipe retrieved on January 31 from http://www.joninge.com/art_recipe.pdf
15. Angelucci, Pam. (2005). *How Can I Serve You? The Delicate Balance of Hotel Staff and Technology Working Together.* Retrieved January 28, 2006 from http://www.hospitalityupgrade.com/Hospitality/Client/Hu/Articles.Nsf/77b53cfa89355b148525688c00608311/30fc24a37ebc03278525703600690a29?OpenDocument

Resources

Internet Sites

www.usfoodservice.com
www.don.com
www.ihmrs.com
www.restaurant.org
www.tsea.org
http://www.posamerica.com/

⚷ Key Words and Concepts

Distribution services
Furniture fixtures and equipment
Peripheral careers
POS
PMS
Purchasing

Contributor Information

The Richard Stockton College—
scalesm@stockton.edu
Michael Scales, EdD is currently an assistant professor at The Richard Stockton College of New Jersey in the Hospitality Tourism Management Program. Prior to joining the college, he had worked in the hospitality industry for over 20 years. Michael worked for Embassy Suites, Boca Raton, and Doubletree Hotel, Fort Lauderdale, Florida, the DuPont Country Club in Wilmington, Delaware, Solitude Ski Resort in Salt Lake City, Utah, and has been involved in opening new food and beverage operations in Key West, Florida, Philadelphia, Pennsylvania, and several towns along the New Jersey shoreline.

The Richard Stockton College—
albanod@stockton.edu
Donna Albano is an instructor of Hospitality Management at The Richard Stockton College in Pomona, NJ. She joined the Stockton Hospitality Management Program in the fall of 2003. Prior to joining Stockton, Donna taught at Atlantic Cape Community College in 1993 as an adjunct faculty member and held that position for three years before being promoted to full-time faculty in 1996. Prior to being an educator, Donna worked in the hospitality industry for 15 years with experience in food and beverage operations, franchise operations, and casino hotel operations. Donna is currently pursuing her EdD at Rowan University in Glassboro, New Jersey in Educational Leadership. Donna holds an MA in Student Personnel Services from Rowan University and a BS in Hospitality Management from Widener University in Chester, PA.

24 Review Questions

1. How would you define distribution services in the hospitality industry?

2. What is meant by "peripheral career opportunities"?

3. Liquor distribution includes beer, wine, and _____.

4. What is wine pairing?

5. Edward Don & Company is a leader in what industry?

6. Why are breweries adding new products such as low carbohydrate beer, non-alcoholic beer, and hard cider?

7. With restaurant patrons wishing to be more educated during their dining experiences, restaurants will be pressured to provide menus offering information about _____ , _____ , and _____ .

8. Equipment distributors play a role in the daily operations of foodservice operations. True or False?

9. What are the career opportunities outlined in this chapter?

10. What are some trends that will affect hospitality operations?

Charles G. Partlow
University of South Carolina

Education Careers

Learning Objectives

✓ To discuss the factors that have had an impact on the growth of the hospitality and tourism industry

✓ To discuss the characteristics that differentiate hospitality and tourism education among the various scope of programs—high school, postsecondary, two-year schools, four-year schools, and graduate programs

✓ To define the three major components of a curriculum vitae

✓ To explain the tenure process and how it works

✓ To describe the differences between faculty at two-year and four-year colleges and universities with regard to level of education, industry experience requirements, and teaching loads

✓ To discuss the benefits of a career in hospitality and tourism education with regard to lifestyle and compensation

Chapter Outline

Growth in Hospitality and Tourism Education

The Scope of Hospitality and Tourism Education

Putting Together a Curriculum Vitae

Tenure and Teaching Load

Lifestyle and Compensation

Tips

*O*ne characteristic that practitioners in the hospitality and tourism industry seem to share is a passion for what they do. Hospitality and tourism educators are no less passionate about what they do.

Growth in Hospitality and Tourism Education

The hospitality and tourism industry has grown tremendously over the past four decades, and it is poised for continued growth. Vacations, time off, or personal time, whatever you choose to call it, has moved from being a privilege to being a right in the minds of most Americans. Travel has become an integral part of the American lifestyle, and that will not be changing any time in the foreseeable future. However, unlike many countries that give their workers four or six weeks for vacation, Americans have shorter vacation times and so tend to use them more frugally. For example, many people will opt for an extra day combining it with a long holiday weekend.

The current demographic profile of the American population points to a continued need for employees in the field of hospitality and tourism. The population is aging, and the baby boomer generation is edging into retirement. Not only will this open jobs for younger people, but retirees are ready to spend money for out-of-home experiences—just the kinds of experiences provided by the hospitality and tourism industry. Never before has any segment of the population been so healthy or wealthy as it moves from age 55 to age 100.[1] With advances in medicine made in the twentieth century, we now have a segment of the population that will spend more years in retirement than working. All this bodes well for both the hospitality and tourism industry and for the educators, teachers, and trainers who help people obtain jobs and launch careers in the industry.

According to the International Council on Hotel, Restaurant, and Institutional Education (I-CHRIE), membership includes approximately 200 institutions that grant four-year and graduate degrees, and about the same number of schools that offer two-year degrees, certificates, or diplomas. I-CHRIE began in 1946 with 10 schools, and the organization continues to grow, just as the number of schools offering a hospitality and tourism curriculum continues to grow. The employment prospects for hospitality and tourism educators are very positive.

The Scope of Hospitality and Tourism Education

The hospitality and tourism industry needs creative, innovative, enthusiastic, and hard-working team players, no matter where on the career spectrum you look—from housekeepers to CEOs. The scope of hospitality education includes in-house training for current industry employees, high school programs to prepare students for entry-level jobs, college or university management degrees to prepare managers, graduate degrees to prepare researchers, educators, and administrators, and executive development educators to prepare upper-level managers for advancement. As a result, there are many different types of careers available from training to research. Your values, interests, and ability to communicate are likely to influence the type of educational career you choose for yourself.

Just as employees at different levels need different skills, so, too, educators must call on different skills. At the entry level, employees need mostly technical skills, and educators must focus on teaching terminology, procedures, day-to-day operations, and specific competencies. To prepare managers, the focus shifts to people skills and planning with more long-term objectives. Students in four-year degree programs are introduced to planning, networking, marketing, finance, strategy, critical thinking, and the principles of team building. Professional development of executives and upper-level managers may concentrate on one of these topics, in addition to helping them develop and communicate their leadership skills and vision. Graduate programs are research oriented and give students the tools to develop innovative ideas to help answer questions or learn about new aspects of the industry.

High School Programs

Most high school programs provide students with training that will enable them to work entry-level positions in foodservice, lodging, or tourism. These skills can include how to clean a room properly to check-in procedures at the front desk to preparing food in the kitchen. In these programs, students participate in hands-on, practical, skill-building exercises.

The Academy of Travel & Tourism® and ProStart® are two programs designed to introduce high school students to the hospitality and tourism industry. These programs benefit high school teachers by providing a well-designed curriculum appropriate for an introduction to the industry. Students in these programs obtain knowledge, skills, and experience that enable them to become superior candidates for jobs in the industry. Students who complete a program and choose to continue with their education in hospitality and tourism may be awarded college credits toward an associate's or bachelor's degree.

Vocational/Technical Schools, Training Institutes

Much like high school programs, the emphasis here is on training. It's likely that the facilities will be more elaborate (commercial kitchens, front desk simulations, even small travel agencies) and allow the students to focus more narrowly on a particular area of interest. Therefore topics for certificates might be how to be a travel agent or tour guide. Many trade associations will offer certificates in their areas to help their members become more knowledgeable and demonstrate their expertise. This means that the instructor, likewise, will need an appropriate background in a specific area. Typically, the instructor will be someone from industry with years of experience who has a special expertise in the certificate area. Students who complete a course of study, typically one year, are awarded a diploma or a certificate.

Two-Year Programs: Community Colleges, Culinary Arts Academies

Most two-year programs award the graduate an associate's degree. However, unlike four-year institutions, courses will be more focused on gaining information that is necessary to get an entry-level job in the field. Many two-year programs have a culinary and/or foodservice management option for students. Many programs have a commercial kitchen, and students are responsible for planning, preparing, and serving meals to the public in a restaurant setting. However, there are very famous programs like CIA or the Cordon Bleu in Paris that develop high-quality chefs.

Typically, a four-year institution will accept transfer credits from a two-year program, thereby reducing the amount of time it will take for a student to obtain a bachelor's degree. An instructor at a community college needs industry experience in their teaching area and usually at least a bachelor's

degree. However, years of experience and reputation can offset a degree.

Four-Year Programs: Colleges, Universities

At a four-year institution, a hospitality and tourism program may be a "college," a "school," or a "department" functioning within a university (e.g., the College of Hospitality, Retail, and Sport Management at the University of South Carolina). Hospitality programs can also be located within other large academic units, such as business (e.g., the Lester E. Kabacoff School of Hotel, Restaurant and Tourism Administration, College of Business Administration, University of New Orleans), consumer and family services, human ecology, health and human development, food and agriculture, or applied science and technology.

Graduates of a four-year program obtain a bachelor's degree. This combines two years of developing a broad liberal arts background with two years of specific hospitality courses. A person should know about the world around them because we don't live in a vacuum. When a manager interacts with other people, he/she is expected to be able to talk intelligently on many different topics outside the realm of the operations. People who teach full-time at this level are required to have at least a master's degree and probably a PhD.

Obtaining a bachelor's degree in hospitality and tourism would require attending a four-year college or university.

Although the industry used to be known for promoting from within—the bellboy who ended up owning a hotel chain with 84 properties—the industry has matured considerably. A bachelor's has become the minimum credential for middle and upper management. We will always have the Rich Melmans—an entrepreneur with no college degree—but more and more, the industry demands a college degree.

Graduate Programs: Universities

Some universities provide the master's student with a choice. A student may choose a degree in hospitality management, often referred to as a professional-degree program, with the emphasis on coursework and a major project, which is most beneficial for returning to industry; or a research-oriented degree (i.e., Master of Science) that concludes with a thesis, which is better for anyone in education or research.

Usually, doctorate programs are designed for people who wish to teach and conduct research at the college or university level. Here, students also have choices. Some universities offer a doctorate in hospitality and tourism management (e.g., PhD in Hospitality Administration at Texas Tech University), whereas others offer a doctorate in a related area with an emphasis in hospitality and tourism management (e.g., PhD in Nutrition and Food Science with an emphasis in Hotel and Restaurant Management at Auburn University). Doctoral programs conclude with a dissertation. Professors who teach at this level must not only have a doctorate but also a stream of research that continually improves their knowledge base.

Putting Together a Curriculum Vitae

To apply for a position within the industry, you should have an excellent resume; for education, you will want an outstanding curriculum vitae. As in a resume, a vitae must be continually updated as you acquire important job-related accomplishments. For an educator, these will fall under three major headings: teaching, research, and service. A different emphasis will be placed on each of these depending on the institution. Furthermore, different institutions define these categories each using its own specifications. Therefore, what is acceptable at one institution may not be acceptable at another.

Student and peer evaluations are an important part of assessing a teacher's performance. High schools, post-secondary programs, and community colleges generally place the greatest emphasis on this aspect of a professional's career.

Research includes the completion of a unique project designed to add knowledge to the field and to disseminate the results, through publication and/or conference presentation. Demonstrating mastery in this category is very important for faculty at research-oriented universities.

Service is primarily to the department/school/college/university, to the profession, and to the community. These activities include being a faculty advisor to student organizations, serving on professional association committees, and donating professional expertise to charitable institutions.

Major research universities require a faculty member to have a track record of research and publications and what is known as a "terminal degree." A terminal degree means the highest degree in that field; it is the end of the line in obtaining degrees. Typically, in a university hospitality and tourism program, you'll find faculty with PhDs (doctorates in philosophy), EdDs (doctorates in education), or JDs (doctorates in law). Some universities are willing to hire a candidate who is "ABD" (all but dissertation) with the stipulation that he must complete the terminal degree within a specified time. Universities that hire an ABD candidate will probably give that teacher the academic rank of instructor. Once the terminal degree is earned, the rank will be changed to assistant professor. It is customary to request promotion to associate professor when tenure is earned. For promotion to full professor, an academic must be considered outstanding in the field, especially in the areas of teaching and research, and to have established a national, if not international, reputation as a leading scholar.

Tenure and Teaching Load

Colleges and universities will place new faculty in "tenure track lines." This means that a faculty member must show development and progress in the three areas of teaching, research, and service to continue in that position. A faculty member will have a periodic review, typically annually, and after the fifth year of employment, a university committee will examine that faculty member's record for a tenure decision. When tenure is granted, this means a faculty member has employment in that department on a continuing basis. Some universities have instituted periodic post-tenure reviews for faculty, to ensure those faculties who continue to develop are rewarded appropriately. Faculty who are expected to conduct research and remain active as scholars will normally be given reduced teaching loads.

Some community colleges offer tenure, some do not. Typically, a master's degree is necessary to teach at a community college. With a decrease in the level of degree required comes an increase in the amount of experience required. Technical schools may require just a bachelor's degree, but they will probably also require years of experience in the industry. In addition, the teaching load also increases as less emphasis is placed on research and service.

High school teacher qualifications are set by each state. The minimum credential is a bachelor's degree, and some states, for instance, New York, require a teacher to earn a master's degree within a set amount of time. High school teachers are typically required to pursue a stated number of hours of professional development.

Lifestyle and Compensation

Hospitality and tourism educators tend to be like their counterparts in the industry: outgoing, enthusiastic, and very busy. For each class taught, it is expected that about two to four hours of preparation are needed. However, when you first start teaching, that time dramatically increases as you select textbooks, outline the chapters, develop class notes, decide how you want to teach the information, find outside materials including video/DVD selections and guest speakers, and create assignments that help students apply what they learn. That is just the teaching side. Then, many professors are expected to write and get published. Depending on the type of publication, it must be accepted by an editorial board, which might take from 6 months to one or two years. Oh, and did I mention, the public service side . . . be on department, school, and university committees, attend/present/be on committees at local national, and international industry meetings and functions, present your research at hospitality education meetings, and be involved in the regional hospitality education chapters. But, one advantage to the profession is that, when not in the classroom or attending a meeting, a professor can arrange her schedule to suit herself. Educators must be able to work autonomously, both inside and outside the classroom. Most educators appreciate this independent aspect of their work.

They also value academic freedom. This gives an educator the right to teach as she sees fit.

If your goal is to become wealthy, education is probably not the career for you. However, if your goal is to be enriched by life-long learning, you will be immensely rewarded. According to a study by Milman and Pizam,[2] salary is affected by academic rank, the average number of courses taught per year, the number of students in the institution, and whether one teaches in a graduate program. Other factors influence salary level, such as the highest degree earned, the type of institution, the extent of administrative responsibilities, geographic location (local cost of living), and the ratio of demand for faculty versus the available supply of qualified candidates. That being said, Milman and Pizam reported average annual salary for faculty with an associate's degree with the academic rank of instructor employed at a two-year institution is $36,750; for faculty with a doctorate and the rank of full professor employed at a four-year institution, it is $87,901. If you are fortunate, when alumni return to campus, you will be seated at a table with your former students who are now making far more money than you are. This is an excellent opportunity to convince them of the value of their education and the benefits of helping other students.

The general public holds the notion that educators have three months of vacation during the summer. This is certainly a misconception. Professional development activities—research, writing, conferences, updating, and revising class material—are time consuming, and there is scant opportunity during the academic year to pursue these. If an educator wants to remain employed, he must be making adequate progress in professional development.

Some Tips for Your Consideration

No matter in which type of institution you wish to teach, experience in the industry combined with teaching experience will always be important. Not only does work experience in the industry provide credibility, but it also adds immensely to a teacher's ability to bring "the real world" into the classroom. Today, however, a growing number of colleges and universities are placing a higher emphasis on research skills and productivity and less emphasis on industry experience when making hiring decisions. Because most college or university programs require at least 400 hours of field experience before graduation, some students who do well academically may decide to go straight through to graduate school. Although this practice was discouraged in the past, it is now being viewed more favorably by colleges and universities that wish to achieve status as major research institutions. The addition of faculty internship programs, like the one sponsored by I-CHRIE, provide educators with valuable industry knowledge and work experience that they can bring back to the classroom.

If you want to attend graduate school, you will be expected to focus on one area of the industry. There will be one functional area of greatest interest to you, and that's the area you should research. That being said, whether you are looking for an honor's thesis advisor or selecting a dissertation committee, find faculty that you respect and can work with. Establishing a good relationship will be of great benefit under the stressful conditions of completing a research project.

Most universities that have graduate programs have graduate student assistantships at both the teaching and research levels. If you plan to pursue a career in education, seek out this opportunity to teach a class or work with a leading researcher in the program. Some universities have support programs for first-time teachers/researchers or for faculty who want to become more effective teachers and researchers. An assistantship, and a course in "how to be the best teacher/researcher you can be," will provide you with additional qualifications for obtaining the position you would most like to have.

To demonstrate your flexibility, adaptability, and willingness to take on new challenges, it is highly recommended that you obtain your credentials from different institutions. It begins to look as if someone who obtains a bachelor's, master's, and PhD from the same place could not possibly be happy (or successful) anywhere else. Also, most institutions have a policy of "not hiring their own." So, if you are a graduate of Penn State, you will not be considered for a faculty position at Penn State until you've spent a few years somewhere else.

Beware of "mail-order" graduate degrees. When applying for a faculty position, you may be removed from consideration because members of the search committee do not consider that you have earned a "real degree." It is becoming more acceptable to do a portion of your coursework as a distance learner, but you should plan to be at an institution that has a campus and plan to spend at least a year there. Your best bet is to begin at an institution that has an accredited hospitality and tourism program. The Commission for Accreditation of Hospitality Management (CAHM) is the organization that evaluates and awards accreditation to two-year programs, and the Accreditation Commission for Programs in Hospitality Administration (ACPHA) is the group that does the same for four-year programs. From there, ask the faculty about their experiences in graduate school, and seek out the program that best suits you. Just as they may wish to "interview" you as part of the application process, so too, you should interview them to see what they have to offer to you as compared to other programs.

If you find that, when shadows lengthen and fall is in the air, you get this feeling, "Perhaps I should be back in school," then perhaps you should be. But, this time, at the front of the classroom.

Endnotes

1. Peterson, P. G. (1999). *Gray Dawn: How the Coming Age Wave Will Transform America—and the World.* New York, Random House
2. Milman, A. and Pizam, A. (2001). Academic Characteristics & Faculty Compensation in U.S. Hospitality Management Programs: 1999–2000. *Journal of Hospitality & Tourism Education, 13*(1). pp. 4–16

Resources

Internet Sites

International Council on Hotel, Restaurant and Institutional Education (I-CHRIE): http://www.chrie.org
The Chronicle on Higher Education: http://chronicle.com/
Accreditation Commission for Programs in Hospitality Administration (ACPHA) and Commission for Accreditation of Hospitality Management (CAHM): http://www.acpha-cahm.org/
Educational Foundation of the National Restaurant Association: http://www.nraef.org/
Educational Institute of the American Hotel and Lodging Association (AHLA): http://www.ei-ahla.org

Supplemental Reading

Peterson, P. G. (1999). *Gray dawn: How the coming age wave will transform America—and the world.* New York, Random House

Sims-Bell, B. (2002). *Career opportunities in the food and beverage industry* (2nd ed). New York: Facts on File, Inc.

☞ *Key Words and Concepts*

A.B.D.
Curriculum vitae
Doctorate
Four-year and graduate programs
High school programs
Master's degree
Postsecondary programs
Tenure
Two-year programs

🗉 *Contributor Information*

Charles G. Partlow is professor and director of Graduate Studies in the School of Hotel, Restaurant and Tourism Management at the University of South Carolina in Columbia. He earned his PhD from Kansas State University and has over 25 years of experience in hospitality management, consulting, and education. He is an active researcher and writer with over 70 article publications.

25 Review Questions

1. Why is "passion" important in a career choice?

2. What impact will the aging baby boomers have on the hospitality and tourism industry?

3. What are career options (locations) for hospitality educators?

4. Explain how the teaching topic needs vary with different levels of hospitality employees.

5. What is the hospitality student exposed to in a postsecondary program such as a vocational/technical hospitality program?

6. What is the hospitality student exposed to in a two-year program such as community colleges or culinary arts hospitality program?

7. What is the hospitality student exposed to in a four-year hospitality program?

8. Describe the different places you might find a hospitality program in a university.

9. What are the components of a teacher's job if he/she works at a major university?

10. What types of service are faculty members at a university likely to engage in?

11. Explain the relationship between advanced education and/or advanced experience in order to teach.

12. What are three of the rewards that come with teaching?

13. How does the salary of educators relate to those in hospitality management?

14. What are some of the duties expected during the summer?

15. What are the advantages of attending graduate school?

16. When should a student consider attending graduate school?

17. Describe the graduate school experience.

18. Explain the advantages and disadvantages to distance learning in advanced degrees.

19. What factors are considered most important in obtaining a faculty position at a major four-year college or university?

G. Burch Wilkes
Pennsylvania State University

Golf Management

Learning Objectives

✓ To learn trends in golf
✓ To learn about career opportunities in the golf industry
✓ To learn what factors motivate customers to play more
✓ To learn why people leave golf

Chapter Outline

The Game of Golf

As an introduction to this chapter, we believe it is important to describe the common rituals of playing the game of golf.

With this common understanding of the culture of golf, it will be possible to introduce golf management and compare it to the more traditional hospitality professions.

Although most of us have seen some professionals play the game on TV, less than one in ten of us has actually experienced play at a golf club. We will use as our example a typical public course at which a fee for play is collected. This could be a resort course, for example, in Florida or the Carolinas or a course that is privately owned at which we can pay to play an 18-hole round of golf.

Prior to the date of play, we would have called to make a reservation, called a "tee time." Without a tee time, it is unlikely one would be able to play on many of the days at a great number of courses. The tee time would usually be made for four people, as the game is commonly played in what is known as "foursomes."

On the day of play and usually about an hour or so before the tee time, we would arrive at the golf course in our car. On arrival, we go to an area called the "bag drop." The bag drop allows outside assistants to help us unload the golf bags and clubs from our cars and put them onto golf cars or take them to a designated place if we are walking and carrying our clubs. Because so few clubs today have an option for the use of caddies to carry the clubs, we will not consider their use. On depositing the clubs and bags at the bag drop, we take our golf shoes and proceed to the "golf shop" to check in. The driver of the car must obviously take the car (unless of course the club provides valet services) to the parking area and then return to the golf shop.

At the golf shop, the assistant behind the counter checks us in and makes sure that our names match the reservation. The check-in process involves paying the daily fee and, if we are riding a golf car, the fee for the golf car as well. On payment, we are given a receipt and told that the receipt will be collected by the "starter." In the golf shop, there are all the accoutrements necessary to outfit us for the game. So if we need apparel, new golf clubs, a golf glove, or golf balls, we can purchase them in the golf shop. If there is enough time before the tee time, usually about a half hour is what is needed, we may choose to practice in an area designated as the practice range and putting green.

To practice on the practice range, a quantity of range practice balls is needed. These balls are rented or provided without charge at the golf shop or at the practice range. If we just practice putting, range practice balls would not be needed. We would use the balls that would be used during our upcoming game.

Prior to moving to the practice range or putting green, we might visit the locker room to change from street shoes to golf shoes and to perhaps change clothes as well. Many clubs make lockers available to players. These lockers can be used to store street shoes and other personal belongings while on the golf course. Many clubs offer complimentary shoe shine service for street shoes while we are playing. Of course, a tip is expected by the person shining the shoes. There is often a locker-room attendant who sometimes serves as the shoe shine person, as well as a provider of towels for the shower and other bathroom amenities. This person expects a gratuity when we exit the locker room at the completion of the game, after perhaps showering and changing back to street shoes.

With golf shoes and proper dress, we proceed to practice at the range and on the putting green until a few minutes before our tee time, when we head to the starter's area. The starter checks that the receipts indicate payment has been made for that day and proceeds to give us instructions about the golf course. These instructions normally consist of rules of golf car use and special local rules of golf affecting the play of the game. The starter also tells us when we can move to the first tee and begin play.

As we play the game of 18 holes of golf, which usually takes about four to five hours in the United States, we may encounter a couple of additional people on the golf course. We often see a food and beverage attendant driving a modified golf car asking us if we would like to buy the products that are for sale. There is also, on most courses, a person employed as a course advisor. This person's job is to make sure that the play of the game proceeds at a pace that will allow everyone to enjoy themselves. This means that the course advisor "polices" the property and "hurries up" those who are taking too long to play the game.

After playing the first nine holes, or the so-called "front nine," we may choose to take a short break before starting play on the "back nine." During this break, food and drink are purchased and consumed. Often there is a facility placed at the convenience of the players called a halfway house.

This is a small food and beverage establishment that services only players between each nine holes.

On completion of the game, we return our golf cars to a designated area where there are attendants to clean the clubs and take them back to the bag drop area. These attendants expect a tip as well.

Now we may visit the "19th hole" to rehash the game, settle our bets, have a liquid refreshment or two, and perhaps have a bite to eat. This activity takes place in a space that many clubs call the "grill room." This is an informal food service and bar area that can accept golf shoes as footwear. It is an area that usually allows smoking; card playing is often seen among the regulars. Often, there is another, more formal, dining room, where such casual attire would not be allowed.

Following the enjoyment of food and drink, we would return to the locker room. Perhaps we would shower and change clothes, change to street shoes, and depart the locker room. We would then return to the car, pick up our golf bags from the bag drop area, and return home.

From this description of a normal day of golf, it is obvious that there are a number of service encounters. Many of these encounters are similar to those in more traditional hospitality professions like food and beverage service or lodging service. We will go into greater detail a bit later in the chapter; however, let's get a sense of the game and the size of the golf industry.

Economics

A study commissioned by GOLF 20/20, the golf industry's initiative committed to growing interest and participation in the game, found that the golf economy in the United States accounted for over $62 billion worth of goods and services in the year 2000.[1] This includes the billions of dollars associated with annual golf travel, that is, lodging, transportation, food and beverage, and entertainment. The number of golf fans increased 36.4 percent since 1999, reaching 106 million people in 2004, thanks in part to Tiger Woods and an increase in media coverage; however, watching does not translate to doing.[2] According to a 2005 GOLF 20/20 industry report by Dr. Joe Beditz, the president of the National Golf Foundation (NGF), participation has grown from 36 million golfers in 2000 to 39 million golfers in 2004; however, rounds played during that time dropped from 518 million rounds in 2000 to just under 500 million in 2004. In line with a de-crease in participation, course construction has significantly slowed in recent years. For several years, the building of new golf courses has exceeded one new golf course each day; however, it appears that supply is now catching up with demand. As reported at the 2005 GOLF 20/20 Conference, there were 398 new courses opened in 2000 and only 150 new courses opened in 2004. Additionally, we have seen an increase in course closings from 32 in 2001 to an estimated 80 in 2005.[3] However, even with the recent economic downturn, rounds appear to have stabilized, and gains in overall participants have been primarily due to junior golf initiatives. Consumers also continue to demonstrate a willingness to spend a sizable portion of their discretionary dollars to join an exclusive country club, play high-end resort properties, or purchase the latest equipment.

The Consumers

The 39 million U.S. golfers are a population overrepresented among higher income households, college graduates, white males, homeowners, and those occupying professional, managerial, and adminis-

According to the National Golf Foundation, the average golfer is a 40-year-old male with an annual income around $68,000.

trative positions. According to the National Golf Foundation (2001[4]), the average golfer is male, approximately 40 years old, has an annual household income of slightly over $68,000, and plays about 21 rounds each year. In addition, when we compare the participation rates of golfers to those engaging in other lifetime recreation activities, we find a marked difference with respect to age. Typically, as individuals age, their tendency is to constrict both the number of leisure pursuits and also the frequency of participation.[5] Whether it's tennis, bowling, jogging, or using exercise equipment, individuals tend to give up these activities in their later years. For the most part, golfers remain with the sport well into their 60s, 70s, and 80s. Some may use larger grips on their clubs to accommodate arthritic conditions. Others may use a golf car to address issues of mobility or use a more flexible shaft or lighter equipment to compensate for a loss of strength or, perhaps, play from the forward tees to compensate for loss of distance.

From the mid-1980s through the 1990s, an additional 6.5 million citizens have joined the golfing community; this translates into a 33 percent increase. The NGF (2001)[6], in its *Trends in the Golf Industry—1986–1999*, noted that during the same period, women's participation only increased 11 percent, whereas juniors' growth rate increased by 43 percent to 2 million. The 1996 NGF trends report predicted significantly greater participation rates among boomers in the 30 to 39, 40 to 49, 50 to 59, and 60 to 64-year-old cohorts through the year 2010.[7] NGF also indicated the echo boomers will represent a significant increase among junior golfers, ages 12 to 17, and young adults, 18 to 29-year-olds. Boomers will also play more frequently and spend more money as they reach their pre-retirement/retirement years with greater discretionary income.

Two additional markets that continue to be untapped are women and minority participants. Although women have represented approximately 36 percent to 40 percent of all beginning golfers, their percentage among all golfers has dropped to approximately 19 percent. Those who stay with the game play fewer rounds than their male counterparts; however, their household income and expenditures on golf are very similar to men. Beginning in the 1980s, African-American golf participation began to grow at a significant rate. For example, the 315,000 African-Americans playing golf in 1980 represented only 2.4 percent of all African-Ameri-

cans.[8] A more recent study by the National Golf Foundation (2001)[9] indicates there are currently 882,000 African-American golfers. This only represents less than 3 percent of the golfing community, but it does represent a 100 percent increase since 1991.

The Venues

By the end of 2001, there were over 17,000 courses throughout the United States. Approximately 71 percent are accessible by the public. This would include daily fee facilities/resorts (approximately 9,300) and municipal courses (approximately 2,700). The remaining 29 percent, nearly 5,000, are private, with nearly three-fourths of the private courses being owned by the membership (equity clubs).

The Business of Golf and Career Opportunities

When most of us think of golf, we think of it as a game, and we do not consider the supporting business organization necessary for us to enjoy the game. From the general manager or club manager to the attendant who drives the food and beverage cart around on the course, all have important service functions that are required for the golf operation to run smoothly and for the players to have an enjoyable experience.

As we discussed earlier, there are a number of different kinds of golf operations. Each type of operation would have an organizational structure necessary to meet the needs of that particular golf entity. Depending on the size of the operation, whether it is a private or public course, and the number of functions or amenities offered to the players, the organization will vary. Therefore, to talk meaningfully about the golfing operation, we will have to generalize a bit. The following positions represent a typical public golf resort operation. Many private clubs and municipal courses have fewer personnel.

Careers in the golf industry fall within three rather distinct tracks: the physical facility, club management and auxiliary services, and management of the game. The career track, which is more closely aligned with what we normally think of as the hospitality industry, involves the management of the club and its various services. The following organizational discussion represents only one of many organizational structures that exist. This one is used for illustrative purposes only and is not meant to indicate a preferred model.

Let's discuss the roles of these employees in delivering the golf experience. That is, what do these people do in their jobs to allow the players to enjoy the game of golf? Like any business or organization, if it is to function well, that is, to make a profit or be successful, all the employees must contribute positively by executing their jobs in the way they were intended to be executed. Each employee is critical to the success of the operation because all the operations are interrelated. As in most organizations, it is often the lowest-paid employee or the employee way down in the organizational structure who has the most contact with the customer and is often the reason why customers (golfers) do not return.

The General Manager or Club Manager

This individual is assigned management responsibility for the complete golf operation. We will abbreviate this role from now on as the GM. The GM is responsible for the bottom line of the operation. People who usually would report directly to the GM are the director of golf and the food and beverage manager. The golf superintendent would also report to the GM or to the director of golf, depending on the operation.

You can see that this person is the executive of the golf operation. It is this person's responsibility to plan so that the organizational goals are met. It is almost always the case that the GM is also responsible to a higher authority. Depending on the type of golf operation, that higher authority could be a board of directors, a corporate office, or a director of parks and recreation.

Traditionally, the career path to the GM has been through more customary hospitality roles like food and beverage manager. Recently, however, the path has become more varied. Directors of golf and club professionals are now moving into GM positions with greater frequency.[10] (See chapter 21, "Private Clubs," for a more detailed discussion of the club manager's position.)

The Director of Golf and Head Professional

Direct provision of golf services is an employment path leading to the position of head professional or director of golf. Among the 17,214 golf courses,

approximately 56 percent are Professional Golfers' Association (PGA) affiliated courses. Those who complete the PGA's requirements for membership can, on average, expect a compensation package that is nearly twice that of the non-PGA member. The average 2004 compensation package for a PGA head professional was $68,447.

In terms of preparation for a career as a golf professional, individuals should consider another option, that of completing a four-year degree program in business or a closely related field, or possibly attend one of the colleges or universities offering a program in Professional Golf Management (PGM). The PGA of America has developed a program that provides each potential member with the most current training in the profession. While attending a PGA accredited college or university, each student is required to complete the PGA of America's Professional Golf Management (PGA/PGM) program. Integrated into the university curriculum, the availability of the PGA/PGM program essentially allows a student to fast-track to PGA membership, thereby reducing the time commitment by approximately three years. Upon graduation, students become members of the PGA of America. The PGA/PGM program is currently accredited at the following colleges or universities: Pennsylvania State University, Florida State University, North Carolina State University, Clemson University, New Mexico State University, Mississippi State University, Ferris State University, Arizona State University, Methodist College, Campbell University, Coastal Carolina University, University of Colorado (Colorado Springs), University of Nebraska (Lincoln), University of Nevada-Las Vegas, University of Idaho, Florida Gulf Coast University, and Sam Houston State University.

Golf Superintendent

For those interested in the golf course itself as the physical facility, their focus must be in agronomy, specifically turf management. With the millions of dollars invested in today's golf courses, formal university training through two- and four-year turf management programs is essential. Individuals interested in this career track should contact the Golf Course Superintendents of America to obtain a list of recognized college and university programs. The importance of a quality agronomy program cannot be overestimated. A recent reader survey of *Golf Digest* subscribers indicated that the golf course su-

Marketing golf as family-friendly raises the value of the time investment required to play.

perintendent was the single most important employee. In addition, as reported at the 2005 GOLF 20/20 Conference, the two highest factors in motivating customers to play more golf are well-maintained greens and bunkers and well-maintained fairways and greens.[11] As we focus on increasing rounds of golf, it is essential for managers to have a well-maintained golf course.

The Food and Beverage Manager

This individual is responsible to the GM for all the food service operations at the club. This position is a bit more varied than that of a food and beverage manager in a restaurant, but it is certainly similar to the food and beverage manager in a hotel. A hotel with its variety of outlets and functions such as room service offers the complexity similar to that of the golf operation. There are many opportunities for a food and beverage manager in golf operations as the business of golf continues to grow.

Trends

One of the most significant trends in the golf industry is the importance for managers to lower the time commitment and raise the value of the golf experience. As reported in a segmentation study at the 2001

GOLF 20/20 Conference, the lack of time is the number one reason people tend to leave the game of golf, followed by family obligations. The golf course building boom of the 1990s has created a surplus of supply and a shortage of demand. The "if you build it, they will come" attitude no longer applies to the industry. Now more than ever, owners and managers need to focus on assessing customer needs and actively improve the pace of play through course advisors, easier pin placements, shorter tees on certain holes, and rewards for faster play. In addition, marketing golf as family-friendly and a way to strengthen relationships, as well as meet new friends, will help raise the value of their time investment.

The second significant trend involves the demand for golf-related housing developments. This is one section of the golf industry that continues to add significant supply. According to Robert H. Dedman, Jr., the Chairman of ClubCorp, Inc., the economics of the real estate profit potential and the ability for golf courses to help developers accelerate sales are a driving force in golf course development.[12]

Another trend that will continue to accelerate in the next five years will be the growth of management companies, such as ClubCorp, to be "one-stop solution providers" to manage golf and the club experiences for members and guests.[12] Mr. Jesse Holshouser, Chief Financial Officer of the PGA of

America, also indicated at the April 1998 general meeting of the Philadelphia PGA Section that approximately 16 percent of all U.S. golf courses were owned and/or managed by management firms. He further indicated that some predict approximately one-half of all courses will fall under management companies within the next decade or two. Management companies such as Club Corporation of America, Marriott Golf, Troon Golf, Heritage Golf Group, Casper Golf, and others are both acquiring and managing golf courses in ever-greater numbers. How this will affect employment opportunities and public access has yet to be determined.

Another significant trend involves the information superhighway. Club managers and golf professionals are only now beginning to realize the significance of the Internet. Golfers are using Web sites not only to see how their favorite tour professional is doing, but also to make vacation plans, decide what courses to play, and perhaps purchase golf equipment. The challenge for those wishing to use the Internet is how they get people to their site. For example, using the Google search engine, this author in January 2006 typed in the term *golf*. The Google search engine identified 465,000,000 Web sites containing the term *golf*!

Summary

We have described the game, its economic impact, and its origins. You have read about the kinds of venues at which golf is played and the people that work to make it happen. The role and impact that each employee has in the golf experience is similar to that of the hospitality employee in the more traditional food and beverage or lodging roles. Each service encounter is important to the success of the operation. It is the intent of professional golf management to make every experience a great one so that we will continue to play the game and continue to provide revenue to those for whom that is important.

Endnotes

1. SRI International. (2002, November). *U.S. golf economy measures $62 billion.* [On-line] http://www.golf2020.com:80/mediacenter/fullView.cfm?aid=70
2. Beckwith, R. (2004, June). *The golf 20/20 industry report for 2003.* Ponte Vedre, FL. The World Golf Foundation
3. Beditz, J. (2005, November). *Rounds played changes.* GOLF 20/20 Conference Report. Ponte Vedre, FL, The World Golf Foundation
4. National Golf Foundation. (2001). [Online] http://www.ngf.org/
5. Guadagnolo, F. (1997). Presentation at PGA merchandise show, Orlando, Florida
6. National Golf Foundation and NFO World Group. (2001, November). *2001 segmentation research: An unprecedented undertaking.* [On-line] http://www.golf2020.com/reports_2001Segmentation.asp
7. National Golf Foundation. (1996, May–June). "A different look at what's up with golf's growth." *Golf Market Today,* 4
8. Warnick, R. (1991, November 21). "On the green." *Black Issues in Higher Education,* 20
9. National Golf Foundation and NFO World Group. (2001, November). 2001 segmentation research: An unprecedented undertaking. [On-line] http://www.golf2020.com/reports_2001Segmentation.asp
10. Gordon, J. (1996). "Making the General Manager Jump." *PGA Magazine* 77 (9), 24–31
11. Last, J. (2005). *Avid golfer research.* GOLF 20/20 Conference Report, Ponte Vedre, FL, The World Golf Foundation
12. Nakahara, K. (2005). "The supply side challenge." *PGA Magazine* (5), 28–47

Resources

Internet Sites

Golf Course Builders Association of America—A nonprofit trade association representing all segments of the golf course construction industry.
http://www.gcbaa.org/

Golf Press Association—A daily transaction golf newsletter, offered through e-mail, that keeps you abreast about equipment, events, players, etc.
http://www.golftransactions.com/aboutgpa.html

Golf Web—A Web site that covers or is linked to most aspects of golf, both as a sport and a business.
http://www.golfweb.com/

Ladies Professional Golf Association—As the official site of the LPGA, everything pertaining to the LPGA is provided—tour schedules, news releases, player standings, etc.
http://www.lpga.com/

Multicultural Golf Association of America, Inc.—The Multicultural Golf Association of America, founded in 1991, is the first national organization to promote opportunities for minorities in golf and is recognized as a leading authority on inner-city junior golf programs with the theme "Golf Is for Everyone."
http://www.mgaa.com/

National Golf Course Owners Association—Represents over 7,200 golf courses with over 5300 members.
http://www.ngcoa.org/

National Golf Foundation—Serves as the primary research wing of the golfing industry. The foundation provides a variety of business and consulting services, houses the largest reference library, and provides an excellent series of links to many aspects of golf.
http://www.ngf.org/

Off the Fringe—This newsletter offers an "unconventional perspective on the world of golf."
http://www.offthefringe.com/

PGA of America—In addition to member services, pgaonline offers current headlines and stories on all the professional tours, tour statistics, instruction, and other industry news.
http://www.pgaonline.com/

United States Golf Association—Serves as the national governing body for the game of golf. The USGA writes and interprets rules, conducts national championships, provides a handicap system, maintains equipment standards, funds turfgrass and environmental research, etc.
http://www.usga.org/

World Golf-Links Around the World—Eighty plus golf links ranging from a history of golf in France to the Association of Left Handed Golfers.
http://www.worldgolf.com/golflinks/golfpages.html

⌐ *Key Words*

19th hole
Bag drop
Club manager
Foursome
Front nine
Golf superintendent
Starter
Tee time

🔳 *Contributor's Information*

G. Burch Wilkes, IV, professor-in-charge, Professional Golf Management, Department of Recreation, Park and Tourism Management, The Pennsylvania State University, 201 Mateer Building, University Park, PA 16802
Phone: (814) 863-8987, Fax: (814) 863-8992, e-mail: gbw104@psu.edu

26 Review Questions

1. Explain the significance of a tee time.

2. Describe the check-in process for playing golf at a club from the point of entering the club for a tee time.

3. How long does it usually take to play 18 holes of golf?

4. Describe the roles of the:

   a. Starter

   b. F&B attendant

   c. Course ranger

5. What is a "grill room"?

6. What is the economic impact of golf?

7. What is the profile of the average golfer?

8. Where and when did golf begin as the game we know today?

9. What is the relationship between age and the continuation of playing golf?

10. What is the fastest-growing population of golfers?

11. What are golfing trends involving females and African-Americans?

12. What are three categories of golf courses?

13. What type of growth has been experienced in golf course development? In what sector of ownership/operation?

14. What are the three distinct tracks of golf industry careers?

15. Identify key responsibilities of the following positions:

a. General manager or club manager

b. Food and beverage manager

c. Director of golf/head professional

d. Golf superintendent

16. What is the impact of PGA membership on the compensation package of a head professional?

17. What are the requirements for PGA membership?

18. What type of academic background is required for a golf superintendent?

19. Discuss three significant trends in the golf industry.

20. Cite at least five of the most referenced golf Web sites.

Cynthia R. Mayo
Delaware State University

Hotel and Lodging Operations

Learning Objectives

After completing this chapter, the student will be able to:

✓ Discuss factors that stimulated the development of hotel and lodging properties

✓ Identify the partners and classifications of hotel and lodging property

✓ Discuss key performance measures used by hotel and lodging managers

✓ Analyze the functions of each department and relate them to guest services

✓ Identify careers found in the hotel and lodging operations

Chapter Outline

A Brief History

Assessing Guests' Needs

The Structure of the Hotel and Lodging Industry

Classifications of Hotel and Lodging Operations

Hotel and Lodging Departments

Careers in Hotel and Lodging Operations

A Brief History

*H*otel and lodging operations have a long history. Generally, an atmosphere of friendliness and care existed throughout the decades. Early hospitality was based on the rules of common courtesy and rank order of guests. Lodging and meals were offered in the homes of private citizens, who designed and offered accommodations for travelers, which included a bed, food, and a place to exchange horses.[1] The advent of railroads stimulated the first grand hotels built in America, such as the Tremont House in Boston, the Astor House (1936) in New York; the Parker House (1936) in Boston, and the Palace House (1975) in San Francisco. During that period, the word "**hotelier**" was developed to refer to the keeper, owner, or manager. After 1908, many hotels were developed to meet the emerging needs of travelers. During the 1920s and 1930s, the number of hotels had grown to over 10,000, with one million rooms.

During the early 1900s, a typical hotel featured such amenities as steam heat, gas burners, electric call bells, baths, and closets. In 1904, the New York St. Regis Hotel provided individually controlled heating and cooling units in each guest room. When the Statler Hotel chain started in 1908, all the guest rooms had private baths, full-length mirrors, radio reception, and telephones. The hotel served as the model hotel for more than 40 years.[2]

Assessing Guests' Needs

Quality service must be promoted by all hotel and lodging operation managers. **Quality** is not an accident. It comes as a result of high intention, sincere effort, intelligent direction, and skillful execution, done from a list of alternatives.[3] Given what is promised, service expectations have proliferated in recent years. Guests' expectations are formed based on the hotel and lodging brand and impressions after staying at a property, as well as viewing the property on the Internet. Managers may be asked two basic questions to determine guests' expectations. What did you like best about your stay? What would make your stay more enjoyable? These questions can be asked through a formal system of evaluation and by managers "walking around" talking to guests. **Line level** employees (employees whose jobs are most often support roles and non-supervisory) can also be asked about guests' expectations

because they provide the products and services to them.

Continuous assessments of guest services can be achieved through benchmarking and cross-functioning teams. **Benchmarking** is a process of knowing what property managers do to deliver guests services and compare the service factors with their competitors. Studying available industry training materials, networking at professional conferences, and analyzing what others are doing to meet guests' expectations are also examples of benchmarking. What works well for one firm may also work with modifications for another firm. **Cross-functioning teams** are groups of employees from various departments who work together to resolve operating problems.

The Structure of the Hotel and Lodging Industry

The structure of the hotel and lodging industry is centered on **hotel owners, management companies, franchising, and ownership**. To understand the structure, one must understand who owns hotels and lodging facilities, who manages them, and who franchises them.

Many individuals and companies invest in hotels and other lodging products. Some **investors** are experienced in the ownership of hotels, whereas others are new to the business. An investor may own all or part of a hotel. Some individual investors take an active role in the management of the property, whereas others purchase the properties for investment purposes only. They have little or no experience in operating and managing a hotel. Therefore, they must rely on a management company to manage the day-to-day operations, based on some predefined goals. **Hotel management companies** are businesses that provide the day-to-day operations of properties. **An owner/operator** is a hotel investor who also manages the hotel or lodging property. The owner/operator may be extensively involved along with family members in the day-to-day operations of the facility. Usually with this type of setup, the property may or may not be one of the national or international brands, such as Marriott, Hilton, or other such brands. **Franchising** is an arrangement where one party (**franchisor**) allows another party (the **franchisee**) to operate a business of a name brand product for a specified period of time for a fee. The brand's logo, trademarks, and operating systems are used exclusively. A network is created of independent business owners sharing a brand name. According to the American Hotel and Lodging Association, hotel and lodging owners have many options to choose from in terms of managing a hotel property. There are a variety of ways hotels and lodging facilities can be owned and managed. They are

- Single-unit property not affiliated with a brand. These single-unit properties are usually historic properties that have been recently renovated. Or the properties may have a city name or some local name.
- Multi-unit properties affiliated with the same brand. The expectations and goals across operations are similar. Some hotel chains are now clustering two or three brands in one location. This allows them to use one general manager for all the properties with assistants operating the day-to-day functions. This saves the company money while meeting service goals.
- Multi-unit properties with different brands. Managing multi-unit properties means the owner must be able to satisfy the owner, operating under different brands and quality standards.
- Multi-unit properties operated by a management company or the brand. These services are offered to the hotel owner for a fee.
- Single or multi-unit properties owned by the brand. This setup is the most widely method in the United States. Many brand hotels hire and develop their own managers. One example is Marriott International. Some properties are company owned, some independently owned, and some are franchised. Regardless of the arrangement, specific standards must be adhered to in order to keep the name and the brand.[4]

Classifications of Hotel and Lodging Operations

Basic classifications and services offered will determine the extent of technical and managerial skills needed. Lodging properties may be classified in many different ways. The typical classifications are based on the following:

Geographical Location: Airport, downtown, highway, financial district, suburbia, others

Service Levels: Limited service, full service, convention, extended-stay, upscale, luxury

Price Levels: Low budget, budget, medium priced, upper scale, upscale, luxury

Rating: Star ratings, ranging from one star to five stars, (Mobil Travel Service), Diamond Rating, ranging from one diamond to five diamonds (AAA Travel)

Number of Rooms: 50 rooms, 51–100 rooms, 101–150, 151–200, 201–250, 251–300, 301–350, 351–400, 401–500, 501–600, 601–1000, mega-size hotels, such as The Opryland in Tennessee, with 3,500+ rooms, MGM Grand with 5,500+ rooms (largest hotel in terms of rooms in U.S.).[5]

The quality of facilities and the services assessment of properties are performed by two organizations: Mobil Travel Services and Automobile Association of America (AAA). The Mobil Travel Guide, a division of the Mobil Oil Corporation, uses the star rating system.[6] The most widely recognized system is the diamond rating issued by the American Automobile Association (AAA). These two classification systems offer brand hotel companies that operate internationally a uniform standard by which to ensure that their guests have comfortable experiences.

Key performance measures are used for hotel and lodging operations. They are Average Daily Rate, Occupancy Rate, and Revenue per Available Room (REVPAR).

- The Average Daily Rate, computed as Total Revenue from Room Sales/Total number of Rooms Sold. If the revenue for a day was $25,000 and the hotel sold 200 rooms, then $25,000/200 = $125.00.
- Occupancy Rate, computed as total rooms sold/total rooms available. If the hotel sells 175 rooms and they have 225 available, the occupancy rate is: 175/225 = 77%.
- Revenue per Available Room (REVPAR) is computed using the average daily rate and the occupancy rate: $125 × .77 = $96.25.[7]

Classifications within Brands

Using Marriott International, Hyatt, and Hilton's classifications of properties, brands are created. The classifications are based on lodging properties (brands) and the services provided. They include:

Marriott International

Full-Service Lodging

Marriott Hotels, Resorts, and Suites include the following. **J. W. Marriott Hotels** is considered the most luxurious brand that carries the Marriott name. These hotels offer a higher level of personal service and amenities. **The Ritz-Carlton Hotel** is the premier global luxury hotel brand owned by Marriott. The Ritz-Carlton is a worldwide symbol of prestige and distinction. The Ritz-Carlton Hotels have won the Malcolm-Baldridge Award for 1992 and 1999.[8] It is the first and only award given to a hotel. **The Renaissance Hotels, Resorts, and Suites** are considered as upscale, full-service lodging properties that provide a distinctive choice to travelers. **Marriott Conference Centers** offer a variety of conference packages.

Select Service Lodging

Courtyard by Marriott, Fairfield Inn, and **Ramada International** are included in this segment. Courtyard by Marriott was designed by and for business travelers. Services include a restaurant, lounge, meeting space, exercise room, and swimming pool. The Fairfield Inn is designed for the mid-tier business and leisure traveler. Clean and comfortable rooms, an exercise room, and enhanced amenities are included. Ramada International provides services for the international business traveler.

Extended-Stay Properties

Some extended-stay and corporate lodgings include the properties **Residence Inn, TownePlace Suites, Springhill Suites, Marriott Executive Apartments**, and **ExecuStay**. The Residence Inn is one of North America's top extended-stay brands, which provides a homelike atmosphere. Features include fully equipped kitchens, space for entertainment or meetings and ample work space, a swimming pool, and an exercise room. Marriott Executive Apartments offers both the ambience and privacy of apartment living, while providing the convenience of hotel-like services and amenities. Most services are offered for 24 hours. ExecuStay by Marriott provides a corporate housing solution for the business traveler in need of a furnished apartment for 30 days or more.

Ownership Properties

Ownership resorts include **Marriott Vacation Club,** the **Ritz-Carlton Club**, and **Horizons**. The Marriott Vacation Club International is a developer and operator of vacation ownership resorts. The resorts feature spacious one-, two- and three-bedroom villas, designed to provide high-quality accommodations in a relaxed atmosphere. Each villa features a spacious living and dining area, master bedroom and bath, and a private balcony, kitchen, and laundry area. The Ritz-Carlton Club is a collection of private residences in highly desirable resort destinations that are reserved for the exclusive use of members and their guests. Horizons, a Marriott Vacation Club, offers value-priced resort communities that emphasize exciting, on-site recreation, planned activities, and entertainment for the entire family.[9]

The Hyatt Corporation

The Hyatt Corporation has specific brands similar to Marriott but offers distinct differences. The Hyatt Corporation opened its first hotel on September 27, 1957. Hyatt's first property at Los Angeles International Airport was originally named the Hyatt House. The owner of Hyatt House was a local entrepreneur, Hyatt R. von Dehn. Hyatt hotels expanded aggressively along the West Coast during the following years. In 1967, Hyatt opened the world's first atrium hotel in Atlanta, Georgia. The Hyatt name became worldwide. The hotel's 21-story atrium tower lobby and dramatic departure from traditional hotel architecture changed the course of the lodging industry. The challenge to hotel architects was no longer to eliminate extra space; rather, to create grand, wide-open public spaces. In 1996, the first international hotel opened, the Hyatt Regency Hong Kong, operated by a newly formed company called Hyatt International.

Full-Service Upscale

Hyatt Regency hotels are Hyatt's core brand of hotels, offering guests opportunities to broaden their horizons and rejuvenate. Lobbies and rooms are designed to reflect the best of the local cultures, inventive food and beverage outlets, and exceptional technology. Meeting and fitness facilities are also available. **Grand Hyatt** and **Park Hyatt** brands were introduced in 1980 to further identify and market the diverse types of Hyatt properties worldwide. Grand Hyatt hotels serve culturally rich destinations that attract leisure and business travelers as well as large-scale meetings and conventions. The hotels, reflecting a grand scale and refinement, include features such as state-of-the-art technology, sophisticated business and leisure facilities, banquet and conference facilities of world-class standard, and specialized programs that cater to discriminating business and vacation guests. Park Hyatts are the company's smaller brand.

Luxury hotels are designed to cater to the discriminating individual traveler seeking the privacy, personalized service, and elegance of a small European hotel. They offer a sense of sanctuary and luxury. In addition to state-of-the-art technology, Park Hyatts offer exceptional food and beverage facilities, intimate, understated surroundings, and 24-hour personalized service.

Hyatt Casino Hotels

Guests can choose from a sophisticated range of gaming titles, slot machines, and other popular games of chance. Each casino destination is unique and offers excellent restaurants, live entertainment, and shopping. Many of the casinos are located in wonderful resorts, complete with challenging sports facilities, recreation, and superb accommodations. Since the opening of the Hyatt Regency Maui in 1980, Hyatt has also become known as a leader in the creation and operation of dramatic luxury resorts as well.

Today, Hyatt specializes in deluxe hotels with meeting facilities and services for the business traveler. In many cities, Hyatt has made a significant contribution to revitalizing the area and stimulating business and population growth. Hyatt Hotels & Resorts have a reputation, not only for their physical distinctiveness, incorporating local art and design, but also for the amenities and services provided. These special services include Hyatt Gold Passport, Hyatt's renowned recognition and award program for the frequent traveler; Regency Club, a VIP concierge floor; complimentary morning newspaper; specialty restaurants; and custom catering.[10]

The Hilton Hotels

Conrad Hilton purchased his first hotel in Cisco, Texas, back in 1919. The first hotel to carry the Hilton name was built in Dallas in 1925. In 1943, Hilton became the first "coast-to-coast" hotel chain in the United States; and in 1949 it opened its first hotel outside the United States in San Juan, Puerto Rico. Hilton went on the New York Stock Exchange in 1946, and Conrad Hilton purchased the Waldorf Astoria in 1949. Hilton has several world-renowned, marquee properties, some of which are Hilton Athens, Hilton San Francisco, and Hilton New York. Hilton Hotel brands are the Doubletree, Embassy Suites, Homewood Suites, Hampton Inn and Suites, and Hilton Garden Inn.

The Upscale Properties

More than 60 years after Conrad Hilton opened his first hotel in Texas, his son, Barron, began another chapter in the innovative history of Hilton Hotels Corporation with the founding of Conrad Hotels in 1982. Conrad Hotels were established with the goal of operating a network of luxury hotels, resorts, and casinos in major business and leisure destinations worldwide. Since then, Conrad has earned a reputation for first-class service and style, as well as, the highest standards of architecture, design, comfort, and cuisine. Such levels of excellence have allowed Conrad hotels to continue to receive numerous awards in prestigious leisure business travel publications around the world.

The Doubletree Hotels are uniquely designed properties ranging from hotels, guest suites, and destination resorts to Doubletree Club hotels. Typical properties offer a full-service restaurant and lounge, room service, swimming pool, health club, complete meeting and banquet facilities, oversized guest rooms, and luxury amenities. This upscale, full-service hotel chain primarily serves major metropolitan areas and leisure destinations, with each unique property reflecting the local or regional environment in its design. From the signature homemade chocolate chip cookies to the deluxe amenities, Doubletree promises travelers a satisfying stay.

Suite Hotels

Embassy Suites Hotels are the nation's largest brand of upscale, all-suite hotels with more total suites than any of its competitors. Embassy Suites Hotels helped create the all-suite segment of the lodging industry and maintain the commanding presence in this segment in terms of system size, geographic distribution, brand-name recognition and operating performance. Created in 1983, Embassy Suites Hotels serve as the pioneer in the all-suite concept and today is a market share leader worldwide.

Upscale Homewood Suites by Hilton is a national brand of upscale all-suite residential-style hotels targeting travelers who are on the road for a few days or more. Homewood Suites are designed to make guests feel at home, providing them with all the comforts, convenience, and privacy of home for the price of a traditional hotel room. **Homewood Suites** hotels feature such amenities as spacious one-bedroom, two-bedroom, and/or studio suites with fully-equipped kitchens, daily complimentary breakfast, and evening Manager's Reception (every Monday–Thursday) with hors d'oeuvres and beverages.

Mid-Price Properties

Hampton Inn Hotels offer value-minded travelers comfortable, well-equipped rooms. Guests will find that friendly service and many extra touches make every stay more enjoyable. A free breakfast bar and a variety of beverages are offered. Local calls are always free, and free in-room movie channels are provided.

Hilton Garden Inns are positioned as the mid-priced brand targeted to today's growing segment of mid-market travelers. Focusing on what guests have said they want and need while traveling, Hilton Garden Inns offer quality accommodations, amenities, and services in a comfortable atmosphere designed for both the business and leisure traveler. From the welcoming Pavilion to the spacious work desk found in each and every guest room, to the Pavilion Pantry selling snacks and sundry items 24 hours a day, guests will feel "at home."

Other Brands

There are other lodging brands, which are classified as follows:

Budget
Super 8
Motel 6
Shoney's Inn
HoJo Inn

Mid-Price
Comfort Inn and Suites
Sleep Inn
Holiday Inn Express

Upscale/First Class
Sheraton
Holiday Inn Select
Doubletree
Radisson

Upper Scale/Luxury
Four Seasons
Independents, such as the Jefferson Hotel, Richmond, VA

Hotel and Lodging Departments

Hotel and lodging departments may be divided into two major components: revenue centers and support centers. The revenue centers are the centers that generate income. In order of predominance, rooms, food and beverage, telecommunications, and rentals receive money from services and products rendered. The support centers are those that provide the support for the revenue centers to earn income. The support centers include marketing and sales, human resources, maintenance, accounting, and security and safety. The departments are designed depending on the size and service levels of properties. Some properties may have two departments, with all the required functions listed under the two departments. Some properties may have a department for each function on the property. It depends on many factors. For the sake of this chapter, the aforementioned departments will be discussed.

Rooms Division/Front Office

The rooms division may consist of guest services, the housekeeping department, and the accounting department. Because selling rooms generates more than 60 percent of the hotel and lodging revenues, the rooms division may be operated in close concert with the front office. Check-in is the first step to selling a room, which is a perishable product. Therefore, the front office staff is usually the first guest encounter. Check-in requires the staff to use some form of technology to record guests' payment method and provide a room key. A property management system (PMS) is the technology used. The front office staff must know the property management system (PMS) well to process guests in a timely manner. Generally, a PMS provides

- Who is scheduled to check in the property?
- What they spend while they are there.
- The form of payment used on departure. Each system depends on the needs of the properties. Franchised properties are usually required to use the brand's PMS.

Guest Services

The front office is responsible for guest services that include welcoming guests, transportation, handling baggage, taking guest messages, delivering newspapers, management of safety deposit boxes, providing information to guests related to the city events, as well as handling concerns and disputes of guests.

Housekeeping Department

The Housekeeping Department is a critical component of providing clean, sanitized rooms for guests. A clean room is the number one request of hotel and lodging guests. Therefore, the housekeeping department must hire and train room attendants who are willing to meet the standards of cleaning rooms in a timely manner, while serving as professional guest servers. The housekeeping department is also responsible for the cleanliness of the public areas, guest areas, and laundry areas.

The housekeeping department must interact with the rooms department daily. Rooms are assigned based on being cleaned and ready to receive guests. Rooms are assigned based on properly cleaned rooms that have been verified as clean and the status correctly reported to the front desk as "clean and vacant." This requires effective and open communications. Many mistakes can be made, thus making guests unhappy, if planning, coordinating, and open lines of communications are flawed. The housekeeping department receives each morning a list of checkouts and those who are expected to stay over. Currently room attendants clean from 13 to 20 rooms a day, depending on the type of property. If the property is a suite hotel, fewer rooms are required for cleaning by each attendant. The housekeeping coding system must be known by all persons in the department. Some typical terms used are

- Clean and Vacant—The room is vacant, has been cleaned and can be assigned to guests.
- Occupied—The room is registered to a guest.
- Stay-over—The guest will stay in the room at least one more night.
- Check-out—The guest has departed.[11]

The housekeeping department must have an open and supportive role with all departments in the hotel. Managing a housekeeping department means that staff must be hired, trained, and developed to become proactive leaders determined to ex-

Room attendants must be willing to clean rooms in a timely manner, while also serving as professional guest servers.

ceed guests' expectations. Room attendants must know what is expected of them. Each room attendant must be able to inspect his or her work and maintain a critical level of assessment to experience success.

Accounting

Rooms' revenue represents more than 60 percent of the total hotel and lodging revenue. Some accountability financial data include REVPAR, Occupancy, and Average Daily Rate. In addition to the three previously mentioned items, **Cost Per Occupied Room** may be determined. Adequate funding is needed to maintain certain quality standards of providing amenities and services.

The accounting department also accounts for all monies received for operations. Analyses of income and expenses are conducted by the department. The analyses serve as a benchmark against standards and goals that have been set by administrators and managers.

Human Resources Department (HR)

The most important asset a hotel and lodging business has is the human resources. The business assets must be managed to realize the "best" possible service and productivity required. The human resources department serves as the key component in recruiting and selecting a productive workforce. The HR department's activities include recruitment, selection, orientation, training and development, developing compensation packages, monitoring the legal aspects of HR, providing safety, and health of employees. Maintaining diversity and employee relations on internal and external components of the industry are also required. The roles and responsibilities of HR present real challenges for the twenty-first century. The challenges become more intense as we realize that for the twenty-first century, ever-changing, dangerous conditions are emerging that require more than the normal solutions.

Sales and Marketing Department

Sales and marketing of hotel and lodging are the systems designed and implemented to lure guests and once they come, ensure that they will return. It is better to keep loyal guests than to try to get new guests. Marketing, then, is a process of creating and sustaining productive relationships with desirable customers. The department managers must be creative and innovative to create brand identities for their market that are different from their competitors. The first step is to decide what the hotel and lodging service and products should be and what to offer to whom. Once this question is answered, the process of marketing involves setting prices, creating an awareness of services and products, making the site available and assessable, managing revenue, preparing and delivering delight, and retaining customers and measuring satisfaction and evaluating performance. If these steps are followed, a sales and marketing plan will be viable and relevant.[12]

Food and Beverage Services

Food and beverage services usually generate the second highest amount of revenue in a hotel and lodging business. The range of services may extend from providing continental breakfasts to operating four or five various types of food and beverage services. Catering services may also be an option for the business. Each service offered depends on the facility, which may range from limited services to full-service venues.

Limited-service hotels typically offer breakfast in the lobby of the property. Some limited-service hotels offer continental breakfasts (juice, muffins, coffee, doughnuts, and other ready-to-eat items). Some limited-service property managers offer "made-to-order hot breakfast items" that may include omelets, bacon, sausage, grits, oatmeal, and other hot items.

Full-service hotels and lodging facilities may offer several menu choices provided by one or two in-house facilities. Full-scale hotels offer convention and banquet services, and there may be two or three themed restaurants on the property. Full-scale properties typically accommodate the diverse needs of a wide range of guests in planning and implementing food and beverage operations.

Depending on the extensiveness of service, the number and types of managers are assigned. If the facility has only breakfast (limited service), one general manager may be assigned to direct the operation of the property and all the components required. Typically, a person is employed part-time to come in and setup and serve breakfast. Full-service properties hire specialized positions that may include chefs, directors and managers of food and beverage services, and directors and managers of convention services. Additional funds can be generated through room service offering food services 24/7 for hotel and lodging guests. Several measures are used to assess operations. **Guest Check Average**—the amount spent by a guest in a room service or dining room service order. **Contribution Margin** is the amount of revenue from food revenue after the cost of the food used to generate the revenue is subtracted.

Safety and Security

Hotel and lodging managers "have a duty of care" to protect guests and their property. This need has heightened since 2001 and the threat of terrorism. Hotel and lodging owners must have systems in place, such as electronic door openers that are programmed and disabled when guests check out. Other systems must be in place to ensure the safety and security of guests. Surveillance and alarm systems must be in place to monitor entrances and exits to doors and other areas that may be vulnerable.

Areas such as food and beverage cashier stations and front desk cashier stations should have alarm systems tied to the police and fire stations.[13]

Careers in Hotel and Lodging Management

Careers in hotel and lodging management are unlimited. Due to the wide number and variety of hotel and lodging operations, the opportunities are phenomenal! Career choices include job titles such as general manager, associate or assistant general manager, shift manager, director of sales and marketing, director of food and beverage services, director of human resources, sales manager, reservations manager, controller, front-office manager, restaurant manager, chief executive housekeeper, supervisor of catering, revenue manager, and director of guest services. This list is by no means exhaustive. Within each department supervisory jobs are available. It is a matter of assessing your interests, finding your niche, and developing into a productive leader. The level of service dictates the responsibilities of each manager. It is wise to learn all you can about the hotel and lodging industry, develop a passion for service and be determined to become a productive, value-added employee. Keep learning and as Bill Marriott says, "Success is never final."[14]

Endnotes

1. Noriega, Pender and Cynthia Mayo, *Contemporary Approaches to Hospitality and Tourism Management.* Hoboken, NJ: Wiley, 2005, p. 4
2. Hayes, David and Jack Ninemeier, *Lodging Management.* Upper Saddle River, NJ: Prentice Hall, 2006, pp. 4–15
3. Willa A. Foster
4. Rutherford, Denny and Michael O'Fallon, *Hotel Management Operations*, 4th ed., New Jersey: Wiley, p. 15
5. Resource Guide for Hospitality Students given out during 2006 NSMH Conference
6. www.hoteltravelcheck.com
7. Schmidgall, Raymond, *Hospitality Industry Managerial Accounting,* 5th ed. Washington, DC: American Hotel and Lodging Association, 2001
8. Ritz-Carlton, International, www.ritzcarlton.com
9. Noriega and Mayo, *Contemporary Approaches*
10. Hyatt Annual Report, 2000
11. Hayes and Ninemeier, *Lodging Management.* chapter 7, pp. 177–200
12. Rutherford and O'Fallon, *Hotel Management Operations*, p. 308
13. Ibid, p. 84
14. Szocki-Foucar, Reginald F., Ronald Cereola, and Stephen D. Wetport, J. W. Marriott: "The Spirit to Serve," *Journal of Hospitality and Tourism Education* 16, no. 4 (2004): 11

Resources

Internet Sites

American Hotel and Lodging Association: www.ahla.com
Marriott International: www.marriott.org
Hotel Related Topics: www.hotel-online.com
e-distribution channels: www.hedna.org-Management
Training Materials: www.ei-ahma.org
Professional Association for Hospitality Sales and Marketing: www.hsmai.org
Chamber of Commerce—Nationally: www.chamberofcommerce.com
Diamond Ratings: www.aaa.com
Hilton Hotels: www.hilton.com
Hyatt Hotels: www.hyatt.com
American Express—wholesale retail travel services: www.travel.americanexpress.com
Computerized Contract Management Systems: www.act.com
Hospitality Educators Resource Organization: www.chrie.org
Summary Results of Individual Properties: www.usfsi.com
Career Opportunities in Hotel Management: www.hcareers.com

Team Building Organization: www.teambuilding.org
Resources Related to Legal Aspects of Hotel and Lodging Forms: www.hospitalitylawyer.com
Fair Labor Standard Laws: www.dot.gov/elaws/flsa.htm
Equal Employment Opportunity Commission: www.eeoc.gov
Immigration Reform and Control Act: www.usda.gov
Society for Human Resource Management: www.shrm.org
Requirements Related to Overtime Pay and Exempt Employees: www.wagehour.dot.gov
Training Resources: www.hoteltraining.com
Hospitality Financial and Technology Professionals: www.htfp.org
Revenue Management Solutions: www.maximrms.com
Ideas for Operation: www.ideas.com
Choice Hotels Site: www.choicehotels.com
Housekeepers' Association: www.ieha.org
Hotel Registry: www.americanhotel.com

☞ Key Words and Concepts

American Hotel and Lodging Association
At-will employment
Average revenue
Benchmarking
Brands
Contract
Cost per room
Cross-functioning teams
Diversity
Duty of care
Geographical locations
Hotelier
Investors
Job description
Job specification
Occupancy rate
Price levels
Ratings
Revenue per available room
Room attendants
Service levels
Structures
Trade and travel
Trade associations
Travel agents

🅐 Contributor Information

Cynthia R. Mayo
Associate Director/Director of Hospitality and
    Tourism Management
Delaware State University
cmayo@desu.edu
www.crmdsc.com
Cynthia Mayo prepared for her career in hospitality and tourism management by receiving a Bachelor of Science degree and a Master of Business Administration degree from Hampton University, and a Master of Arts and Master of Education degrees in Economics and Education from Virginia State University. She received her Doctor of Philosophy degree from Virginia Polytechnic Institute and State University. She has worked as a middle and high school teacher, a food services supervisor, a director of food services, and she taught at Virginia State University for more than 13 years. She has worked in hotels, restaurants, and currently owns a catering business.

Dr. Mayo is the coauthor of several textbooks, and she has published many articles related to competencies needed by hospitality graduates and leadership development. She resides in Glen Allen, Virginia, and is an active community volunteer.

27 ▊ Review Questions

1. Explain the factors that contributed to the development of hotel and lodging operations in the United States.

2. Design a chart with the names and dates of the hotel and lodging companies that were termed the "first" to offer a service, technique, or product.

3. Explain the techniques of determining REVPAR, Occupancy, and Average Daily Rate.

4. Evaluate and summarize the duties of each department described in the chapter. Conduct research and determine requirements of departments not included in the chapter.

5. Visit three properties' Web sites and map out the products offered. Identify their brands and the key aspects of each brand. Describe what is being marketed.

6. Visit www.hcareers.com and write a summary of the careers available in hotel and lodging management.

7. Research using Internet sites to determine the number of hotel properties and rooms available today. Determine the average occupancy and average room rate. Determine the top five management companies in terms of revenue, property, and rooms.

8. Explain why all partners in the hotel and lodging industry must work together. Explain why diversity initiatives are important today.

9. Analyze and explain the types of ownership that can exist for hotel and lodging operations.

Ken Myers
University of Minnesota, Crookston

Gail Myers
Suite Harmony Corporation

Hospitality Layout and Design

Learning Objectives

After reading this chapter, the student will be able to:

✓ Explain the role of the many professionals involved on a design team

✓ Explain the basic design elements that are part of all design projects

✓ Describe what "universal design" is and how it affects the planning and design of a hospitality establishment

✓ Explain the design considerations and how those considerations work together in creating the desired environment

✓ List organizations that rate hotels and restaurants on specific criteria and how hospitality establishments can use these criteria as they plan design projects

Chapter Outline

Rating Systems
Function, Flow, and Aesthetics
Interior Design
The Design Project

*I*t all begins with the concept. Every aspect of layout and design is driven by that central idea that will make your establishment an exciting place. Whether it be a southern-style barbeque restaurant, a Far Eastern–inspired spa, or a historical building turned hotel, every choice of lighting, place of furniture, choice of linens, and even exterior signage will signal to potential guests who you are. The design and layout of the property also sets the stage for guest expectations and behaviors. Do you want guests to wear suits and ties? Do you want guests to stay a long time or move in and out quickly? Do you want your guests to have romantic memories of your establishment, or do you want them to remember you as a hot, trendy new property? Elements like color, traffic flow, and music can all communicate strong messages to the guests. You control those messages by proper use of layout and design. Layout refers to the flow, placement, and routing of both people and product. Design refers to the placement and selection of your building and its colors, fixtures, walls, ceiling and floor treatments, furniture and equipment, lighting, and all the accessories in between. Creating ambience, providing for safety, buffering sound, and increasing efficiency and comfort for the guest are some of the goals of layout and design in the hospitality industry.

In this day of online restaurant reviews, hotel reservations, and general entertainment planning on the Internet, layout and design now play a key role in consumer choice because it can be available to them before they ever take a step inside the establishment. Online tours and 360-degree exterior and interior room views allow guests to make determinations before they venture outside. The décor creates an ambience or atmosphere that reflects the quality of the food, the pricing, and the level of service. The environment is important because it influences a patron's expectations, their mood, and their responses. If the planning has been successful, the guest will pull out their credit card and book a reservation.

Rating Systems

The two most highly regarded rating companies for hospitality establishments base a large portion of their criteria on layout and design elements. Mobile Travel Guide and AAA base their ratings for hotels on criteria they have established with layout and design specifics for the exterior, public areas, guestrooms, bathrooms, and hotel amenities in addition to service. Other rating services, such as American Express, examine restaurant quality with criteria covering ambience, lighting, traffic flow, and general comfort, in addition to the quality of the food and service. Management in the hospitality field is well aware that even service and food quality are largely affected by the layout and design of the kitchen and related production and storage areas.

Whether the rating symbols are diamonds, keys, or stars, upscale hotels usually have some common characteristics. Some of the rating companies use words like *luxurious*, *superior*, and *well appointed* to describe the layout and design of a four-star hotel. Yahoo travel ratings describe their four-star hotel as having "upscale facilities, a well integrated design, stylized room décor, excellent restaurant facilities and landscaped grounds." Some of the larger companies use very specific descriptions, such as:

- A roomy registration area located away from the main traffic flow, with multiple conversation areas and several furniture groupings
- Sheetrock as a ceiling material with trims or moldings

Hotels must plan for the rating they wish to receive well before construction begins.

- Decorative tissue boxes
- More luxurious guest room floor coverings such as marble, granite, carpet, or wood

Hotels must actually plan the rating they wish to achieve well in advance of construction because revisions in layout and design after the hotel is built can be costly. For example, one hotel chain saved money by installing vinyl bathroom flooring that resembled tile, only to find later that they met all the four-star criteria except for that flooring. Most highly rated hotels have wide corridors and spacious bathroom layouts that are difficult to change once the hotel is built.

Function, Flow, and Aesthetics

Function, flow, and aesthetics are the important factors in making a decision about how a hospitality facility should be planned and maintained. Yes, guests need a comfortable bed to sleep on (function), but is the layout arranged so that they can get to the bathroom in the night without tripping on a chair or escape to a nearby stairway in case of fire (flow)? In addition, is the bed well appointed with dust ruffle, extra pillows, and coordinating bed linens (aesthetics)? Guest perception is always the first consideration in function, flow, and beauty. Just any bed serves the function of a place to sleep, but quality hotels are concerned about upgrading function to achieve a higher level of comfort. Radisson Hotels have been switching some of their conventional mattresses to the "Sleep Number Bed," a specific brand name that consumers recognize and associate with increased comfort. Some luxury hotels are offering a more customized approach to function that allows guests to choose from a selection of pillows. How a person sleeps directly affects their perception of the hotel in the morning. An appropriate traffic flow pattern is essential in a family dining establishment. For example, guests expect they will not have to take their kids through the bar to get to the restroom. Esthetics or beauty plays a primary role in touching the emotions of people. A café seems a little more upscale . . . a little more pleasant if there are flowers on the table. A beautiful environment keeps the guests coming back.

It is hard to place an order of importance on function, flow, and aesthetics. Once again, guest perception and expectations play a part in the layout and design choices. Great food served on picnic tables squeezed into a small space where elbows touch, waitstaff have a hard time maneuvering, and the noise of pots and pans blends in with loud music may be acceptable at an outdoor barbeque, but will leave a bad taste in the mouths of guests at most restaurants who expect adequate aisles, private space, a low noise level so that they can hear conversation, and comfortable seating.

Interior Design

Interior design has come to be much more than selecting carpet or wall coverings to meet fire codes. The elements of interior design can be used to create theatrics, special effects, or historic restoration. When you walk into a restaurant, whether it is freestanding, at the casino, or on a cruise ship, interior excitement is created by the materials on the walls, ceilings, and floors; the psychological effect of color; and the level and type of lighting. A jazz club may use bold and unique color combinations, small halogen track lighting, and contemporary furniture to promote its on-the-edge feel. The flow-through of the concept should enter into every design detail, including the furniture, menu, and centerpiece. Even the switch plate covers are preplanned to become part of a total design concept.

Hospitality facilities are known to remodel every five to seven years. No matter how old or new, the design of the inside of the building affects every aspect of the comfort and enjoyment of guests. In fact, design involves the stimulation of the five senses. How does the food smell in conjunction with the flowers on the table, the aromatherapy, and the smell of wood or leather? How does the texture of the carpet or the flooring work with the wall covering, the texture of the tablecloth and linens, and the ceiling materials? Is the room acoustically balanced so that guests can hear the music playing and hear the conversation of the partner next to them without hearing the conversation of the next table? Do the guests feel soothed by the colors so that they are encouraged to linger over many courses, or are the colors passionate and brash, encouraging a fast-food approach? We will leave the sense of taste and the blend of exquisite flavors to the chef, but when it comes to artistic taste for the environment, the interior designer reigns. Do the styles mix: the furniture, the waiter's uniform, the china, glass, and silver? Can a new layout increase business by adding more seats? Will a new layout train customers to stand in line, to order at a particular place, to become part of the flow of service? A key ingredient in making these decisions is whether all these aspects of the décor blend together into a consistent whole. When one of these factors is different from the rest, a discord is created that results in guests feeling that something is not quite right. It may not be enough to make them leave, but it can be a reason to select another restaurant next time without them even being aware of why.

These questions are answered with careful planning and a project design team that follows through from developing the very concept of the hospitality establishment to making that concept a physical reality. Add to that the responsibilities of health and safety standards required by building codes, analyzing specifications of products for use and wear, planning for the efficiency necessary for any services that are provided, and of course, close attention to a budget, and you can begin to understand the knowledge required by a design team.

Design Team Professionals

Architects: These professionals prepare and review plans for the overall construction. Qualified architects will have an AIA (American Institute of Architects) appellation.

Interior Designers: These professionals design interior spaces involving materials, finishes, colors, space planning, and layout. This person may be employed by the architects or may be freelance. The interior designer in this case should be a commercial interior designer, as residential design is very different. A qualified applicant will have an ASID appellation. See American Society of Interior Designers Web site.

Electrical Engineers: They assist with all electrical planning. They may have to prepare and stamp electrical plans to obtain building permits and are usually employed by the architects.

Contractors: They are the builders of the project. The general contractor will oversee specialty subcontractors needed for the project. Specialty contractors include tradespeople like cabinetmakers, carpet and tile installers, and painters. Contractors are hired by bid and recommendation and are licensed by the state.

Acoustical Engineers: They offer advice and planning for acoustical or sound issues and suggest materials to solve noise problems or enhance sound. They are usually employed by the architects.

Interior Plantscapers: They advise on the proper selection and positioning of plants and their maintenance. Usually they are hired by recommendation.

Commercial Kitchen Designers: They provide planning and drawings for commercial kitchens as well as specifying equipment. They will begin with the menu and the number of seats to make appropriate determinations of the kitchen layout and design. Often these kitchen designers are freelance or are employed by equipment sales companies. There is no professional appellation here, so check for appropriate hospitality background and equipment knowledge.

Health Inspector: Inspectors are employed by the state and interpret state codes. They will inspect existing facilities and must review and approve plans for new or remodeled food preparation areas, service areas, and restrooms. In addition, they will want to approve selections of interior finishes and equipment.

Hospitality Manager: This essential part of the team represents the owners of the facilities. They coordinate the design team and keep them on track with the concept and budget. They will be the final decision maker and/or represent investors, developers, or board members of the company. The manager will follow every detail of the plan. The manager may involve other company personnel including the purchasing agent.

The Design Project

Once you have a well-defined concept, and you have selected your design team, you can begin on the new or remodel project. Every project is different and will require a different combination of members, depending on what is to be accomplished.

Basic Design Elements

Color: Color trends change dramatically every decade, but the psychology of color remains constant. Warm colors like yellows, oranges, and reds excite our passions, make us hungry, and energetic, or they can make us feel cozy, cocooned in a warm glow. Warm colors can make a space seem smaller. Cool colors like blues, greens, purples, and pastels relax us and are peaceful and restful. Cool colors tend to widen a space so we perceive it as bigger than it really is. Neutrals such as brown, khaki, gray, black, or white can be soothing because they do not stimulate the brain in the way that other colors do. Low-stress establishments like spas often use a monochromatic (one color) or neutral color scheme to reduce stress. Color has such a strong effect on us that it can affect our feelings and affect how our physical bodies function. For example, rose tones have been known to lower blood pressure; reds and oranges make us hungry. Color can create a dramatic fast-paced atmosphere or a passive place where we want to linger. Color can communicate to guest the intent of the hospitality establishment.

Flow: This includes considerations like traffic flow and design transitions from one space to another. The flow affects how equipment will be placed, adjacencies of rooms and functions, or how one hallway transitions into another. Flow also directs the eye where to look with the use of lines and patterns. Vertical lines are strong and sophisticated, horizontal lines are relaxing, and curved lines create a harmony, an almost maternal rocking motion when they are used as patterns in wallcoverings, as part of the traffic flow in the layout, or as a design element or characteristic of the furnishings. Flow helps hospitality patrons understand how to move from one space to another, it makes work more efficient, and it helps guests understand the concept you are creating.

Style: These are characteristics that pull a visual presentation together. It can be a period style and can be defined as a room designed with characteristics from the Victorian period or from the reign of Louis the XIV. It can also mean an artistic style such as contemporary or traditional. Often style includes a portrayal of good taste that is associated with a particular look.

Design Considerations

Each part of the hospitality establishment has different design considerations and priorities. In some areas safety and function come before beauty. In other areas pure drama is the most important element. The right interior design for your concept can allow guests to perceive the value of your services as much greater than the competition. Some specific design considerations are as follows.

The Guest Room

The guest room influences the perception of all of the hotel's facilities. Guests spend more time in their room than anywhere in the hotel. Rooms should accommodate the physical needs and comfort of a diverse group of people. Layout considerations include

The guest's room influences the perception of all the hotel's facilities.

planned spaces to accommodate the five functions of a guest room: sleeping, bathing/grooming, dressing, and entertainment activities. Some guest rooms also become workspace. Trends for guest room design include increased comfort and spa-like details such as elaborate showerheads and featherbeds. Room design can be more fluid than other areas in a hotel as accessories can be changed frequently.

Food/Beverage Service Areas
(includes dining areas, bars, and meeting rooms/banquet areas)

Design concepts in these areas portray to guests the type of service offered and even the pricing. Chandeliers may cue guests as to menu prices and even their attire in this setting. Design characteristics for fast food include easy maintenance, elements that encourage fast turnover, and lots of energy (see Table 28.1). Some restaurants soften the hard edge of fast-food design by adding plants, skylights, and play areas. Contrast this environment with tableside dining, where there are often barriers for privacy and a high level of comfort that makes guests want to stay. Theme restaurants are not just about food but also about creating an experience. Theatrical food and beverage areas allow guests to "see the show" from all areas. Open kitchens may be part of the show as are animatronics, displays, actors and acrobats, or television. Trends for food and beverage areas run from casual and trendy European styling to the nostalgic craze from the 40s and 50s. Lots of props add to the ambience. Multi-tasking including eating, drinking, and socializing has now expanded to include entertainment, games, and Internet surfing all while you're still at the table or bar.

Kitchen/Food Production Areas

The kitchen square footage is planned at one-third to one-half of the dining area square footage. Ignoring this rule can cause a restaurant to fail, as adequate space is needed for the manufacturing processes surrounding food. Workstations are established based on the menu: salad station, grilling station, etc. Tasks are analyzed and placed in efficient adjacencies. For example, baking areas can be next to roasting areas so that ovens are accessible to both. Areas to be considered are: hot foods, cold foods, beverage, service, warewashing, storing and receiving, offices, and employee areas. Health and sanitation requirements will dictate some of the placement and the materials used for walls, floors, and so forth. Equipment selection and traffic patterns in the kitchen and to the dining room are important decisions that will affect success.

Common Areas
(including corridors, elevators, stairways, lobbies, public restrooms)

The hallways in any hospitality establishment are not only the primary circulation areas, but also the escape system. The design must actually point the way in the form of directional cues, including wallpaper patterns, handrails, colors, and signage. Illumination of the walls and floors is also of primary importance, as long narrow dark hallways trigger negative emotional responses. Trends include hallways wide enough to provide niche seating areas as accommodation for those guests with reduced strength and endurance.

The number of seats in a restaurant will dictate the number of restrooms that are needed. Good restroom design is a way to communicate goodwill to guests by adding colorful tiles, easy-to-clean

Table 28.1 ⫴ Fast-Service Design vs. Table-Service Design

Fast-Service Restaurant	Table-Service Restaurant
Bright warm colors Bright overhead lighting	Soft peaceful colors/trendy special effects Low-level lighting with some lighting specifically for mood or atmosphere
Short seat depth and upright back on chairs Non padded or partially padded seating Hard surface low-cost floors Limited noise reduction	Long seat depth/angled back Thickly cushioned seats and back Multisurface flooring including carpets, tile, wood Finishes chosen to reduce noise including wall fabrics, linens, carpets, ceiling treatments
Line stanchions, condiments stations, open beverage dispensers for self-service	Wide aisles to accommodate waitstaff, tableside cooking, tray stands

beautiful wallcoverings, flowers, and makeup areas. Certainly, the appearance of cleanliness is part of good design.

Lobbies communicate the identity of the establishment to guests as well as provide adjacencies to all other public areas. Guests are encouraged to socialize, transact business, and linger. Typically there are changes in materials, lighting, and signage in lobby areas as directional cues to other main areas of the hotel. Trends for design include mixing a multitude of textures such as glass, wood, and even concrete with fabrics, leathers, and metal. Custom designs are often used in flooring such as logos created with tile or carpet, exotic lighting, and high ceilings.

Mechanical Equipment and Special Systems

The internal workings of the facility are usually unseen by the guests but are essential to their needs and comfort. Architects and technicians are involved in planning security systems, audio visual equipment and use, telephone and computer accessibility for the guests and for the business of the hotel. Mechanical equipment planning and maintenance is also essential. Plumbing, electrical, and HVAC systems (heating, ventilation, and air conditioning) must be efficient and meet environmental standards for the health and safety of everyone. Sprinkler systems, elevators, and fire extinguishers are inspected periodically to make sure they are working correctly.

Air quality in a hotel or restaurant can make or break what should be a pleasant experience, even if the food and furnishings are of the highest standards; sewer smells, kitchen grease, or mildew would be offensive and would ruin the occasion. One new restaurant was constantly filled with smoke, as their hood system in the kitchen was inadequate. Potential diners, enticed by a unique concept and a great menu, were uncomfortable with an atmosphere that was environmentally unfriendly and left guests smelling badly when they left. Hood systems, air exchange systems, and exhaust fans must be properly sized, installed, and maintained to create the desired environment.

Universal Design

The importance of access to the environment for all physically challenged people began to be regulated in 1990 with the Americans with Disabilities Act. That act listed specific regulations that affected building codes and new construction all over the country. Increased awareness of the growing aging population of the baby boomers and the variety of physical challenges affecting the entire population caused those in the design industry to develop products that would allow accessibility to all kinds of people, including adults, children, and the elderly. The term "Universal Design" was used to convey the idea that products (furnishings, hardware, etc.) and architectural changes could be made to make life easier for all people, whether or not they have a disability. Some of those design changes today include barrier-free rooms and lobbies, lever faucets and door handles, 34- to 36-inch door openings, grab bars in restroom stalls and shower areas, water fountains at different height levels, and self-flushing toilets. Although hotels are required to have a certain percentage of handicapped rooms to be ADA compliant, the concept of Universal Design is that of inclusion to have all rooms as barrier free and accessible as possible. Some efforts to create universal accessibility are as simple as wider aisles in a restaurant or full-size mirrors in restrooms.

Summary

The entire interior design industry is committed to making the hospitality experience more efficient, more beautiful, more exciting, and more profitable. Your layout and design choices communicate to the guest your commitment to their enjoyment and pleasure. Good design will keep guests coming back.

Resources

Internet Sites

American Institute of Architects (AIA): www.AIA-online.org
American Society of Interior Designers (ASID): www.asid.org
The International Facility Management Association (IFMA): www.ifma.org
Three links for AAA Diamond Criteria: http://www.aaanewsroom.net/Main.asp?SectionID=&SubCategoryID=22&CategoryID=9&

http://www.aaanewsroom.net/Main.asp?CategoryID=9&SubCategoryID=22&ContentID=62&
http://www.aaanewsroom.net/Main.asp?CategoryID=9&SubCategoryID=22&ContentID=63&
Mobil Stars Criteria: http://www.mobiltravelguide.com/mtg/
Travelocity: http://svc.travelocity.com/info/info_popup/0,,YHOE:EN%7CRATINGS,00.html
Yahoo Travel: http://travel.yahoo.com/

🔑 Key Words and Concepts

Acoustical engineers
Aesthetics
Architects
Color
Commercial kitchen designers
Contractors
Electrical engineers
Function
Flow
Health inspectors
Hospitality managers
Interior designers
Interior plantscapers
Style
Universal design

👤 Contributor Information

Ken W. Myers
Associate professor and program leader of Hotel, Restaurant, & Institutional Management with the University of Minnesota, Crookston. Professor Myers teaches several courses in hospitality management including Facility Layout & Design plus consults on design projects with the Suite Harmony Corporation.

Gail J. Myers, Allied ASID
Senior Interior Designer with the Suite Harmony Corp. and adjunct professor at the University of Minnesota, Crookston. Ms. Myers consults on commercial and residential designs, has taught Facility Layout and Design, and is a noted speaker.

28 Review Questions

1. What is the role of the architect, interior designer, electrical engineer, contractor, acoustical engineers, interior plantscapers, the commercial kitchen designer, the health inspector, and the hospitality manager in a design project?

2. Explain the design elements of color, flow, and style.

3. List the five functions of a hotel guest room.

4. Why can the design be considered more fluid than other areas in a hotel?

5. If a restaurant's dining room was 2,500 square feet, how many square feet would you expect the kitchen to be?

6. What term is used to convey the idea that product and architectural changes can make life easier for all individuals?

7. What are two organizations that rate hotels and restaurants on specific criteria?

8. How frequently do many hospitality establishments remodel?

9. How can design impact the guest room, food and beverage areas, and common areas of a hospitality establishment?

10. Compare and contrast how design considerations may affect guests at a fast-service vs. a table-service restaurant?

Ernest P. Boger
University of Maryland,
Eastern Shore

International Tourism

Learning Objectives

- ✓ To provide an introductory acquaintance with the landscape of tourism across national borders
- ✓ To emphasize breadth of coverage at the expense of depth in any particular area
- ✓ To lead/stimulate investigation of one or more of these areas as a prelude to lucrative and fulfilling career pursuit
- ✓ To articulate the definitional parameters of international tourism
- ✓ To summarize historical evolution
- ✓ To discuss size and scope
- ✓ To reference the marketing/regulatory organizations
- ✓ To explain approaches to the study of, debate the challenges, and assess career opportunities

Chapter Outline

Background and Definition

Historical Evolution/Development of International Tourism

Size and Scope of International Tourism Today

Organizations for Regulation and Marketing of International Tourism

Dimensional Approaches to the Study of International Tourism

International Tourism Challenges

Career Opportunities

Background and Definition

*T*he working definition of tourism, historically advanced by the author, is "Voluntary and temporary alternate environment encounter for the purpose of enrichment." The tourist is necessarily, then, a "traveler" and a "visitor." By extension, international tourism refers to the visitor's movement or "travel" across sovereign national borders. Many definitions of tourism abound, but all have common components. First, they are always voluntary movements. Second, they require going beyond the traveler's every day surroundings. Third, they are focused on some form of experiential growth (i.e., enrichment). And finally, the traveler must return home, usually within a year. The World Tourism Organization (WTO)[1] provides detailed recommendations on definitions of tourism, tourists, and travelers that permit standardization for research, measurement, and application in varying jurisdictions.

Historical Evolution/ Development of International Tourism

Ancient Times—Heroic Figures

Human wanderlust is well documented in the archeological record, which stretches back at least 150,000 years to the African continent. However, the continental shifts of humanoids from Africa to Europe to Asia were motivated by a search for more accommodating surroundings for survival, rather than enrichment as we know it today. Also, going back (i.e., returning home), was not an option. As such, those movements would be classified as migration. No doubt, the seeds of exploration were planted in the human psyche as individuals reached out to define the "cutting edge" of their existence.

The invention of money as a medium of representational exchange by the Sumerians (Babylonians) around 4000 BC is recognized as a benchmark in international travel/tourism in that "value" became portable. Thus money represented a quantum leap from the barter system, which limited mobility and distance, because actual goods or services had to be present and/or performed. An updated, albeit substantially less revolutionary, comparison would be the substitution of credit cards, which eliminates the need to carry large quantities of cash.

Early travelers who we recognize as "heroic figures" today include the journey of the Sumerian King set forth in the Epic of Gilgamesh (ca. 2000 BCE) and Egyptian Queen Hatshepsut, whose journey in 1480 BCE to the land of Punt is well documented on the walls of temple Deir el-Bahri at Luxor. The Nile Valley burial tombs of the pharaohs punctuated by the great pyramids and the Sphinx were built between 2700 BCE and 1700 BCE and were well established as

The great pyramids and Sphinx were established as major attractions by 1200 BCE.

major attractions by 1200 BCE. Around the same time, 1760 BCE–1027 BCE, the Shang Dynasty pioneered trade routes to far-flung locales throughout what is present-day China. The jungles of Mexico and South America continue to reveal the ancient travel routes of Mayan and other ancient civilizations. The thirteenth century CE journey of Marco Polo from Italy to China and back must certainly be included in chronological benchmarking for international tourism.

The Roman Era—Order, Roads

Beginning around 150 BCE and by 117 CE, "Roman roads comprised a network of some 50,000 miles. They girdled the Roman Empire, extending from near (what is now) Scotland and Germany in the North, to the south well within Egypt and along the southern shores of the Mediterranean Sea. To the east, roads extended to the Persian Gulf in (what is now) Iraqi and Kuwait."[2] At that time, movement throughout that vast network would not have been considered "international" travel, as all fell within the Roman empire. A glance at the map of 2006 reveals a staggering conflagration of national boundaries and barriers as well as historical and contemporary animosities that severely restrict international travel in a region that was once united, albeit by force of arms.

The Grand Tour, Sixteenth through Nineteenth Centuries

The phrase "Grand Tour" entered the lexicon of travel as the sons of English nobility and wealthy aristocracy were escorted or sent abroad to the "finishing school" of the European continent to be enriched by the arts, science, language, and culture of the so-called civilized world. These tours often spread over several years, thereby overlapping into the time period usually associated with migration. However, the "must return home" caveat overrules in this case and clearly stamps this historical movement as international tourism. The most ambitious itinerary began with France including a heavy infusion of Paris. Italy, including Florence, Genoa, Venice, and hopefully Rome, came next. Return to England was through Germany and the Low Countries via Switzerland, should the Alps not prove too daunting. Today, variations of this itinerary are popular among U.S. international travelers, generally presented as a 21-day experience. It is not, however, uncommon for some to attempt this journey over a "long weekend" and report back that, "I've done Europe!" Serious travel professionals lament the disingenuousness of such claims.

Thomas Cooke—1841

Any discussion of international travel must recognize Thomas Cooke, generally regarded as the father of the packaged tour or excursion. His prominence began with a 1-shilling, 12-mile, round-trip rail excursion from Leicester to Loughborough, England. Amenities included a picnic lunch and a brass band. He moved on to develop escorted tours to the European continent, to the Americas, and beyond. Like all good ideas, imitation becomes the sincerest form of flattery, and so his pioneering techniques and styles of international tourism servicing were emulated worldwide. Today the company continues to be a major player in the international travel/tourism marketplace. Indeed, the *Thomas Cooke European Timetable* is still today considered the definitive source of information about European rail service.[3]

World War II—National and International Mobility

World War II fueled the largest people movement across the United States and the Americas on to Europe and related theaters of war. Travel was mostly by troopship, although airlift became increasingly reliable and available as the war wore on. This was not tourism as it was neither voluntary nor for enrichment. Survival was at the high stakes table in this case, and return home was not guaranteed. By the end of the war, however, more than 17 million U.S. and Canadian citizens had been exposed to Europe, Asia, and Africa via military assignments and were anxious to share these experiences with relatives and friends in the relative affluence of peacetime that ensued. Thus, 1945, the end of the war, represents a benchmark in the explosion of mass tourism on the international scene.

The Jet Age—1960

The most extraordinary quantum leap in international tourism occurred with the initiation of intercontinental jet passenger air service by American Airlines on January 25, 1959. The Boeing 707, utilizing jet engines proven in military aircraft of WWII, made the trip from Los Angeles to New York City in about four hours. A decade later, Pan American World Airways debuted the Boeing 747 whiffing 352 passengers from New York City to London in about seven hours, giving birth to the jumbo jet era. Now international tourists could think in terms of hours versus days or months of travel via steamship to foreign lands.

The Twenty-First Millennium

The introduction of supersonic flight, via the Concorde collaboration between British Airways and Air France, provided a glimpse of what the international traveler/tourism can expect as the twenty-first century gets underway. A Concorde flight including a mixture of subsonic and supersonic flight reduced the travel time from London to New York to three and one-half hours. With the time zone changes, one popular trick was the ability to ring in the New Year in London, board Concorde. Ring the New Year in again while crossing the international dateline (Greenwich meridian), and then pop the final champagne cork upon landing in New York City. Unfortunately for the intrepid and relatively well-heeled international traveler, all Concorde service, and with it all supersonic passenger flight, was retired in 2000 after a fatal crash on takeoff from Orly Airport in Paris. This was the only serious accident in the history of the aircraft and resulted from a combination of once-in-a-lifetime circumstances. In reality, the Concorde was an extremely unprofitable program for the airlines to maintain, given the economics and technology of the times.

It is relatively certain that the resumption of supersonic flight awaits only a matter of time and cost-effective technology. This will be followed in a geometrically reduced time frame by full space-based passenger flight. This will represent a quantum leap in international travel where transcontinental travel will be reduced from hours to minutes.

Size and Scope of International Tourism Today

The all-encompassing pervasiveness of tourism is a classic case of the forest being obscured by the trees. When international and domestic tourism are taken together, they represent the largest industry in the world, both in terms of income dollar volume and people employed.

Some 808 million international tourist arrivals were recorded for the 2005 calendar year. The WTO

Web site (www.world-tourism.org) has the most current and extensive data.[4] *Tourism 2020 Vision* is the WTO's long-term forecast and assessment of the development of tourism up to the first 20 years of the new millennium, or the year 2020. That report projects world tourist arrivals to grow from 3.2 percent per annum to 4.5 percent by 2020. This translates into 1.56 billion international arrivals worldwide, with 1.2 billion intraregional and .4 billion long haul (between regions). The top three recipient destinations are outlined in Figure 29.1.

Figure 29.1 | **Top 3 International Recipient Destinations— 2020 (WTO)**

Region	(Millions)	
	Projected Arrivals	Market Share %
Europe	717	46
East Asia/Pacific	397	25
Americas	282	18
Africa	<164	<11
Middle East	<164	<11
South Asia	<164	<11
All Regions	1560	100

WTO data further indicates uneven distribution in regional arrivals. In 2000, Africa received 1 percent of international arrivals, the Middle East followed with 3 percent, East Asia/Pacific 16 percent, the Americas 19 percent, and a whopping 57 percent to Europe. WTO estimates that these shares will equalize over the next two decades with Europe settling to about 45 percent of the total.

Figure 29.2 | **Worldwide Spending 2004 International Tourist Receipts (WTO)**

Region	(US$ millions)	
	International Tourist Receipts	% World Market Share
Europe	326,693	53
Americas	131,682	21
Asia/Pacific	124,960	20
Middle East	21,005	3.0
Africa	18,335	2.9
Total	622,675	100

In addition to regional receipts as shown (Figure 29.2), WTO data are available for individual countries within those regions. From that data one can make interesting comparisons. For example, tourism receipts for the entire continent of Africa are approximately the same as the Caribbean.

Figure 29.3 **Primary Originating Destinations 2004 Outbound Tourism (WTO)**

	(Millions)	
Region	Tourist Departures	Market Share %
Europe	431.2	56.5
Asia/Pacific	151.1	19.8
Americas	127.5	16.7
Middle East	22.1	2.9
Africa	18.3	2.4
All Regions	763.2	100

As the data in Figures 29.1–29.3 illustrate, any way one wants to track it, international tourism continues to live up to top billing as "the world's largest industry."

Organizations for Regulation and Marketing of International Tourism

World Tourism Organization (WTO)

The World Tourism Organization has been cited several times in previous parts of the chapter. Now it is time for a fuller understanding of its functions. The World Tourism Organization (WTO), or sometimes (UNWTO), is an international intergovernmental body hosted by the United Nations as a special agency and is entrusted with the promotion and development of responsible and sustainable tourism

Tourism as Instrument of Global Tolerance, Peace, and Understanding—World Tourism Organization

Tourism for Prosperity and Peace

At the start of the new millennium, tourism is firmly established as the number one industry in many countries and the fastest-growing economic sector in terms of foreign exchange earnings and job creation.

International tourism is the world's largest export earner and an important factor in the balance of payments of most nations.

Tourism has become one of the world's most important sources of employment. It stimulates enormous investment in infrastructure, most of which also helps to improve the living conditions of local people. It provides governments with substantial tax revenues. Most new tourism jobs and businesses are created in developing countries, helping to equalize economic opportunities and keep rural residents from moving to overcrowded cities.

Intercultural awareness and personal friendships fostered through tourism are a powerful force for improving international understanding and contributing to peace among all the nations of the world.

The UNWTO recognizes that tourism can have a negative cultural, environmental and social impact if it is not responsibly planned, managed and monitored. The UNWTO thus encourages governments to play a vital role in tourism, in partnership with the private sector, local authorities and non-governmental organizations.

In its belief that tourism can be effectively used to address the problems of poverty, UNWTO made a commitment to contribute to the United Nations Millennium Development Goals through a new initiative to develop sustainable tourism as a force for poverty elimination. The programme, known as ST-EP (Sustainable Tourism-Eliminating Poverty), focuses the longstanding work of both organizations on encouraging sustainable tourism with a view to alleviating poverty and was implemented in 2003.

worldwide. It is headquartered in Madrid, Spain. Perusal of the Web site (www.world-tourism.org) reveals some of the vehicles available for accomplishing that mission. They include business council, a Global Code of Ethics for Tourism, market intelligence, statistics, and publications. In 2005, membership included 145 countries, seven territories, and more than 300 affiliate members representing the private sector, educational institutions, tourism associations, and local tourism authorities. WTO is the unquestioned leading organization in fostering international tourism.

World Travel & Tourism Council (WTTC)

Unlike WTO, whose core membership group consists of sovereign governments, the World Travel & Tourism Council (WTTC) is more private-sector focused.

As reproduced from the WTTC Web site:

The World Travel & Tourism Council (WTTC) is the forum for global business leaders comprising the presidents, chairs and CEOs of 100 of the world's foremost companies. It is the only body representing the private sector in all parts of the Travel & Tourism industry worldwide.

WTTC's mission is to raise awareness of the full economic impact of the world's largest generator of wealth and jobs—Travel & Tourism. Governments are encouraged to unlock the industry's potential by adopting the Council's policy framework for sustainable tourism development—*Blueprint for New Tourism*.[5]

In addition to publications and logistical support from the Web site, WTTC activities include hosting a lodging investment summit, a world tourism forum, and a time share/resort investment conference.

International Air Transport Association (IATA)

The International Air Transport Association, or IATA, is the trade association for the world's largest airlines. Like all trade associations, they provide opportunities for their member organizations to collaborate and achieve high standards of operations, marketing, and cost control. For the international traveler/tourist, the two passages from their website are instructive:

Continual efforts by IATA ensure that people, freight and mail can move around the vast global airline network as easily as if they were on a single airline in a single country. In addition, IATA helps to ensure that members' aircraft can operate safely, securely, efficiently, and economically under clearly defined and understood rules.

For **consumers**, IATA simplifies the travel and shipping process. By helping to control airline costs, IATA contributes to cheaper tickets and shipping costs. Thanks to airline cooperation through IATA, individual passengers can make one telephone call to reserve a ticket, pay in one currency, and then use the ticket on several airlines in several countries—or even return it for a cash refund.

Cruise Line International Association (CLIA)

Today's cruise ship excursions present an excellent multi-dimensional opportunity to observe international tourism in action. The ship itself as a floating destination hotel and resort[6] provides an instantaneous "alternative environment encounter" the minute one steps onboard. More alternate environments are encountered as the ship moves in and out of the various ports comprising its itinerary. "Enrichment" can range from touring an archeological dig to swimming with sharks to attending a service in a 500-year-old church and everything in between. Since 1980, nearly 100 million persons have taken a deep-water cruise of 2+ days. However, this represents only 16 percent of the U.S. population. Thus, the market potential remains strong.

It is therefore expected that there would be a strong trade association. The Cruise Line International Association (CLIA) is that body. It is the official trade organization of the North American cruise industry. As announced on the CLIA Web site www.cruising.org.[7]

Cruise Lines International Association is a marketing and training organization composed of 19 of the major cruise lines serving North America. CLIA was formed in 1975 in response to a need for an association to promote the special benefits of cruising. CLIA exists to edu-

Cruise ship excursions present an excellent opportunity to observe international tourism in action.

cate, train, promote and explain the value, desirability and affordability of the cruise vacation experience.[8]

In addition, CLIA offers support and training for the travel agent professional community and administers the Cruise Counselor Certification Program.

Dimensional Approaches to the Study of International Tourism

The great fascination and challenge in studying tourism is the many points of departure from which study can be launched. Goeldner[8] proposed eight approaches, as follows.

Geographical

From prehistoric times to present, "alternative environment enrichment" provided by the magnetic attraction of topography continues to be a compelling reason for crossing national borders. As Goeldner[10] elaborated, "The geographer's approach to tourism sheds light on the location of tourist areas, the move-

ments of peoples created by tourism locales, the changes that tourism brings to the landscape in the form of tourism facilities, the dispersion of tourism development, physical planning, and economic, social and cultural problems." An illustration of the marketing value of geographical analysis lies in a promotional slogan from the island country of Jamaica, which promises the opportunity to experience the topography of a continent in an area the size of Rhode Island.[11] This is indeed the case, because one can go from a 7,400-ft. mountaintop to sea level in a few hours.

Sociological

Sociology is the study of people in groups and group behavior. Tourism movements frequently take place with affinity groups. International tourism invariably brings unfamiliar nationalities in contact with each other. Such international encounters are generally pleasant and without friction, given proper preparation on both sides. Occasionally, diplomatic and social conditions are such that international travel is a non-starter. Currently, regular Americans cannot vacation in the ancient city of Baghdad, due to the existence of wartime conditions and dangerous pockets of anti-U.S. sentiment.

Economic

International tourism revenue streams are highly desirable for their ability to "multiply" as their flow infuses throughout international destination communities. Indeed, tourism revenues often represent the only, or major, opportunity for nations to acquire hard or key currency, which is necessary to purchase goods and services not produced in that particular country. The Caribbean/Atlantic country of Cuba continues at this writing to be off limits for regular U.S. travel. However, special licenses are available and special exceptions are made. Upon arrival, travelers find a warm welcome for the U.S. dollars and the tourists who will leave them behind.

Historical

This approach to the study of international tourism relies on making comparisons of tourism movements as they have evolved over time. The State of Florida, for example, enjoys a healthy influx of international tourists going to and from the various cruise ships that depart from the state. This target population grows in direct proportion to the annual increase in ships calling Florida homeport.

Institutional

In this instance, focus is on the facilities such as hotels, ground transportation, restaurants, travel agencies, and other intermediaries that facilitate the experience of the international traveler. These also include governmental agencies like customs and immigration and their role in managing entry to the country's frontier. A few countries are authorized to operate U.S. pre-clearance facilities on their soil, thereby enabling visitors returning to the U.S. to immediately depart the airport as easily as when traveling domestically. The Bahamas is one such favored nation.

Product

The step-by-step design, creation, and distribution of tourism products are at the heart of the product approach to international tourism study. These include airline seats and guided tours, and well as native crafts and deep-sea fishing.

Managerial

Management by definition involves planning, organizing, staffing, directing, and controlling. These functions are constantly under scrutiny as professionals strive to provide positive, profitable, and sustainable experiences for the international traveler.

Interdisciplinary and Systems Approaches

Because tourism in general and international tourism in particular cuts across all aspects of society as noted earlier, tourism philosophers are calling for a systems approach that coordinates all the approaches and derives a unified whole.[12]

International Tourism Challenges

The multidimensional nature of tourism as detailed in the foregoing section presents distinct challenges that are exacerbated significantly when international boundaries are crossed as the tourists seek that alternative environment encounter and attendant enrichment. Some of the more challenging aspects follow.

Language

Naturally, communication is vital for the full absorption of new experience. Tourists who would seek out an international adventure are sometimes shocked when they experience difficulty or are unable to communicate altogether with individuals in countries that speak the same language, for example, the U.S. traveler's encounter with the Irish brogue, British Cockney, or Virgin Islands word inflections and rhythms. Completely "foreign" languages create even more challenges but are sometimes welcome as a part of the "exotic" experience. Traveling in guided tour groups admirably solves each of these potentially troublesome scenarios.

Customs/Culture

To prevent embarrassment, disgust, or even hostility, it is always essential to study the "do's and taboos" of the receiving culture. Over the millennia, human societies have evolved meaning and substance for an incredible variety of dress patterns, hand gestures, seating arrangements, body language, and hygienic practices. Nothing could be worse than unintentionally offending a gracious international host with a mistaken act or hand motion that would seem perfectly natural at home. The ancient adage, "When in Rome, do as the Romans do," continues to serve as a practical mantra for international travel. It is also important to resist the urge to force one's culture on the visiting culture. This is illustrated by the requirement of women to walk behind men when in the presence of a certain king in the African country of Ghana.

Currency

Currency in recent years has become less of a challenge in international travel due to the worldwide use of the credit card. Charges encountered in the currency of the realm are instantly or eventually translated into one's home currency, and the bill is paid accordingly at some future date. Also, the introduction of the euro as the standard currency of the major countries on the European continent has mitigated some historical traveler dismay in constantly needing different local currencies to function in countries that are in close proximity. A standard practice has been to "convert at the border" and start the recalculation. The introduction of the euro has eliminated that process.

Politics

In all countries politics create passion and polarization sometimes spilling over into internal hostility that creates unsafe conditions for international travel. Governments of the world usually issue "Travel Advisories" to alert its nationals that travel is unsafe to certain destinations. In some cases, travel is forbidden to such areas until further notice.

Security

Although adventure travel is more popular than ever, the threat to personal safety is the fastest way to kill international travel. This begins with the transportation mode, particularly aircraft, which were proven vulnerable to highly motivated terrorists in the 2001 attacks of 9-11 on New York City and Washington, D.C. Occasionally, hotels catering to international travelers are singled out as targets of terrorists who want to "make a point" against a particular country's citizens. Happily, these are rare expectations, and tourists taking reasonable precautions specific to the destination are unlikely to experience tragic unpleasantries.

Sustainable Development and Ecotourism

One dilemma of international tourism is that the uniqueness of the destination that attracts the tourist can be destroyed by these same tourists if proper management of the environmental encounter is not in place. This is particularly acute for nature-based or natural attraction tourism. International destinations sometimes in lesser-developed countries eager for the hard currency of the tourist fail to provide the safeguards that will protect and sustain the environment and experience. Ecotourism places emphasis on embracing a tourism experience that is also benevolent to the host environment. Sustainable development is a concept that requires the design and developmental pacing of infrastructure and superstructure to enhance the carrying capacity of the supporting area but not at the expense of the environmental attraction that fuels development in the first place. The requirement that no structure can be built higher than the tallest palm tree in Negril, Jamaica, is a case in point.

Career Opportunities

Following are some institutions that provide excellent opportunities for careers in international tourism.

- Travel agencies
- Tour companies
- Hospitality service institutions (airlines, hotels, foodservice)
- Umbrella marketing agencies (CVB, national tourism offices)
- Immigration, customs, embassy postings

The actual job responsibilities are as diverse as the phenomenon of tourism itself. An excellent source of related career information is *Travel Perspectives: A Guide to Becoming a Travel Professional*, written by two seasoned professionals who also operate a specialized school and training program.[13]

Summary

This chapter set out to present broad and reasonably comprehensive introductory exposure to the subject of international tourism. Discussion opens with a working definition of tourism that contains all the elements critical to any definition of tourism and travelers. The historical perspective follows, with a listing of benchmark international travels and travelers. Recent statistical data establishing the legitimacy of tourism's claim to be the "world's largest industry" appears in the third section. Regulatory and marketing agencies facilitating international tourism are introduced with Web sites for further study. A popular academic listing of approaches to the study of tourism are referenced and comments offered to heighten their importance as components of international tourism. International tourism challenges including language and security lead into a final section on international careers. An essay on prospects for world peace via tourism reproduced from the World Tourism Organization Web site is shared.

Accordingly, it is the author's expectation that the reader has gained substantial insight and awareness of the exciting journeys, both personal and professional, that lie along the pathways, seaways, and airways of international tourism.

Endnotes

1. World Tourism Organization (WTO). www.world-tourism.org
2. Goeldner, C., & Brent Ritchie, J. R. *Tourism. Principles, Practices, Philosophies,* 9th ed. Hoboken, NJ: John Wiley, 2003, p. 45
3. *Thomas Cook European Timetable.* Timetable publishing office, Peterborough England, 2006
4. World Tourism Organization (WTO). www.world-tourism.org
5. World Travel and Tourism Council (WTTC). www.wttc.org
6. International Air Transport Association. www.iata.org
7. Boger, E. P. "Conflict or Compliment? Marketing Strategies of Caribbean Tourist Boards vs. Cruise Ship Lines." In *The Practice of Hospitality Management,* edited by A. Pizam, R. C. Lewis, and P. Manning, Westport, CT: AVI Press, 1983, Chapter 42, pp. 413–426
8. Cruise Line International Association (CLIA). www.cruise.org
9. Goeldner, C., & Brent Ritchie, J. R. *Tourism,* p. 45
10. Ibid
11. *Destination Jamaica (Official Visitor's Guide).* Kingston, JA: 2005. Jamaica Hotel & Tourist Association
12. Todd, G. & Rice, S. *Travel Perspectives: A guide to becoming a travel professional,* 3rd ed. Albany, NY: Delmar, 2002, pp. 1–16
13. Ibid

Resources

Internet Sites

Cruise Line International Association (CLIA): www.cruise.org
International Air Transport Association: www.iata.org
U.S. Treasury, Customs Division, "Know before You Go": www.customs.tres.gov/travel/know/htm
World Tourism Organization (WTO): www.world-tourism.org
World Travel and Tourism Council (WTTC): www.wttc.org

⚷ Key Words and Concepts

Concorde	Supersonic flight
Cruise line	Sustainable tourism
Grand tour	Tourism
Jet age	Travel
Offshore	WTO
Passport	

Contributor Information

epboger@umes.edu

Ernest P. Boger, II (CHA, FMP, CHE, MHCIMA), a native of Tampa, Florida, is the University of South Florida's first Black graduate. Dr. Boger is CEO of the consulting company VIP Hosts Internationale, Inc. and is associate professor in Hospitality Management with (IMCA)-Revans University, serving as advisor to the Caribbean Doctoral Set. He is widely published on Hospitality Education, Marketing, and Tourism, including an anthology (1975–2004), *Selected Readings in Hotel, Restaurant and Tourism Administration*. He was appointed by the Governor of Florida to the Citizens Advisory Committee on Coastal Resource Management. He is a founding board member of the Multicultural Food Service & Hospitality Alliance (MFHA). For the past five consecutive years, he has been named "One of the most influential African/Americans in Travel/Tourism" by *Black Meetings & Tourism Magazine*. The National Coalition of Black Meeting Planners bestowed its "Pioneer" award on him in 1996. In 2002 he was presented with the "Steve Fletcher Achievement Award." It is the second-highest award established by International CHRIE.

29 Review Questions

1. Discuss the three common components of the definition of tourism.

2. How did the invention of "money" stimulate the growth of international tourism?

3. Compare the original "Grand Tour" with the Grand Tour of today.

4. Identify three benchmarks in the evolution of international air travel.

5. Select five pieces of statistical evidence indicators to make the case for tourism.

6. Visit the Web sites of WTO, WTTC, and IATA. Compare and contrast.

7. Explain the ease of multinational travel via a cruise.

8. Identify and interview an individual actually holding one of the positions noted in the career opportunities section.

Joe Hutchinson
The University of Southern Mississippi

Management Consulting

Learning Objectives

- ✓ To learn about different types of consulting firms
- ✓ To understand what it means to be a management consultant
- ✓ To know skills requirements and personality traits
- ✓ To understand the ethics
- ✓ To learn how to develop a career path

Chapter Outline

Types of Management Consulting Firms
The Nature of the Work
The Consultant's Lifestyle
Consulting Skill Requirements
Personality Traits
Ethics, Certification, and Professional
    Development

A person with years of experience, a talent for identifying problems, and the ability to find creative solutions may want to become a consultant. The consulting industry is a rapidly growing segment in the service sector of the U.S. economy. Consultants offer a wide range of professional services to clients in many different fields.

A consultant may be any individual who has a specific area of expertise and is compensated for providing advice or other services to a client. Sometimes people are hired as consultants after firms downsize and then hire them back as independent contractors. This allows the firm the advantage of retaining the expertise without the former budgetary constraints or expenses. Other times, a firm may be looking for an objective viewpoint to convince the board of directors or upper-level management that their plans and strategies are sound and feasible.

There is a saying that experts are people who live more than 50 miles away. Sometimes we tend to give consultants more credibility if they are not part of the company or community. In any case, a consultant can work independently or they can join a firm. Correspondingly, a client may be served by an individual, a group of persons, or an organization that compensates the consultant in exchange for the advice or other services received.

Hospitality management consulting is an industry-specific form of consulting that may be included under the broader umbrella of business or management consulting. Management consultants often focus their services in specific functional areas, such as general management, human resources, marketing, management information systems, operations, administration, and finance/accounting. Most management consultants who serve clients in the hospitality industry also serve clients in numerous other industries. A hospitality management consultant would be a consultant who serves only hospitality industry clients and provides services in one or more functional areas.

Hospitality organizations may hire an external consultant because specialized expertise may be unavailable within their organizations to complete the specific tasks within the necessary time frame. For example, consultants may be hired to design a foodservice facility or to conduct a hotel feasibility study. Even when an organization has adequate internal expertise to complete the necessary tasks, an outside consultant may be hired because of the sensitive nature of the issues involved, the objectivity provided by an outsider, and/or the reputation and credibility of the consultant or the firm that he or she represents.

This chapter provides an overview of the management consulting profession. Topics discussed include the types of management consulting firms, the nature of the work, the consultant's lifestyle, consulting skill requirements and personality traits, ethics and professional development, and the consulting career.

Types of Management Consulting Firms

Management consulting firms may be classified according to a number of characteristics, such as their size, level of specialization, industries served, geographical location, or types of clients/industries that they serve. Consultants who provide services to clients in hospitality organizations are often found in the following types of firms.

General Management Firms

These firms provide general management consulting services to international clients in many different industries. Consultants in these firms may be referred to as generalists who provide a broad range of services to their clients and tailor their services to the specific needs of each client. In some cases, they can assess an organization's structure and recommend restructuring and position cuts and/or additions. Other times, they can examine management practices or organizational efficiencies. With today's prevalence of corporate mergers, consultants provide an objective approach to blending companies together with services that may include strategic planning, psychological testing for compatibility, skill assessments, or recommendations for department restructuring. The better-known international firms that provide general management consulting services to a diverse base of clients include McKinsey and Company, Boston Consulting Group, and Booz Allen Hamilton.

Management Consulting Divisions of Certified Public Accounting (CPA) Firms

Large international CPA firms may have a consulting presence in the hospitality industry. These firms are staffed with consulting professionals who have backgrounds, experiences, and education in the hospitality industry. These firms often perform project feasibility studies or recommend improvements in areas such as strategic planning, operating efficiencies, product/service quality, or customer service. PricewaterhouseCoopers is an example of a larger international accounting/consulting firm that includes a consulting division specializing in the hospitality industry. Hospitality consultants in these larger firms often focus on the lodging industry, particularly with respect to hotel development.

Functionally Specialized Firms

A number of consulting firms may serve clients in the hospitality industry and many other industries by providing their expertise in a specific functional area. Specialists in these firms focus on their narrow area of expertise. For example, a firm that specializes in management information systems may develop the system requirements for a large hotel. Another consultant may be the advertising agency that creates the media campaign for the company.

Industry-Specific Firms

Some firms serve only the management of organizations in the hospitality industry. These firms often provide specialized consulting services to their clients by focusing on a specific industry segment (i.e., foodservice industry), an industry subsegment (i.e., full-service restaurants), and/or a specific functional area in certain industry organizations (i.e., facilities/equipment layout and design in foodservice operations). PKF Consulting is a national consulting firm that specializes in the lodging industry. Some of you may have seen their reports on salaries for different positions in different segments of the hotel industry across the nation. They also track and report various lodging statistics for various regions of the United States. On the other hand, Cini-Little International serves clients in a wide variety of foodservice operations. A large number of small firms and sole practitioners also specialize in the layout and design of kitchen facilities. In fact, most consultants specialize in hospitality industry consulting do work for either small firms (2 to 10 employees) or operate as sole practitioners (one-person firms).

Internal Consultants

External consultants serve clients of different hospitality firms, whereas internal consultants serve only one hospitality organization. These consultants may be on the payroll of the organization or they may serve on a contract basis exclusively with that one organization. These individuals are often referred to as "troubleshooters" or "field consultants" and perform many of the functions that external consultants perform. Most large restaurant and lodging chains have in-house personnel who provide operational support and assistance to both company-owned and franchised units of those organizations. For example, chain hotels or restaurants often have in-house consultants or troubleshooters who conduct on-site visits to specific units or properties in the chain to identify problems and develop solutions for implementation. Others might locate sites for new development and evaluate their feasibility for success.

The Nature of the Work

Although the work of a consultant varies significantly among individuals and firms, there are three major steps in the consulting cycle that are common to most consultants: marketing, the consulting engagement, and administration.

Marketing

The marketing of consulting services is usually designed to build the reputation of an individual or a firm as a leading expert in a specific area. Every consulting firm, irrespective of size, must generate and sustain enough work to stay in business. Marketing in consulting involves the direct or indirect solicitation of new clients and/or efforts to generate additional business from existing or previous clients. Forms of indirect marketing include active membership in trade associations, serving on industry boards and panels, writing books and articles, making conference presentations, or conducting workshops and seminars. More direct forms of marketing would include advertising, direct mail, and meetings with potential clients.

The Consulting Engagement

Each new consulting project is typically referred to as a consulting engagement. Most engagements begin with an initial client meeting to discuss the scope and nature of the client's needs. The consultant may have responded to a phone call or a request for proposal (RFP). An RFP is a document, frequently used by government organizations, that

An oral presentation discussing the findings and recommendations outlined in the report is usually included in the final report to the client.

outlines the nature of the work requested and other project details. Following an initial client meeting or the receipt of an RFP, the consultant often prepares a formal proposal. This proposal will clarify the details of the engagement by outlining the project background and objectives, the approach and work plan that will be used to complete the engagement, the final deliverables that will be provided to the client (i.e., oral presentations and written reports), and other project details (i.e., project fees, billing procedures, timing, and qualifications of consultants). After completing all the work steps outlined in the proposal, the consultant usually presents a final report to the client, in addition to an oral presentation discussing the findings and recommendations outlined in the report.

Administration

Consultants must perform other duties in addition to soliciting clients, writing proposals, meeting with clients, and completing consulting engagements. A number of administrative tasks must be completed in every consulting firm. In large firms, there usually will be a project manager who directs the work of the consultants on the project, maintains an ongoing dialogue with the client, and ensures that payments for services are received in a timely manner. These consultants may also be responsible for establishing a project budget and ensuring that each

consulting engagement is completed within the allocated amount of time and dollars. Larger firms have support staff to perform necessary administrative and clerical tasks within the firm (report production, telephone calls, graphics, copy services, payroll, benefits, professional development, taxes, etc.). In small firms or sole proprietorships, consultants typically will be responsible for completing all relevant administrative tasks required to operate the business.

The Consultant's Lifestyle

There is no common lifestyle shared by all individuals in the consulting profession. The lifestyle of a consultant may differ significantly from one firm to another. Factors that may influence a consultant's lifestyle include the size of the firm, the type of services provided, the geographical area covered, and the industries served. For example, sole practitioners may shape their own working conditions to match their desired lifestyle by limiting travel, selecting only certain clients to serve, determining their own work hours, setting their own fees, working out of their own home, or working part-time. Conversely, consultants in large firms usually have little input into the services they provide, the hours they work, the type of clients they serve, the fees they charge, or the geographical locations where they work.

The consulting profession may be very rewarding for certain individuals. Consultants have the opportunity to help and influence others and may derive a great deal of satisfaction from making a positive contribution to both clients and society. There is also the potential of high earnings, status, and respect. Many consultants thrive on the constant new challenges they are faced with and the opportunities to learn so much in a short period of time.

Despite the many rewards of consulting, there are lifestyle trade-offs involved. Although these job benefits are enjoyed by some consultants, the actual working conditions are usually much different from what they appear to outsiders. Most consultants are required to meet difficult project deadlines by working long hours under intense pressure to complete their tasks. The consultant must become absorbed in these projects and may be required to spend days, weeks, or months of sustained focus on a project until problems are diagnosed and appropriate solutions are generated. This lifestyle can be physically and mentally fatiguing.

Travel demands and uncertain living conditions also present a challenge for most consultants. Significant amounts of a consultant's time may be spent in travel. This often requires an individual to spend weeks at a time away from home. Although a sole practitioner may have greater control over travel demands, most successful independent consultants will be required to travel frequently over a wide geographic area.

Consulting Skill Requirements

The skill requirements of a consultant will vary according to the nature of services provided, the industries served, or size of the firm. However, a number of skills are required for all consultants. These skills are discussed next.

Technical Skills

All consultants must have a certain level of expertise in a particular industry, function, or technique. However, it takes more than just experience, education, and skills to be a successful consultant. All consultants must have the unique ability to translate their knowledge base into applications that provide value to their clients.

Communication Skills

The ability to communicate both orally and in writing is one of the most critical skills needed to be a successful consultant. All consultants must communicate with other individuals on a regular basis. This communication may take the form of telephone conversations, meetings, interviews, presentations, or written proposals and reports. Consultants must have the ability to convey information clearly and professionally through every step of a consulting engagement.

Interpersonal Skills

The relationship between the client and the consultant is critical to the successful completion of all consulting engagements. The consultant must have strong interpersonal skills that create a mutual sense of trust and openness with clients. This requires that the consultant remain sensitive to the client's needs and feelings.

Administrative Skills

In addition to performing the tasks of a consulting engagement, a consultant may be required to maintain regular communication with clients, review the work quality of other consultants, keep projects within budgeted hours and costs, and manage the client billing and collection process. As a sole practitioner, these responsibilities are magnified, because one individual is responsible for completing all project tasks and managing the business.

Marketing and Selling Skills

A consultant's ability to market and sell a firm's consulting services is essential to the promotion to upper-level positions in a large firm. To build and sustain a viable consulting business, a firm must maintain a strong relationship with existing and previous clients, while continually adding new clients.

In large firms, a progression usually occurs in terms of a consultant's skills development. New consultants are typically hired on the basis of their technical expertise. An individual will usually first work on technical-related tasks relevant to his or her expertise. After this stage is mastered, the consultant will progress into a supervisory role. In this capacity, more emphasis will be placed on communication, administration skills, and interpersonal skills. As the consultant advances in the firm, he or she will become more involved in marketing and sales.

Personality Traits

Although a consultant may meet the skill requirements to complete all necessary tasks effectively, certain personality traits are necessary to pursue a career in the consulting profession. The following personality traits are usually required for all consultants, irrespective of the work settings.

Ambition and Self-Motivation

A consultant must have a high desire for personal success and must be internally driven, as there is often little outside motivation or direction. This requires an individual to have the initiative to start and complete tasks in an effective and efficient manner with little oversight and guidance.

Ability to Work with Others

A consultant is required to work with other consultants, clients, and employees of a client's organization on an ongoing basis. Thus, the individual must be able to get along with others and enjoy participating in a team-oriented process. Quite often, this includes active listening to hear what the other person is saying. Once you understand the other person's point of view, you can discuss some creative intermediary step. Along with active listening comes the skill to mediate different viewpoints so that consensus of opinion for new directions can be implemented.

A consultant is also a marketer who must both create and sell the product to the client. Like any good salesman, they must be able to adapt and modify proposals to address specific client concerns and to know when the sales job is finished.

Self-Fulfillment

Despite the many benefits that a consultant may provide to his or her clients, their contributions often are unrecognized. Consultants usually receive few tangible forms of personal recognition (i.e., certificates and awards) for their accomplishments. This requires the individual to have a strong sense of self-fulfillment.

Mobility, Flexibility, and Tolerance for Ambiguity

Because most successful consultants serve clients dispersed across wide geographic regions, the traveling demands can be rigorous. Further, the nature of projects and the work settings may change on a regular basis, with roles and client problems not well defined. An individual who does not have the mobility to travel extensively, the flexibility to shift directions on short notice, or the tolerance to work in ambiguous situations may have difficulty coping with the challenges of consulting.

High Energy and the Ability to Work under Pressure

The numerous demands and challenges of the consulting profession provide a great deal of excitement but also require high and sustained levels of energy. Most consultants must be able to work long hours on a regular basis. Projects often must be completed under significant pressure to meet multiple deadlines and to satisfy prior commitments made to clients. Although individuals may enjoy the challenges of consulting, it is difficult to maintain such a demanding pace over a sustained period of time.

Self-Confidence

Consultants must be confident in themselves, and they must be able to instill in their clients a strong sense of confidence in them. This often requires an ability to deal with rejection and failure due to lost proposals, mistakes, or a client's unwillingness to accept their recommendations. A consultant must overcome these barriers and continue to move on confidently to each new engagement with a fresh start. A consultant also must have enough self-confidence to think outside the box and be creative in recommending the best possible solutions to a problem or issue, even when those recommendations are not popular.

Ethics, Certification, and Professional Development

Unlike many other professions, there are no government regulations, certification requirements, or codes of ethics that universally apply to all consultants. Because consulting applies to all fields, it is not possible to have one general licensing procedure. However, most major professional consulting associations and large consulting organizations have a code of ethics that outlines the consultant's responsibilities to the client and to the public.

Consultants are often faced with a number of ethical dilemmas that are not regulated by law and are not that obvious. Some ethical issues common to the consulting profession include confidentiality, conflict of interest, objectivity, and professional involvement. Specific examples of the type of ethical dilemmas consultants are often faced with include:

- The client seeks assistance for services outside the consultant's scope of competence.
- The consultant has an existing relationship or other interests with the client that would influence his or her objectivity in completing the work.
- The client requests the consultant to manipulate the results to favor the client's position.
- The client requests that the consultant omit, conceal, or revise certain information.
- The client requests that the consultant obtain proprietary information from a former client.

Professional development opportunities are available to enhance and refine an individual's technical expertise and consulting skills. Because technical skills can become obsolete quickly, successful consultants stay current by attending workshops, seminars, lectures, and professional meetings. These skills are further updated by reading current books, periodicals, and newspapers. To improve their consulting skills, consultants may attend professional association consulting skills workshops. Large consulting firms usually conduct their own in-house training to further enhance the consulting skills of their professionals.

Summary

The consulting industry is anticipated to continue to outpace the growth of the U.S. economy by a wide margin. This provides a bright outlook for those individuals who desire to pursue a career in management consulting. Consulting can be a re-warding profession for individuals at all ages and career stages, such as recent MBA graduates, individuals in midcareer, retirees, or part-time consultants searching for other outlets to use their skills. The appeal of a career in consulting has continued to grow, as an increasing number of individuals enters the field to utilize their knowledge, skills, and experience.

Individuals who are considering a career in management consulting should take a personal inventory of their interests, skills, and personality traits. Although a person may desire a career in consulting initially, a more thorough examination of the skill requirements, lifestyle, and personality traits of successful consultants may reveal a lack of compatibility with a person's actual needs and desires. However, an individual's talents, interests, and personal situation may change a number of times during his or her career. As these changes occur, each individual should reevaluate his or her fit with a consulting career.

There are many different career paths that people take to become a consultant. These paths depend on a number of factors, such as age, education, experience, interests, and skills. Many sole practitioners have begun consulting careers after being laid off as part of company downsizings, restructurings, or mergers. Conversely, MBA graduates who lack the experience, skills, or capital to start their own firm often seek positions with national or regional consulting firms or as internal consultants to large companies. Even in these situations, it is usually desirable to have at least five years of management experience to establish credibility among clients. The expertise demonstrated through business management experience and the knowledge gained through education and other professional development opportunities should serve as assets for those interested in pursuing a career in management consulting.

☛ *Key Words and Concepts*

Consultant
Consulting careers
Consulting firms
Consulting qualifications

Consulting skills
Hospitality consultant
Management consultant

🏛 *Contributor's Information*

Dr. Joe Hutchinson has been an associate professor in the Department of Tourism Management at the University of Southern Mississippi since 1998. Prior to that, he was a faculty member in the Department of Hotel, Restaurant, and Institution Management at Iowa State University. Dr. Hutchinson received a BS degree in Hotel and Restaurant Management from the University of Houston, an MBA degree from Southwest Texas State University, and a PhD degree in Hospitality and Tourism Management from Virginia Polytechnic Institute and State University.

Dr. Hutchinson has taught courses in the introduction to hospitality and tourism management, human resources management, financial management, strategic management, quality service management, hospitality law, gaming law, casino operations management, and strategic planning for public and nonprofit organizations. He has conducted research in the areas of customer satisfaction and service quality. Prior to his academic background, Dr. Hutchinson served as a management consultant with KPMG Consulting and two other international accounting/consulting firms. He continues to provide management consulting services to public- and private-sector clients throughout the United States. Prior to his management consulting career, Dr. Hutchinson served for seven years as a general manager of independent and chain-operated casual-themed restaurants.

30 ▌Review Questions

1. Define "consultant."

2. Describe the profile of a "management consultant."

3. Describe the profile of a "hospitality consultant."

4. When is it most likely for a hospitality business to hire a consultant? List three situations.

5. How are management consultant firms classified?

6. Define "generalist."

7. In which hospitality segment is one most likely to find a CPA consultant?

8. Describe the role of an internal consultant.

9. For whom does an internal consultant most likely work?

10. What are the three major steps in the consulting cycle?

11. What is the goal of the marketing phase?

12. What are several forms of direct marketing?

13. What are several forms of indirect marketing?

14. What is an RFP?

15. What are some of the administrative duties of a consultant?

16. Who performs the administrative duties in a large consulting business? In a sole practitioner's business?

17. What are five of the factors that influence a consultant's lifestyle?

18. How does the lifestyle/workstyle vary between the sole practitioner and the consultant who works for a large firm?

19. What are the rewards associated with a consulting career?

20. What are the drawbacks associated with a consulting career?

21. List the skills required for working as a consultant. What is the progression of skills from the newly hired consultant stage to that of being more experienced?

22. What types of communication skills do consultants need?

23. Why are communication skills particularly important?

24. How do interpersonal skills influence the building of trust with the client?

25. What personality traits are important for success as a consultant?

26. Why is "tolerance for ambiguity" important to a consultant's success?

27. What are some ethical dilemmas common to consultants?

28. What are the projections for careers as consultants?

29. How do consultants stay current in their area of expertise?

30. How many years of work experience does one need before embarking on a career as a consultant?

31

George G. Fenich
University of New Orleans

Meetings, Expositions, Events, and Conventions (MEEC)

Learning Objectives

✓ To define and discuss the major segments of meetings, expositions, events, and conventions

✓ To understand why meetings, expositions, and conventions occur

✓ To have a basic acquaintance with key industry indicators and statistics

✓ To have a basic understanding of the economic impact at the national, regional, and local levels

✓ To have a familiarity with the basic types and formats of meetings, expositions, events, and conventions, including

→ Conventions

→ Seminars

→ Workshops

→ Congresses

→ Symposia

→ Expositions

→ Events

→ Trade shows

Chapter Outline

Organizational Structure
Background
Economic Impact
Career Opportunities
Professional Associations

One of the major components of the MEEC industry is putting on a convention. A three-day convention for a national association held at a single resort hotel could include roughly 1,900 people (participants and exhibitors) who will have flown on approximately nine different major airlines and regional carriers on 200 different flights, covered 4 million air miles, consumed 1,000 airline snacks, thousands of bags of candy or snacks grabbed on runs through airports, sat through 60,000 people hours of presentations and education, played 4,000 person hours of golf, and eaten approximately 12,000 catered meals. They will have made about 80,000 telephone calls, purchased and read 5,700 newspapers, transmitted and received more than 500 faxes, and injected about $5,000,000 into the local economy. Their presence will generate about $500,000 in taxes toward state and local coffers. Countless local business owners will make sales in everything from clothing to artwork to souvenirs. Dry cleaners, cab drivers, area restaurateurs, sports facilities, attractions, and hotels will all see jumps in their average weekly revenue. There may also be a significant boost to the local underground cash-only economy, with contributions made to the seamier side of this phenomenon, such as drugs and prostitution. In total, the convention-related activities for this single event will touch more than 250 local jobs.

This scenario is only a brief glimpse of the multitude of complexities that support the planning and management and of the jobs that employ those who work in and around the **MEEC** industry, all of which contribute to a meeting's success.

Performing poorly at any of the hundreds of potential failure points can cause dramatic immediate financial loss to the geographic area. In addition, the financial impact could result in positive or negative impact for years to come: A good experience by each delegate will result in praise to many others; a negative experience will result in even more people hearing the results of the stay in that destination. Each of these people can bring or deny more business to the destination and the resort.

Organizational Structure

MEEC is a part of, and encompasses, many elements of the hospitality and tourism industry. To understand how MEEC is related, one must understand the organization and structure of the tourism and hospitality industry.

There are six major divisions, or segments, of the tourism and hospitality industry:

1. Lodging
2. Food and beverage
3. Transportation
4. Attractions
5. Entertainment
6. Shopping

It would seem, then, that the MEEC industry is involved with all segments of the hospitality and tourism industry. Understanding the interactions and complexities of the hospitality and tourism industry, along with MEEC, helps explain why it is difficult to determine the size and scope of these industries. Until the late 1990s, the U.S. government, using its Standard Industry Classification (SIC) codes, did not even track many elements of these industries. For example, the government did not even list "meeting planner" as a recognized profession until the late 1980s.

Background

Gatherings, meetings, events, and conventions (of sorts) have been a part of people's lives since the earliest recorded history. Archeologists have found primitive ruins of ancient cultures that were used as meeting areas where citizens would gather to discuss common interests such as government, war, hunting, or tribal celebrations. Once humans developed permanent settlements, each town or village had a public meeting area, often called a town square, where residents could meet, talk, and party! Under the leadership of Alexander the Great, over half a million people traveled to what was then Ephesus (now Turkey) to see exhibitions that included acrobats, magicians, animal trainers, and jugglers. Andrew Young, the former U.S. ambassador to the United Nations, said at an MPI (Meeting Professionals International) meeting in Atlanta in the middle 1990s that he was sure there would have been a meeting planner for the Last Supper and certainly for the first Olympics. In Rome, the Forum was a type of organized meeting to discuss politics and decide the fate of the country. Ancient Rome had the Coliseum, which was the site of major sporting events such as gladiatorial contests— someone had to organize them. In Old England, there are stories of King Arthur's Round Table, another example of a meeting to discuss the trials and tribulations of the day. Religious gatherings of various faiths, pilgrimages to Mecca, and others are examples of ancient religious meetings and festivals. The Olympics are an ancient sporting event that was organized just like similar events today. World's fairs and expositions are still another piece of the MEEC industry.

The MEEC industry has also been a part of American culture and development. In one of the oldest communities in North America, Santa Fe, the square not only houses the seat of government but also has been used traditionally as a festival marketplace. Even today, Native Americans can be seen around the perimeter of the square displaying their handicrafts for sale. The First Continental Congress in Philadelphia is an example of a "formal meeting," in this case to decide on governance of the thirteen colonies. Political conventions have a long history in the United States and are part of the MEEC industry. Americans have made festivals and celebrations of every sort, such as St. Patrick's Day, Thanksgiving, and Mardi Gras in New Orleans, part of their lives since the early days of this country.

Today, structures supporting the MEEC industry are integral parts of major cities. It is a well-known fact that to be considered a "world-class city" a community must possess a convention center and a stadium or arena for sports and events. The largest cities all have them, including New York, Los Angeles, Chicago, Washington, San Francisco, and even New Orleans. The hope is that these public facilities will attract out-of-town attendees for conventions and events and that they will spend money in the community.

Since its founding in New York in 1949 by four organizations—the American Society of Association Executives (ASAE); American Hotel and Motel Association (AH&MA, now the American Hotel Lodging Association); Hospitality [then Hotel] Sales and Marketing Association International (HSMAI); and the Destination Marketing Association International (DMAI, which was IACVB)—the Convention Industry Council (then the Convention Liaison Council) has traditionally followed the lead of its constituent organizations, which now number 31.[1] In 1895, "[t]he roots of present-day convention & visitor bureaus (CVBs) [were] planted when journalist Milton Carmichael suggest[ed] in The Detroit Journal that local businessmen band together to promote the city as a convention destination, as well as represent the city and its many hotels to bid for business. Two

weeks later, what [became] the Detroit Convention and Businessmen's League form[ed] to do just that. Carmichael head[ed] the group, which . . . later evolve[d] into the Detroit Metro CVB."[2]

The role of CVBs has changed over time. As in Detroit, most began by trying to attract only conventions and business meetings to their community. Later, they realized leisure visitors were an important source of business and added the "V" for visitors to their name. Today, virtually every city in the United States and Canada, and many cities throughout the world, has a CVB or convention and visitors association (CVA). CVB or CVA is a membership organization that helps promote tourism and meetings and related business for their cities.

Economic Impact

The MEEC industry is diverse. As a result, it is hard to estimate the size, magnitude, and impact of the MEEC industry. Further, only limited research has been done in the field. The CIC commissioned Deloitte & Touche, LLP, to study the economic impact of the meetings and hospitality industry. The study, from the mid-1990s, states that the industry encompassing meetings, conventions, expositions, and incentives contributed more than $82.8 billion to the U.S. economy, making it (then) the 22nd largest contributor to the gross domestic product of the United States.[3]

One of the most comprehensive accounts of the impact of the MEEC industry is published biannually in the "Meetings Market Report" in Meetings & Conventions Magazine. It shows that in 2003 there were 891,000 corporate meetings, 155,600 association meetings, and 12,200 conventions for a total of 1,058,800 meetings held in the year. The number of people attending MEEC is also significant. In 2003, 56,400,000 attended corporate meetings, 15,800,000 attended association meetings, and 12,400,000 attended conventions for a total meeting attendance of 84,600,000 in the year. Total expenditures included $15 billion for corporate meetings, $13.7 billion for association meetings, $16 billion for conventions, and $44.7 billion aggregate expenditures for all meetings in 2001. Readers are reminded that these figures are for direct spending and do not include the "multiplier effect." When the latter is considered, the preceding amounts are doubled. Thus, the "total impact" of the MEEC industry sector studied by this magazine is $93.6 billion.

In 2003, 12,400,000 people attended conventions, spending $16 billion.

Another source of information on the impact of MEEC is provided by the Trade Show Exhibitors Association. They found that in 2001 trade shows and exhibits alone had total direct spending amounting to $20.5 billion, whereas spending by exhibitors totaled $3.6 billion. There were 4,983 events at an exhibition or convention center, 1,070 events at a conference center or seminar facility, 4,870 events at a hotel, and another 2,262 that were not classified. Of all the direct spending, 63.1 percent was done at conventions and expositions, 32.7 percent was done at meetings, and 4.2 percent was on incentive travel. The recipients of direct spending included hotels with 32.5 percent, air transportation with 22.3 percent, restaurants with 12.1 percent, ground transportation with 8.6 percent, retail trade with 6.7 percent, business services with 6.6 percent, and entertainment with 4.5 percent; the remainder was unspecified.

Career Opportunities

The meetings, expositions, events, and conventions industry is a subsegment of the hospitality industry, which itself is part of the larger services industry. It encompasses many areas of the hospitality industry. Thus, the readers are challenged to conceptualize their personal ideal job and then determine how and where in the MEEC industry they could be employed doing what they dream of.

Some of the careers in MEEC include the following.

- *Event Planner:* Puts together special events like the Super Bowl of football, the Final Four in basketball, festivals, and celebrations.
- *Meeting Planner:* Organizes meetings and other gatherings for companies, corporations, and associations. These gatherings can range from a small board of directors meeting, a stockholders meeting, and new product introductions to educational seminars and national conventions.
- *Wedding Planner:* Did you ever think that *someone* needs to organize all the weddings that occur each year?
- *Hotel Sales:* The majority of positions in hotel sales deal with groups, and MEEC covers most of those groups.
- *Restaurant Sales:* Although most people think of restaurants attracting walk-in clientele, many rely heavily on the MEEC industry for business. Food and beverage (F&B) venues employ significant numbers of people on their group sales staff. In New Orleans, Arnaud's, Emeril's, and even the Crescent City Brewhouse have convention sales teams.
- *Entertainment Venue Sales:* Although these places attract individual patrons primarily, most also devote much time and effort to selling and producing events for groups. Further, groups have lots of money and can afford lavish productions.
- *Destination Management:* Destination Management Companies (DMCs) function as the "local experts" for companies and associations in organizing gatherings and events. People employed for DMCs usually work in either sales or production.
- *Hotels:* Hotels are one of the primary locations where MEEC events are held using ballrooms, meeting rooms, and break-out rooms for their

gatherings along with sleeping rooms and F&B for their attendees. The two departments in hotels that deal with the MEEC industry are sales and convention services.

■ *Convention Centers:* These venues include dedicated facilities like McCormick Place in Chicago, the Jakob Javits Convention Center in New York, and the Sands Expo in Las Vegas. Also included in this category are multipurpose venues like the Superdome in New Orleans or the Astrodome in Houston. Once again, careers are found in either sales or operations.

■ *Exposition Services Contractors:* Do you like to build things? Have you thought about being an engineer or architect? Well, exposition services contractors (ESCs) may be the place for you. These businesses design and erect the booths, backdrops, and staging, for meetings and conventions. The decorations and backdrops for your school prom may have been done by an ESC. Again, career paths exist in sales and in production.

■ *Convention and Visitor Bureaus:* CVBs serve to represent a wide range of MEEC companies and market the destination to business and leisure travelers. CVBs have many departments and careers, including convention sales, tourism sales, housing bureaus, convention services, marketing, research, and member services.

As you can see, MEEC is a vibrant, dynamic, and exciting part of the hospitality industry. It may also serve as an ideal work environment for someone who has tried or worked in many different areas and likes them all. Many careers in MEEC involve multiple aspects of the hospitality industry. For example, someone who works in convention or group sales in a hotel must interface with and be knowledgeable about hotel sleeping rooms, front desk, food and beverage, catering, and all the meeting facilities. Further, unlike at a front desk, hotel convention employees develop long-term friendships and relationships with their MEEC clientele. These hotel employees have been known to be invited to clients' homes, vacation retreats, birthdays, weddings, and so forth. In fact, one of the most important considerations for anyone involved in MEEC is the building of long-term relationships with clientele. In marketing jargon, this is called "relationship marketing."

Is there anyone who does not have some influence on the MEEC industry? A case can be made that every person has an impact, in some way, on each and every meeting or event—even those gatherings of two or three that take place in an office or restaurant. Take a few minutes and add to the jobs or functions listed earlier that might affect a meeting or event. Then think again. Even the president of the United States and all members of Congress affect our industry by determining trade regulations, security issues, and whether or not our country goes to war.

Meeting/Event Planner

When asked about a "typical day," there are few if any meeting professionals, whether they work in an organization or operate an external meeting/event planning company, who could say that any day is "typical." These jobs are ideal for those who love to multitask, who have broad interests, who enjoy problem solving, and who care passionately about building community through meetings and events.

Doug Heath, Certified Association Executive (CAE) and Certified Meeting Planner (CMP), who was the second executive director of MPI, said many years ago, "Meeting planners have to be more than coffee-cup counters." When Mr. Heath said that, it was a time when most meeting planners were concerned only with logistics—"ensuring room sets, coffee and refreshment breaks, meals, and audiovisual setup."[4]

Today, this job is strategic. Event planners are charged with supporting the work toward an organization's bottom line. To do that, and in the course of planning a meeting or event, a planner may do any or all of the following, and more:

■ Define meeting goals and objectives.

■ Develop a request for proposal (RFP) based on a meeting's objectives, audience profile, budget, and program.

■ Send the RFP to national sales offices of hotel and conference center companies, to convention and visitors bureaus, and to external meeting planning companies.

■ Prepare and manage a budget and expenditures that can range from a few hundred dollars to well over $2 million.

■ Negotiate contracts with a facility, transportation providers, decorators, speakers, entertainers, and all the vendors and venues that will support a meeting or event.

- Market the event electronically and in print and track results.
- Invite and manage needs (travel, lodging, registration, room setup, and audiovisual) for all speakers, trainers, and facilitators involved in delivery of information and knowledge for the meeting.
- Invite and manage contracts and needs for entertainers.
- Design food and beverage events and negotiate contracts for these events. To do so, a planner must know the audience (age of participants, gender, abilities, allergies, geographic location, and more) and timing for the program.
- Prepare a crisis management plan in conjunction with other staff, facilities, vendors, and emergency personnel.
- Register participants, ensuring data is accurately entered.
- Manage the multitude of changes that happen from first conceptualizing a function to the execution.

If you are extremely organized, you may have the aptitude to be a good meetings professional.

- Monitor industry and business publications for strikes and other issues.
- Calm others' nerves and remain calm.

The following are some questions you might answer to determine if you have what it takes to be a successful meetings or events professional.

- Do you like to plan parties, work schedules, your day, and so forth?
- Do you have a date book or personal digital assistant (PDA) that you update regularly and that includes everything you need to do for weeks or months into the future?
- Do you like to organize your bedroom, car, workplace, and so on? Is your idea of fun organizing a closet for someone?
- Are you very organized, almost to the point of obsession?

If you answered "yes" to all those questions, you have the aptitude to be a good meetings professional.

To be prepared for short- and long-term change, *meeting professionals*—a term that encompasses those who plan and execute meetings, those who work for and in facilities in which meetings are held, and the many vendors who supply services for meetings—must begin to anticipate changes that will occur as the nature of meetings changes. In the scenario at the beginning of the chapter, there is a designated vendor to work with satellite and other e-communication tools. In the future, meeting/ event professionals will need a greater working knowledge and will be charged with selecting meeting destinations (cities) and sites that can facilitate distance learning and e-communications.

Professional Associations

The Association MEEC Industry

Association meeting planners join professional associations in greater numbers than their corporate counterparts. Those associations include the American Society of Association Executives,[5] Meeting Professionals International,[6] Professional Convention Management Association,[7] International Association for Exhibition Management,[8] Greater Washington Society of Association Executives,[9] and the Society of Government Meeting Planners.[10] There are also many local organizations of meeting planners that provide support and professional development opportunities for them.

The Government MEEC Industry

Meeting planners who work for the government and/or independent meeting management companies are likely to join associations to support their professional development. These associations include the Society of Government Meeting Planners[11] and its local or regional chapters, Professional Convention Management Association[12] and Meeting Professionals International.[13] Those who have responsibility for organizing exhibitions are likely to join the International Association for Exhibition Management.[14]

The Exposition Management Industry

The associations that support the exhibition management industry include the International Association for Exhibition Management[15] for the production side of the business and the Trade Show Exhibitors Association[16] for the exhibitor side of the business. Other related associations include the Exhibit Designers and Producers Association,[17] the Exposition Service Contractors Association,[18] and the Healthcare Convention and Exhibitor Association.[19]

Independent Planners

The type of company individuals are associated with will dictate the type of association that they would likely join to support their professional development. Many of them will join the Professional Convention Management Association[20] or Meeting Professionals International.[21] Others will choose to join organizations like the International Special Event Society,[22] the National Association of Catering Executives,[23] the American Rental Association,[24] or the Association of Bridal Consultants.[25]

Summary

Industry Terminology and Practice

The MEEC industry has struggled for years, before and since the founding of the Convention Industry Council, with terminology and practices that are specific to the work we do. **CIC**'s APEX[26] is attempting to put into place words that will help all those in the United States, and eventually in all North America, "speak the same language" as it pertains to types of meetings and events as well as to other aspects of our industry. This is no easy task. However, it will make it easier for people who work in the MEEC industry to define and recognize each other once the terminology is standardized.

In this chapter, you were introduced to the world of meetings, expositions, events, and conventions—MEEC. As can be seen, MEEC is multifaceted and exciting and offers diverse career opportunities. MEEC is also very large and incorporates many facets of the hospitality industry. It has tremendous economic impact. For a more complete insight into the MEEC industry, refer to *Meetings, Expositions, Events, and Conventions: An Introduction to the Industry* by George G. Fenich, published by Prentice Hall and on which much of this chapter is based.

Endnotes

1. CIC Web site: http://www.conventionindustry.org
2. From *EXPO Magazine* at http://www.expoweb.com/expomag/BackIssues/2001/Apr/feature2.htm
3. From PCMA at http://www.pcma.org/resources/industry/research/clc_study.asp
4. Fenich, G. G. (2005). *Meetings, Expositions, Events and Conventions: An Introduction to the Industry*, (1st ed., p. 27), Upper Saddle River, NJ: Prentice Hall
5. http://www.asaenet.org
6. http://www.mpiweb.org
7. http://www.pcma.org
8. http://www.iaem.org
9. http://www.gwsae.org
10. http://www.sgmp.org
11. http://www.sgmp.org
12. http://www.pcma.org
13. http://www.mpiweb.org
14. http://www.iaem.org
15. http://www.iaem.org
16. http://www.tsea.org

17. http://www.edpa.com
18. http://www.esca.org
19. http://www.heca.org
20. http://www.pcma.org
21. http://www.mpiweb.org
22. http://www.ises.com
23. http://www.nace.net
24. http://www.ararental.org
25. http://www.bridalassn.com
26. http://glossary.conventionindustry.org

☞ Key Words and Concepts

APEX
BEO
CIC
Conference
Convention
Convention services
CSM
Destination
DMC
Exhibition
IACVB
MEEC
Meeting
Outlet
Sales and marketing

For definitions, refer to
http://glossary.conventionindustry.org

🖹 Contributor Information

George G. Fenich, PhD, is a professor in the Lester E. Kabacoff School of Hotel Restaurant and Tourism Administration at the University of New Orleans. Dr. Fenich was a practitioner for 15 years before joining academe in 1985. He is a well-known expert on the MEEC industry, having written over 25 articles and made numerous presentations at industry conferences. He is the author of the text on the subject and was awarded PCMA Educator of the Year in 1995.

31 ▌Review Questions

1. What are meetings? Expositions? Events? Conventions?

2. Describe some events from the past that were "meetings."

3. Describe some current aspects of MEEC industry jobs.

4. Who attends meetings? Events? Conventions?

5. What can be accomplished by convening or attending a meeting?

6. What are five key jobs in a facility (hotel, resort, conference center) that contribute to the successful outcome of a meeting or event?

7. What is CIC?

8. What is APEX, and what does it hope to accomplish?

9. What is the impact on the U.S. economy of meetings?

10. What is the future of electronic meetings?

Nancy Swanger
Washington State University

Quick-Service Restaurant (QSR) Operations and Management

Learning Objectives

✓ To understand how the quick-service restaurant (QSR) segment came to be and identify some of its key players

✓ To identify the quick-service restaurant segment based on its characteristics

✓ To describe chain operations and their relationship to QSRs

✓ To explain the role of the QSR manager

✓ To discuss the trends and challenges of the QSR industry

Chapter Outline

History
Characteristics
Quick-Service Categories
Chain Operations
Role of the Manager
Trends/Challenges

As today's hospitality student, you have grown up with industry icons like McDonald's, Pizza Hut, Subway, and Taco Bell being an integral part of everyday life. You have never known a life without fast-food restaurants. Quick-service restaurants (QSRs) and visits to them are so commonplace in today's society (the average QSR user eats 6.2 dinners from fast-food/pizza restaurants each month[1]) that their existence is often taken for granted. However, nearly one-third of all adults in the United States have worked in the restaurant industry at some time during their lives.[2] Specifically, one of every eight Americans has worked at McDonald's.[3] This segment of the restaurant industry provides endless opportunities for the student serious about the hospitality business.

History

Quick-service restaurants got started back in the 1930s and 1940s with White Castle, A&W, and Dairy Queen. However, it wasn't until the 1950s when Ray Kroc met the McDonald brothers that the face of the restaurant industry was changed forever. Kroc was not a restaurateur; he sold milkshake machines. In fact, he sold milkshake machines to the McDonald brothers for their fast-food hamburger restaurant in San Bernardino, California. The fact that their concept often needed to produce up to 40 milkshakes at a time caught Kroc's eye, and because the brothers had no desire to expand, they sold Kroc the rights to the name and system they had developed.

In his early days with McDonald's, Ray Kroc established the standards of quality, service, cleanliness, and value (QSCV) that to this day, serve as the benchmarks for others in the quick-service industry. Because of his early jobs in sales, Kroc fully understood the importance of a first impression. He, himself, was always meticulously groomed and carried that standard forward with the employees of his own company. Today, McDonald's is the most recognized brand in the world.[4]

Quality, service, cleanliness, and value (QSCV) have become synonymous with today's quick-service restaurants. In a recent study of students on the campus of Michigan State University, the number one factor influencing which fast-food restaurant they patronized was cleanliness. Friendliness, price, speed, consistency, menu variety, and location followed, in that order. Merely having QSCV guarantees a quick-service restaurant operator nothing; however, lack of them almost surely guarantees failure. What separates the winning restaurants from the others is hospitality—the delivery of genuine, caring, personable service to the guests from each of the employees.

Characteristics

Quick-service restaurants are identified based on some common characteristics. They include limited menu, service style, size, location, and check average.

Limited Menu

QSR menus typically center on a common menu theme—pizza, tacos, burgers, sub sandwiches, or chicken, etc. Although many chains have expanded menu offerings to attract a larger customer base, most can still be identified by their core menu. For example, Arby's has added chicken choices to its line; however, roast beef remains its signature product. Items are generally prepared in less than five minutes and use a few key ingredients in multiple combinations for the appearance of a broader menu.

Service Style

Customers inside the restaurant generally place their order at the counter prior to settling at a table or booth. The meal is usually paid for before it is prepared and eaten and is often picked up from the same counter where the order was placed. The restaurant business is very labor-intensive, and as a result, many operators have converted to self-service drink stations and condiment bars in an effort to reduce the number of employees required per shift.

Drive-thru windows provide a convenient way for customers to enjoy their favorite fast-food meals without ever leaving their cars. In the most recent report of the *QSR Drive-Thru Time Study* conducted by g[3] Mystery Shopping, Rally's had the best overall ranking, edging out Chick-fil-A, who held the number one spot for the previous three years. The survey measured the following attributes: speed, order accuracy, menu board appearance, and speaker clarity.[5] The demand for convenience by customers has seen a modification of service style to include take-out and delivery options at many locations. Pizza has been delivered to the customer's door for years, but recently, chains like KFC and Subway have experimented with delivery in certain areas of

Customers in a QSR generally order, pay, and pick up their food at the same counter.

the country with success. The challenge with both take-out and delivery is in maintaining the quality of the product while in transit.

Size

The size of the QSR can vary; however, those including seating generally accommodate less than 100 patrons. Because of the need for speed and efficiency, unit layouts are designed to maximize productivity and reduce unnecessary steps for the employees. Operations can range from small, single employee carts or kiosks to large freestanding units with a drive-thru and inside seating, which may require double-digit numbers of employees per shift.

Location

As the number of people working continues to climb, the demand for convenience has also risen. Quick-service restaurants locate where the consumers can access them easily. As America moved to the suburbs in the 50s and 60s, so did fast food. Units can be freestanding, part of a strip mall, in a convenience store, inside the mall, at the airport, inside a grocery or department store—virtually anywhere traffic patterns have dictated a need. Because the reasons for choosing a quick-service restaurant are not the same as those for choosing a special occasion or destination restaurant, location is key. The cur-

rent trend favoring take-out food puts those restaurateurs with the most desirable locations in the best position to compete.

Check Average

Generally, prices in QSRs are lower than those found in full-service restaurants, and as a result, quick-service restaurants depend on high seat turnover to generate the necessary volume. In the late 1980s and early 1990s, Taco Bell turned the industry upside down with the introduction of its value menu. All items were less than $1, and many were priced at 49, 59, or 69 cents. To remain competitive, other quick-service restaurants soon followed, and value menus, meal deals, and daily specials remain a part of most major chains today. As a result, check average (Total Sales divided by Number of Guests/ Transactions) can be pretty low (less than $5) in comparison to other segments of the foodservice industry.

Quick-Service Categories

Quick-service restaurants are classified, and sometimes compared, based on the category they represent. Those categories may include burgers, pizza/ pasta, chicken, seafood, snacks, sandwiches, Mexican, and Asian.

The burger chains dominate the industry in market share and system-wide sales.[6] McDonald's is the leader in the burger category and in the QSR industry as a whole. Based on 2004 sales, the top performers in this category, following McDonald's, include Wendy's, Burger King, Sonic Drive-In, and Jack in the Box.

Pizza Hut is the leader in the chain pizza/pasta category—followed by Domino's Pizza, Papa John's Pizza, Little Caesars Pizza, and Sbarro.

In the chain chicken category, KFC is the long-standing leader, with Chick-fil-A, Popeyes, Church's Chicken, and Boston Market following.

Chains in the seafood category, a smaller segment overall, include Long John Silver's, Captain D's Seafood, Ivar's Seafood, and Skipper's.

Starbucks dominates the snack category, along with players such as Dunkin' Donuts, Baskin-Robbins, Jamba Juice, and Cold Stone Creamery.

Heading up the sandwich category is Subway, followed by Arby's, Quiznos, and Panera Bread.

Mexican quick-service restaurants are very popular and include the category-leading Taco Bell, Chipotle, Del Taco, Baja Fresh Mexican Grill, and Taco John's.

A relatively new category for QSRs, Asian, continues to grow in popularity. Panda Express is far and away the leader, followed by Noodles & Co., Yoshinoya, and Manchu Wok.

Chain Operations

The key to success in quick-service operations is consistency—consistency of product, consistency of service, and consistency of facilities. One of the ways this is achieved is through tight controls established by the chain's corporate headquarters. Because the vast majority of quick-service restaurants are part of a chain, a brief discussion of what that means follows.

Defined

According to Jaffe,[7] a chain is defined as "any single restaurant concept with two or more units in operation under the same name that follow the same standard operating procedures."[8] Many of the chain operations franchise their business format. This allows the business owner (franchisee) to use the name, logo, recipes, system, products, and marketing of the particular chain (franchiser).

Advantages and Disadvantages

One of the biggest advantages of being involved with a chain is that because the concept has been tested and proven, the risk of failure is greatly reduced. When nearly 40 percent of all new businesses fail within the first year and about 75 percent fail within the first five years of operation, buying into a system can be very beneficial. According to the U.S. Department of Commerce, less than 5 percent of franchised businesses fail within the first year.

Other advantages include help from the franchiser with site selection, design, and possibly financing. The purchasing power of a chain is greater than the purchasing power of a single operator, helping the franchisee to keep costs and quality under control. Systems of budgeting, inventory control, and accounting are generally available for immediate use by the new franchisee.

Although operators of QSRs enjoy many benefits being associated with a chain, there are some negative considerations as well. First, there is not a lot of room for creativity and, second, decision-making opportunities are limited. Independent operators have complete freedom and autonomy, but QSR operators are generally governed by the chain's corporate office.

Another disadvantage of being part of a chain is that the chain is only as strong as its weakest operator or its current place in the media. Wendy's "finger-in-the-chili" incident is a perfect example of how damaging negative press can be. A person claimed that they found part of a finger in their chili. Even though it was determined the entire story was a hoax (and arrests were made), the store involved, along with the entire chain, suffered through a period of declining sales from the unfavorable publicity.

Costs

The costs involved in franchising include the franchise fee (usually between $7,500 and $50,000), development costs (sometimes up to $1 million), royalties (usually between 3 percent and 8 percent of gross sales), and advertising fees (usually between .5 percent and 5 percent of gross sales.)

Franchise Fee

The franchise fee is a sum of money paid to the franchiser for the rights to use their system. This fee includes training in the system and a copy of the company's Operations Manual. This manual includes all the information necessary for the franchisee to operate the business, and its contents are invaluable to the new owner or manager. As part of the franchise agreement and included in the franchise fee, the parent company may also send an "opening team" (a group of employees trained in operations and new store openings) to assist the franchisee during the critical first days of operation. Once the restaurant is open, the franchiser may send people to inspect the store on a regular basis to make sure the franchisee is adhering to the chain's standards and offer any necessary support.

Development Costs

Development costs are those associated with the land, the building, the furnishings, and the equipment necessary for operation of the restaurant. There can be a huge variation in these costs, depending on the particular situation. For example, will the land be purchased or leased? What are the current land values or lease rates in the area? Is this a remodel of an existing building or a new structure created from the ground up? Is there a level of décor packages available from the franchiser based on price or is there a standard, one-price package required for all units? Is the required equipment very specialized and unique to the concept or is the equipment more generic and easily purchased? Although these considerations are by no means complete, you can see that many factors contribute to the development costs of the restaurant.

Royalties

Royalties are monies paid to the franchiser at regular intervals once the restaurant is open for business. Generally, the amount due is calculated as a percentage of gross sales for the period.

Advertising Fees

Monies for national and regional/area advertising are calculated and collected in the same manner as royalties. These fees are used to create and produce promotional materials and buy media, as examples, to help drive sales for the chain. Many times, each restaurant will also set aside an additional percentage of gross sales to support local store marketing efforts.

The Role of the Manager: A Personal Perspective

It can be argued that the unit manager is the most important factor in the success of a quick-service restaurant. The following focuses on the three areas of the manager's position felt to be most critical—their focus on hiring, their role in training, and their influence on the environment.

Hiring

One of the biggest challenges facing this industry is in finding quality employees. As mentioned earlier, this is a very labor-intensive business, and finding enough people to fill all the available positions is almost impossible. Even with the tight labor market, it is imperative the unit manager be very selective about the employees. Managers must "Hire the smile and train the technical." A manager can teach a new employee how to make a sandwich or take an order, but he/she cannot teach the person how to smile and be nice to people.

Unit managers must be familiar with all legal and human resource issues involved in hiring; the process must be defined and implemented for each prospective employee. Having said that, it is important to remember that each new employee must "fit" with the other members of the staff. Because the success of the restaurant is based on the efforts of the team, it is essential to keep the chemistry of the team in balance.

Standards of grooming and behavior must be addressed in the employee handbook and discussed during the interview and orientation sessions. The unit manager must "walk the talk" and always provide the example. Selecting the right people makes the manager's job much easier and sets the stage for building positive employee/guest relations.

Training

The time spent by the unit manager in the training of the employees is vital to the long-term success of the business. Too many times new employees come to work, it's busy, and they are left to flounder on their own or told to follow so-and-so and do what they do. The best training programs are structured in their content and are scheduled during non-peak times to allow for maximum attention to the trainee. Taking the time to teach the new employee right the first time saves the manager from having to go back and try to correct established bad habits.

Training is not a one-shot deal; effective managers are constantly coaching even their veteran staff members for improved performance. Winning managers are continually raising the bar for productivity and performance through on-going training and feedback.

Environment

It is the job of the manager to create an environment in which the employees feel motivated. A survey conducted by Rice found the unit manager to be the most critical element in employee satisfaction.[9] To help ensure employee satisfaction, it is important that the manager prove competency, show interest, and be sincere.

Prove Competency

Employees need to know the unit manager is on top of things. The manager doesn't necessarily have to be the best at every single position in the restaurant; however, they need to be good enough to hold their own and able to teach the position to others. Effective managers never ask an employee to do something that they are not willing or able to do themselves. One advantage to starting at the entry level and working up is the knowledge gained along the way about how the entire operation functions. Managers must demonstrate their ability.

Show Interest

Great managers get to know their employees as people. They build relationships with them that foster trust and loyalty. One way to do this is to spend some time with new employees on their first day doing a task where it is possible to chat while working. A good icebreaker question involves the employee telling the manager about their family. Usually, family is a topic people are comfortable with, and it generally leads to other discussion topics such as interests or hobbies. During these informal visits, attempts are made to connect the new employee to others on the shift with whom they may have things in common. Great managers know their people.

Be Sincere

Managers with credibility avoid saying things to employees they don't mean. Employees know phony praise and false promises. Honesty and integrity are everything when it comes to managing people. Character leads by example.

Trends and Challenges

The past few years have fared well for quick-service restaurants in comparison to some other segments of the hospitality industry. With rising gas prices and other pressures on the economy, the amount of disposable income in many households has been challenged. However, because we have become a nation that is used to dining away from home, we may have scaled back our choices but have continued to eat out. While fine dining and upscale eateries have shown limited or no growth in sales, the quick-serve segment has been able to maintain and even show sales increases in many areas.

Events currently in the news that may have an impact on the industry include the use of irradiated and genetically modified foods, banning the use of latex gloves in certain states, minimum wage hikes, and state smoking bans. However, the emergence of the fast casual segment, an emphasis on nutritional offerings, the rise of co-branding, and staffing may have the most profound effects on the QSR industry.

Fast Casual

Fast casual restaurants, those perceived to be a step above the traditional QSR but not quite a casual restaurant (due mainly to the service style), are growing in numbers of concepts and popularity. Players in the emerging fast casual arena include companies like Panera Bread, Chipotle, Corner Bakery, Qdoba Mexican Grill, and Buffalo Wild Wings. More upscale décor, prepared-to-order items using high-quality ingredients, and a pricier menu distinguish this segment of the QSR industry.

Nutritional Emphasis

To combat the negative press from obesity lawsuits, recently published childhood obesity rates, and Morgan Spurlock's documentary "Super Size Me," the QSR industry has begun to reevaluate some of its menu offerings. Although some chains have created entirely new items that promote healthier eating (McDonald's Fruit and Walnut Salad), some have chosen to reposition items already on their core menu (Subway's "8 Under 6" campaign—eight sandwiches under 6 grams of fat). Whether employing either strategy the goal is to provide customers healthy choices, with the hope of growing or at the very least—maintaining sales volumes. The QSR industry, in general, targets 18- to 34-year-old males;

however, expanding menu choices may attract additional users from other target markets.

Co-Branding

In an attempt to draw a larger share of the foodservice dollar, many QSRs are entering into co-branding agreements. These agreements are an arrangement between two or more concepts to operate at one location. One of the more common co-branding arrangements involves KFC and Taco Bell, as they have the same parent company (YUM! Brands). Patrons visit one location and have the choice of ordering from either or both menus with one transaction. Kitchens, signage, and menu boards have been retooled to accommodate both concepts, and employees are trained to prepare and serve all food. Oftentimes in a co-branding arrangement, the menus are a bit more limited than would be found at a traditional, one-concept-only location.

As KFC and McDonald's recently celebrated their 50th anniversaries, many quick-service restaurants are making improvements they feel are necessary to enhance their own longevity. In addition to new menu items, those improvements include upgrades to facilities such as new designs, remodeling or rebuilding of older units, improved signage, enhanced technology, and updated décor options.

Staffing

The National Restaurant Association projects the restaurant industry, as a whole, will add 1.9 million jobs by 2016. Many QSRs are having a difficult time attracting people to fill current position vacancies; thus, who will fill the 1.9 million new positions? The QSR segment has traditionally drawn its workers from the 16- to 24-year-old age group; however, that group, demographically, is shrinking in size. In addition, the QSR segment has suffered from an image problem—a reputation of providing minimum-wage, dead-end jobs—which compounds the problems of attracting new workers. Several studies in recent years cite staffing as the biggest challenge facing operators both now and in the future. Successful operators have incorporated a variety of strategies to recruit and retain employees including targeting older workers, offering referral bonuses, providing incentives and bonuses, using tuition reimbursement, and other creative methods.

Summary

What are the opportunities for you in quick-service restaurants? As an industry segment, quick-service restaurants are projected to do sales just over $142.4 billion in 2006, according to the National Restaurant Association, which represents about 5 percent real growth over the year 2005.[10] The number of managers is forecasted to increase 12 percent from 2006 to 2016. These unit managers will earn between $25,000 and $50,000 and may be eligible for bonus compensation equal to an additional third of their base salary. This bonus is often centered on goals in relation to sales volume, food/beverage/labor costs, customer count/ticket average, and profit. What other industry allows young people in their 20s the chance to be responsible for hundreds of thousands of dollars (even millions of dollars) in assets and sales? The opportunities are endless—go out and be great!

Endnotes

1. From Business Wire. (2000, November 7). *Dick Wray Executive Connections, 3,* (24), 2
2. National Restaurant Association. (2000). *Industry at a glance* [On-line]. Available Internet: http://www.restaurant.org/research/ind_glance.html
3. A & E Television Networks. (1996). Ray Kroc: Fast food mcmillionaire. In *Biography*. New York: New Video Group
4. Ibid
5. Baker, B. (2005, October). Why accuracy matters. *QSR,* 35–37
6. Nuckolls, M., Davis, L., Cuthbert, W., & LeClaire, J. (2005, August). The QSR 50. *QSR,* 37–69
7. Jaffe, W. (1995). Chain operations in the hospitality industry. In R. Brymer (Ed.), *Hospitality management: An introduction to the industry* (pp. 94–108). Dubuque, IA: Kendall/Hunt
8. Ibid
9. Rice, G. (1997, January). *Industry of choice: A report on foodservice employees.* (Available from The Educational Foundation of the National Restaurant Association, 250 S. Wacker Drive, Suite 1400, Chicago, IL 60606)
10. National Restaurant Association. (2006). *2006 Restaurant Industry Forecast* [On-line]. Available Internet: http://www.restaurant.org. Accessed on January 17, 2006

Resources

Internet Sites

National Restaurant Association: www.restaurant.org
QSR (online): www.qsrmagazine.com
Nation's Restaurant News (online): www.nrn.com
McDonald's: www.mcdonalds.com
Subway: www.subway.com
KFC: www.kfc.com
Taco Bell: www.tacobell.com
Pizza Hut: www.pizzahut.com

⌐ *Key Words and Concepts*

Chain
Check average
Co-branding
Fast casual
Franchise
Franchisee
Franchiser
Franchise fees
Quality, service, cleanliness, value (QSCV)
Quick-service restaurant (QSR)
Royalties

▣ *Contributor Information*

Dr. Nancy Swanger, FMP is an Associate Professor at Washington State University, where she teaches the introductory classes. Nancy has over 30 years of restaurant experience as a coworker, manager, district manager, and owner. She and her husband have owned and operated Subway restaurants since 1988. Her research interests lie in the areas of quick-serve restaurant operations and hospitality curriculum. Dr. Swanger received the Dean's Excellence Fellow Award in both 2004 and 2005 from Washington State University's College of Business and Economics. She also received the President's Award for Outstanding Teaching from Lewis-Clark State College in 1998 and the Associated Students of Lewis-Clark State College Outstanding Instructor Award in 1999.

32 ▌Review Questions

1. What is QSCV and why is it important for successful operations?

2. Choose a QSR in your area and explain how the operation compares to the characteristics presented in the chapter.

3. Define a chain and provide three examples of one.

4. Why can it be argued that the unit manager is the most important factor in the success of a QSR?

5. Of the trends and challenges facing the QSR industry, which do you feel is the most important and why?

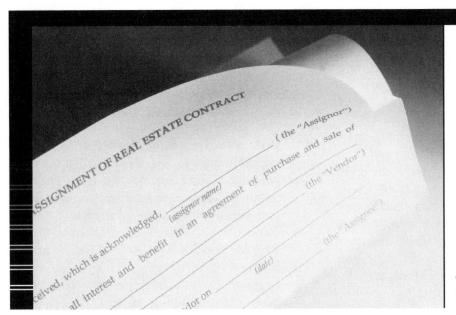

John M. Stefanelli
Karl J. Mayer
University of Nevada, Las Vegas

Real Estate Opportunities in the Hospitality Industry

Learning Objectives

✓ To familiarize the student with an important and dynamic sector of the hospitality industry—the real estate area

✓ To understand the importance of real estate

✓ To understand the variety of career choices that are available for those students who wish to focus on hospitality real estate

✓ To identify the skills, background, and experience required to effectively engage in the real estate field

✓ To distinguish which hospitality programs offer specific classes in real estate at the present time

Chapter Outline

Typical Hospitality Real Estate Positions

Preparing for Hospitality Real Estate Positions

Your Future in Hospitality Real Estate

*W*hen one thinks about a job in hospitality, real estate is usually not one of the career opportunities that comes to mind. However, one of the advantages of working in the hospitality industry is the availability of a wide array of career options. Although most of the jobs are in operations (that is, production and service positions), several support staff positions are available for persons who want to be in the hospitality industry, but who are not interested in operations. Support staff refers to people who work with hotels and restaurants to aid in their endeavors. For example, a firm can have its own hospitality accounting staff or it can outsource the effort. In real estate, some corporate headquarters may have a person who does site selection, or they may hire different contractors to aid them in evaluating sites depending on the location.

Many avenues can lead to working in a staff role. Some people enter these positions while going to school. Some move into them on graduation. Others move into them only after working in several operations positions. A few find themselves thrust into these jobs through a combination of circumstances. An internship, if your program of study offers one, is often an excellent way to explore whether a staff position would be a feasible career option for you.

Hospitality real estate offers interesting and rewarding career opportunities. Several hospitality firms employ real estate specialists, such as market analysts, location analysts, and lease negotiators. However, you do not have to be employed by a hospitality company to work in this field. For instance, you could be an independent appraiser or work for a lender, private investor, or real estate brokerage firm. The next section of this chapter will discuss the typical positions that are available for those who are interested in a real estate career in hospitality.

Typical Hospitality Real Estate Positions

Several career options relate directly or indirectly to the hospitality industry. Persons wishing to work in this area may find employment with real estate departments in multi-unit hospitality corporations, appraisal firms, real estate brokerages, vacation-ownership firms, business brokerages, site selection firms, and lending institutions. The skills needed to perform well in hospitality real estate are very diverse and depend on the specific area of emphasis that a person chooses. These areas are discussed next.

Company Real Estate Representatives

Many large multi-unit hospitality corporations employ a real estate director and one or more real estate representatives. These persons are usually responsible for the following activities:

1. Performing location analyses (i.e., evaluating real estate sites to determine whether the company should construct new businesses in these locations). Some considerations would be traffic patterns, visibility, and current or potential competition. After all, think about when you see a McDonalds. How far away is the nearest Burger King? Why is that?
2. Evaluating existing business locations from the perspective of acquiring and managing the business that is situated there. One of the questions that can be raised is why is the business selling or closed? Was there a problem with the site? If so, can the problem be resolved? Problems can be something as simple as being on the wrong side of the highway.
3. Working with a variety of external agents, for example, negotiating lease or purchase agreements with brokers and/or owners.
4. Interfacing with the company's legal, construction, operations, and financial personnel.

Company real estate representatives typically travel a great deal. It is usual for them to be on the road four days a week. Such extended travel, however, is necessary to evaluate a site properly. If insufficient time is spent researching a location, the company may make a rash decision. Because location is a critical factor influencing a hospitality property's success, it is very important to make good, well-informed site-selection decisions.

Appraisers

Real estate appraisers are employed to render estimates of value. They are trained to value real estate (i.e., land and buildings); furniture, fixtures, and equipment (FFE); collectibles and artifacts; and going-concern businesses. One of the concerns that we don't often think about is the aspect of goodwill; that is, what is the name and reputation of a going concern restaurant worth? How do you appraise the intangibles?

Commercial lenders, investors, sellers, insurance companies, contractors, attorneys, accountants, pension funds, and other entities having a financial stake in a project engage appraisers. For example, before a commercial lender, such as a bank or savings and loan, can lend money, it must have the collateral appraised by an independent appraiser it selects. A hospitality firm that needs to borrow money to build a new property must pay the cost of the appraisal needed to satisfy this regulatory requirement.

Some appraisers specialize exclusively in the hospitality industry. The major one, *Hospitality Valuation Services* (HVS), was founded in 1980. HVS has offices in New York, San Francisco, Miami, Dallas, Chicago, Phoenix, and Denver in the United States, as well as offices in eight other countries. Although its array of client services has expanded in recent years, HVS's major focus is the appraisal of lodging properties.

It is unusual, however, for individual appraisers to specialize in hospitality because there may be insufficient work available to make it a full-time job. Generally speaking, appraisers tend to specialize in a particular category and not in a particular industry. For instance, a business valuation specialist who appraises restaurants will typically appraise related businesses, such as taverns, liquor stores, bakeries, and food marts.

In other cases, appraisers may be part of a larger consulting practice. The firm *Ernst & Young* is representative of these types of appraisers and has consultants who are specifically designated to serve the hospitality industry through its Real Estate, Hospitality and Construction Group. Besides their appraisal work, these firms also conduct a wide variety of other assignments designed to assist their client companies.

In addition to appraisal assignments, appraisers usually counsel clients. For example, a motel owner may hire an appraiser to estimate the most likely sales price for the property. He or she may also ask the appraiser to suggest things the owner could do to make the motel more attractive to potential buyers. In this role, the appraiser is required to draw on his/her considerable expertise in the real estate field to make sound recommendations to the property owner.

Lastly, over and above an appraising or counseling role, some appraisers also get involved with real estate sales, property management (such as overseeing a shopping center complex), and loan brokerage (such as helping clients search for and secure the most favorable debt financing available). It is important to note, however, that in all aspects of appraisal work, it is essential for appraisers to render objective, unbiased advice. To do otherwise would severely impair their reputations.

Real Estate Sales

Although property owners are free to sell their properties without help from other professionals, most prefer using a third party to represent their interests. The same is true for potential buyers. Thus, brokers play a valuable role by serving as an intermediary in a real estate sales transaction.

Several brokerages specialize in the sale of lodging properties. For example, there are consortiums of brokerages in the United States that account for a majority of all lodging properties sold nationwide.

A brokerage office may also specialize in the sale of restaurants, taverns, liquor stores, and other similar hospitality businesses. In large cities, it is not unusual to find offices that deal exclusively with the sale and purchase of restaurants or with tavern operations.

Persons working in a sales office generally are in business for themselves; that is, they are independent contractors. Their livelihood depends on the amount of property sold, in that their main (and most often, only) source of income is sales commissions generated when deals are concluded.

Some sales associates represent sellers, and some represent buyers. Few represent both parties because doing so may be a conflict of interest.

Although sales commissions are their primary source of income, some sales associates prefer to operate as independent consultants. In the typical sales transaction, the seller pays the commission, which is then divided among the relevant sales offices that helped consummate the deal. However, some salespersons work strictly for hourly fees and are paid regardless of the outcome of a transaction. In effect, they sell their time and are compensated accordingly.

A day in the life of the typical real estate sales associate finds him or her showing property to potential buyers, gathering pertinent data, suggesting appropriate sales and purchase strategies, recommending alternative financing arrangements, estimating the most likely sales prices, organizing and completing deal-related paperwork, negotiating contract terms and conditions, and shepherding the deal to ensure that it stays on track and is finalized.

It should be noted that the role of a real estate sales associate is evolving due to the impact of tech-

In large cities, it is not unusual to find offices that deal exclusively with the sale and purchase of restaurants.

nology and growth of the Internet. The Internet is making it possible for companies to circumvent intermediaries and "go direct" to potential buyers and sellers on a worldwide basis. Although many aspects of being a real estate sales associate will not be affected by these developments, students who are interested in this area should carefully explore the impact of these trends on the future of working in a real estate sales position.

Vacation Ownership Sales

A vacation-ownership firm is in business to sell long-term vacation packages to guests. They sell "slices of time," in that they normally sell a guest the right to use a vacation apartment, hotel room, or condominium for a specified time period per year (usually two weeks) for several years (usually 7 to 20 years) at a specific property. In some cases, a person can buy two weeks of a condominium timeshare. The sales pitch is that a family of four may never have to pay for a vacation again. This type of timeshare also means that this vacation ownership can be passed on to your children and grandchildren without any additional costs, except for fairly nominal annual fees as discussed later. Guests who prepay for these vacations usually have the option of swapping their time at one location for comparable time at other vacation locations that are part of a

timeshare exchange network. Normally the guest pays a small fee for this exchange privilege.

In most cases, the prepaid vacation is an economical alternative to paying for vacations every year. Usually the guest needs to pay only a relatively modest maintenance fee each year to defray the cost of routine repairs, necessary remodeling, and so forth. In addition, the guest will pay local property taxes on a proportionate basis—normally, these annual tax payments are also relatively modest.

At one time these "timeshare operations" had a seedy reputation. Most of them were high-pressure sales operations that generated numerous consumer complaints. For example, in New York City, one firm sold timeshare units to people who had never been to the site. How did they sell? They invited couples to a black tie dinner at the Waldorf Astoria. Between each couple, a real estate broker was seated who kept the conversation going. The strategy was that people are on their best behavior when they are dressed up. So, they are not rude. In a crowd of 500 people, the dinner ended and a speaker stepped up to the podium. He thanked everyone for coming and said that of course everyone knew why they were there . . . to buy real estate, if anyone was not interested, they could get up and leave. Because people were on their best behavior and not rude especially after being treated to the best dinner in the city, no one got up. After several minutes, the speaker replied, "Well, let me show you what you have decided to buy." Of course, if anyone had had the nerve to get up and leave, the game would have been over.

However, although a few of these boiler-room operations probably still exist, generally speaking the industry is considered quite aboveboard today. This is due primarily to the involvement of major lodging firms in the field, such as Disney, Hilton, and Marriott. Their participation has legitimized the industry. In addition, other large firms, such as Fairfield and Cendant, have specialized in providing high-quality timeshare properties for guests. Today, this sector represents a growth area in the hospitality field. It offers excellent opportunities for hospitality students who are interested in the variety of careers available in vacation ownership sales. For those uninterested in sales, there are many positions in operations, such as housekeeping, maintenance and engineering, and property management.

Business Opportunity Sales

A business opportunity is an ongoing business located in leased real estate facilities. The owner typically sells the furniture, fixtures, and equipment (FFE); leasehold improvements (i.e., interior finishing of the leased premises); the business's name and reputation; and perhaps some other types of assets, such as inventory or a valuable liquor license. The business opportunity purchase usually includes everything but the real estate.

A business opportunity brokerage is very similar to the typical real estate brokerage. Although business brokers do not normally sell real estate, they do sell businesses that must be transferred to buyers. In effect, the work performed by business sales associates parallels almost exactly that performed by most real estate sales associates. However, like the role of the real estate sales associate, this intermediary role will likely be evolving due to technology and the Internet, so students should be mindful of the potential impact of these trends on future careers in this area.

Site Analysts

Some research firms, real estate brokerages, and business brokerages provide location analysis for persons or firms unable or unwilling to do the work themselves. These companies typically maintain computerized databases that can be adapted to suit any need

or answer any question. Their reports help clients make sound real estate and business decisions.

Some hospitality firms prefer to contract out this type of work to independent firms because it is more economical than maintaining their own real estate divisions. This concept is known as outsourcing. However, even those large hospitality companies that have real estate divisions are apt to use an outside firm on occasion because it is not always feasible for them to study every potential site.

Financial Positions

Many lending institutions are active in hospitality finance. These lenders provide the discretionary capital that allows new properties to be conceived and developed or existing properties to be refinanced. The major players include the following organizations.

1. Life insurance companies that specialize in financing lodging properties
2. Pension funds that invest in lodging properties or lend to them
3. Banks and savings and loans that make real estate and business loans to qualified hospitality operators
4. Government agencies (such as the Small Business Administration) that make direct loans or guarantee loans made by a third party
5. Leasing companies that will construct a property and/or provide all necessary equipment and lease these assets to a hospitality operator (especially in the gaming or restaurant sector of the industry) on a rent-to-use or a rent-to-own plan

Lenders must qualify potential borrowers. Before recommending a loan, the lender must ensure that there is a high probability that the money will be repaid in a timely manner. Lenders must perform "due diligence," which means that they must evaluate a borrower's credit worthiness, character, reputation, capacity to repay, business skill, and collateral. These evaluations require that a skilled financial professional be involved.

Lenders who are heavily involved in hospitality finance may employ real estate experts on their own staffs to perform these functions. For example, DePfa Bank AG (Deutsche Pfandbriefbank) is a German-based institution that has a specialized hotel financing team. This team has financed first-class hotels all over Europe and the United States, including properties such as the Plaza Hotel in New York City and the Adam's Mark Hotel in Dallas. In other cases, a lending institution may outsource these tasks to appraisers or consulting firms on an as-needed basis. Whichever approach is taken, it creates an opportunity for you to build a hospitality real estate career in a financial position.

Preparing for Hospitality Real Estate Positions

If these career opportunities seem exciting, you should begin to prepare for them now. It is never too early to select the right college courses and work experiences most likely to give you an edge when applying for this type of work.

These positions are very academically oriented, in that a great deal of research, writing, and computer skills are needed to succeed. You should take college courses designed to develop and enhance these skills.

You should also take a basic real estate course, a real estate investments course, and a real estate appraisal course. These classes will give you the best perspective of the industry, as well as highlight the various career opportunities that may exist in your local area. The next section of this chapter discusses which hospitality programs presently offer such courses.

Accounting and finance courses are also necessary. At the very least you should take the basic accounting and financial principles classes. Generally, however, additional finance courses are necessary to acquire the techniques needed to prepare the types of research projects you will encounter.

Computer literacy is a must. You should be very familiar with word processing, database, and spreadsheet software. In addition to working with your own computer files, you must be able to use the computerized databases most offices subscribe to. For instance, a real estate sales office usually subscribes to a computerized multiple listing service (MLS). Sales offices also typically use services that provide demographic data and updated lists of lenders and their current loan terms and conditions. The number of service firms offering these data has expanded significantly in recent years to meet the industry's ever-increasing demand for information. Also, geographic mapping software is now available, offering detail that can be used to examine a potential site on-screen before ever leaving the office for a site inspection.

Computer literacy is also needed to efficiently access information available on the Internet. In recent years, there has been an explosion of real estate information that can be downloaded from the World Wide Web (WWW). This information could include such things as local market data and reports, national economic trends and conditions, financing availability and terms, and federal and state guidelines for site development activity. Thus, a broker, appraiser, or real estate director can now obtain a great deal of pertinent information without ever leaving the office. However, because real estate is inherently a localized business opportunity, there is no substitute for on-site visits by a trained real estate professional.

Many real estate positions require licensing or certification, or both. For instance, if you want to be an appraiser, you will likely need a state license as well as certification from a nationally recognized appraisal association.

Finally, you should acquire a reasonable amount of operations experience before tackling one of these staff positions. If you want to work in a hospitality company's real estate division, you should have a basic understanding of how the company's food or lodging units are operated and managed. This provides the perspective needed when wrestling with decisions that can make or break your employer's bottom line.

Hospitality Programs Offering Real Estate Courses

The top 25 hospitality programs in the United States were surveyed to determine whether they offered specific real estate courses or a concentration (specialization) in the real estate area. During the year 2006, only six of these leading programs offered at least one real estate course (Cornell, Michigan State, UNLV, Penn State, University of Central Florida, and Florida International University) as a part of their hospitality programs. Further, Cornell and Michigan State appear to be the only two hospitality programs that also offer a specialization, or concentration, in this area. Other schools, such as Virginia Tech and Florida State, have real estate courses available through the university's College of Business, but do not currently offer them within their hospitality programs.

The results of this survey were very comparable to a similar survey that was conducted in 2001, so not much has improved in terms of the availability of specific real estate coursework in most hospitality programs. Thus, students who are serious about a career in hospitality real estate may want to carefully consider their choice of a program and select one that offers a real estate curriculum, either in the hospitality program itself or in a related business program at the university.

Your Future in Hospitality Real Estate

Research and experience have shown that for every four people graduating with a degree in hospitality administration, one of them leaves operations within one year or leaves the industry entirely. Interestingly enough, for every four who leave operations or the hospitality industry, one of them ends up in some type of financial management career. In a nutshell, then, the odds are about one in eight that you will end up in one of the careers discussed in this chapter.

Hospitality is a people industry, and so is real estate. The skills, education, and work experience you have already earned and will earn in the future will qualify you for many types of careers. Take the time to explore the many options that are available. Hospitality is a field that can accommodate many career interests and many different backgrounds. If you choose a career in hospitality real estate, you can be assured that many exciting challenges and new opportunities will lie ahead.

Summary

This chapter introduced you to the opportunities that are available for hospitality students who have an interest in real estate. Real estate is a vitally important aspect of most sectors of the hospitality industry, and those students who decide to pursue a career in this area will find it to be a rewarding and challenging career option. They would be well advised to take full advantage of the quantitative courses that are available in the hospitality school in which they are already enrolled. Alternatively, they may choose to attend one of the hospitality programs that offer either specific real estate courses or a concentration in this unique and exciting area.

Resources

Internet Sites

Hospitality Valuation Services: www.hvsinternational.com
Ernst & Young: www.ey.com/global/content.nsf/International/Industries_-_REHC
Fairfield Resorts vacation ownership: www.fairfieldresorts.com
Real estate terms and definitions: www.realestateabc.com/glossary

☞ Key Words and Concepts

Appraisers—Professionals who are trained to value land and buildings, hired to render estimates of value.

Brokers—A professional who serves as an intermediary in a real estate sales transaction.

Real estate representative—A person who works for the hospitality firm that specializes in real estate transactions, including site location and analysis.

Support staff—Professionals who work in hospitality and tourism but not in operations.

Vacation-ownership firm—A business focused on selling long-term vacation packages to guests; these "slices of time" may be hotel rooms or condominium units at a specific property.

Contributor Information

john.stefanelli@unlv.edu

John Stefanelli is a professor in the Department of Food and Beverage Management, William F. Harrah College of Hotel Administration, at the University of Nevada, Las Vegas (UNLV). He earned his PhD from the University of Denver, MBA from Michigan State University, BS from the University of Illinois, and AAS from the College of DuPage. He has been at UNLV since 1978, serving in teaching and administrative positions, including chair of the Department of Food & Beverage Management and associate dean of the College. Over the years he has authored or coauthored several publications, among them many textbooks that are widely used in hospitality education. In addition to his academic responsibilities, Stefanelli has consulted for many restaurant companies and individuals. He recently completed his duties as department chair and has returned to full-time teaching status, with a special focus on developing distance education classes. A Vietnam veteran, Stefanelli and his wife of 35 years, Deanna, have two children and four grandchildren. They live in Henderson, Nevada.

karl.mayer@unlv.edu

Karl J. Mayer is an accomplished academic researcher and a skilled business practitioner with more than 20 years of experience in various sectors of the economy. Dr. Mayer is an associate professor at the William F. Harrah College of Hotel Administration at the University of Nevada, Las Vegas, where he teaches graduate and undergraduate hospitality accounting, finance, and marketing courses. During 2000–2001, he served as assistant professor with Temple University's School of Tourism and Hospitality Management. He received his PhD in Hotel Administration from UNLV in 1999, where he was the recipient of the Ace Denken fellowship award. Dr. Mayer received an MBA in Business Administration from Harvard University in 1984. He also earned an MS in Engineering from Columbia University in 1976 and a BS in Engineering from the University of Wisconsin in 1974. Dr. Mayer has published in a wide variety of academic and trade journals, including the *Journal of Services Marketing* and the *Cornell HRA Quarterly*. Dr. Mayer's research interest areas include hospitality real estate and finance, casino gaming, and services marketing and management.

33 ▌Review Questions

1. List the typical hospitality-related real estate positions.

2. What are the functions of a real estate director and real estate representatives who work for large multi-unit hospitality corporations?

3. Discuss the importance of real estate representatives making well-informed site selection decisions when working with hospitality companies.

4. What functions are performed by real estate appraisers? Who would typically hire an appraiser? How do most appraisers handle areas of specialization? In what types of counseling do appraisers sometimes engage? What are other possible roles of the appraiser?

5. Explain the concept of "independent contractor" as applied to persons working in real estate sales. How are these people usually compensated?

6. List what is typically included in a business opportunity purchase. What is the function of the business opportunity brokerage?

7. What types of businesses may be involved in conducting a site analysis?

8. What is a vacation ownership firm? How has the vacation ownership industry been legitimized?

9. List the types of organizations that are most active in hospitality finance and are major lenders in this industry.

10. Describe the type of skills and experience that would be beneficial for someone seeking a career in hospitality real estate.

Sherie Brezina
Florida Gulf Coast University

Resort Operations and Management

Learning Objectives

✓ To understand how resorts are differentiated from traditional hotel properties
✓ To understand how resorts seek to satisfy resort guest needs
✓ To understand the variables that determine resort profits
✓ To understand the importance of spa amenities and other recreational activities in providing the resort experience to the guest

Chapter Outline

Types of Resorts
The Resort Guest
Resort Characteristics
Resorts versus Traditional Hotel Management
Resort Operations
Resort Economics
Industry Trends

In Roman times resorts typically centered around public baths for relaxation and social interaction. In the United States the early resorts were established around spas, often at seaside locations in the East. The first resort city was Atlantic City touting sunshine and fresh air along the boardwalk and amusement pier. Most early resorts were either summer operations or winter ski resorts. As transportation improved and more people had automobiles, warm winter resorts developed in places like California and Florida. By the 1960s the four-season resort concept took hold, offering year-round attractions to minimize the financial risk of relying on one season a year for business.

Resorts are the fusing of traditional food, beverage, and lodging hospitality with recreational amenities that offer activities to guests. The variety and complex nature of the food, beverage, lodging, and recreational amenities found at resorts demand sophisticated management practices to be successful.

Resorts are a combination of three elements:

1) Recreational attraction that draw the guest
2) Housing/lodging, food, and beverage services that cater to people away from home
3) Activities that occupy guests during their stay[1]

Resorts can be characterized in terms of

- Location relative to the primary market—how far guests travel and by what means, car, airplane, or train
- Primary amenities, setting, and climate
- Mix of residential, lodging, and community properties[2]

Resorts are typically associated with specific types of recreational amenities and are defined by the activity, such as golf resorts; tennis resorts; skiing resorts; mountain resorts; fishing resorts; health, wellness, and spa resorts. Resorts often earn a reputation and image for their superior facilities for equestrian, sporting, gaming, and entertainment activities.

Resorts are often differentiated as destination or non-destination resorts. Destination resorts tend to be found in more remote locations, are self-contained, and the recreational amenities that the resort offers are the motivating factors for people to travel, often long distances, to the destination. Non-destination resorts are usually found close to a primary natural or man-made attraction, and although they may offer many of the same amenities found in resort hotels, the resort is not the primary motivation for travel to the location; the attraction is the motivation. Non-destination resorts are often frequented by visitors within a two- or three-hour drive and often repeat visit several times a year. Resorts may fit both categories depending on where they are located and the nature of the recreational attraction. They appeal to residents in the nearby primary market and also to longer-stay visitors that may come from as far away as overseas. Disney World in Florida and ski resorts in Colorado are examples of resorts that are both destination and non-destination resorts.

Types of Resorts
Hotel Resorts

Hotel resorts are the most common resort product. Resort hotels attract guests that are seeking relaxation and an array of recreational and leisure activities. These properties are also popular choices to host business meetings because the self-contained

Resorts are the fusing of traditional food, beverage, and lodging hospitality with a recreational amenity such as golf.

environment provides everything needed for a successful meeting, including recreational activities with few outside distractions to pull the attendees away from the business meeting.

Resorts are found in all size categories from a few rooms or bungalows up to hundreds of rooms, suites, or housing units.

Small resorts with 25 to 125 lodging units are often specialty "boutique" resorts catering to a small upscale market niche. Mid-size properties of 125 to 400 rooms are typically chains and located in mega resort areas offering more space and amenities than the traditional commercial brand hotel.

Large resorts have more than 400 rooms and are often located in primary resort locations offering ski facilities, beach frontage, theme parks, gaming, spa, golf, or a combination of these amenities.[3]

Vacation Ownership and Timeshare Resorts

One of the fastest growing segments of the hotel and resort market is time shares, also referred to as vacation ownership or vacation clubs. Timesharing was introduced to the United States in the 1970s. The term timeshare is defined as "the right to accommodations at a vacation development for a specified period each year for a specified number of years or for perpetuity."[4] Owners of timeshares purchase a time period or fraction of a unit in the resort development either by a lump sum payment or financed over a number of years. Timeshare owners pay a yearly maintenance, management, and operation fee. Many timeshares allow the purchaser to exchange or trade the timeshare through exchange companies.

Over time the timeshare option has evolved from a set week that was purchased to the addition of floating week options and most recently the more flexible option of vacation club points, which are purchased and can be redeemed at resorts within the brand or a vacation time period.[5]

In the past few years most major hotel companies have developed timeshares. Marriott, Hyatt, Hilton, and Disney are in the timeshare business. Having well-known brands involved has helped to bolster consumer confidence in the timeshare product. The timeshare concept continues to evolve offering a wider range of products and choices for consumers. At many resorts the distinction between timeshare and hotel at the resort is becoming blurred. Guests often rent out timeshare units in the same way as they book a hotel room at the resort. The timeshare unit has become another resort lodging offering. Management of the resort timeshare unit is particularly complex, as the manager often is responsible to three or four bosses, the developer selling the units, the owners, the timeshare association board, which governs the timeshare community, and the guest who is renting the unit.

Current demographic and vacation trends suggest that the timeshare concept is filling a market need for people desiring a resort or second home experience, but do not want the financial or maintenance responsibilities of year-round ownership because they only plan to spend a few weeks or long weekends on vacation. With the flex point system vacations are not restricted to one location, and the desire to experience new places is appealing to many people. The United States dominates the timeshare market worldwide. The outlook for continued robust growth in the resort timeshare industry is strong.

Second Home Developments

Resort communities that are primarily second home developments are becoming popular. Fee simple, individually or family owned, attached, detached, or multi-family homes are often found in resort communities. These are best combined with primary and retiree residences to provide a mix of full- and part-time residents. These private residences are provided with all the comforts and ambience of a resort. These resort communities may be characterized by high-rise condominiums on beach front locations, mid-rise low-density residential communities near lakes or ski areas, single family developments with golf courses and a clubhouse, or large planned communities with a variety of housing types and recreation activities. The recreational activities and amenities offered to the residents mimic those found in resort hotel developments. These communities often have a resort hotel and retail found in traditional resorts complete with concierge services. For the property owners, resort living becomes a lifestyle.

Multi-Use Resorts

Resorts often offer a combination of facilities, resort hotels, timeshare units, residential single or multi-family homes. The recreational amenities are available to all owners and visitors to the resort. This type of resort requires skilled management at every level.

Resort Cruise Ships

Cruise ships are large floating resorts with many of the same concerns as land-based resorts. Sophisticated food, beverage, lodging, recreation, entertainment, and security are the expectation of the cruising guest. Many of the newer cruise ships are the size of a small city, with 5,000 or more people sailing at a time. New cruising products include timeshare cruising, with unit and package offerings modeled after the resort timeshare concept. Cruise ships compete with land-based resorts offering amenities, entertainment, and vacation appeal, typically at very competitive pricing.

The Resort Guest

The fundamental needs that resorts seek to satisfy for guests are

- Desire for change of pace, to get away from the familiar
- Desire to satisfy recreational needs while being entertained and stimulated
- Desire to travel to interesting places[6]

The primary resort guest market in season is the leisure traveler seeking to vacation in a recreational and entertainment rich environment, in a relaxing atmosphere. Resort hotels often extend their season and fill the property in the months on either side of high season, called the "shoulder season," with group business.

Resort Characteristics

The resort, particularly those referred to as mega-resorts offer more recreational activities and amenities than typical lodging properties. Location is critical to both destination and non-destination types of resorts. The surrounding scenery, environment, or close proximity to the region's natural or man-made attractions providing recreation offerings are what people travel and stay at resorts to experience.

The time and money that guests spend at a resort is discretionary, meaning freely chosen. Because of this, resorts are affected by demand elasticity to a much greater extent than traditional commercial hotel properties.[7]

Superior quality food and beverage choices, high service expectations, and a variety of recreation experiences and planned activities are expected by

the resort guest. The foundation of modern day resorts is built on the provision of a wide variety of recreational and spa amenities that allow for a longer or year-round resort operation.

Employees often need housing, and the resort must offer or make arrangements for housing in these often high value housing markets to hire and maintain staff.

In the United States, many times resorts recruit a number of their seasonal employees from outside the country and provide housing for them while they work for the resort.

Resorts versus Traditional Hotel Management

Resorts differ from traditional hotel properties in the following ways.

1) Resorts are typically self-contained. This means every need that the guest may have while on-site must be taken into consideration, planned for, and provided as needed. Basic needs such as laundry and maintenance must be done at the resort, rather than contracted out. Transportation for employees and guests must be provided. Shuttle service to and from the airport is important.

2) Recreation offerings are the reason people come to resorts. The resort room to get a night's sleep is not the motivation to purchase a room, it is all that comes with the room, golf, tennis, skiing, spa services, or beautiful location to hike or swim. Attractive amenities are essential to the resort's success.

3) Seasonality has a significant impact on resorts. High season is when demand peaks. Low season is when demand is low and resorts often struggle to attract guests. Most resorts are year round having developed recreation attractions to bring business to the resort in the off season. Though less and less common, some resorts only operate a few months of the year, around the primary recreation activity. The rest of the year the resort is closed or has very few people staffed to operate and manage it. This means that every new season, new employees must be hired and trained. Security during off-season is a concern.

4) The average length of stay is longer in a resort. Rooms are typically larger, with more closet or

storage space to accommodate more luggage. Resorts are spread out over a large land area to accommodate the variety of recreational amenities.

5) Resort guests have always been and continue to be more sophisticated consumers and have higher expectations of service and quality standards.

6) Resorts cater to repeat guests, annually or several times a year. Oftentimes the annual traditions and festivals attract and keep guests returning time after time to the resort. This must be incorporated with new offerings that keep the experience fresh for the guest.

7) The resort, especially those found in more remote locations, may be a primary employer in a community and as such the economic driver of the region's economy. The communities' dependence on the resort for economic vitality adds an additional consideration for the resort in being a conscientious community partner in making decisions to lay people off or close the resort during slow season. Many resorts do their best to make use of their full-time employees in the off-season by assigning them to maintenance detail.

8) Resorts, especially those with timeshare units that can be sold prior to development, have a much quicker return on investment (ROI) for the project's investors in the resort than traditionally financed property.

Resort Operations

The staff and line positions found in the front of the house and back of the house in a typical hotel are also found in resorts. Resorts have a third position type, recreation personnel. Recreation and activity planning in a resort is a management concern and function. Recreation, social, and entertainment activities are planned 24/7 for guests. Skilled recreation oriented and trained staff are responsible for running activities, guest relations, and guest services. One size does not fit all for resorts; each property develops a particular structure that fits its mission and needs.[8]

Resort Economics

Four variables determine a resort's profit: capacity, length of season, amount of capital investment, and amount of revenue per guest per visit.[9] How well a

Recreation and activity planning in a resort is a management concern and function.

resort maximizes these four variables determines the resort's economic success or failure.

Capacity

Capacity is determined by a number of factors. Physical and ecological capacity are determined by the limitations of the site. Comfortable carrying capacity is defined as "the maximum number of participants who can utilize the facility at any one time, without excessive crowding and without danger to the quality of the environment."[10] At a resort, safety for guests is the responsibility of management and not jeopardizing safety is considered in the carrying capacity maximum and minimum usage standards. Support facilities must be in place to contribute to full capacity at a resort. Support facilities at a resort include restrooms, foodservice, transportation, first aid, bars, lounges, and retail sales. Capacity is also determined by the design or footprint of the facility, number of available lodging units, meeting rooms, and banquet space and how many people they can hold for events and functions.

Length of Season

Weather and climate dictate what is considered "high season" depending on the nature of the recreational activity that drives guest demand. At most resorts in the United States, across the country, high season is usually a 90 to 120 day period. Much marketing effort is given to boost occupancy levels during shoulder season. Full capacity is the norm during season; it is in the off season that a good marketing strategy can bring needed guests to the resort, extending the year and the profitability of the resort.

Capital Investment

The amount of available money to develop the resort is important. The capital budget is specific to the design, site, and primary recreational activities the resort will offer. Millions and millions of dollars are typically needed in developing a large destination resort.

Revenue Per Guest Usage

The amount of revenue generated by each guest to the resort is a critical variable. This number is calculated by adding all total revenue during a specified time period, divided by the number of guest visits. The revenue comes from recreation amenities and activities and all supporting services that the guest has purchased.[11]

Revenue-Generating Programs, Amenities, and Activities

People often pursue recreation to satisfy needs and wants important to them. Common reasons often cited for recreation participation are to make new friends, belong to a group, experience competition, learn a new skill, share a talent or hobby, gain prestige, and get in shape.[12] The guest activity director and staff services are crucial to providing the guests with the benefits they seek in staying at a resort. Resorts often do best by recognizing guests as consumers of recreation products and services. Guest activity programming that is done well satisfies some or most of the needs and wants important to resort guests.[13]

In today's competitive marketplace the resort must perform at many levels. Guest activities and recreational amenities are not simply part of the supporting services available to the guest, but also must be revenue-generating functions for the resort. As such management at a resort is concerned that any space allocated to recreation offerings is also a

producer of revenue for the resort. Golf, tennis, water-based recreation, skiing, and retail have traditionally generated revenues for resort operations. In the past few years, with people's concerns for health and wellness, spas have emerged as a lead revenue generating amenity for resorts. Resorts and many hotels across the country are racing to benefit from this trend by upgrading, enlarging spa space, and embracing stand alone spa facilities, often bringing well-recognized branded spa companies on-site.

The three types of spas are

1. Resort Spa: The resort spa is located at the property of a resort hotel with other sports and recreation activities offered besides the spa program itself. Spa guests and hotel guests intermingle.
2. Amenity Spa: Similar to a resort spa, the amenity spa is an added amenity to the hotel. The distinction is its unimportance as a profit center when compared to the resort spa.
3. Destination Spa: The destination spa is a hotel property targeted to the spa guest and program. Outside guests are not part of the program.[14]

The International Spa Association reports that spas are big business with revenues estimated at 15 billion dollars annually. The United States has over 12,000 spas. The fastest five year growth rate for spas occurred in the hotel/resort segment. "A full service spa contains a full compliment of facial devices, a comfortable facial bed or chair in each room, massage tables for a full body treatment, and a range of hydrotherapy treatment options"[15]

Industry Trends

Resorts will continue to evolve to accommodate the changing vacation patterns of guests. Currently, shorter, long weekend vacation patterns have replaced longer stays. Packaging is the key to providing the resort guest with myriad recreation and activity choices over relatively small time periods. As the baby boomer generation turns 60, the sheer magnitude of numbers of people will make this generation's needs and wants dominate the resort market's attention. Resort offerings and services have spawned resort residential communities offering all the amenities of a resort. This resort lifestyle is a growing trend with appeal to affluent baby boomers and the generation following them.

Consumers are willing to pay more money than ever before for a powerful and truly positive emotional experience. They crave experiences that are more spiritual, educational, and "feeling good" in nature. Eulogio Bordas refers to this notion as the Dream Society. For resorts, creating value is key to playing to the "it may be expensive, but it is worth it" mentality. Resort guests continue to like to take home "conversational currency," bragging rights to their latest resort experience.[16]

The economics of the industry suggest that as the resort market matures, consolidation will continue, with a few industry players owning a large number of resort properties. Independent resorts have the position of being unique, a desired characteristic; however, they will struggle to compete with the capital and marketing network the corporate-owned resorts have available to develop and sell their properties.

Resorts are typically found in communities and locations with high real estate values compared to national averages, often out of the financial reach of resort staff. Affordable employee housing will continue to plague the resort industry. The resort industry will need to be creative to meet the challenges of recruiting, training, and keeping skilled employees.

As the resort market becomes more competitive, constant re-evaluation by management of what services, experiences, and amenities guests are seeking is crucial to success. Rapidly changing lifestyles and needs are forcing operators to adapt to the sophisticated wants and needs of the resort guest, creating a fluid total resort experience.

Endnotes

1. Robert Christie Mill, *Resort: Management and Operation* (New York: John Wiley & Sons, 2001), prefix XV
2. Dean Schwanke et al., Urban Land Institute, *Resort Development Handbook* (Washington, DC: Urban Land Institute, 1997), p. 4
3. Mill, *Resorts: Management and Operation*, pp. 15–16
4. *The United States Timeshare Industry: Overview and Economic Impact Analysis* (Washington, DC: American Resort Development Association, 1997), p. 5
5. M. A. Baughman, "New Points System Points Industry in Right Direction," *Hotel and Motel Management*, 17 (May 1999): p. 22
6. Mill, *Resorts: Management and Operation*, p. 25
7. Robert A. Brymer, *Hospitality and Tourism*, 11th ed. (Dubuque, IA: Kendall/Hunt Publishing Company, 2004), p. 307
8. Ibid., p. 337
9. Mill, *Resorts: Management and Operation*, p. 296
10. Patrick L. Phillips, *Developing with Recreational Amenities: Golf, Tennis, Skiing, Marinas* (Washington, DC: Urban Land Institute, 1986), p. 126
11. Mill, *Resorts: Management and Operation*, pp. 297–98
12. Patricia Farrell and Herberta M. Lundegren, *The Process of Recreation Programming: Theory and Technique*, 3rd ed. (State College, PA: Venture Publishing, 1991), p. 43
13. Mill, *Resorts: Management and Operation*, p. 326
14. Ibid, p. 397
15. Ibid, p. 417
16. Levitan Katz, "Dream Theme: What Timeshare Europe Discovered," *Developments* (February 2006); pp. 34–36

Resources

Internet Sites

International Resort Managers Association: www.resortmanagers.org/resort_links.htm
American Resort Development Association: www.arda.org
International Spa Association: www.experienceeispa.com

🔑 Key Words and Concepts

Comfortable carrying capacity
Conversational currency
Destination resort
High season
Low season
Multi-use resorts
Non-destination resort
Recreational amenities
Resort
Resort cruise ships
Resort hotels
Revenue per guest usage
Second home development resort
    communities
Vacation ownership/timeshare resorts

🖼 Contributor Information

In May of 2003, Dr. Sherie Brezina was hired as the director of the Resort & Hospitality Management Division at Florida Gulf Coast University in Fort Myers, Florida, to develop and implement the new Resort and Hospitality Management degree. The program has grown rapidly and has over 300 majors. Dr. Brezina teaches resort courses at FGCU, works closely with the regions resort and club industry, and speaks on resort and tourism issues. She is an active member of numerous professional hospitality and tourism industry associations and environmental organizations.

Sherie Brezina received a BA and an MA from the University of Florida and a PhD from Michigan State University, specializing in natural resource-based tourism and the convention industry. She has held faculty positions at The University of New Haven and The University of West Florida. Prior to joining academia, Dr. Brezina worked for the City of Tampa as a budget analyst and later Marketing Director for the Convention Facilities Department. Other work experience includes national feasibility and management consulting for convention centers, hotels, convention bureaus, and stadiums and experience as a Mainstreet Project Manager.

34 Review Questions

1. What are the advantages of being a four-season resort?

2. Explain the appeal of the timeshare or vacation ownership/club to the purchaser.

3. How has branding affiliation helped push timeshare or vacation club sales in the past few years?

4. Explain the meaning of resort lifestyle in second home development communities.

5. Why are cruise ships called "floating resorts"?

6. What fundamental needs are resort guests seeking?

7. List at least five common characteristics resort properties share.

8. How do resorts differ from traditional hotels?

9. What four variables determine resort profit? Briefly explain each variable.

10. Identify several trends that are affecting the resort industry.

Constantine Vlisides
University of New Haven

Restaurant Operations

Learning Objectives

✓ To better understand the restaurant industry
✓ To understand the difference between proactive and reactive management techniques
✓ To identify the different types of restaurant classifications
✓ To understand the importance of management functions, such selection of employees
✓ To better understand the need to control labor and food costs
✓ To consider a career in restaurant management

Chapter Outline

Classification of Restaurants
Selection of Personnel

*E*veryone has been in a restaurant. There are up-scale dining operations and then quick-service places like McDonald's. Many people believe that it is pretty easy to run a restaurant because there are waiters and cooks. In addition, although restaurants are great places to work in college because of the tips, you wouldn't want to make a career out of it. Some people have told me that "a restaurant would be a great thing to do when I retire. After all, I like to cook. And you only have to work from 5:00 until 9:00 because that's when the restaurant is open. So I would have plenty of time to do other things. How hard can it be?"

This public perception of running a restaurant is why many people open restaurants and many fail. Restaurants are one of the hardest professions and require the most dedicated people in operations. Contrary to popular opinion, depending on the type of restaurant operation, a kitchen crew can start at 8:00 am or earlier getting ready for a 5:00 pm opening. There are perishable items that must be purchased each day and inventories to check in. Everything must be cleaned and cut to order. Broths, sauces and soups have to be prepared early so that other last minute preps will be ready. An inventory of leftovers from last night and possible re-use must be determined. For example, baked potatoes last night can be mashed potatoes today or fried wedges. In Valencia, Spain, I was told that paella is only ordered at lunch time in restaurants. Paella takes a long time to prepare and cook so it is served fresh at lunch. Then according to my friends, if there are leftovers, it is re-heated for dinner. Therefore "only tourists" order paella for dinner. So, as you can see from just a very brief list of things—and the list goes on for a long time—working and managing a restaurant is a very time consuming occupation.

Therefore, the restaurant business is a challenging and unique profession. The challenges come from two main components, labor and perishable products. In the back of the house, people who work in the kitchen are usually skilled labor, but there is room for entry-level people to learn. Depending on the quality of foodservice, the skill level can be superior with graduates from the CIA (Culinary Institute of America) or the Cordon Bleu in France who train for years mastering their craft for taste and presentation. Blending the skill levels of different people can be a challenging experience. The front of the house waitstaff can be unskilled labor, depending on the level of service the restaurant desires. However, the higher the quality of the restaurant, the more skilled the waitstaff and the more training is required. Think how you would react if you wanted to impress your girlfriend by taking her to an upscale restaurant, and the waiter sat down at the table and started jabbering away about her day.

The second concern is perishability of the food. For example, take something simple like lettuce. How much lettuce do you order? Think about what happens to lettuce that you bring home and cut up for dinner. What happens to it tomorrow? Wilted and brown spots do not allow the product to be served at its optimum nutritional value nor does it look appetizing. Would you want that served to you at a restaurant? Another consideration is the quality of a hamburger that has been reheated with a microwave. These are just some basic problems with handling food. Why should you be concerned? It goes back to revenue management. These two crucial issues cause restaurateurs to seek out individuals that are motivated by their abilities to react to many different factors that cannot be pre-planned in advance. The satisfaction of working in the restaurant industry comes from the inherent joy one receives when making others happy.

To be able to manage these different skill levels, there are two recognizable styles of leadership:

1. Proactive leadership means that the one in charge forecasts what will happen. Forecasting can include, but is not limited to, the volume of business, safety and sanitation measures, or the ordering of food and supplies. As much as possible, managers try to anticipate guests' needs and plan accordingly. For example, when a waiting line begins to form, what can you do to plan for this expected occurrence to make the guest satisfied? There is more to proactive management than this brief overview. In essence, proactive management attempts to thwart any issues that may negatively affect the operation before such an occurrence takes place.

2. Reactive management is the opposite of proactive. A leader is forced to come to a reasonable conclusion that will avert a negative action and lessen its impact on the operation. For example, a customer falls in your restaurant and requires immediate attention to make sure the patron is made comfortable. They will also know that you are personally concerned about their welfare. This is also known as crisis management—the art of handling problems.

Defining these terms is not difficult, practicing them is. It is in the nature of the restaurant business that reactive management skills are as important as proactive skills because of the two crucial items mentioned before. Careers are made or broken on how well your leadership style accommodates these two principles.

Classifications of Restaurants

The selection of which restaurant classification you choose makes a critical difference in your career advancement possibilities. There are several different classifications (Figure 35.1). The quick-service restaurant (QSR) has been examined and discussed in detail earlier in this book. A second classification is the specialty quick-service restaurant. These are specialty QSRs that specialize in coffee or sandwiches such as a Krispy Kreme Doughnut Shops or Mr. Goodcents submarine sandwich shops. A third classification is that of coffee shops. These are operations that provide all three meals per day. Breakfast, lunch, and dinner items appear on their menu. The fourth level is that of dinner house. A dinner house operation usually operates through two meal periods, lunch and dinner. The last classification is that of a luxury or fine dining establishment. This operation is usually open for dinner only and is very formal in its types of service and food. There will be more detailed examples of these types of restaurants later in this chapter.

The National Restaurant Association claims that 12.5 million people are currently employed in the restaurant industry.[1] The restaurant business continues to grow on a yearly basis, and more restaurants are being built. The devastating effects of September 11th, 2001, had negative implications to most of the hospitality industry. However, the restaurant segment continues to grow as more and more people are eating outside their homes.[2]

Types of Service

Quick-Service Restaurants (QSRs)

The classification of the restaurant profession is dependent on the type of service the operation desires. A rule of thumb is that the less formal the service, the quicker the food is delivered. Therefore, QSRs create limited menus and develop architectural styles that allow for a quick turnover of cus-

Figure 35.1 ||| **Classification of Restaurants**

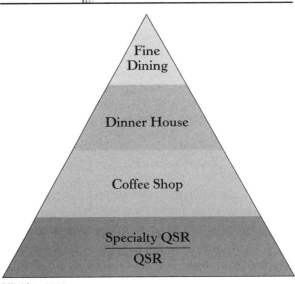

Vlisides, 2002

tomers. The key to their profitability is the amount of volume of customers served. The higher the customer count, the more revenue is generated. The more revenue that is generated leads to greater profitability. As a note, revenue is based totally on sales. Therefore, QSRs require a heavier flow of customer traffic through their doors.

Quick-Service Specialty Restaurants

The classification of specialty QSRs is new to the industry. The segmentation of QSRs has created this category. As reported on the A&E network *Food Show* in December 2002, these operations have limited their menu offerings to a few specific items. The customer can pick and choose what they desire, and their orders are filled most rapidly. Variations of the items that are available may be offered but only to what the operation can provide.

For example, Dunkin' Donuts specializes in coffee drinks and a limited number of pastries and bagels. Customers are most generally aware of the menu choices before entering the door. Dunkin' Donuts operators know that their prime business hours will be early in the morning. Therefore, the bulk of their employees and products are consumed at that time. Managing a QSR or specialty QSR is not easy. Customer satisfaction, employee efficiency, and product quality are keys to success.

The same can said of Mr. Goodcents, a submarine sandwich shop found mostly in the Midwest. The principles are still the same. In this case, customers order their food choices and the amounts they desire to be placed on a roll. Each item placed on the sandwich is weighed and a price per ounce determines the cost of the sandwich. The customization of each customer's sandwich makes Mr. Goodcents unique. The same principles of this type of operation hold true as described in the QSR chapter.

The largest of these chains is Subway. This is a global operation that has 25,329 units in 83 countries.[3] The cost per unit is dependent on its size, location, and regional construction costs. Estimates to own one of these units range from $70,000 to several million dollars, as underscored by the units operating near Times Square in Manhattan, New York City. The responsibilities of a unit manager are very well described in the QSR chapter.

Coffee Shops

The coffee shop concept is not one to be taken lightly. Each of us has been at Denny's or Big Boy restaurant. The type of service that is used to deliver the food is performed by a server who waits on each customer. This is a key difference from the QSR operations. The interaction between the customer and the server is critical because the customer's perception of service makes this an experience that is either enjoyable or not. Therefore, the selection of servers that can interact with people is absolutely critical.

The type of menus found in the coffee shop is larger and more expansive then that of the QSRs. This requires managers to seek out, hire, train, and motivate individuals that can create, prepare, and present food within the confines of a standardized recipe. Coffee shops generally try to get the food from the time the order is taken to the table in 10 minutes at breakfast time, 10 to 12 minutes at lunch and 15 to 20 minutes at dinner. These are rules of thumb that have been learned from 25 years in the restaurant business. Of course, some menu items may take more time or less time, depending on the customer's desire.

Because there is more food variety on the menu, there are more specialized requests. These requests oftentimes determine the success of the coffee shop. All customers have the right to request what they wish to be served. The successful operator makes most of those desires come true. This level of customer expectation and perception of the operation separates the good from the best. It is easy to be per-

ceived as good; it is difficult to be perceived as great. It is most difficult to remain being perceived as great.

The coffee shop is open more hours and more days per week than any of the other concepts. They offer more variety of menu items and offer them any time of the day or night. They rely on their hours of operations and their diverse menu to bring in their revenue. They have increased expenses because they have more employees than QSRs. Therefore, their menu prices are higher, because the customer is getting more service and more food choices.

Dinner House

The dinner house concept is fashionable and can be the most profitable. The impact that the dinner house restaurant segment has had on the entire American dining experience is quite remarkable. The largest dinner house chain in America is Red Lobster with nearly 700 units.[4] The Olive Garden Restaurant chain continues to grow with nearly 500 units. Darden Restaurants, Inc. owns both of these chains. The reason they are named Darden is because Mr. Bill Darden created the original Red Lobster concept and restaurant. Each unit within the chain generates approximately $4 to $5 million per year. The total revenue between these two concepts is then approximately equal to $5 billion per year. The responsibility of a general manager and his or her subordinate management team is obviously heavy.

Each unit is constructed at an average cost of between $2 and $4 million dollars. This does not include any of the inventories that are needed to supply the restaurant for its initial operation. Having opened two units in Las Vegas, Nevada, and Houston, Texas, it was a very interesting experience. There must be coordination among the architect, the general contractor (who is charge of construction), and the operator. The two restaurants were remodeled from former restaurant operations, and so they needed to look and "feel" like currently operating Olive Garden Restaurants. The reason for this is that the customers from the East knew from their experiences what to expect from the new operations in the West.

Las Vegas was especially important because as a destination point for travelers and conferees, the expectation for nation-wide acceptance of this chain was critical. The selection of the management team and their training was done in a meticulous fashion.

A dinner house operation usually operates through lunch and dinner.

Management teams were pre-selected to open Olive Garden units in the western United States. Orlando was the selected training site, as it was the area that Olive Garden first opened and subsequently succeeded. Therefore, their operating and training systems were proven to be successful. To secure restaurant chain continuity, the training was done in operating units as well as the corporate training headquarters.

The training proved to be invaluable, as those who participated in the intense management-training program were certified as qualified Olive Garden managers. It is noteworthy that not all participants were successful, and many were eliminated from the program before anyone left Orlando. That was just the beginning because after training, the management teams were sent to their opening sites.

Construction Complications in Houston

The completion of construction had to be overseen. The experience of being in the Orlando units was needed to secure the same environment in Las Vegas and Houston. Construction does not often match up with architectural plans because remodeling took place after each of the units was originally built. The architects in Orlando had no knowledge of the remodeling that took place before the building was to become an Olive Garden. The general contractor was forced to make decisions that were inherent with property. A prime example would be that either the cook's line would be two feet wide or the server's aisle would be less than three feet wide.

The architect was called immediately to help remedy the situation. The results took several weeks to resolve. Although the ultimate resolution to this problem was found, it pushed back the opening date and cost over $40,000 to remedy. The purpose for this example is to underscore the necessity of leadership within the industry. Someone has to make decisions that affect organizational resources. These resources include fiscal, physical, and human, which are considered assets of an organization. Each leadership decision, on whatever level, affects these assets. Good decision-making skills are a necessity within the restaurant profession at all levels and classifications.

Luxury and Fine Dining Segment

There will always be the need for fine and luxurious dining. This segment of the restaurant industry generally caters to those who can afford it. Normally, these dining establishments are open in the evening and on special holidays. They may cater to specific clientele as seen in a previous chapter. The type of service and menu must meet or exceed customer expectations and enjoy an excellent recommendation in the form of word-of-mouth marketing made by customers. These recommendations are crucial for this type of operation's long-term success. Each detail of the operation must be overseen, as it is essential that nothing is overlooked. Of course, this argument may be said of each of the other previously mentioned segments. However, it is imperative in this restaurant segment. You may be thinking to yourself, why?

A Perception Ruined

Simply put, because the customers pay top dollar, they expect top-of-the-line service and products in an exceptional environment. As an illustration to this point, a visit was made to a fine city club that will remain unnamed. Upon entering the club, you received a warm and personable greeting from the door person; one could feel their feet sink into the plush carpet. The foyer was elegant with richly decorated hand-carved oak wood panels, staircase, and front desk area. The tile was marble, and the chandeliers were made of exquisite imported crystal. The paintings that hung from the walls were original oils by well-known artists. The entire building was immaculate, and service was outstanding.

Upon entering the sanitized restrooms, one could not help but see the luxurious accoutrements that were in place. For example, there were gold spigoted faucets on marble sinks. More original oil paintings and other accent pieces were to be marveled by all who saw them. The linens were thick and fresh, laid out so everyone who entered would be assured of receiving a fresh towel. This entire experience was beyond compare until one looked at the soap dispenser. It was totally out of place. It was plastic, and the 79-cent price tag was still on it and could be viewed by all. That one item destroyed the perception of exquisite surroundings and left the patrons with the perception that if this was done, where else were cost-saving measures occurring?

It is the attention to small details that make or break any restaurant operation: cleanliness, uniforms, plate presentations, personnel selection, floor and wall coverings, music selection, interior and exterior lighting, interior and exterior landscaping, purveyors, bar and food menus, and more. Each of these items must be specified clearly and concisely for operational uniformity and confor-

mity. These become expected standards of operation for the restaurant unit or chain.

Fine operations will deviate very little from established standards because their patrons expect quality and consistency in service, atmosphere, and product. To deliver that kind of quality and consistency every time requires vigilance by restaurant leadership.

Selection of Personnel

As mentioned earlier in this chapter, one of the critical issues that faces restaurant managers/leaders is the selection of people that will impact their business operation in the near and distant future, especially the front-line people that take care of the customers. Within the restaurant industry it is common that these are the least-paid employees and yet have the most interaction with the customers. Therefore, the selection of these individuals is critical to the long-term success of the operation. When opening the Las Vegas Olive Garden in 1986, 1,800 people were interviewed for 108 positions. When the operation was running at peak efficiency, the number of employees dropped to 88. These remaining individuals stayed with the operation for a longer than normal period of time.

When Houston opened its Olive Garden in the Baybrook Mall, the same scenario was needed. It began as a larger unit, as its seating capacity was nearly 300. The number of individuals interviewed was over 2,200 for 135 to 140 positions. These statements are actual activities and counts, which are made to underscore the need for the creation of a team of employees that will meet or exceed your customers' perception of quality of service.

Summary

The restaurant profession is a most honorable one that demands individual excellence. Personality, decision-making skills, and the inherent joy of making other people happy is the ultimate reward. Can you make a good living and earn enough money to enjoy a wonderful lifestyle? Yes. In a survey done of 23 corporate and partnership restaurant operations, the average number of years to make it to senior level management was 11.2. If you are in charge of an organization that employs over 1,000 people, your earnings will exceed six figures.[5] The ability to influence and affect many peoples' lives from either a customer and employee standpoint is incredible.

Endnotes

1. National Restaurant Association. (2002). Forecast material. [http://www.restauarant.org]
2. Orilio, W. (2002, December 9). Hospitality bubble may have burst, but aim of operators still should be customers first. *Nation's Restaurant News, 36,* (49)
3. Subway, Inc. (2002). Company Web site statement. [http://www.subway.com/development/]
4. Red Lobster: Our Company. Fact Sheet [http://www.redlobster.com/discover/our_company/fact_sheet.asp]
5. Vlisides, C. E. (1993). *Personal value systems of senior corporate and partnership restaurant managers and higher education program implications.* University of North Texas. Denton: TX

Resource

Internet Site

www.nationalrestaurantassociation.org

☞ Key Words and Concepts

Coffee Shop restaurants are establishments that serve breakfast, lunch and dinner in an informal manner. Many are open 24 hours per day.

Dinner house restaurants are open for dinner and many times lunch. They have a varied menu selection and offer alcoholic beverages.

Proactive management is the technique of forecasting problems and creating a plan for their resolution.

Reactive management is the technique of resolving unexpected problems that ensures customer retention and satisfaction.

Quick-serve restaurants are considered informal dining establishments that specialize in delivering food quickly.

Quick-serve specialty establishments are food-service entities that offer very limited menu offerings.

🖾 Contributor Information

Constantine Vlisides has worked in the restaurant business for 25 years, beginning with his father's restaurant in Ann Arbor, Michigan. Subsequently, he went on to become a Top 400 Franchise operator as named by Restaurants USA. He has worked in several U.S. cities and was general manager for the Good Earth Restaurant, an opening manager for the Olive Garden Restaurant, and a district troubleshooter for Smitty's of Arizona and its 22 restaurants.

He has served on the Missouri Restaurant Association Board, was invited to serve on the Texas and Nevada Restaurant Association Boards, and was a participant in the Connecticut Restaurant Association's Education Committee. He is a professor and has taught at the University of New Haven for the past 11 years and has served as the chair or program director.

35 ▮ Review Questions

1. Why is it important to define proactive and reactive management techniques in the restaurant industry? What are the strengths of these concepts? Conversely, what are their weaknesses?

2. Identify the different classifications of restaurants. Why are there so many? Which are most attractive to you? Why?

3. Someone once said that the strength of a restaurant lies in the selection of its staff. Do you agree or disagree with this statement? Why?

4. How can a manager influence staff selection? Why is this a most critical task?

5. Construction of a new restaurant is costly. What can a manager do during construction that can offset future problems?

6. What are the most interesting aspects of a restaurant manager's position? What kind of individual attributes must an individual possess to have a successful restaurant management career?

Bradley Beran
Syracuse University

Senior Living Centers

Learning Objectives

✓ To define and identify the different types of senior assisted-living centers

✓ To identify job requirements that are similar to other segments within the hospitality industry

✓ To identify job requirements that are unique to senior assisted-living centers

✓ To understand and identify define the career positions, scope, and growth potential of careers within senior assisted-living centers

✓ To understand the market needs and trends of senior assisted-living centers

✓ To identify specific guest needs, demands, services, and requirements and the types of centers that fill these needs

Chapter Outline

Types of Living Centers
Market Outlook and Cost Support
Development and Ownership of Senior Living Centers
Employment in Living Centers

*I*n the aftermath of WWII, thousands of soldiers came home to start their lives and families. With this momentous occasion came the influx of thousands of babies within a short time span. The "baby boomers," as they were called, set records at every stage of their lives because they were the largest percentage of the population. In their teenage years, they created movies stars their own age and rock stars with their own brand of music. As they reached maturity, new product lines and new ideas about growing old were created. Baby boomers did not want to rock their lives away and grow old gracefully. They wanted to stay young and active, and they demanded scientific solutions to aid in their quest. As a result, it was discovered that if you use your muscles and maintain fitness, you look younger, and the health and fitness boom was born. Baby boomers invented strollers to jog with and health clubs to get fit. No longer was the health club a place for men only to lift weights. Spas became all the rage, as those with sore muscles needed a place to relax. Spas were not just for movie stars anymore. New products reduced wrinkles, and hair dyes created a youthful color and appearance. Men and women paid attention to taking care of their bodies and their appearances. "You are what you eat." This phrase started people thinking about organic foods and healthy eating habits.

Now, the baby boomer generation is getting ready to retire. This group of future retirees will be the healthiest, most financially well off, most independent and mobile, and longest living of any group to date. The 2000 census data from the U.S. Department of Commerce (2005) provides the following data:

- 12.4 percent of the population is 65 years old or older representing about 35 million
- 21 percent of the population is 55 years old or older representing about 60 million
- 34.4 percent of the population is 45 years old or older representing about 97 million people, just over one-third of the total population of the United States

The potential market for senior living centers is enormous. Senior living centers provide many services to attract and support the needs of this population. The potential clientele have many different needs and goals for their golden years. This includes people who no longer have the ability and/or desire to maintain a private residence because they want greater flexibility and/or fewer responsibilities. One option that meets their residential and personal needs is senior living centers.

Senior living centers are filling the need of retirees by offering a multitude of services and conveniences that are as minimal or as extensive as retirees desire. Minimal services can be limited to living space and basic interior and exterior maintenance at one end of the spectrum to full-service living centers offering restaurants and meal plans, laundry, cleaning, pharmacy and basic medical services, transportation, activities and entertainment, and more. As the level and amount of service increases, so does the cost to the living center resident.

Senior living centers can be categorized by the amount and level of service they provide ranging from at-home and independent living centers to full-care living centers.

Types of Living Centers
Independent Living Communities

Independent living communities are for the most healthy and independent residents. These residents typically own a car, are in good health, drive often, and come and go as they please. If they require any medical support at all, it is minimal and usually not much more than pharmacy support for medications. These people may be living in their own house alone and find that taking care of the lawn and house maintenance is getting to be too much. In addition, many of their friends have moved away to be with family, and the neighborhood has changed. Therefore, they are isolated and lonely. They may not want to move in with their family because they value their independence, but concerns about living alone are strong. Especially women worry about being robbed or worse, and the thought that perhaps they will fall and can't get up and no one will find them for days troubles them. Therefore, these communities offer an alternative to living alone and yet maintain their freedom.

Independent living communities for self-sufficient residents like these offer the fewest services and are the lowest cost. Typical services at this level are lawn care, snow removal, and similar outdoor maintenance. Other services often include a community center and/or recreation center and may offer food services (restaurant or catered meals) and/or home replacement meals and laundry services. These centers may resemble apartment complexes.

Independent living communities for self-sufficient residents like these offer the fewest services at the lowest cost.

Newly built facilities are usually no more than two stories high and look more like a small community of duplex or multiplex housing, thus giving a more homey feel to the community.

One example of high-level services at the independent level is Sunrise Independent Living Communities. Services for residents include exercise and wellness programs, outings to local events and attractions, on-site entertainment, programs and activities, fine dining, landscaped grounds, barber and beauty shops, housekeeping, linen, transportation services, and more.[1]

The price for independent living communities ranges from just over $1,000 per month to upward of $2,500 per month, depending on location and the number of services offered and selected by the resident. The resident pays for the fees with possibly some government assistance.[2]

At-Home Assisted Living

For some seniors who are healthy and relatively independent, the prospect of giving up their home is unacceptable, yet they need assistance in certain tasks. Sometimes this is a good possibility when spouses are still active outside the home but are not strong enough to bathe and get their loved ones out of bed and dressed. A small but growing area known as at-home assisted living fills this need. This service provides support for a multitude of needs such as light housekeeping, meal preparation and planning, bathing and grooming assistance, medication management, errands and shopping services, and more.[3]

Assisted-Living Centers

The typical resident of assisted-living centers either drives minimally, or does not drive at all and often needs varying degrees of assistance due to various limitations such as medical, physical, or mental conditions. They are not as healthy or independent as residents of independent living centers and may be in declining health. These residents value their independence, but are not capable or comfortable living completely independently. Typically, the longer these residents stay at a center, the more services they require as they age. These centers are often set up as smaller efficiency apartments, or as group units with a central common area and bedrooms for 8 to 20 residents with several units per center.

Assisted-living centers offer more services at a greater cost to their residents. In addition to the services offered at independent centers, assisted centers generally add or offer assistance with medications, meal preparation and/or feeding, personal care (shaving, showering, dressing, etc.), ambulatory care, and transportation services. Medical care may be on site, but is minimal, usually provided by a licensed practical nurse (LPN) or registered nurse

(RN), is often not available 24 hours per day, and is generally for minor injuries, consulting, and referrals. Some assisted-living centers provide specialty care for residents with Alzheimer's and other debilitating, non-communicable diseases. Coordination with external physician and pharmacy services are provided as the medical needs of this group are much greater than in independent living centers.[4] Living center administration must be aware of special medical requests, such as "Do Not Resuscitate" orders, visitation restrictions, hospital preference in case of emergency transport, personal physician information, and the like.

Services available for assisted-living are usually offered in one of three ways.

1. A resident may select from a menu of services and pay a fee based on the number and type of services selected.
2. A resident selects one of several service programs or packages, each offering more services at different price points.
3. An assisted-living center may offer only one set of services at one price. In this instance, if a resident requires more services than are available, they must to move to another center to have their needs met, which is usually a transfer to a full-service center/nursing home.

At Sunrise Assisted Living Centers, services include three meals per day served in a restaurant-style setting, health and wellness assessments, scheduled transportation, activities programs, weekly housekeeping and linen service, and personalized levels of care based on each resident's needs.[5]

The price for assisted-living centers ranges from about $1,800 per month to upward of $3,500 per month, depending on services used. Alzheimer's care is more expensive, from nearly $3,000 per month to around $4,000 per month. The resident most often pays for these costs with possibly some assistance from Medicaid.[6]

Full-Care Living Centers

Full-care living centers are most commonly known as nursing homes. Residents are unable to live by themselves and, at best, can only provide minimal care for themselves. These residents may require feeding assistance, may be bedridden, and may need continual observation and care.

These centers provide full service for those seniors least able to care for themselves. All services are provided for these residents, which includes all meals, housekeeping, laundry, personal care, medication, and other services. Medical personnel are on staff 24 hours each day, including registered nurses (RNs), licensed practical nurses (LPNs), and certified nursing assistants (CNAs). Doctors are on call and often maintain a regular schedule. Pharmacy services are provided, and some medical testing is often available on-site.

Sunrise Senior Living nursing homes offer 24-hour nursing, post-hospital care, post-surgical care, physician and pharmacy coordination, family counseling and other support services, and emotional and physical health and well-being.[7] Nursing home prices will range from around $3,000 per month to around $6,000 per month depending on services needed by the resident. Residents pay these costs themselves, and Medicare or Medicaid can supplement the costs.[8]

Respite Care

Many assisted-living centers and full-service centers offer respite care as an option if there is space available. Respite care is a short-term, temporary use of assisted-living center resources and services. This care is designed to fill the needs of an individual who may need assistance in recovery from surgery, injury, or other ailment and only needs temporary assistance during recovery and rehabilitation. Respite care generally lasts from one week to a few months and is usually billed by the day and/or week. Typical services for respite care can include medical and pharmacy services, physical therapy, meals, laundry and housekeeping services, and other services as needed, depending on each situation.[9] Respite care fees are usually paid for through some combination of insurance, Medicare, Medicaid, and personal funds.[10]

Market Outlook and Cost Support

Expected Demand

The 2000 census lists 1,720,500 residents in nursing homes. By 2010 it is projected that there will be 36,818,000 Americans aged 65 or older, and by 2020 the estimate increases to 47,338,000 and to 81,999,000 by 2050.[11] To meet the expected demand for senior living centers, an additional 1.25 million units will need to be built. Put another way, the construction of one unit capable of housing 600 residents must be built each week for the next 40 years to fill the expected demand. Private companies are building and/or completely renovating apartments and other buildings into senior living centers to begin to meet the demand through private investment and federal programs.

Government Support

Medical costs have risen drastically over the last several years, with costs for seniors accounting for a significant portion. To address and contain these costs and to help improve the quality of life for seniors, the federal government is also expanding the market for living centers. To reduce costs while still providing services, seniors who meet certain eligibility criteria are encouraged to consider assisted-living centers instead of more expensive nursing home care. To accomplish this, two programs have been developed. First, Medicare has developed the PACE program. PACE has an option that allows qualified seniors to receive assistance while remaining in their own homes, adult day health centers, and inpatient facilities.

From the Medicare WEB site:

Program of All Inclusive Care for the Elderly (PACE)

PACE is unique. It is an optional benefit under both Medicare and Medicaid that focuses entirely on older people, who are frail enough to meet their State's standards for nursing home care. It features comprehensive medical and social services that can be provided at an adult day health center, home, and/or inpatient facilities. For most patients, the comprehensive service package permits them to continue living at home while receiving services, rather than be institutionalized. A team of doctors, nurses and other health professionals assess participant needs, develop care plans, and deliver all services, which are integrated into a complete health care plan. PACE is available only in states, which have chosen to offer PACE under Medicaid.[12]

A second program is matching government funding under the HUD Section 202 grants program.[13] This program provides matching funds at an assortment of levels to individuals and companies for supportive housing for the elderly and persons with disabilities. Eligibility requirements apply based primarily on income level.

Several Web sites and other forms of assistance in defining, identifying, and selecting a senior living center and/or determining the level of service needed are available. One site, A Place for Mom,[14] offers a complete and free consulting service and advice to families considering senior living center alternatives.

Development and Ownership of Senior Living Centers

Religious Groups

Senior living center residents do not own their apartments. They are tenants who contract for the space and services they receive. Senior living centers have several types of ownership. Some are owned by religious orders, such as Menorah Park, which is owned by the Jewish Orthodox. Religious-based living centers are operated for members of their religion, and costs can be subsidized by the religion.[15]

Charities and Foundations

Charities and foundations, such as the Bethesda Living Centers owned by the Bethesda Foundation, also own and operate living centers. Like religious owned living centers, resident fees are often subsidized to some degree. Residents generally must meet certain criteria to belong to these living centers, such as income guidelines or specific medical needs.

Private Businesses and Corporations

Private companies and corporations, such as Sunrise Assisted Living, Inc. and Southern Manor Living Centers, LLC, provide a third type of ownership. These are usually for-profit companies supported by private investment, returning dividends or tax deductions to investors, often through Real Estate Investment Trusts or REITs.[16] Government agencies also own retirement centers; however, this type of ownership is declining and most often was limited to nursing homes. As local and state governments cut costs and move toward the privatization of services, many community/government owned senior centers are being sold to private concerns or closed.

For more information please visit any of the sites listed at the end of the chapter providing information and services for seniors or complete an Internet search on your favorite search engine for "Senior Living Centers."

Employment in Living Centers

The Nature of Work in Assisted-Living Centers

By their needs, characteristics, and service to residents, assisted-living centers have career tracks that share many similarities to other hospitality venues. For example, private clubs cater to their members with a few outsiders for the occasional parties. One challenge is to create interesting and creative opportunities for members from menus to activities. Assisted-living centers have this same challenge, a consistent clientele. Therefore, employees must be creative and appreciate the challenges of working with the same people day after day.

Hotels are 24 hour a day, seven day per week operations with on-site residents who may need services at any time. When problems occur, employees must be ready to be pleasant, courteous, and willing to make things better. Assisted-living centers are in the same situation. Problems can be basic needs such as heat, light, and power or more urgent requirements for security or medical emergencies. It is important for people who work in this field to be truly caring people who want to help.

As we mentioned earlier, it is important to be creative because you have the same people all the time. Therefore, events planning and activities are part of the services to meet guest needs. Whether it is a personal event like a birthday or planning special activities and trips, an employee must have the ability to take everyone's needs into consideration when making arrangements. This could include making sure that there are transportation vehicles for everyone to go or planning enough time for people with special needs to be able to enjoy themselves without rushing.

Restaurant operations and management are part of assisted-living centers. Therefore, menus have to be planned, dining rooms must be set up, waitstaff and kitchen staff must be organized. However, whereas restaurant menus have some items that cater to special needs like low calories or low carbs, our menus must include all these and more. Everyone must be able to have a selection to eat. This requires a large knowledge base of medical problems and their dietary needs. In addition, anytime new guests are introduced into the community, the restaurant must make sure that their needs are met as well, even if it is at the last minute.

Resort operations tasks are also part of assisted-living centers including recreation services, grounds maintenance, snow removal, mowing, gardens, and walkways.

Assisted-living centers are diverse places to work. Some centers have residency requirements for managers who may receive living quarters for themselves and their families as part of their job compensation.

Service Coordination

Part of the manager's job is to coordinate multiple services from external providers for the residents. This often includes medical scheduling and doctor visits, pharmacy services, transportation, through self-operated or contracted services, nursing and other medical care, grounds and maintenance issues, ambulatory services, emergency services, including medical emergencies, natural disasters, security issues, and physical plant maintenance and repair. All this involves good planning and scheduling, contacts with different vendors, contract analysis, bidding and procurement systems, a high level of organization, and more.

Positions in Living Centers

Positions in living centers are as varied as the nature of the work. Living centers can provide jobs in many different areas of interest, of which many are hospitality related. Some positions include

- Administrative
  - Executive director
  - General manager
  - Regional director (for multi-unit operations)
  - Purchasing director
  - Information systems
  - Business director
  - Marketing

- Foodservice
  - Food and beverage director
  - Catering manager
  - Nutritionist
  - Executive chef
  - Station chef
  - Cook
  - Dining room manager
  - Host/hostess
  - Server
- Residence
  - Director of residence services
  - Activities director
  - Housekeeping manager
  - Housekeeper
  - Facility maintenance
  - Grounds keeper

Summary

In closing, senior assisted-living centers offer stable careers in a growing and high demand field with jobs similar to those found in a broad assortment of hospitality venues. These positions tend to not have the stress and pressure of other operations, like restaurants, offer good pay and benefits, and are often overlooked by hospitality professionals as solid and stable career choices.

Endnotes

1. Sunrise Senior Living, Inc. (2003). *Sunrise Living Centers*, Retrieved on January 2, 2006, from http://www.sunriseseniorliving.com/Home.do

2. A Place for Mom. (2002). *The search for senior care*, Retrieved December 28, 2005, from http://www.aplaceformom.com/default.htm

3. Sunrise Senior Living, Inc. (2003). *Sunrise Living Centers*, Retrieved on January 2, 2006, from http://www.sunriseseniorliving.com/Home.do

4. Saint Barnabas Health Care Systems, Inc. (1998). *Saint Barnabas Health Care*, Retrieved January 2, 2006, from http://www.saintbarnabas.com/locator/index.html

5. Sunrise Senior Living, Inc. (2003). *Sunrise Living Centers*, Retrieved on January 2, 2006, from http://www.sunriseseniorliving.com/Home.do

6. A Place for Mom. (2002). *The search for senior care*, Retrieved December 28, 2005, from http://www.aplaceformom.com/default.htm

7. Sunrise Senior Living, Inc. (2003). *Sunrise Living Centers*, Retrieved on January 2, 2006, from http://www.sunriseseniorliving.com/Home.do

8. A Place for Mom. (2002). *The search for senior care*, Retrieved December 28, 2005, from http://www.aplaceformom.com/default.htm

9. Bethesda Adult Communities. (2005). *Where life blooms again*, Retrieved December 28, 2005, from http://www.bethesdalivingcenters.org/home/index.cfm?flash=1

10. A Place for Mom. (2002). *The search for senior care*, Retrieved December 28, 2005, from http://www.aplaceformom.com/default.htm

11. U.S. Department of Commerce. (2005). *Census Bureau online*, Retrieved December, 26, 2005, from http://www.census.gov

12. U.S. Department of Health, Education and Welfare. (2005). *Medicare online*, Retrieved December 28, 2005, from http://www.medicare.gov

13. U.S. Department of Housing and Urban Development. (2006). *Section 202 grants*, Retrieved January 7, 2006, from http://www.hud.gov/news/release.cfm?content=pr06-003.cfm

14. A Place for Mom. (2002). *The search for senior care*, Retrieved December 28, 2005, from http://www.aplaceformom.com/default.htm

15. Menorah Park. (2002). *Menorah Park Center for Senior Living online*, Retrieved December, 29, 2005, from http://www.menorahpark.org/

16. Harper, D. (2004). *What are real estate investment trusts (REITs)*, Retrieved January 2, 2006, from http://www.investopedia.com/articles/04/030304.asp

Resources

Internet Sites

Medicare Nursing Homes: http://www.medicare.gov/Nursing/Overview.asp
Medicare Nursing Home Alternatives: http://www.medicare.gov/nursing/alternatives/PaceSites.asp
Saint Barnabas Health Care Systems: http://www.saintbarnabas.com/locator/index.html
Menorah Park Center for Senior Living: http://www.menorahpark.org/
Life Care Centers of America: http://www.lcca.com/
American Senior Living Centers: http://www.aslc.net/
Bethesda Living Centers: http://www.bethesdalivingcenters.org/home/index.cfm?flash=1
Southern Living Centers: http://www.southernlivingcenters.com/
Sunrise Senior Living Centers: http://www.sunriseseniorliving.com/Home.do
Hallmark Senior Communities: http://www.hallmarksenior.com/

Supplemental Reading

A Place for Mom. (2002). *The search for senior care*, Retrieved December 28, 2005, from http://www.aplaceformom.com/default.htm

Bethesda Adult Communities. (2005). *Where life blooms again*, Retrieved December 28, 2005, from http://www.bethesdalivingcenters.org/home/index.cfm?flash=1

Harper, David. (2004). *What are real estate investment trusts (REITs)*, Retrieved January 2, 2006, from http://www.investopedia.com/articles/04/030304.asp

Menorah Park. (2002). *Menorah Park Center for Senior Living online*, Retrieved December 29, 2005, from http://www.menorahpark.org/

Saint Barnabas Health Care Systems, Inc. (1998). *Saint Barnabas Health Care*, Retrieved January 2, 2006, from http://www.saintbarnabas.com/locator/index.html

Sunrise Senior Living, Inc. (2003). *Sunrise Living Centers*, Retrieved on January 2, 2006, from http://www.sunriseseniorliving.com/Home.do

U.S. Department of Commerce. (2005). *Census Bureau online*, Retrieved December 26, 2005, from http://www.census.gov

U.S. Department of Health, Education and Welfare. (2005). *Medicare online*, Retrieved December 28, 2005, from http://www.medicare.gov

U.S. Department of Housing and Urban Development. (2006). *Section 202 Grants*, Retrieved January 7, 2006, from http://www.hud.gov/news/release.cfm?content=pr06-003.cfm

☞ Key Words and Concepts

At-home living
Assisted-living communities
Careers and jobs
Costs and reimbursement
Forms of ownership
Full-care centers/nursing homes
Growth and demand for living centers
Similarities to other hospitality venues
Support services

🖳 Contributor Information

bcberan@syr.edu

Dr. Bradley Beran is the Director of the Hospitality and Food Service Management program at Syracuse University. His background includes a PhD from Syracuse University, an MBA from Northern Michigan University, a BA in Hotel, Restaurant, and Institutional Management from Michigan State University, and a Certificate in Culinary Arts from the Culinary Institute of America. Dr. Beran's experience includes country club management, catering, food sales and marketing, product research, development, and testing, and consulting in the areas of cost control, finance, menu analysis, product development and marketing, hotel development, design, operations, equipment design and testing restaurant planning, and operations. He has worked with assisted-living centers, purveyors, hotels, restaurants, caterers, sports arenas, and other hospitality venues.

36 Review Questions

1. What are the characteristics of a senior for:

   ■ At-home assisted-living

   ■ Assisted-living communities

   ■ Full-care living centers

   ■ Respite care

2. Describe the type of services offered at each of the following:

   ■ At-home assisted-living

   ■ Assisted-living communities

   ■ Full-care living centers

   ■ Respite care

3. What types of support services are provided to members of full-service assisted-living communities?

4. Describe the expected assisted-living potential market and explain what factors contribute to this market.

5. What types of careers and work experiences are available at assisted-living communities?

Patrick T. Tierney
San Francisco State University

Travel Management Companies and Tour Operators

Learning Objectives

✓ To be introduced to services provided by travel management companies and tour operators
✓ To know differences in traditional, contemporary and electronic travel and tour agencies
✓ To learn about consumer trends related to travel bookings and tours
✓ To learn about management issues and techniques
✓ To learn types of jobs in travel management companies and tour operators

Chapter Outline

Travel Management Company Operation
Tour Operators
Future of Travel Management Companies and Tour Operators

*I*ncreasing demand by both domestic and international tourists and the travel industry complexity have led to an increasing desire by many travelers for highly specific travel information, help in making their travel plans, and convenient packages of travel services. Out of these needs have evolved *travel management companies*, including *electronic travel agencies* and *tour operators*. *Travel management company* (TMC) is a more contemporary and accurate term for the new travel agency because it reflects less of a ticketing role and more consulting and management functions that successful agencies now provide. According to a leading travel industry research group Yesawich, Pepperdine, Brown & Russell,[1] travel management companies are shifting into sellers of "complex" and "high risk" travel products and services, such as cruises, all-inclusive vacations, multi-stop tours, and group packages; and away from selling airline tickets. *Travel agents* within a travel management company act to match the travel desires of leisure and business travelers with the most appropriate suppliers of tourist services. Agencies do not normally own the means of production, that is the lodging facilities, restaurants, or attractions that will used by travelers, but act as agents for the suppliers. So what do travel management companies provide? Information to plan an optimal trip; arrange an individualized coordinated itinerary; and secure tickets for transportation, lodging, receptive services, resorts and cruise lines, and recreation attractions. TMCs still play a key role in the travel industry representing about 70 percent of the U.S. travel market sales.[2]

Electronic travel agencies, such as Travelocity.com, have developed from the Internet revolution and communicate entirely via Web sites and e-mail. They do not have physical locations where clients can go, but they employ extensive databases and online booking technology and are open seven days a week and 24 hours per day. They have taken away a significant amount of travel industry sales, especially domestic airline ticketing, and are projected to reach 40 percent of the U.S. travel market by 2007, according to PhoCusWright, a leading Internet research firm.[3]

Tour operators organize complete travel programs for groups or individuals to every continent, by all kinds of transportation modes. Perish the thought of tour operators only offering sedate sightseeing to groups of senior citizens in buses, today there are a vast array of tour itineraries and formats that appeal to youthful and mature audiences alike. Tour operators are different from travel agents and individual suppliers in that they plan, arrange, and market pre-established *packages* at a *set price* that include, to varying degrees, transportation, lodging, educational opportunities, recreation, meals, and entertainment. Many, but not all, tour companies operate substantial portions of the tour package. They make their profit from operations, markup, and/or buying other accommodations, meals, and necessary services at discount rates. Through volume buying power they can offer competitive rates. The importance of the tour industry is underscored by the fact that residents of the United States and Canada spent a total of approximately $166 billion on packaged tours worldwide.[4]

Travel Management Company Operation

In 1867 Thomas Cooke introduced the first hotel coupon and started the travel agency business. The modern travel agency era really began with the advent of the airline industry in the 1960s. Since that time the number, roles, and types of travel agencies have mushroomed. Some travel agencies specialize in one type of travel service, whereas others, as exemplified by the country's largest travel agency conglomerate, American Express, are active in multiple markets. Over 85 percent of travel agencies today are considered small independently owned businesses. Most (57 percent) TMCs are single-location businesses but over half (73 percent) are affiliated with or buy the services of a consortium or association. The average independent TMC receives 68 percent of their revenue from leisure sales (see Figure 37.1), 25 percent from business, and 7 percent from combination business and leisure buyers.

Types of Travel Agencies

Corporate Agencies

Those agencies specialize in serving business clients, often with little or no walk-in clientele. They cater to corporations on the telephone or through e-mail, often working under contracts that provide for exclusivity but also require the return of a portion of the normal travel agent commission or on a fee-based arrangement. They rely heavily on revenue from airline tickets, hotel rooms, and rental cars.

Figure 37.1 ‖ Sources of Travel Management Company Revenue, 2005

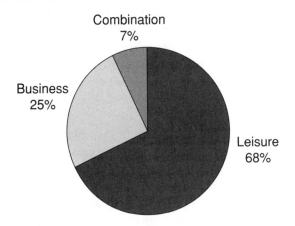

Source: Travel Weekly.com. October 27, 2005

Leisure Agencies

Tourists going on vacation are the primary clients of this agency. Clients have traditionally gone to the agency office to discuss options and to look at brochures and videos. This business relies heavily on cruise sales, resort packages, airline tickets, rental cars, tours, and hotel room sales.

Wholesalers

These organizations sell primarily to travel agents and not to the general public. They organize and promote specific types of travel services, but do not operate the tours or facilities. Wholesalers contract with suppliers for blocks of tickets or rooms in anticipation of future sales.

Specialized Leisure Agencies

A growing trend in the travel agency business is shops that specialize in one category of leisure product, such as cruise or drive agencies, or in one region of the world. By limiting what they sell, these agents can become experts on unique products, services, and destinations.

Incentive Travel Houses

These agencies develop customized programs for corporations who offer incentives for high employee productivity by providing deluxe travel rewards. They set up and administer reward contests, inform

eligible staff, and contract with suppliers. Incentive agencies earn their profits from supplier commissions and management fees.

Consolidators

These are businesses that purchase large blocks of airline seats or cruise berths at a substantial discount and resell them to travel agents or the general public for a lower than normal fare. They may also have contracts with certain airlines for larger commissions on certain routes. Consolidators, also known as "Bucket Shops," advertise to the public in the travel sections of metropolitan newspapers, whereas others deal exclusively with travel agents.

Electronic Travel Agencies

As a result of the Internet revolution and communication advances, a growing number of companies sell travel products entirely via Web sites. There are no human travel agents to talk with, and they do not have physical locations where clients can go, but they employ extensive databases, and online booking technology. Some electronic travel agencies are independently owned, like Travelocity,[6] whereas others are owned and/or controlled by the airlines, such as Orbitz.[7] Initially these businesses only offered airline tickets, but now they offer a wide range of travel services and have moved aggressively into booking hotel rooms and rental cars.

How Travel Management Companies Get Paid

Because TMCs do not own the facilities or equipment used to operate destination services, they are paid only when they make a sale. Payment is in the form of a commission, based on a percentage of the sale price, or increasingly payment is by an additional ticketing charge. The cost of the agent commission was built into the sales price so in the past it did not cost the consumer more to use the travel agent than if they went direct to the supplier. Commissions historically have been about 10 percent for airline tickets and other services, but on February 9, 1995, Delta Airlines announced it would pay travel agents no more than $25 on any one-way domestic ticket. Since then all major U.S. airlines have discontinued paying commissions on domestic flights altogether. The main exception to this no-commission policy is where the airlines and large travel agencies have a preferred-provider contract that allows for a small commission. In contrast to the airlines, other segments of the travel industry, such as cruise lines announced at the same time it would increase its travel agent commission from 10 percent to 12 percent. The end result has been that more travel agencies are seeking other sources of revenue besides the sales of airline tickets, such as commissions from cruise lines, tours, resorts, and international air carriers. In fact, many travel suppliers offer agents *over-ride commissions* of an additional 2 percent to 5 percent to encourage group sales or to introduce new travel products or services. A large number of agencies have diversified and are starting to develop and market their own tour packages, others like Corniche Travel has also started an event planning company.[8] Still other experienced agents charge *hourly fees* for the time they spend developing complex customized vacation packages. A *ticketing fee* of from $15 to $40 in addition to airline ticket price is being charged customers by an increasing number of agencies. Even electronic travel agencies are charging a ticketing fee. For example, Expedia.com has a $5 ticketing fee, but they show it in the ticket price, rather than as a separate charge. Another way to increase profits has been by reducing their operational costs through increased automation. TMCs offer their own online booking, and many use "robotics" software programs that handle automated ticketing, check for compliance with corporate travel policies, and e-mail a complete

itinerary. Lastly, more travel agents are quoting lower fares to consumers than the public can find on the Internet by becoming or using consolidators.

Certainly one of the most desired benefits of being a travel agent is discount travel to destinations worldwide. Suppliers wanting to promote new travel services are often willing to provide familiarization trips at little or no cost to agents. Airlines, cruise lines, and resorts provide very low cost tickets or ticket class upgrades. An inclusive five-day stay at a new resort in Brazil for only the cost of taxes, for example, is a unique opportunity available to travel agents. These benefits tend to make up for the rather low wages that travel agents receive, which average about $40,000 per year for an agent with three years of experience. Some agents are paid a monthly salary, some only commission, others a combination of these. So persons considering becoming a travel agent must weigh their financial goals against the excitement and low cost of travel that are available to agents.

From the outside a travel agency in your neighborhood appears to be a lucrative, if not glamorous, business. But increasing competition from larger agencies with volume discounts and lower overhead, electronic travel agencies, the Internet (see following section), elimination of airline commissions, and generally increasing costs of doing business have resulted in low profitability, distressed sales, and business failures, especially small inde-

One of the most desired benefits of being a travel agent is discount travel.

pendent neighborhood companies. To increase profitability, three-quarters of TMCs have joined consortiums, groups of agencies that combine strength to negotiate lower rates for clients and higher commissions for their agencies. A member agency is often required to use a limited number of *preferred providers* who have contracts with the consortium. With such contracts the agency must offer a fare quote from their preferred supplier first, but can sell to any supplier the consumer wishes.

Automation and Certification

Precise accurate information on schedules, availability, and rates is critical for a travel agent to know, but the scope and amount of information on the global travel industry is overwhelming. Therefore, computerized databases are a basic tool of the travel agent. *Global Destination Systems* (GDS), such as Apollo, Sabre, World Span, and Amadeus, list over 12 million fares, a quarter of which are updated daily. These systems were started by airlines and at one time carried just airline schedules and inventory, but today they have become full-scale travel information systems that also contain lodging, tours, and attraction information. Effective data search and ticketing with a GDS are critical skills for agents.

To be able to issue domestic tickets, an agency must be approved by the *Airlines Reporting Corporation* (ARC). This organization is an association of U.S. airlines who facilitate funds transfer and ensure that travel agencies have experienced management. For sale of international airline tickets, a travel agency may also be approved by the *International Airlines Travel Agent Network* (IATAN), who has similar responsibilities to the ARC. These licensing agreements limit companies who can sell travel to legitimate businesses and help protect the consumer from fraud. Individual travel agents must show proper identification to receive travel discounts and promotions. The most accepted form of credential is a photo identification card issued by IATAN. Some travel agencies, but not all, require that their senior agents be a *Certified Travel Counselor* (CTC). The later credential, issued by the Institute of Certified Travel Agents, is awarded to persons who pass rigorous examinations and have five years full-time experience in a travel agency.

Although the full-time in-office travel agent will continue to be the backbone of any TMC, there are a growing number of *Outside Sales Agents* (OSA) who are affiliated with the company, but are independent contractors not employees. The OSA provides work at their home, provides their own telephone, and pays employment taxes, but shares commissions with their affiliated agency.

Information Revolution

Travel agencies no longer have exclusive access to the myriad schedules, fares, and destination information that are found in a GDS. One of the most popular types of sites on the World Wide Web provides travel ticketing. The electronic travel agency Travelocity,[9] for example, allows booking reservations on most domestic and international flights for a $5 booking fee. It also has content on destinations, an area where viewers can ask questions about travel providers, and a shopping "mall" with specialized travel merchandise for sale. Suppliers have also embraced the Internet as a way to lower their travel sales distribution costs. Hilton Hotels, for instance, was one of the first lodging chains to place all its properties world-wide on the Internet.[10] Travelers themselves, especially business travelers, have gone directly to supplier Web sites, bypassing the middle organization. Obviously, this type of free service is in direct competition with some of the services that both traditional and electronic travel agencies have provided. The travel agency business has been undergoing a radical transformation due to changes brought on by the Internet and air carrier payment policies.

But the Internet revolution is also threatening other "middle men," and it is leading the push toward a more direct consumer–supplier link. For example, in January 1999 Delta Airlines announced that it will require anyone not booking directly with only the Delta Web site to pay a $2.00 per ticket surcharge. Subsequently, Delta and other airlines have backed off requiring surcharges, but instead are offering lower priced "Internet only" fares to drive traffic to their Web sites. The percentage of travelers viewing fare information and booking through the Internet continues to grow, and this suggests further changes in the travel services sales and distribution system in the future.

Tour Operators

The most basic functions of a tour operator are to bundle together a *package* of travel services, offer it at a fixed price, and provide some or all of the services during a tour itinerary. To develop and operate exciting and safe tour programs the tour operator staff must have a very good understanding of what consumers desire, outstanding knowledge of destinations, keen negotiating skills to secure reasonable supplier prices, sophisticated marketing skills, exceptional guides, a strict trip budget, and a well-constructed risk management plan for each tour. They usually provide and operate transportation equipment, such as a motorcoach, van, raft, or ship. Describing exactly what a tour operator offers can be tricky because there are many types of tours. Following is a listing of the most common tour formats.

In a *group tour* clients travel with a number of individuals sharing similar interests and have the potential for substantial savings and unique opportunities. *Escorted tours* offer a professional guide who remains with a tour group for the entire package. This escort takes care of travel problems that may arise and usually is knowledgeable about the culture and natural history of the area being traversed. A fully *inclusive tour* provides everything that a traveler will need for a set price, except for shopping, gambling, and personal needs. This type of tour is the most convenient because the escort facilitates and pays for all included services.

A *foreign independent tour* or *FIT* is a travel package that normally includes some lodging and a rental car or train pass, but they are not just to foreign countries. It can also include airline tickets and specialty recreation activities, like rafting trips or attraction admissions. The traveler is independent when it comes to travel and must get from destination to destination on their own by driving a rental car or catching trains and buses.

A *fly-drive package* is a common tour in the United States and includes flights, motels, and a rental car. Mass marketing companies, such as Pleasant Hawaiian Holidays, specialize in this type of tour. Such a package allows the traveler to enjoy volume discounts but have the freedom to travel where they wish in between specific meeting dates.

Types of Tour Operators

The escalating demands of sophisticated travelers and the competitive nature of the travel industry have resulted in the tour operator business becoming more specialized with many types of tour services. Some companies engage in only a narrow niche in the tour market, such as Adrift Adven-

Rafting tour, Green River, Dinosaur National Monument, Utah.

tures, a white-water rafting outfitter in Jensen, Utah,[11] whereas other large organizations, such as Maupintour,[12] operate tours throughout the world via multiple transportation modes. To further confuse things, some air carriers and travel management companies also act as tour operators. Described are the most well recognized types of tour operators.

Wholesale Tour Company

Arranges and promotes tour packages, but sells them primarily to travel agents or international tour operators, and not the general public. They often do not operate any portion of the tour. Marketing to the travel trade is one of the strengths of this type of firm. Revenues come primarily from markup of tours they represent.

Receptive Operator

This type of company, also called a ground operator, may meet and greet groups at airports, make arrangements for lodging, and shuttle them to the lodging at one particular destination. They also frequently offer foreign language interpreters, sightseeing tours, or step-on guides.

Specialty Travel Tour Operators

Organizations who possess highly specialized equipment and guides for unique tours, such as diving, rafting, biking, and photography programs. Tours may be geared toward adventure and risk activities, nature or eco-tourism, skills development, or simply sightseeing in unique settings. Clients are often younger than for other tours, averaging 40 years old.

Motorcoach Tour Operators

These companies own and operate deluxe motorcoaches holding up to 52 passengers, with some costing over $250,000. Sightseeing via a motorcoach is still the most popular and economical tour both domestically and internationally. Operators may provide long-distance or local tours, with and without narration. Some motorcoaches have two levels for sightseeing and sleeping on-board; others have bars, and gambling tables.

Types of Jobs with a Tour Operator

Tour Escort/Guide

The tour guide job provides exciting opportunities to enter the travel profession and for a career traveling the globe. This occupation can require the skills of a teacher, entertainer, accountant, doctor, and psychologist. Tour conductor and guide schools provide training and certification to get a start in the field. Guides lead everything from adventure travel, like rowing a raft through the Grand Canyon, to sightseeing tours in the wine country of Italy.

Operations Manager

This professional manages the logistics of equipment and staff scheduling, as well as coordination with other suppliers. This person must also be proficient in budgeting. He or she works primarily in the office and not on the road.

Tour Planner

Designing a new tour, contracting with appropriate suppliers, testing the itinerary, and costing the program are the duties of a tour planner. This person must be in touch with changing client wants and supplier status. Such a position usually involves a balance between business travel and office work.

Sales and Marketing Manager

He or she works with key trade industry and client accounts and develops promotions directed at consumers. They must be very familiar with company services and the competition. Personal sales skills are very important in this position.

Future of Travel Management Companies and Tour Operators

Despite being battered by global changes in the marketplace, travel management companies and tour operators will continue to provide needed services to business and leisure clients in the future. Undoubtedly, there will be consolidation through attrition and independent agencies joining consortiums. Travel agencies have shifted away from their traditional dependence on domestic airline ticket sales and look for more profitable opportunities, as consumers are better able to book flights directly, and revenues from commissions decline. More agencies will rely on outside sales associates to reduce employment costs and enlarge their reach in the marketplace. The shear magnitude of travel services available and the need for expert advice will continue to push small agencies to specialize and large firms to hire agents who are experts in a segment of the industry.

The rebound in U.S. and global economies in 2004–2005, the lack of other highly publicized airplane hijackings after the tragic events of September 11, 2001, at the World Trade Center in New York, more sophisticated marketing, and the increasing use of technology to lower costs has resulted in growth for many larger TMC organizations. Most industry analysts agree that there will be continued consolidation in the industry, but TMCs and tour operators will not disappear because they add value through personalized service and are increasingly savvy businesses. Many people with Internet hookups, simply do not have the time or desire to conduct an extensive search of the Internet, and these folks will continue to look to travel agents for assistance with lengthy and expensive travel plans. Others will still value the specialized expertise that experienced agents possess. The days of agents simply being "order takers" are nearly gone, and they are being quickly replaced by true *travel consultants*. Revenue growth in electronic travel agencies will continue, and this will provide exciting opportunities for sales, programming and operations jobs with these companies.

Tour operators will need to design new tours that cater to changing customer demands, such as family travel, more independence, and participation. Aging of the population will provide expanding opportunities for senior travel, served by new and exciting tour programs. Demand for eco-tourism and other specialty travel tours are predicted to experience rapid growth. But managers will need to contend with increased access restrictions and regulations. They must develop ways to assure clients their deposits are secure and satisfaction guaranteed.

Summary

Travel by U.S. and international residents has recovered from the September 11, 2001, events in New York, and by 2006 it is booming. Travel management companies and tour operators provide needed services and are well positioned to increase sales. But both will have to reduce overhead and increase profitability. Enlightened TMC and tour operator managers see substantial future business opportunities, although the way they conduct their affairs will need to evolve to keep pace with changing consumer demands and technological changes.

Endnotes

1. Yesawich, Pepperdine, Brown & Russell. 2005. "Ten Trends to Watch in the Year Ahead." In http://ehotier.com/browse/news_more_.pdp?id=D721301100M. December 30, 2005
2. PhoCusWright. 2006. "U.S. Online Travel Market Fueled by Supplier Sites, Though Growth Slows." Press release at http://www.phocuswright.com/press/releases.php, dated November 28, 2005
3. PhoCusWright. 2006. "U.S. Online Travel Market Fueled by Supplier Sites, Though Growth Slows." Press release at http://www.phocuswright.com/press/releases.php, dated November 28, 2005
4. National Tour Association. 2001. "2001 Packaged Travel In North America." Lexington, Kentucky
5. Travel Weekly. 2005. "Travel Agencies are Solo, Small and Selling Hard." In www.travelweekly.com, October 27, 2005
6. www.travelocity.com
7. www.orbitz.com
8. Terro, Ruthanne. 2005. "Anastasia's Way: Corniche Travel Carves an Artful Path Through the Word of Luxury." *Luxury Travel Advisor*, October, 2005
9. www.travelocity.com
10. www.hilton.com
11. www.adrift.com
12. www.maupintour.com

Resources

Internet Sites

Adrift Adventures: www.adrift.com
American Society of Travel Agents: www.asta.org
PhoCusWright Travel Research: www.phocuswright.com
National Tour Association: www.nta.org

☛ Key Words and Concepts

Airlines reporting corporation—A non-profit organization representing U.S. airlines that facilitates funds transfer between suppliers and agents and ensures that travel agencies have experienced management through licensing.

Consolidators—Businesses that purchase large blocks of airline seats or cruise berths at a substantial discount and resell them to travel agents or the public at lower than normal fare.

Electronic travel agencies—Providing extensive information and on-line ticketing via the Internet.

Foreign independent tour (FIT)—A travel package that normally includes airfare, lodging, and some recreational activities, but is not necessarily just in foreign countries. The traveler is independent when it comes to travel and must get from destination to destination on their own by driving a rental car or catching trains and buses.

Global destination systems—Powerful database systems, such as Apollo, Sabre, and Amadeus, that list and offer ticketing for millions of air, hotel, and rental car services and provide world-wide attraction information.

Incentive travel houses—These agencies develop customized programs for corporations who offer incentives to induce high employee productivity by providing deluxe travel rewards.

Outside sales agents—Individual who is affiliated with the travel agency, acting as an independent contractor, not employee, who sells travel products and shares commissions with their affiliated agency.

Preferred providers—Agencies sign contract with specific suppliers to try and sell their services first and in return receive a large sales commission.

Receptive operator—A company may meet and greet groups at airports, make arrangements for lodging, and shuttle them to the lodging at one particular destination and offer foreign language interpreters.

Sales commission—A percentage of the sales price paid by the supplier to the agent on the purchase of a travel product or service.

Ticketing fee—An additional charge above the base cost of the ticket that is charged by a TMC to cover their ticketing costs.

Tour escort—A person who travels with a group and acts as guide and business manager, using the skills of a teacher, entertainer, accountant, doctor, and psychologist.

Tour operators—Organize market and operate packages of travel services with a variety of themes, ranging from adventure to sightseeing, for groups or individuals.

Travel agent—Individuals within a travel management company that match and ticket the travel desires of leisure and business travelers with most appropriate suppliers of tourist services.

Travel management company—A contemporary term for travel agencies that provide consulting, ticketing, and management of travel products for leisure and business travelers.

Contributor Information

Patrick Tierney received a PhD in recreation resources with a concentration in tourism from Colorado State University in 1991. Currently he has a joint appointment in the Departments of Hospitality Management and Recreation-Leisure Studies at San Francisco State University, where he is a professor teaching classes in recreation, tourism, travel management, resort management, and eco-tourism. Dr. Tierney is also actively involved in tourism research. He is recipient of the 1997 Best Tourism Research Award from the California Division of Tourism, the 1991 Excellence In Research Award from the Commercial Recreation and Resort Association, as well as co-recipient of the 1990 Colorado Rural Tourism Achievement Award.

In addition to his academic pursuits he is actively involved in tourism, through being co-owner, for 25 years, of Adrift Adventures, an eco-tourism adventure recreation business offering summer white-water learning adventure vacations in Colorado, Utah, and Alaska. Pat serves on the Board of Directors of the California Travel Industry Association and the Board of the Bay Area Partners in Responsible Tourism.

37 Review Questions

1. What is the name of the privately operated global ticketing system used extensively by travel agents for airline tickets? Why are these organizations so important to travel management companies?

2. An FIT package usually includes what services and products?

3. Can anyone sell airline tickets? What are two organizations that have a licensing requirement for a company to be able to sell domestic and international airline tickets?

4. What is the difference between travel agencies who are primarily order takers, in comparison to travel consultants?

5. Why have travel management companies shifted from "order takers" to travel consultants and managers?

6. Are tours just for seniors on motorcoach-based sightseeing trips? What types of tours are available in major tourist destinations?

Glossary

A la Carte—Every item on the menu is priced independently, including side items and salads

AAHOA—Asian American Hotel Owners Association

ABC—The Alcoholic Beverage Commission; the state agency that enforces restrictions on methods and hours of operation, records, and expansion, concerning the sale and service of alcohol

Academic Freedom—The educator has the right to teach as he/she sees fit

ACF—American Culinary Federation

ACPHA—The Accreditation Commission for Programs in Hospitality Administration; evaluates and awards accreditation to four-year programs

Aft—Rear of the ship

AHLA—American Hotel and Lodging Association

AIA—American Institute of Architects

Ambience—The overall décor, sound, lighting, and furniture of an establishment

Americans with Disabilities Act—A law that calls for "reasonable" accommodations for both employees and customers who are functionally challenged; became law on July 26, 1990

Amusement Parks—A collection of rides and food stands located in one central area; most of the time each ride requires its own ticket or admission fee

Anti-Gaming Advocates—Those individuals who protest against gaming and try to deter people from voting for gaming

Appraisers—Professionals who are trained to value land and buildings, hired to render estimates of value

Apprenticeship—The European model for training chefs, where a chef gains employment and through the tutelage of the chefs on premises hones one's skills and progresses through the ranks of a single kitchen

ARDA—American Resort Development Association began in 1969

ASID—American Society of Interior Designers

Assisted-Living Centers—Centers for senior citizens that offer more services and moderate costs (medications, meals, transportation); designed for the senior residents that cannot fully live on their own, but do not need full care

Associations—A body that is made up of individual, organizational, and allied or affiliated members, who are drawn together to promote and develop a specific industry through a variety of services (including continuing education) and benefits to the membership

ASTA—American Society of Travel Agents formed in 1931

Audit—Another individual checking the cash handling often of a subordinate

Autonomy—The ability to work well and productively yet primarily alone; make decisions with little to no supervision

Bacchus—The Roman god of wine and indulgence

Back-of-the-House—Refers to positions whose worksite is removed from the customers' view

Bag Drop—A location where golf assistants help golfers unload golf bags from their cars and place them in waiting golf carts

Balance Sheet—Measures the flow of money, showing a business's net worth; it shows total assets, total liabilities, and owner's equity; shows the performance of a business at a snapshot in time

Balance—A delicate mixture of your time spent at work and off; one needs to spend enough time at work to succeed and achieve personal goals, but time off work is important to maintain good health and get sufficient exercise and rest

Base Fee—A percentage of total revenue paid by the host organization to the management company; trends show these are declining

Bed and Breakfast Inns—Started in the early 1800s as overnight stays in private homes

Benefits—Traditionally a motivational tool, though now often expected; often includes health insurance, vacation pay, sick time off with pay, dental insurance, retirement, 401k plans, etc.

Berth—A sufficient distance for maneuvering a ship; also a place to sit and sleep on a ship

Blind Spot—"When you don't know what it is that you don't know"; can be a handicap to people in their careers, especially if there is limited feedback

Bow—Front of the ship

Brand Identification—The symbol or trademark of a company, which consumers recognize, such as the swoosh of Nike or the golden arches of McDonald's

Branding—Taking a known brand, like McDonald's or Pizza Hut, and opening that facility in a hospital, B&I, or school

Brokers—A professional who serves as an intermediary in a real estate sales transaction

Cages—Mini banks within a casino

CAHM—The Commission for Accreditation of Hospitality Management; evaluates and awards accreditation to two-year programs

Capital—Money used to build a new business venture, or make long-term improvements

Captain—The top leader, person in charge, of the ship

Captive Foodservice—Where the customer has little or no choice in his/her decision to pay for and consume the food services; examples are elementary schools, hospitals

Career Fair—An event where many recruiters come together on a college or university campus to meet and interview students for employment opportunities—often internships and entry-level management

Cash Handling Procedures—The proper way an employee is trained to handle cash transactions

Catering—The service of food for a group of people coming together for a reason, may be on-premise (at the site where the food was prepared) or off-premise (when the food is prepared at one location and served at a different location)

Chains—Often referred to as multi-unit operations; a business with three or more separate outlets bearing the same name, concept style of service and systems of operation

Chief Purser—The position responsible for accounting, personnel services, and the concessions

Chief Steward—The position that is responsible for the dining room and food services

Chips—Small round plastic disks used in lieu of money

CHRIE—International Council on Hotel, Restaurant, and Institutional Education

CIC—Convention Industry Council, founded in 1949; provides the CMP (Certified Meeting Planner) designation

City Clubs—Establishments that are in urban areas and cater to the businessmen or women, provides dining services and occasionally athletic events

Civil Rights Act—A law signed in 1964 that prohibits discrimination on the basis of race, color, religion, sex, or national origin

Classification by Location—The lodging industry can be classified many ways including the location of the property: City Hotels, Suburban Hotels, Highway Hotels/Motels, Airport Hotels

Classification by Price—The lodging industry can be classified many ways including the price likely to be paid for one night stay at that property: Luxury and Deluxe Hotels, Midmarket and Commercial Hotels, Budget and Economy Hotels

Classification by Service—The lodging industry can be classified many ways including the degree of services to be found at that property: Luxury Hotels and Resorts, Deluxe Hotels, Midmarket Hotels and Commercial Hotels, Full-Service Hotels, Limited-Service Hotels, All-Suite Hotels/Extended Stay Hotels

Classification by Unique Characteristics—The lodging industry can be classified many ways including the types of facilities: Bed and Breakfast Hotels, Casino Hotels, Convention Hotels, Residential Hotels, Resort Hotels

CLIA—Cruise Line International Association

Club—A group of persons organized for social, literary, athletic, political, recreational or other purposes

CMAA—Club Managers Association of America formed in 1920

Coffee Shops—These restaurants provide waiter/waitress service, larger menu variety, and service takes longer; open more hours and more days of the week than any other restaurant concept

Coles Ordinary—The first American tavern, opened in 1634; the term "ordinary" soon changed to "inn"

Commercial Kitchen Designers—Professionals who provide planning and drawings of commercial kitchens, and specify equipment

Communication Skills—The ability of one to spell well and clearly, and write succinctly and correctly

Comparative Negligence—Where a jury or judge must determine the percentage of fault applicable to the parties in a negligence action to apportion financial liability

Comps—Free enticements given to gamblers while in the casino to encourage more or repeated play at a later date; usually includes free meals, room nights, or special event tickets

Conceptual Skills—The ability to see the company or department as a whole and understand how the different parts work together

Connectivity—The fact that many business systems or units are now connected electronically and can communicate with relative ease, regardless of geographic location

Consolidation—Often the result of buy-outs and takeovers, several (what were) independent businesses are merged together within the same company

Consolidators—Businesses that purchase large blocks of airline seats or cruise berths at a substantial discount and resell them to travel agents or the general public for a lower than normal fare

Consultant—An individual who has a specific skill set or area of expertise and is compensated for providing advice or other services to a client

Contract Management—When a mutually binding legal document has been negotiated between the operator who furnishes management services and the owner who pays for these services

Contractors—The professional builder of the project

Control—Comparing the performance of employees in a workforce against the objectives and goals that have been set by the company

Controlling the Money—The focus of casino management; securing the flow of cash; uses computers, accounting departments, security and surveillance

Convention Hotels—Those hotels with added features such as the removal of interior posts, barrier-free space, flexible walls, blackout window treatments, and improved lighting

Conversion Rate—The percentage of Web visitors that actually buy a product online

Core Menu—The main "signature" item line of a restaurant, such as pizza, hamburgers, roast beef

Costs—The outflow of dollars

Country Clubs—Hospitality establishments that provide elaborate social events, offer dining, pool, tennis and golf

Creativity—The leading core characteristic that research has shown is vital in determining success or failure of an entrepreneur; the ability to create innovative ideas sets one business apart from the others

Cruise Director—The position that is responsible for securing and procuring continuous entertainment for the ship

Cruise Ship Market—A major segment of the travel and tourism industry, which has increased more than 800 percent from 1970 to 2000

Cultural Attractions—Anything made by humans that draws people to it; sites set up to preserve or further the culture of the community

Customer Relationship Management—Software that enables the company to track customers' preferences, enhancing their hospitality experience and ultimately increasing the customers' loyalty to the brand

Daily Fee Course—These are golf courses that are privately owned, but open to the public, and require a fee be paid for each round of golf

Development Costs—Those costs associated with the land, the building, the furnishings, and the equipment necessary for operation of the restaurant

Dinner House—Waiter/waitress service is provided, more upscale, menu variety and better service is received, open for lunch and dinner

Dionysus—The Greek god of wine

Direct Marketing—Sales force reaches potential customers through personal interactions and increasingly through technology

Discretionary Dollars—Those that the customer has a choice about spending; vacation and resort revenues are typically from a person's discretionary dollars

Distribution Services—The chain of operational products that are produced, handled by a middleman, then delivered to the operator

Domestic—Within the country

Dram Shop Laws—Laws that impose penalties on the establishment if guests leave intoxicated and are involved in an accident

Drop—Total amount of cash plus the value of the markers (credit slips) the casino takes in

E-Business—Companies that expand the use of technologies to include all major stakeholders in their business: customers, employees, management, government, business partners, bankers, suppliers/vendors, and stockholders. The focus is on synergy, integration, and collaboration.

E-Commerce—Focuses only on the customers and suppliers and the transactions with them that occur online; is concerned with enabling and successfully completing sales transactions online efficiently

86ed—When the operation has run out of an item; a slang term

Emergency Maintenance—Breakdowns that are unpredictable and often expensive; requires immediate attention of maintenance and engineering

Empowerment—Where a contemporary leader has created the organizational work environment in which staff members are trained in necessary skills, and management delegates a certain degree of power and decision-making authority to the employees, often on the front line; to establish ownership in the position and organization, and ultimately better achieve the company's goals—usually improving guest service; management must support the decisions made by the staff members

Energy Management—The effective management that monitors both consumption and costs of energy, and climatic conditions

Enterprise Resource Management—Inventory management software that manages information across the enterprise so that the same information is available to all parties

Entrepreneur—Someone who starts, manages, and assumes the risks and rewards of a new business enterprise; he/she also strives to achieve business growth and possible expansion into new markets or geographic locations

E-Procurement System—When purchasing transactions are conducted in an electronic environment, such as the Internet

Equity Clubs—Those facilities owned by their membership, are nonprofit; oldest form of clubs

Ethics—A set of principles that managers apply when interacting with people and their organizations; fair and equal treatment, truth, lack of bias, consistency, and respect of others

Expatriate—A foreign citizen

Extended Stay—A segment of the lodging industry, which accounts for most of the new construction of properties built from 1998–2001; consumers want the luxuries of home in space and design

Fabricators—These companies take one or more manufactured products and "assemble" them or add more "value" by creating a new product; sometimes called processors

Fast Food—The traditional name for QSRs, limited menu, counter service, so the consumer is served their food very quickly

Feedback—The exchange of words, used often to provide praise, or constructive remarks

FF and E—An abbreviation for furniture, fixtures, and equipment

Fine Dining—Dinner only typically, very formal waiter/waitress service; often used for special occasions

Fiscal—Financial; often used as "fiscal year" for financial records

"Fit"—What you and potential employers want to know—do your values line up with their organization, and how successful will you be in their work environment

Food/Beverage—One of the four major subdivisions of hospitality and tourism, this segment includes taverns, restaurants, bars, catering, and vending

Food Cost—The cost of the food being prepared

Food Quality—The utmost expectation of a chef, food quality must taste good, be appealing to the eye, and appeal to the specific customers of the business

Foursome—A term used to describe the golfing party; usually four people

Franchise System—Comprised of properties that have the same name and design, but are owned and operated by different parties; this group is characterized by tight performance standards; and where the franchisee pays a fee to open and operate a unit

Franchise—Owned by an individual (the franchisee) who pays for the rights to operate, including the operating systems, standardized policies and procedures, and agrees to maintain the performance standards of the larger group (the franchisor)

Franchising—The process of selling a "prepackaged" brand of restaurant or hotel to an entrepreneur for a fee

Full Membership—Entitles a member to full use of the club, all amenities during any hour of operation

Full-Service Living Centers—These centers are more commonly known as nursing homes, they provide full services (medical, personal care—bathing, etc.) for senior citizens who cannot care for themselves, high cost; designed for the most needy senior resident

Fusion—The blending together of two traditionally different styles

Gaming—The industry built around gambling; casino industry; generates huge money for state government

GCSA—Golf Course Superintendents Association of America

Generalist—One who provides a broad range of services to their clients

GOLF 20/20—The golf industry's initiative committed to growing the game of golf

Golf Professional—The head of the golf department; oversees the pro shop, gives lessons, manages golf tournaments, usually is PGA certified

Golf Superintendent—The professional who is educated in agronomy and oversees the care of the golf course and surrounding property

Grill Room—An informal dining facility in the club house where golf attire is appropriate

Gross Registered Tonnage (GRT)—A classification for ships that gauges the volume of public space; the greater the GRT the greater number of passengers it can carry

Halfway House—A small food and beverage facility that serves food between the "front nine" holes and the "back nine" holes of golf

HAMA—Hotel Asset Managers Association

Hard Products—Products sold online, often outside the hospitality industry, which must be physically shipped to the buyer, such as chemicals or apparel

Haute Cuisine—A high-end, lavish style of cooking, elegantly prepared and served

High Rollers—People who gamble large amounts of money at the tables, the target market profile of a casino

High Season—When demand is at its peak

Hospitality—An environment of friendliness, warmth, cheer, graciousness, and conviviality

House—The particular casino; chips from one casino may not be used at another casino

Hub-and-Spoke System—A system created by the airlines after deregulation, where a carrier has a "hub" in certain cities in which most flights pass through

Human Resource Management—The management of people, who work for the organization, includes recruiting, training, maintaining extensive records, and ensuring all workforce laws are adhered to

HVAC—The heating, ventilation, and air-conditioning system; delivers heating and cooling on demand while maintaining the proper humidity and air quality

IAAPA—International Association of Amusement Parks and Attractions founded in 1918

ICCA—The International Congress and Convention Association founded in 1965

IFMA—The International Facility Management Association

Impersonal Marketing—Sales force reaches potential customers through marketing promotional tools such as advertising or public relations

Incentive and Special Event Producers—Usually sponsored by corporations are reward-based programs for top employees; utilize resorts, tours, and recreation facilities, with a high degree of social interaction

Incentive Fees—A fee based on performance improvement(s) after at least a year, usually a percentage of the amount over a specific goal, paid by the host organization to the management company

Income Statement—Also known as the profit and loss report; although the format may vary, it includes a record of accounts including: total sales, cost of goods sold, gross profit, expenses, taxes, and net income

Independent Living Centers—Centers for senior citizens that offer few services and the lowest cost (lawn care, housekeeping); designed for the most independent senior resident

Independent Operations—Owned and operated by an individual or group of individual investors; owns one or two operations and enjoys greater business decision-making freedom than that of the franchisee; a person who maintains a limit to the size and scope of the business operation; the owner directs a business that has no affiliation with any other facilities or operations

Indirect Marketing—Sales force reaches potential customers through wholesale intermediaries, such as tour operators or meeting planners, who in turn sell to retail travel agencies or the customer

Institutional Foodservice—A term no longer used, now called contract food services

Intellectual Capital—The combined knowledge of all knowledge workers (employees) working to improve a business, thinking outside the box

Interior Designers—Professionals that design interior spaces involving materials, finishes, colors, space planning, and layout

Intermediaries—These are distributors, wholesalers, suppliers, dealers, purveyors, and vendors that buy products from manufacturers and sell them to hospitality and tourism providers; sometimes called middlemen

International Exchange Agreements—Articulation agreements between two schools or universities that allow its student to attend the other school, in a different country, and receive credit toward graduation

International—Outside one's home country; within many countries

Interpersonal Skills—The ability to understand people and work well with them on an individual basis and in groups

Interval-Ownership Properties—Property developers sell a fraction of a designated space, such as a 30-day slice or 7-day slice of a condominium

Job Analysis—The process to determine the tasks and skills necessary to complete the job

Job Descriptions—A tool used to identify the purpose, duties, and conditions under which jobs are performed

Job Design—Determines how the job is organized, and how it can be planned to provide both productivity to the organization and job satisfaction to the employee

Job Specifications—The qualifications, knowledge, and skills necessary to perform the position

Just-in-Time—When an item of inventory (food, airline seat, hotel room) becomes available just before the next consumer wants to rent/buy it; ultimately reduced capital is tied up in inventory

Knowledge Worker—A person who knows how to access, where to search, and how to get base knowledge in real time

Labor Intensive—The business or industry that employs a large number of employees to provide customers with a product or service

Labor Relations—Specialized area of the law devoted to unionized workplaces

Leadership—The influencing of others to channel their activities toward reaching the goals of the business

Learning Organization—A business that encourages (and often rewards) learning, accessing new information, and applying it toward achieving the company's goals

Lease—A legal document outlining usually the rental of space from a landlord

Leisure Activities—Entertainment, attractions, recreation, cruises, gaming, and shopping

Lido Deck—A deck that offers informal activities such as indoor and outdoor buffets

Liquor Liability—State laws that govern the selling of alcohol and its licensing

Lodging—One of the four major subdivisions of hospitality and tourism, this segment includes hotels, motels, resorts, and vacation ownership

Low Rollers—People who play the nickel, dime, and quarter slots; only gamble a small amount of money

Low Season—The lowest business demand time

Macro View—A perspective outside the immediate geographic location of the business to include any company or customer that may do business with them online; understanding the large scope of the competitive environment

Management Control System—Records to track the costs of the operation; can document the responsibility and accountability for all items

Management—The process of getting tasks accomplished through people

Manufacturer—Sources of the product supply; sometimes referred to as "growers"

Manufacturing Economy—Businesses that contribute to the gross national product (GNP) that are manufacturing in type—such as the automobile or chemical industry

Marketing Mix—A blending of several inducements designed to create and keep customers

Meeting and Convention Managers—These professionals are most often associated with conferences, seminars, conventions, training programs, and new product introductions; events with a strong focus on education

Mega-Ships—Those ships built in the very recent past that are extremely large and offer amenities similar to a resort

Member—Regardless of type of club, each is made up of members, who have applied for and been accepted into membership

Mentor—Someone who is experienced in the business that one can talk to for advice and counsel; usually not one's immediate supervisor

Merit Pay—Providing increased wages based on an employee's performance that is at or above expected levels

MGM Grand Hotel and Theme Park—The largest resort in the world, and the dream of pioneer Las Vegas hotel developer, multi-millionaire, Kirk Kerkorian

MICE Industry—Meetings, Incentive, Convention, and Exposition Industry

Mid-Ship—Middle of the ship

Military Clubs—Cater to enlisted men and women and the non-commissioned officer; provides a social outlet, often has golf

Moments of Truth—Any time a guest comes in contact with anything that represents the operation; may be positive or negative

Motel—Also known as a motor hotel, provides a room and parking available near the room as many motels did not have uniformed staff or bell persons; flourished as the Interstate highway system grew

MPI—Meeting Planners International

Multiculturally Aware—A person who is sensitive and tolerant of other cultures and customs

Multinational Company—A business with locations in more than one country

Multiple Service Centers—Centers for senior citizens that offer all types of service centers—Independent Living, Assisted Living, and Full Service—at one site or campus

Municipal Course—Golf courses that are owned and operated by a tax-supported entity, such as a city or county, open to the public

National—A local citizen

Natural Attractions—Nature's beauty; often protected by the government or special interest groups

NCA—National Club Association

Negligence—The area of the law that attempts to define who is legally responsible for a particular accident and to make that person, or entity, pay for the reasonable costs of the accident victim

Net Income—All the inflows of dollars, minus the outflows of dollars

Networking—The process of meeting and getting to know other people; usually people with similar interests and share information that is beneficial to all parties, often making contacts for future employment opportunities

NGF—National Golf Foundation

Non-Commercial Foodservice—Those food-services that are in businesses whose primary function is not food and beverage (schools, hospitals, businesses, or universities); profit is not always a motive

NRA—National Restaurant Association

Occupational Safety and Health Act—Mandates safety regulations and practices at the federal level, so that businesses in the United States provide a safe property and safe work environment

Onsite—The operation of services within the physical structure of the host organization

Operations—The day-to-day managing and running of the business; great career opportunities for people who get fired up by the day-to-day contact with customers and the myriad challenges and surprises that arise in the business

Organizing—The efforts involved with determining what activities are to be done and how employees are grouped together to accomplish specific tasks

Owner's Equity—The portion of the assets that the company owns

PACE—Program of All Inclusive Care for the Elderly, developed by Medicare, provides comprehensive care for the elderly

Paradigm—An environment, example, pattern

Paradigm Shift—The changing environment, when the notion that "we always did it this way" no longer is sufficient, and often for growth or survival, a company must change the way it is doing business

Partnership—Owned by two or more people

Pathological Gambler—Problem gamblers who get caught up in trying to win the jackpot and stay too long; less than 2 percent of the population is at risk

PCMA—The Professional Convention Management Association

People Person—In the hospitality business one is surrounded by people: employees and customers; a manager must be able to communicate effectively with individuals in the different roles of subordinates/superiors and guests

Performance Clause—A clause in the contract that states if the management company does not perform to a pre-agreed-upon level, the owner has the right to terminate the contract

Performance Standards—Guidelines created by a franchisor to ensure consistency in products and customer service experience in each operation, regardless of franchisee

PGA—Professional Golfers' Association

Phoenicians—Among the first real travelers

Physical Plant—The facility in which the products or services that guests purchase are created, delivered, and generally consumed

Picea—The earliest known version of today's pizza, consumed by Roman soldiers during the approximate year of 1000

Pineapple—Not only a delicious fruit, but now recognized as the international symbol of hospitality

Placement Office—An office on most college and university campuses that helps students develop resumes, helps practice interviewing skills, and can assist with job searches

Planning—The establishment of goals and objectives and deciding how to accomplish these goals

POM—An accounting abbreviation for property, operation, and maintenance accounts

Port—Left side of the ship

Ports of Call—Cities that cruise ships enter into and dock so their patrons can visit the city

Ports of Embarkation—Cities from where cruise ships take off (embark) on their voyage

Practice Range—An area near the pro shop and first tee to practice hitting golf balls

Pro Shop—A small retail establishment, boutique style as it is highly specialized in golf apparel, equipment, and tools for the game

Proactive Management—The leader forecasts what may occur within the business such as volume of business, safety issues, ordering supplies as to not get caught off guard or unprotected

Professional Associations—These associations hold meetings and conventions often annually and are a major source of revenue for the MICE Industry

Professional Certification—Offered through associations in a specific area or field, usually a culmination of work experience, continuing education, and passing a comprehensive examination. It validates one's knowledge and demonstrates one's commitment to lifelong learning, and the industry.

Professional Development—Continuing education in a specific industry, often in the form of seminars, workshops, or distance education

Project Design Team—A group of professionals who are brought together because of their individual and varying skill sets to create a new facility or remodel an existing one

Project Manager—One who directs the work of the consultants on a project, maintains an ongoing dialogue with the client, and ensures that payments for services are received/paid on a timely basis

Promotions—Short-term inducements such as coupons or drawings for free prizes

Proprietary Clubs—Those owned by a corporation, company, business, or individual; they are for-profit businesses

Prove Competency—A QSR manager should be able to work in each position to prove to his/her employees he/she has a working knowledge of the operation; they do not need to be the best at each job

Publicity—Unpaid communication about the firm or its products

Purchasing Agent—Someone who works for the hospitality business who purchases and receives the products

Purchasing Economics—The purchasing of products in larger volume to gain substantial discounts, then redistributing these products to the units

Putting Green—A putting surface used by golfers to practice putting

QSR Location—Where people can easily access them; virtually anywhere traffic patterns have dictated a need; suburbs, malls, grocery stores

Quality Assurance—Specific operating standards that must be met, often enforced through regular inspections

Quick-Service Restaurants—A very large segment of the restaurant industry, which provides a limited menu, counter service, yet prepares the food quickly; often used interchangeably with "Fast Food," though many would argue these terms are not synonymous

Ranger—A person who monitors the pace of playing golf and may tell a foursome to speed up if need be

Rating Services—The two primary services in the United States are the American Automobile Association (AAA) and Mobil Travel Guide. These businesses rate restaurants and hotels on specific criteria to render judgment on its property level of services to the guest; consumers who are seeking consistency while traveling use these

Reactive Management—Being able to "think on your feet" and react well to changes and unpredictable events, such as a slip and fall accident

Real Estate Representative—A person who works for the hospitality firm that specializes in real estate transactions including site location and analysis

Real-Time—Current time, immediate

Recreation Services—A department typically found in a resort hotel that manages the recreational facilities and possible youth programs at the resort, such as golf, tennis, horseback riding

Recreation—One of the four major subdivisions of hospitality and tourism, this segment includes festivals, parks, gaming, and attractions

Referral Associations—Comprised of properties that have the same name and design, but are owned and operated by different parties; this group is characterized by greater owner autonomy. Benefits include international marketing and a central reservation system, while maintaining the independence of an individual hotel.

Refrigeration Systems—A system that maintains the temperature of a space by removing any heat that enters the space

Regional Carriers—Those airlines that operate within a certain geographic area or region

Representative—A company that provides advertising services and books reservations for independent hotels; receives a commission on each reservation it books, but imposes no quality assurance standards on its properties

Respite Care—Short-term, temporary use of assisted living center resources and services

Retention—Keeping employees employed; the best method to enhance retention is an atmosphere of fair treatment, where employees enjoy working, where they feel they make a difference and are rewarded based on their own individual performance

Revenue—Money flowing into the business

RFP—Request for Proposal; a document that outlines the nature of the work requested and other project details

Routine Maintenance—General upkeep, occurs regularly, requires little skill

Royalties—Monies paid to the franchisor at regular intervals once the franchised business is operating

Sales—The inflow of dollars into the business

Saloons—America's first bars, they provided the community a place to spend leisure time and even hold trials

Sanitation—A key component to any kitchen, employees must be trained in safe food handling practices to prevent food poisoning and meet heath code requirements

Scheduled Maintenance—Initiated by formal work order and attempts to meet a known need in an orderly and timely manner

Security—The task of protecting people—both guests and employees, and protecting assets

Self-Managed Teams—A group of employees, often with technical skills, which work as a team to accomplish the company's goal(s) with little or no close supervision

Self-Op or Self-Operating—The parent company chooses to take full responsibility and operate the integrated services (food, lodging) themselves

Service Economy—Businesses that contribute to the gross national product (GNP) that are service oriented in type—such as the restaurant or lodging industry

Service—The reason why private clubs exist; members receive high-end, personalized service at their club

Slots—Games that include slot machines, video poker, and other computerized games; the 25-cent slot machine is the most popular

Small Business—Currently accounts for 9 million self-employed Americans, this segment created more than 63 percent of all new jobs and is responsible for 43 percent of the gross national product (GNP)

Social Membership—Entitles a member to limited use of a country club, typically dining, pool, and tennis, but not golf; reduced initiation fee and dues structure

Soft Products—Digital products that hospitality companies sell online such as airline tickets that lend themselves well to online distribution channels

Sole Proprietorship—Owned by one person

Special Events—Food services at specialty events such as outdoor concerts, tennis or golf tournaments, or extensive events like the Olympics

Specialty Quick-Service Restaurants—Very limited menu, orders are filled most rapidly, such as Krispy Kreme Doughnuts or Subway

Staff or Support—Those positions that exist to provide assistance to managers in operations, such as human resources, training, accounting, and marketing; without operations these positions would not exist

Staffing—Supplying the human requirements necessary to service guests

Starboard—Right side of the ship

Starter—A person at the starting location of a golf course who verifies payment has been received and gives any instructions for the course

Stern—Extreme rear of the ship

Super-Service Industries—Telecommunications, information technology, and tourism, the three areas that futurist John Naisbitt stated would drive the global economy in the 21st century

Supply Chain Management—The management of information related to the flow of material along the entire production cycle

Support—Professionals that work in hospitality and tourism but not in operations

Surveillance—A department that operates above the gaming floor; utilizes hundreds of cameras embedded in the ceiling of the casino

Table Games—Any game played on a table

Tangible—Touchable, something that can be seen and felt

Task Force Team—A group of employees who come together to address and solve a specific task for the organization; often made up of one person per department affected by the task

Taverns—First found in the U.S. in 1770s, built in the colonies and became the focal point of the community

Technical Skills—The skills involving knowledge of and the ability to perform a particular job or task

Tee Time—A reservation for a specific time to start a round of golf

Tenure—A faculty member has employment on a continuing basis

Terminal Degree—The highest degree offered in that field

Theatrical Food and Beverage—Areas that allow guests to see the show in the kitchen

Theme Parks—Strive to create a fantasy atmosphere that transports the visitor to another place and time; closed geographical boundaries exist with an admission price at the gate

Thinking Outside the Box—Looking to other non-related industries or businesses to improve one's operation, taking another business's model and applying it to a similar situation to improve operations

Third-Party Liability—Imposes penalties on those who sell or serve alcohol when certain circumstances exist

360-Degree Evaluation—The most optimal method of performance evaluation, yet time consuming and costly; where the supervisor evaluates the employee performance as do the employees they supervise, peers, and customers

TIA—Travel Industry of America formed in 1941

Toque—The traditional tall white hat worn by chefs

Total Assets—The possessions of the business

Total Liabilities—What the company still owes on its possessions or has already used

Tour Operators—Professionals that organize complete travel programs for groups or individuals to every continent and by all modes of transportation

Tradeshow or Exposition Managers—Events where there are booth-displays of products and services, focus is on marketing

Travel Agents—Professionals within an agency that act to match the travel desires of leisure and business travelers with the most appropriate suppliers of tourist services

Travel—One of the four major subdivisions of hospitality and tourism, this segment includes railroads, automobiles, cruise ships, and airlines

Troubleshooter—An internal consultant, one who works for a single company but goes to different units as they have problem areas; also called a field consultant

Turnover—A term used to describe the cycle of when an employee leaves for any reason (fired or quit) and must be replaced; an expensive occurrence

Vacation Clubs—Similar to interval ownership, this plan allows for maximum flexibility as the owner earns points for the value of his/her time that is owned and trades those points for space elsewhere

Vacation-Ownership Firm—A business focused on selling long-term vacation packages to guests; "slices of time," can be hotel room or condominium at a specific property

Value-Added Relationship—The ideal relationship between an employee and his/her employer; mutually beneficial to both parties

Wage and Hour Law—Requires the employer pay at least a minimum wage, pay extra for overtime work, and pay for all the work that was completed

Wastewater Systems—Systems that remove and sometimes treat wastewater (sewage)

WATS—Wide Area Telephone System—allows leasing of telephone lines, which dramatically reduces the cost of high volume use

"We work, so others can play"—This motto depicts the type of work done in the hospitality industry, it often includes nights and weekends when a lot of other people are off work

Whole-Ownership Condominium Hotels—These facilities are usually sold outright, and the owners generally have year-round occupancy

Word-of-Mouth Marketing—Recommendations from friends and relatives; far and away the best way to generate interest and business

Workers' Compensation—State-regulated insurance programs that are meant to compensate employees for medical expenses, lost wages, and rehabilitation costs that may be incurred as a result of work related injuries

Working Capital Management—The short-term management of what the company owns and what the company owes

"WOW"—A term coined by Tom Peters when describing a business that effectively thinks outside the box to improve its core operation and ultimately better reach its goals

WTO—World Tourism Organization

WTTC—The World Travel and Tourism Council

Yacht Club—Establishments near or on the water, activities center on sailing and boating, dining also available

Zoning—Regulations that specify how land might be used

Index